Rockin' in Time

Rockin' in Time

A Social History of Rock-and-Roll

Seventh Edition

David P. Szatmary

Prentice Hall
Upper Saddle River London Singapore
Toronto Tokyo Sydney Hong Kong Mexico City

To My Father and Mother

Editor in Chief: Sarah Touborg
Editorial Assistant: Carla Worner
Executive Editor: Richard Carlin
Director of Marketing: Brandy Dawson
Marketing Assistant: Suzanne Jalaiel
Senior Marketing Manager: Kate Mitchell
Senior Managing Editor: Ann Marie McCarthy
Assistant Managing Editor: Melissa Feimer
Project Managers: Fran Russello/Jean Lapidus
**Composition/Full-Service
   Management:** Prepare/Emilcomp
Production Editor: Assunta Petrone

Senior Art Director: Pat Smythe
Interior Designer: Dutton & Sherman Design
Cover Designer: Ray Cruz
Chapter-Opening Art styled by: Cory Skidds
Senior Operations Specialist: Brian Mackey
Color Scanning: Cory Skidds
Manager, Rights & Permissions: Zina Arabia
Image Permission Coordinator: Craig A. Jones
Lead Media Project Manager: Rich Barnes
Senior Media Editor: David Alick
Printer/Binder: Quebecor World Book Services
Cover Printer: Lehigh-Phoenix Color

This book is set in 10/12 Ehrhardt.

Credits and acknowledgments borrowed from other sources and reproduced, with permission, in this textbook appear on page 388.

Library of Congress Cataloging-in-Publication Data

Szatmary, David P.
   Rockin' in time: a social history of rock-and-roll/David P.
Szatmary.—7th ed.
      p. cm.
   Includes bibliographical references and index.
   ISBN 0-205-67504-2
1. Rock music—United States—History and criticism.   2. Rock music—Social aspects—United States.   I. Title.
   ML3534.S94 2010
   781.660973—dc22

                                                                    2008055213

10 9 8 7 6 5 4 3 2 1

Prentice Hall
is an imprint of

PEARSON

www.pearsonhighered.com

Student edition:
ISBN-10   0-205-67504-2
ISBN-13   978-020-567504-3

Exam copy:
ISBN-10   0-205-67506-9
ISBN-13   978-020-567506-7

Contents

Preface

❝ Rock-and-roll will be around for a long, long time. Rock-and-roll is like hot molten lava that erupts when an angry volcano explodes. It's scorching hot, burns fast and completely, leaving an eternal scar. Even when the echoes of the explosion subside, the ecstatic flames burn with vehement continuity. **❞**

—Don Robey, owner of Peacock and Duke Records,
in *Billboard,* March 1957

This book is a social history of rock-and-roll. It places an ever-changing rock music in the context of American and, to some extent, British history from roughly 1950 to 2008. *Rockin' in Time* tries to explain how rock-and-roll both reflected and influenced major social changes during the last six decades. As Ice-T explained in 1997, "Albums are meant to be put in a time capsule, sealed up, and sent into space so that when you look back you can say that's the total reflection of that time."

This book deals with rock music within broad social and cultural settings. Rather than present an encyclopedic compilation of the thousands of well-known and obscure bands that have played throughout the years, it examines rock-and-rollers who have reflected and sometimes changed the social fabric at a certain point in history. It does not focus on the many artists, some of my favorites, who never gained general popularity or who achieved commercial success with a sound that either reinvigorated an older style or who did not encapsulate the times. *Rockin' in Time* concentrates on rock musicians who most fully mirrored the world around them and helped define an era.

Rockin' in Time emphasizes several main themes, including the importance of African-American culture in the origins and development of rock music. The blues, originating in the work songs of American slaves, provided the foundation for rock-and-roll. During the early 1950s, southern African Americans who had migrated to Chicago created an urbanized, electric rhythm and blues that preceded rock-and-roll and served as the breeding ground for pioneer rock-and-rollers such as Little Richard and Chuck Berry. African Americans continued to create new styles such as the Motown sound, the soul explosion of the late 1960s, the disco beat in the next decade, and, most recently, hip-hop.

The new musical styles many times coincided with and reflected the African-American struggle for equality. The electric blues of Muddy Waters became popular amid the stirrings of the civil rights movement during the 1950s. During the early 1960s, as the movement for civil rights gained momentum, folk protesters such as Bob Dylan and Joan Baez sang paeans about the cause. In 1964 and 1965, as Congress passed the most sweeping civil rights legislation since the Civil War, Motown artists topped the pop charts. When disgruntled, frustrated African Americans took to the streets later in the decade, soul artists such as Aretha Franklin shouted for respect. During the late 1980s and into the 1990s, hip-hoppers such as Public Enemy rapped about inequality and renewed an interest in an African-American identity.

As the civil rights struggle began to foster an awareness and acceptance of African-American culture, rock-and-roll became accessible to white teenagers. Teens such as Elvis Presley listened to late-night, rhythm-and-blues radio shows that started to challenge and break down racial barriers. During the 1960s, African-American performers such as the Ronettes, the Crystals, the Temptations, and the Supremes achieved mass popularity among both African Americans and whites. By the 1980s, African-American entertainers such as Michael Jackson achieved superstar status, and rap filtered into the suburbs. Throughout the last six decades, rock music has helped integrate white and black America.

A dramatic population growth during the postwar era, the second theme of this book, provided the audience for an African-American-inspired rock-and-roll. After World War II, both the United States and Great Britain experienced a tremendous baby boom. By the mid-1950s, the baby boomers had become an army of youngsters who demanded their own music. Along with their older brothers and sisters who had been born during the war, they latched onto the new rock-and-roll, idolizing a young, virile Elvis Presley who attracted hordes of postwar youth.

Rock music appealed to and reflected the interests of the baby-boom generation until the end of the 1970s. The music of the Dick Clark era, the Brill Building songwriters, the Beach Boys, the Motown artists, and the early Beatles showed a preoccupation with dating, cars, high school, and teen love. As this generation matured and entered college or the workforce, the music scene became more serious and was dominated by the protest music of Bob Dylan and psychedelic bands that questioned basic tenets of American society. The music became harsh and violent, when college-age baby boomers were threatened by the Vietnam War military draft and the prospect of fighting in an unpopular war. During the 1970s, after the war ended and when many of the college rebels landed lucrative jobs, glitter rock and disco exemplified the excessive, self-centered behavior of the boomers. During the 1980s, artists such as Bruce Springsteen, who matured with his audience and celebrated his fortieth birthday by the end of the decade, reflected a yearning for the 1960s' spirit of social change.

New generations began to carry the rock-and-roll banner. By the mid-1970s, disaffected youths created a stinging punk rock to vent their emotions. A decade later Generation X, confronted by sobering social conditions, turned to hardcore punk, thrash metal, grunge, death metal, and rap. In the late 1990s and into the new century, yet another generation of young teens embraced hip-hop pop, and then nu-metal, and three variants of the blues as their music.

The roller-coaster economic times during the post–World War II era serve as a third focus of this book. A favorable economic climate initially allowed rock to flourish among the baby-boom generation. Compared to the preceding generation, which had been raised during the most severe economic depression of the twentieth century, the baby boomers in the United States lived in relative affluence. In the 1950s and early 1960s, many youths had allowances that enabled them to purchase the latest rock records and buy tickets to see their favorite heartthrobs. During the next fifteen years, unparalleled prosperity allowed youths to consider the alternatives of hippiedom, and led to cultural excesses and booming record sales during the 1970s.

When the economic scene began to worsen during the mid-to-late 1970s in Britain, a new generation of youths created the sneering protest of punk that reflected the harsh economic realities of the dole. A decade later, American youths, who had few career prospects and little family stability, played shattering hardcore punk, a pounding industrial sound, bleak grunge music, a growling death metal, and a confrontational rap. When the economy brightened on both sides of the Atlantic by the late 1990s, teens turned to a bouncy, danceable hip-hop pop and an optimistic nu-metal.

Advances in technology shaped the sound of rock-and-roll and provides another framework for *Rockin' in Time*. The solid-body electric guitar, developed and popularized during the 1950s by Les Paul and Leo Fender, gave rock its distinctive sound. Mass-produced electric guitars such as Fender's Telecaster, appearing in 1951, and the Stratocaster, first marketed three years later, enabled blues musicians and later white teens to capture the electric sound of the city and the passion of youth. Later technologies such as the synthesizer, the sequencer, and the sampler allowed musicians to embellish and reshape rock-and-roll into different genres.

Several technological breakthroughs helped popularize rock-and-roll, making it easily and inexpensively accessible. Television brought, and still brings, rock to teens in their homes—Elvis Presley and the Beatles on *The Ed Sullivan Show*, Dick Clark's *American Bandstand*, and currently MTV. In Britain, television programs such as *Thank Your Lucky Stars, Ready Steady Go!*, and *Juke Box Jury* played the same role. The portable transistor radio, the portable cassette tape player-recorder, the portable CD player, and, most recently, the iPod provided teens the opportunity to listen to their favorite songs in the privacy of their rooms, at school, or on the streets. The inexpensive 45-rpm record, introduced in 1949 by RCA, allowed youths to purchase the latest hits and dominated rock sales until the 1960s, when the experimental psychedelic sound fully utilized the more extended format of the long-play, 12-inch, 33-1/3-rpm record. Advances in the quality of sound, such as high fidelity, stereo, component stereo systems, and the digital compact disc, brought the immediacy of the performance to the home and helped further disseminate rock-and-roll. By the late 1990s, the Internet enabled youths to listen, trade, download, burn their favorite music, and learn about and contact their favorite bands from their personal computer.

The increasing popularity of rock music has been entwined with the development of the music industry, another feature of this book. Rock-and-roll has always been a business. At first, small, independent companies such as Chess, Sun, Modern, and

King recorded and delivered to the public a commercially untested rock. As it became more popular among teens, rock-and-roll began to interest major record companies such as RCA, Decca, and Capitol, which in the 1960s dominated the field. By the 1970s, the major companies aggressively marketed their product and consolidated ranks to increase profits and successfully create an industry more profitable than network television and professional sports. In 1978, as the majors experienced a decline in sales, independent labels again arose to release new rock styles such as punk, rap, grunge, and techno. At the end of the 1980s and 1990s, the major companies reasserted their dominance of the record industry, buoyed by the signing of new acts that had been tested by the independents and by the introduction of the compact disc, which lured many record buyers to purchase their favorite music in a different, more expensive format. As the new century unfolded, the major record labels confronted and protested against the Internet, which created a fundamentally new business model for the music industry by allowing musicians to release and distribute their music inexpensively to a worldwide audience without an intermediary.

Though a business, rock music has engendered and has been defined by rebellion, which manifested itself through a series of overlapping subcultures. Youths used rock-and-roll as a way to band together and feel part of a community. As Bruce Springsteen mentioned about his own experience, rock music "provided me with a community, filled with people, and brothers and sisters who I didn't know, but who I knew were out there. We had this enormous thing in common, this 'thing' that initially felt like a secret. Music always provided that home for me, a home where my spirit could wander."

During the last six decades, identifiable rock-and-roll communities took on specific characteristics and styles. Fueled by uncontrolled hormones, rockabilly greasers in the 1950s and early 1960s came together and challenged their parents by wearing sideburns, long, greasedback hair, and driving fast hot rods. Their girlfriends sported tight sweaters, ratted hair, pedal-pusher slacks, and screamed to the hip-shaking gyrations of Elvis Presley. In the 1960s, conservatively dressed, college-aged folkniks directed their frustration and anger at racial and social injustice, taking freedom rides to the South and protesting against nuclear arms. A few years later, the hippies flaunted wild, vibrant clothing, the mind-expanding possibilities of LSD, sexual freedom, and a disdain for a warmongering capitalism, which they expressed in their swirling psychedelic poster art. In the next decade, the rock lifestyle changed once again, as some baby boomers discoed to dee-jays and others crammed into stadium concerts to collectively snort cocaine and celebrate sexually ambiguous, theatrical, and extravagant superstars.

During the late 1970s, two angry rock subcultures emerged. Sneering British punks grew spiked hair, wore ripped, safety-pinned T-shirts, and pogoed straight up and down, lashing out against economic, gender, and racial inequities. About the same time, a hip-hop subculture started, that unabashedly condemned racial prejudice and its effects on African Americans in the inner cities, highlighting the racial injustice that the civil rights movement of the sixties had not erased. Within a decade and into the new century, the inner-city b-boy subculture had spread to the white suburbs, where gun-toting teens looked for ho's and wore Adidas, saggy pants, baseball caps (preferably New York Yankees) turned backward, loose T-shirts, and, depending upon the year, gold chains.

In the 1980s and 1990s, Generation X youth voiced a passionate frustration and despair through a series of subcultures that included a slam-dancing, Mohawked hardcore punk; a gothic-looking industrial style; a long-haired, leather-jacketed thrash and death metal; and the self-described "loser" community of grunge, which adopted the idealized look of the working class: longish, uncombed hair, faded blue jeans, boots, and T-shirts. Other Generation Xers faced their problems differently by refashioning the hippie lifestyle for the nineties. Joining together at updated love-ins called raves, they favored Ecstasy over LSD, put on their smiley faces, and hugged their fellow techno-travelers as demonstrations of peace in a war-filled, terrorist-riddled world. Though less confrontational than its grunge counterpart, the techno subculture directly challenged and shocked mainstream society as each rock subculture has done during the last sixty years before being subverted and incorporated into the mainstream by fashion designers, Hollywood, and big business.

By the start of the new century, rock-and-roll took on different cultural forms. Laid-back jam bands and their followers congregated at festivals such as Bonnaroo, wearing casual clothes and adopting a Grateful Dead–like ethos. Confronted by a seemingly never-ending war in Iraq and the prospects of rapid climate change, collegiate-styled youths listened to socially conscious singer-songwriters and the twenty-first-century blues of the White Stripes. Still others rocked to black metal, espousing paganism and wearing facial corpse paint, studded black leather outfits, and long hair to denote their disgust with current cultural mores. As it has done during the past six decades, rock-and-roll continues to rebel against injustice and question conservative and constraining social norms.

History seldom can be separated into neat packages. Many of the different rock genres and their accompanying subcultures overlapped with one another. For example, from 1961 to the advent of the British invasion in 1964, the Brill Building songwriters, surf music, and Bob Dylan coexisted on the charts. Though sometimes intersecting and cross-pollinating, the different subcultures of rock-and-roll have been divided into distinct chapters to clearly distinguish the motivating factors behind each one.

Rockin' in Time attempts to be as impartial as possible. Even though a book cannot be wrenched from the biases of its social setting, I have tried to present the music in a historical rather than a personal context and to avoid any effusive praise or disparaging remarks about any type of rock. As Sting, lead singer of the Police, once said, "there is no bad music, only bad musicians."

These pages explore the social history of rock-and-roll. During the last six decades that it has been an important and essential part of American and British culture, rock-and-roll has reflected and sometimes changed the lives of several generations.

New to this seventh edition

- A new chapter about folk rock
- A new section on death metal
- A new section about hip-hop pop, including Kanye West
- Material about Radiohead and Tool

- A new chapter dealing with
  - Music and the Internet
  - The change in the music industry
  - Jam bands
  - Singer-songwriters such as John Mayer and Jack Johnson
  - The new garage rock of the White Stripes
  - Black metal

MyRockKit

Every student who purchases a copy of this book gets free access to Prentice Hall's new online resource, MyRockKit. MyRockKit includes complete self-assessment tools, including chapter summaries and questions, to help improve your class performance. It also includes valuable additional information about rock and roll:

- Documentaries on key eras of rock history
- An interactive introduction to rock styles
- Flashcards on key terms with pronunciation and musical examples
- Videos of key performances
- An interactive timeline

Acknowledgments

Thanks to several people who helped me with this book: Bill Flanagan, Timothy Leary, Michael Batt, Jamie Steiwer, Peter Blecha, Chris Waterman, Charles Cross, Gene Stout, Jeff Taylor, Dave Wolter, Adam Bratman, Artur Sedov, Don Hood, Carl Krikorian, Rob Innes, Anthony Allen, Howie Wahlen, John Shannon, Gary June, Arnie Berger, Marty Jack Rosenblum, David Webb, Joe Moore, Dave Rispoli, Jerry Schilling, Keith John, Joel Druckman, W. Michael Weis, and Sonny Masso offered perceptive comments and constant help on various drafts of the text. I also thank Robert Palmer, Bob Guiccione, Jr., Alan Douglas, Mike Farrace, Gregg Vershay, and Bob Jeniker for their encouragement. Thanks to Gerald Barnett for finding the seven deadly typos in the fourth edition. I especially thank Stewart Stern, Richard Hell, Sebastian, Frank Kozik, Mark Arminski, Emek, and rapper Ed "Sugar Bear" Wells for their insights. Special thanks to Richard Carlin who did a masterful job editing this seventh edition. Obviously, none of those who provided assistance can be held responsible for the contents of this book.

As in previous editions, I have others to thank. Jerry Kwiatkowski (Kaye) introduced me to the world of rock and prodded me to listen to everyone from Captain Beefheart to Eric Clapton. Mike Miller helped me explore the summer concert scene in Milwaukee. Ramona Wright, Neil Fligstein, Eileen Mortenson, Gail Fligstein, and Tom Speer did the same for me in Tucson and Seattle. On the East Coast, Dave Sharp fearlessly accompanied me on journeys to see Sid Vicious and explore the mantra of Root Boy Slim.

I acknowledge former coworkers at Second Time Around Records in Seattle— owners Wes and Barbara Geesman, Dan Johnson, Mike Schwartz, Michael Wellman, and Jim Rifleman—for adding to my understanding of rock music and the rock business. At the University of Arizona, Donald Weinstein graciously allowed me to teach a class on the social history of rock-and-roll, the beginnings of this book; Rick Venneri did the same at the University of Washington. Students in those classes added to my knowledge of rock music. Thanks to Dudley Johnson at the University of Washington for putting me in contact with Prentice Hall.

I owe a special debt to Bob "Wildman" Campbell, the king of psychedelia, who spent many hours with me analyzing the lyrics of Larry Fischer, the nuances of Tibetan Buddhists chants, Bonzo Dog Band album covers, and the hidden meaning behind the grunts of Furious Pig. Besides reading and commenting on this manuscript, he expanded my musical horizons with a series of demented tapes and letters, which twisted this book into shape. Such a debt can never be repaid.

I thank my parents, Peter and Eunice, for instilling in me a love of music and the written word. My appreciation goes to my mother, who commented on the manuscript and gave me suggestions for a title.

My daughter Sara brought me back to reality when I became overly absorbed in the manuscript and showed me that energy can be boundless. She provided needed guidance about music in the new century and gave me hope that rock-and-roll will never die. In the last three editions, she offered insightful comments about the newest music on the charts and provided invaluable research.

Most of all, I thank my wife Mary for her love and companionship, her openness to all types of music, her editorial comments, and her indulgence of my vinyl and rock-poster addictions. I could not have completed the seven editions of this book without her understanding, interest, encouragement, and love.

Credits

Grateful acknowledgment is made to the following copyright holders for permission to reprint their copyrighted material.

Bruce Springsteen Music: Lyrics from "My Hometown," words and music by Bruce Springsteen, copyright © Bruce Springsteen Music. Used with permission of Bruce Springsteen Music.

Irving Music: Lyrics from "White Rabbit," lyrics and music by Grace Slick, copyright © 1967 Irving Music, Inc. (BMI). All rights reserved—International Copyright Secured.

Jondora Music: Lyrics from "Fortunate Son" by John Fogerty, copyright © 1969 Jondora Music. Courtesy of Fantasy Inc.

All photographs are copyrighted by the photographer or company cited in the credit lines beneath each picture, all rights reserved.

I thank the following individuals and companies for use of photos and help in finding them: Alligator Records, especially Bruce Iglauer; Peter Asher Management, with special help from Ira Koslow; Atlantic Records; Roberta Bayley; David Bowie; Bill Graham Presents (BGP) Archives; Capitol Records; Chrysalis Records; Columbia Records; Delmark Records and Bob Koester; Brian O'Neal at D.M.B.B. Entertainment; Alan Douglas and the staff at Are You Experienced?; Elektra Records; the Estate of Elvis Presley, especially Marc Magaliff; Don Everly; Cam Garrett; Richard Hell; Isolar Enterprises; Jeff Kleinsmith; Marilyn Laverty at Shore Fire; the Library of Congress; Living Blues Archival Collection, University of Mississippi Blues Archive; London Records; MCA Records; Q Prime; RCA Records, especially J. Matthew Van Ryn; Rush Artist Management; *The Seattle Times*; Sire Records; Beverly Rupe at Specialty Records; Chris Stamp; Sun Records; Virgin Records; and Warner Brothers Records.

I especially thank Barbara Krohn of *The Daily* of the University of Washington for her help in locating photos.

Special thanks to Frank Kozik, Mark Arminski, Emek, Jeral Tidwell, and Jeff Wood and Judy Gex at Drowning Creek for use of their posters.

Every effort has been made to locate, identify, and properly credit photographers, songwriters, and song publishers. Any inadvertent omissions or errors will be corrected in future editions.

The Blues, Rock-and-Roll, and Racism

1

> 66 It used to be called boogie-woogie, it used to be called blues, used to be called rhythm and blues. . . . It's called rock now. 99
>
> —Chuck Berry

A smoke-filled club, the Macomba Lounge, on the South Side of Chicago, late on a Saturday night in 1950. On a small, dimly lit stage behind the bar in the long, narrow club stood an intense African American dressed in an electric green suit, baggy pants, a white shirt, and a wide, striped tie. He sported a 3-inch pompadour with his hair slicked back on the sides.

He gripped an oversized electric guitar—an instrument born in the postwar urban environment—caressing, pulling, pushing, and bending the strings until he produced a sorrowful, razor-sharp cry that cut into his listeners, who responded with loud shrieks. With half-closed eyes, the guitarist peered through the smoke and saw a bar jammed with patrons who nursed half-empty beer bottles. Growling out the lyrics of "Rollin' Stone," the man's face was contorted in a painful expression that told of cotton fields in Mississippi and the experience of African Americans in Middle America at midcentury. The singer's name was Muddy Waters, and he was playing a new, electrified music called rhythm and blues or R&B.

The rhythm and blues of Muddy Waters and other urban blues artists served as the foundation for Elvis, the Beatles, the Rolling Stones, Jimi Hendrix, Led Zeppelin, and most other rock-and-rollers. A subtle blend of African and European traditions, it provided the necessary elements and inspiration for the birth of rock and the success of Chuck Berry and Little Richard. Despite their innovative roles, R&B artists seldom received the recognition or the money they deserved. Established crooners, disc jockeys, and record company executives, watching their share of the market shrink with the increasing popularity of R&B and its rock-and-roll offspring, torpedoed the new music by offering toned-down, white copies of black originals that left many African-American trailblazers bitter and sometimes broken.

The Birth of the Blues

The blues were an indigenous creation of black slaves who adapted their African musical heritage to the American environment. Though taking many forms and undergoing many permutations throughout the years, the blues formed the basis of rock-and-roll.

Torn from their kin, enduring an often fatal journey from their homes in West Africa to the American South, and forced into a servile way of life, Africans retained continuity with their past through music. Their voices glided between the lines of the more rigid European musical scale to create a distinctive new sound. To the plantation owners and overseers, the music seemed to be "rising and falling" and sounded off-key.

The music involved calculated repetitions. In this call-and-response, often used to decrease the monotony of work, one slave would call or play a lead part, and fellow slaves would follow with the same phrase or an embellishment of it until another took the lead. As one observer wrote in 1845, "Our black oarsmen made the woods echo to their song. One of them, taking the lead, first improvised a verse, paying compliments to his master's family, and to a celebrated black beauty of the neighborhood, who was compared to the 'red bird.' The other five then joined in the chorus, always repeating the same words." Some slaves, especially those from the Bantu tribe, whooped or jumped octaves during the call-and-response, which served as a basis for field hollers.

Probably most important, the slaves, accustomed to dancing and singing to the beat of drums in Africa, emphasized rhythm over harmony. In a single song they clapped, danced, and slapped their bodies in several different rhythms, compensating for the absence of drums, which were outlawed by plantation owners, who feared that the instrument would be used to coordinate slave insurrections. One ex-slave, writing in 1853, called the polyrhythmic practice "patting juba." It was performed by "striking the right shoulder with one hand, the left with the other—all the while keeping time with the feet and singing." In contrast, noted President John Adams, whites "droned out [Protestant hymns] . . . like the braying of asses in one steady beat."

African Americans used these African musical traits in their religious ceremonies. One writer in the *Nation* described a "praise-meeting" held in 1867: "At regular intervals one hears the elder 'deaconing' a hymn-book hymn which is sung two lines at a time, and whose wailing cadences, borne on the night air, are indescribably melancholy." The subsequent response from the congregation to the bluesy call of the

On the cotton plantation, 1937. Photo by Dorothea Lange. *Permission by Library of Congress, F34-17335.*

minister, along with the accompanying instruments, created the rhythmic complexity common in African music.

Such African-inspired church music, later known as gospel, became the basis for the blues, when singers applied the religious music to secular themes. Bluesman Big Bill Broonzy, who recorded nearly two hundred songs from 1925 to 1952, started as "a preacher—preached in the church. One day I quit and went to music." Broonzy maintained that "the blues won't die because spirituals won't die. Blues—a steal from spirituals. And rock is a steal from the blues. . . . Blues singers start out singing spirituals."

From the Rural South to the Urban North

During and after World War I, many southern African Americans brought the blues to northern cities, especially Chicago, the end of the Illinois Central Railroad line, where the African-American population mushroomed from 40,000 in 1910 to 234,000 twenty years later. Many African Americans left the South to escape the boll weevil, a parasitic worm that ravaged the Mississippi Delta cotton fields in 1915 and 1916. Some migrated to break loose from the shackles of crippling racial discrimination in the South.

As Delta-born pianist Eddie Boyd told *Living Blues*, "I thought of coming to Chicago where I could get away from some of that racism and where I would have an opportunity to, well, do something with my talent. . . . It wasn't peaches and cream [in Chicago], man, but it was a hell of a lot better than down there where I was born." Once in Chicago, migrating African Americans found jobs in steel mills, food-processing plants, and stockyards that needed extra hands because of the wartime draft and a sudden restriction on European immigration. They settled in Chicago's South and West Side neighborhoods.

The migrants to the Windy City included guitarist Tampa Red, who moved from Florida to Chicago in 1925. Pianist Eurreal Wilford ("Little Brother") Montgomery, born in 1907 on the grounds of a Louisiana lumber company, performed at logging camps until he ended up in Chicago. Big Bill Broonzy, an ex-slave's son who worked as a plow hand in Mississippi and laid railroad track in Arkansas, headed for the same destination in 1916, when drought destroyed the crops on his farm. In 1929, pianist Roosevelt Sykes, "The Honeydripper," took the same route. A few years later, harmonica wizard John Lee ("Sonny Boy") Williamson, the first Sonny Boy, migrated from Jackson, Tennessee. And around the same time, guitarist Sleepy John Estes, the son of a Tennessee sharecropper, moved to the Windy City. George Leaner, who began selling blues discs in Chicago during the 1930s, recalled, "The Illinois Central Railroad brought the blues to Chicago. With the thousands of laborers who came to work in the meat-packing plants and the steel mills came Peetie Wheatstraw, Ollie Shepard, Blind Boy Fuller, Washboard Sam, Little Brother Montgomery, Blind Lemon [Jefferson], Memphis Minnie, and Rosetta Howard."

These migrants played different styles of blues. At first, most brought country blues to the city. By the early 1940s, when the urban setting began to influence the music, they recorded a hybrid of blues, vaudeville styles, and newer swing rhythms, which included the boogie-woogie, rolling-bass piano, a sound that had been associated with the jump blues band of Louis Jordan. Some dubbed the early Chicago blues the "Bluebird Beat" because many of the blues artists recorded for RCA Victor's Bluebird label, formed in 1933.

Lester Melrose, a white music talent-scout producer, documented the Chicago blues scene during the 1930s and 1940s. As Willie Dixon, bassist, songwriter, and talent scout, told *Living Blues*, "I started goin' up to Tampa Red's house where a lot of the other blues artists was, on 35th and State Street. He had a place up over a pawnshop. And a lotta the musicians used to go up there and write songs, lay around in there, and sleep. Lester Melrose always came there when he was in town. That was his kind of headquarters, like. And whenever he was in town, and different people had different songs that they wanted him to hear, they came by Tampa's house. . . . Big Bill Broonzy and a bunch of 'em would hang around there. And we get to singing it and seein' how it sounds. If it sounded like it was alright, then Melrose would say, 'Well, looky here, we'll try it out and see what happens.'" Melrose himself boasted that "from March 1934 to February 1951 I recorded at least 90 percent of all rhythm-and-blues talent for RCA and Columbia Records." He included on his roster Big Bill Broonzy, Tampa Red, Sleepy John Estes, Roosevelt Sykes, Sonny Boy Williamson, and many others. By using several of his artists in one session, Melrose featured vocals, a

Listening to the blues. The South, early 1940s. Photo by Russell Lee. *Permission by Library of Congress, F34-31941.*

guitar, and a piano to create a Chicago blues sound more enlivened and sophisticated than the more subdued country blues.

The blues became even more entrenched in northern urban areas during and after World War II, when thousands of Southerners in search of work streamed into the cities. "World War I started bluesmen up North and No. II made it a mass migration," pointed out Atlantic Record executive Jerry Wexler. Mechanical cotton pickers and the need for workers in wartime industrial factories pushed many African Americans northward.

From 1940 to 1944, estimated *Time* magazine, more than 50,000 African Americans from Mississippi alone headed for Chicago. They paid about $15 for the trip on the Illinois Central Railroad to the Windy City, the home of *The Defender,* the widely read, black-owned newspaper that encouraged southern sharecroppers to migrate to the North. From 1940 to 1950, 214,000 southern African Americans arrived in Chicago, an increase of 77 percent in just one decade, and the African-American population in Chicago increased to nearly a half million. About half of the new migrants came from the Mississippi Delta region, which stretched 200 miles from Memphis to Vicksburg.

Many of the Delta migrants had heard a propulsive, acoustic, personalized style of blues on their plantations. On Saturdays, at parties, at picnics, and in juke joints, they listened to the moans, the heavy bass beat, and the bottleneck slide guitar of local musicians. Their favorites included Charley Patton, the king of the Delta blues, who played around Will Dockery's plantation during the 1920s, and in 1929 recorded his classics "Pony Blues," "Pea Vine Blues," and "Tom Rushen Blues." He played with Eddie ("Son") House, a Baptist preacher who taught himself how to play the guitar at age twenty-five and in the 1930s cut such discs as "Preachin' the Blues." Robert Johnson, one of the most celebrated and legendary Delta blues artists, learned his guitar technique from Patton disciple Willie Brown and picked up Delta stylizings from Son House. During his brief recording career, which began in 1936, he released such gems as "I Believe I'll Dust My Broom," "Sweet Home Chicago," "Cross Road Blues," "Love in Vain Blues," and "Rambling on My Mind."

Muddy Waters and Chicago R&B

Muddy Waters (a.k.a. McKinley Morganfield), who grew up in Clarksdale, Mississippi, listening to Johnson, Patton, and Son House, merged his Delta influences with the urban environment of Chicago. He had his first introduction to music in church. "I used to belong to church. I was a good Baptist, singing in church," he recollected. "So I got all of my good moaning and trembling going on for me right out of church."

Muddy bought his first guitar when he was thirteen. "The first one I got," he told writer Robert Palmer, "I sold the last horse we had. Made about fifteen dollars for him, gave my grandmother seven dollars and fifty cents, I kept seven-fifty and paid about two-fifty for that guitar. It was a Stella. The people ordered them from Sears-Roebuck in Chicago." A young Muddy played locally around his home base, a plantation owned by Colonel William Howard Stovall. In 1941, on a trip to the Mississippi Delta in search of Robert Johnson, musicologists Alan Lomax and John Work discovered Waters, then a tenant farmer, and recorded him for the Library of Congress.

Two years later, Muddy moved to Chicago "with a suitcase, a suit of clothes, and a guitar," hoping to "get into the big record field." He told a journalist, "I wanted to get out of Mississippi in the worst way. They had such as my mother and the older people brainwashed that people can't make it too good in the city. But I figured if anyone else was living in the city, I could make it there, too." Muddy worked in a paper-container factory and then as a truck driver by day, playing at parties in the evenings.

In 1944, Muddy bought his first electric guitar, and two years later, he formed his first electric combo. Possibly the archetype of Chicago R&B artists, Muddy Waters felt compelled to electrify his sound in Chicago. "When I went into the clubs, the first thing I wanted was an amplifier. Couldn't nobody hear you with an acoustic." At least partly out of necessity, Muddy combined his Delta blues with the electric guitar and amplifier, which blasted forth the tension, volume, and confusion of the big-city streets.

By combining the sounds of the country and city into a nitty-gritty, low-down, jumpy sound, Muddy Waters reflected the optimism of postwar African Americans,

The Muddy Waters band, 1954. From left to right: Muddy Waters (guitar), Jerome Green (maracas), Otis Spann (piano), Henry Strong (harmonica), Elgin Evans (drums), and Jimmy Rogers (guitar). Photo courtesy of Living Blues Archival Collection, University of Mississippi Blues Archive/MCA Records.

who had escaped from the seemingly inescapable southern cotton fields. The urban music contrasted sharply with the more sullen country blues, born in slavery. Willie Dixon, a bassist from Vicksburg, Mississippi, and composer of blues-rock classics such as "(I'm Your) Hoochie Coochie Man," "I'm a Man," and "I Just Want to Make Love to You," recalled, "There was quite a few people around singin' the blues but most of 'em was singing all sad blues. Muddy was giving his blues a little pep." The peppy blues of artists like Muddy Waters became known as rhythm and blues.

After three years of perfecting his electric sound in Chicago clubs, Muddy signed with Aristocrat Records, owned by local entrepreneur Evelyn Aron in partnership with Jewish immigrant brothers Leonard and Phil Chess, who had operated several South Side bars, including the Macomba Lounge. At first, as Muddy told journalist Pete Welding, Leonard Chess "didn't like my style of singing; he wondered who was going to buy that. The lady [Evelyn Aron, a partner of the Chess brothers] said 'You'd be surprised.' . . . Everybody's records came out before mine. [Macomba house vocalist] Andrew Tibbs had two records before me. . . . But when they released mine, it hit the ceiling." Muddy remembered about his first disc, "I Can't Be Satisfied," backed with "Feel Like Going Home" [September 1948]. "I had a hot blues out, man. I'd be driving my truck and whenever I'd see a neon beer sign, I'd stop, go in, look at the jukebox, and see my record on there. . . . Pretty soon I'd hear it walking along the street. I'd hear it driving along the street."

Encouraged by success and the abandonment of the blues market by RCA and Columbia, in December 1949 the Chess brothers bought out their partner Evelyn Aron, changed the name of the company to Chess, and released a series of Muddy Waters sides that became hits on the "race" charts. They first cut "Rollin' Stone" backed by the Robert Johnson tune "Walkin' Blues," followed the next year with "Long Distance Call" and "Honey Bee." By the mid-1950s, Waters had defined the raucous, urbanized, electric Delta blues, recording "Got My Mojo Working," the Delta standard "Rollin' and Tumblin'," "Mad Love," "(I'm Your) Hoochie Coochie Man," "I Just Wanna Make Love to You," and "I'm Ready," among many others. His group in the early 1950s, which included Otis Spann on piano, Little Walter on harmonica, Jimmy Rogers on guitar, and Leroy ("Baby-Face") Foster on drums, stands out as one of the most explosive R&B units ever assembled.

The Wolf

Chester ("Howlin' Wolf") Burnett, another Chess discovery, rivaled Muddy Waters with a raw, electrified Delta blues. A teenaged Burnett, living on Young's and Morrow's plantation near Ruleville, Mississippi, in 1926, met Charley Patton, who lived nearby on Will Dockery's plantation. As he told writer Pete Welding, "Charley Patton started me off playing. He took a liking to me, and I asked him would he learn me, and at night, after I'd get off work, I'd go and hang around." A few years later he listened to the country yodeling of another Mississippian, Jimmie Rodgers, and he decided to emulate the white singer. Never mastering the yodeling technique with his harsh, raspy voice, the blues singer earned a series of nicknames for his distinctive style, which included "Bull Cow," "Foot," and "The Wolf." "I just stuck to Wolf. I could do no yodelin' so I turned to howlin'," remembered Burnett. To perfect his raspy blues, Howlin' Wolf traveled across the Delta during the next two decades and played with the legendary blues artists of the area, including Robert Johnson and Rice Miller (also known as Sonny Boy Williamson II).

In 1948, at age thirty-eight, the Wolf plugged his Delta blues into an electric amplifier and in West Memphis formed an electric band, the House Rockers, who at times included harp players James Cotton and Little Junior Parker. The Wolf and his band landed a regular spot on radio station KWEM and began to attract attention.

Four years later, the Wolf joined the exodus to Chicago. At first, remembered Burnett's guitarist Hubert Sumlin, "He stayed at Muddy [Waters'] house for about two months. And Muddy introduced him around. Muddy was on the road a good bit in those days, so he took Wolf and introduced him to Sylvio, Bobby, and Mutt at the Zanzibar, and Ray and Ben Gold at the 708 Club. When Muddy went on the road, Wolf just stepped in his shoes in [those] three places."

A competition began to develop between Waters and the Wolf, who quickly established himself among the Chicago R&B crowd. Sumlin pointed out that, "Ever since the Wolf came to Chicago and started taking over, Muddy didn't like him too well. A kind of rivalry started up between them about who was the boss of the blues."

Willie Dixon, hired by the Chess brothers in 1950 as a songwriter and talent scout, recalled "Every once in a while [the Wolf] would mention the fact, 'Hey man, you wrote that [song] for Muddy. How come you won't write me one like that?' But when you write one for him he wouldn't like it." Dixon "found out that all I could do was use backward psychology and tell him, 'Now here's one I wrote for Muddy, man.' 'Yeah, man, let me hear it. Yeah, that's the one for me.' And so, I'd just let him have it."

The Wolf scored a series of hits with Dixon's songs and traditional blues standards that would influence the course of rock-and-roll. He recorded his calling card, "Moanin' at Midnight"; "Killing Floor," later recorded by Jimi Hendrix; "How Many More Years," which became Led Zeppelin's "How Many More Times"; "I Ain't Superstitious," covered by Jeff Beck; and "Smokestack Lightnin'," later popularized by the Yardbirds.

Wolf's stage performances presaged later rock-and-roll antics. At the end of one performance, he raced toward a wing of the stage, took a flying leap, and grabbed onto the stage curtain, still singing into his microphone. As the song built to a climax, the Wolf scaled the curtain; as the song drew to a close, he slid down the drapery. He hit the floor just as the song ended, to the screams of the audience. Recalled Sam Phillips, the genius behind Sun Records who recorded a few Howlin' Wolf songs and sold them to Chess, "God, what it would be worth on film to see the fervor in that man's face when he sang. His eyes would light up, you'd see the veins come out on his neck and, buddy, there was nothing on his mind but that song. He sang with his damn soul."

Bo Diddley and Other Chess Discoveries

The Chess brothers recorded other hard-driving rhythm-and-blues performers from the Delta. Born Otha Ellas Bates McDaniel in McComb, Mississippi, on December 30, 1928, Bo Diddley moved to the Windy City with his family when he was eight years old. "Oh, I played street corners until I was nineteen or twenty, from about fifteen on," he told rock critic and musician Lenny Kaye. "Then I walked the streets around Chicago for about twelve years, before I got somebody to listen to me." Eventually, he landed a job at the 708 Club, and in June 1955, he signed with Chess Records, where reputedly Leonard Chess named him Bo Diddley after a local comedian. That year, Diddley hit the R&B charts with "Bo Diddley" and "I'm a Man" and subsequently with "Mona," "You Can't Judge a Book by Its Cover," and "Say Man." Though appealing to rock-and-roll fans, Diddley stood firmly rooted in the electrified Delta sound. The striking similarity between his "I'm a Man" and Muddy Waters's "Mannish Boy," both recorded in 1955, attests to Bo Diddley's Delta underpinnings.

Chess also recorded two pioneers of the amplified harmonica: Aleck "Rice" Miller (Sonny Boy Williamson II) and Marion Walter Jacobs, otherwise known as Little Walter. Miller was the undisputed king of the blues harmonica, who gained popularity through his long-running *King Biscuit Time*, a daily fifteen-minute radio show on station KFFA, broadcast from Helena, Arkansas. Although already a popular artist when signing with Chess in 1955, Sonny Boy cut a number of now-classic singles for the Chicago label including "One Way Out," which the Allman Brothers later covered. Walter grew up in the cotton fields of Louisiana. He learned to play the harmonica (the harp, as he called it) during his teens, patterning himself after Miller. A year

Little Walter Jacobs at the Chess Studios, circa 1960. Photo courtesy of Living Blues Archival Collection, University of Mississippi Blues Archive/MCA Records.

after World War II, Little Walter left home and reached Chicago, where he joined the Muddy Waters band. In 1952, backed by the Muddy Waters group, he hit the chart with "Juke," which remained in the R&B Top Ten for fourteen weeks. Little Walter quickly formed his own band, the Night Cats, and followed with several others culminating in 1955 with his biggest commercial success "My Babe," a Willie Dixon composition based on the gospel song "This Train."

Leonard Chess snagged Aleck "Rice" Miller (Sonny Boy Williamson II), the idol of Little Walter and the undisputed king of the blues harmonica. His band included the Muddy Waters outfit and, sometimes, Robert Jr. Lockwood, who had learned guitar from Robert Johnson and for two years had played with Williamson on *King Biscuit Time* radio show. Though already a popular artist when signing with Chess in

1955, Sonny Boy cut a number of now-classic singles for the Chicago label including "One Way Out," which the Allman Brothers later covered.

By the mid-1950s, the Chess brothers had offered a new blues sound to record buyers. As Billy Boy Arnold, the harp player who backed Bo Diddley on his first Chess recording explained, blues "changed drastically from 1940 to 1950. . . . The saxophone players couldn't hardly get jobs. And piano was just about obsolete," with the notable exception of Otis Spann in the Muddy Waters band. In their place, continued Arnold, Chicago blues during the 1950s featured "that harmonica blastin' on the amplifiers. Two guitars strumming behind 'em. . . . Electric blues and harmonica and Muddy's type of country singing and low-down blues was at its pinnacle at that time." In the Windy City, the entrepreneurial Chess brothers had captured the new sound on vinyl and helped make popular the guitar-driven, amplified blues, which reflected postwar America and formed the bedrock of rock-and-roll.

Modern Records: B. B. King, Elmore James, and John Lee Hooker

Other Jewish immigrants, who lived in many of the same poor urban areas as African Americans and started R&B record labels in other cities, competed with the Chess brothers to popularize electric blues. They included Syd Nathan, who established the King label; Herman Lubinsky, who started Savoy Records; and Hy Weiss, a onetime distributor of Chess Records, who opened Old Town Records in New York City with his brother Sam. "We were people who had an understanding" with the African-American musicians, asserted Dave Usher, a Jewish music entrepreneur who worked as a talent scout for the Chess brothers.

Modern Records and its various subsidiaries, owned by two Jewish brothers, Saul and Jules Bihari of Los Angeles, gave Chess Records its stiffest competition in the search for R&B talent. During the late 1940s and early 1950s, the Bihari brothers made numerous scouting trips to the Mississippi Delta. They also commissioned pianist Ike Turner as a talent scout. Turner was then the leader of the Rhythm Kings, and he later gained fame as half of the Ike and Tina Turner duo.

The Biharis signed one of the most successful rhythm-and-blues artists, Riley "Blues Boy" King. Born on a cotton plantation near Indianola, Mississippi, the heart of the Delta, King was forced into the fields at age nine, working for $15 a month. "I guess the earliest sound of blues that I can remember was in the fields while people would be pickin' cotton or choppin' or somethin,'" King told *Living Blues*. "Usually one guy would be plowin' by himself or maybe one guy would take his hoe and chop way out in front of everybody else and usually you would hear this guy sing most of the time. No special lyrics or anything. Just what he felt at the time. When I sing and play now I can hear those same sounds that I used to hear as a kid," he said.

As with many R&B performers, King began his musical career in the church. "Singing was the thing I enjoyed doing, and when I started in school, I sang with a group: a quartet singing spirituals," King told *Downbeat*. From his father, the fifteen-year-old King received an $8 guitar, which became the boy's constant

B. B. "Blues Boy" King. Sidney A. Seidenberg Inc.

companion. He continued to "sing gospel music, using the guitar to tune up the group I played with," he related. "When I was introduced into the army at the age of eighteen, I started playing around little towns, just standing on the corner. People asked me to play gospel tunes and complimented me real nicely: 'Son, if you keep it up, you're going to be real good someday.' But the people who asked me to play the blues tunes normally tipped me, many times getting me beer. So that motivated me to play the blues, you might say."

In 1946, after being discharged from the army, King hitchhiked to Memphis, Tennessee, and moved in with a cousin, Booker T. ("Bukka") White, a renowned Delta blues figure. He found a job at the Newberry Equipment Company, and in early 1949, he began singing Peptikon commercials on the black-owned radio station WDIA. The guitarist remembered: "This Peptikon was supposed to be good for whatever ails you, y'know, like a toothache. Anyway, they put me on from 3:30 to 3:40 P.M. and my popularity began to grow. I sang and I played by myself and I later got two men with me . . . Earl Forrest playing drums and Johnny Ace playing piano."

After nearly a year on WDIA, King, now called "Blues Boy," or "B. B." for short, signed a contract with Modern Records and its subsidiaries, RPM, Kent, and Crown. His music, now almost fully developed, fused his Delta influences with a piercing falsetto vocal style and a jazzy, swinging, single-note guitar attack borrowed from jazz guitarist Django Reinhardt and Texas bluesman Aaron (T-Bone) Walker, who himself had electrified the technique he had learned from country bluesman Blind Lemon Jefferson. Within a few years, King's new style produced dozens of R&B classics that subsequent rock guitarists have either copied or stolen, including "Everyday I Have the Blues," and "You Upset Me Baby."

Elmore James eventually joined B. B. King at Modern Records. Born on a farm near Richland, Mississippi, on January 27, 1918, James taught himself guitar by stringing a broom wire to a wall of his cabin and plunking on it. He listened to Delta giants such as Robert Johnson and Charley Patton; by the late 1940s, he had become a master of the slide guitar. Trumpet Records, started in Jackson, Mississippi, by Lillian McMurry, first recorded James. In 1952, the company released James's gut-wrenching, slashing version of Robert Johnson's "Dust My Broom." The next year, the Bihari brothers lured Elmore to Chicago, where he began to record for the Meteor label, another subsidiary of Modern. His output included a number of now-classic tunes such as "It Hurts Me Too," "The Sky Is Crying," and "Hawaiian Boogie."

As with his fellow Delta performers, Elmore James captured in his music the pain and anguish of three centuries of slavery and tenant farming. As African-American producer Bobby Robinson suggested, listen "to the raw-nerved, spine-tingling picking of the guitar and the agonized screams and the soul-stirring of Elmore James. Close your eyes, you'll see the slave ships, the auction blocks, the cotton fields, the bare backs straining, totin' that barge and liftin' that bale. You will smell the sweat, feel the lash, taste the tears and see the blood, and relive 300 years of the blues."

The Biharis also recorded John Lee Hooker, the Delta-born guitarist who traveled north to Detroit during the postwar era. Hooker learned guitar from his stepfather Will Moore, who had performed with Charley Patton on Dockery's plantation. He sang with various gospel groups in the Delta, left home by age fourteen, and in 1943 moved to Detroit. "At that time jobs weren't hard to get, it was during the war," recalled Hooker. "Good money, too. You could go anywhere any day and get a job, nothing to worry about too much." In the Motor City, Hooker worked by day as an orderly, and as a janitor at the Dodge automobile factory and Comco Steel, and at night played in various Detroit nightclubs. After a few years, he boasted, "I became the talk of the town around at the house parties. Finally I met this very, very great musician, who I loved so much, I treasured him like I would a piece of gold, the great T-Bone Walker. He was the first person to get me my electric guitar."

In October 1948, he was spotted by record distributor Bernie Besman, who recorded Hooker on his Sensation label. For his first single, he recorded "Boogie Chillin'," an electric, chantlike, dark, superstitious-sounding stomp that vividly described black Detroit's main thoroughfare, Hastings Street. According to Hooker, the single "caught fire. It was ringin' all around the country. When it come out, every juke box you went to, every place you went to, every drug store you went, everywhere you went, department stores, they were playin' it in there." Hooker followed with such rhythm-and-blues chart climbers as "Hobo Blues," "Crawling King Snake," and "I'm in the Mood," which label owner Besman leased to Modern Records.

Other Independents

African-American disc jockey Vivian Carter and her husband James Bracken founded Vee Jay Records of Chicago in 1953. Noting the success that Chess and Modern had achieved with the electrified Delta blues, they jumped into the R&B field with Jimmy Reed. Born on a plantation near Dunleith, Mississippi, Reed discovered the guitar with friend and later backup musician Eddie Taylor, whose style derived from Charley Patton and Robert Johnson. He learned harmonica by "listening to Sonny Boy Williamson [Rice Miller]. . . . I'd slip out of the fields and go up to the house to listen to them do the fifteen minutes he had to do over the radio show. He was broadcastin' for King Biscuit flour out of Helena, Arkansas." In 1941, Reed headed toward Chicago, where he worked at various steel mills and foundries. During his breaks and lunch hours, he practiced one-chord, Delta guitar shuffles and a laid-back vocal style that masked the biting lyrics of songs like "Big Boss Man." In 1953, after being rejected by Leonard Chess, Reed signed with the newly organized Vee Jay Records. He first topped the R&B charts in 1955 with "You Don't Have to Go" and followed with a series of hits that included "Ain't That Lovin' You Baby," "Hush-Hush," "Honest I Do," and "Take Out Some Insurance on Me Baby," the last covered by the Beatles in their early years. By the early 1960s, Reed had charted on the pop chart with eleven songs.

Small, independent record companies in Los Angeles, the new home of thousands of African Americans who had migrated to the city during World War II to secure jobs, specialized in different styles of the new R&B music. Aladdin Records, begun by brothers Leo and Edward Mesner, recorded a postwar sound that spanned the relaxed vocal stylings of Charles Brown and the more jumpy blues of Amos Milburn, who hit the charts in the early 1950s with songs about alcohol. In 1956, the company released Shirley and Lee's "Let the Good Times Roll," which became a rallying cry for rock-and-rollers.

In 1945, Lew Chudd established Imperial Records in Los Angeles and achieved success with the barrelhouse, rolling piano of Antoine "Fats" Domino. Born in New Orleans, Domino learned to play piano at age nine, and as a teenager worked in a bedspring factory by day and in local bars at night. He quickly mastered the New Orleans piano style and in 1949 signed with Imperial. He debuted with the single "Fat Man," which sold one million copies. Domino followed with a string of hits, including "Ain't That a Shame," "Blueberry Hill," "Blue Monday," and "I'm Walkin'." From 1949 to

1962, Fats had forty-three records that made the *Billboard* charts, twenty-three gold records, and record sales of sixty-five million units.

R&B record companies arose in cities other than Chicago and Los Angeles. In Cincinnati, Syd Nathan set up King Records in an abandoned icehouse and recorded the jump blues of Bill Doggett and big band–influenced vocalists such as Lonnie Johnson, Ivory Joe Hunter, and Wynonie "Mr. Blues" Harris. In 1952, African-American entrepreneur Don Robey bought the Memphis-based Duke Records and scored hits with the smooth-voiced, gospel-influenced Bobby "Blue" Bland and teen star Johnny Ace, a former member of the B. B. King band. In Newark, New Jersey, Herman Lubinsky jumped into the R&B field, adding rhythm-and-blues vocalists like Nappy Brown and Big Maybelle to his jazz record label, Savoy.

By the mid-1950s, dozens of independent companies in the major urban areas of the United States had begun to grab a market share of the record industry through R&B. In 1953, the independents already accounted for more than 80 percent of the R&B product. In just two more years, they produced 92 percent of all R&B releases, cornering an emerging market.

The R&B Market

The market for the new sound expanded with the number of African Americans who flooded into northern and western cities during and after World War II. The migrants, some of them having extra cash for the first time, looked for entertainment but faced a number of obstacles. "Harlem folks couldn't go downtown to the Broadway theaters and movie houses," recalled Ahmet Ertegun, cofounder of Atlantic Records. "Downtown clubs had their ropes up when they came to the door. They weren't even welcome on Fifty-Second Street where all the big performers were black. . . . Even radio was white-oriented. You couldn't find a black performer on network radio. And when it came to disc jockeys on the big wattage stations, they wouldn't play a black record. We had a real tough time getting our records played—even Ruth Brown, who didn't sound particularly black."

For their leisure, some African Americans in urban areas frequented segregated clubs such as the Roosevelt in Pittsburgh, the Lincoln in Los Angeles, the Royal in Baltimore, Chicago's Regal, the Howard in Washington, and the now-famous Apollo Theater in New York City. The owners of Town Hall, the only large dance hall in Philadelphia that admitted African Americans, claimed that "swollen Negro paychecks at local war plants and shipyards" helped increase their profits. Other African Americans went to segregated taverns and demanded music by African-American artists on the jukeboxes.

The majority of migrants, bound closer to home by their families, found entertainment through the record. As Ahmet Ertegun suggested, most "black people had to find entertainment in their homes—and the record was it." They bought 78-rpm discs by their favorite artists in furniture stores, pharmacies, shoeshine stands, and other local businesses. Most favored the electrified R&B sound. "The black people, particularly the black people I knew," Art Rupe, the owner of Specialty Records, recalled of the late 1940s, "looked down on country music. Among themselves, the blacks called country blues 'field nigger' music. They wanted to be citified."

At first, only African Americans bought R&B discs. Johnny Otis, a white band-leader who grew up in a black section of Berkeley, California, and later helped many African-American artists rise to stardom, noticed the trend: "As far as black music was concerned we had what was known as race music. Race music was Big Bill Broonzy, Peetie Wheatstraw, and things like that. Now, these things were very much part of the black community but they didn't occur anywhere else and these cats could hardly make a living plying their trade." A successful rhythm-and-blues recording generally sold a maximum of 400,000 copies and, according to Jerry Wexler of Atlantic Records, "Sales were localized in ghetto markets. There was no white sale, and no white radio play."

During the early 1950s, more and more white teenagers began to become aware of R&B and started to purchase the music. At first, young southern whites began to buy records by African-American artists. As Jerry Wexler observed about his experience in the early 1950s, "We became aware that Southern whites were buying our records, white kids in high school and college." In California, at the same time, Johnny Otis saw the changing demographics of the R&B audience, which was becoming dotted with white faces. In 1952, the Dolphin Record store in Los Angeles, which specialized in R&B records, reflected the trend by reporting 40 percent of its sales to whites. Eventually, white teens in all parts of the country turned to rhythm and blues. In April 1955, Mitch Miller, then head of Columbia Records and later famous for the sing-along craze he masterminded, complained that "rhythm-and-blues songs are riding high." This "'rock-and-roll' began among Negro people, was first recorded by Negro performers and had its following among Negroes in the South and also Negro urban areas in the North." But Miller noticed that "suddenly millions of white teenagers who buy most of the 'pop' records in America have latched onto rhythm and blues."

From R&B to Rock-and-Roll: Little Richard and Chuck Berry

The white teens who bought R&B records favored a few showmen who delivered the most frenetic, hard-driving version of an already spirited rhythm and blues that became known as rock-and-roll. They especially idolized young R&B performers with whom they could identify. By 1955, Muddy Waters had turned forty, Howlin' Wolf was forty-six, Sonny Boy Williamson was fifty-six, John Lee Hooker was thirty-five, B. B. King was thirty, and Elmore James was thirty-seven.

Little Richard and Chuck Berry, significantly younger and wilder than most R&B performers, became heroes to white teens who had discovered rhythm and blues. Little Richard, born Richard Penniman in Macon, Georgia, on December 5, 1932, sang in a Baptist church choir as a youth and traveled with his family gospel troupe, the Penniman Family. He joined various circuses and traveling shows, and in the Broadway Follies met gospel/R&B shouter Billy Wright, who secured a recording contract from Camden Records for the eighteen-year-old Little Richard. In October 1951, Richard cut eight sides for Camden, which featured boogie-woogie and urban blues numbers in the style of Billy Wright.

The next year a local tough shot and killed Little Richard's father, the owner of the Tip In Inn. To support the family, Richard washed dishes in the Macon

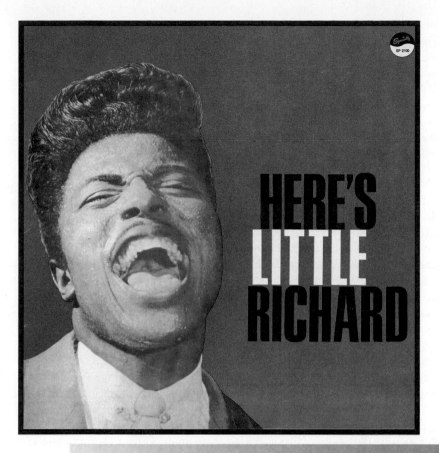

The fabulous Little Richard. *Permission by Specialty Records*.

Greyhound Bus station by day and at night sang with his group, the Upsetters, at local theaters for $15 a show. "We were playing some of Roy Brown's tunes, a lot of Fats Domino tunes, some B. B. King tunes and I believe a couple of Little Walter's and a few things by Billy Wright," remembered Little Richard.

After a few years of one-night stands in southern nightclubs, Penniman began to change his style. He transformed himself from a traditional R&B singer into a wild-eyed, pompadoured madman who crashed the piano keys and screamed nonsensical lyrics at breakneck speed. Richard later recalled that "it was funny. I'd sing the songs I sing now in clubs, but the black audiences just didn't respond. They wanted blues stuff like B. B. King sings. That's what they were used to. I'd sing 'Tutti Frutti' and nothing. Then someone would get up and sing an old blues song and everyone would go wild."

On the advice of rhythm-and-blues singer Lloyd Price of "Lawdy Miss Clawdy" fame, Richard sent a demo tape of two rather subdued blues tunes to Art Rupe at

Specialty Records in Los Angeles, which had recorded Price as well as R&B artists like Roy Milton. The tape, according to Specialty's musical director Bumps Blackwell, was "wrapped in a piece of paper looking as though someone had eaten off it." Blackwell opened the wrapper, played the tape, and recommended that Rupe sign Little Richard.

Richard arrived in New Orleans on September 14, 1955, for his first Specialty recording session. Little Richard reminisced: "I cut some blues songs. During a break in the session, someone heard me playing 'Tutti Frutti' on the piano and asked about the song. We ended up recording it and it sold 200,000 copies in a week and a half." And a legend was born. During the next three years, Richard cut a wealth of rock standards, which defined the new music: "Long Tall Sally," "Slippin' and Slidin'," "Rip It Up," "Ready Teddy," "The Girl Can't Help It," "Good Golly Miss Molly," "Jenny, Jenny," "Keep a Knockin'," and "Lucille."

Little Richard, dressed in flamboyant clothing with a pompadour hairstyle and makeup, delivered his music accompanied by a wild stage show. His band "the Upsetters wasn't just a name; when we'd go into a place, we'd upset it! We were the first band on the road to wear pancake makeup and eye shadow, have an earring hanging out of our ear and have our hair curled in process," said drummer Charles Conner. "Richard was the only guy in the band that was actually like that, but he wanted us to be different and exciting."

If anyone besides Little Richard could claim to be the father of rock-and-roll, it would be Chuck Berry. Berry, unlike almost all other R&B musicians, spent his youth in a sturdy brick house on a tree-lined street in the middle-class outskirts of St. Louis. He first sang gospel at home with his family. As he wrote in his autobiography, "Our family lived a block and a half from our church, and singing became a major tradition in the Berry family. As far back as I can remember, mother's household chanting of those gospel tunes rang through my childhood. The members of the family, regardless of what they were doing at the time, had a habit of joining with another member who would start singing, following along and harmonizing. Looking back I'm sure that my musical roots were planted, then and there."

The young Berry soon heard a different music on the radio. "The beautiful harmony of the country music that KMOK radio station played was almost irresistible," recalled Berry. By his teens, Berry also had become a fan of Tampa Red, Arthur Crudup, and, especially, Muddy Waters.

After a stay in reform school from 1944 to 1947 and having held various jobs, which included work as a cosmetologist and an assembler at the General Motors Fisher Body plant, Berry turned to rhythm and blues. He obtained his first guitar from St. Louis R&B performer Joe Sherman and, in the early 1950s, formed a rhythm-and-blues trio with Johnnie Johnson on piano and Ebby Harding on drums that played "backyards, barbecues, house parties" and at St. Louis bars such as the Cosmopolitan Club.

In the spring of 1955, a twenty-eight-year-old Berry and a friend traveled to Chicago, then the mecca of urban blues. He watched the shows of Howlin' Wolf, Elmore James, and his idol, Muddy Waters. After a late-night set, Berry approached Waters for his autograph and got "the feeling I suppose one would get from having a word with the president or the pope." When Berry asked Muddy about his chances of making a record, Waters replied, "Yeah, see Leonard Chess, yeah. Chess Records over on Forty-Seventh and Cottage." To Berry, Waters "was the godfather of the blues. He was perhaps the greatest inspiration in the launching of my career."

Chuck Berry took Muddy Waters' advice. The next day he rushed to the Chess offices and talked with Leonard Chess, who asked for a demo tape of original songs within a week. Berry returned with a tape that included a country song, "Ida Red." Chess, recalled Berry, "couldn't believe that a country tune (he called it a 'hillbilly song') could be written by a black guy. He wanted us to record that particular song." In the studio, on the advice of Willie Dixon, Berry added "a little blues" to the tune, renamed it "Maybelline," after the trade name on a mascara box in the corner of the studio, and backed it with the slow blues, "Wee Wee Hours."

Berry convinced Chess to release "Maybelline," a country song adapted to a boogie-woogie beat, which hinted at the marriage between country and R&B that would reach full fruition with the rockabillies. Within weeks, Berry's upbeat song had received national airplay and by the end of August hit the Top Five Pop chart in *Billboard*. The guitarist-songwriter followed with "Roll Over Beethoven (Dig These Rhythm and Blues)," "School Day," "Rock and Roll Music," "Sweet Little Sixteen," "Johnny B. Goode," "Reelin' and Rockin'," and an almost endless list of other songs. He embarked on a whirlwind tour of the country, playing 101 engagements in 101 nights, during which he perfected antics such as the duck walk.

By 1956, Chuck Berry and Little Richard had bridged the short gap between rhythm and blues and what became known as rock-and-roll, originally an African-American euphemism for sexual intercourse. They delivered a frantic, blues-based sound to teens, who claimed the music as their own.

Social Change and Rock-and-Roll

The popularity of a wild, teen-oriented rock-and-roll can be attributed to a number of social changes that occurred during the 1950s. Television made radio space available to more recording artists. Before the 1950s, network radio shows, many of them broadcast live, dominated the airwaves and, as Johnny Otis argued, "in the thirties and forties, black music was summarily cut off the radio." Music by African Americans "simply was not played, black music of any kind—even a Louis Armstrong was not played on the air."

After World War II, television became more popular and affordable. By 1953, more than three hundred television stations in the United States broadcast to more than twenty-seven million television sets. By absorbing the network radio shows to fill a programming void, television created airtime for a greater variety of records, including discs by African-American artists.

Many of the disc jockeys who spun R&B records became die-hard advocates of the music. B. Mitchell Reed, who jockeyed on the leading Los Angeles rock station KFWB-AM, became "enthralled with rock" during the 1950s and convinced the management to switch from a jazz format to rock when he "realized that the roots of the stuff that I was playing—the rock—had come from the jazz and blues I'd been playing before." Even earlier than Reed's conversion to rock, the Los Angeles "dean of the DJs," Al Jarvis, "wanted the black artists to be heard" and introduced them on his show.

Rock-and-roll's superpromoter was Alan Freed. Freed, a student of trombone and musical theory, began his broadcasting career in New Castle, Pennsylvania, on the classical station WKST. After a stint on a station in Akron, Ohio, in 1951, he landed a job in Cleveland on the independent station WJW. Prodded by record-store owner Leo Mintz, Freed began to play R&B records on his program. He picked the howling "Blues for the Red Boy," a release by Todd Rhodes on King Records, for his theme song and named his show *The Moondog Rock 'n' Roll House Party*.

Freed ceaselessly marketed the new music. In 1952 and 1953, the disc jockey organized increasingly racially integrated rock-and-roll concerts in the Cleveland area that met with enthusiastic responses. For the first, the "Moondog Coronation Ball," he attracted 18,000 teens to an auditorium that seated 9,000 and was forced to cancel the show. By late 1954, the successful Freed landed a key nighttime spot on New York station WINS. While there, the DJ introduced thousands of young whites on the East Coast to African-American music, consistently befriending African-American artists who recorded on small, independent labels. Freed also managed several R&B acts and appeared in movies such as *Don't Knock the Rock*, *Rock, Rock, Rock* and the now-famous *Rock Around the Clock*, which caused riots in the United States and Europe and further familiarized white youths with R&B, now being called rock-and-roll by Freed.

Young teens listened to disc jockeys such as Freed on a new gadget, the portable transistor radio. First developed in 1947 at the Bell Laboratory in New Jersey, it reached the general public by 1953. Within a decade, more than twelve million consumers, many of them teens, bought the handheld radios each year. It offered teens on the move an inexpensive means of experiencing the exciting new music called rock-and-roll.

The car radio served the same purpose as the portable transistor model. Marketed initially in the 1950s, it became standard equipment within a few years. By 1963, music blasted forth from the dashboards of more than fifty million automobiles speeding down the highways and back roads of the country. The car radio introduced rock-and-roll to many teens, who used the automobile in such rites of passage as the school prom and the first date. In 1956 a nervous, clammy-palmed youth, sitting next to his girlfriend and behind the wheel of his father's El Dorado, could hear Chuck Berry detail his exploits with Maybelline that occurred in a similar car. The car radio helped deliver rock-and-roll to a mobile, young, car-crazy generation.

The civil rights movement helped make possible the acceptance of African American–inspired music by white teens. In 1954, at the advent of rock-and-roll, the Supreme Court handed down *Brown* v. *Board of Education of Topeka*. Convinced by the arguments of Thurgood Marshall, counsel for the National Association for the Advancement of Colored People (NAACP) and later a Supreme Court justice himself, the Court unanimously banned segregation in public schools and ordered school districts to desegregate. "In the field of public education," Chief Justice Earl Warren contended, "the doctrine of 'separate but equal' has no place. Separate educational facilities are inherently unequal." By overturning the "separate but equal" doctrine of

Elizabeth Eckford ignores the hostile screams and stares of fellow students on her first day of school, September 6, 1957. She was one of the nine negro students whose integration into Little Rock's Central High School was ordered by a Federal Court following legal action by the NAACP. CORBIS—NY. © Bettmann/CORBIS All Rights Reserved.

the 1896 *Plessy* v. *Ferguson* case, the Court had strongly endorsed African–American rights and had helped start a civil rights movement that would foster an awareness and acceptance of African-American culture, including the African American–based rock-and-roll.

The number of youths who would feel the impact of the *Brown* decision was growing rapidly. In 1946, about 5.6 million teenagers attended American high schools. Ten years later, the number climbed to 6.8 million; and in 1960, the number of teens increased to 11.8 million. Observers called it the "wartime baby boom."

Many of these teens enjoyed prosperous times and had money in their pockets to spend on records. Between 1940 and 1954, the average yearly family income increased from about $5,000 to $6,200. In general, Americans had more leisure time than during the war and started to use financial credit, which had been extended to them for the first time since before the Great Depression. Most Americans spent much of this extra money on consumer items such as paperback novels, television sets, cameras, and electrical appliances. Teenagers received sizable allowances totaling more than $9 billion in 1957 and $10.5 billion in 1963, some of which was spent on records. In a 1960 survey of 4,500 teenaged girls conducted by *Seventeen* magazine, the average teen had "a weekly income of $9.53, gets up at 7:43 A.M., and listens to the radio two hours a day." Wanting to own the songs they heard, more than 70 percent of the girls bought records with their allowances. Along with other factors, an increasingly affluent and consumer-based society paved the way for the mass consumption of rock music.

By 1954, rock-and-roll was beginning to achieve widespread popularity among white youths. Teens bought discs by Chuck Berry and Little Richard and soon started to dance to the music. While touring with Fats Domino, Chuck Berry saw audiences beginning to integrate racially: "Salt and pepper all mixed together, and we'd say, 'Well, look what's happening.'" When Ralph Bass, a producer for Chess Records, went on the road with African-American acts during the late 1940s and early 1950s, "they let the whites come over once in a while. Then they got 'white spectator tickets' for the worst corner of the joint." "By the early fifties," continued Bass, "they'd have white nights, or they'd put a rope in the middle of the floor. The blacks on one side, whites on the other, digging how the blacks were dancing and copying them. Then, hell, the rope would come down, and they'd all be dancing together." The producer concluded, "You know it was a revolution. Music did it. We did as much with our music as the civil rights acts and all of the marches, for breaking the race thing down."

R&B and early rock-and-roll helped racially integrate America as white teens began to accept aspects of African-American culture. "By their new-found attachment to rhythm and blues," suggested Mitch Miller in April 1955, "young people might be protesting the Southern tradition of not having anything to do with colored people." *Cashbox* had come to the same conclusion a few months earlier. Rock-and-roll, it editorialized, "has broken down barriers which in the ordinary course of events might have taken untold amounts of time to do." R&B "is doing a job in the Deep South that even the U.S. Supreme Court hasn't been able to accomplish," the jazz magazine *Downbeat* contended the same year. "In some areas, areas where segregation is the most controversial, audiences will often be half colored and half white, not in separate accommodations either."

Racist Backlash

The integration of white and black youths elicited a racist response from many white adults. In 1956, as white Southerners lashed out against desegregation and attacked civil rights workers, Asa "Ace" Carter of the White Citizens Council of Birmingham, Alabama, charged that rock-and-roll—"the basic, heavy-beat music of the Negroes"—appealed to "the base in man, brings out animalism and vulgarity" and, most important, represented a "plot to mongrelize America."

Other whites expressed their fear of race mixing by complaining about the sexual overtones of rock. Testifying before a Senate subcommittee in 1958, Vance Packard—author of *Hidden Persuaders*—cautioned that rock-and-roll stirred "the animal instinct in modern teenagers" by its "raw savage tone." "What are we talking about?" Packard concluded, quoting an article from a 1955 issue of *Variety*. "We are talking about rock-'n'-roll, about 'hug' and 'squeeze' and kindred euphemisms which are attempting a total breakdown of all reticences about sex." *Cashbox* similarly editorialized that "really dirty records" had been "getting airtime" and suggested that companies "stop making dirty R&B records." Russ Sanjek, later vice president of Broadcast Music, Inc. (BMI), which initially licensed most rock songs, explained the white fear of possible white and African-American sexual relations: "It was a time when many a mother ripped pictures of Fats Domino off her daughter's bedroom wall. She remembered what she felt toward her Bing Crosby pinup, and she didn't want her daughter screaming for Fats."

A few adults defended the music of their children. In 1958, one mother from Fort Edward, New York, found that rock eased the boredom of her housework: "After all, how much pep can you put into mopping the floor to 'Some Enchanted Evening,' but try it to 'Sweet Little Sixteen' by Chuck Berry and see how fast the work gets done. (I know the above is silly, but I just had to write it because it really is true, you know.)" She added, "Rock-and-roll has a good beat and a jolly approach that keeps you on your toes."

To jazz innovator William "Count" Basie, the uproar over rock reminded him of the racist slurs hurled at his music two decades earlier. After living through the "swing era of the late 1930s when there was a lot of screaming, pretty much like the furor being stirred up today," he remembered "one comment in the 1930s, which said 'jam sessions, jitterbugs, and cannibalistic rhythm orgies are wooing our youth along the primrose path to hell.' The funny thing is, a lot of the kids who used to crowd around the bandstand while we played in the 1930s are still coming around today to catch us. A lot of them are parents in the PTA, and leading citizens."

Many whites, rejecting the Count's logic, tried to waylay expected integration by outlawing rock-and-roll. In 1955, the Houston Juvenile Delinquency and Crime Commission sent local DJs a list of nearly 100 songs that it considered objectionable, all of them by African-American artists. Their list included "Honey Love" by the Drifters, "Too Much Lovin" by the Five Royales, "Work with Me Annie" by Hank Ballard and the Midnighters, and Ray Charles's "I Got a Woman." R&B/blues singer Jimmy Witherspoon, living in Houston at the time, felt that "the blacks were starting a thing in America for equality. The radio stations and the people in the South were fighting us. And they were hiring program directors to program the tunes. . . . They banned Little Richard's tune ("Long Tall Sally") in Houston."

The same year, anti-R&B crusaders in other cities followed the Houston example. In Memphis, station WDIA, the station that B. B. King had helped to popularize, banned the recordings of thirty African-American rock-and-roll singers. Radio program managers in Mobile, Alabama, similarly pledged that "the offensive will be discarded." In Long Beach, the sheriff banned "offending" records from the town's jukeboxes. In nearby Los Angeles, twenty-five disc jockeys agreed to "do everything possible to avoid public airing of records which [were] believed to be objectionable."

In some cases, racist violence erupted over the new music. In April 1956, at a Nat King Cole concert, members of the White Citizens Council of Birmingham, equating jazz with R&B, jumped on the stage and beat the performer. Explaining the incident, Ray Charles said it happened because "the young white girls run up and say, 'Oh, Nat!' and they say, 'No, we can't have that!' Come on man, shit, that's where it is." At other rock-and-roll shows, Bo Diddley reminded an interviewer that "we used to have funny things like bomb scares and stuff like that because we were in South Carolina where the Ku Klux Klan didn't want us performing."

The Music Industry versus Rock-and-Roll

The music industry also organized against rock-and-roll. Crooners whose careers had taken nosedives because of the new music bitterly condemned it. Testifying before Congress in 1958, Frank Sinatra called rock "the most brutal, ugly, desperate, vicious form of expression it has been my misfortune to hear." He labeled rock-and-rollers "cretinous goons" who lured teenagers by "almost imbecilic reiterations and sly— lewd—in plain fact dirty—lyrics." By such devious means, he concluded, rock managed "to be the martial music of every sideburned delinquent on the face of the earth." A year earlier, Sammy Davis, Jr., an African American who had achieved success with a smooth crooning style, put it more succinctly: "If rock-'n'-roll is here to stay I might commit suicide." At the same time, crooner Dean Martin cryptically ascribed the rise of rock to "unnatural forces."

Disc jockeys who lost listeners from their pop and classical programs to rock-and-roll stations similarly spoke out against their competition. In 1955, Bob Tilton of WMFM in Madison, Wisconsin, called for "some records for adults that don't rock, roll, wham, bam, or fade to flat tones." To Chuck Blower of KTKT in Tucson, the year 1955, "with the tremendous upsurge of R&B into the pop crop—the almost complete absence of good taste, to say nothing of good grammar—this has been the worst and certainly the most frustrating pop year I have ever known." A *Billboard* survey in the same year indicated that "many jockeys believe the quality of the pop platter has seriously deteriorated in the past year. . . . Several jockeys are strongly opposed to the rhythm-and-blues influence in pop music."

Songwriters in the American Society of Composers, Authors, and Publishers (ASCAP) exhibited an equal disdain for rock. Because the new music usually was written by the performers themselves, professional songwriters who had been dominant in the music industry since the days of Tin Pan Alley began to scramble for work and soon complained. Lyricist Billy Rose, then a board member of ASCAP, labeled rock-and-roll songs "junk," and "in many cases they are obscene junk much on the level with dirty comic magazines." Meredith Wilson, the songwriter of *Music Man* fame, charged that "rock-and-roll is dull, ugly, amateurish, immature, trite, banal and stale. It glorifies the mediocre, the nasty, the bawdy, the cheap, the tasteless."

To reassert their control, in November 1953, ASCAP songwriters initiated a $150 million antitrust lawsuit against the three major broadcasting networks,

Columbia Records, RCA, and Broadcast Music, Inc. (BMI), a song performance/licensing competitor that had been formed in 1941 by broadcasters and catered to R&B, country music, and the new rock-and-roll. The battle eventually ended in a congressional subcommittee, but it did little to squelch the popularity of rock music.

The Blanching of Rock

Many record executives complained about and successfully undermined African-American rockers and their music. Some leaders of the music industry personally disliked rock-and-roll. RCA vice president George Marek did not "happen to like [rock] particularly, but then I like Verdi and I like Brahms and I like Beethoven." Explained Ahmet Ertegun, who had recorded R&B artists on his Atlantic Records: "You couldn't expect a man who loved 'April in Paris' or who had recorded Hudson DeLange in the '30s when he was beginning in the business, to like lyrics like 'I Wanna Boogie Your Woogie,' and 'Louie, Louie.' He had always thought race music and hillbilly were corny, and so he thought rock-'n'-roll was for morons."

More important than their personal tastes, established record executives feared the economic consequences of a new popular music that they did not control. Outdistanced by new, independent labels that had a virtual monopoly on rock acts by 1955, they worried about their share of the market, especially when white teens started to buy rock-and-roll records en masse.

To reverse this trend, larger companies signed white artists to copy, or "cover," the songs of African-American artists, sometimes sanitizing the lyrics. Charles "Pat" Boone, a descendent of pioneer Daniel Boone, became the most successful cover artist of the era. He wore a white sweater and white buck shoes, had attended college, and idolized Bing Crosby. After hosting the "Youth On Parade" radio program on Nashville station WSIX, Boone signed with Dot Records in early 1955. The singer, though speaking out against racism, refused "to do anything that will offend anybody. If I have to do that to be popular, I would rather not be an entertainer. I would rather not have a voice."

In September 1955, Boone first hit the top of the charts with a cover of Fats Domino's "Ain't That a Shame." He continued to score hits during the next two years with other covers such as "At My Front Door" by the El Dorados, Big Joe Turner's "Chains of Love," "Tutti Frutti" and "Long Tall Sally" by Little Richard, and Ivory Joe Hunter's "I Almost Lost My Mind," among many others. All told, Boone recorded sixty hit singles, six of them reaching the number-one spot. Boone many times toned down the originals; he reworked T-Bone Walker's "Stormy Monday," substituting the phrase "drinkin' Coca-Cola" for "drinkin' wine." When covering "Tutti Frutti," Boone explained, "I had to change some words, because they seemed too raw for me. I wrote, 'Pretty little Susie is the girl for me,' instead of 'Boys you don't know what she do to me.' I had to be selective and change some lyrics, but nobody seemed to care," the singer recalled. "It made it more vanilla."

Boone, like some of the other cover artists, believed that their versions furthered the development of rock-and-roll. "R&B is a distinctive kind of music; it doesn't appeal to everybody. So if it hadn't been for the vanilla versions of the R&B songs in the 1950s, you could certainly imagine that rock-'n'-roll, as we think of it, would never have happened," argued Pat Boone. "Imitation may be the sincerest form of flattery, but that kind of flattery I can do without," countered LaVern Baker, who hit the R&B chart in 1955 with "That's All I Need" and "Tweedle Dee" and saw her songs covered by white singers.

To sell these imitations, Columbia, Capitol, Decca, and RCA employed new marketing techniques. The companies placed their product on racks in suburban supermarkets, which by 1956 sold $14 million worth of records and within a year sold $40 million of records, almost 20 percent of all record sales. In addition, Columbia and then RCA and Capitol started mail-order record clubs to further increase sales.

Many disc jockeys aided the major companies in the purge of the independent labels. Although a few such as Alan Freed refused to spin covers, most DJs gladly played "white" music. "It was a picnic for the majors," Ahmet Ertegun of Atlantic Records told an interviewer. "They'd copy our records, except that they'd use a white artist. And the white stations would play them while we couldn't get our records on. 'Sorry,' they'd say. 'It's too rough for us.' Or: 'Sorry, we don't program that kind of music.'" Danny Kessler of the independent Okeh Records also found that "the odds for a black record to crack through were slim. If the black record began to happen, the chances were that a white artist would cover—and the big stations would play the white records. . . . There was a color line, and it wasn't easy to cross."

Industry leaders even succeeded in banning some African-American artists from the airwaves. In one instance, CBS television executives discontinued the popular *Rock 'n' Roll Dance Party* of Alan Freed when the cameras strayed to a shot of African-American singer Frankie Lymon of the Teenagers dancing with a white girl.

The introduction of the 45-rpm record by the major companies helped undermine the power of the independents. Leon Rene of the small Exclusive Records outlined the effects of the new format: "We had things going our way until Victor introduced the 7-inch vinyl, 45-rpm record, which revolutionized the record business and made the breakable, 10-inch 78-rpm obsolete overnight. . . . [We] had to reduce the price of R&B records from a $1.05 to 75 cents, retail. This forced many independent companies out of business." By 1956, the new 7-inch records accounted for $70 million in sales, mostly to teenagers who preferred the less breakable and the more affordable record.

Through all of these efforts, business people at the head of the major companies suppressed or at least curtailed the success of the independents and their African-American performers. The McGuire Sisters' copy of "Sincerely," for example, sold more than six times as many records as the Moonglows's original. In 1955 and 1956, the covers by white artists such as Pat Boone climbed to the top of the charts, while most African-American artists received little fame or money for their pioneering efforts. By the early 1960s, Wynonie Harris tended bar, Amos Milburn became a hotel clerk, and Muddy Waters, Howlin' Wolf, and Bo Diddley were forced to tour constantly to make a living. "With me there had to be a copy," complained Bo Diddley twenty years later. "They wouldn't buy me, but they would buy a white copy of me. Elvis got me. I don't even like to talk about it. . . . I went through things like, 'Oh, you got a hit record but we need to break it into the white market. We need to get some guy to cover it.' And I would say, 'What do you mean?' They would never tell me it was a racial problem." Johnny Otis put the problem succinctly: African-American artists developed the music and got "ripped off and the glory and the money goes to the white artists."

The Story of Arthur "Big Boy" Crudup

The saga of Arthur "Big Boy" Crudup bears testimony to Otis's charge. Crudup, born in Forest, Mississippi, on August 24, 1905, worked as a manual laborer in the fields, logging camps, sawmills, and construction projects until his thirties. In 1941, he

Arthur "Big Boy" Crudup. Photo by George Wilkinson. *Permission of Delmark Records.*

headed to Chicago and signed a contract with RCA. Between 1941 and 1956, Crudup released more than eighty sides, which included "Mean Ole Frisco Blues," "Rock Me Mama," "So Glad You're Mine," "Who's Been Foolin, You," "That's All Right Mama" and "My Baby Left Me," which have been subsequently reworked by Elvis Presley, Creedence Clearwater Revival, Elton John, Rod Stewart, Canned Heat, Johnny Winter, and many others. By the late 1950s, Crudup quit playing. "I realized I was making everybody rich, and here I was poor."

In 1968, Dick Waterman, an agent and a manager for many blues artists, began the fight for Crudup's royalties through the American Guild of Authors and Composers. After two years, he reached an agreement for $60,000 in back royalties with Hill and Range Songs, which claimed ownership of Big Boy's compositions. Crudup and his four children traveled from their home in Virginia to New York City and signed the necessary legal papers in the Hill and Range office, a converted four-story mansion. John Clark, the Hill and Range attorney, took the papers to Julian Aberbach, head of Hill and Range, for his signature, while Waterman, Crudup, and his children "all patted each other on the back and congratulated Arthur that justice had finally been done." But, according to Waterman, "The next thing, John Clark comes back in the room, looking stunned and pale, and says that Aberbach refused to sign because he felt that the settlement gave away more than he would lose in legal action. We all waited for the punch line, for him to break out laughing and whip the check out of the folder. But it wasn't a joke. We sat around and looked at each other." Crudup, who once said, "I was born poor, I live poor, and I'm going to die poor," passed away four years later, with little money.

Though Crudup did not reap the benefits of his innovations, his voice did not go unheard. Years later, one rock-and-roll star confessed his debt to Crudup. "If I had any ambition, it was to be as good as Arthur Crudup." This admission came from Elvis Presley.

Elvis and Rockabilly

❝ I love the rhythm and beat of good rock-and-roll music and I think most people like it too. After all, it's a combination of folk or hillbilly music and gospel singing. ❞

—Elvis Presley

Rockabilly Roots

Elvis Presley, a kinetic image in white suede shoes, an oversized, white-checkered jacket over a jet-black shirt with an upturned collar and *no tie*. He violently shook his black zoot-suit pants as he gyrated his hips and legs. A sneering, rebellious expression covered Presley's face, and his greased hair fell over his sweat-drenched forehead. The singer grabbed a microphone as though he were going to wrench it from its metal base, and he barked, snarled, whimpered, and shouted into it. Elvis warded off screaming fans who pulled at his loose pants, his suit, and his shirt, lusting to tear off a piece of the raw energy that burst forth. Swaggering across the stage, he sang a sexually charged music that fused a white country past with African-American sounds. Elvis Presley, singing to hordes of adoring, frantic teens, delivered a sound called "rockabilly" that would change the direction of popular music.

White teenagers from poor southern back-grounds, growing up in the border states where black-and-white cultures stood face-to-face over a seemingly impassable chasm, concocted the pulsating mixture of African American–inspired rhythm and blues and country and western known as rockabilly. They were teenagers such as Jerry Lee Lewis, who leapt on his piano, banged the keys with his feet, and heaved his jacket, and sometimes his shredded shirt, to the audience; the more subdued Carl Perkins, writer of "Blue Suede Shoes," "Boppin' the Blues," and many other classics; Johnny Cash; who launched his career with several rockabilly gems; Johnny Burnette, the cofounder of the crazed Rock and Roll Trio with brother Dorsey and Paul Burlison; the quiet, bespectacled Texan, Charles ("Buddy") Holly; and, of course, Elvis Presley, the pacesetter of the new music, whose raw edge drove crowds to a frenzy. Despite the warnings of many horrified adults, these poor southern whites spread the message of rock-and-roll to millions of clamoring teenage fans and vaulted to the top of the national charts.

Most rockabillies never dreamed of such success. Presley, the king of swagger, the musical embodiment of James Dean's celluloid image, grew up in a 30-foot-long, two-room house in the poor section of Tupelo, Mississippi. His father Vernon share-cropped and worked odd jobs, while his mother Gladys did piecework as a sewing machine operator. When Elvis was born on January 8, 1935, one neighbor remembered that his parents "didn't have insurance and the doctor didn't believe in carrying his expectant mothers to the hospital, so Gladys stayed at home." During Elvis's childhood in Tupelo, noted a friend, the Presleys "lost their house and moved several times. They lived in several houses this side of the highway, on Kelly Street, then on Barry. Later the house on Barry was condemned. They was real poor. They just got by." In September 1948, the Presley family moved from Mississippi. As Elvis told it: "We were broke, man, real broke, and we left Tupelo overnight. Dad packed all our belongings in boxes and put them on the top and in the trunk of a 1939 Plymouth. We just headed to Memphis. Things had to be better."

In Memphis, the standing of the Presleys did not improve initially. Vernon worked for a tool company, as a truck driver, and finally, in 1949, landed a job as a laborer at the United Paint Company. Earning less than $40 a week, he paid the rent on an apartment in Lauderdale Courts, a federally funded housing project. Elvis attended the nearby L. C. Humes High School, "a lower poverty-type school, one of the lowest in Memphis," according to one of Presley's classmates. After graduating from Humes High in 1953, he did factory work at M.B. Parker's Machinists' Shop, then worked at the Precision Tool Company, and finally drove a small truck for the Crown Electric Company until he turned to music. Jane Richardson, one of two home-service advisors working for the Memphis Housing Authority, summed up the condition of the Presleys during their first years in Memphis: "They were just poor people."

Other rockabilly stars came from similarly impoverished backgrounds. Jerry Lee Lewis, who scored hits with "Great Balls of Fire" and "Whole Lotta Shakin' Goin' On," was born on September 29, 1935, on a farm outside of Ferriday, Louisiana. His father, the gaunt-faced Elmo, eked out a living by doing carpentry work and growing surplus produce on the farm. Johnny Cash was born on February 26, 1932, into a poor country family in Kingsland, Arkansas. When Franklin D. Roosevelt's New Deal came to the South, the Cash family moved to Dyess, Arkansas, as part of a resettlement program for submarginal farmers. Johnny later enlisted in the U.S. Air Force and after his discharge sold refrigerators in Memphis. The boredom of the sales job prompted him to write the classic "I Walk the Line." Carl Perkins grew up only a few miles from Johnny Cash. According to Cash, "He on the Tennessee side of the Mississippi, I on the Arkansas side. We both lived on a poor cotton farm." At age six, Perkins began picking cotton and worked in the fields for years until he could fill five 65-pound bags in one day. When writing "Blue Suede Shoes," Perkins recounted, "Me and my wife Valda were living in a government project in Jackson, Tennessee. Had the idea in my head, seeing kids on the bandstand so proud of their new city shoes—you gotta be real poor to care about new shoes like I did—and that morning I went downstairs and wrote out the words on a potato sack—we didn't have reason to have writing paper around."

The Rockabilly Sound

These poor youths combined the two indigenous musical forms of the rural American South: the blues and country music. Like the Delmore Brothers in the 1930s and Arthur "Guitar Boogie" Smith in the 1940s, Elvis Presley looked to both African-American and white music for inspiration.

Elvis listened to bluesmen of the Mississippi Delta such as B. B. King, John Lee Hooker, and Chester ("Howlin' Wolf") Burnett, hearing them on late-night radio and in the clubs along Beale Street in Memphis, one of the main thoroughfares of African-American musical culture in the South. According to blues great B. B. King, "I knew Elvis before he was popular. He used to come around and be around us a lot. There was a place we used to go and hang out on Beale Street. People had pawn shops there and a lot of us used to hang around in certain of these places and this was where I met him."

"The colored folks been singing it and playing it just like I'm doin' now, man, for more years than I know," Elvis contended in 1956. "Down in Tupelo, Mississippi, I used to hear old [bluesman] Arthur Crudup bang his box the way I do now, and I said if I ever got to the place where I could feel all old Arthur felt, I'd be a music man like nobody ever saw."

The Presley sound also was steeped in the country-and-western tradition of the South—Roy Acuff, Ernest Tubb, Ted Daffan, Bob Wills, and Jimmie Rodgers. In late 1954, Elvis, then called the King of the Western Bop, played at the Bel Air Club in Memphis with bassist Bill Black and guitarist Scotty Moore in Doug Poindexter's Starlite Wranglers. At that time, recalled Poindexter, "We were strictly a country band. Elvis worked hard at fitting in, but he sure didn't cause too many riots in them days."

Presley's first recordings revealed his dual influences: a "race" number written by Arthur ("Big Boy") Crudup, "That's All Right, Mama," and a Bill Monroe country tune, "Blue Moon of Kentucky." As Presley indicated at the time, "I love the rhythm and beat of good rock-and-roll music and I think most people like it too. After all, it's a combination of folk or hillbilly music and gospel singing." In 1954, *Billboard*, noticing the singer's musical hybrid, referred to Presley as "the youngster with the hillbilly blues beat."

Ironically, at least to self-righteous Northerners, southern whites incorporated African-American sounds into their music. "The breakthrough didn't come, as you might expect, in the North," observed Atlantic Records cofounder Ahmet Ertegun. "No, it was 'prejudiced' white Southerners who began programming R&B. They began playing Fats Domino, Ivory Joe Hunter, Roy Milton, Ruth Brown, Amos

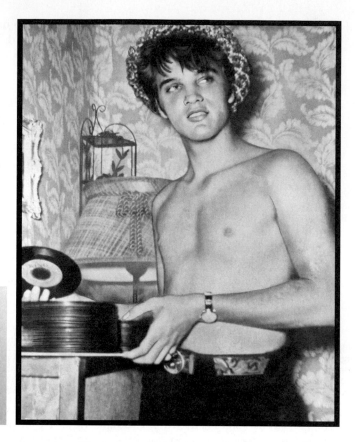

Elvis Presley was as much a fan of rock as the teenagers who adored him. Here he goes through his collection of 45s at home. Young Elvis, 1953. Corbis/Bettmann.

Milburn, because young white teenagers heard them on those top-of-the-dial stations and began requesting them. What the hell was Elvis listening to when he was growing up?" Added Jerry Wexler, another force behind Atlantic: "Despite the Ku Klux Klan and bloodshed, the southern white is a helluva lot closer to the Negro psyche and black soul than your liberal white Northerner."

As with most blues artists, Elvis and the rockabillies first found music in the southern churches. A member of the evangelical First Assembly of God Church, Elvis "used to go to these religious singings all the time. There were these singers, perfectly fine singers, but nobody responded to them. Then there was the preachers and they cut up all over the place, jumpin' on the piano, movin' ever' which way. The audience liked 'em. I guess I learned from them." At church, he listened to spirited white gospel singers, especially the Blackwood Brothers Quartet who performed and were members of the First Assembly of God Church in South Memphis.

For a few wild rockabilly musicians such as Jerry Lee Lewis, the close connection to the church not only provided musical bedrock but also engendered a sense of guilt when they turned to rock-and-roll. "Jerry, he thought he was going to hell for not preaching," mused Johnny Cash years later. "He had gone to a seminary to be a preacher, but he turned to rock-and-roll. He went on a tangent one night backstage and told us we all were going to hell for singing the kind of music we were singing. I said, 'Maybe you're right, Killer, maybe you're right.'"

Sun Records and Elvis

Many southern rockabillies recorded their brand of raucous black-and-white blues at the Sun Record Company in Memphis, which was owned by Sam Phillips. Phillips, growing up near Florence, Alabama, and working in the cotton fields as a boy, seldom noticed "white people singing a lot when they were chopping cotton, but the odd part about it is I never heard a black man who couldn't sing good. Even off-key, it had a spontaneity about it that would grab my ear." He "got turned on to rock-and-roll immediately, when it was still rhythm and blues," he later related. "I always felt that rhythm and blues had a special viability." During the early 1940s, a young Phillips landed a job as a disc jockey at WLAY in Muscle Shoals, Alabama, moved to WLAC in Nashville, and ended up at WREC in Memphis.

Phillips, earning his certification as a radio engineer through a correspondence program, built his own recording studio in a converted radiator shop at 706 Union Avenue in Memphis to record R&B artists, since, in his words, "There was no place in the South they could go to record. The nearest place where they made so-called race records—which was soon to be called rhythm and blues—was Chicago." He cut sides for such independent companies as Chess and Modern with such performers as Howlin' Wolf, Big Walter Horton, Joe Louis Hill, Rosco Gordon (who began to

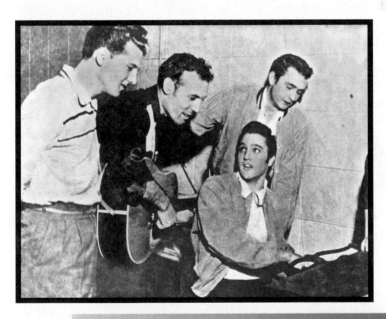

Million-dollar quartet of Sun Records. From left to right: Jerry Lee Lewis, Carl Perkins, Elvis Presley, and Johnny Cash. *Permission by Sun Entertainment Corporation.*

combine R&B and country), B. B. King, and Jackie Brenston, who with the Ike Turner band cut "Rocket 88."

The R&B orientation of Sun Records began to change during the early 1950s. Many of the best African-American performers in Memphis, such as Howlin' Wolf, moved to Chicago, the rhythm-and-blues capital of the world, and the artists remaining at Sun sold only a few discs. Phillips, still in his twenties, also sought a younger audience. As he told *Rolling Stone* magazine, he wanted his records to appeal "most especially to young whites, young blacks, and then thirdly to the older blacks. . . . There was just no music for young people then except for a few little kiddy records put out by the major labels." Faced with a declining business in R&B, Phillips confided to his office manager that, "If I could find a white man who had the Negro sound and the Negro feel, I could make a billion dollars."

Elvis Presley walked into the Sun Records studio and gave Sam Phillips the sound he sought. On July 18, 1953, eighteen-year-old Presley recorded "My Happiness," a 1948 pop hit for Jon and Sandra Steele, and the Ink Spots' "That's When Your Heartaches Begin" as a present for his mother at the Memphis Recording Service, a service of the Sun studio in which anyone could record a 10-inch acetate for $4. On Friday, January 4, 1954, he returned and cut his second disc—a ballad, "I'll Never Stand in Your Way," and a Jimmy Wakely song, "It Wouldn't Be the Same Without You." Marion Keisker, a Memphis radio personality and a front office staff person at the studio, taped the takes and rushed them to her boss.

In April 1954, Phillips first brought in Presley for an unsuccessful session on a ballad, "Without You." In late June, the Sun owner teamed Presley with guitarist Scotty Moore and bass player Bill Black and on July 5 recorded the trio. The combo struggled without results until finally a disgusted Phillips "went back to the booth. I left the mikes open, and I think that Elvis felt like, 'What the hell do I have to lose? I'm really gonna blow his head off, man.' And they cut down on 'That's All Right, Mama,' and, hell, man, they were just as instinctive as they could be." The next day, Presley and his group cut a rockin' version of the country song "Blue Moon of Kentucky."

Dewey Phillips, the WHBQ disc jockey who hosted the R&B radio show *Red Hot and Blue*, received an advance acetate of the record from the Sun owner four days later. On the evening of July 10, 1954, recalled Sam Phillips, Dewey "played that thing, and the phones started ringing. Honey, I'll tell you, all hell broke loose." Locating the teenager in a local Memphis movie house after a frantic search, the disc jockey rushed the new sensation into the radio studio. In Dewey's words, "I asked him where he went to high school and he said Humes. I wanted to get that out, because a lot of people listening thought he was colored." In the nine days before the release of the Presley record on July 19, more than 5,000 orders streamed into the Sun offices for the disc that hit the top position on the Memphis chart by the end of the month.

Elvis's live performances contributed to the hysteria. "In his first public show," Phillips remembered, "we played him at a little club up here at Summer and Medenhall. I went out there that night and introduced Elvis. Now this was kind of out in the country and way out on the highway, as they say. It was just a joint. Here is a bunch of hard-drinking people, and he ain't necessarily playing rhythm and blues, and he didn't look conventional like they did. He looked a little *greasy*, as they called it then. And the reaction was just *incredible*."

The wild reaction over Presley intensified during Elvis's tour of the South during the summer of 1955. In Jacksonville, Florida, at the Gator Bowl on May 13, rabid fans chased Elvis backstage and cornered him. According to Mae Axton, a concert promoter, substitute English teacher, and cowriter of "Heartbreak Hotel," "at least fifty girls were tearing at Elvis. They'd pulled off his coat and shirt and ripped them to shreds. They all wanted a souvenir. Elvis started running and climbed on top of the shower stall. They pulled his shoes and socks off and were even trying to get his pants off when I finally arrived with the security guard." Afterward, Presley told country singer Faron Young, who also appeared on the bill at the concert, that "them little girls are strong." "Yeah," agreed Young, "one of them you can whip; but fifty of 'em get a hold of your ass, and it's just like a vacuum cleaner sucking on you. You can't get away." Young remembered, "From then on, that was the thing to do—just to get him, tear his clothes off, pull out his hair, or something."

As Faron Young suggested, the Presley mania continued unabated. On July 4, 1955, in DeLeon, Texas, fans shredded Presley's pink shirt—a trademark by now—and tore the shoes from his feet. One female admirer from Amarillo, Texas, suffered a gash in her leg at the concert. "But who cares if it left a scar," she told a *Newsweek* reporter. "I got it trying to see Elvis and I'm proud of it. This must be what memories are made of."

Country singer Bob Luman recalled a similar scene at Kilgore, Texas. "The cat came out in red pants and a green coat and a pink shirt and socks," he told writer Paul Hemphill, "and he had this sneer on his face and he stood behind the mike for five minutes, I'll bet, before he made a move. Then he hit his guitar a lick, and he broke two strings. So there he was, these two strings dangling, and he hadn't done anything yet, and these high school girls were screaming and fainting and running up to the stage, and then he started to move his hips real slow like he had a thing for his guitar. That was Elvis Presley when he was about nineteen, playing Kilgore, Texas."

Presley also appealed to African-American teens. In 1956, Presley agreed to appear at Ellis Auditorium at the WDIA Goodwill Revue to benefit needy African-American children. "For a young white boy to show up at an all-black function took guts," asserted B. B. King, who also played at the event. When Presley took the stage, remembered emcee Rufus Thomas, "people just leapt out of their seats and started screaming. They came running down the aisles trying to get Elvis. There was complete pandemonium."

The extreme reaction to Presley came from teens, especially teenaged girls, born during and immediately after World War II, who had just reached adolescence. They perceived Elvis's stage act as a sexual call to arms. "The girls went crazy!" remembered guitarist Scotty Moore. "Elvis didn't know why; none of us knew why. When we came off the stage, somebody told Elvis it was because he was shaking his leg. That was the natural thing for him. It wasn't planned. . . . Naturally, once he found out what was happening, he started embellishing on that real quick." To the adolescent girls in the audience, like one screaming, teary-eyed Florida fan, Elvis became "just a great big, beautiful hunk of forbidden fruit."

A regional radio show helped spread Presley's fame. On October 16, 1954, he started a thirteen-month-long stint on the influential *Louisiana Hayride* radio show, which had brought initial popularity to country stars Hank Williams, Webb Pierce, Faron Young, and others. Broadcast on KWKH in Shreveport, Louisiana, to listeners as far away as California and televised locally on the weekends, by the end of 1955 the *Hayride* helped propel Presley's "Baby, Let's Play House" to number ten and "I Forgot to Remember to Forget" to the top slot on the national country-and-western chart. In 1955, observed the *Memphis Press-Scimitar*, "A white man's voice singing Negro rhythms with a rural flavor has changed life overnight for Elvis Presley."

"The Killer"

Sam Phillips, buoyed by his success with Presley, began to record other young Southerners who had the same gritty, jumpy sound. A persistent Jerry Lee Lewis, nicknamed "The Killer" in high school, joined Sun in 1956. First playing piano publicly at age fourteen with a local country band in a Ford dealership parking lot, Lewis had his musical roots in the blues and country music. As a young boy, he snuck into Haney's Big House in Ferriday, Louisiana, where blues artists such as B. B. King performed. He also listened to such country stars as Jimmie Rodgers and southern gospel music. "He'd play a lot of boogie woogie and blues, and some country" in the house, his sister Linda Gail remembered of her brother in his early years. "Other times the whole family would gather round the piano and sing gospel songs." Mickey Gilley, Lewis's cousin and later a country musician himself, remembered the same influences on Jerry Lee. "With his left hand, he'd play what the black rhythm 'n' blues players used to do, with the boogie beat," he explained. "On the right hand, you'd hear the old [country] Moon Mullican style. He put those things together."

At nineteen, a determined Jerry Lee headed for Memphis with his musical gumbo and met Jack Clement, the producer at the Sun studio. According to Lewis, Clement "told me he didn't have time to make a tape with me, but I told him he was going to do it or I'd whip him. I had driven up to Memphis from Ferriday, Louisiana—286 miles. I sold thirty-nine dozen eggs to pay for the gas. I said, 'You've got the time. I'm going to play the piano and you're going to put it on tape for Sam Phillips.'" Clement said, "Well, if you feel that strongly about it, you must be good."

When Phillips returned from a long-deserved vacation in Daytona Beach, Clement put Lewis's "Crazy Arms" on the sound system, and the Sun owner screamed, "Where the *hell* did that man come from? He played that piano with abandon," Phillips later remembered. "A lot of people do that, but I could hear between the stuff that he played and he didn't play, that spiritual thing. Jerry is very *spiritual*."

In December 1956, Sun released Lewis's "Crazy Arms," which entered the lower reaches of the charts. For the next year, Jerry Lee backed a few lesser-known Sun acts and added drummer James Van Eaton and guitarist Roland James to his band. In 1957, Sam Phillips recorded Jerry Lee Lewis and his new band ripping through an earth-shattering version of "Whole Lotta Shakin' Goin' On" for his second Sun disc, which sold 60,000 copies regionally soon after its release.

Phillips, in dire financial straits, decided to put Sun's efforts behind the single. "I knew the only hope to make Sun a successful and big company was that we take Jerry Lee Lewis and put everything behind him and use his talent to create all the other Sun personalities," remarked Judd Phillips, Sam's brother and a Sun executive. The promotion package included a spot on the popular *The Steve Allen Show*—close

Jerry Lee Lewis in Sun Records' studio with Sam Phillips. c. 1970.
Michael Ochs Archives/Getty Images.

rival of *The Ed Sullivan Show*—which on July 28, 1957, showcased Lewis frantically banging the keys, kicking the piano stool into the audience, and shaking his mop of curly blonde locks until he looked like Lucifer's incarnation. The teens in the audience erupted, while the stage crew peered in disbelief. After the performance, the switchboard lit up: Scandalized voices screamed their dissatisfaction, and shaky-voiced teenagers called to find out more about their new idol. In an uncharacteristic understatement, Lewis related: "Then I got on *The Steve Allen Show* and it busted wide open." By September, "Whole Lotta Shakin' Goin' On" reached number three on the *Billboard* singles chart. In another month, Lewis neared the top of the chart with "Great Balls of Fire."

"Blue Suede Shoes"

Lewis's success was matched by a steady stream of Sun rockabilly talents, among them guitarist-songwriter Carl Lee Perkins. Born near Tiptonville, Tennessee, on April 9, 1932, as a youth Perkins constructed his first guitar and began to perfect a unique style. Since he seldom had the cash for new strings, he once told a reporter, "I'd slide along to where I'd had to tie a knot and push up on a string 'cause I couldn't jump over the knot. Maybe if I'd been wealthy and could have bought new strings, I'd have slid down it and not developed the pushing up on the strings and I'd have sounded like everyone else."

Carl produced a sound that resembled the music of other rockabillies. He "liked Bill Monroe's fast stuff and also the colored guys, John Lee Hooker, Muddy Waters, their electric stuff. Even back then, I liked to do Hooker's things Monroe style, blues with a country beat and my own lyrics." He soon began to play music that sounded very much like Presley's. Bob Neal, then a disc jockey at Memphis radio station WMPS and later Presley's manager, recalled that he and Elvis saw Perkins perform "in the fall of 1954 and we were both struck by the sound Perkins was getting. It was very similar to Elvis' own." After hearing Presley's first Sun recording, Perkins him-

Carl Perkins with his band in 1957 on the set of the Hollywood film *Jamboree*; from left to right: Clayton Perkins (bass), W. S. Holland (drums), and J. B. Perkins (guitar). Michael Ochs Archives/Getty Images.

self felt that "it was identical to what our band was doing and I just knew that we could make it in the record business after that."

Perkins and his band, which included his brothers Clayton and Jay as well as W. S. (Fluke) Holland, signed with Sun in October 1954 and began touring from the back of a truck, charging $1 to watch the show. In 1955, the Perkins band released "Movie Magg," backed by "Turn Around"; and "Let the Jukebox Keep Playing," with the hard-bopping "Gone, Gone, Gone." On December 16, 1955, Perkins cut the smash "Blue Suede Shoes," which within four months topped country-and-western and R&B charts and reached the number-three slot on the pop chart.

As he vied for the rockabilly crown, Perkins faced tragedy on March 22, 1956. On the way to New York City for an appearance on the television show *The Perry Como Hour*, outside of Dover, Delaware, he was involved in a car crash with a pickup truck that nearly killed his brother Jay and hospitalized him with a broken collarbone. "I was a poor farm boy, and with 'Shoes' I felt I had a chance but suddenly there I was in the hospital," Carl recalled bitterly.

Perkins never attained the stardom of Presley, who, according to Perkins, "had everything. He had the looks, the moves, the manager, and the talent. And he didn't look like Mr. Ed, like a lot of us did. Elvis was hitting them with sideburns, flashy clothes, and no ring on the finger. I had three kids," added Carl. After Presley hit the chart with his version of "Blue Suede Shoes," Perkins became known more for his songwriting than for his performing and worked in the shadow of the King.

Johnny Cash

Johnny Cash became the other stellar Sun rockabilly beside Elvis Presley, Jerry Lee Lewis, and Carl Perkins. The son of a sharecropper, Cash joined the U.S. Air Force when, in his words, "I started writing songs. I wrote 'Folsom Prison Blues' in the Air Force in 1953. I played with a little group of musicians in my barracks. I was singing Hank Snow and Hank Williams songs with them before I ever tried to sing my own songs."

Cash also was attracted to the blues. "My favorite music," he recalled, "is people like Pink Anderson, Robert Johnson, the king of the Delta blues singers, Howlin' Wolf, Muddy Waters. . . . Those are my influences in music, those are the ones I really loved."

The songwriter signed with Sun Records in early 1955 and developed his own sound. As Cash told *Musician* magazine, "I kind of found myself in those first months working in the studio at Sun. I discovered, *let it flow*." He first hit the country-and-western chart with "Cry, Cry, Cry." Convincing Sam Phillips that *he* should record his next song rather than baritone singer Tennessee Ernie Ford, Cash followed with "Folsom Prison Blues." In May 1956, Cash released his signature song "I Walk the Line," which by November hit the Top Twenty. As Cash told it, "Elvis asked me to write him a song. . . . I just told a story about a shoeshine boy. I put it down and Elvis loved ['Get Rhythm']. But it came time for my next single release and Sam said, 'Elvis can't have that!' . . . So Sam released it with 'I Walk the Line,' which got the most play for a long time."

The Sun Rockabilly Stable

The Big Four of Sun—Presley, Lewis, Perkins, and Cash—supported a battalion of lesser-known but nonetheless hell-bent rockabillies. Billy Lee Riley was probably the most promising. The wild Riley, part Native American who played guitar, harmonica, drums, and bass, formed the Little Green Men in 1955. He scored hits with "Flying Saucers Rock and Roll" and "Red Hot" and drove crowds to a frenzied pitch with his onstage antics. During one memorable performance, he hung from the water pipes near the stage with one hand and clutched the microphone with the other, screaming the lyrics of a song until his face turned bright pink.

Sonny Burgess, another slightly crazed rockabilly in the Sun fold, produced raw rock that attracted a local audience. A farm boy from Newport, Arkansas, Burgess traveled to Memphis in 1955. His music, best exemplified by his minor hit "Red-Headed Woman," which sold 90,000 copies, combined a country Arkansas heritage and African-American rhythm and blues: "Yes, I really liked R&B, Fats Domino, Jimmy Reed, Muddy Waters," Burgess told a reporter.

Ray Harris, who cut "Come On Little Mama" for Sun in 1956, exhibited an intensity similar to other rockabillies. Bill Cantrell, then a Sun employee, felt that "Ray wanted to be another Elvis. He couldn't sing and he wasn't good to look at but he didn't care. Man, he was crazy. You would go to visit him and hear him practicing there on Ogden from two blocks away. He would open the door wearing nothing but his overalls and dripping with sweat. He had an old portable tape recorder and he'd go back to singing and playing and sweating. In the studio he would throw himself around with his arms like windmills. That record 'Come On Little Mama' was a triumph for the guitar man Wayne Powers and drummer Joe Riesenthal. They had to keep up with the guy." In an understatement, *Billboard* referred to his hit "Little Mama" as "excitable."

Some Sun rockabillies took a more subdued approach to their music. Roy Orbison, raised in Wink, Texas, formed the Wink Westerners, later renamed the Teen Kings, while in high school. After a year of college, the singer remembered, "I met a couple of guys who had written 'Ooby Dooby' and what convinced me I was in the wrong place at the wrong time was I heard a record by a young fellow on the jukebox called 'That's All Right.'"

Orbison headed for Memphis and in March 1956 recorded the Sun-issued "Ooby Dooby." It sold nearly a half million copies and reached number fifty-nine on the *Billboard* singles chart, which was the best chart position of a Sun disc other than hits by the Big Four of Sun. The singer, identifiable by his sunglasses, black clothes, and a near-operatic, high-pitched, ethereal voice, followed with "Rockhouse," but only reluctantly. Said Jack Clement: "I recorded 'Rockhouse' with Roy and it was good but Roy was not into what the Sun studio was capable of back then." Roy confirmed, "I was writing more ballads then [1957], but I didn't bother to ask Sam to release them. He was the boss and there was no arguing. I made some demos of things like 'Claudette,' but that was about it. I would never have made it big with Sun. They just didn't have the ways to get into the audience I wanted to go for." Orbison eventually signed with Monument Records and during the early 1960s achieved popularity with a series of songs that built to powerful, dramatic, emotional crescendos: "Only the Lonely," "Running Scared," "Crying," and "Oh, Pretty Woman."

The Decca Challenge

The major record companies competed with Sun for the rockabilly market. Decca Records took the lead, signing Bill Haley and the Comets. Born in Detroit, Michigan, Haley in 1948 formed a band, the Four Aces of Western Swing, that played on a radio show that he hosted on station WPWA in Chester, Pennsylvania. As the Ramblin' Yodeler, he recorded country music with the Four Aces and subsequently with the Saddlemen. "My mother was a piano teacher," he told an interviewer. "My dad, who was from Kentucky, played mandolin. And I suppose that was where the country influence came from."

In 1951, Haley released a cover version of Jackie Brenston's "Rocket 88," which convinced him to combine country swing music with the R&B "jump beat" of Louis Jordan. "We'd begin with Jordan's shuffle rhythm," said Milt Gabler, the Comets' producer at Decca. "You know, dotted eighth notes and sixteenths and we'd build on it. I'd sing Jordan riffs to the group that would be picked up by the electric guitar and tenor sax, Rudy Pompilli. They had a song that had the drive of [Jordan's] Tympany Five and the color of country and western. Rockabilly was what it was called back then."

"We started out as a country western group, then we added a touch of rhythm and blues," Haley recalled. "It wasn't something we planned, it just evolved. We got to

Bill Haley, 1970. Michael Ochs Archives/Getty Images.

where we weren't accepted as country western or rhythm and blues. It was hard to get bookings for a while. We were something new. We didn't call it that at that time, but we were playing rock-and-roll."

After a minor success with "Crazy Man Crazy" in 1953, Haley and the Comets signed with Decca. On April 12, 1954, they recorded "Rock Around the Clock" and followed with a remake of Joe Turner's "Shake, Rattle, and Roll," which hit the Top Ten in both the United States and Britain. In early 1955, the Comets rereleased "Rock Around the Clock," which hit the top of the chart and caused riots worldwide when it was included on the soundtrack of *Blackboard Jungle*, a movie that captured the spirit of teenage rebellion embodied by rock during the mid-1950s. The furor over "Rock Around the Clock," according to rock critic Lillian Roxon, "was the first inkling teenagers had that they might be a force to be reckoned with, in numbers alone. If there could be one song, there could be others; there could be a whole world of songs and, then, a whole world."

Haley continued to churn out hits. During 1955 and 1956, he scored with twelve Top-Forty records, including "See You Later Alligator," "Burn That Candle," "Dim, Dim the Lights," "Razzle-Dazzle," and "R-O-C-K." In 1957, he appeared in two movies, *Rock Around the Clock* and *Don't Knock the Rock*, which featured his music.

Though predating Elvis and laying claim to the first rockabilly success, Haley never wrenched the rock crown from Presley. He delivered a smoother sound than the jagged-edged music of Presley. The singer and his Comets also offered a tamer stage show. In 1956, Haley warned that "a lot depends on the entertainer and how he controls the crowd. The music is stimulating enough without creating additional excitement," an apparent jab at Elvis. Just as important, Haley's age and appearance—pudgy, balding, and thirty-two years old in 1957—compared unfavorably to that of the young, virile, swivel-hipped Elvis in the eyes of teenaged rock-and-rollers driven by raging hormones.

Decca, hoping for a larger share of the teen market, signed brothers Johnny and Dorsey Burnette along with their friend Paul Burlison who called themselves the Rock 'n' Roll Trio. Growing up in Memphis, the three met in 1953 at the Crown Electric factory, the same company that employed Presley as a truck driver. Initially they played in a Hank Williams style. But when Burlison backed Howlin' Wolf on a radio broadcast in West Memphis, the group started to blend country music with electric blues.

Beale Street in Memphis "was really happening in those days, and my dad and his friends would go down there a lot and listen to the blues guys," remembered Billy Burnette, the son of Dorsey, who continued the rockabilly tradition of his father. "They'd buy their clothes on Beale Street, at Lansky Brothers, where all the black people shopped. Right outside Memphis, there was a voodoo village, all black—real mystic kind of people. . . . A lot of real old line southern people called my dad and my uncle white niggers. Nobody was doing rock-and-roll in those days except people they called white trash. When my dad and uncle started doin' it, they were just about the first."

The pathbreaking Trio caused disturbances throughout the South with "The Train Kept a Rollin'," "Rock Billy Boogie," "Tear It Up," and "Rock Therapy." In one incident, reported the Evansville, Indiana, *Courier* in late 1956, "All during Burnette's performance, the crowd of about 2,000 people kept up a continuous howl that all but drowned out the singer's voice." When Johnny Burnette tried to leave the stage, hundreds of wild-eyed girls attacked him and "tore his shirt to bits for souvenirs." According to the *Courier*, "the singer, who had all but exhausted himself in the performance, was in sad shape when he reached the car. 'I should'a laid off that last 'Hound Dog,'" he panted. In 1956, the Trio decided to quit their jobs and moved to New York City with hopes of national success. After winning first prize on Ted Mack's *Amateur Hour*, Decca signed the group, and they recorded one seminal album before disbanding.

That same year, Decca discovered Charles "Buddy" Holly, a skinny teenager from Lubbock, Texas, who wore thick-rimmed glasses and a shy grin. Holly had heard R&B through records and on radio programs such as *Stan's Record Rack*, broadcast from Shreveport, Louisiana. As Holly's friend Bob Montgomery explained, "Blues to us was Muddy Waters, Little Walter, and Lightnin' Hopkins."

As with other rockabillies, Holly also was influenced by white country music, especially bluegrass and western swing. He listened to performers such as Hank Snow and Hank Williams and, in 1953, with friends Bob Montgomery and Larry Welborn, formed a country music trio that performed at the Big D Jamboree in Dallas and regularly played on the radio as *The Buddy and Bob Show*. By his sixteenth birthday, Buddy already had "thought about making a career out of western music if I am good enough but I will just have to wait and see how that turns out."

The new music of rock-and-roll changed Buddy's plans. In early 1955, when Elvis arrived in Lubbock for an engagement at the Cotton Club, Holly and Bob Montgomery drove the new sensation around town. Later that night at the concert, recalled a Lubbock local, Buddy and Bob "went over to talk to Elvis. Later, Buddy said to me, 'You know, he's a real nice, friendly fellow.' I guess Buddy was surprised that Elvis was so normal and would talk to him so easily, because Buddy thought of Elvis as a big star and really admired him." The next day, Holly and his group backed Elvis at the grand opening of a local Pontiac car dealership. "And when the next KDVA Sunday Party rolled around, Buddy was singing Elvis songs." Added Larry Holly, Buddy's brother, "He was on an Elvis Presley kick—he just idolized the guy. And, I mean, he sounded exactly like him. He did Elvis Presley things on the Jamboree." Holly, interested in leatherwork at the time, even crafted a wallet with "ELVIS" emblazoned in pink letters on it, and in early 1956 he left the wallet at Sun Studios as a present for Presley.

Holly incorporated Presley's style to create a unique sound. By early 1957, when he formed the Crickets with Joe B. Maudlin on stand-up bass and Jerry Allison on drums, he had perfected a light, bouncy, bright rockabilly that bore traces of the unique Presley sound.

Holly took his distinctive music to the small studio of producer Norman Petty, who had already recorded hits for the Rhythm Orchids—"Party Doll" and "Stickin' with You," released under the names of singer Buddy Knox and bassist Jimmy Bowen. With Petty's help, the Crickets hit the charts in 1957 with "That'll Be the Day," the title taken from a John Wayne line in the movie *The Searchers*. They followed with a series of fresh rockabilly tunes that became rock-and-roll classics: "Peggy Sue," "Maybe Baby," "Not Fade Away," "Rave On," and "Oh Boy."

Rockabilly Sweeps the Nation

Other record companies searched for their own acts to enter the rockabilly market. Capitol Records, a major label, signed Gene Vincent, a Korean War veteran who was born Eugene Vincent Craddock in the southern Navy town of Norfolk, Virginia. In 1956, with his band the Bluecaps, Vincent released the unforgettable "Be-Bop-a-Lula." According to the singer, he wrote the classic one day when he "and Don Graves were looking at this bloody comic book. It was called Little Lulu and I said, 'Hell, man, it's bebopalulu.' And he said, 'Yeah, man, swinging,' and we wrote the song. Just like that. And some man came to hear it and he bought the song for $25. . . . And I recorded it and told my friends that I was going to get a Cadillac, because all rock-and-roll singers had Cadillacs." From 1956 to 1957, in quest of his Cadillac, Vincent cut such boppers as "Dance to the Bop," "Bluejean Bop," "Race with the Devil," and "Crazy Legs."

Cadence Records, a small, New York–based independent company owned by Archie Bleyer, scored with the Everly Brothers. Sons of country stars Ike and Margaret Everly, the two brothers, Don and Phil, toured with their parents and performed on a family radio show that aired on several stations. In 1955, the duo headed for Nashville, where they sold a few songs to a country music publishing firm owned by country guitarist extraordinaire Chet Atkins. Later in the year, they signed with Columbia Records, which in February 1956 released two songs that flopped.

In March 1957, the Everly Brothers signed with Cadence Records after being spotted by music publisher Wesley Rose. By June, the duo neared the top of the chart with "Bye Bye Love." Their sound, dominated by bright, warm, country-style harmonies that they had learned from their father, had an R&B influence. As Don pointed out, "I loved Bo Diddley; I told Chet Atkins, 'That's what I want my guitar to sound like.' I said, 'Chet, have you heard Bo Diddley?' he said, 'Yeah.' 'What's he doing?' He said, 'Well, he's got an amplifier, but he's also got a tuned guitar.' The intro to 'Bye Bye Love' was inspired by Bo Diddley." Don added: "Phil and I are really a strict mixture of rhythm 'n' blues and country." After appearances on *The Ed Sullivan Show* as well as on other television variety programs in 1957, the Everlys followed with the now-classic "Wake Up Little Susie," "All I Have to Do Is Dream," and "Bird Dog," racking up sales of $35 million by 1962.

Imperial, the label that featured Fats Domino as its star, snagged Ricky Nelson in the rockabilly sweepstakes. The son of jazz bandleader Ozzie Nelson and singer Harriet Hilliard, the young Nelson "used to listen to the radio and longed to be a recording artist. I wanted to be Carl Perkins. I used to go and buy every Sun record that I could get my hands on back in the Fifties 'cause they were such a really good sound."

Beginning in October 1952, Ricky played himself on his parents' television series, *The Adventures of Ozzie and Harriet*. In April 1957, he covered Fats Domino's "I'm Walkin'" on the show and, after a wild teenage response to the program, Verve Records released the song. Attesting to the importance of television, the song sold 60,000 copies in three days. Ricky continued to sing one of his songs on each subsequent episode of the show, ending the segments by belting out a song at the sock hop of his television high school. When Verve Records withheld royalties, Nelson signed with

Imperial Records in September 1957 and racked up a series of hits such as "Be-Bop Baby," "Stood Up," "Travelin' Man," "Poor Little Fool," "Lonesome Town," and "Hello Mary Lou." He also scored with songs written by Johnny and Dorsey Burnette, such as "Waiting in School," "Believe What You Say," and "A Little Too Much."

Liberty Records jumped onto the rockabilly wagon with Eddie Cochran. The son of two Oklahoma City country-western fans, in 1949 Eddie moved with his family to Bell Gardens, California. While thumbing through the racks of a local record store in October 1955, Cochran met Jerry Capehart, who would become his songwriter-collaborator throughout his career. In 1956, Capehart wrote and Cochran performed "Skinny Jim," which flopped. Several months later, a movie producer in Los Angeles spotted Cochran and offered him a small part in the film *The Girl Can't Help It*, in which he sang "Twenty Flight Rock." Trying to secure better distribution for their discs, Capehart convinced Si Waronker, president of Liberty Records, to invest in the rockabilly talent of his partner. After releasing a few unsuccessful singles, in late 1958,

Cochran alternated between an Elvis-like whimper and a gravel-voiced growl in an anthem of teenage frustration, "Summertime Blues." Cochran's bopping call to arms, nearing the top of the chart, struck a chord among teenagers, who were gaining increasing power through their numbers.

The Selling of Elvis Presley

RCA Victor lured to its label the performer who became known as the king of rock-and-roll. In 1955, amid a competitive bidding war for Presley, Steve Sholes, who produced country-and-western acts for RCA, convinced his company to offer Sun Records $35,000 plus $5,000 in back royalties owed by Sun to Elvis for the rights to Presley's recorded material. Sam Phillips accepted the money and surrendered all of the Presley tapes that Sun had produced. "I looked at everything for how I could take a little extra money and get myself out of a real bind," explained Phillips. "I mean I wasn't broke, but man, it was hand-to-mouth."

Elvis had been sold to RCA by a new manager, Colonel Tom Parker. Born in 1909 in the Netherlands, Parker got his start in carnivals. Since the circus life, according to the Colonel, "was a day-to-day living," he used his ingenuity to make money. For one of his ploys, he rented a cow pasture adjacent to the circus grounds and during the night herded the cows on the only road through the field, which served as the sole exit from the carnival. When unsuspecting circus goers reached the exit the next day, they could either walk through ankle-deep manure or pay the Colonel a nickel for a pony ride through it.

By the 1950s, Parker had abandoned the circus and applied his ingenious techniques to the careers of such country singers as Roy Acuff, Minnie Pearl, Eddy Arnold, and Hank Snow. On November 21, 1955, Parker signed the new sensation to an exclusive contract. As one of Elvis's neighbors remembered, the Colonel, "in the most polished Machiavellian way," convinced Vernon to sign his son to the Colonel's management company. "Colonel Tom was a salesman, I'll give him that. He sure knew how to sell."

Almost immediately, the Colonel began to market Elvis Presley to the media. "The Colonel doesn't sell Elvis to the public, dig?" Jon Hartmann, one of Parker's employees, later observed. "He sells Elvis to the people who sell to the public, and those are the media people—the television and motion picture personalities, the executives and businessmen who control the networks, the important radio people. It's like an endless trip for the Colonel. Elvis, as a product, always in the state of being sold."

As part of his media strategy, Parker tried to sell Presley on the powerful new medium of national television. Developed during the 1920s, televised images had first been offered to the public at the end of the 1930s. In 1948, the Columbia Broadcasting System (CBS) and the National Broadcasting Company (NBC) began to offer regular television programming, soon followed by the American Broadcast Company (ABC). By 1950, more than 7.3 million Americans had bought television sets, prodded by the lure of short-term consumer credit, which had increased from $8.4 billion in 1946 to more than $45 billion twelve years later. By the time Colonel Parker began to manage Presley, there were thirty-seven million TV sets in American homes, with nearly 628

stations televising many programs that previously had been aired on radio. Americans could watch television while feasting on TV dinners, introduced in 1954, and read about their favorite programs in the newly published magazine *TV Guide*.

Parker immediately attempted to slot the photogenic Elvis on television. After being rejected by every other variety show on national television, Presley landed a spot on the January 28, 1956, airing of *Stage Show*, a half-hour variety program hosted by jazz band leaders Tommy and Jimmy Dorsey and produced by Jackie Gleason as a lead-in to his popular *Honeymooners* comedy show. Though some organizers of the show objected to the rock-and-roller, Jackie Gleason backed Elvis. Supported by Gleason, Presley appeared five more times on *Stage Show*, last appearing on March 24, 1956. On April 3, as a favor to Colonel Parker, comedian Milton Berle scheduled the singer for his program in the first of two appearances. On July 1, impressed by the reaction to Presley on *The Milton Berle Show*, Steve Allen featured Presley on his prime-time program.

Ed Sullivan, who earlier had condemned Presley as "unfit for a family audience," noticed the reaction to Presley on *The Steve Allen Show*, his prime-time competitor. He agreed to pay the new rock star $50,000 for three appearances on his show,

The new sensation. RCA Victor ad for Elvis Presley, appearing in *Billboard*, December 3, 1955. *Permission by RCA Records/Estate of Elvis Presley.*

one of the two most popular television programs in America at the time. Sullivan booked Presley for a first appearance on September 9, 1956. Fearing a backlash from his usual viewers and prodded by the publicity-hungry Colonel Parker, the television host ordered that Elvis be filmed from the waist up, allowing the teenaged television audience to only imagine the pelvic gyrations that took place off screen. Creating one of the most legendary moments in television history, Sullivan attracted nearly fifty-four million viewers, or almost 83 percent of the television audience, to his show and helped lift Presley into national prominence.

Presley's televised appearances exemplified the power of national television. By the time he finished his six appearances on *Stage Show* in March 1956, Presley had sold nearly one million copies of "Heartbreak Hotel" and generated more than 300,000 advance orders of his first, self-named album. On May 5, less than a month after appearing on the influential *The Milton Berle Show*, which attracted 25 percent of the viewing public, "Heartbreak Hotel" became Presley's first number-one single. A few weeks after singing "Hound Dog" and "I Want You, I Need You, I Love You" on *The Milton Berle Show* and *The Steve Allen Show*, Presley again hit the top of the singles chart with both songs. After Elvis debuted "Love Me Tender" on his first *Ed Sullivan Show*, RCA was forced to advance ship the single to demanding fans who made the record another number-one smash.

During the next few months, Presley continued his domination of the singles chart with a number of songs, many of which he had sung during his television appearances: "Too Much," "Don't Be Cruel," and "All Shook Up," the last two written by African-American songwriter Otis Blackwell, who had penned "Great Balls of Fire" for Jerry Lee Lewis. "It was television that made Elvis' success possible," related Steve Allen. "What his millions of young fans responded to was obviously not his voice but Elvis himself. His face, his body, his hair, his gyrations, his cute, country-boy persona."

Film became another medium to plug Presley, as it had for other male singers, from Rudy Valle to Frank Sinatra. "I knew there was an acting possibility from the beginning," explained RCA publicist Anne Fulchino. "He understood all this. He wanted it, and he had the talent." In 1956, Elvis told a television interviewer that he "wanted to go out to Hollywood and become the next James Dean." First enthusiastic about his acting career, Presley started in August 1956 on the production of his first feature-length film, *Love Me Tender*. Director and cowriter Hal Kanter expanded a role to fit Presley and included songs to help sell the picture. On November 15, 1956, the film opened in 550 theaters across the country to enthusiastic crowds, despite poor reviews of Elvis's performance.

A new Top-Forty format on radio also helped promote Presley. It was pioneered in 1954 by radio-chain owners Todd Storz and Gordon McLendon to rescue radio from a five-year decline caused by the popularity of television. Top-Forty radio involved an instant news concept, disc jockey gags and patter, and a limited play list of roughly forty hits that disc jockeys spun in a constant rotation.

Top-Forty radio, promoting the songs of only a few artists, fueled the meteoric rise of Elvis. "There was a huge change overnight," recalled Russ Solomon, founder of the Tower Records chain. "Everybody was interested [in Presley]. At the same

moment, Top-Forty radio came into play. As a result there was a very dramatic change in the way you perceived selling records. Your hit titles became more and more important."

In mid-1956, Hank Saperstein joined Colonel Parker in the Presley media blitz. Saperstein had become successful in the advertising industry through his marketing efforts for television creations such as *Lassie*, *Wyatt Earp*, and *The Lone Ranger*. Not to be outdone by his competitors, he had even stuffed plastic blowguns in cereal boxes to increase the sales of Kellogg's Cornflakes. Saperstein recognized the "universality" of the Presley appeal and began to plaster Elvis's name and picture on all types of products. "We wanted to manufacture a phenomenon," said Saperstein. "My mission was to create someone whose name and image flashes in your mind without having to think. If you have to ask, 'Who?' then we did *not* do our job." By 1957, Saperstein and Parker had saturated the American market.

If a loyal fan so desired, she could put on some Elvis Presley bobby socks, Elvis Presley shoes, skirt, blouse, and sweater, hang an Elvis Presley charm bracelet on one wrist, and with the other hand smear on some Elvis Presley lipstick—either Hound Dog Orange, Heartbreak Hotel Pink, or Tutti Frutti Red. She might put an Elvis Presley handkerchief in her Elvis Presley purse and head for school. Once in the classroom, she could write with her green Elvis Presley pencil, inscribed "Sincerely Yours," and sip an Elvis Presley soft drink between class periods. After school, she could change into Elvis Presley Bermuda shorts, blue jeans, or toreador pants, write to an Elvis Presley pen pal, or play an Elvis Presley game, and fall asleep in her Elvis Presley pajamas on her Elvis Presley pillow. Her last waking memory of the day could be the Elvis Presley fluorescent portrait that hung on her wall. All told, the fan could buy seventy-eight different Elvis Presley products that grossed about $55 million by December 1957. In addition to 25 percent of Elvis's performance royalties, Colonel Parker received a percentage of the manufacturer's wholesale price on each item.

Reactions Against the Presley Mania

The national press disparaged Presley's success, criticizing him for his sexual innuendo. In one review, Jack Gould, television critic for *The New York Times*, wrote: "Mr. Presley has no discernible singing ability. His specialty is rhythm, songs which he renders in an undistinguished whine; his phrasing, if it can be called that, consists of the stereotyped variations that go with a beginner's aria in a bathtub. . . . His one specialty is an accented movement of the body that heretofore has been primarily identified with the repertoire of the blonde bombshells of the burlesque runway. The gyration never had anything to do with the world of popular music and still doesn't." Jack O'Brien of the *New York Journal-American* agreed that "Elvis Presley wiggled and wiggled with such abdominal gyrations that burlesque bombshell Georgia Southern really deserves equal time to reply in gyrating kind. He can't sing a lick, makes up for vocal shortcomings with the weirdest and plainly planned, suggestive animation short of an aborigine's mating dance." *Time* magazine called Presley a "sexibitionist," who lived "off what most parents would agree is the fat of teenagers' heads," and *Look* accused him of dragging "'big beat' music to new lows in taste."

Government officials similarly blasted the singer for his role in the moral corruption of youths. Addressing the U.S. House of Representatives, Congressman Robert MacDonald of Massachusetts viewed "with absolute horror" performers "such as Elvis Presley, Little Richard . . . and all the other hundreds of musical illiterates, whose noises presently clutter up our jukeboxes and our airways." In 1956, U.S. Senator Allen Ellender tended "to be convinced that Americans are barbarians if the best we can offer as a symbol of our culture is bebop and rock-and-roll music."

Religious leaders, guarding the moral fabric of America, especially felt compelled to speak out against Presley. Reverend William Shannon commented in the *Catholic Sun* that "Presley and his voodoo of frustration and defiance have become symbols in our country, and we are sorry to come upon Ed Sullivan in the role of promoter. Your Catholic viewers, Mr. Sullivan, are angry." Although he had never seen Elvis, evangelist Billy Graham was "not so sure I'd want my children to see" him. Reverend Charles Howard Graff of St. John's Episcopal Church in Greenwich Village called Elvis a "whirling dervish of sex," and Reverend Robert Gray of the Trinity Baptist Church in Jacksonville, Florida, believed Presley had "achieved a new low in spiritual degeneracy. If he were offered salvation tonight, he would probably say, 'No thanks, I'm on the top.'" In his sermon "Hot Rods, Reefers, and Rock-and-Roll," Gray warned the youth in his congregation not to attend an upcoming Presley show.

Fear of increasing juvenile delinquency underlaid much of the backlash against Presley. The dark image of the alienated, shiftless, and violent street tough in a black leather jacket who dangled a cigarette from his lips had been popularized in books and films. The preoccupation with the teenage delinquent was reflected in paperbacks such as *Blackboard Jungle, Gang Rumble, The Hoods Ride In*, and countless others. It also appeared in movies such as *The Wild One* (1954), which showcased Marlon Brando as the leader of a heartless motorcycle gang, and *Rebel Without a Cause*, released the next year, which starred James Dean, who with Brando symbolized teenage rebellion.

Rebel Without a Cause, explained Stewart Stern, who wrote the screenplay, dealt with "the phenomenon of what was called in those days juvenile delinquency, happening not in families that were economically deprived but in middle-class families that were emotionally deprived. Partly, people felt it had to do with the war, the fact that so many women were working for the first time away from the home, that older brothers and fathers who would have been role models for the young weren't there, and the tremendous drive for material 'things.' When the kids saw that the material goods that were supposed to make their parents happy really didn't, they began to doubt their parents' authority," said Stern. "The lesson of *Rebel*," concluded the screenwriter, "was that if the kids could not be acknowledged or understood by their parents, at least they could be acknowledged by each other."

The "generation gap" between the baby boomers and their parents fueled a fear among adults for their children. As teens began to listen to a music based on African-American and poor white southern cultures, parents worried about the social implications of race mixing and violence. When one southern teen in 1958 declared that "I'm not afraid of Negroes, I'm afraid of parents," the fabric of society seemed to be unraveling for many adults, who had lived in a more stratified, racist society.

Many worried adults also linked the poor southern style of Presley, including his wild clothes, swagger, slicked-back hair and sideburns, to the violence of juvenile delinquency. On April 11, 1956, *Variety* connected a Presley-driven rock to a "staggering wave of juvenile violence and mayhem. . . . On the police blotters, rock-'n'-roll has been writing an unprecedented record. In one locale after another, rock-'n'-roll shows, or disc hops where such tunes have been played, have touched off every type of juvenile delinquency." The Pennsylvania Chief of Police Association contended that rock music provided "an incentive to teenage unrest," and Pittsburgh Police Inspector Fred Good felt "wherever there's been teenage trouble lately, rock-and-roll has almost always been in the background."

Teen riots increased the fear of rock-and-roll delinquents and prompted officials to bar promoters from holding rock concerts in civic buildings. In San Jose, rock fanatics routed seventy-three policemen and caused $3,000 in damage, convincing the mayor of nearby Santa Cruz to ban rock concerts. On May 3, 1958, violence erupted after an Alan Freed–hosted rock revue that headlined Jerry Lee Lewis. When police turned on the house lights before the show ended, Freed huffed, "I guess the police here in Boston don't want you kids to have a good time," and teens streamed into the street. As *Time* reported, "All around the arena common citizens were set upon, robbed and sometimes beaten. A young sailor caught a knife in the belly, and two girls with him were thrashed. In all, nine men and women were roughed up enough to require hospital treatment." Though, as *Time* admitted, "the arena site had been the site of frequent muggings in the past" and teens probably did not participate in the violence, Boston Mayor John Hynes barred rock-and-roll shows from the city. Officials in New Haven and Newark followed the Boston example, canceling scheduled Freed-sponsored shows. After a melee among 2,700 fans at a rock show, Mayor Roland Hines of Asbury Park, New Jersey, banned all rock concerts from city dance halls. Officials in nearby Jersey City did the same a few days later.

Others mobilized against Elvis Presley. In Nashville and St. Louis, angry parents burned effigies of Presley. In Ottawa, Canada, eight students of the Notre Dame convent were expelled for attending a local Elvis show. Yale University students handed out "I Like Ludwig [Beethoven]" buttons to counter the sale of "I Like Elvis" buttons. And a Cincinnati used-car dealer tried to increase business with a sign that read: "We Guarantee to Break fifty Elvis Presley Records in Your Presence If You Buy One of These Cars Today."

Disc jockeys who broadcast classical and pop music also took action. In Halifax, Nova Scotia, station CJCH rigidly forbade the airplay of any Elvis discs. Nashville jockey "Great Scott" burned 600 Presley records in a public park, and a Chicago station manager smashed Elvis 45s during a broadcast. In Wildwood, New Jersey, a local disc jockey started an organization to "eliminate certain wreck and ruin artists" such as Elvis. For many, the rock-and-roll embodied in Elvis Presley had become a menace to society that needed to be eradicated.

Elvis Goes to Hollywood

RCA Victor and Colonel Parker responded to the reaction against Presley by modifying the singer's wild act. Presley's appearance on *The Steve Allen Show* provides an early example. "We'd recognized the controversy that was building around Elvis and so we took advantage of it," said Allen. The host dressed Presley "in a tuxedo—white tie and tails—and [took] away his guitar. We thought putting Elvis in formal wardrobe to sing the song was humorous. We also asked him to stand perfectly still, and we positioned a real hound dog on a stool next to him—a dog that had been trained to do nothing but sit and look droopy." Elvis's respectable behavior on the show stood in marked contrast to his earlier hip-shaking performances and foreshadowed a change in image.

Throughout the late 1950s and into the 1960s, Presley became more subdued and more popular. In September 1957, the rising star split with two members of his original band, Scotty Moore and Bill Black, who had helped pioneer the distinctive Presley sound. Elvis recorded with them only sporadically during the next decade. After his return from the army in 1960, Presley recorded an operatic ballad "It's Now or Never," based on the Italian standard "O Sole Mio," which separated the singer even further from his rockabilly roots. "After the Army you had a totally polished performer," explained RCA executive Joan Deary. "These records ['It's Now or Never' and the 1961 number-one hit 'Are You Lonesome Tonight'] were not at all based on the same appeal as 'That's Alright (Mama)' and 'Hound Dog' and 'Don't Be Cruel.' Suddenly Elvis was just not for kids."

With an expanded audience, Presley began to sell more records. He sold more than 20 million copies of "It's Now or Never," his best-selling single. Though briefly revisiting his rock roots in his 1968 television comeback, in the 1960s and 1970s Elvis followed with thirty gold records, which were mostly pop ballads. Appealing to a wide

Elvis Presley in a promotional picture for the 1966 film *Paradise Hawaiian Style*. It is typical of the teen-action films that Elvis made in the mid-'60s. Photo by Hulton Archive. Getty Images, Inc.—Hulton Archive Photos. Hulton Archive/Getty Images.

range of record buyers, Presley sold a total of more than 250 million records by the end of his career. In the history of recorded music, only Bing Crosby neared Elvis's mark with about 200 million records sold. Frank Sinatra, the bobby-socks sensation of the 1940s, sold only about 40 million discs.

Presley also broadened his fan base by opting for a safe, clean-cut image in the movies. He starred in thirty-one feature films such as *G.I. Blues, Flaming Star, Wild Star, Blue Hawaii, Follow That Dream, Kid Galahad*, and *Girls! Girls! Girls!* Though offered dramatic roles in films such as *Thunder Road, Midnight Cowboy*, and *West Side Story*, Elvis obeyed Colonel Parker and settled for parts in movies written around songs, which for the most part abandoned gut-bucket rockabilly for a soothing ballad style that reinforced his new image. "Elvis would go ahead with the program and get the picture done," remembered D. J. Fontana, the drummer who played with Elvis from 1954 to 1968. "You see, the Colonel's thought was *don't make any waves*; don't let me have to make a deal with these people." Gene Nelson, director of two Elvis movies, recalled, "The Colonel's stock answer was just 'You come up with the money; we'll do the picture.' He wasn't interested in Elvis' latent dramatic abilities."

Presley, appealing to a wider audience, began to receive awards of all types. In 1959, the Mississippi legislature passed a resolution that lauded Elvis as a "legend and inspiration to tens of millions of Americans," who "reaffirms a historic American idea that success in our nation can still be attained through individual initiative, hard work, and abiding faith in one's self and his creator." A few months later, a joint session of the Tennessee legislature honored Presley.

The young, working-class Presley, ceaselessly marketed by RCA and Colonel Parker, was swept away by stardom. "My daddy and I were laughing about it the other day," he told a reporter in late 1956. "He looked at me and said, 'What happened, El? The last thing I remember is I was working in a can factory and you were still driving a truck.' We all feel the same way about it still. It just caught us up."

The famous star enjoyed a newfound wealth. Elvis bought a fleet of Cadillacs, including one in his favorite color—pink; a $40,000, one-story ranch house in Memphis; and then a $100,000 mansion, Graceland, for himself and his parents. He purchased an airplane, a truckload of television sets, a horse ranch, dozens of motorcycles and cars, and hundreds of gadgets, which he freely gave as gifts to his friends and employees.

The rock star paid dearly for his fame. As his popularity increased, Elvis found it difficult to protect his privacy. "Even today [late sixties] I'd be willing to bet a thousand dollars he could draw a hundred people in five minutes anywhere he went," mused Neal Matthews, one of the Jordanaires, Elvis's backup singing group. "And he knows this. It's bound to make him unhappy. He'd like to be able to walk down the street like a normal human being. He can't be a person like anybody else." The "only time he could get out, really, was at night, or if he had the night off. He'd rent a skating rink or a movie house and rent it for the whole night and he and whoever'd be around would go to two, three movies after the movie theater had closed. That's the only kind of entertainment he had. He couldn't go out."

On his 1969 tour of Hawaii with Minnie Pearl, Minnie related, "There were five hundred women there and as we got out of the taxi, Elvis grabbed my arm and the women broke and mobbed us. I felt my feet going out from under me. . . . You know, everyone wants to be number one, but that one experience was enough to convince me I don't want it." As Minnie Pearl and her husband enjoyed the Hawaiian sun, "Elvis never got out of his room except to work. They say he came down in the middle of the night to swim. He couldn't come down during the day. He had the penthouse suite on the top of that thing there and we'd get out and act crazy, having the best time in the world, and we'd look up there and Elvis would be standing at the window, looking down at us."

Eventually the isolation began to affect Presley. As early as 1956, he told the pastor of the Assembly of God Church that "I am the most miserable young man you have ever met. I have more money than I can ever spend. I have thousands of fans out there, and I have a lot of people who call themselves my friends, but I am miserable." Trapped in a creative wasteland by Colonel Parker who forced him to keep churning out B-grade movies, Elvis progressively became more despondent. "You know, you all are lucky," Presley told D. J. Fontana and his wife in 1968. "I'm so tired of being Elvis—I don't know what to do. I just wish I could do something else."

A depressed Elvis resorted to drugs. Even early in his career, Presely like many other performers at the time turned to amphetamines to deal with the hectic touring and movie schedule that he had been asked to meet. As the years progressed and his fame overwhelmed him, he turned to a smorgasbord of pills. "The drugs were a band-aid for a lack of a creative outlet," explained Elvis's friend Jerry Schilling.

Elvis's drug habit and the constant pressure of his fame sometimes led to violence. He destroyed television sets, pool cues, jukeboxes, and cars. "The temper was the hardest thing to take," one friend recalled. "One day he'd be the sweetest person in the world, the next day he'd burn holes in you with his eyes."

In the end, Elvis Presley became a larger-than-life icon to the world, which looked at him in superhuman terms. Elvis the man, a small-town Southerner with a cornball sense of humor and a sense of evangelical religion, became superceded by media expectations, which his handlers had created and which could never be fulfilled by any human being. He became the premier American icon, known in nearly every part of the globe, who could find little human interaction or peace and who needed to piece together a lonely, isolated life to exist. As singer Johnny Rivers concluded, Elvis "had created his own world. He had to. There was nothing else for him to do." His retreat into himself ended with an untimely death on August 16, 1977, at the age of forty-two.

Elvis Presley had been trapped by success. The gyrating, sneering Elvis, who taunted his audiences and worked them to a fevered pitch, had given way to a more haggard, bloated performer adorned by extravagant, sequined costumes, singing ballads to the well-dressed clientele of Las Vegas nightclubs. Sometimes the old magic sneaked through the weary flesh, but most of the original vibrancy and vitality had disappeared. Elvis was transformed from an innocent country boy who belted out a new kind of music with animalistic intensity to a well-groomed, multimillion-dollar product. The change, starting when Presley signed with RCA and becoming more pronounced during the 1960s after Presley returned from the Army, signaled the end of rockabilly. Soon teenaged crooners schooled by Dick Clark would vie for the mantle of the King.

The Teen Market: From *Bandstand* to Girl Groups

>**❝** I hope someday that somebody will say that in the beginning stages of the birth of the music of the Fifties, though I didn't contribute in terms of creativity, I helped keep it alive. **❞**
>
> —Dick Clark

"Elvis in the army, Buddy dead, Little Richard in the ministry, and Berry nabbed by the Feds," became the chant of a bewildered rock-and-roll generation. An important part of American culture just three years earlier, by 1959, rock-and-roll had lost many of its heroes. Elvis Presley had been inducted into the army, Buddy Holly had been tragically killed, Little Richard had suddenly joined a fundamentalist religious sect, and Chuck Berry had been arrested and stood trial.

Two young entrepreneurs—Dick Clark and Don Kirshner—produced a new crop of idols and a fresh batch of songs for rock-starved teens. Beginning in 1957, Clark found photogenic, well-groomed Italian teens, promoted them on his television show, and almost single-handedly created the Philadelphia sound. Only the payola scandal slowed Clark's success. A music publisher in the Tin Pan Alley tradition, Kirshner assembled teams of young, talented songwriters in the Brill Building in New York City and from 1960 to 1963 churned out hundreds of tunes that he placed with scores of budding girl groups. For nearly three years he helped set the direction of rock-and-roll. From 1958 to 1963, in the absence of Presley and other rock pioneers, two businessmen reshaped rock-and-roll and made it respectable.

Lost Idols

During the late 1950s, rock-and-roll fans either lost or rejected their heroes. On October 12, 1957, the flamboyant Little Richard renounced his jeweled bracelets and wild parties for the ministry of the Seventh Day Adventist Church. Richard had frequently threatened to quit rock. Chuck Conners, the drummer in Little Richard's band, remembered that Richard "had been talking about giving up rock-'n'-roll and devoting his life to God for a long time." Then, on his way to Australia, as Little Richard looked out the window of the plane, the engines seemed to burst into flames, doused only by the saving efforts of yellow angels. A few days later in Sydney, on the fifth day of a two-week tour, Richard walked away from rock-and-roll in the middle of a show and in front of 40,000 fans. As he told it, "That night Russia sent off the very first *Sputnik* [the Soviet Union's first satellite in outer space]. It looked as though the big ball of fire came directly over the stadium about two or three hundred feet above our heads. . . . It really shook my mind. I got up from the piano and said, 'This is it. I am through. I am leaving show business to go back to God.'" True to his word, Richard deserted his fans for Jehovah. Said the singer: "If you want to live for the Lord, you can't rock-and-roll, too. God doesn't like it." Not until 1964 during a tour of England did Little Richard again raise the standard of rock.

Two months later, twenty-two-year-old Jerry Lee Lewis married his thirteen-year-old third cousin, Myra Gale Brown, who was the daughter of Lewis's bass player. It was Lewis's third marriage. The marriage caused promoters to cancel thirty-four of the thirty-seven scheduled shows for Jerry Lee's 1958 tour of England. During his first performance, the crowd greeted the rockabilly star with silence and then sporadic heckling. "I sho' hope yawl ain't half as dead as you sound," Lewis shouted to the crowd. "Go home, crumb, baby snatcher," the audience yelled back. For more than a decade, the public censured the "Killer," who gravitated more and more toward country music.

On March 24, 1958, the king of rock-and-roll, Elvis Presley, entered the armed forces for a two-year stint and became U.S. Private 53310761. On orders from his manager, Colonel Tom Parker, he refused to sing for the army and spent his time in Bremerhaven, Germany, where he met his future wife, Priscilla Beaulieu. When discharged in January 1960, Presley concentrated his efforts on motion pictures and only in 1968 returned to the stage.

In 1959, two of rock's pioneers left the stage. On February 3, tragedy struck. Rockabilly singer and songwriter Buddy Holly, the shy, bespectacled youth from Texas, died when his plane crashed in a cornfield near Mason City, Iowa, after a show during a midwestern tour. J. P. Richardson, the disc jockey known as the Big Bopper, who in 1958 hit the chart with "Chantilly Lace," and the seventeen-year-old sensation Richie Valens (a.k.a. Richard Valenzuela), who had just scored hits with "La Bamba" and "Donna," were killed in the same crash.

Chuck Berry was forced from the music scene by a federal court. On December 23, 1959, a fourteen-year-old girl accused Berry of transporting her from El Paso, Texas, to St. Louis for immoral purposes after Berry fired her as a hatcheck girl in his St. Louis club. Testimony at the trial revealed that the girl had been a prostitute when Berry first met her and that she had come willingly to St. Louis. A judge initially found Berry guilty, but a retrial was scheduled because the magistrate referred to the performer as "this Negro." The jury in a second trial convicted Berry of a violation of the Mann Act and in 1962 sentenced him to three years in the federal penitentiary at Terre Haute, Indiana.

An automobile accident robbed rock-and-roll of two other hit makers. On April 17, 1960, after a successful tour of England, Eddie Cochran, Gene Vincent, and Sharon Sheely, Cochran's girlfriend, who subsequently wrote many of Ricky Nelson's hits, rode to the airport in a chauffeured limousine. En route near Chippenham, Wiltshire, a tire blew out, the driver lost control, and the car smashed into a lamppost. Within hours, Cochran died of multiple head injuries at Bath Hospital. Sheely and Vincent survived, but the accident destroyed Vincent's career.

The Booming Teen Market

Rock-and-roll tragedy occurred amid booming economic conditions. During the 1950s, the gross national product (GNP), the indicator of U.S. economic growth, rose from $213 billion to $503 billion. The personal per capita income in the country increased from $1,526 in 1950 to $2,788 ten years later, an increase of 82 percent. Throughout the decade, unemployment fluctuated between 4 percent and 5.5 percent.

The recording industry, reinvigorated by rock-and-roll, shared in the general prosperity. Record sales in the United States skyrocketed from $189 million in 1950 to nearly $600 million by the end of the decade. The industry sold almost half of all discs through mail-order clubs and in supermarkets, which by the 1950s had replaced neighborhood stores. In 1959, the industry chalked up almost $200 million in sales of 45-rpm records, which usually were manufactured for teens, who could afford the comparatively inexpensive discs. Though over 5,000 record labels competed for a share of the market, four major companies—RCA Victor, Columbia, Decca, and Capitol—racked up nearly 75 percent of total sales.

Reflecting a postwar trend in U.S. business, the record industry expanded into the international market with rock-and-roll. RCA vice president George Marek observed in 1959 that "rock-and-roll is popular not only in this country but it has swept the world, the world where there are no broadcasting stations even: It is relatively popular in conservative England, in Australia, India, Germany, wherever you go." An early 1960s' Decca press release described the state of the music business: "The recording industry, a fledgling during the heyday of vaudeville, has shown a steady, remarkable growth until today it stands as a major factor in the world's economy."

Dick Clark and *American Bandstand*

Dick Clark, a marketing genius from upstate New York, delivered new stars to the increasing number of rock-and-rollers. Born in 1929, Clark attended Syracuse University and studied advertising and radio, getting, in his words, a "sound education in business administration." In 1951, he landed a part-time job as an announcer for station WOLF and then worked for his father, who was station manager at WRUN in Utica, New York. A short time later, Clark decided to accept a job at WFIL in Philadelphia, at first announcing a radio show of popular and classical music. He later wrote: "I was a great pitchman. I sold pots and pans, vacuum cleaners, diamond rings, Mrs. Smith pies, the works. Eventually I landed the Schaefer Beer account. I did one hell of a beer spot."

In July 1956, Clark moved to WFIL's television station and hosted Philadelphia *Bandstand*, which showcased local high school students dancing to popular hit records. He replaced disc jockey Bob Horn, who, in October 1952, had launched the program, but four years later was forced to resigned due to adverse publicity surrounding two drunken driving citations.

Dick Clark initially knew little about the rock-and-roll music that the program highlighted. During his first *Bandstand* appearance as the regular host, Clark said he arrived on the "set at two that afternoon with only a foggy notion of what the kids, music, and show were really about. I don't understand this music."

The new host of *Bandstand* quickly became familiar with the commercial potential of the new music. "The more I heard the music, the more I enjoyed it; the more I enjoyed it, the more I understood the kids," Clark later related. "I knew that if I could

Dick Clark counts down the hits on the set of "American Bandstand," c. 1958. Photo by Hulton Archive/Getty Images.

tune into them and keep myself on the show, I could make a great deal of money."
Clark—voted by his high school classmates as the "Man Most Likely to Sell the
Brooklyn Bridge"—felt that behind his "bland twenty-nine-year-old face lay the heart
of a cunning capitalist" who wanted to "defend my right and your right to go to a
church of our choice, or to buy the record of our choice."

Clark's business savvy transformed a local telecast into a national phenomenon.
To get sponsors for the show, he "traveled the advertising agency circuit on Madison
Avenue" and eventually snagged the lucrative Beechnut Spearmint Gum account.

Bandstand, built on a solid advertising base by Clark, was nationally televised as
American Bandstand, premiering on August 5, 1957, on sixty-seven stations coast to
coast to more than eight million viewers. The show aired from Philadelphia for ninety
minutes every weekday afternoon and on Monday nights from 7:30 to 8:00 P.M. It featured 150 teenagers in the audience, many of whom danced to the popular hits and listened to the smooth patter of Dick Clark. "It's been a long, long time since a major network has aimed at the most entertainment-starved group in the country," Clark told
Time magazine. "And why not? After all, teenagers have $9 billion a year to spend."

Droves of teenaged girls responded to Clark's brand of rock-and-roll. After
school hours, hordes of pubescent girls rushed home and feverishly tuned into
American Bandstand. Usually with their best girlfriend or sister, they danced to the
music on their living-room floors, identified with the regular dancers, and fantasized
about stardom on the dance floor of *American Bandstand*. The girls flooded the show
with up to 45,000 letters a week and helped the program gross $500,000 a year and net
ratings that equaled the combined ratings of the shows telecast by two rival networks.
"We love it," gushed one girl from Charleston, West Virginia. "When I hear a
Beethoven symphony I don't feel anything. When I hear our kind of music, I feel
something way down deep, like oatmeal." In the absence of major rock stars and working on the new medium of television, the farsighted Clark had created a rock-and-roll
that emphasized the audience as much as the music.

Clark and *American Bandstand* brought a respectability to rock-and-roll that had
not existed with the suggestive, greasy rockabillies. Clark himself portrayed a prim, clean-
cut image. *Newsweek* referred to him as "genial and softspoken," and *Time* characterized
the announcer as "personable and polite, he manages to sound as if he really means such
glib disc jockey patter as, 'Let me pull up a hunk of wood and sit down with you.'"

The dancers and performers featured on *American Bandstand* mirrored the
clean-cut demeanor of the host. Clark insisted on a dress code, forcing boys to "wear a
jacket and tie, or a sweater and tie. Nobody dressed that way in real life, but it made the
show acceptable to adults who were frightened by the teenage world and their music.
Girls couldn't wear slacks, tight sweaters, shorts, or low-necked gowns—they had to
wear the kind of dresses or sweaters and skirts they wore in school. No tight toreadors
or upturned collars." *Newsweek* approvingly reported that "Clark enforces strict rules:
No smoking, no tight sweaters or dresses, no slacks, no hats or overcoats, no gum
chewing. He also carries a supply of safety pins for 'sent' kids who come undone."
"We've never had an incident," Clark boasted to *Time* in 1958.

To further purge sexuality from the airwaves, the announcer refused to say "going
steady" and banned the Alligator and Dog dances as "too sexy." "We just didn't deal with

sex," Clark later wrote. As music writer Arnold Shaw concluded, "Clark was, in fact, the great tranquilizer of the era, reassuring parents by his suave manners that rock-and-roll was not bad and transforming the youngsters on his show into sunshine biscuits."

One of Clark's books about teenage etiquette, *To Goof or Not to Goof*, exemplified his dampening of teenage rebellion. The dust jacket read: "How to have morals and manners and still have fun." The contents dealt with such burning questions "to successful teenaging" as "Where do your elbows go when you're not eating?" "How long should it take to say good night to a girl? To her father?" "Do nice girls call up boys?" and "How far is friendly?"

Clark's Creations

Dick Clark, though showcasing a variety of rock-and-roll acts on *American Bandstand*, created a stable of mostly Italian, Philadelphia-bred youths whom he groomed, promoted, and cast as the stars of his show. One such idol was Fabian. One day in 1957, a South Philadelphia policeman, Dominick Forte, suffered a heart attack on the street. Bob Marcucci, co-owner of Chancellor Records, offered help and noticed Forte's fourteen-year-old son Fabian. Impressed with Fabian's resemblance to Elvis Presley, the manager gave the youth voice and etiquette lessons for two years and then tried to sell the teen by buying full-page ads in the music industry trade papers. "I was molded, manufactured to fit a certain ideal, and I'll probably wind up with a plastic tombstone," complained Fabian years later.

In 1959, Dick Clark agreed to promote Fabian, who lip-synced "Turn Me Loose," "Tiger," and the Elvis Presley imitation, "Hound Dog Man" on *American Bandstand*. Though believing that the singer "got screams though he couldn't sing a note," Clark transformed Fabian from a $6-a-week drugstore clerk into an overnight sensation. Within a year, Clark had helped the Philadelphia teen to sell almost one million copies of his signature song "Tiger," appear on *The Ed Sullivan Show*, and receive coverage in *Time* magazine. "Dick Clark was the only way to get your artist to be seen throughout the entire country in the matter of one day," commented Bob Marcucci on the importance of *American Bandstand*.

Dick Clark also launched the career of Frankie Avalon, another regular on *American Bandstand*, who was managed by Bob Marcucci. Born Francis Avallone, Avalon played trumpet for the Philadelphia group Rocco and the Saints, and in 1958 debuted his solo single "DeDe Dinah," which reached the number-seven slot on the chart. Through repeated appearances on *American Bandstand*, the teen scored hits with songs such as "Venus" and "Why." Remarked Frankie about "Venus": "Dick got behind it and it sold a million and a half copies. He's the greatest."

Bobby Rydell, born Robert Ridarelli in Philadelphia, followed his friend Frankie Avalon on the path to stardom. Also a member of Rocco and the Saints, Rydell started a solo career in 1958 that was unsuccessful until he joined *American Bandstand* a year later. In 1959, he scored hits with "Kissin' Time," "Volare," and "Swingin' School," and within four years, he chalked up nineteen Top-Thirty chartbusters. Rydell's music was a teenaged version of the smooth ballads delivered by Italian crooners of the 1940s and early 1950s such as Frank Sinatra, Perry Como, and Dean Martin.

Chubby Checker dances the "Twist" with a model in this staged PR shot, c. 1961. Photo by Hulton Archive/Getty Images.

Clark also brought fame to Ernest Evans, another Philadelphian who became known as Chubby Checker and popularized an international dance craze. In the summer of 1960, Clark noticed an African-American couple on *American Bandstand* "doing a dance that consisted of revolving their hips in quick, half-circle jerks, so their pelvic regions were heaving in time to the music." Clark screamed to his producer, Tony Mammarella, "For God's sake, keep the cameras off that couple. . . . It looked like something a belly dancer did to climax her performance."

The announcer soon realized the commercial potential of the dance and suggested that Cameo Records—a company that he owned partially—cover Hank Ballard's 1959 "The Twist." For a singer the company chose Chubby Checker, an African American who had attended high school with Fabian and Frankie Avalon and already had cut a novelty disc for Cameo. At the time, he was working in a butcher shop cleaning chickens. In 1960, *American Bandstand* played Checker's "The Twist" until it hit the top of the chart. By 1963, Checker had sold 70 million singles, 30 million albums, and had starred in two movies, *Twist Around the Clock* and *Don't Knock the Twist*.

A new dance craze, started on the program, accompanied the song. To do the dance, instructed rock critic Lillian Roxon, "You put one foot out and pretend you're stubbing out a cigarette butt on the floor with the big toe. At the same time, you move your hands and body as though you're drying every inch of your back with an invisible towel. That's the twist." The twist craze reached international proportions and spawned a series of records: "Twist with B. B. King," the Isley Brothers' "Twist and Shout," "Twist with Bobby Darin," Sam Cooke's "Twistin' the Night Away," "Twistin' with Duane Eddy," and many others.

Dick Clark marketed other dances and their theme songs on his television show. "Many of these dances," admitted the announcer, "came out of Philadelphia and were associated with songs done by artists on Cameo Records." Chubby Checker instructed fans to dance to the Hucklebuck, the Pony, the Limbo, and the Fly. Bobby Rydell popularized the Fish. The white Philadelphia doo-wop group the Dovells introduced the Bristol Stomp and the Continental, and singer Dee Dee Sharp exhorted television viewers to do the Mashed Potato.

Though creating teen idols and dance steps for his television viewers, Clark remained at center stage. He received the attention of the trade publications and the popular press. *Time* labeled him "the Pied Piper of the teenagers." Even the teens themselves swooned over Clark. During the first year of *American Bandstand*, more than 300,000 fans requested Clark's photo, and in 1958, *Life* printed a revealing shot of an awestruck sixteen-year-old, June Carter, during "her great moment, touching the cheek Dick Clark has just kissed."

For Clark, popularity led to wealth. The announcer collected a sizable salary each year for his work on television programs such as *American Bandstand* and *The Dick Clark Show*, a concert format started in 1958, and *Dick Clark's Caravan of Stars*, begun in 1959. In addition to the income from his work on shows, he earned $50,000 a year spinning discs at record hops, which led to the formation of his first corporation, Click. Clark slowly gained interest in local record companies such as Chancellor, which featured Fabian and Frankie Avalon; Cameo-Parkway, which recorded Bobby Rydell, Chubby Checker, and the Dovells; Swan Records in Philadelphia; and Jamie Records. He also owned the copyrights to over 160 songs, including "At the Hop," "Party Time," and "Sixteen Candles." During the 1950s, Dick Clark held at least some share in thirty-three corporations. By April 8, 1958, *Time* reported that "television's newest rage consists of a jukebox full of rock-'n'-roll records, a studio full of dancing teenagers, and Dick Clark, a suave young (twenty-eight) disc jockey full of money."

The Payola Investigation

Clark's interlocking interests became painfully public during the payola investigations of 1959 and 1960. Payola, or "play for pay," had been an accepted practice in the music industry, dating back to the vaudeville era. "Historically, payola is an outgrowth of a music business tradition—song promotion," noted Paul Ackerman, music editor of *Billboard*.

The payola investigations of 1959–1960 began with fraud on television. In November 1959, Charles Lincoln Van Doren admitted before the House Special Committee on Legislative Oversight that he had been given answers in advance as a contestant on NBC's *Twenty-One* quiz show. Reeling from the revelation, the networks discontinued many game programs. NBC canceled *Tic Tac Dough* and *The Price Is Right*; CBS eliminated all quiz shows from its schedule and fired the president of the network, who had been closely associated with *Quiz Kids, Stop the Music*, and *The $64,000 Question*, the most popular show in America.

The scandal spread to the music industry with the prodding of the American Society of Composers, Authors, and Publishers (ASCAP), a song/performance-licensing concern that, through the 1950s, had attacked the interlocking interests of radio, network television, and the record companies represented by the rival licensing agent, Broadcast Music, Inc. (BMI). Concerned about rock performers such as Little Richard and Chuck Berry, who wrote their own material, the professional songwriters of ASCAP used the payola investigation to lash out bitterly against BMI and the rock-and-roll it licensed. The songwriters hired Vance Packard, author of *Hidden Persuaders*, who tried to demonstrate that the rock-and-roll was "largely engineered, manipulated for the interests of BMI, and that would be the point, that the public was manipulated into liking rock-and-roll." ASCAP member and well-known Broadway songwriter Oscar Hammerstein asked, "What do you think is going to happen to rock-and-roll songs? There seems to be something funny to me that these songs have been so popular, so much more popular than any other new songs that have been produced, and yet don't live. They die as soon as the plug stops."

Congressmen in charge of the investigation, hoping to impress their conservative constituencies during an election year, joined in the attack on rock-and-roll. "Suppose John Smith owns a record company and then buys a broadcast station," postulated the counsel for the committee. "Suppose he dumps its personnel and its good music format to put on his own label, generally only rock-and-roll. . . . Now, that's not in the public interest." Without payola, "a lot of this so-called junk music, rock-'n'-roll stuff, which appeals to the teenagers would not be played," stressed Congressman John Bennett of Michigan. Such "trash" as rock music had been "pushed" on unsuspecting teens, agreed Representative John Moss of California.

The committee focused on disc jockeys who played rock-and-roll. Boston jockey Norm Prescott told the House committee that "bribery, payola, has become the prime function of this business to get the record on the air at any cost" and that he had taken almost $10,000 from various record distributors. Another Boston announcer, WBZ's Dave Maynard, admitted that a record distributor had helped finance his purchase of two cars and had given him $6,817 in cash. Alan Dary, also of WBZ, received cash, a hi-fi, liquor, and carpeting for his master bedroom. By 1960, investigators announced that 207 rock disc jockeys in forty-two states had accepted more than $263,000 in payola. President Dwight Eisenhower instructed the committee, headed by Oren Harris of Arkansas, "to clean up this whole mess."

Some rock DJs immediately felt repercussions from the payola investigation. In Detroit, WJBK's Tom Clay was fired after he admitted to taking $6,000 in a year and a half. In Boston, three top disc jockeys on the rock station WILD—Stan Richards,

Bill Marlowe, and Mike Eliot—found themselves unemployed. And in New York, premier rock announcer Alan Freed was dismissed by WABC when he admitted that he had taken $30,650 from six record companies. Complained a bitter Freed, "What they call payola in the disc jockey business they call lobbying in Washington."

Dick Clark came under especially close scrutiny. As Representative John Bennett of Michigan put it: "I think it is pretty convincing that Clark was involved with payola as all other disc jockeys, but on a much larger scale." Illinois Congressman Peter Mack called him "the top dog in the payola field," and Representative John Moss of California began to refer to the investigations as "Clarkola."

However, Clark escaped the payola investigation with his job and reputation intact. Wearing a blue suit, a button-down shirt, and black loafers, the announcer uncategorically informed the House committee in April 1960 that, "I have never agreed to play a record in return for payment in cash or any other consideration." When grilled about promoting artists who recorded for companies in which he owned an interest, a cool Clark replied softly that, "I did not consciously favor such records. Maybe I did so without realizing it." The host of *American Bandstand*, projecting an air of respectability to the congressional investigators, slipped through the committee unscathed. At the end of his testimony, he was told by Chairman Oren Harris: "You're not the inventor of the system or even its architect. You're a product of it. Obviously, you're a fine young man."

Alan Freed, a tireless champion of black performers who wrote their own songs and had created rock-and-roll, did not fare as well. As the payola investigation ended in 1960, an unemployed Freed was charged with commercial bribery in connection with payola by an eight-member grand jury in New York. Blackballed by the music industry after the payola scare, the former disc jockey, penniless, stood trial in December 1962 and pleaded guilty to two counts of commercial bribery. He was fined $300 and given a six-month suspended sentence. Less than two years later, on March 16, 1964, Freed was charged with income tax evasion from 1957 to 1959 by another grand jury, which ordered him to pay the Internal Revenue Service almost $38,000 in back taxes. Later in the year, a broken, unemployed, despondent Alan Freed entered a California hospital, suffering from the effects of alcoholism. On January 20, 1965, he died at age forty-three.

Don Kirshner Takes Charge

The payola investigation had an immediate impact on rock-and-roll. As the established tunesmiths in ASCAP had hoped, songwriters became a dominant force in the new music. Ironically, from 1960 to 1963, a new breed of songsmiths nurtured by New York music publisher Don Kirshner outdistanced recognized Tin Pan Alley songwriters to corner the teen market. They produced romantic lyrics and upbeat melodies for and about teenagers and placed the songs with gospel-influenced, African-American girl groups, who gradually became more popular than the white, male, Italian teen idols of the Dick Clark era.

Don Kirshner masterminded the takeover of rock by the songwriters. The son of a Bronx tailor, Kirshner began to write songs professionally in 1958 and hoped to reshape Tin Pan Alley for the expanding teen market. As he remembered, "My idols at the time were Max and Louis Dryfuss, who had built [the music publishing firm of] Chappell Music. I had watched some of the old movies they were in, like *Night and Day* and *Rhapsody in Blue*, and had observed them molding the greats like Gershwin, Rodgers and Hammerstein, and Lerner and Lowe. My philosophy—my dream—was that we were approaching a new era in the music business with room for new people to accomplish what the Dryfusses had," he related. "And I believed that if I got the chance to sit behind a desk in the music business, I'd be the guy to accomplish that."

Chasing his dream, a twenty-one-year-old Kirshner, along with Al Nevins, guitarist for the pop group the Three Suns, established Aldon Music in 1958. "Our concept," pointed out Kirshner, "was to build new writers." The business partners rented office space across the street from the famed Brill Building at 1619 Broadway, which housed the well-known publishing firms so important to Tin Pan Alley pop music. "The Brill Building," reminisced songwriter Mike Stoller, who collaborated with Jerry Leiber on a number of songs recorded by Elvis Presley, the Coasters, and many others, "had music publishers on every floor. Frequently . . . writers would go [there] to peddle their songs, and they'd go from door to door trying to sell them."

Kirshner quickly discovered teams of young songwriters who challenged the established firms across the street. One afternoon, just two days after he had opened his door for business, two aspiring writers who had been high school chums, Neil Sedaka and Howie Greenfield, walked into the office. As Kirshner recalled, "They had just been turned down by Hill and Range [publishers] upstairs. They asked to see me. I said, 'I'm the guy!' They said, 'Come on, you're kidding us.' But they figured they had nothing to lose, so they proceeded to play six incredible songs: 'Stupid Cupid,' 'The Diary,' and 'Calendar Girl' and a few others." Kirshner took the team to the home of a friend, pop singer Connie Francis, who recorded and in September 1958 hit the Top Twenty with "Stupid Cupid."

Neil Sedaka, unlike almost all of the other songwriters at Aldon, began to record his own material. After the Connie Francis hits, Sedaka, who was a classically trained pianist, believed that the singers who recorded his songs "couldn't feel it the way I could. I used to play songs for people and then play the record, and they would say, 'We like the way you do it better.'" In 1959, Al Nevins took Sedaka to RCA, which signed Sedaka. The label recorded "The Diary," which, after a $100,000 promotional campaign, became Sedaka's first hit as a singer. During the next three years, Sedaka followed with the chartbusters "Breaking Up Is Hard to Do," "Calendar Girl," "Happy Birthday, Sweet Sixteen," and "Oh! Carol," the last written in 1959 for his girlfriend, Carole Klein.

The Sounds on the Streets

Don Kirshner found some successful songwriters who helped extend the boundaries of doo-wop. Doo-wop originated on the streets of New York City, where groups of young African-American males, too poor to afford instruments, started to sing in harmony. Many groups fashioned themselves after the Ravens. Formed in 1945, the six-man group featured the deep bass tone of leader Jimmy Ricks; they released singles for several independent labels before signing with Columbia in 1950. They hit the R&B Top Ten with "I Don't Have to Ride No More" and "Rock Me All Night Long." During the 1950s, the Ravens inspired dozens of groups named after birds, including the Larks ("Heaven and Paradise"), the Swallows ("Itchy Twitchy Feeling"), the Cardinals, the Robins ("Smokey Joe's Cafe"), the Jayhawks ("Stranded in the Jungle"), and the Penguins, who perhaps achieved the greatest commercial success with "Earth Angel."

Doo-wop groups also looked to Clyde McPhatter and the Drifters for inspiration. As with most doo-wop harmonizers, McPhatter first joined a gospel group, the Dominoes, which was managed by Billy Ward. Soon after their television debut on *The Arthur Godfrey Show*, the Dominoes began to record R&B numbers, and in May 1951, they released the classic "Sixty Minute Man." Within two years, McPhatter bolted from the Dominoes to form the Drifters, settling on the name because the members "drifted" from one group to another. The group signed with Atlantic Records and immediately scaled the chart with the million-selling "Money Honey." In 1954, they followed with such hits as "Such a Night," "Honey Love," and "Bip Bam."

Influenced by the success of the Ravens and Drifters, several new doo-wop groups were promoted by New York music entrepreneur George Goldner. Originally in the garment business, Goldner began recording Latin acts in the late 1940s, and then, in March 1954, he took a chance on the doo-wop group the Crows, which unexpectedly attracted an R&B and pop following with "Gee."

Encouraged by his success with the Crows, Goldner signed several now-legendary harmonizers, including Frankie Lymon and the Teenagers. The Teenagers, fronted by twelve-year-old Lymon, practiced on street corners, in a junk-filled backyard, and on the top of a Harlem tenement house. One day, Richard Barrett, the lead singer of another Goldner act, the Valentines, overheard the Teenagers as he passed by a street corner. Excitedly, he brought the boys, all in their teens except Lymon, to Goldner's offices, where they sang "Why Do Fools Fall in Love." Goldner asked Lymon if he had the sheet music for the song. "Nope," replied Frankie, "we don't know anything about written down music." The next day, the Teenagers recorded the song. Released in January 1956, the song became a national hit within a few months. Goldner followed with many other doo-wop groups such as the Wrens, the Flamingos, and the Channels. "His gift was that he could recognize and manipulate talent with an uncanny ear for commercial potential," remarked Herb Cox, lead singer of the Cleftones, who hit with "Little Girl of Mine."

By the mid-1950s, hundreds of young African-American males, most of whom had just graduated from high school, harmonized on the streets of urban America. Most came from New York City, including the Paragons ("Florence"), the Jive Five ("My True Story"), the Jesters ("The Plea"), the Chords ("Sh-Boom"), and the Charts ("Desirie"). Other cities contributed to the movement as well. From Los Angeles came the Penguins, the Olympics ("Western Movies"), the Hollywood Flames ("Buzz-Buzz-Buzz"), and the Jacks ("Why Don't You Write Me"). The Five Satins, who hit with "In the Still of the Night," came from New Haven; the Charms ("Hearts of Stone") sang on the streets of Cincinnati; the Monotones ("Book of Love") grew up in Newark; and the Dells ("Oh, What a Night") came from Chicago.

Frankie Lymon and the Teenagers on tour shortly after scoring their major hit, "Why Do Fools Fall in Love?" January 1, 1970. Photo by Michael Ochs Archive/Getty Images.

Many of the doo-wop groups named themselves after hallmarks of the urban streets. Some borrowed their names from the automobiles that glided past the streets on which they sang: the El Dorados, the Cadillacs, the Edsels, the Fiestas, the Impalas, the Imperials, and the Belvederes. Dion and the Belmonts ("I Wonder Why" and "Teenager in Love"), one of the few white doo-wop groups, named themselves after Belmont Avenue in the Bronx near their home. Reflecting life in 1950s' urban America, these teens created a sound that would reverberate throughout the history of rock-and-roll.

The Girl Groups

Don Kirshner hired teams of young New York City songwriters who built on the doo-wop tradition by writing teen-oriented songs. Carole Klein, the subject of a Neil Sedaka song ("Oh! Carol"), who later became known as Carole King, helped write Aldon Music's first smash hit, which set the direction of the company for the next three years.

King had learned piano at age four and in high school formed her first band, the Co-sines. While attending Queens College in New York in 1958, she met lyricist Gerry Goffin, who started to write songs with her. The King–Goffin team joined Aldon Music and began to compose Tin Pan Alley songs designed especially for teens. Goffin told *Time*, "Lyrics will hurt a song if they're too adult, too artistic, too correct. You should shy away from anything too deep."

In 1960, the King–Goffin duo composed the teen ballad "Will You Love Me Tomorrow." Initially, Kirshner brought the song to Mitch Miller, then the head of Artists

Gerry Goffin and Carole King working on a song at the Aldon offices.
Photo of Gerry Goffin, 1970. Photo by Michael Ochs Archives. Getty
Images, Inc.—Michael Ochs Archives.

and Repertoire (A&R) at Columbia Records, but the conservative Miller rejected the song.
Turning away from the musical establishment, Kirshner took the song to a New
Jersey–based independent company, Scepter Records. He approached its owners and rec-
ommended the song "for a group they had called the Shirelles," an African-American, all-
girl act that was signed to the label. Kirshner convinced them to record "Will You Love Me
Tomorrow," which in January 1961 became a number-one hit, a first for an all-girl group.

Kirshner hired other teams of songwriters who worked side by side to compose
teenage-oriented tunes for other doo-wop–influenced, African-American girl groups
who became some of the first female rock-and-roll performers. Paying his composers
about $150 a week, he snagged the songwriting teams of Barry Mann–Cynthia Weil and
Ellie Greenwich–Jeff Barry, who joined about thirty other young tunesmiths at Aldon
Music during the early 1960s. "It was insane," recalled Barry Mann. "Cynthia and I
would be in this tiny cubicle, about the size of a closet, with just a piano and chair; no
window or anything. We'd go in every morning and write songs all day. In the next room
Carole [King] and Gerry [Goffin] would be doing the same thing, and in the next room
after that Neil [Sedaka] or somebody else. Sometimes when we all got to banging on our
pianos you couldn't tell who was playing what. All of us—me and Cynthia, Carole King
and Gerry Goffin, Neil Sedaka and Howie Greenfield—were so insecure that we'd never
write a hit again that we constantly wrote in order to prove we could," added Mann.

The two teams of Mann–Weil and Greenwich–Barry crafted a number of songs
during 1962–1963 for two of the premier African-American girl groups, the Ronettes
and the Crystals. Mann and Weil wrote the hits "Uptown" and "He's Sure the Boy I
Love" for the Crystals and "Walking in the Rain" for the Ronettes. The more prolific

Greenwich–Barry team authored "Baby, I Love You" and "Be My Baby" for the Ronettes, "Da Doo Ron Ron" and "Then He Kissed Me" for the Crystals. They also composed "Today I Met the Boy I'm Gonna Marry" and "Wait Till My Baby Gets Home" for Darlene Love, who sang lead vocal on many of the Crystals' hits.

Darlene Love (born Darlene Wright) infused the girl-group sound with a gospel flavor. "My father was a minister, and I used to sing all the time in the church choir," remembered Love. At age sixteen, she joined the Blossoms, a racially integrated female vocal group in Los Angeles that also included Annette, Nanette, and Fanita James and Grazia Nitzsche. In 1962, Darlene Love sang lead vocal on the Crystals' "He's a Rebel," instilling the song with a gospel sound. With the Blossoms, the singer cut many other gospel-influenced records officially released under the Crystals' name. Ellie Greenwich described Love as "a typical sixties soulful street gospel singer."

Despite her success singing Aldon's material, Darlene Love complained that "many of the singers [in the girl groups] that sung those songs didn't really want to sing them. We called them bubblegum songs. The lyrics were really not even teenage. I say kid, you know ten to twelve, the market was geared for them."

Phil Spector, owner of Philles Records, which recorded the Crystals and the Ronettes, surrounded the teen-oriented, gospel-flavored tearjerkers of Aldon Music with a "wall of sound" to create distinctive, girl-group music. Spector, born in the Bronx, moved to Los Angeles with his mother when his father died. After a short-lived success with the rock combo the Teddy Bears, he found employment with independent producers Lester Sill and Lee Hazelwood, who in 1960 sent Spector to New York. In 1961, the twenty-one-year-old Spector and Lester Sill, a former promotion man for Modern Records, formed the New York–based Philles Records, which Spector owned solely by 1962.

While recording the Crystals and the Ronettes for Philles, the producer perfected his now-famous wall of sound, which involved multiple instrumentation. Ronnie Bennett, the lead singer of the Ronettes, who later married and then divorced the producer, remembered that "everything was done double. I mean where most people have one guitar or one drummer we had two of everything, so that's what made that wall of sound." Spector took this lush instrumentation and doubled it through an elaborate echo system. "You had live sound going to the [echo] chamber and you had a delayed sound going to the chamber at the same time, and the result was that it repeated in the chamber, so when it came back it was just a big blur," explained music engineer Bones Howe who worked with Spector on several songs.

The resulting music sounded heroic and mounumental "Well, I know that Phil's favorite composer was Wagner, no question, power, bigness," commented Ellie Greenwich. "And a few times when I'd gone over, Phil had an office on the main floor of a building and he had an apartment upstairs, and very often he would be upstairs in his one room listening with the speakers blasting, conducting. Wagner was his idol and Wagner was power and bigness and heavy and all that and I think he was going after that in his records." Spector himself called the new sound "a Wagnerian approach to rock-and-roll; little symphonies for the kids." The power of Spector's production that surrounded gospel-flavored songs of teenage romance resulted in the bright, upbeat, almost ethereal girl-group sound.

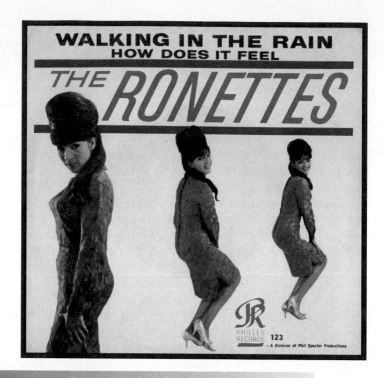

WALKING IN THE RAIN
HOW DOES IT FEEL

THE RONETTES

PHILLES RECORDS 123
– A Division of Phil Spector Productions

Photo sleeve for "Walkin' in the Rain," a major hit for the Ronettes.
Ronnie Spector, with her characteristic beehive hairdo, stands at the left.
Photo of Ronettes, c. 1970. Photo by Michael Ochs Archives. Getty
Images, Inc.—Michael Ochs Archives.

The Dream

The rags-to-riches success stories of the girl groups added to the romantic appeal of
the music for thousands of school-age girls. The Crystals, a group of Brooklyn teens,
had been discovered by Phil Spector while auditioning in New York City. The
Shirelles had begun singing at school shows and at parties, and in 1958 had been
signed to Scepter Records by Florence Greenberg, the mother of one of their high
school classmates. The Chantels, five New York teens who sang in the youth choir of a
local Catholic grade school, were signed to a contract when a talent scout inadvertently
heard them harmonizing at a Frankie Lymon concert. In 1958, they hit the chart with
"Maybe."

Other groups had similar stories. The Chiffons, a group of high school friends
who sang during lunch breaks and in the neighborhood after school, were discovered
by songwriter Ronnie Mack, who groomed the girls until they made their chart-topping "He's So Fine." The Dixie Cups, singing together since grade school, were
spotted at a local New Orleans talent contest by singer/pianist Joe Jones, who became
their manager and helped them chart with the Greenwich–Barry song "Chapel of

Love." The Shangri-Las, one of the few white girl groups of the era, grew up in a tough section of Queens, New York, and began singing together as teenagers. One day, producer Shadow Morton, a friend of Ellie Greenwich, happened to hear the four girls—Mary Weiss and her sister Betty and the Ganser twins, Marge and Mary Ann—and signed them to the new Red Bird label, which had been started by doo-wop impresario George Goldner and R&B songwriters Jerry Leiber and Mike Stoller. In late 1964, when Mary was only fifteen, the group hit the Top Ten with "Remember (Walkin' In the Sand)" and later the same year topped the singles chart with "Leader of the Pack."

The discovery of the Ronettes—sisters Veronica and Estelle Bennett and cousin Nedra Talley—probably offered teenage girls the most encouraging story. In 1961, the three girls became resident dancers at the Peppermint Lounge, the focus of the twist craze in New York City. In August, the group signed with Colpix Records and released four unsuccessful songs. After a show at the Peppermint Lounge in June 1963, Ronnie Bennett casually walked into a bar and saw Phil Spector sitting at the piano. Their eyes fastened on one another, and Spector softly asked Ronnie to sing. After a few bars, the producer exclaimed, "That's the voice, that's the voice I've been looking for."

Such tales of instant stardom, coupled with the dramatic, romanticized music of the girl groups, created the fantasy among many young girls that they too could become famous. "You see them coming from the cities, mostly groups, off the streets, hanging around Tin Pan Alley on Broadway near the Brill Building," noticed Phil Spector at the time. "They're usually between sixteen and nineteen, anxious to record, anxious to be a singer." Although few traveled to New York in search of their dreams, millions of girls lay on their beds, listened to their transistor radios, and fantasized about impending stardom. Songwriter Jerry Leiber characterized the era as "very naive, very innocent, full of hope, full of fantasy, full of promise." *Life* magazine referred to the new sound as "a fairy tale called the pop-record business" and identified Don Kirshner as "the grand wizard of the fairy tale."

The fantasies of teenage girls helped Don Kirshner establish a music publishing empire. "The fastest rising phenomenon in the business is a Tin Pan Alley octopus called Aldon Music Inc., which has thirty-five boys and girls busy night and day composing songs," reported *Time* in March 1963. A few months later, *The Saturday Evening Post* renamed Tin Pan Alley, "Teen Pan Alley," and told its readers that "Broadway's Brill Building, once the home of jelly-jowled, gray-headed music publishers, is now being refurbished with youthful executives who have grown up to no other kind of music than the beat of today. . . . One of the typical—and prime—figures in youth's takeover of the pop–record business is a onetime unsuccessful songwriter named Don Kirshner." By the end of the year, Kirshner had sold hundreds of songs that dominated the music charts and grossed millions of dollars.

In 1963, Don Kirshner and his partner Al Nevins sold Aldon Music. "The money just kept rolling in, and the hits kept rolling in," shrugged Kirshner, "and you walk away at twenty-eight years of age with a $2 million check with your partner, it's difficult to turn down." Kirshner left for a lucrative job in the Columbia Screen Gems Television Music Division, where he supervised the record and music publishing interests of the company. He had left Aldon just when the surf had begun to rise.

4 Surfboards and Hot Rods: California, Here We Come

❝ We sang about California and being young. ❞

—Dean Torrence

Eureka, a Greek word meaning "I have found it," was selected by state legislators as a motto in 1850, at the end of the great gold rush, when California became the thirty-first state. Especially during the late 1950s and early 1960s, it aptly characterized the sentiments of the droves of migrants from the Midwest and the East Coast who traveled to California with hopes of sun, fun, and jobs. A new indigenous music, a bright, bouncy sound that glorified beaches, bikinis, and hot rods, embodied and promoted the California myth.

Postwar California had advantages over most other states. It enjoyed an abundance of natural resources, including lumber, oil, and many minerals. In 1961, the state produced more fruit, vegetables, and nuts than any other state and topped the number-two farm state, Iowa, by more than $700 million in total produce. Ushering in the computer age, in 1961 the state procured almost half of the $6 billion in Defense Department research-and-development contracts, and during the 1950s, it had attracted 200 electronic firms, such as Western Electric, Raytheon, Remington Rand, Zenith, and Motorola, to the aptly named Silicon Valley, which contained deposits of silica used in manufacturing transistors and computer chips. Probably most important, third only to Alaska and Texas in size, California boasted a wide range of terrains and climates from the desert of Death Valley to the damp, forested mountains in the north and from the central farm valley to the beaches of Malibu.

The resources of California, especially a healthy economy and the sunny, balmy climate of the southern part of the state, drew throngs of migrants after World War II. In 1940, the population of the state stood at almost 7 million. Within ten years, it had increased to 10.6 million, bolstered by many Texans and Oklahomans who had come there during the war for employment in government factories. People continued to stream into California during the next decade, until, by late 1962, with its population expanding by 1,700 daily, California had more than 17 million inhabitants and had become the most populous state in the country. About 60 percent of the people lived in the ten southernmost counties of the state.

Many of the migrants looked for the mythical California of fun and prosperity that had been promulgated by the press. In a late 1962 article, "What to Know About and Look For," *Life* focused on California's "bigness, bustle, and boom." The reporter described a state with a per capita income 25 percent above the national average, a "wide open" job market, "plenty" of houses equipped with swimming pools, 160 state parks (a third of which were beaches), and supermarkets and roadside stands that would "stagger most Easterners." At the same time, *Newsweek* emphasized the "happy hedonism" of the California transplants. "Californians take their relaxation seriously," it asserted. "Unassuming and carefree, they break with the staid ways of their former communities, dip freely into credit for financing luxury items, and start experimenting in weird and wonderful ways." California, concluded a writer in a September 1962 issue of *Look*, "presents the promise and the challenge contained at the very heart of the original American dream."

Several homegrown California attractions and consumer items symbolized the fairyland aura of fun, sun, and whimsical hope of the nation's largest state. Disneyland, a 160-acre theme park, opened to the public on July 18, 1955. The brain-child of animation king Walt Disney, it featured fantasy neighborhoods such as Frontierland, Adventureland, Fantasyland, and Tomorrowland, the last of which Disney described as "designed to give you an opportunity to participate in adventures that are a living blueprint of our future." Each section of the $17 million, dazzling-colored extravaganza included theme-inspired rides on rivers, waterfalls, mountains, spaceships, and spinning teacups with employees dressed in larger-than-life cartoon costumes greeting the visitors. By 1965, more than 50 million children and their parents had entered the gates of the magic kingdom to enjoy an otherworldly and unforgettable experience. A television show, *The Mickey Mouse Club* series, which premiered on October 3, 1955, and featured Mouseketeers such as Annette Funicello, added to the California-centered Disney craze.

Toy manufacturer Mattel, producing Disney-licensed merchandise, created another product that pandered to the idealized image that California backers promulgated. In 1958, Ruth Handler, the wife of one of Mattel's cofounders, unveiled an 11.5-inch fashion doll, which she dubbed "Barbie" after her daughter. Unlike stuffed animals or traditional porcelain dolls, Barbie sported anatomically unrealistic measurements of 39-21-33, if magnified to human proportions. Debuting at the 1959 New York World's Fair, the Mattel doll gave young girls an impossible goal and provided boys with a buxom, blonde, ever-smiling, and totally passive ideal. "That's a doll for little girls?" blurted future Beach Boy Dennis Wilson, then a young boy in

Hawthorne, California, where Mattel had its headquarters. "Whoa! I'd rather have this in my room than a stag magazine!" In 1961, Ruth Handler developed a trim, muscular male counterpart of Barbie, which she named "Ken" after her son.

Surfing U.S.A.

A buoyant surf music, born amid the California boom, reflected and promoted the myth of the California wonderland. It glorified one of the most attractive elements of the California myth: the sun-drenched Southern California beaches dotted with tanned, blonde, bikini-clad, Barbie-like beauties.

Surfing, the sacred sport of Hawaiian kings that began in the fifteenth century, was introduced to California at the turn of the twentieth century. In 1959, the sport received a boost from the movie *Gidget*, a tale about a young girl who spends a summer on the beach and falls in love with two surfers.

The same year, the innovations of two surfboard companies, Hobie Surfboards in Dana Point and Sweet's Surfboards in Santa Monica, further popularized the sport. Hobie Alter and Dave and Roger Sweet replaced the heavy wooden board with a light-weight polyurethane foam strip coated with fiberglass and glossed with a polyester resin that could be handled more easily, an important consideration for the teen market.

Almost immediately, young people in Southern California started to buy the new plastic boards and took to the waves. In late September 1961, *Life* commented that "now the surf that sweeps in on the beaches bears flotillas of enthusiasts standing on long buoyant boards. . . . Surfing has become an established craze in California. There are some 30,000 [teenagers who] revel in the delights of mounting their boards on waves hundreds of feet out and riding them in." "If you're not a surfer," explained one high school boy, "you're not 'in.' If you're a good surfer, you're always in. All you've got to do is walk up and down the beach with a board and you've got girls."

By August 1963, reported *Time*, "every weekend an estimated 100,000 surfers paddle into the briny on 7 ft. to 12 ft. balsa or polyurethane boards, struggle upright into a precarious balance with nature, and try to catch the high breakers coming in." Bill Cooper, executive secretary of the U.S. Surfing Association, calculated, "Ninety percent are beginners. Half of them give it up in a year or two, but then there are more."

The new legion of predominantly male, teenage surfers began to develop its own culture, dressing and speaking in a distinctive way. At high school, the bleached-blonde surfers wore Pendleton shirts, sandals, white, tight, and somewhat short Levis, and baggies—very large, loose boxer-style shorts. After school, they jumped into an oversized station wagon with wooden sides (a "woodie"), which transported their "polys" (surfboards), drove to the beach, and dashed toward the ocean. They ran with their "sticks" (surfboards) into the "soup" (the foaming water near the beach) and tried to catch a wave. Some would only "fun surf" on 3- to 6-foot waves. Other more daring surfers would carry their "big guns" (surfboards designed for riding tall waves) into the water, pick up a "hairy" wave (a fast wave that is difficult to surf), and "shoot" (ride) it, sometimes "hot dogging" (performing tricks) to impress the "bunnies" (girls) on shore. All surfers showed disdain for the poorly skilled or fraudulent, to whom they referred to as "gremlins" or "kooks." After packing up and going home, they could read magazines such as *Surfer* and *Surfer Illustrated* or watch surfing films by director Bruce Brown such as *Slippery When Wet* (1960) and *Barefoot Adventure* (1962), or the more commercial *Beach Party* (1963), *Muscle Beach Party* (1964), and *Bikini Beach* (1964), which starred two Dick Clark regulars, Frankie Avalon and former Mouseketeer Annette Funicello.

The Sound of the Surf

Surfers listened to their own music, which originated with Dick Dale and his Del-Tones. Born in Beirut, Lebanon, a teenaged Dale (b. Richard Monsour) moved with his family to El Segundo on the Southern California coast and joined the hordes of young surfers. Also a guitar enthusiast who had released a few unremarkable singles on his own label in 1959 and 1960, Dale worked closely with Leo Fender, the manufacturer of the first mass-produced, solid-body electric guitar, to improve the Showman amplifier and to develop the reverberation unit that would give surf music its distinctively fuzzy sound.

Dick Dale fused his two passions—surfing and the guitar—to create a new music for surf fanatics. "There was a tremendous amount of power I felt while surfing and that feeling of power was simply transferred into my guitar when I was playing surf music," he recalled. "The style of music I developed, to me at the time, was the feeling I got when I was out there on the waves. It was that good rambling feeling I got

Dick Dale (seated with the yellow Stratocaster) and his group in the early '60s. Michael Ochs Archives/Getty Images.

when I was locked in a tube with the white water caving in over my head. I was trying to project the power of the ocean to the people," added the guitarist. "I couldn't get the feeling by singing, so the music took an instrumental form."

During the summer of 1961, Dale and his band unveiled the new surf sound during weekend dances at the Rendezvous Ballroom in Balboa, California. The Rendezvous, remembered Pete Johnson, later a member of the surf group the Belairs, "held well over 1,000 and Dale's sound was, in a word, awesome! The music was huge and throbbing, especially when combined with all those sandals stomping on the wooden floor." By late 1961, when he first arrived on the West Coast, disc jockey and producer Jim Pewter found that "the word was 'Let's go to a Dick Dale dance,' so my girl and I motivated to the Rendezvous and checked it out, only to return again and again."

Dick Dale and the Del-Tones released records for the surf crowd. In late 1961, "Let's Go Trippin'" topped the California charts and a few months later edged toward the national Top Fifty. Dale followed with "Surfbeat," and in May 1962 produced the classic surf instrumental "Miserlou." In March 1963, Capitol Records recorded Dale and pegged him as the "King of the Surf Guitar." The same year, the guitarist landed a spot in the William Asher–directed movie *Beach Party*, and by the end of 1963, he had become a California celebrity.

The Beach Boys

The Beach Boys brought surf music to national prominence. Raised in the suburb of Hawthorne, California, the boys—leader Brian Wilson, his brothers Carl and Dennis, cousin Mike Love, and Al Jardine, a classmate of Brian's at El Camino Junior College—began to play in 1961. After trying out several names, they settled on the Pendletones, a play on the Pendelton shirts that were favored by California teens.

The band smoothed the rough edges of the fuzzy, twanging surf instrumental. As with Dick Dale, the boys favored a swinging, 1950s' electric guitar sound. "'Rock Around the Clock' shocked me," Brian Wilson once told a reporter. "I mean, I was so electrified by the experience—that song was really it." The group combined the rawness of 1950s' rock with glossy harmonies gleaned from white vocal groups such as the Four Freshmen. The blend resulted in a bright, airy, snappy sound that embodied the California myth and, as with the girl-group sound, reflected the general optimism of the Kennedy presidency.

These California teens recorded their new sound with the help of their domineering, sometimes abusive, father, Murry Wilson, who managed a heavy machinery import business and in his spare time composed songs. Murry introduced the boys to music publisher Hite Morgan who was looking for new material. In October 1961, the band auditioned for Morgan. "We've written a song about the surfing sport and we'd like to sing it for you," pestered the Wilson brothers. Morgan quietly listened to the tune and exclaimed, "Drop everything; we're going to record your song. I think it's good." Within two hours, the group recorded "Surfin'." Morgan took the demo to the local Candix label, which released the record in December 1961 and changed the group's name to the Beach Boys. Commented Mike Love about the name change: "We

The Beach Boys perform onstage c. 1964 in California. From left to right: Dennis Wilson, Al Jardine, Carl Wilson, Brian Wilson, Mike Love. Photo by Michael Ochs Archives/Getty Images.

didn't even know we were the Beach Boys until the song came out." Within weeks, "Surfin'" topped the California charts and reached number seventy-five on the national Top One Hundred.

Good luck temporarily deserted the Beach Boys. Two months after the success of "Surfin'," the Beach Boys recorded four more songs, but before they could be released, Candix Records, plagued by financial difficulties, ceased operations. Murry Wilson, by this time the manager of the group, played the demos to a variety of labels, all of which rejected the songs because, in the estimation of an executive at Dot, "surfing music was a flash in the pan." Al Jardine, disgusted with the failures, quit the band to begin dental school but would rejoin the group nearly a year later.

Murry Wilson finally brought the demos to Nick Venet of Capitol Records. After listening to the songs, the producer rushed into the office of his supervisor and boasted, "Boss, I've got a double-sided smash for Capitol." The label signed the Beach Boys and in June 1962 released "Surfin' Safari," which reached number fourteen on the national singles chart. Later in the year, Capitol followed with an album of the same name, which cracked the Top Thirty-Five.

In May 1963, Capitol released the breakthrough Beach Boys' album *Surfin' U.S.A.*, whose cover featured an action photo of a surfer cutting a path across a 30-foot wave and included a headline that hailed the Beach Boys as "the number-one surfing group in the country." "Surf's Up! Here Come the Beach Boys," Nick Venet proclaimed in the liner notes on the album. "Here's the group that started the surf-dancing craze all over the country—even in places where the nearest thing to surf is maybe the froth on a chocolate shake." Venet promoted the "brawny, sun-tanned" Beach Boys as "nationwide symbols for the exhilarating sport that has taken America by storm."

The Beach Boys applied their trademark harmonies to the title track on the album *Surfin' U.S.A.*, a note-for-note reworking of Chuck Berry's "Sweet Little Sixteen," which hit the number-three slot on the national singles chart. The other selections on the album included covers of Dick Dale's "Miserlou" and "Let's Go Tripping" and other odes to surfdom such as "Lonely Sea," "Surf Jam," and "Noble Surfer." The album established the Beach Boys as the kings of surf, and *Surfin' U.S.A.* helped spread the surfing craze across the nation.

During the next few months, the Beach Boys fortified their reputation. In late 1963, they scored with "Surfer Girl," and in 1964, they topped the singles chart with "I Get Around." The group reflected and enforced the California myth with their chartbusters "Fun, Fun, Fun" (1964) and "California Girls" (1965). By the mid-1960s, the Beach Boys had brought a bright, bouncy surf music that extolled sun and fun to teens throughout the country.

Jan and Dean

Jan and Dean delivered the same message of the California surf to American teenagers. Becoming friends at Emerson Junior High School in Los Angeles, Jan Berry and Dean Torrence began their partnership by recording teen ballads. In October 1959, they reached the Top Ten with "Baby Talk" and appeared on the nationally televised *American Bandstand*. Further paeans to teenage love followed, until the duo joined the ranks of surfdom with the help of the Beach Boys. "When 'Surfin' came out," recalled Dean, "we heard it and liked it. I think we sensed that it was going to be good for business." Because "Jan and I were physically involved with surfing, it was just natural that we became involved with the music."

In late 1962, Jan and Dean became converts to surf music after performing with the Beach Boys. At one show, the Beach Boys first played a few songs, including "Surfin'" and "Surfin' Safari," and Jan and Dean followed with three or four songs. After receiving an enthusiastic reaction from the crowd, Jan and Dean asked the Beach Boys, "Hey, do you want to do your set again, and we'll sing with you guys?" "Gee, you'll sing our songs," responded an awestruck Brian Wilson. "Sure," replied Dean, "I think your songs are really fun to sing." Jan and Dean backed the Beach Boys on two numbers, and the crowd went wild.

The collaboration convinced Jan and Dean to include a surf song on their upcoming album, which featured the song "Linda." As Dean told it, their record producer and manager Lou Adler suggested, "Why don't you take Linda surfing . . . That gets it all in there." Dean agreed but "didn't know any surfing songs except the two that the Beach Boys had done." He called Brian Wilson and asked if the group would play the instrumental parts to "Surfin'" and "Surfin' Safari" on the album. Dean recalled

Jan and Dean, *Drag City* album cover, Liberty Records, 1963. *Permission by EMI/Capitol Records.*

that Brian "was just totally knocked out that we were going to record his songs! He said, 'Sure, I'll get the guys,'" who dashed to the studio. While at the session, Brian sang the opening line of a new song, which he offered to Jan and Dean. The duo added lyrics and recorded it as "Surf City," a tune that in 1963 went to the top of the charts. As part of the California myth of abundance, the lyric promised "two girls for every boy." The next year, they followed with "Ride the Wild Surf" and "Sidewalk Surfin'."

By the end of 1963, surf music had become a national craze. The Surfaris recorded "Wipe Out," which reached number two on the national chart. Modeling their sound after Dick Dale, the Chantays hit the Top Five with "Pipeline." Duane Eddy, the king of twang, recorded "Your Baby's Gone Surfin'," the Trashmen from the Midwest cut "Surfin' Bird," and the Astronauts from Colorado released "Surfin' with the Astronauts." A spate of other surf-inspired albums emerged: *Surfin' with the*

Challengers, Surfin' Bongos, Surfin' with the Shadows, the Marketts' *Surfers Stomp, Surfbeat* by the Surfriders, and *Surf Mania* by the Surf Teens. Chess Records even released the album *Surfin' with Bo Diddley,* without informing the R&B guitarist. By the mid-1960s, the California surf had risen.

Drag City

Many of the surfer groups glorified another aspect of the sprawling Southern California landscape: the automobile. By the early 1960s, a maze of highways connected the inhabitants of Southern California. "California," *Life* informed its readers in October 1962, "has 1,000 miles of freeways and blueprints for many more. It has 850 miles of expressways and 2,400 miles of multi-lane highways."

The tangle of roads forced most Californians to own at least one automobile. "In California, a car is like an extra, highly essential part of the human anatomy," explained *Life,* which estimated that the 8.5 million cars in the state, positioned bumper-to-bumper, would extend more than 27,000 miles. The magazine equated life in California without an automobile to "a fate roughly equal to decapitation."

The importance of cars in California led to a subculture that, as with the surf ethos, involved distinctive dress and language. Teenagers, mostly males, lusted for their first automobile. Rather than a staid station wagon, they cast their eyes upon "asphalt eaters" (dragsters) such as Cudas (Plymouth Barracudas) or GTOs (Grand Turismos), propelled by huge engines such as the rat motor (a 427-cubic-inch Chevy engine) or the Chrysler Hemi (a 426-cubic-inch engine equipped with hemispherical combustion chambers). Like cowboys on their horses, teens with greased hair and tight black pants drove their machines to seldom used roads and waited for a competitor to drag (race). They anticipated the flash of a light, "dropped the hammer" (released the clutch quickly), and sped away, "shutting down" (defeating) an opponent. By the end of the 1950s, the dragsters could race legally on such strips as the one at the Orange County Airport near Santa Ana. "Kids love dragging a car," gushed auto customizer Ed Roth.

The hot rod subculture was promoted through the press and on film. *Hot Rod* magazine, which would become standard reading for car-crazed California youth, first rolled off the presses in 1947. Casting hot-rodders as juvenile delinquents on wheels, movies such as *Hot Rod Girl* (1956), *Dragstrip Riot* (1958), and *Teenage Thunder* (1959) further popularized drag racing among an element less clean-cut than the surfer crowd.

Roger Christian, a Los Angeles disc jockey who was tagged "Poet of the Strip," helped surfer bands such as the Beach Boys write songs about dragsters, even though die-hard surfers considered hot-rodders, or "ho-dads," as they called them, rivals. "Roger was a guiding light for me," revealed Brian Wilson of the Beach Boys. After Christian's late-night radio show, Brian and the disc jockey would "go over to Otto's, order a hot fudge sundae, and just . . . whew! talk and talk." He told *Life* in 1964, "Roger is a real car nut. His normal speech is only 40 percent comprehensible. And he has a tremendous knack for rhyming things with *carburetor.*" In early 1963, Christian and Brian Wilson first collaborated on "Shut Down," which backed "Surfin' U.S.A." and became a Top-Twenty hit. They continued their partnership with "Little Deuce

Coupe," "Don't Worry Baby," and "Spirit of America," the last of which celebrated Craig Breedlove's three-wheeled, 7,800-pound jet car.

Roger Christian also began to compose songs for Jan and Dean. In 1963, at Jan's request, Christian and Brian Wilson wrote "Drag City" for the duo, which reached the Top Ten. The disc jockey penned most of the other songs on the album of the same name, including "Hot Stocker," "I Gotta Drive," "Schlock Rod," and "Dead Man's Curve," the last which became prophetic in 1966 when Jan Berry smashed his Stingray into a parked truck at 65 mph. "For the finest reproduction," wrote Roger Christian in the liner notes for the album *Drag City*, "this recording should be played on a chrome reversed turntable driven by a full-blown turntable motor equipped with tuned headers. Transmission of power should be through a four-speed box with a floor stick." The "Poet of the Strip" had, in his own words, effected "the merger of Jan and Dean and the car craze."

By 1964, several other bands had jumped on the car-craze bandwagon. The Rip Chords, a studio band formed by Bruce Johnston, a neighbor of Jan Berry and later a Beach Boy, scored with "Hey, Little Cobra." The Nashville-based Ronny and the Daytonas hit with "G.T.O." Dick Dale and his Del-Tones checked in with the album *Mr. Eliminator*; Jerry Kole and the Stokers released the album *Hot Rod Alley*; the Hot Rodders cut "Big Hot Rod"; and the T-Bones cut *Boss Drag at Hot Rod Beach*. Even artist Ed "Big Daddy" Roth who had provided the car culture with such graphic art images as Rat Fink, recorded an LP, *Rods and Ratfinks*, under the name Mr. Gasser and the Weirdos. In November 1964, *Life* noted the proliferation of "love songs to the carburetor."

By 1964, jangling harmonies celebrated the California myth. "I think we had a lot to do with the population rush to California," asserted Beach Boy Al Jardine. "People hearing the Beach Boys' songs envisioned California as sort of a golden paradise where all you did was surf and sun yourself while gorgeous blondes rubbed coconut oil on your back." Dean Torrence agreed, "We sang about California and being young. They seemed to go together. In the sixties everyone wanted to go to California, or so it seemed, and it was the time of the youth movement, too. Our records, of course, were directed at the young; they were obviously teenage songs. Who else would be hanging out at the beach or driving hot rods around?"

However, as Jan and Dean promoted "Surf City," folk singers in New York City such as Bob Dylan were singing about another America where African Americans protested and died for their civil rights.

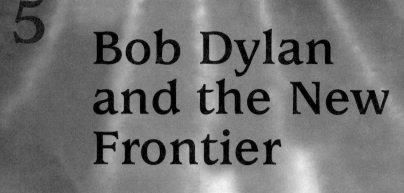

5

Bob Dylan and the New Frontier

> " There's other things in this world besides love and sex that're important. "
>
> —Bob Dylan

Early on a Saturday night in April 1961, a twenty-year-old singer carrying an oversized guitar case walked into a dimly lit folk club, Gerde's Folk City in Greenwich Village, New York City. He was dressed casually: worn brown shoes, blue jeans, and a black wool jacket covering a plain yellow turtleneck sweater. A jumble of rumpled hair crowned his head, which was topped by a black corduroy Huck Finn cap. He pressed his lips together tightly and glanced at the tables of patrons, who sipped espresso and seemed to be arguing feverishly about current events. The singer looked serious and exhibited a nervousness that a friend had earlier tried to calm with four jiggers of Jim Beam bourbon. He slowly mounted the stage, opened his guitar case, and carefully took out an old, nicked, six-string acoustic guitar, which he treated like an old friend. He fixed a wire harmonica holder around his neck and pushed a harmonica into place. As the singer stood alone on stage, motionless, a hush descended upon the coffeehouse.

The audience, mostly white middle-class college students, many of them attending nearby New York University, politely applauded the singer. For a moment, the scene appeared to epitomize Eisenhower gentility and McCarthy repression: boys with closely cropped hair, button-down shirts, corduroy slacks, Hush Puppy shoes, and cardigans; and rosy-cheeked girls dressed in long skirts, bulky knit sweaters, and low-heeled shoes, who favored long, straight, well-groomed hair.

The singer shattered the genteel atmosphere when he began to strum a chord and sing. He was young Bob Dylan, who had just recently arrived in New York City to sing songs of social protest. As civil rights marchers protested in Birmingham and as President John F. Kennedy announced plans for a new frontier, many college-age youths heard the stirring message of Bob Dylan, who leveled his guitar at racism and the hypocrisy of corporate America. By 1963, the first baby boomers had entered college and were starting to become aware of the world around them.

Songs of Protest

The foundation for 1960s' protest music was laid at the turn of the century by the International Workers of the World (IWW). Members of the group, known as Wobblies, first penned protest songs in the United States as part of their drive to achieve equality for American workers. While marching in demonstrations, the radical unionists sang from the *Little Red Songbook*, first published in 1909 and compiled by organizers Ralph Chaplin and the legendary Joe Hill, a Swedish immigrant who later was executed in Utah for his political beliefs. The Wobblies adopted as their anthem Chaplin's "Solidarity Forever," a protest song set to the music of the "Battle Hymn of the Republic": "They have taken untold millions that they never toiled to earn/ But without our brain and muscle not a single wheel can turn/ We can break their haughty power, gain our freedom when we learn/ That the Union makes us strong/ Solidarity forever!" However, the union was crippled when federal and state authorities raided and closed IWW offices during the Red Scare that followed World War I.

Woody Guthrie continued the IWW's legacy of the protest song. Born on July 14, 1912, to a poor family in Okemah, Oklahoma, Woodrow Wilson Guthrie left home at age sixteen and drifted through the Southwest during his teens, working as a newsboy, sign painter, and farm laborer. While visiting his uncle, Jeff Guthrie, in Pampa, Texas, in 1929, the young Woody learned to play guitar. The youth performed on street corners and continued to work odd jobs until 1937, when he became a performer and the host for a program on Los Angeles radio station KFVD, on which he read radical newspapers over the air. Within two more years, he moved to New York City and began writing a daily column for the Communist party's newspaper *People's Daily World* and the *Daily Worker*. In 1940, Guthrie recorded for folklorist Alan Lomax, who taped the singer for the Library of Congress.

After a two-year stint in the merchant marine and the army during World War II, Guthrie returned to New York City, where he penned many of his 1,000 songs, including "This Land Is Your Land," "Tom Joad," "Billy the Kid," and "Pastures of Plenty." He later explained, "I don't sing any songs about the nine divorces of some millionaire play gal or the ten wives of some screwball. I wouldn't sing them if they

The Almanac Singers, c. 1942. Left to right: Woody Guthrie, Millard Lampbell, Bess Lomax Hawes, Pete Seeger, Arthur Stern, and Agnes "Sis" Cunningham. Michael Ochs Archives/Getty Images.

paid me $10,000 a week. I sing the songs of the people that do all of the little jobs and the mean and dirty hard work in the world and of their wants and their hopes and their plans for a decent life." The motto emblazoned on his guitar summed up his message: "This Machine Kills Fascists."

Pete Seeger joined Woody Guthrie, roaming the countryside to sing songs to and about the American worker. Born on May 3, 1919, in New York City to a musical family, Seeger quit Harvard University during the late 1930s and worked with folk-lorist Alan Lomax at the Library of Congress. In 1940, he founded the Almanac Singers with Guthrie, Lee Hays, and Millard Lampell. After serving in World War II, Seeger established a musician's union and booking agency, People's Songs, Inc., which attracted 3,000 members. Seeger formed the Weavers with Lee Hays, Ronnie Gilbert, and Fred Hellerman, who found work by late 1948 at the Village Vanguard and popu-larized folk songs such as "On Top of Old Smokey" and "Good Night Irene," Guthrie's "So Long, It's Been Good to Know You," and "The Hammer Song" writ-ten by Seeger and Hays. "Like the Almanac Singers," recalled Seeger, "the Weavers also hoped to sing for peace and civil rights." Gilbert added about the Weavers, "We were four very politically motivated people interested in doing what we could for the music we loved and for social action."

Protest singers such as Seeger and the Weavers fell into disrepute during the McCarthyite witch hunt. During the 1950s, until his Senate censure in late 1954, Senator Joseph McCarthy of Wisconsin doggedly pursued the shadows of Communist sympathizers. He progressively accused more and more public figures of Communist tendencies, eventually creating a hysterical crisis atmosphere throughout the nation. The Wisconsin senator criticized politically minded entertainers like Woody Guthrie and Pete Seeger, who were blackballed by the networks and the recording industry. "In the summer of 1950," remembered Seeger, "'Goodnight Irene' [by the Weavers] was selling two million copies. It was the biggest hit record since the end of World War II. We were offered a coast-to-coast network TV program sponsored by Van Camp's Pork and Beans, half an hour a week. The contract came in, we signed it. The next day, when they were supposed to sign, an outfit called the Red Channels came out with an attack on us. Called us 'commie fellow-travelers,' and Van Camp's never signed the contract. The jobs started vanishing, and pretty soon we were down to singing at Daffy's Bar and Grill on the outskirts of Cleveland." Though the destructive effects of McCarthyism abated for the Weavers by December 1955, when they triumphantly performed at Carnegie Hall, the group never regained its pre–Red Scare popularity until the early 1960s on the college campuses.

The Folk Revival

Folk music reappeared around 1960, when the number of college students increased. In 1954, three million students attended college across the country; six years later, almost four million studied within the ivy halls.

These college-age youths searched for an alternative to the popular, romanticized hit singles of Don Kirshner's songwriters who composed for the young teen market. "Today," observed *Look* in early 1961, "the fifteen- to twenty-year-olds, especially those in college, are showing their musical curiosity in ways that don't appear on single-record popularity charts." A few issues later, the magazine reported that college students were "weary of the more and more juvenile level of 'pop' music, frustrated by the dearth of good Broadway show tunes, and slightly befuddled by the growing complexity of jazz, [and were] ready to turn solidly folknik."

The Kingston Trio started the folk revival. Formed in 1957 by three college students—Bob Shane, Nick Reynolds, and Dave Guard—the Trio scored a number-one hit in 1958 with "Tom Dooley," based on a version of the song by North Carolina banjo player Frank Proffitt. The threesome followed with a series of successful albums for Capitol Records, which in four years grossed $40 million, and they surpassed Frank Sinatra as Capitol's number-one moneymaker. By June 1960, *Time* called the "rockless, roll less and rich" trio the "hottest group in U.S. popular music."

The Kingston Trio projected a safe, corporate image. "They are 'sincere' without being 'serious,'" reported singer Will Holt about the Trio in 1961. "They are the kids who sing Saturday nights at fraternity house parties, and the audience gets the comfortable feeling that anyone can do it." Pictures in national magazines featuring the well-groomed, well-dressed Trio at poolside with their wives further promoted the image of stability.

The wholesome Trio profited from their success. In 1962, the threesome averaged $10,000 per concert in a large hall, earned nearly $300,000 in record sales, and grossed $1.7 million in total earnings. The group established Kingston Trio Inc., a ten-company investment firm that owned an office building in San Francisco, a land-development concern, a restaurant, a concert-promotion agency, and a group of music publishing companies. "When we fight nowadays," one of the Kingston Trio told *Time* in 1960, "it's mostly about business—what to invest in."

The commercial success of the Kingston Trio encouraged other apolitical, clean-cut folkies to form singing groups. In July 1959, thirty-six-year-old Lou Gottlieb, an arranger for the Kingston Trio who had earned a Ph.D. in musicology from UCLA, Alex Hassilev, an actor and a University of Chicago graduate, and thirty-nine-year-old Glenn Yarbrough began to sing as the Limeliters. Within a year, the group commanded $4,000 a week for their performances and recorded their debut. In 1961, they hit the Top Five with their *Tonight in Person*. "If the button-down, scrubbed-looking, youthful Kingston Trio are the undergraduates of big-time U.S. folksinging," *Time* reported in June 1961, "the Limeliters are the faculty."

As the Limeliters scaled the chart, ten folksters banded together into the blatantly commercial New Christy Minstrels. "When I chose our people," explained founder Randy Sparks, "I made it a point to shy away from questionable people. I looked for the all-American boy or girl who had no political complaints and no sexual problems anyone would be interested in." The "sporty, clean New Christy Minstrels," reported *Time*, offered "a bland mix of broad harmonies, familiar tunes, corny humor and just enough of the folk music spirit to cash in on the most avid adult record buyer." The group sold over 100,000 copies of its first album and in 1963 hit the Top Twenty with "Green Green." In 1964, Sparks sold his interest in the group for $2.5 million.

The commercial folk boom ironically led to the rediscovery of traditional folk. "Commercialization has actually helped folk music," claimed Pete Seeger in 1963. "It revived interest in it in the cities, where it had almost died. Country interest never really stopped. Now, there are kids all over the nation plinking their banjos, and folk music is a living, vibrant thing again." College-age youths began to listen to Seeger, the re-formed Weavers, the spiritual, operatic singing of Odetta, and Jean Ritchie, who sang Appalachian folk ballads to her own accompaniment on the dulcimer. They became interested in the spirited bluegrass style of pickers, such as Bill Monroe, Doc Watson, and Earl Taylor, and discovered the blues of Muddy Waters, John Lee Hooker, and Howlin' Wolf.

By the early 1960s, folk music in its varied forms had become a craze. Coffeehouses opened in Boston, Chicago, Minneapolis, Denver, and San Francisco. College-age folk fans, having more money than young teens, abandoned 45-rpm hit singles for long-playing albums (LPs) of their favorite groups, which helped double sales of LPs from 1956 to 1961. Beginning in early April 1963, eleven million folk fans watched *Hootenanny*, an ABC nationally broadcast, Saturday night television show that each week took viewers to a folk concert on a different campus. They bought hootenanny sweat shirts, played hootenanny pinball games, read hootenanny magazines, and even watched the feature film *Hootenanny Hoot*. "Yesterday, it was the esoteric kick of history buffs and music scholars. Today, it's show business," *Look* told its readers in 1963. "With a hoot and a holler, folk music has taken over from coffeehouse to campus to prime-time television."

Civil Rights in a New Frontier

The growing clamor of African Americans for civil rights coincided with and shaped the burgeoning folk music scene. On February 1, 1960, four African-American freshmen from the Agricultural and Technical College in Greensboro, North Carolina, entered a Woolworth's variety store, made several purchases, and sat down at the lunch counter reserved for whites to order coffee. Although they were refused service and told to leave, the students remained at the counter until the store closed. The next day, the four freshmen were joined by twenty other students. By the end of the week, nearly a thousand students, both African American and white, crowded around the lunch counter until Woolworth's closed its doors to business until further notice. This tactic of passive resistance, the sit-in, attracted national attention to the civil rights movement, which for the first time challenged segregation in privately owned facilities.

The next week, African-American students in Nashville, schooled in the teachings of Gandhi and emboldened by the recent African liberation movements in countries such as Ghana, organized a protracted sit-in effort. On February 13, hundreds of students sat in white-only sections of restaurants and department stores. Though confronted by police, white violence, and negative public opinion, on May 10 they successfully desegregated lunch counters at three variety stores, a drugstore, and two department stores.

Sit-ins spread to other cities. African-American students in North Carolina staged them in Raleigh, Durham, Charlotte, and Fayetteville. On October 19, 1960, a group of seventy-five African Americans marched into the all-white Magnolia Room of Rich's Department Store in Atlanta and refused to leave, singing "We Shall Overcome." Leader Martin Luther King, Jr. was sentenced to four months of hard labor in Reidsville State Prison for his part in the incident. As some African Americans warned in the *Atlanta Constitution*, "We do not intend to wait placidly for those rights which are already legally and morally ours to be meted out to us one at a time." By the end of 1960, 70,000 African Americans had participated in sit-ins in more than a hundred cities.

The next year, sit-ins, picketing, and boycotts ended segregation in restaurants and at beaches. In Oklahoma City, Savannah, Atlanta, Louisville, and Norfolk, African Americans used sit-ins to desegregate lunch counters and restaurants. In Chicago, passive resistance opened a beach that had previously been available to whites only. A weekend sit-in around the courthouse square in Monroe, North Carolina, successfully ended segregation in city facilities.

In 1961, civil rights demonstrators employed another tactic, the freedom ride. Early that year, two veterans from the sit-in movement, Gordon Carey and Tom Gaither, hatched an idea while stranded on a bus in a snowstorm on the New Jersey Turnpike on their way to New York. "Reading about Gandhi's march to the sea got us talking about an analogous march to the sea in the South," remembered Carey. "We began talking about something that would be a bus trip, and of course we were also inspired by the Journey of Reconciliation, which the Congress of Racial Equality (CORE) and the Fellowship of Reconciliation had sponsored back in 1947. Somehow the drama of the whole thing caught us up, and the two of us planned most of the freedom ride before we ever got back to New York."

On May 4, the CORE, an interracial direct-action group founded in 1942 and headed by James Farmer, Jr., boarded members on buses in Washington, D.C., and sent them on a "freedom ride" into the South to challenge the segregation of interstate travel and terminals that recently had been declared illegal by the Supreme Court. "We planned the freedom ride with the specific intention of creating a crisis," remembered Farmer. "We were counting on the bigots in the South to do our work for us. We figured that the government would have to respond if we created a situation that was headline news all over the world, and affected our image abroad."

The white segregationists played into Farmer's hands. Despite the warnings of federal officials to Alabama Governor John Patterson, the riders were brutally attacked by white racists in Anniston, Birmingham, and Montgomery, Alabama. "I was beaten—I think I was hit with a sort of crate thing that holds soda bottles—and left lying unconscious there, in the streets of Montgomery," recalled rider John Lewis. When they arrived in the segregated bus terminal in Jackson, Mississippi, more than 300 freedom riders, mostly college students, ministers, and professors, were arrested and jailed. Though the freedom riders never reached their New Orleans destination, they attracted the attention of the nation and forced the intervention of federal troops two weeks before a Kennedy–Krushchev summit in Vienna.

Trouble exploded next in Albany, Georgia. On December 10, 1961, youths in the Student Non-Violent Coordinating Committee (SNCC) walked into the all-white lobby of the Albany railway station, sat down, and waited until local authorities arrested them on charges of disorderly conduct. The next week, Martin Luther King, Jr. traveled to Albany and led 700 civil rights adherents in a march to protest the arrest of the students. After authorities arrested King, African Americans in Albany boycotted the local bus system, which relied heavily on these riders. Within forty days, they successfully forced the bus company to cease operations.

The demand for civil rights among African Americans escalated, turning violent in 1963. On April 3, protesters in Birmingham, Alabama, marched for fair employment and desegregation, led by Martin Luther King, Jr. and Reverend Fred Shuttlesworth, the head of the Birmingham chapter of the Southern Christian Leadership Conference (SCLC). The demonstrators slowly increased in numbers, reaching more than 3,000 in a month. On May 3, the marchers, many of them schoolchildren, were assaulted by police, who unleashed dogs, wielded electric cattle prods, and used fire hoses to disperse them and to achieve an uneasy peace. Police arrested thousands of demonstrators, including King, and seriously injured Shuttlesworth. A week later, when racists bombed the house of a demonstrator and an African American–owned motel, African Americans spilled out into the streets and confronted police who pelted them with bricks and bottles. By May 12, when the violence ended, Birmingham officials had agreed to desegregate most of the downtown public facilities, to hire and promote African Americans in local businesses, and to establish a permanent biracial committee to deal with future problems. The riot in Birmingham quickly spread to other cities such as Tallahassee, Nashville, New York, and Cambridge, Maryland.

Racist-inspired violence erupted in June. That month, racists in Jackson, Mississippi, ambushed and killed Medgar Evers, the Mississippi field secretary of the National Association for the Advancement of Colored People (NAACP), near his home. Police in Danville, Virginia, arrested 347 protesters and injured 40 others, when they turned fire hoses on the crowd. Racists shot and killed white civil rights crusader William Moore, who was walking near Attalla, Alabama, with a sign demanding equal rights. They pelted 10 freedom riders with rocks and herded them into jail as they attempted to continue Moore's march. By early July 1963, authorities had arrested almost 15,000 civil rights advocates, who participated in 758 demonstrations in 186 cities.

On August 28, 1963, 250,000 white and African-American civil rights partisans converged on Washington, D.C., a march conceived by A. Philip Randolph, who had envisioned the event as early as 1941. "Black people voted with their feet," civil rights leader Bayard Rustin recollected. "They came from every state, they came in jalopies, on trains, buses, anything they could get—some walked." They marched to the steps of the Lincoln Memorial to listen to ten civil rights leaders, including Martin Luther King, Jr. "I have a dream," intoned King, "that one day this nation will rise up and live out the true meaning of its creed . . . 'we hold these truths to be self-evident that all men are created equal.' I have a dream," King continued in a mounting fervor, "that one day on the red hills of Georgia the sons of former slaves and the sons of former slave owners will be able to sit down together at the table of brotherhood. I have a dream that one day even the state of Mississippi, a state sweltering with the heat of injustice, sweltering with the heat of oppression, will be transformed into an oasis of freedom and justice."

President John F. Kennedy, elected in 1960 and a passive supporter of the March on Washington, offered civil rights crusaders hope that King's dream could become reality. The young, energetic Kennedy assured the nation that the United States was approaching a "new frontier . . . a frontier of unknown opportunities and perils—a frontier of unfulfilled hopes and threats" that was "not a set of promises—it is a set of challenges. It sums up, not what I intend to offer the American people, but what I intend to ask of them." In his inaugural speech, the president specifically focused on "human rights to which this nation has always been committed."

Kennedy supported the demand for equal rights. On September 20, 1962, as part of an ongoing effort to desegregate public schools, Kennedy sent federal troops to the University of Mississippi in Oxford, at which James Meredith, an African-American Air Force veteran, attempted to enroll. When resisted by state troops mobilized by the governor, Kennedy federalized the Mississippi National Guard and on national television appealed to the students at the university to accept desegregation. After a racist-inspired riot left two dead, the president ordered a guard of U.S. marshals to protect Meredith, who began to attend classes.

In June 1963, the president sent federal troops to the University of Alabama to safeguard two new African-American enrollees, Vivian Malone and James Hood. He ordered federal marshals to dislodge Alabama Governor George Wallace, who physically positioned himself in the front doorway of a university building and denounced "this illegal and unwarranted action of the Central Government." In a televised broadcast after the Wallace incident, Kennedy told the nation that the civil rights question was "a moral issue . . . as old as the Scriptures and . . . as clear as the American Constitution." He committed his administration to the proposition "that race has no place in American life or law."

Kennedy took further action the same year. The protests for civil rights, he declared, "have so increased the cries for equality that no city or state or legislative body can prudently choose to ignore them." The president proposed wide-reaching civil rights legislation to guarantee equal access to all public facilities, to attack employment discrimination based on race, and to empower the attorney general to file suit on behalf of individuals whose civil rights had been violated.

Many college students pledged their energies to the new frontier of racial equality. They perceived Kennedy, the youngest elected president in U.S. history, as an energetic visionary who stood in sharp contrast to the grandfatherly Dwight Eisenhower. College-age youth felt an affinity to the Harvard-educated president, who surrounded himself with academics such as Harvard professor Arthur Schlesinger, Jr., and in his inaugural address, had told a national audience that "the torch has been passed to a new generation of Americans."

College students devoted themselves to Kennedy's program for civil rights. "This generation of college students has begun to react against being treated like adolescents," reasoned a writer in a 1961 issue of *The New Republic*. "They have been willing to associate themselves with nonconformist movements, despite warnings by parents and teachers that such activities will endanger their personal as well as their job security." Driven by a Kennedy-inspired idealism, college students became freedom riders, marched for desegregation, and gathered in Washington, D.C., to demand equality.

Student civil rights activism led to one of the first major campus protests, the free speech movement. As they returned to school on October 1, 1964, students at the University of California at Berkeley discovered that tables, which previously had been reserved for the distribution of political leaflets, had been banned on the Bancroft Strip at the Telegraph Avenue entrance to the campus. "We knew at the time that it was aimed at the civil rights movement and at progressive organizations and at those of us interested in the peace movement and civil rights," recalled Jackie Goldberg, who participated in the subsequent protests. When authorities arrested CORE activist Jack Weinberg, who ignored the new policy and would coin the phrase "Don't trust anyone over thirty," the Berkeley students began a three-month protest. Sparked by Mario Savio, who had participated in civil rights activities in Mississippi and headed the Campus Friends of SNCC, the students occupied campus buildings and eventually found faculty support for their free speech demands. "Last summer I went to Mississippi to join the struggle there for civil rights," Savio shouted to his fellow students during one demonstration. "This fall I am engaged in another phase of the same struggle, this time in Berkeley. The two battlefields seem quite different to some observers, but this is not the case." Students, uniting for their rights at Berkeley, had been mobilized by the struggle for African-American civil rights.

Bob Dylan: The Music of Protest

The convergence of the civil rights movement and folk music on the college campuses led to the mercurial rise of Bob Dylan and his brand of protest folk music. Born on May 24, 1941, to the owner of a hardware store in Hibbing, Minnesota, Robert Allen Zimmerman grew up near the Mesabi copper range. Being Jewish in an area that, in his words, "had a certain prejudice against Jews," Dylan felt isolated. As Dylan's high school girlfriend later confided: "The other kids, they wanted to throw stones at anybody different. And Bob was different. He felt he didn't fit in, not in Hibbing." Dylan told a reporter from *The Saturday Evening Post*, "I see things that other people don't see. I feel things that other people don't feel. It's terrible. They laugh. I felt like that my whole life. . . . I don't even know if I'm normal."

To cope with the isolation, Dylan turned to music. He first listened to "Hank Williams one or two years before he died. And that sort of introduced me to the guitar." As with thousands of other youths at the time, Dylan "late at night used to listen to Muddy Waters, John Lee Hooker, Jimmy Reed, and Howlin' Wolf blastin' in from Shreveport. It was a radio show that lasted all night. I used to stay up until two, three o'clock in the morning."

A fan of both country and R&B, Dylan almost naturally embraced the new music of rock-and-roll. When the film *Rock Around the Clock* showed in Hibbing, Dylan shouted to a friend outside of the theater, "Hey, that's our music! That's written for us." He began to idolize Little Richard and then Elvis Presley and "saw Buddy Holly two or three nights before he died. I'll never forget the image of seeing Buddy Holly on the bandstand. And he died—it must have been a week after that. It was unbelievable." By his freshman year in high school, Dylan formed "a couple of bands," including the Golden Chords, which played rock-and-roll at local functions.

Dylan turned to folk music when it reached the Midwest. "I heard a record—the Kingston Trio or Odetta or someone like that," he remembered, "and I sort of got into folk music. Rock-and-roll was pretty much finished. And I traded my stuff for a Martin [acoustic guitar]." In 1959, he began to perform traditional folk music and

Bob Dylan. *Permission by* The Daily *of The University of Washington*.

bluegrass in coffeehouses around the University of Minnesota under the name Dillon and then Dylan.

Bob Dylan encountered his most important early influence while in Minneapolis. As he told it, "I heard Woody Guthrie. And when I heard Woody Guthrie, that was it, it was all over. . . . He really struck me as an independent character. But no one ever talked about him. So I went through all his records I could find and picked all that up by any means I could. Woody was my god." In December 1960, Dylan traveled from Minnesota to New York City and frequently visited the dying Guthrie at a state hospital in nearby New Jersey. Dylan's first album, recorded in October 1961 for $402, included a song dedicated to Woody.

In Greenwich Village, at clubs such as Gerde's Folk City, the Gaslight Coffeehouse, and the Village Gate, Dylan began to sing his own songs of social protest. Remembered Terri Thal, manager of several folk acts and married (at the time) to folk guitarist Dave Van Ronk: "He was beginning to think about and talk about people who were being trod upon [by 1961]. Not in any class way, but he hated people who were taking people. He had a full conception of people who were being taken, and he did read the newspapers, and that's what came through in 'Talkin' Bear Mountain' and 'Talkin' New York,'" both in the Guthrie style of talking blues.

Some observers suggested that Dylan's girlfriend also influenced him. Thal remarked that "Dylan's girlfriend at the time, Suze Rotolo, worked as a secretary for the civil rights group CORE and probably caused Dylan to write 'The Ballad of Emmett Till,'" a song about the brutal murder of a fourteen-year-old African American from Chicago, who in August 1955 traveled to Money, Mississippi, to visit relatives. As one observer in the Village mentioned, "Suze came along and she wanted him to go Pete Seeger's way. She wanted Bobby to be involved in civil rights and all the radical causes Seeger was involved in." By 1962, Dylan had become friends with civil rights activists such as James Forman, Bernice Johnson, and Cordell Reagon of the Student Non-Violent Coordinating Committee and began publishing his songs in *Broadside*, a mimeographed newsletter printed by folksters Agnes Cunningham and Gordon Friesen, to encourage young folk singers to compose topical songs.

Composing songs about current social issues, rather than singing traditional or commercialized folk, Dylan politicized the 1960s' folk music scene with his second album, *The Freewheelin' Bob Dylan*. The album, released in May 1963, featured "Blowin' in the Wind," a song based on the melody of an old spiritual, which became an anthem for the civil rights movement. "The idea came to me," Dylan said, "that all of us in America who didn't speak out were betrayed by our silence. Betrayed by the silence of the people in power. They refuse to look at what's happening. And the others, they ride the subway and read the *Times*, but they don't understand. They don't know. They don't even care, that's the worst of it." Dylan told of the ordeal of James Meredith at the University of Mississippi in "Oxford Town" and composed "Hard Rain's A-Gonna Fall" about the Cuban missile crisis, which occurred in October 1962, when the United States threatened nuclear warfare if Russia did not remove its missiles from Cuba. He penned "Talkin' World War Three Blues," a humorous but somber picture of life after a nuclear holocaust and blasted government leaders in the vitriolic "Masters of War." At the time, the singer felt that "there's other things in this world besides love and sex that're important, too. People shouldn't turn their backs on them just because they ain't pretty to look at. How is the world ever going to get better if we're afraid to look at these things?"

Dylan continued to pen protest songs for his next album, *The Times They Are A-Changin'*, released in February 1964 and hitting the Top Twenty the next month. The title song became a battle cry of the emerging social revolution. He wrote about the murder of civil rights leader Medgar Evers in "A Pawn in Their Game." Dylan chronicled the plight of African Americans in "The Lonesome Death of Hattie Carroll," based on the 1963 killing of an African American barmaid by a white Maryland tobacco farmer who received a sentence of only six months in prison and a $500 fine for the murder.

Dylan reinforced his politicized music through a number of public demonstrations. On May 12, 1963, he refused to perform on *The Ed Sullivan Show* when CBS censors banned him from singing "Talkin' John Birch Society Blues." On July 6, he gave a concert outside Greenwood, Mississippi, with Pete Seeger to promote African-American voter registration initiated by the Student Non-Violent Coordinating Committee. Later in the month, he appeared on a local New York television program dealing with "freedom singers." On August 28, Dylan performed at the famous March on Washington, D.C., headed by Martin Luther King, Jr.

Bob Dylan began to serve as the focal point for a community of protest singers. To Joan Baez, herself active in the protest movement, "Bobby Dylan says what a lot of people my age feel but cannot say."

Joan Baez

Joan Baez was Bob Dylan's female counterpart in folk protest. The daughter of a Mexican-born physicist and a Scotch-Irish mother who taught English drama, the dark-skinned Baez faced racial discrimination at an early age. As a girl in Clarence Center, New York, a town of 800 people, she felt that "as far as the [townspeople] knew we were niggers."

Baez moved with her family to Boston, where, during the late 1950s, she began to perform traditional folk songs in coffeehouses around Harvard, such as Club 47, the Ballard Room, and Tulla's Coffee Grinder. In 1959, Baez debuted to 13,000 people at the first Newport Folk Festival. "A star was born," wrote Robert Shelton in *The New York Times* after the performance, "a young soprano with a thrilling lush vibrato and fervid and well-controlled projection." Baez continued to attract a following, selling out a Carnegie Hall performance two months in advance. From 1960 to 1962, she recorded three albums, all of which hit the Top Twenty. By 1962, *Time* referred to Joan "as the most gifted of the newcomers to the folk scene" and featured her on the cover of its November 23 issue.

The singer, though composing few of her own songs, took a decidedly political stance. She sang topical songs such as the antiwar "Strangest Dream" and a parody of the House Un-American Activities Committee, which ceaselessly tracked supposed Communist sympathizers. The singer refused to appear on ABC's *Hootenanny*, when the show blacklisted Pete Seeger, and rejected more than $100,000 in concert dates

Folk singer Joan Baez sings and plays her guitar in front of a crowd at a freedom rally in front of Sproul Hall at the University of California, Berkeley, California, December 2, 1964. © Bettmann/CORBIS.

during a single year because, as she told *Time*, "folk music depends on intent. If someone desires to make money, I don't call it folk music." In 1963, Baez demonstrated in Birmingham for desegregation and in August marched on Washington, D.C. "I feel very strongly about things," Joan told *Look* in 1963. "Like murdering babies with fallout and murdering spirits with segregation. I love to sing and, by some quirk, people like to hear me. I cannot divide things. They are all part of me."

The Singer-Activists

Other folk singers followed the path of protest. Texas-born Phil Ochs, the son of a Jewish army physician, became a journalism major at Ohio State University, where he won his first guitar by betting on John Kennedy in the hotly contested 1960 presidential election. A year later, he composed his first song, "The Ballad of the Cuban Invasion," about the American invasion of Cuba at the Bay of Pigs, and joined a radical singing group called the Sundowners or, sometimes, the Singing Socialists, with roommate Jim Glover, who later became half of the pop duo Jim and Jean. In 1962, Ochs dropped out of Ohio State and journeyed to New York City to start his folk-protest career in earnest, describing himself as a "singing journalist." He performed at the 1963 Newport Folk Festival with the Freedom Singers, Dylan, Baez, and the songwriters' workshop, where, according to Phil, "the topical song suddenly became the thing. It moved from the background to the foreground in just one weekend."

Ochs, looking for a forum to propagate his radical ideals, churned out protest songs dealing with the issues of the day. His first album, *All the News That's Fit to Sing*, released by Elektra in April 1964, included "Too Many Martyrs," "Talking Cuban Crisis," and "Talking Vietnam." Said Ochs: "I was writing about Vietnam in 1962, way before the first antiwar marches. I was writing about it at a point where the media were really full of shit, where they were just turning the other way as Vietnam was being built." Subsequent albums delivered other protest hymns, such as "Ballad of Oxford, Mississippi," "Draft Dodger Rag," and "I Ain't Marching Anymore."

Phil Ochs backed his words with action. In 1964, when he heard that the bodies of three murdered civil rights workers had been found buried under an earthen dam, he headed for Mississippi. Ochs later traveled to Hazard, Kentucky, to help striking miners, who were engaged in a bloody struggle with mine owners who were trying to bypass provisions of the Mine Safety Act. Phil's song "No Christmas in Kentucky" became a battle cry among the workers. When Phil and folk singer Tom Paxton played a benefit for the miners, members of the John Birch Society and the Fighting American Nationalists picketed the concert with placards that read "Agrarian Reformers Go Home."

Tom Paxton raised his voice in protest for similar causes. Born in Chicago, a young Paxton traveled to Oklahoma with his family. At the University of Oklahoma, Paxton discovered the music of Woody Guthrie and, like Dylan, became radicalized. "Woody was fearless; he'd take on any issue that got him stirred up . . . and he became one of my greatest influences," explained the folk singer. After a stint in the army, in the early 1960s Paxton moved to New York City, where he started to write songs and perform at the Gaslight Café in Greenwich Village with Bob Dylan, Phil Ochs, and others. In 1963, he appeared at the Newport Folk Festival, and Pete Seeger recorded a few of his songs, including "What Did You Learn in School Today." By 1964, Paxton landed a recording contract with Elektra Records and offered a series of protest songs in *Ramblin' Boy*. The next year, he recorded one of his most political albums, *Ain't That News*, which included "Lyndon Johnson Told the Nation," "Buy a Gun for Your Son," and "Ain't That News." Explained Paxton about the title song: "When the poor (again, with the help of the students) are making the first hesitant steps toward organization; when Negroes, disenfranchised for years, are lining up by the thousands to register to vote; when mass demonstrations and teach-ins protest this government's foreign policy; when after the long sleep of the Eisenhower years you find heated dialogues and demonstrations throughout the country—that's news."

By 1964, the protest songs of Bob Dylan and others such as Tom Paxton climbed the charts, telling of racial injustice and the need for change. Their songs reverberated throughout the campus halls of the country, reaching college students who listened to their words and sometimes took action. As Dylan preached his message of social change, a small African American–owned record company in Detroit, motivated by the same concerns, sought to integrate America by appealing to a younger audience more interested in pop music. Owner Berry Gordy, Jr. called his company Motown and his music the Sound of Young America.

6

Motown: The Sound of Integration

❝ This organization is built on love. **❞**

— Berry Gordy

"This organization is built on love," thirty-five-year-old Berry Gordy, Jr., the founder of Motown Records, told *Newsweek* in early 1965. "We're dealing with feeling and truth."

Gordy, sounding much like Martin Luther King, Jr., created a music empire that exemplified the peaceful integration advocated by King and reflected the progress of the civil rights movement. The African American–owned and operated Motown was established a year before the first sit-in demonstration and achieved moderate success during the civil rights strife of the early 1960s. The Detroit-based company, using the assembly-line techniques of nearby auto factories, became a major force in popular music from late 1964 to 1967, when civil rights partisans won a series of significant legislative victories. At a time when the civil rights of African Americans began to be recognized, Motown became the first African American–owned label that consistently and successfully groomed, packaged, marketed, and sold the music of African-American youths to the white American masses.

Motown: The Early Years

Berry Gordy, Jr. started his career in the music industry as a producer and songwriter. Born in Detroit on November 28, 1929, Gordy became interested in songwriting as a youth. "I did other things," he remembered. "I was a plasterer for a while in my father's business, took a job on an automobile assembly line. But I always wrote songs." In 1957, Gordy had his first success with the song "Reet Petite," which was recorded by Detroit-born Jackie Wilson, who at one time had replaced Clyde McPhatter as the lead singer of the Dominoes. The next year he penned the million-selling

"Lonely Teardrops" for Wilson and established the Jobete Music Publishing Company. At the same time, Gordy began to produce records such as the Miracles' "Got a Job."

In January 1959, the same year that Don Kirshner started Aldon Music, Berry Gordy borrowed $800 from his family, rented an eight-room house at 2648 West Grand Boulevard, and founded the Motown Record Corporation, which would issue records under a variety of labels. "If I ever get this house and get it paid for," Gordy told his sister Esther at the time, "I'll have it made. I'll live upstairs, I'll have my offices down in the front part, and I'll have a studio out back where I can make demonstration records or masters to sell to record companies."

Gordy initially recorded rhythm-and-blues artists on Tamla Records. He signed Mable John, the gospel-trained sister of blues singer Little Willie John, who described herself as "basically a blues singer." Gordy scored a minor hit with the first Tamla release, R&B singer Marv Johnson's "Come to Me." Later during his first year of operation he cowrote and released "Money," which was recorded by Barrett Strong and climbed to the number-two position on the R&B chart. In September 1959, the Motown founder recorded "Bad Girl" by young William "Smokey" Robinson and the Detroit-born Miracles, a song that reached number ninety-three on the pop charts with the help of national distribution by Chess Records.

Gordy became convinced by Smokey Robinson that Motown should distribute its own records. "When I started," Gordy told *Black Enterprise*, "we licensed our singles to other companies such as United Artists. Smokey Robinson gave me the idea to go national with my own product; my attorneys and other people said it was madness, that I shouldn't do it because a hit would throw me into bankruptcy since [we were] undercapitalized." In 1960, Gordy cowrote and distributed "Shop Around" by Smokey Robinson and the Miracles that hit the top of the R&B chart and the number-two slot on the pop chart to establish Motown as an important independent company.

Throughout the next four years, Berry Gordy continued to produce hits by capitalizing on the girl-group craze. In 1959, sixteen-year-old Mary Wells approached the Motown founder with a song she had written for Jackie Wilson. Unable to write music, she sang the song to Gordy, who immediately signed the teenager and released her version of "Bye Bye Baby," which hit the Top Ten on the R&B chart in 1960. Two years later, Wells teamed with Smokey Robinson, who by now wrote and produced for Tamla, and hit with "The One Who Really Loves You," "You Beat Me to the Punch," and "Two Lovers," all of which hit the Top Ten on the pop chart. After a few minor hits, in 1964 Wells topped the pop chart with her signature song, "My Guy."

Gordy also charted with the Marvelettes. "We were discovered at a talent show in Inkster [Michigan]," recalled Wanda Young, who founded the group with Gladys Horton. "One of our teachers arranged an audition for us with Motown, even though we didn't even win the contest. This was around 1961 and there were five of us then." The group signed with the label and released "Please Mr. Postman," written by Marvelette Georgia Dobbins, a song that became Motown's first number-one hit. The next year, the Marvelettes hit the Top Twenty with "Playboy" and "Beachwood 4-5789." In November 1962, the group toured the South in a bus and five cars as part of the first Motortown Revue and, according to Katherine Anderson of the Marvelettes, "did what we could to play for integrated audiences."

Martha and the Vandellas on stage in Chicago, c. 1963. Raeburn Fleriage/Cache Agency.

Berry Gordy, Jr., encouraged by his success with the Marvelettes, recorded another group of girls from Detroit—Martha and the Vandellas. Martha Reeves, influenced by the gospel sound of Clara Ward and jazz singer Billie Holiday, joined with Annette Sterling and Rosalind Ashford to sing as the Del-Phis while in high school and recorded the unsuccessful "I'll Let You Know" for Chess. In 1961, Reeves accepted a job at Motown as a secretary and, by July 1962, had convinced the company to use her group. The persistent trio sang backup vocals on a number of Motown hits, including "Hitch Hike" and "Stubborn Kind of Fellow" by Marvin Gaye, a romantic balladeer who had sung in the doo-wop group the Moonglows and in 1961 had joined Motown. In late 1963, amid the girl-group explosion, Martha and the Vandellas hit the chart with the million-selling, Top Ten "Heat Wave" and "Quicksand." The next year they recorded the memorable "Dancing in the Street," which neared the top of the pop chart and, along with hits by Mary Wells and the Marvelettes, positioned Motown as a major source of the girl-group sound.

Civil Rights in the Great Society

The civil rights movement, which began in the 1950s and escalated during the early 1960s, resulted in significant achievements in 1964 and 1965 that would coincide with the Motown heyday.

On July 2, 1964, Congress passed the most sweeping civil rights legislation since the Civil War. The Civil Rights Act established a sixth-grade education as a minimum voting requirement and empowered the attorney general to protect the voting rights of all citizens. It forbade discrimination in public places such as restaurants, hotels, bathrooms, and libraries; created an Equal Employment Opportunity Commission and a Community Relations Service to help communities solve racially based problems; banned discrimination in federally funded programs; and authorized technical and financial aid for school desegregation. Also in 1964, Congress ratified the Twenty-fourth Amendment to the U.S. Constitution, which outlawed the poll tax in federal elections.

Congress enacted the Voting Rights Act the next year, after violence erupted in Selma, Alabama. Early in 1965, Sheriff James G. Clark forcibly resisted a voter registration drive in Dallas County, Alabama, where no African Americans had voted in years. He collected a posse wielding whips, clubs, and canisters of tear gas to disperse peaceful demonstrators, two of whom were murdered. Martin Luther King, Jr. and 3,200 equal rights partisans, protected by the Alabama National Guard, marched 50 miles from Selma to Montgomery to protest the blatant discrimination and violence. "No tide of racism can stop us," King exhorted 25,000 listeners in Montgomery after the completion of his five-day march.

Disturbed by the events in Selma, President Lyndon Johnson proposed greater voting safeguards for African Americans and, in the words of the civil rights anthem, promised Congress that "We shall overcome." Congress responded with a law that banned the unfair literacy tests used in the South to disenfranchise African Americans and authorized the attorney general to dispatch federal examiners to register voters in areas where local examiners discriminated on the basis of color. By the end of the year, nearly 250,000 African Americans had registered to vote for the first time.

President Lyndon Johnson also promised a Great Society "where the city of man served not only the needs of the body and the demands of commerce but the desire for beauty and the hunger for community." He encouraged America to ask "not only how much, but how good; not only how to create wealth, but how to use it; not only how fast we are going, but where we are headed."

To achieve his dream, Johnson pushed through Congress a series of bills designed to eradicate economic inequality. In 1964, Congress passed the Economic Opportunity Act, which declared a "war on poverty." It created the Office of Economic Opportunity, which included a Job Corps for high school dropouts, a Neighborhood Youth Corps for unemployed teens, the Volunteers in Service to America (VISTA), which was a domestic version of the Kennedy-established Peace Corps, the Head Start Program for disadvantaged children, and the Upward Bound Program, which prepared the poor to attend college.

That same year, Congress enacted the Criminal Justice Act, which provided the indigent with adequate legal representation. It passed the Food Stamp Act to provide groceries to needy families and ratified the Housing Act, which authorized $1 billion for the urban renewal of inner cities. Congress also agreed to cut taxes by $11.5 billion in two years, which Lyndon Johnson called "the single most important step that we have taken."

In 1965, Congress continued to legislate reforms. It passed the Elementary and Secondary Education Act, which earmarked more than $1.3 billion for the improvement of school districts that had desegregated. Congress also created Medicare, which provided medical and hospital insurance to the aged. Coupled with civil rights legislation, the new laws of the Great Society provided African Americans with hope for a better future and seemed to be a giant step toward realizing the dream of Martin Luther King, Jr.

The Sound of Integration

In 1964, Berry Gordy, Jr. assembled the parts of a music machine to create a distinctive Motown sound, which reflected and furthered the integration of African Americans into white America. Gordy had always supported the peaceful integrationist program of Martin Luther King, Jr., who once had paid a brief visit to the Motown offices. In 1963, he had released a recorded version of King's "I Have a Dream" speech, delivered on the steps of the Lincoln Memorial at the end of the March on Washington, D.C. He also recorded another album of King's speeches, *Great March to Freedom*, which captured the civil rights leader in a Detroit march. "Motown was a very strong backer of Martin Luther King's total program," asserted Motown producer Mickey Stevenson. "Berry felt that our job in Detroit was to make blacks aware of their culture, of the problems and some of the ways out of the problems. We'd showcase our artists to young kids at the Graystone Ballroom and it gave us a chance to get the youngsters off the street and see what our image was about . . . inspiring them a little to maybe live up to that imagery. Motown was a tremendous avenue of escape and hope." Gordy explained, "I saw Motown much like the world Dr. King was fighting for with people of different races and religions, working together harmoniously for a common goal."

Gordy, the son of an African–American entrepreneur, who hoped for the upward mobility of African Americans, specially groomed and cultivated streetwise teens from Detroit to make them acceptable to mainstream America. In 1964, he hired Maxine Powell, who formerly had operated a finishing and modeling school, to prep his performers. "The singers were raw," remembered Powell. "They were from the streets, and like most of us who came out of the [housing] projects, they were a little crude: some were backward, some were arrogant. They had potential, but they were not unlike their friends in the ghetto. I always thought of our artists as diamonds in the rough who needed polishing. We were training them for Buckingham Palace and the White House, so I had my work cut out for me."

Powell tried to transform the Motown artists into polished professionals. "Many of them had abusive tones of voice, so I had to teach them how to speak in a nonthreatening manner," she explained. "Many of them slouched, so I had to show them what posture meant. Some were temperamental and moody; I would lecture them about their attitude. . . . I chose which clothes were best for them as well. We used to call them 'uniforms,' and before we had them specially made, I would have to choose outfits that would complement all of the people in a group, which wasn't easy. As far as makeup, I worked with all of the girls on wigs, nails, and that sort of thing. And on stage technique, I taught them little things like never turning their backs to an audience, never protruding their buttocks onstage, never opening their mouths too wide to sing, how to be well-rounded professionals." She also taught them the art of the inoffensive interview. "I had to force these lessons," Powell concluded. "The youngsters often had to be pushed and shoved."

A few months after adding Maxine Powell to the staff, Berry Gordy, Jr. hired choreographer Cholly Atkins. Atkins, a well-known dancer in the 1930s and 1940s who had performed in the Cotton Club and the Savoy Ballroom, tried to teach the Motown groups to move gracefully. "What I was really trying to do with them was to teach them physical drama, which most of them had no respect for," he said. "My method for the Motown artists was that I always wanted them coming from someplace and going to someplace." Within a year, boasted Atkins, "we had the best-looking artists in the record business."

Atkins worked with Maurice King, who served as the executive musical director. King, who had arranged shows at Detroit's Flame Show Bar for years and had worked with jazz artists such as Billie Holiday and Dinah Washington, taught the Motown acts about stage patter. "My rehearsals were conducted like a class, a noninterrupted class," he recalled. "When we were through with them, they could play any supper club in the country and shine."

By the mid-1960s, Berry Gordy, Jr. had assembled a Motown team that could take poor African-American youths from Detroit and teach them to talk, walk, dress, and dance like successful debutantes and debonair gentlemen. "I'm sure that blacks were wearing tuxedos, top hats, wigs and eyelashes before Berry Gordy came along but not with the popular music we were recording, and not for the same reasons," observed one Motown staffer. "We really wanted young blacks to understand that you do not have to look like you came out of the ghetto in order to be somebody other blacks and even whites would respect when you made it big. They'll believe you had a rough childhood; you don't have to prove it to them by looking like hell."

Berry Gordy, Jr. combined the polished image of the Motown acts with a gospel-based music that could appeal to the American mainstream. "Blues and R&B always had a funky look to it back in those days, and we at Motown felt that we should have a look that the mothers and fathers would want their children to follow. We wanted to kill the imagery of liquor and drugs and how some people thought it pertained to R&B," explained Motown producer Mickey Stevenson. "I did not like blues songs when choosing material for our artists, and Berry agreed with that," continued Stevenson. "We enjoyed John Lee Hooker and B. B. King just as much as the next guy, but we would reject anything that had a strong blues sound to it."

In place of blues and R&B, Gordy favored a distinctive music grounded by an insistent, pounding rhythm section, punctuated by horns and tambourines and featuring shrill, echo-laden vocals that bounced back and forth in the call-and-response of gospel. Building upon his experience with girl groups, he produced a full sound both reminiscent of and expanding upon Phil Spector's wall of sound. Aiming for the mass pop market, Gordy called the music "The Sound of Young America" and affixed a huge sign over the Motown studio that read "Hitsville U.S.A."

The Supremes on the Assembly Line

The Supremes fulfilled Berry Gordy's dream of a polished African-American act that sang gospel-based pop to both African Americans and whites. Born in Detroit and meeting in the low-income Brewster housing project, Diana Ross, Mary Wilson, Florence Ballard, and Betty Travis began singing together in high school "when groups were becoming very popular with teenagers," recalled Wilson. They sang as the Primettes at sock hops and in 1960 won the first prize at the Detroit/Windsor Freedom Festival talent contest. Late that year, after pestering Motown staffers for a few months, the group, which included Barbara Martin, who replaced Betty Travis, signed to Motown and on the advice of Berry Gordy, Jr. changed their name. "One day I was working at my desk," recalled Motown songwriter Janie Bradford, "and Berry came up to me and said, 'I'm changing the name of this group called the Primettes, four giggly little girls. Come up with a name.' So I thought it over and came up with three names, put them in a hat on little slips of paper. Florence picked the Supremes."

The Supremes performing in London in 1965; Diana Ross is at the microphone. Photo by Michael Ochs Archives. Getty Images, Inc.—Michael Ochs Archives.

The newly signed act had little success initially. In December 1960, the Supremes recorded "I Want a Guy," which attracted so little attention that Barbara Martin quit the group. During the next three years, the group recorded more than forty songs, of which only twelve were released and met with limited success.

Around 1964, when Mary Wells left the company, Motown began to polish the Supremes. It sent the girls to Maxine Powell, who taught them about proper etiquette and attire. "We spent only about six months working with Mrs. Powell, but anything we learned would be incorporated the same day," recalled Mary Wilson. "We would be out eating something, and if one of us accidentally picked up her chicken with her fingers, the other two would say, 'remember what Mrs. Powell said.'" The company also provided the group with lessons from music director Maurice King and choreographer Cholly Atkins.

The Supremes, groomed by the Motown organization, scaled the charts in 1964. After cracking the Top thirty with "When the Lovelight Starts Shining Through His Eyes," the group recorded "Where Did Our Love Go," which was released just fifteen days after the passage of the momentous Civil Rights Act. In the summer, Gordy secured a spot for the Supremes on Dick Clark's Caravan of Stars tour. "We need Dick Clark for the white people," Gordy asserted. "I gotta have that tour." Prepared by Gordy and promoted by Clark, the Supremes' "Where Did Our Love Go" topped both the pop and R&B charts by the end of the year. On December 27, 1964, the Supremes made their first of twenty appearances on *The Ed Sullivan Show*, which had introduced Elvis Presley to the American public. The Supremes, appearing in sleek, light-blue chandelier gowns, embodied the Motown image of the slick, cultivated African-American entertainer and became overnight pop stars.

Berry Gordy, using methods practiced in the Detroit auto factories, ensured the continued success of the Supremes by assembling the parts of a hit-making machine that included standardized songwriting, an in-house rhythm section, a quality control process, selective promotion, and a family atmosphere reminiscent of the paternalism fostered by Henry Ford in his auto plant during the early twentieth century. "I worked in the Ford factory before I came in the [record] business, and I saw how each person did a different thing," Gordy reasoned. "And I said, 'Why can't we do that with the creative process?' It was just an idea of coming in one door one day and going out the other door and having all these things done."

The songwriting team of Brian Holland, Lamont Dozier, and Eddie Holland, joining forces in 1962, perfected the formula of success that they discovered with their composition "Where Did Our Love Go." From late 1964 to early 1967, they wrote a series of number-one hits for the Supremes, which included "Baby Love," "Come See About Me," "Stop! In the Name of Love," "Back in My Arms Again," "I Hear a Symphony," "You Can't Hurry Love," "You Keep Me Hangin' On," and "Love Is Here and Now You're Gone." "When 'Where Did Our Love Go' hit for the Supremes," remembered Lamont Dozier, "we knew we had stumbled onto a sound. You'll notice that we patterned 'Baby Love' and 'Come See About Me' right after the first hit. In fact, all the Supremes' big hits were really children of 'Where Did Our Love Go.'"

Lamont Dozier explained the creative process of the team. "I was basically the idea man in the group, and I came up with a good 70 or 75 percent of all the ideas for the songs," he explained. "Brian was a recording engineer as well as a melody man, and so I would team up with him to produce the track, and then I would start a lyrical idea and give it to Eddie to finish. He in turn would teach the song to the artist. You might say that we had our own little factory within a factory," he concluded. "We were able to turn out a lot of songs that way."

The different singles sounded remarkably similar because of the in-house rhythm section known as the Funk Brothers, who played on most of the Supremes' recording sessions. In 1964, Earl Van Dyke, a former be-bop jazz pianist who had toured with R&B singer Lloyd Price, became the leader of the studio band. He played with drummer Benny Benjamin, Robert White or Joe Messina on guitar, and bassist James Jamerson, who had backed Jackie Wilson and the Miracles. Along with a few other musicians who joined them occasionally in the studio, the Funk Brothers provided the trademark percussive beat of the Motown sound.

Berry Gordy, Jr. attempted to maintain the consistent quality of Motown material by conducting weekly meetings that scrutinized possible releases. "The quality control meetings on Fridays were real intense," remarked Motown songwriter Ron Miller. "All of the writers, producers, and many of the executives gathered in Berry's office, and he would play everyone's songs. And then he went around to everyone there and asked them for their opinion. It was brutal."

Berry Gordy, Jr. carefully promoted the songs, which were released through a marketing strategy that kept the slick Motown image intact. Besides spots on *The Ed Sullivan Show*, he snagged appearances for the Supremes on mainstream television programs such as *The Dean Martin Show, The Tonight Show, Hollywood Palace*, a special presented by African-American crooner Sammy Davis, Jr., and the Orange Bowl

Parade. For concerts, Gordy favored posh settings such as the Copacabana in New York, which hosted the Supremes for three weeks in July 1965; the Yale University prom of 1965, which featured jazz great Duke Ellington as well as the Supremes; and exclusive Las Vegas hotels such as the Flamingo, where the Supremes performed in 1967. He even asked established entertainers such as Sammy Davis, Jr. and Broadway star Carol Channing to write the liner notes for the Supremes' albums.

Gordy retained control of the successful group by creating a family atmosphere at the company. In 1965, like a watchful father, he limited each Supreme to a $100 weekly allowance and funneled the remainder of their $300,000 profit for the year into a joint bank account. The Motown owner refused to allow the girls to date and, to fend off possible suitors, gave each girl a diamond ring. "They're Christmas presents from Gordy," Florence Ballard told *Newsweek* about her ring in 1965. "Someone saw mine the other week," chimed in Mary Wilson. "He said, 'Oh, you're engaged.' I said, 'Yeah. To Motown.'" Sounding like a stern father, Gordy asserted, "You have to be very strict with young artists. That instills discipline."

The Motown Stable

Berry Gordy, Jr.'s paternal, production-line approach produced other successful performers such as the Temptations. In 1957, the eighteen-year-old, Detroit-raised, gospel-schooled Otis Williams started a street-corner doo-wop group, the Distants, with a few friends, including Elbridge Bryant and teenager Melvin Franklin who released "Come On" on Warwick Records. Three years later, the Distants joined forces with Eddie Kendricks and Paul Williams to become the Elgins.

In 1960, between sets at a local club, Williams walked into the bathroom of the Stevens Community Center in Detroit, where he met Berry Gordy, Jr., who complimented the group and signed them to Motown. Renamed the Temptations after Gordy signed them, from 1961 to 1963 the group released seven singles, which met with only moderate success.

Berry Gordy shaped the Temptations into the Motown image and placed them on the charts by 1964. He replaced their processed hair styles with carefully cropped Afros, discarded their casual clothes for top hats and tails, inserted such standards as "Old Man River" into their repertoire, and added the precise choreography of Motown dance master Cholly Atkins to their stage show.

In 1964, the Temptations enjoyed their first U.S. hit, "The Way You Do the Things You Do," which peaked at number eleven. When lead singer David Ruffin replaced Elbridge Bryant in March 1965, the refurbished Temptations recorded the Smokey Robinson composition "My Girl," an answer to the Mary Wells hit "My Guy," which topped both the pop and R&B charts. During the next eighteen months, the group remained on the charts with a series of songs, including "Since I Lost My Baby" and "Get Ready" by Smokey Robinson and "Ain't Too Proud to Beg," "Beauty Is Only Skin Deep," and "(I Know) I'm Losing You," all by Eddie Holland and Norman Whitfield who, with Robinson and the Holland-Dozier-Holland team, formed the legendary Motown songwriting production crew.

This Motown team revived the careers of other former doo-woppers, the Four Tops. The group—Levi Stubbs, Renaldo Benson, Lawrence Payton, and Abdul

Fakir—grew up together in Detroit during the late 1940s. In 1954, they banded together as the Four Aims and in 1956 released "Kiss Me Baby" on Chess Records. The vocal group began to back jazz vocalist Billy Eckstine and in 1960 signed with Columbia to record the unsuccessful "Ain't That Love." In 1962, the group signed with Riverside Records and recorded "Where Are You?," which also failed to chart. "We were working," recalled Abdul Fakir, "perfecting our craft and just out there hustling. Guess you could say we were getting ready for the Chairman."

Chairman Berry Gordy signed the group in 1963, dressed them in tuxedos, and within a year paired them with the songwriting team of Holland-Dozier-Holland, who wrote "Baby I Need Your Loving," a smooth, gospel-flavored composition that hit the number-eleven slot on the pop charts. Gordy continued to provide the Four Tops with Holland-Dozier-Holland material, including the number-one pop hits "I Can't Help Myself" and "Reach Out I'll Be There" as well as other chartbusters such as "Shake Me, Wake Me (When It's Over)," "Standing in the Shadows of Love," and "It's the Same Old Song."

As with the Supremes and the Temptations, the Four Tops benefited from the Motown finishing school, the dance classes, the musical direction, and the promotion to become a slick, popular act, which appealed to both white and African-American audiences. "Our pop sound [and] our visual performance, especially the dancing, was such that people were comfortable with us," explained Levi Stubbs. "Because of Motown the music merged, black-and-white music was brought together and solidified. The mixture was a turning point in our country—the music melted together, and that was great for social relations."

The integration of Motown's version of R&B pop into the white mainstream of rock-and-roll did not come easily. The Motown tours throughout the American South consistently met opposition. "The Motown Revue was on tour somewhere, and we were staying down South at the Daniel Boone Hotel," remembered the Temptations' Otis Williams. "We had performed and these white guys drove by in a car, called us the 'n' word, shot at us and the [Four] Tops and other Motown acts." Though no one was hurt, the Temptations, the Four Tops, and other Motown artists suffered similar degradation each time they toured the southern states.

Despite the roadblocks, Berry Gordy, Jr. persisted and established a music empire, which included eight record labels, a management service, and a publishing company. From 1964 through 1967, Motown placed fourteen number-one pop singles, twenty number-one singles on the R&B charts, forty-six more Top Fifteen pop singles, and seventy-five other Top Fifteen R&B records. In 1966 alone, 75 percent of all Motown releases hit the charts. The next year Motown grossed $21 million, selling 70 percent of its records to whites. "It is no coincidence," observed a British newspaper columnist in 1965, amid a Motown tour of England, "that while 10,000 Negroes are marching for their civil rights in Alabama, the Tamla-Motown star is on the ascendent." Berry Gordy, Jr., putting into action the program of peaceful integration, had created one of the most commercially successful African American–owned enterprises and certainly the most successful African American–owned record company. In his heyday, he had almost no rivals except a sprightly group of four lads from Liverpool who in early 1964 took the United States by storm.

The British Invasion of America: The Beatles

7

66 We were just the spokesmen for a generation. **99**

— Paul McCartney

On Friday, February 7, 1964, at Kennedy International Airport in New York City, a mass of screaming teenagers covered the rooftop on one of the airport wings. The crowd, mostly pubescent girls, had been waiting for more than eight hours in the frosty winter air. They considered themselves lucky: Only those with special passes had been permitted on the roof, patrolled by dozens of uniformed security police.

Inside the terminal, huddled around the gate that admitted incoming passengers from London, more than 9,000 teenage girls, adorned with bouffant hairdos, oversized jewelry, and their mothers' makeup, shoved, clawed, and pushed each other in a mad attempt to get to the arrival entrance. They were separated from their goal only by a thin white nylon rope and a few airport guards. As the minutes passed slowly and the intensity mounted, the crowd was comforted by a voice from a transistor radio: "It is now 6:30 A.M. Beatle time. They left London thirty minutes ago. They're out over the Atlantic Ocean heading for New York. The temperature is 32 Beatle degrees."

Four of the passengers on Pan American flight 101 felt uneasy. "We did all feel a bit sick," remembered one. "Going to the States was a big step. People said just because we were popular in Britain, why should we be there?" Asked another: "America's got everything, George, so why should they want us?" A third: "I was worrying about my hair as well. I'd washed it, but when it had dried, it had gone up a bit." The fourth, the oldest and the leader of the group, sat silent and motionless in his seat.

As the plane neared its destination, a few wild screams from the airport broke the tense silence. Then an entire chorus of cries from girls on the rooftop alerted the crowd inside of the group's arrival. In a few moments, the frenzied wails of pent-up teenage passion sent tremors throughout Kennedy International Airport, increasing at a deafening rate. The girls started to half chant, half sing, "We love you Beatles, oh yes we do."

The plane landed safely and reached the hangar. Scurrying attendants pushed a platform toward the jet, the door swung open, and passengers started to descend the steps. Employees of Capitol Records shoved Beatle kits complete with wigs, autographed photos, and a button with the message "I Like the Beatles" at them. At last, four young Englishmen, who sported button-down, Edwardian suits from Pierre Cardin and mushroom-shaped haircuts, walked out. After almost 150 years, the British had again invaded the United States. This time they would emerge as the victors. The Beatles had arrived in America.

The four lads from Liverpool—John, Paul, George, and Ringo—dashed toward a chauffeured airport limousine. They leapt in the car, locked the doors, and rode toward the terminal, assaulted by hundreds of girls who hurled themselves at the slow-moving automobile, clinging to the hood, the roof, and the sides. As they inched away, the foursome saw, pressed against the windows, the contorted faces of teenage fans who tried to catch a glimpse of their heroes before a fellow Beatle maniac pulled them away.

The foursome broke loose from the crowd and headed toward the airport complex. After a short press conference, the Beatles jumped back into the limousine and sped down the Van Wyck Expressway, reaching Manhattan about an hour and a half later. Though swarmed by hundreds of fans when the car stopped at New York's plush Plaza Hotel, the Beatles managed to pry the doors open and somehow make it into the hotel lobby, where they were escorted to a twelfth-floor room. There they discovered three screaming girls in the bathtub and called the service desk for help. Throughout the night and for the next few days, the Beatles were protected by armed guards from ingenious girls, who climbed the fire escapes, and from conspiring groups of teens, who checked in at the hotel, using the names of their well-to-do parents to penetrate the twelfth floor. Outside, the Liverpool lads heard fans keep a twenty-four-hour vigil by chanting, "We want the Beatles, we want the Beatles."

On Sunday night, the new idols from across the Atlantic came into full view. Late in 1963, Ed Sullivan, the square-faced, stocky show business impresario, had witnessed a near riot at the London airport, where more than 15,000 screaming fans descended upon the terminal, delaying the Queen and Prime Minister Sir Alec Douglas-Home in order to welcome the Beatles back from a trip abroad. Impressed, Sullivan told *The New York Times*, "I made up my mind that this was the same sort of mass hit hysteria that had characterized the Elvis Presley days." He hurriedly located Brian Epstein, the dapper, brilliant manager of the group, and for less than $20,000 booked the Beatles for three appearances on his show.

On February 9, 1964, Sullivan showcased the Beatles. Packed into the studio from which *The Ed Sullivan Show* was broadcast were 728 wild teenagers who had battled 50,000 others for tickets to the show that featured their heroes. When Sullivan

The Beatles with Ed Sullivan after performing for the first time on his program on February 9, 1964. Photo by Bernard Gotfryd. Getty Images. Premium Archive/Getty Images.

introduced the foursome—"and now, the Beeeatles!"—the room erupted. Girls with checkered skirts and Macy blouses let out primal screams and pulled their hair, thrusting themselves toward the front of the stage or leaning perilously over the balcony. Some simply fainted. Few noticed that one of the microphones had gone dead. All eyes fastened on Paul, bobbing back and forth as he played a left-handed bass guitar; Ringo, smiling as he brushed the drumskins; John, yelling the lyrics over the din; and a rather dour, flu-stricken George, the youngest, skinniest member of the group, just looking down at the neck of his lead guitar. The screaming intensified. Explained one girl in the crowd: "You really do believe they can see you and just you alone, when they're up on stage. That's why you scream, so they'll notice you. I always felt John could see me. It was like a dream. Just me and John together and no one else." The show, ending amidst the wails, had been phenomenally successful. It had been witnessed by more than seventy-three million people across the country, more than 60 percent of all television viewers.

From New York City, the Beatles rode the King George train to Washington, D.C. On Wednesday, February 11, at 3:09 P.M., amid a storm that dropped 10 inches of snow, they arrived in the nation's capital. The band emerged from the train, hurriedly made their way down a platform "behind a wedge of Washington's finest," and reached the main concourse of Union Station. "For hours," the *Washington Post* wrote, "teenagers had been drifting into Union Station—many of them from National Airport, where the Beatles before the show had been scheduled to arrive. . . . In the concourse, the teenagers, perhaps 2,000 strong, lined the barriers, breathed on the glass, hung through the bars, even climbed the gates." The Beatles, heads down in combat fashion, snaked through the crowd with the help of the police, who pushed and shoved the oncoming torrent of fans. Screamed one girl to the police as they dragged away her friend, "You can't throw her out, she's president of the Beatles Fan Club." Finally John, Paul, Ringo, and George broke through the crowd and leapt into a waiting limousine. They sped toward the Washington Coliseum, which was jammed with 8,092 wild-eyed teens. "From the moment the Beatles were led to the stage by a phalanx of policemen," the *Post* informed its readers, "the din was almost unbearable." Reporter Leroy Aarons compared the noise to "being downwind from a jet during takeoff." During the performance, frantic, distraught girls mercilessly began to pelt their heroes with jelly beans. Explained George: "It was terrible. They hurt. They don't have soft jelly babies in America but hard jellybeans like bullets. Some newspaper had dug out the old joke, which we'd all forgotten about, when John had once said I'd eaten all his jelly babies."

From Washington, the Beatles flew to Miami, where they were greeted by four bathing beauties, a four-mile-long traffic jam, and seven thousand screaming teens, who shattered twenty-three windows and a plate glass door in a tumultuous attempt to touch their idols. The group played for a raucous audience in Miami, then headed toward New York City, where they upstaged President Lyndon Johnson. In an article entitled "LBJ Ignored as New York Crowds Chase Beatles," *Billboard* reported that "President Lyndon B. Johnson visited here late last week, but the arrival was over-shadowed by the Beatles invasion. Few were aware of the president's presence in their midst, but no one could miss the fact that Britain's Beatles had descended upon the town. Radio, TV, and all other communication media were filled with Beatle clamor. At Kennedy Airport here, Beatle greeters began lining up at 4:00 A.M. Friday to await the group's arrival this afternoon."

By the time the Beatles left New York for London on February 16, the entire nation had become aware of Beatlemania. Headlines in the staid *Billboard* told the story: "The U.S. Rocks and Reels from Beatles Invasion"; "Chicago Flips Wig, Beatles and Otherwise"; "New York City Crawling with Beatlemania"; and "Beatle Binge in Los Angeles." In the nine days during the Beatles' brief visit, Americans had bought more than two million Beatles records and more than $2.5 million worth of Beatles-related goods. They purchased blue-and-white Beatles hats; Beatles T-shirts and beach shirts; Beatles tight-fitting pants; Beatles pajamas and three-button tennis shirts; Beatles cookies; Beatles egg cups; Beatles rings, pendants, and bracelets; a pink plastic Beatles guitar with pictures of the four lads stamped on it; and a plethora of Beatles dolls, including inflatable figurines, 6-inch-tall hard rubber likenesses, painted wooden dolls that bobbed their heads when moved, and a cake decoration in the form of the Beatles. Others snapped up Beatles nightshirts, countless Beatles publications, Beatles ice-cream sandwiches covered with a foil Beatles wrapper, Beatles soft drinks, and Beatles wigs, which Lowell Toy Company churned out at the rate of 15,000 a day. Seltaeb (Beatles spelled backward), the American arm of the Beatles manufacturing company, even planned for a Beatles motor scooter and a Beatles car.

The Beatles promotion photo, c. 1964. *Permission by Capitol Records.*

The Mods, the Rockers, and the Skiffle Craze

Beatlemania had its genesis in a wartime and postwar baby boom and in an economic depression that spawned gangs of British working-class youths. As with the United States, England experienced a baby boom after World War II. "That was the Bulge, that was England's Bulge," Pete Townshend, lead guitarist for the Who, told a reporter. "All the war babies, all the old soldiers coming back from the war and screwing until they were blue in the face—this was the result. Thousands and thousands of kids, too many kids, not enough teachers, not enough parents." By the late 1950s and early 1960s, many English baby boomers had become teenagers, who were ready for rock-and-roll.

At the same time, England faced economic hardships. Crippled by the war, it continued to enforce wartime rationing until 1954 and tried to rebuild with little help from wartime allies. "World War II went on there for another nine years after it finished everywhere else," recalled Keith Richards of the Rolling Stones. "I remember London, huge areas of rubble and grass growing."

During the mid- to late 1950s, many British teens, unlike their American counterparts, faced hard times upon finishing school at age fifteen or sixteen. By March 1964, Harold Wilson, a Labour Party leader from Liverpool and later prime minister, regarded "as deserving of the utmost censure and condemnation a system of society which, year in, year out . . . cannot provide employment for its school-leavers." British youths felt especially directionless due to the change in English conscription laws. The draft ended in 1960, remembered Ringo Starr, "and so at eighteen you weren't regimented. Everyone was wondering what to do."

Idle working-class teens began to form rival gangs: the Rockers and the Mods. The Rockers, modeling themselves after the tough Teddy Boys of the 1950s, wore black leather jackets, tight-fitting pants, and pointed boots or suede shoes. They greased back their hair in a pompadour style and sometimes donned sunglasses in beatnik fashion, roaring down the streets on motorcycles.

The Modernists, shortened to Mods, favored "teenage Italian-style clothes," according to Townshend, himself a Mod. They had "short hair, money enough to buy a real smart suit, good shoes, good shirts; you had to be able to dance like a madman. You had to be in possession of plenty of pills all the time and always be pilled up [especially with Drynamil, an amphetamine commonly known as a "purple heart"]. You had to have a scooter covered in lamps. You had to have like an army anorak [parka] to wear." The Mods sometimes adopted different fashions weekly. "One outfit might be twelve quid, a week's wages, and the next week you'd have to change the whole lot," recalled Townshend. Reacting against the generic simplicity necessitated by the impoverished conditions following World War II, they especially favored brightly colored, eye-catching styles. "I remember growing up as a kid in black and white," explained Kenny Jones, a Mod who played in the band the Small Faces. "We were the people to wear color, and it was amazing. We started to wear all these bright things, and it was alright to dye your hair then. A lot of Mods actually dyed their hair blonde." The fashion-conscious Mods fueled the rise of the now-famous alternative clothing district at and near Carnaby Street in London, where music blared from shops packed with teens searching for the newest trend.

As with the Rockers, the Mods "were nothing. They were the lowest, they were England's lowest common denominators. Not only were they young, they were also lower-class young," recalled Pete Townshend. "Most Mods were lower-class garbage men, you know, with enough money to buy himself Sunday's best."

The lower-class Mods, buying snappy, preppy clothes, for the first time took away the fashion mantle from the British upper crust. "Once only the rich, the Establishment, set the fashion. Now it is the inexpensive little dress seen on the girls in the High Street," asserted 1960s' fashion queen Mary Quant. "The voices, rules, and culture of this generation are as different from those of the past as tea and wine. And the clothes they choose evoke their lives . . . daring and gay, never dull," she continued. "They represent the whole new spirit that is present-day Britain, a classless spirit that has grown out of the Second World War."

The Mods, blurring the class lines in British society, fostered a sense of belonging among some lower-class British youths. Pete Townshend knew "the feeling of what it's like to be a Mod among two million Mods and it's incredible. It's like suddenly you're the only white man in the Apollo [Theater in Harlem]. Someone comes up and touches you and you become black. It's like that moment, that incredible feeling of being part of something. It covered everybody, everybody looked the same, and everybody acted the same and everybody wanted to be the same. It was the first move I have ever seen in the history of youth toward unity, toward unity of thought, unity of drive and unity of motive. Any kid, however ugly or however fucked up, if he had the right haircut and the right clothes and the right motorbike, he was a Mod. He was a Mod!" exclaimed Townshend.

The Mods and the Rockers, each group bound by a common appearance, fought one another for dominance. During the Easter weekend of 1964 at Clacton-on-Sea, Essex, a few hundred "young scooter riders" from the eastern and northeastern parts of London attacked motorcycle gangs of Rockers. According to D. H. Moody, chairman of the Urban District Council, "they insulted passersby, lay in the middle of the road to stop traffic, jumped onto cars, and destroyed and damaged property. The girls were almost as bad, and [one witness] had seen five of them try to knock a child off his bicycle." Reported the *London Times*, "At one stage, there was almost a battle on the seafront with missiles of all descriptions being thrown." The police intervened and arrested more than a hundred rioters, whom the *Times* called a "collection of uncivilized youths with no respect for persons, property, or the comfort of other people." Explaining the incident, Labour's chief front bench spokesman, Fred Willey, observed that the "general complaint of those who took part was that there was nothing for them to do. They came from housing estates with far too few social amenities and were expected to spend their time in amusement arcades. . . . The present government regarded working-class adolescents as fair game for blatant exploitation by commercial interests."

On May 17, 1964, trouble broke out in the Kent resort of Margate and at Brighton. More than 800 Mods, arriving "on scooters bristling with headlights and badges," fought 200 leather-jacketed Rockers. The *Daily Express* painted a terrifying picture: "There was dad asleep in a deck chair and mum making sandcastles with the children when the 1964 boys took over the beaches at Margate and Brighton yesterday and smeared the traditional scene with more bloodshed and violence." Fumed Dr. George Simpson, Margate Court Chairman, "these long-haired, mentally unstable petty little sawdust Caesars seem to find courage, like rats, by hunting only in packs." By Tuesday, May 18, when the clashes subsided, "at least forty youths had been arrested," the *Daily Mirror* informed its readers. "And there was blood on the sand."

Many of these warring youths, having time and lacking direction, turned to music. "My opinion why music suddenly shot out of England in the sixties is that we were the first generation that didn't get regimented and didn't go into the army," explained Beatles drummer Ringo Starr. "Music was a way out. We all wanted to leave. Everyone wanted to fly. Music was my way. Back then every street had a band. You could hear it all over. Everyone was playing, and mostly it sounded real bad, but we were playing. We all picked up guitars and drums and filled our time with music." Echoed Dave Clark, "Had not the government stopped the draft there would have been no Dave Clark Five, no Beatles, no Stones."

Skiffle, a mixture of Dixieland jazz and country blues, first attracted British youths. The music originated from British Dixieland, or traditional jazz, which reached the height of its popularity with a group that included trombonist Chris Barber, banjo and guitar player Tony "Lonnie" Donegan, and Harold Pendelton, co-owner of the

Marquee Club with Chris Barber. "We discovered that our trumpet player, Ken Coyler, had a weak lip which gave out on him, so he needed an occasional rest," remembered Pendelton. "As a solution, Chris [Barber] devised a little four-piece band within his band to perform as a novelty respite while Ken's lips recovered. This little band was composed of a crude guitar, a homemade bass, a suitcase that was played with whisk brooms and a washboard strummed with thimbles. Chris called it his skiffle group. He got the name from having read about the rent parties that used to be given in poor, Negro quarters to raise money—that blacks of New Orleans called them skiffle groups."

Soon Barber's novelty skiffle act became more popular than his traditional jazz band and engendered an accessible, participatory musical style. According to Barber, "The way Lonnie [Donegan] did it was a way that anyone could join in with, and they did it with homemade guitars, tea chest and broom handle string bass and all this stuff. Just singing any kind of song." In 1956, Lonnie Donegan climbed the chart with skiffle versions of two Leadbelly songs, "Rock Island Line" and "John Henry," and started a skiffle craze in Britain among poor youths who could start bands with homemade instruments and little musical schooling. "Skiffle bands sprung up everywhere because the kids didn't have to learn how to play difficult instruments like the trombone or trumpet or clarinet. Anybody could skiffle." Pendelton added, "Out of this skiffle craze, the new rock groups like the Beatles began to emerge. The Beatles began as a skiffle group."

The Early Beatles

The four rowdy Rockers from Liverpool, who banded together as the Beatles during the skiffle craze, changed rock-and-roll history. Formed in 1959, the Quarrymen, as they were first called, then Johnny and the Moondogs, then the Silver Beatles, and finally just the Beatles, started their musical careers as a skiffle band in the Cavern Club of Liverpool. The next year, they traveled to Hamburg, Germany, to back up singer Tony Sheridan, who helped the group on their first record "My Bonnie," released in 1961. A year later, the Beatles had become the rage of England, and by 1964, they had become worldwide celebrities.

The Beatles came from working-class families. Abandoned by his father and mother, John Winston Lennon grew up with his Aunt Mimi and as a boy joined a Rocker gang that "went in for things like shoplifting and pulling girls' knickers down." Paul McCartney, the son of a cotton salesman, lived in a half house—"They were such small, diddy houses, with bare bricks inside," he later reminisced. The youngest of the Beatles, George Harrison, was the son of a bus driver and began an apprenticeship as an electrician at age sixteen. Drummer Ringo Starr, born Richard Starkey, told a reporter that his family had "always been just ordinary, poor working class." When her husband deserted the family, Ringo's mother worked as a barmaid to support her child. At age fifteen, Ringo landed a job as a messenger boy for the British Railways.

The four Liverpool youths adopted a Rocker image. To his aunt, Lennon seemed to be "a real Teddy boy." Lennon insisted, "I wasn't really a Ted, just a Rocker. I was imitating Teds, pretending to be one. I was never a real one, with chains and real gangs. If I'd met a proper Ted, I'd have been shit-scared." Paul spent hours styling his pompadoured hair and choosing the clothes that fit Rocker fashion. Worried that his son would "turn out a Teddy boy," Jim McCartney "said over and over again that [Paul] wasn't going to have tight trousers. But he just wore me down." George Harrison "used to go to school with his school cap sitting high on top his hair. And very tight trousers," remembered his mother. "Unknown to me, he'd run them up on my machine to make them even tighter. I bought him a brand-new pair once and the first thing he did was to tighten them. When his dad found out, he told him to unpick them at once. 'I can't Dad,' he said. 'I've cut the pieces off.' George always had an answer." As a band, the Beatles affected a Rocker image, wearing black-and-white cowboy shirts with white tassels dangling from the pockets, leather jackets, and pointed cowboy boots.

The quasi-western attire indicated a major musical influence on the Beatles: American rockabilly. Although first drawn to music through skiffle and covering Chuck Berry tunes such as "Rock and Roll Music" and "Roll Over Beethoven," the early Beatles modeled their sound after Elvis Presley. "Nothing really affected me until Elvis," John Lennon remembered. "I had no idea about doing music as a way of life until rock-'n'-roll hit me. It was *Rock Around the Clock*, I think. I enjoyed Bill Haley, but I wasn't overwhelmed by him. It wasn't until 'Heartbreak Hotel' that I really got into it." McCartney felt that Presley "was the biggest kick. Every time I felt low I just put on Elvis and I'd feel great, beautiful. I'd no idea how records were made and it was just magic. 'All Shook Up'! Oh, it was beautiful." Ringo Starr added, "Elvis changed my life. He was the first teenager in my life. Johnnie Ray, Frankie Laine, and Bill Haley were my early heroes, around 1954. But they were always a bit like me dad. Elvis was the first real *lad* who came out. The kid. He totally blew me away, I loved him so." When Malcolm Evans, later a road manager for the Beatles, first heard the group at the Cavern Club, he felt that they "sounded a bit like Elvis."

The Beatles idolized other rockabilly stars as well. In 1959, as a Silver Beatle, George Harrison changed his name to Carl Harrison after one of his heroes, Carl Perkins. On tour with Perkins in 1964, John Lennon told the rockabilly star, "We've got all your records! We slowed 'em down from 45 to 33 rpm [to learn them]." After telling the Beatles that they sounded "a lot like the old Sun Records," remembered Perkins, John jumped off the couch, put "both arms around me and kissed me on the jaw." At another point during their early years, the foursome called themselves the Foreverly Brothers in honor of the Everly Brothers. *Variety* spotted the influence years later. "Malarkey," read one story. "The Beatles are dishing up a rock-and-roll style that was current in this country ten years ago and that is still typical of such groups as the Everly Brothers." The name the group eventually adopted reflected the rockabilly connection. As John told a reporter, "I was looking for a name like the Crickets [Buddy Holly's band] that meant two things. From Cricket I went to Beatles. . . . When you said it, people thought of crawly things; when you read it, it was beat music."

The Beatles' passion for rockabilly may have come from the popularity of country music in Liverpool. Years later, Ringo Starr unabashedly gushed that "Hank Williams was my hero." He noted that "at one point, Liverpool was the capital of country 'n' western music in England."

Manager Brian Epstein

This Rocker band, playing an English brand of rockabilly influenced by R&B and skiffle music, became famous through the efforts of Brian Epstein. Epstein, born in September 1934 into a wealthy family, was raised in a five-bedroom house in Childwall, one of Liverpool's most exclusive residential areas. He began a successful career as a salesman in two of his father's stores: a furniture shop and the North End Music Enterprises. "I enjoyed selling, watching people relax and show trust in me," he explained. "It was pleasant to see the wary look dissolve and people begin to think there were good things ahead for them and I would be the provider." After expanding his father's record retailing business, Epstein turned his attention to the Beatles, a group he had heard about in one of his music stores. As he told it, "I suppose it was all part of getting bored with simply selling records. I was looking for a new hobby. The Beatles at the same time, though I didn't know it and perhaps they didn't either, were also getting a bit bored with Liverpool." In 1961, Brian Epstein became the manager of the Beatles, getting a 25 percent share of their net revenues.

To make the band more palatable to the general public, Epstein changed their Rocker image. When he first saw them at the Cavern Club, he thought "they were a scruffy crowd in leather." The Beatles "were not very tidy and not very clean. They smoked as they played and they ate and talked and pretended to hit each other." Brian tried to "clean our image up," John Lennon later remarked. "He said our look wasn't right. We'd never get past the door at a good place. We just used to dress how we liked, on-and-off stage. He talked us into the suit scene." Said Epstein himself: "First I got them into trousers and sweaters and eventually into suits." Besides changing their appearance, said Pete Best, the Beatles' drummer before Ringo joined the group, the manager forced the band to "work out a proper program, playing our best numbers each time, not just the ones we felt like playing." After Epstein had finished molding the four Liverpudlians, noticed Malcolm Evans, "the image of the Beatles was so good and nice."

To sell the band, Epstein brought in other professionals from the music business. After being rejected by nearly every British label, he approached George Martin, an executive with the Parlophone branch of the Electrical Music Industry (EMI), who on September 11, 1962, recorded the Beatles' first British release, "Love Me Do" and "P.S. I Love You." Epstein, who "didn't know how you promoted a record," enlisted the services of Tony Barrow, a publicity man for Decca Records. By May 1963, the manager had set up the machinery to make the Beatles a national sensation.

The Toppermost of the Poppermost

As with most working-class youth, the Beatles initially wanted money and fame. Scarred by the insecurity of his childhood, John "wanted to be popular. I wanted to be the leader. It seemed more attractive than just being one of the toffees." Paul later confessed, "All I wanted was women, money, and clothes." In discussing his financial future with Paul, George said that he "felt he was going to make a lot of it [money]. He was going to buy a house and a swimming pool, then he'd buy a bus for his father." As a group, the Fab Four dreamed of stardom. In 1961, remembered George, "we still used to send up the idea of getting to the top. When things were a real drag and nothing happening, we used to go through this routine: John would shout, 'Where are we going, fellas?' We'd shout back, 'To the Top, Johnny.' Then he would shout, 'What Top?' 'To the Toppermost of the Poppermost, Johnny!'"

The Beatles soon achieved their goal. They first became well known in Liverpool. By late 1962, remembered Maureen Cox, Ringo's first wife, admirers "used to hang around the Cavern all day long, just on the off chance of seeing them. They'd come out of the lunch time session and just stand outside all afternoon, queuing up for the evening show. . . . It was terrible, the mad screams when they came on. They went potty." News spread quickly. More than 5,000 squealing teens mobbed a Beatles performance and caused a riot in Manchester. At Newcastle-upon-Tyne, more than 4,000 diehards lined up in front of a concert hall at 3:00 A.M. to secure tickets for an evening Beatles show. Dr. F. R. C. Casson, a psychologist who tried to explain the phenomenon for the readers of the *London Times*, likened Beatlemania "to the frenzied dancing and shouting of voodoo worshippers and the howls and bodily writhing of converts among primitive evangelical sects in the southern states of America. Beat music has a rhythmic stimulation on the brain. A similar result of rhythmic stimulation is seen in some types of epileptic fit, which may be caused by rapidly flickering light."

British television helped propel the Beatles into the spotlight much like American television had helped make Elvis a star. "Television was the key media, massive," contended Sean O'Mahony, publisher of the *Beatles Monthly*. "One little airing and you could sell an awful lot of records very quickly." In early 1963, Beatles music publisher Dick James called television host Philip Jones, who had produced James's radio sing-alongs, and convinced the TV personality to include the Beatles on his influential variety show, *Thank Your Lucky Stars*. On January 19, 1963, the program helped launch the foursome and their new song, "Please Please Me."

On October 13, 1963, the band gained national exposure when it headlined at the London Palladium on a show called *Sunday Night at the London Palladium*. More than fifteen million television viewers watched thousands of young Londoners claw at each other to get a glimpse of the Beatles. "From that day on," insisted press agent Tony Barrow, "everything has changed. My job has never been the same again. From spending six months ringing up newspapers and getting no, I now had every national reporter and feature writer chasing *me*." During one number, John asked the audience to clap. "Those upstairs, just rattle your jewelry," he added, looking up toward the royal box. The following Sunday, twenty-six million Britons witnessed the escapade while sitting in front of their television sets.

By December 1963, manufacturers started to offer Beatles products with one firm in Peckham selling Beatles sweaters "designed specially for Beatles people by a leading British manufacturer with a top-quality, two-tone Beatles badge." The Beatles Fan Club swelled to more than 800,000 members, and the foursome sold a million copies of two singles that featured "I Want to Hold Your Hand" and "She Loves You." The band's first British album, *Please Please Me*, topped the British chart for more than six months. By the end of 1963, the Fab Four had sold eleven million records and $18 million worth of Beatles goods.

British public opinion responded favorably to the Beatles. The *Daily Mirror* argued that "you have to be a real sour square not to love the nutty, noisy, happy, handsome Beatles." From a different political perspective, *The Daily Worker* of the British Communist Party commented that the "Mersey sound is the voice of 80,000 crumbling houses and 30,000 people on the dole." Although Conservative politician Edward Heath first criticized the Beatles' language as "unrecognizable as the Queen's English," he later told an interviewer: "Who could have forecast only a year ago that the Beatles would prove the salvation of the corduroy industry" as thousands emulated the band in its trouser style. Prime Minister Sir Alec Douglas-Home called the group "our best export" and "a useful contribution to the balance of payments." Even the Queen complimented the Beatles. "So young, fresh, and vital," she cooed.

Amid such praise, Brian Epstein began to question his marketing tactics. He feared overexposure: "At first sight the endless discussion in the newspapers of the Beatles' habits, clothes, and views was exciting. They liked it at first and so did I. It was good for business. But finally it became an anxiety. How long could they maintain public interest without rationing either personal appearances or newspaper coverage? By a stringent watch on their bookings and press contacts we just averted saturation point. But it was very close. Other artists have been destroyed by this very thing."

The band members started to doubt the value of stardom as they began to pay the price of success. Ringo Starr complained about the loss of friendships and the diminishing control he exercised over his own life. "There were so many groups in Liverpool at one time that we often used to play just for each other, sitting in on each other's sessions, or just listening. It was a community on its own, just made up of groups." But when the Beatles became popular nationally, "it broke all the community up. People start hating each other." Moreover, Ringo felt slighted when George Martin replaced him with session drummer Andy White on "P.S. I Love You." "Nobody said anything. What could the others say, or me? We were just lads, being pushed around. You know what I mean. They were so big, the London record company and all that. We just did what we were told." At about the same time, John believed that the band had relinquished too much control. In Liverpool, he later told an interviewer, the Beatles "felt embarrassed in our suits and being very clean. We were worried that our friends might think we'd sold out—which we had, in a way."

The Beatles Invade America

Despite their doubts, the Beatles prepared for even greater success in America. Epstein paved the way for the British invasion, convincing Capitol Records to spend $50,000 on a "crash publicity program." The company plastered five million "The Beatles Are Coming" stickers on buildings, fences, and telephone poles in every state and printed a million copies of a four-page tabloid about the Fab Four. Capitol executives pressed one million units of a promotional, 7-inch Beatles interview record, which gave radio listeners the impression that the Beatles had personally contacted every disc jockey in the country. They also convinced many of the major weekly publications to run stories on the British foursome before their arrival: *Time* covered the group in its November 15, 1963, issue; *Newsweek* did so three days later; and on January 31, 1964, *Life* published a color spread entitled "Here Come the Beatles." By February 7, 1964, Brown Meggs, director of eastern operations for Capitol Records, told *The New York Times* that, "I have been on full-time Beatles duty since—the date is indelibly imprinted on my mind—January 6, when I returned from vacation. All this came at once, everything happened in a tremendously concentrated period. I'm awfully tired, but Beatles only come once in a decade, if that." Voyle Gilmore, a vice president of Capitol, summed up the efforts of his company in an understatement: "There was a lot of hype."

Radio also plugged the Beatles. During February 1964, one record executive in a company that had no Beatles releases complained that "stations are playing our records like spot commercials between Beatles tunes." Explained Brown Meggs of Capitol, "What sells records is radio. The Beatles got unbelievable radio play. There wasn't a single market in the country in which airplay wasn't simply stupendous."

By the time the Beatles arrived in New York City on February 7, 1964, Beatlemania had swept the United States. Entering the charts at number eighty-three, by February 1 "I Want to Hold Your Hand" had replaced Bobby Vinton's "There! I've Said It Again" in the number-one slot. The song remained in the top position for seven weeks. The third week of February 1964, contended *Billboard*, "was the week that was the Beatles.' First in the platter polls, first in the press, first in police protection, and the first in the hearts of New York teenagers who upset the mechanics of John F. Kennedy Airport, the Plaza, a CBS-TV studio, Penn Station, and Carnegie Hall ever since the foursome arrived from London."

Some adults disapproved of the new rage. After the *Sullivan* show appearance, the *Herald Tribune* called the Beatles "75% publicity, 20% haircut, and 5% lilting lament." To the *Daily News*, "the Presleyan gyrations and caterwauling were but luke-warm dandelion tea compared to the 100-proof elixir served up by the Beatles." Disregarding his personal ban on Sunday television viewing, evangelist Billy Graham watched the Beatles on *The Ed Sullivan Show* and believed that the performance revealed "all the symptoms of the uncertainty of the times and the confusion about us." Ray Block, orchestra leader on the *Sullivan* program, prophesied that the band "wouldn't last longer than a year," and actor Noel Coward said, "I've met them. Delightful lads. Absolutely no talent." Concert critic Louis Biancolli summed up the adverse reaction to the Beatles: "Their effect is like mass hypnosis followed by mass nightmare. I never heard anything like what went around me. I've read about the bacchantes and corybantes in wild Greek rites screaming insensately. They were antique squares compared to these teenage maenads."

Most media commentators, however, welcomed the clean-cut, well-tailored Beatles and their aristocratic manager. *Time* wrote that "the boys are the very spirit of good clean fun. They look like shaggy Peter Pans, with their mushroom haircuts and high white shirt collars, and onstage they clown around endlessly." The 1964 *Yearbook of World Book Encyclopedia* singled out the Beatles' "rambunctious and irreverent sense of fun" and the *Yearbook of Collier's Encyclopedia* likened the foursome to "Little Lord Fauntleroys."

Newsweek probably best captured the majority opinion when it labeled the Beatles "a band of evangelists. And the gospel is fun. They shout, they stomp, they jump for joy, and their audiences respond in a way that makes an old-time revival meeting seem like a wake. . . . The Beatles appeal to the positive, not negative. They give kids a chance to let off steam and adults a chance to let off disapproval. They have even evolved a peculiar sort of sexless appeal: cute and safe. The most they ask is: 'I Want to Hold Your Hand.'" The fun-loving Beatles seemed a perfect antidote to the pessimism that had engulfed America after John F. Kennedy's death a few months earlier.

The "cute and safe" Beatles, appealing to a vast audience, scored fantastic successes in America. Shortly after their tour of the United States, John Lennon released his book *In His Own Write*, which nudged Ian Fleming's latest James Bond thriller from the top of the best-seller list and won Lennon an invitation to the prestigious Foyles Literary Lunch on Shakespeare's 400th birthday. Some compared the book to James Joyce's classic *Finnegan's Wake*. On July 6, 1964, the Beatles premiered a full-length motion picture, *A Hard Day's Night*. "The idea was to make it as quickly as possible and get it out before their popularity faded," admitted director Richard Lester. The timing was superb. Even historian and John F. Kennedy speechwriter Arthur Schlesinger, Jr. lauded the movie as "the astonishment of the month" by a band that embodied the "timeless essence of the adolescent effort to deal with the absurdities of an adult world." During its first six weeks, the film earned $5.6 million in rental fees.

In August 1964, the Beatles returned to the States for another series of concerts. The second American tour started at the Cow Palace in San Francisco on August 19 and ended a month later in New York with a charity benefit.

In Seattle, on August 21, a typical explosion of mayhem erupted over the second coming of the Beatles. When the foursome arrived in town, they faced screaming, clawing teenagers. Escorted by a police motorcade, the band stopped for a fourteen-minute press conference and then sped to Room 272 of the Edgewater Inn, which had been secured with barbed wire and sawhorse barricades. While in their room, Ringo, George, Paul, and John sorted through hundreds of letters from their fans, ate a few of the cookies and pieces of cake that Beatles diehards had baked, and fished from a window that overlooked Elliot Bay.

The Beatles emerged from the hotel to play an afternoon and an evening show, running from the Edgewater Inn lobby and jumping into a limousine bound for the Seattle Coliseum. Marty Murphy, a twenty-five-year-old switchboard operator at the Edgewater Inn, rode with the Beatles, dragged into the car by Brian Epstein, who desperately needed help with two terrified Beatles secretaries. According to her account, "the limousine started moving. Now I could understand why the Beatles had looked so scared when they arrived. When we got to the barricade, I have never been so frightened in my life. These children had their faces pressed up against the car, all bent out of shape. They were crying, screaming, 'Touch me! Touch me!' They were saying that to me, and they didn't even know who I was. Finally, the limousine got to the Coliseum." When the Beatles leapt onstage and started to play, remembered police officer Noreen Skagen, "I only sort of heard the music; the screaming was just too loud. The Beatles themselves looked very tense, pale, scared. . . . We had to have a regular flying wedge with our then-TAC squad to bring them into the Coliseum and onstage. The entire audience charged the stage when the Beatles were ready to leave. We were constantly dragging hysterical youngsters who had gone berserk. Back then, it wasn't a matter of drugs or alcohol. It was hysteria. The girls were in love. They would say, 'I have to talk to them! You don't understand!'"

After the evening performance, the police bundled the Fab Four in blankets, put them on stretchers, and carried them through the crowd to a Red Cross van, which escaped the wild hordes of fans, who demanded their heroes. About the entire episode, the *Seattle Times* reported: "Seattle seethed with uncontrollable hysteria, terrifying noise, and danger in a real-life nightmare last night. This was the Beatles' show. For thirty incredible minutes, those in the jam-packed Seattle Center Coliseum had the feeling of being sealed in a crazed capsule pitching through the chasms of space."

A similar hysteria gripped other cities on the four Beatles' tours of America, which by the end of 1965 had reaped more than $56 million.

The intensity and magnitude of Beatlemania in America can be attributed, at least in part, to the postwar baby boom. In 1964, millions of pubescent and prepubescent Beatlemaniacs were part of the more than forty-three million youths who had been born between 1947 and 1957. They searched for an identity and collectively latched onto the Beatles as a symbol of unity. As one Beatles fan told a reporter as she stood vigil in 1964 outside of a hotel where her heroes resided, "I'm here because everyone else is here." Though youths had idolized Elvis Presley, the mass hysteria of Beatlemania could only have occurred during the mid-1960s, when the majority of baby boomers were old enough to become interested in music and seventeen-year-olds became the largest age-group in the United States. "We were just the spokesmen for a generation," explained Paul McCartney.

The Mersey Beat

In the mid-1960s, the Beatles, who had conquered the American music market by appealing to the baby boom generation, paved the way for other British groups, some of them linked to Brian Epstein. "The biggest thing the Beatles did was to open the American market to all British artists," contended British promoter Arthur Howes, who planned the early Beatles' tours of England. "Nobody had ever been able to get in before the Beatles. They alone did it. I had brought over lots of American stars, but nobody had gone over there." By February 1965, *Variety* told its readers, "Britannia ruled the airwaves. The advent of the [Beatles] now has shattered the steady, day-to-day domination of made-in-America music here and abroad." During 1964, British rock bands sold more than $76 million worth of records in the United States.

Some of the British groups had grown up with the Beatles in Liverpool. In 1959 Gerry Marsden, a truck driver, who was a neighbor of one of the Beatles, formed a band called the Pacemakers. Under the watchful eye of manager Brian Epstein, who signed the group in June 1962, Gerry and the Pacemakers established a following at the Cavern Club in Liverpool, frequently playing on the same bill as the Beatles. In 1963, they climbed to the top of the British chart with a song recorded by the Beatles, "How Do You Do It?," and followed with the chart-toppers, "I Like It" and "You'll Never Walk Alone," ending the successful year with an appearance on the British television show *Sunday Night at the London Palladium*. On May 10, 1964, Gerry and the Pacemakers debuted in America on *The Ed Sullivan Show*, which helped promote the group's best-selling U.S. single, "Don't Let the Sun Catch You Crying." They capped their career in 1965 by starring in the movie *Ferry Across the Mersey* and scoring with a Top-Ten single of the same name.

Members of another Epstein act, Billy J. Kramer and the Dakotas, rose from their working-class backgrounds to stardom. Billy J. Kramer (a.k.a. William Ashton), a worker for the British Railways, originally sang with a group called the Coasters but teamed with a Manchester combo, the Dakotas, on the advice of Epstein, who signed the Liverpudlian in late 1962. Observed *The Big Beat*, an English fanzine: "The marriage of the zing singing of Billy J. to the true-beat accompaniment of the Daks has proven a brilliant stroke on the part of Epstein. These boys just have to step onto the stage and the fans go wild!" Though not having "the greatest voice in the world," according to producer George Martin, Billy J. Kramer hit the chart in June 1963 with "Do You Want to Know a Secret?," a track from the Beatles' first album, and the same month toured the United Kingdom with the Beatles. Two months later, he followed with the chart-topper "Bad to Me," a song written by John Lennon specifically for Kramer. Within a year, the group hit the British Top Ten with two Lennon/ McCartney originals, "I'll Keep You Satisfied" and "From a Window," and in mid-1964 broke into the American Top Ten with "Little Children."

The Searchers, another Liverpool group, rode the crest of the Beatles' success. Formed in 1961 and named after a John Wayne movie, the group began performing regularly at Liverpool clubs such as the Cavern, the Casbah, and the Hot Spot, eventually becoming the house band at the Iron Door. "We copied such people as Buddy Holly, Eddie Cochran, and Gene Vincent," related John McNally, one of the founders of the band. In August 1963, they topped the British singles chart with a remake of the Drifters' "Sweets for My Sweet" and followed later in the year with the British chart-topper "Sugar and Spice." After an April 1964 appearance on *The Ed Sullivan Show*, and amid Beatlemania, the Searchers scaled the U.S. charts with their best-selling record, a remake of "Needles and Pins."

Along with the Beatles, these Liverpool groups delivered the "Mersey sound." Alexis Korner, a British blues innovator, found that "there was a certain brashness about the Liverpool music, which stamped it almost immediately—they played it the way they speak English, you know! You could definitely tell a Liverpool group. The Mersey sound was basically a guitar sound: lead guitar, rhythm guitar, bass guitar, and drums was the basic Liverpool setup."

Groups from other parts of Great Britain invaded America with a sound similar to the Mersey beat. From Manchester, a dingy, smokestacked industrial center much like Liverpool, came Freddie Garrity and the Dreamers. Quitting his job as a milkman, Freddie and his Dreamers hit the British Top Five in 1963 with "If You Gotta Make a Fool of Somebody," "I'm Telling You Now," and "You Were Made for Me," becoming popular on English television for their comedy act. In February 1965, the band appeared on the U.S. television programs *Hullabaloo* and *Shindig*, and "I'm Telling You Now" promptly topped the U.S. chart.

In early 1965, Wayne Fontana and the Mindbenders, another band of Manchester youths, scored a number-one hit with "The Game of Love." Fontana (a.k.a. Glyn Geoffrey Ellis), a former telephone engineering apprentice, took his stage name from his record company and named the group after a horror film that was then playing in a local theater. Besides their smash hit, the next year the Mindbenders neared the top of the U.S. chart with a sequel, "A Groovy Kind of Love."

The Hollies proved to be more long lasting than most other Manchester beat bands. The group was started by Graham Nash and singer-guitarist Allan Clarke, who first met in grammar school and later became the Two Teens. After a few name changes, the duo added three other members in 1962 and labeled themselves the Hollies after their musical hero, Buddy Holly. "We were Buddy Holly crazy," recalled Nash, who, as with other Merseybeats, was influenced by such rockabillies as the

Everly Brothers. Signed by EMI producer Ron Richards, who saw them perform at the Cavern Club in Liverpool, the band first hit the British Top Ten in January 1964 with "Stay" and followed in the next several months with the chartbusters "Just One Look," "Here I Go Again," "Yes I Will," "I'm Alive," and the Beatles' "If I Needed Someone." In 1966, during a tour of America, they worked fans into a frenzy at New York City's Paramount Theater and on such television shows as *Shindig*, *Hullabaloo*, and *The Smothers Brothers Show*, and that year hit the American Top Ten with "Bus Stop" and "Stop! Stop! Stop!"

Herman's Hermits, another Manchester band, capitalized on the beat music craze. Formed in 1962 with Peter Noone as the front man, the band was signed two years later to EMI Columbia by producer Mickie Most, who noticed the facial resemblance of Noone to John F. Kennedy. "When Most finally agreed to help us," recalled Noone, "he found this Carole King song, 'I'm into Something Good,'" which featured Noone backed by such session musicians as Jimmy Page and John Paul Jones, later of Led Zeppelin. "Once we recorded it, and I heard it on the radio, I said, 'That's it, my life's complete.' Then we did some TV shows, and in three weeks we were number one. It was unbelievable." In 1965, Herman's Hermits followed with a string of upbeat hits that included "Silhouettes," "Mrs. Brown You've Got a Lovely Daughter," "Wonderful World," and a revival of the British music hall tune, "I'm Henry the Eighth, I Am."

The Dave Clark Five (DC5), from the Tottenham section of London, initially posed the most serious threat to the commercial dominance of the Beatles. Teaming together to raise money for Dave Clark's rugby team, in 1964 the Five toured America, appearing on *The Ed Sullivan Show* on May 31. "Within the course of seven days, we were household names and ended up having five records on the charts at once," explained Clark, who, like the Beatles, had been inspired by "Little Richard, Elvis Presley, Fats Domino, all those great rockers." The DC5 hit the charts on both sides of the Atlantic with "Glad All Over," "Bits and Pieces," "Can't You See That She's Mine," and "Because." The liner notes on their American debut album predicted that "the Tottenham sound of the Dave Clark Five is on its way toward overthrowing the reign of the Beatles in this country." In 1965, they copied the Fab Four by releasing the film *Catch Us If You Can*. The band also charted with "Over and Over" and "I Like It Like That." All told, the group sold fifty million records, placing eight singles in the Top Ten.

The Monkees

Two American producers took advantage of the Mersey beat craze by creating the Monkees, a prefabricated American version of the Beatles. Observing the success of Richard Lester's Beatles film *A Hard Day's Night*, Bob Rafelson and Bert Schneider, the son of then-president of Columbia Pictures, Abe Schneider, formed Raybert Productions. They placed an ad in the major Hollywood trade papers for "four insane boys, age seventeen–twenty-one, want spirited Ben Frank types" for "acting roles in new TV series." In a month the duo auditioned 437 hopefuls, including folk rocker Stephen Stills.

Mike Nesmith, Davy Jones, Mickey Dolenz, and Peter Tork on the set of the television show *The Monkees* in August 1967. Photo by Michael Ochs Archives. Getty Images, Inc.—Michael Ochs Archives.

The producers picked four photogenic, energetic, largely inexperienced applicants: Robert Michael Nesmith, an unknown folk singer; Mickey Dolenz, who as a child had played Corky in the TV children's series "Circus Boy," and more recently had played in a California garage band; Greenwich Village folk singer Peter Thorkelson, shortened to Tork; and David Jones, the most experienced of the four, who had appeared on Broadway as the Artful Dodger in *Oliver*, had played a drug-crazed husband on the TV program *Ben Casey*, and had released an album of pop songs, some of which he performed on the same *Ed Sullivan Show* on which the Beatles had debuted.

In late 1965, Rafelson and Schneider secured $225,000 from Jackie Cooper, the former child actor who headed the television subsidiary of Columbia Pictures, for a pilot TV series. "It all went great," Rafelson told *Time*. "NBC bought the series twenty-four hours after it saw the pilot and sold it to two sponsors seventy-two hours later."

The producers quickly began to groom their new product. They hired underground film director James Frawley to provide intensive acting lessons for the group. "At first they were embarrassed, they were stiff, and they were a little raw," Frawley told *The Saturday Evening Post*. "We would roll over on the floor, sometimes, and do animals. 'You're a crab. Talk the way a giraffe would talk. Deal with an elephant. Now, talk the way a teapot would talk.' It was like a training period to free them physically, to start to use their bodies in a new way."

Rafelson and Schneider also shaped the Monkees musically. Besides enlisting the help of songwriters Tommy Boyce and Bobby Hart, the team approached former Brill Building music publisher Don Kirshner, the president of the music division of Columbia Pictures/Screen Gems TV and its new record label, Colgems. "The boys didn't relate," explained Kirshner at the time. "I was looking for a driving, exciting, frantic young sound. There was no sound to the Monkees." Having little time to develop and record twenty-two songs for an album and five TV shows, he "brought in Goffin and King, Mann and Weil, Sedaka and Greenfield, the Tokens and Neil Diamond and created songs for the group. On most of the records I did with the Monkees, Carole King and Neil Diamond would sing background." Studio musicians such as Glen Campbell, Leon Russell, and James Burton would play the instruments. "The music had nothing to do with us," complained Michael Nesmith.

Though prefabricated, the look and sound of the Monkees started to sell. After their television debut on September 12, 1966, the group attracted ten million viewers every Monday night and received 5,000 fan letters a day. Just as they launched their television show, the group hit the top of the singles chart with their debut "Last Train to Clarksville" and three months later did the same with "I'm a Believer." In October 1966, the Monkees scored with a number-one, self-titled album, and within the next year released three more chart-topping LPs. During less than a three-year period from 1966 to 1968, the band sold more than $20 million in Monkees merchandise, including shirts, slacks, raincoats, sweaters, comic books, trading and playing cards, dolls, lunch boxes, stuffed animals, games, hats, bubblegum, shoes, charms, guitars, and puppets. "We're advertisers," enthused Mickey Dolenz. "We're selling a product. We're selling Monkees."

The successful Monkees had been patterned after the Beatles. Before releasing the Monkees debut LP, the band's label spent $100,000 on an ad campaign that involved seventy-six advance men, who distributed thousands of posters proclaiming "The Monkees Are Coming" and provided preview records to 6,000 disc jockeys. The name of the group had been calculatedly misspelled, as had the Beatles, and the first Monkees single included several "no-no-no" choruses to substitute for the Beatles' "yeah-yeah-yeah" chants. The group's management even published a *Monkees Monthly* magazine, similar to the many fanzines dealing with the Beatles, such as *Beat Monthly* and *Beatles Monthly*. "The teens have bought the Monkees," a Raybert official proclaimed in early 1967. "They're the American Beatles." *Newsweek* called the band members "direct videological descendants of the Beatles," and *Time*, in early 1967, commented that "less than a year ago, a team of wily promoters ran the Beatles through a Xerox machine and came up with the Monkees."

During the mid-1960s, the Beatles and their American counterpart faced competition from another group of bands. Coming from London and its suburbs, groups of British youths adopted American electric blues and its underdog image to blast out a siren call to teens across the Western world. Headed by the Rolling Stones, these bands formed the second prong of the British invasion.

The British Blues Invasion and Garage Rock

> **❝** We wanted to sell records for Jimmy Reed, Muddy [Waters] and John Lee Hooker. We were disciples. **❞**
>
> —Keith Richards

British Blues and the Rolling Stones

English groups playing American electric blues formed a second flank of the British invasion, led by the Rolling Stones. "By 1962 it became clear to me that the music scene was in a real rut, and a new twist was needed. Blues was the answer," recalled Giorgio Gomelsky, the first manager of the Stones.

The British fascination with American blues and the seeds of the Stones' success began during the late 1950s, when American bluesmen finally were allowed to perform in England. When the British Musicians Union ended its ban on American musicians in 1956, skiffle innovator Chris Barber and his bandmates began to invite American blues artists to England. Remembered Harold Pendelton: "Muddy Waters came out on stage [in 1958] and played an electric guitar. This was the first electric guitar anyone in Britain had ever seen. . . . When we opened the Marquee Club in 1960, skiffle was on the way out so we were able to occasionally feature a rhythm and blues group."

Alexis Korner and Cyril Davies, two members of the Chris Barber band, helped popularize American blues among British youths. "Alexis and Cyril Davies were the only ones really playing blues in London at that time," remembered Rolling Stones drummer Charlie Watts, who originally played with them. "Cyril was a great harmonica player; he made a couple of very good records—'Country Line Special' was one. He and Alexis got together while playing with Chris

Barber" and occasionally played a blues set, when Barber's skiffle group took a break. By 1962, the two left the Barber band, formed Blues Incorporated, and landed a regular Saturday night job at the Ealing Club, a crowded basement venue, which attracted youths such as Keith Richards, Mick Jagger, and Brian Jones, who occasionally performed with Korner and Davies.

Like the Beatles, Richards, Jagger, and Jones started with an interest in American rockabilly. Mick Jagger "had been singing with some rock-and-roll bands, doing Buddy Holly," guitarist Keith Richards remembered. "Buddy Holly was in England as solid as Elvis. Everything that came out was a record smash number one," Richards himself was "really listening to what was coming over the Atlantic. The ones that were hitting hard were Little Richard, and Presley, and Jerry Lee Lewis." He "was rockin' away, avoidin' the bicycle chains and razors in those dance halls." When the movie *Blackboard Jungle*, with the music of Bill Haley and the Comets, showed in London, Richards found that "people were saying 'Did ya hear that music, man?' Because in England we had never heard anything: the BBC controls it and won't play that sort of music. But everybody our age stood up for that music, and the hell with the BBC."

They soon began to uncover the blues roots of rockabilly. Keith Richards heard "[Big Bill] Broonzy first. . . . Then I started to discover Robert Johnson and those cats." The multi-instrumentalist Brian Jones, initially the impetus behind the group, one day heard "Elmore James, and the earth seemed to shudder on its axis. . . . The blues was real. We only had to persuade people to listen to the music, and they couldn't help but be turned on to all those great old blues cats." When Jones saw Muddy Waters perform, recalled Jones's friend Richard Hattrell, "It was as if Brian had found his mission in life. He got himself electrified and he never stopped practicing." Mick Jagger similarly "was crazy over Chuck Berry, Bo Diddley, Muddy Waters, and Fats Domino, not knowing what it meant, just that it was beautiful."

In London, recalled Richards, "I get on this train one morning and there's Jagger—and under his arm he has four or five albums. . . . He's got Chuck Berry, Little Walter, Muddy Waters." The two talked about their mutual passion for Chicago blues and in a few weeks, with friend Dick Taylor, they formed a band called the Glimmer Twins, which laid "down some of this Chuck Berry and Little Walter stuff. No drummer or anything, just two guitars and a little amplifier." Remarked Dick Taylor: "We'd sit around and listen to Mick's records, and then our little skiffle group would try to imitate what we were hearing."

In mid-1963, Keith Richards, Mick Jagger, and Brian Jones, along with Dick Taylor and drummer Tony Chapman, formed the Rolling Stones and moved into a rundown apartment in the downtrodden district of King's Road. They debuted on July 12 at the Marquee Club in London as a replacement for Blues Incorporated and landed a steady gig at the Crawdaddy Club. By the end of the year, jazz aficionado Charlie Watts replaced Chapman as drummer and bassist Bill Wyman joined when Taylor quit to form the blues-driven band, The Pretty Things, solidifying a lineup that would remain intact for over forty years. "We wanted to sell records for Jimmy Reed, Muddy, John Lee Hooker," explained Keith Richards. "We were disciples—if we could turn people on to that, then that was enough. That was the total original aim."

"The Fabulous Rolling Stones" performing on British TV, c. 1965. Left to right: Bill Wyman, Brian Jones, Mick Jagger, Charlie Watts, and Keith Richards. Photo by Michael Ochs Archives. Getty Images, Inc. —Michael Ochs Archives.

The material chosen by the early Stones showed their Chicago blues orientation. For their first single, recorded in early 1963, they covered Chuck Berry's "Come On" and Muddy Waters' "I Wanna Be Loved." Their first American album, *England's Newest Hitmakers*, included Slim Harpo's "I'm a Kingbee," "Carol" by Chuck Berry, Willie Dixon's "I Just Wanna Make Love to You," and Jimmy Reed's "Honest I Do." Subsequent albums exposed teenage record buyers to Chicago blues classics such as "You Can't Catch Me" (Chuck Berry), "Little Red Rooster" (Willie Dixon), "Mona" (Bo Diddley), and "Look What You've Done" (Muddy Waters). The Stones recorded many of these cuts at the Chess studio in Chicago. "Chuck Berry wandered in while we were recording 'Down the Road Apiece,'" a wide-eyed Bill Wyman told a reporter from *New Musical Express*, "and he said to us: 'Wow, you guys are really getting it on.' Muddy Waters was also there." The band even took its name—the Rolling Stones—from a track on Muddy Waters' debut album, "Rollin' Stone."

By April 1963, the *Record Mirror* characterized the Stones as "genuine R&B. As the trad scene gradually subsides, promoters of all kinds of teen-beat entertainment heave a long sigh of relief that they have found something to take its place. It's rhythm and blues . . . and at the Station Hotel, Kew Road, the hip kids throw themselves around to the new jungle music like they never did in the more restrained days of trad. And the combo they writhe and twist to is called the Rolling Stones."

The Stones Turn Raunchy

Andrew Loog Oldham, a former employee of fashion queen Mary Quant and publicity man for Bob Dylan and the Beatles, became the manager of the Stones on May 6, 1963. He helped propel the blues-based group to fame by creating a raunchy, crude, offensive image that contrasted sharply with the reputation of the Beatles.

At first, the band appeared like most other British invasion bands. When debuting on the influential British television show *Thank Your Lucky Stars* on July 7, 1963, the Stones wore checkered suits with velvet collars and matching ties and trousers. "You have to make some compromises," Oldham instructed the group, sounding like his one-time boss, Brian Epstein. As Keith Richards later told it, the manager "tried to tidy us up. . . . There are photographs of us in the suits he put us in, those dog-toothed checked suits with the black velvet collars." He explained, "You've done it because you want to get into the studio, you want to make a record no matter what it takes, even to the point of wearing hounds tooth suits."

Oldham quickly changed his strategy and manufactured an opposite to the neat, smiling Beatles. "The overall hustle I invented for the Stones was to establish them as a raunchy, gamy, unpredictable bunch of undesirables. I decided that since the Beatles had already usurped the clean-cut choirboy image with synchronized jackets, I should take the Stones down the opposite road. Rejecting matching clothing was one step, emphasizing their long hair and unclean appearance was another, and inciting the press to write about them, using catchy phrases that I had coined, was yet another. . . . I wanted to establish that the Stones were threatening, uncouth and animalistic," said Oldham. "It was perfect, just perfect," he told Jagger after a press conference at which the Stones had given flippant and insulting replies to journalists. "They're going to plaster your pictures and your terrible, terrible statements all over the papers. Those dirty Rolling Stones, that's what you are. The opposite of those nice little chaps, the Beatles. . . . We're gonna make you famous."

To refine the image, Oldham engineered a few changes. He downgraded piano player Ian Stewart to roadie. "Well, he just doesn't look the part, and six is too many for [fans] to remember the faces in the picture," Oldham told Richards at the time. The manager shaved a few years off the ages of each Stone in their official biography, making them teens again. He then convinced his label, London Records, to blitz the media. As one ad read in *Billboard*: "They're great! They're outrageous! They're rebels! They sell! They're England's *hottest*."

The rest of the media soon picked up the cue. In 1964, *Melody Maker* carried an article headlined "Would You Let Your Daughter Go Out with a Rolling Stone?" and described the band as "symbols of rebellion . . . against the boss, the clock, and the clean-shirt-a-day routine." The Stones, it continued, looked like "five indolent morons, who give one the feeling that they really enjoy wallowing in a swill-tub of their own repulsiveness." *New Musical Express* labeled the group as "the caveman-like quintet." The British *Daily Express* characterized the band as "boys any self-respecting mother would lock in the bathroom." In 1964, *Time* interviewed Keith Richards, who told the magazine that he hoped "to be sitting in a country house with four Rolls-Royces and spitting at everyone."

Success

The raunchy Rolling Stones soon achieved success in England. Reaching a national audience through appearances on the British television shows in September 1963 the band hit number twenty-one on the British singles chart with a remake of Chuck Berry's "Come On." The same year, Oldham introduced the Stones to the Beatles, who gave the Stones the song "I Wanna Be Your Man," which neared the Top Ten on the British chart. In March 1964, the Stones added a Bo Diddley beat to Buddy Holly's

"Not Fade Away" to reach number three. By May, the group got 100,000 advance orders for its first British album, which immediately topped the chart on its release.

The British success of the Stones probably stemmed from their youth and good looks, appealing to the growing legion of U.K. baby boomers. "The Stones were the first people into the blues in England. Alexis Korner and Cyril Davies were, but the Stones were the first ones who were young, you know," recalled Giorgio Gomelsky, the first manager of the Stones. "I like to think we became popular," agreed Charlie Watts, "because we played music to dance to, which was a massive appeal to the young people. In addition, we weren't bad looking."

The Stones initially had more difficulty igniting the youth in the United States. During their first U.S. tour, which started in June 1964, the Stones received scant notice. On June 13, they appeared on a segment of *The Hollywood Palace* television show, which was hosted by crooner Dean Martin. After the Stones chugged through their versions of "I Just Want to Make Love to You" and "Not Fade Away," a twisted-faced Martin, eyes rolling upward, asked the audience, "Aren't they great?" He continued: "They're off to England to have a hair-pulling contest with the Beatles. . . . Their hair is not that long—it's just smaller foreheads and higher eyebrows." When a trampolinist finished his act, Martin added: "That's the father of the Rolling Stones. He's been trying to kill himself ever since." To a distraught Brian Jones, Dean Martin "was just a symbol of the whole tour for us."

On the remaining dates of the tour, the band mostly played to empty seats. In San Antonio, Texas, the crowd clamored for an encore by a trained monkey rather than one by the Rolling Stones. "We all wanted to pack up and come home," confessed Bill Wyman. The colorful Keith Richards remembered, "Nebraska, we really felt like a sore pimple in Omaha. On top of that, the first time we arrived there, the only people to meet us off the plane were twelve motorcycle cops who insisted on doing this motorcade thing right through town. And nobody in Omaha had ever heard of us. We thought, 'Wow, we've made it. We must be heavy.' And we get to the Auditorium and there's 600 people there in a 15,000-seat hall."

The Stones conquered America on their second tour, which began on October 24, 1964, and featured a spot on *The Ed Sullivan Show*. During the 1950s and 1960s, Ed Sullivan provided the means for teens across the United States to hear rock-and-roll. He had helped promote Elvis Presley, had fostered Beatlemania, had publicized Motown acts, and had provided the springboard for British invasion groups such as Gerry and the Pacemakers, the Searchers, and the Dave Clark Five. "The power of the man [Sullivan] and his show was unbelievable," enthused Dave Clark, who appeared on the show seventeen times. "He was responsible for the success of the British invasion."

On *The Ed Sullivan Show* of October 25, 1964, American teens were introduced to the Stones as a raunchy, hip alternative to the Beatles. After the appearance by the Stones, the host publicly proclaimed: "I promise you they'll never be back on our show. . . . Frankly, I didn't see the Rolling Stones until the day before the broadcast. They were recommended by my scouts in England. I was shocked when I saw them. It took me seventeen years to build this show; I'm not going to have it destroyed in a matter of weeks." Privately, remembered Mick Jagger, "Ed told us it was the wildest, most enthusiastic audience he'd seen any artist get in the history of his show. Got a message a few days later saying: 'Received hundreds of letters from parents complaining about you, but thousands from teenagers saying how much they enjoyed your performance.'" Sullivan hosted a return engagement by the Stones on May 2, 1965.

A critical American press also helped publicize the Rolling Stones. *Newsweek* pegged the Stones as a "leering quintet" obsessed with pornographic lyrics. *Time* magazine printed the letter of one concerned woman, who wrote: "We like the Beatles because they have rhythm, enthusiasm, and a good sound. After listening to the groans, pants, and frankly dirty words of the Rolling Stones and a few other sick groups, one begins to wonder where they dig up a DJ to play such garbage."

Such adult criticism of the band predictably pushed rebellious American teenagers into the Stones' camp. Beatle George Harrison noticed that "it's become the in thing for adults to say the Beatles are good or the Beatles are funny, it's in for adults to like us. So the real hip kids—or the kids who think they are—have gone off us. The in thing for those kids now is to be a Stones fan, because their parents can't stand the Rolling Stones." Agreed Sean O'Mahony, publisher of the *Beatles Monthly*, "The Stones and the Beatles had quite different fans. The Beatles were thugs who were put across as nice blokes, and the Stones were gentlemen who were made into thugs by Andrew [Loog Oldham]."

Throughout the remaining dates of their second American tour in 1964, the Stones played to enthusiastic crowds. Keith Richards at the time felt an "energy building up as you go around the country. You find it winding tighter and tighter, until one day you get out halfway through the first number and the whole place is full of chicks screaming. We'd walk into some of these places and it was like they had the Battle of the Crimea going on—people gasping, tits hanging out, chicks choking, nurses running around. . . . There was a period of six months in England we couldn't play ballrooms anymore because we never got through more than three or four songs every night," added Richards. "Chaos. Police and too many people in the places fainting. They used to tell us, 'There's not a dry seat in the cinema.' And the bigger it got, America and Australia and everywhere it's exactly the same number." Ian Stewart, who now traveled with the band as a roadie, added, "There sure as hell weren't any empty seats this time. Wherever we went, it was bedlam."

The Stones' success coincided with a new, less blues-dominated sound. "I was convinced they couldn't make it as a top group by just playing old rhythm and blues tunes," recalled Andrew Loog Oldham. "We had all witnessed with our own eyes and ears how easy Lennon and McCartney had knocked off 'I Wanna Be Your Man,' and I felt that Mick and Keith could do the same for us once they got the hang of it."

Encouraged by Oldham, Richards and Jagger pushed aside the versatile Brian Jones and began to concentrate on their own material, which combined pop conventions with Chicago-style blues. "Andrew literally forced Mick and me to start writing songs," remembered Richards. "Andrew presented the idea to us, not on an artistic level, but more money." At one point, the dictatorial Oldham locked Jagger and Richards in a room and instructed them to write. Oldham "told Mick and Keith I was going to my mother's to eat—I was locking them in a flat and when I came back I expected a song, and they'd better have one if they expected me to bring them any food." When the manager returned, "Mick was pissed off and hungry, and told me they'd 'written this fucking song and you'd better fucking like it.'" "One thing I can never thank Andrew Oldham enough for—it was more important to the Stones than anything and probably his main achievement," asserted Richards, "was that he turned Mick and me into songwriters."

The Jagger–Richards songwriting team quickly became prolific. On their first three albums, Jagger told interviewer Ed Rudy, the Stones found "that American songs are better for ourselves. The songs that Keith and I write . . . we give to other people. They're mostly ballads." By their fourth LP, *Out of Our Heads*, which was recorded in mid-1965, the band had moved toward the R&B-influenced hard rock songs of Jagger–Richards, such as the rebellious, chart-topping "Satisfaction." According to Mick Jagger, the song dealt with "my frustration with everything. Simple teenage aggression."

With the 1966 *Aftermath*, Jagger–Richards compositions, such as the murky incantations of "Paint It Black" and the misogynist venom of "Under My Thumb" and "Stupid Girl," had almost totally replaced R&B covers. "That was a big landmark record for me," explained Jagger. "It's the first time we wrote the whole record and finally laid to rest the ghost of having to do these very nice and interesting, no doubt, but still cover versions of old R&B songs." By the end of the year, the Rolling Stones vied with the Beatles for the rock-and-roll crown.

The Who

The Who made a similar transition from the Chicago blues to their own songs. As the Detours, the band covered American blues such as Jimmy Reed's "Big Boss Man," Bo Diddley's "I'm a Man," and Willie Dixon's "I Just Wanna Make Love to You." The group, changing its name to the High Numbers, reworked bluesman Slim Harpo's "Got Love If You Want It" for its first single, "I'm the Face."

Pete Meaden, the archetypical Mod and a freelance publicist who had worked with Andrew Loog Oldham, first managed and reshaped the R&B cover band. To distinguish the leather-clad boys from other blues cover bands in Britain, Meaden grafted a Mod image onto the group. "I had this dream of getting a group together that would be the focus, the entertainers for the Mods; a group that would actually be the same people onstage as the guys in the audience . . . an actual representation of the people," remembered Meaden. "Our Mod image was engineered by our first manager, a very bright boy named Peter Meaden," recounted singer Roger Daltrey. "At the time in England, 90 percent of the bands resembled either the Rolling Stones or the Beatles. If anything, we were similar to the Stones. . . . The Mod look was very clean-cut, Ivy League, fashion conscious, which was exactly opposite from the Stones."

The band quickly adopted the clean-cut Mod style. "The original idea was for Roger [Daltrey] to dress up as a sharp top Mod, a face; and the rest of the band to be in T-shirts and Levis, boxing boots and the current 'in' clothes of a typical street Mod, a ticket," remarked Richard Barnes, an early confidant of the band. "Pete Meaden introduced the Who to the very hub of this exclusive group. He took them to the Scene Club in Ham Yard in London's Soho. This dark, dirty, dingy basement not far from Piccadilly Circus was the 'in' place. Top Mods would check each other out and dance or stand around looking cool until about 4 o'clock in the morning," recalled Barnes. Guitarist Pete Townshend even "practiced the complicated steps to the two main Mod dances, the 'block' and the 'bang.' He rehearsed the Mod way of walking and tried to pick up the correct way of standing around."

In 1964, Meaden promoted the reworked blues single of the High Numbers as a Mod anthem. He titled the song "I'm the Face," a reference to a sharply dressed, top Mod. His press release called the record "the *first authentic* Mod record, a hip tailored-for-teens R&B–oriented shuffle rocker . . . with a kick in every catch phrase for the kids of the fast-moving crowd . . . to cause an immediate rapport between the High Numbers and the thousands of young people like themselves. In a nutshell—they are the people." In the summer of the same year, Meaden negotiated with filmmakers Kit Lambert and Chris Stamp, the brother of actor Terence Stamp, to feature the group in a film about the Mods.

After working on the film, the band fired Meaden and hired as managers Lambert and Stamp, who reinforced the Mod image of the group. On the advice of their new managers, recalled drummer Keith Moon, the band members went "to Carnaby Street with more money than we'd ever seen in our lives, like a hundred quid each. . . . We weren't into clothes, we were into music. Kit thought we should identify more with our audience. Coats slashed five inches at the side. Four wasn't enough. Six was too much. Five was just right." The band returned with garb that would become their trademark: bull's-eye T-shirts, and pants, shirts, and jackets cut from the British flag. The group renamed themselves the Who and played for sixteen consecutive Tuesdays at the new London Marquee Club, a Mod hangout owned by Ziggy Jackson.

To complete the reshaping of the Who, Pete Townshend began to write original material for the band on the advice of the managers. He first penned "I Can't Explain." Though "Roger in particular wanted the band to be a blues-based band and thought that 'I Can't Explain' was too pop sounding," mentioned Richard Barnes, Townshend followed with "Anyhow, Anyway, Anywhere." As his third song, he wrote "My Generation," which became the battle cry of the Mods. "That's my generation, that's how the song 'My Generation' happened, because of the Mods," Townshend explained.

The Who in their "mod" days; note John Entwistle's coat made out of the British flag. Left to right: Keith Moon, Pete Townshend, John Entwistle, Roger Daltrey. United Kingdom—c. 1965. Photo by Michael Ochs Archives. Getty Images, Inc.—Michael Ochs Archives.

The members of the Who grew up in the same working-class neighborhoods as other London Mods. Roger Daltrey, lead singer and organizer of the group, Pete Townshend, and bassist John Entwistle were raised in Shepherd's Bush, a dilapidated suburb of West London. Before the Who gained notoriety, band members worked as manual laborers—Daltrey for five years as a sheet metal worker, and Townshend and Entwistle at various odd jobs. Keith Moon, the ebullient madman of the Who, who met an untimely death in 1978, grew up in Wembley and joined the band when he wandered into the Oldfield Hotel one day to listen to their show. Standing out with his "dyed ginger hair and a ginger cord suit," Moon asked the band if he could play with them during one number. In the words of the drummer, "they said go ahead, and I got behind this other guy's drums and did one song—'Road Runner.' I'd several drinks to get me courage up and when I got onstage I went arrgggGhhhh on the drums, broke the bass drum pedal and two skins, and got off. I figured that was it. I was scared to death. Afterwards I was sitting at the bar and Pete came over. He said: 'You . . . come 'ere.' I said, mild as you please: 'Yes, yes?' And Roger, who was the spokesman then, said: 'What are you doing next Monday?' I said: 'Nothing.' I was working during the day, selling plaster. He said: 'You'll have to give up work . . . there's this gig on Monday. If you want to come, we'll pick you up in the van.' I said: 'Right.' And that was it."

The Who's sound captured the anger and rebelliousness of the English Mods. Daltrey screamed the lyrics of a song, backed by Townshend's crashing chords, the thumping bass of Entwistle, and Moon's propulsive drumming. Townshend, who wrote most of the band's material, felt that the Who's brand of rock-and-roll "is a single impetus and it's a single force which threatens a lot of crap which is around at the moment in the middle class and in the middle-aged politics or philosophy." Townshend's guitar-smashing antics and Moon's destruction of his drum kit accentuated the rebellious spirit of the band. Though reaching the height of their popularity during the late 1960s with the rock opera *Tommy*, the R&B-influenced group became the most popular band among British Mods. "The groups that you liked when you were a Mod were the Who," bragged Pete Townshend. "That's the story of why I dig the Mods, man, because we were Mods and that's how we happened."

The British Blues Onslaught

Other British bands, enamored of Chicago blues, gained the allegiance of British and American teens. The Yardbirds learned about the power of the blues from the Rolling Stones. Around 1963, singer Keith Relf and drummer Jim McCarty "went to see the Rolling Stones because they started playing in Richmond, which was quite near . . . and we gradually listened to more of this R&B stuff, got more records," recollected McCarty. That year, McCarty's band, which included guitarists Chris Dreja and Top Topham, merged with Relf and bassist Paul Samwell-Smith, both of whom wanted to play more R&B "like Jimmy Reed, Howlin' Wolf, and Chuck Berry."

The Yardbirds first performed as a backup band for Cyril Davies, and in 1963, replaced the Rolling Stones as the house band at the Crawdaddy Club, owned by the first manager of the Stones, Giorgio Gomelsky. In June 1964, they debuted on record with a cover of Chicago bluesman Billy Boy Arnold's "I Wish You Would" and first charted in Britain a few months later with Don & Bob's R&B standard, "Good Morning Little School Girl." On a December 1963 tour of England, booked by Gomelsky, the band backed Sonny Boy Williamson and a few months later played at the Rhythm and Blues Festival in Birmingham. "A lot of the basis of our act was rearranged rhythm and blues," commented Dreja.

The Yardbirds featured a series of guitar wizards steeped in the blues. When lead guitarist Top Topham left for college in 1963, the band hired blues purist Eric Clapton, who "grew up loving black music." Clapton left the group in 1965, when he felt that the hit "For Your Love" sounded too pop. "I went back to Skip James and Robert Johnson—I spent years in that field and then I came back to the city blues, worked around there for a while, and I guess that's where my heart really still is," explained the guitarist. "When the Yardbirds decided to record 'For Your Love,' I knew it was the beginning of the end for me, as I didn't see how we could make a record like that and stay as we were. It felt to me that we had completely sold out," he concluded.

After the departure of Clapton, the Yardbirds added the more rockabilly-influenced Jeff Beck. "We still played the blues—Jeff could play a great blues—but at the same time we were always looking to something new, something fresh," remarked McCarty. In June 1966, Jimmy Page, who would later help invent heavy metal with Led Zeppelin, joined the group. By July 1968, when they disbanded, the Yardbirds had scored blues-inspired hits in Britain and America with "Heart Full of Soul," "Shapes of Things," and "Over Under Sideways Down."

From the Muswell Hill region of London, a northern working-class suburb, came the Kinks. The band was formed in late 1963 by R&B enthusiasts Ray and Dave Davies, Peter Quaife, and Mick Avory, who had briefly played with the Rolling Stones. In February 1964, they unsuccessfully debuted with Little Richard's "Long Tall Sally." By September of the same year, the group topped the British chart and entered the U.S. Top Ten with "You Really Got Me," which defined power-chord rock. Dave Davies explained to *Melody Maker* that the distinctive sound originated because "I was never a very good guitarist . . . so I used to experiment with sounds. I had a very small amplifier which distorted badly." Two months later the Kinks followed with the crunching "All Day and All of the Night" before turning toward a softer, music-hall style. Although charting in America, the group met disaster when the American Federation of Musicians instituted a four-year ban on them for unprofessional conduct during their first American tour in June 1965.

Spencer Davis, a teacher and blues enthusiast, formed another R&B-based band. In August 1963, he joined with drummer Peter York and the Winwood brothers, Steve and Muff, to start the Spencer Davis Group, which debuted with a remake of John Lee Hooker's "Dimples." "We were really heavily into the blues, blues singers and blues writers," remembered Davis. "Basically what we used to do was more or less copy—or do our own arrangements of—blues and rhythm 'n' blues records, which at the time were fairly unheard of," agreed Steve Winwood. Within two years, added Winwood, "we had an idea that we no longer wanted to actually copy, [we wanted] to write; we felt we could contribute ourselves toward the material." From 1965 to 1967, the band members scored on both sides of the Atlantic with their own blues-drenched compositions such as "I'm a Man," "Gimmie Some Lovin'" and "Somebody Help Me."

The Kinks, c. 1966. Back row: Dave Davies, Mick Avory; front row: Ray Davies, Peter Quaife. Michael Ochs Archives. Getty Images, Inc.

In 1962, a budding jazz pianist Manfred Mann (a.k.a. Manfred Lubowitz) teamed with Mike Hugg to become the Mann–Hugg Blues Brothers. After being greeted by wild receptions at the London Marquee Club, the duo added three more members to emerge as Manfred Mann and the Manfreds or, in the United States, as simply Manfred Mann. In early 1964, the band scored in Britain with "5-4-3-2-1," the theme of the popular British rock television show *Ready, Steady, Go!*, and by August topped the U.S. charts with a remake of the Exciters' "Do Wah Diddy Diddy." The band subsequently covered R&B standards such as Muddy Waters' "I've Got My Mojo Working," "Smokestack Lightnin'" by Howlin' Wolf, and Willie Dixon's "I'm Your Hoochie Coochie Man."

The Animals, a group of poor youths from a mining town in northern England, named for their wild stage behavior, played a convincing brand of British R&B to both British and American fans. In 1962, jazz organist Alan Price joined with lead guitarist Hilton Valentine, bassist Bryan "Chas" Chandler, drummer John Steel, and Eric Burdon, who had become captivated by Chicago blues after witnessing a Muddy Waters performance. Price was pushed in the direction of rhythm and blues by the new musicians, especially Burdon, who, according to the *New Musical Express*, had "written out hundreds of lyrics by artists like Mose Allison and Chuck Berry. On the first page, he had written the word *blues* in his own blood. He had cut his finger especially for it." During their first two years, the Animals attracted a following at the Club-a-Go-Go in their hometown of Newcastle-on-Tyne. Price remembered that "we used to play everything from the blues to Chico Hamilton, and it used to swing like the clappers." After moving to London in 1964, the band reworked the folk blues number "The House of the Rising Sun" into a number-one, million-selling hit on both sides of the Atlantic. They then revived John Lee Hooker's "Boom Boom" and "I'm Mad Again," and singer Sam Cooke's "Bring It on Home to Me," and in September 1964, they triumphantly toured the United States.

George Ivan Morrison and his group, Them, were equally dedicated to American R&B. Raised in Ulster by parents who were blues and jazz enthusiasts, Van Morrison grew up listening to John Lee Hooker, Muddy Waters, Leadbelly, and Sonny Boy Williamson. At age fifteen, he dropped out of school to join a band called the Monarchs, which headlined at the R&B Club in Belfast. In 1963, Van Morrison formed the group called Them, who charted in Britain and America with "Here Comes the Night." Though hardly cracking the U.S. charts with "Gloria," a song that Van Morrison attributed to "listening to all those old blues records," the band defined a sound that would be emulated by thousands of garage bands in the United States during the next few years.

American Garage Rock

The British blues invasion of America prompted young American teens to embrace their blues heritage. The British covers of American originals began to offer notoriety for some blues pioneers among a white audience. "We still have mostly Negro adults at our gigs," remarked B. B. King in 1966, "but I've noticed in the last year or so I've had a lot [more] of the white kids come than ever before. When the British bands came over," he added, "they made the U.S. as a whole aware of the blues." Muddy Waters noticed the same trend: "The Rolling Stones came out named after my song, you know, and recorded 'I Just Wanna Make Love to You' and the next thing I knew [white youths] were out there. And that's how people in the States really got to know who Muddy Waters was." In the mid-1960s, the sound of Chicago blues ironically had been introduced to American youths by British bands.

British blues also influenced a generation of American youths, who bought electric guitars and drums, formed bands, practiced in their garages, and sometimes had gut-bucket, primal, proto-punk regional hits. From 1964 to 1966 after the Stones and other British blues invasion acts toured the United States, garage bands formed in nearly every part of the country.

Los Angeles and other parts of California nurtured several prominent garage groups. Assembled by former folkie Sean Bonniwell in 1966, the Music Machine exploded on the scene with the hard-hitting anthem "Talk Talk." The group, referred to as "the American Rolling Stones" according to Bonniwell, "really wanted that bottom power punch." In 1965, the Stones-influenced Seeds formed in Los Angeles around Sky Saxon (a.k.a. Richard Marsh). They delivered garage-rock hits such as "Pushin' Too Hard" and "Can't Seem to Make You Mine." The same year, the Los Angeles–based Electric Prunes joined with Rolling Stones engineer Dave Hassinger to hit the chart with "I Had Too Much to Dream Last Night." The band also charted with the Bo Diddley–inspired "Get Me to the World on Time." "We loved Bo Diddley," explained singer James Lowe. Just like the Rolling Stones, he "grew up on that beat, I ate to that beat."

In San Jose near San Francisco around 1965, the Chocolate Watchband started performing with vocalist Dave Aguilar and Sean Tolby on guitar. The British blues–influenced group quickly became a regional sensation with "The Blues Theme." On stage, the band, according to Aguilar, played "some rather obscure stuff by probably—it would range from Muddy Waters to the Yardbirds or an occasional very obscure Stones song." They also selected the Chuck Berry song "Come On." "Hell, if it worked for the Stones, it might work for us," reasoned the lead singer. Ed Cobb, the manager of the Chocolate Watchband, also refashioned the Los Angeles pop group the Standells into a garage band with the 1966 classic "Dirty Water." San Jose also yielded the Count Five, a Yardbirds–inspired outfit that in 1966 hit the Top Five of the national chart with the churning, raucous "Psychotic Reaction."

In the Midwest, bands seemed to be coming from nearly every garage. Chicago, the epicenter of electric blues, listened to the Shadows of Knight, which modified the British blues for the Windy City. "The Stones, the Animals and Yardbirds took the Chicago blues and gave it an English interpretation," observed the group. "We've taken the English version of the blues and re-added a Chicago touch." In late 1965, they remade the Them's "Gloria" for a Top Ten national hit.

Detroit spawned a series of garage bands that added a touch of soul to the British blues. With earth-shattering shrieks and flying-knee drops in concert, Mitch Ryder (a.k.a. William Levise) and the Detroit Wheels defined a gut-bucket, propulsive sound. He scaled the chart with such raves as "Jenny Takes a Ride!," "Little Latin Lupe Lu," and "Devil with a Blue Dress On." Question Mark and the Mysterians played a more straightforward, Stones–influenced style. After topping the regional chart, the Latino band had a national number-one smash in 1966 with the rowdy "96 Tears."

A more original, wilder, and definitive garage band sound emanated from the Seattle area. Getting together well before the Rolling Stones, the Wailers met at an officers' club outside Tacoma, Washington. They originally listened to blues and early rock-and-roll. "We used to go to the Evergreen Ballroom to see R&B shows. The first night we went in there it was Bobby 'Blue' Bland and Little Junior Parker, and I just went nuts," remembered bassist Buck Ormsby. "We'd go see Little Richard and the Upsetters every time they came through, and we were the only white guys there." Soon the band began to play covers of the songs that they liked. "There were all these old ballrooms left over from the big band era, and we just sort of took them over," continued Ormsby. "When we had a dance up there at the Spanish Castle [the subject of Jimi Hendrix's "Spanish Castle Magic"], we had like two or three thousand kids. We were doing Freddie King songs like 'Stumble' and 'San-Ho-Zay' before anybody had ever heard of them." In 1959, the Wailers had a hit with the original "Tall Cool One," appearing on *American Bandstand* and the *Alan Freed Show* to promote the record.

In 1960, the Wailers, unhappy with their record contract, decided to start their own label, calling it Etiquette. They released what would become the all-time classic garage single, "Louie Louie." The group followed with the raw abandon of *The Fabulous Wailers at the Castle*. Though having some early local competitors, only the Wailers transformed an instrumental rhythm and blues into the nitty-gritty sound of the garage. The group provided an inspiration to such soon-to-be stars as the Rolling Stones, Pete Townshend of the Who, and the Kinks.

Buck Ormsby also sought other local bands for his label, finding the Sonics in a Tacoma garage practicing in 1963. "My thing was not just recording the Wailers, it was recording other groups," he explained. "I went out to a garage and heard 'em [the Sonics] and they sounded O.K. but they were doing all these Wailers cover songs. Then they started playing 'The Witch' and I went, 'Man this is it! Let's go record that!'" The Sonics acknowledged their debt to the Wailers. "Overall, the Wailers were our biggest influence always!" confessed bass player and Sonics leader Andy Parypa. "Other influences were people like James Brown and Freddie King, the blues guitarist, [organist] Bill Doggett was a big influence on all the Seattle groups." The group took these influences, revved them up and distorted them, adding the bloodcurdling screams of Gary Rosalie for vocals. In songs such as "The Witch," "Psycho," and "Strychnine," and with two unforgettable albums on Etiquette, the band defined garage rock and presaged heavy metal and punk with its nearly uncontrollable music. "It's raw, it's forceful, it's energetic," explained Parypa about his band's sound. "I mean the Sonics were savage!"

The Tacoma crunch of the Sonics was commercialized by other Northwest bands. Formed in Portland, Oregon, in 1959, the Kingsmen spent $50 to cut a demo audition tape of "Louie Louie" in a Portland recording studio. Jerry Dennon, the owner of Jerden records, bought the song and rushed it to market. By the end of the month, the Kingsmen version of the Northwest classic had become a number-two national hit and raised the ire of adults who imagined obscene lyrics in the obscured vocals of Jack Ely. The governor of Indiana even banned the record from the state, and the Federal Bureau of Investigation began to investigate the band. With their newfound fame, a revamped Kingsmen lineup scored again with two covers, Barrett Strong's "Money" and the Olympics's "Big Boy Pete," which they titled "Jolly Green Giant."

Paul Revere and the Raiders, an Idaho band coming together in 1959, scored even greater success as they built upon the Wailers' and Sonics' sound. "It was the Wailers who really inspired everybody," remembered Paul Revere (a.k.a. Paul Revere Dick). "Everyone wanted to be like the Wailers." Sporting Revolutionary War costumes after 1963, the band offered a slightly more accessible version of Northwest garage rock and hit regionally with "Louie Louie."

In 1964, the band opened for the Rolling Stones and attracted the attention of Columbia Records. In early 1965, they just missed the Top Ten with "Just Like Me," characterized by singer Mark Lindsay as "a rip-off. Sounded to me like the Kinks and the Stones." By June 1965 with the help of Beatles publicist Derek Taylor, the Raiders achieved national stardom, becoming the house band for the weekday, Dick Clark–inspired television show *Where the Action Is*. Within a year, they hit the Top Ten with "Kicks" and "Hungry." "We were in the right place at the right time with the right name with the right costumes, just in time for the British invasion, just in time [when] Dick Clark happened to have a television show where he needed something visual, colorful with three-cornered hats," explained Revere.

By the mid-sixties, garage bands played in nearly every major American city. The Litter covered the songs of the Yardbirds in Minneapolis; the Human Beinz sang their hit "Nobody But Me" in Youngstown, Ohio; the Nightcrawlers emerged from Daytona, Florida; the Moving Sidewalks wailed their "99th Floor" in Houston, Texas; the Strangeloves from Brooklyn snarled their "I Want Candy"; and the Mojo Men covered the Stones' "Off the Hook" in San Francisco. Throughout the country, hundreds of garage bands scored regional and sometimes national hits with the raw, many times British-inspired, blues-based rock, which would pave the way for later developments such as punk and grunge.

9 Folk Rock

❝ Ours is happy music—we haven't any message to impart. **❞**

—Sonny Bono

In early 1964, Gene Clark sat in a bar in Norfolk, Virginia, and looked at the selections on the jukebox. In August of the previous year, he had been recruited by the folk group, the New Christy Minstrels, and was touring with them. Unsuspectingly, he chose the song "She Loves You" by a new group from Liverpool called the Beatles. "I might have played it 40 times in the two days the New Christy Minstrels were playing that town," he later enthused. "I knew, I *knew* that this was the future." After hearing the Fab Four, Clark quit the New Christy Minstrels and moved to Los Angeles where he went to the Troubadour folk club and met Roger McGuinn, another folkie who had been converted by the Beatles. Within months, the duo joined together with a few other former folk musicians and started a band that they called the Byrds, intentionally misspelled to emulate the spelling error of the Beatles' own animal moniker. By 1965, the group topped the charts with a combination of Dylanese folk, vocal harmonies and Beatles music to create a sound called folk rock.

By 1965, folk music changed fundamentally. Bands such as the Byrds took the introspective songs of an electrified Bob Dylan and combined them with the jangly sound of the British Invasion to create a new music. Following Dylan in his abandonment of the protest song for Beat-inspired, personal lyrics and influenced by the dizzying success of the lads from Liverpool, these groups combined two of the dominant trends of the early 1960s for an escapist music that the nation embraced following the assassination of President John F. Kennedy.

Dylan's Disenchantment

Folk music began to change during late 1963. On November 22, in Dallas, a rifleman shot and killed President John Kennedy, who was riding in a motorcade with his wife Jackie and Texas Governor John Connally and his wife. The assassination shocked and horrified the nation, which mourned a president who had symbolized energy, action, and optimism.

Folk musicians felt especially disillusioned by the assassination. Phil Ochs sensed "a definite flowering-out of positive feelings when John Kennedy became president. The civil rights movement was giving off positive vibrations. There was a great feeling of reform, that things could be changed, that the government cared, that an innovator could come in. . . . Things looked incredibly promising. Then came the Bay of Pigs, the beginnings of Vietnam and the assassination. It ruined the dream. November 22, 1963, was a mortal wound the country has not yet been able to recover from."

Dylan experienced the same pain and confusion over Kennedy's death. As folk singer Eric Andersen told it, "You can't separate Dylan from history in the sense of what was going down, the way he reacted to a chain of events. The first being Kennedy's death; I think that got him out of politics. . . . Kennedy, he was sort of like the shadow of the flight . . . and then that bird got shot out of the sky and everyone was exposed, naked to all the frightening elements, the truth of the country. It had flown, that force had lost out. And people were depressed."

Dylan, though depressed over the Kennedy assassination, started to become more commercially successful. The national press began to notice Dylan during the early 1960s. In 1962, *Newsweek* tagged him "the newest rage" in folk music, and *Time* sarcastically mentioned that Bob Dylan delivered "his songs in a studied nasal that has just the right clothespin-on-the-nose honesty to appeal to those who most deeply care." The next year, the influential folk magazine *Little Sandy Review* called him "our finest contemporary folk songwriter."

Bob Dylan attracted national prominence after he signed with manager Albert Grossman, who was a major impetus in the folk revival. In 1957, Grossman opened one of the first folk clubs, the Gate of Horn, in Chicago; two years later, he collaborated with George Wein to launch the first Newport Folk Festival. In 1960, he met folk singer Peter Yarrow, whom he signed to a management contract. Grossman introduced Yarrow to onetime Broadway singer Mary Travers and stand-up comic Paul Stookey, who began to perform as Peter, Paul, and Mary. "It was Albert's idea to make a group, and it was Albert's suggestion that it contain a comedian, a very strong energetic woman's voice—ballsy is I guess the term that you might use—and that I would be the serious presenter onstage and the sensitive male lead singer," explained Yarrow. "Albert Grossman," added Stookey, "had a vision of a more accessible form of folk entertainment."

Left to right: Noel Paul Stookey, Mary Travers, and Peter Yarrow from the photo session for their debut album, 1962. Photo by Michael Ochs Archives. Getty Images, Inc.—Michael Ochs Archives.

The folk trio, propelled by Grossman's vision, hit the chart in April 1962 with "Lemon Tree" and six months later cracked the Top Ten with Pete Seeger's and Lee Hays's "If I Had a Hammer," which brought folk protest to a national audience. The group's debut album, which included both hits, topped the album chart in late October and would eventually sell two million copies. The next year, the trio reached number two on the singles chart with Dylan's "Blowin' in the Wind," which had been given to them by their manager, who had signed Dylan in June 1962. Along with an appearance at the 1963 Newport Folk Festival, which also featured Peter, Paul, and Mary, the success of the folk trio's version of the song lifted Dylan into the national spotlight.

After gaining national exposure, and in the wake of the Kennedy assassination, Dylan started to become somewhat disillusioned with political activism. "I agree with everything that's happening," he told writer Nat Hentoff over dinner in October 1964, "but I'm not part of no Movement. If I was, I wouldn't be able to do anything else but be in 'the Movement.' I just can't sit around and have people make rules for me. . . . Those [protest] records I already made," said Dylan, referring to his first three albums, "I'll stand behind them, but some of that was jumping on the scene to be heard and a lot of it was because I didn't see anybody else doing that kind of thing. Now a lot of people are doing finger-pointing songs. You know—pointing at the things that are wrong. Me, I don't want to write for people anymore. You know—be a spokesman." Dylan began to criticize Joan Baez for her involvement with the Institute for the Study of Nonviolence at Carmel, California, established to "root out violence in ourselves and in the world." By 1965, Dylan abruptly informed a *Newsweek* reporter that "I've never written a political song. Songs can't save the world. I've gone through all that. When you don't like something, you gotta learn to just not need that something."

In place of social protest, Dylan crafted complex, personal, and sometimes cryptic songs. "I have to make a new song out of what *I* know and out of what *I'm* feeling," he told Nat Hentoff. "I once wrote about Emmett Till in the first person, pretending that I was him. From now on, I want to write what's inside *me*." *Another Side of Bob Dylan*, recorded on a single night in June 1964, featured such nonpolitical poetry as "Chimes of Freedom" and more pop-oriented tunes such as "All I Really Want to Do" and "It Ain't Me Babe." It explicitly repudiated the composer's folk protest in "My Back Pages." "I think it is very, very destructive music," complained Joan Baez at the time, regarding Dylan's new orientation. "I think he doesn't want to be responsible for anybody, including himself."

Dylan's next album, *Bringing It All Back Home*, released in early 1965, edged toward an electrified rock. On one side backed by the Chicago-based electric blues of the Paul Butterfield Blues Band, it highlighted bitter, dark songs such as "Subterranean Homesick Blues," "She Belongs to Me," and "Maggie's Farm." The other acoustic side included "Mr. Tambourine Man," "Gates of Eden," and "It's All Right, Ma (I'm Only Bleeding)." Also released in 1965, *Highway 61 Revisited* featured an all-out rock sound with the impressionistic, beat-inspired poetry of "Desolation Row," "Ballad of a Thin Man," and "Like a Rolling Stone."

On July 25, 1965, at the Newport Folk Festival, Dylan unveiled his new electric sound and brand of songwriting to the folk community. Behind the stage, some of the folk performers tried to prevent Dylan from playing his electric music with the Paul Butterfield Blues Band. "On one side you had Pete Seeger, [concert organizer] George Wein, the old guard," remembered Paul Rothchild, who mixed the Dylan set and had recently recorded the Butterfield band. "Pete is backstage, pacifist Pete, with an ax saying, 'I'm going to cut the fucking cables if that act goes onstage.'" Eventually, Seeger dashed to his "car and rolled up the windows, his hands over his ears." When Dylan unleashed the electrified "Maggie's Farm," recalled Elektra Records owner Jac Holzman, "suddenly we heard booing, like pockets of wartime flak." Irwin Silber, editor of the radical folk magazine *Sing Out!*, lamented "I wouldn't mind so much if he sang just one song about the war." Peter Yarrow later related, "People were just horrified. It was as if it was a capitulation to the enemy—as if all of a sudden you saw Martin Luther King, Jr. doing a cigarette ad."

Dylan, angry and shaken, stormed off the stage. Encouraged backstage by Johnny Cash and prodded from onstage by Peter Yarrow, he returned a few minutes later, alone. Dylan asked for a D harmonica from the crowd, which soon carpeted the stage with the instrument and hoped that the request signaled a victory for acoustic music. He sang "Mr. Tambourine Man" and "It's All Over Now, Baby Blue" and walked off the stage for the last time. "To me, that night at Newport was as clear as crystal," explained Paul Rothchild. "It's the end of one era and the beginning of another."

Though ridiculed by old-time folksters, Dylan secured a national audience with the electric sound. He snagged the number-two spot with "Like a Rolling Stone," his first hit single. He also first hit the Top Ten with *Bringing It All Back Home* and neared the top of the chart with *Highway 61 Revisited*. In 1966, the singer again cracked the Top Ten with *Blonde on Blonde*, which made the transition complete from folk protest to an electrified poetry inspired by the Beatniks, and raised the bar for anyone who hoped to write rock lyrics. Dylan had become a commercial success with a sound that would inspire a folk-rock boom.

Folk Rock

Many groups added vocal harmonies and the jangly sound of the early Beatles to Dylan's electrified folk sound and sometimes used his songs to create what critics termed *folk rock*. The Byrds, probably the premier folk rockers, were formed in 1964 by Roger McGuinn, who had backed the Limeliters and the Chad Mitchell Trio. Besides McGuinn, the group consisted of bassist Chris Hillman, drummer Michael Clarke and guitarist Gene Clark, who had met the other member of the group, David Crosby, at the Troubadour Club in Los Angeles on a hootenanny night.

The Byrds combined their folk background, which had been rooted in Dylan, with the Beatles. "I did feel that the real folk scene was in the Village," remembered Roger McGuinn. "But the Beatles came out and changed the whole game for me. I saw a definite niche, a place where the two of them blended together. If you took Lennon and Dylan and mixed them together, that was something that hadn't been done." Though believing that "Dylan was real and the Beatles were plastic," McGuinn and his band grafted the bouncy, jangling harmonies of the mop-tops from Liverpool onto Dylanesque folk.

In 1965, after obtaining a test pressing of Dylan's "Mr. Tambourine Man" from Dylan's producer Tom Wilson, the Byrds meteorically rose to the top of the chart with a version of the song that featured bouncy vocal harmonies and a ringing twelve-string Rickenbacker guitar. Two months later, the group neared the top of the chart with the Dylan composition, "All I Really Want to Do." The group followed with electrified, harmony-rich versions of Dylan's "Spanish Harlem Incident," "The Times They Are A-Changin'," and "Chimes of Freedom," as well as chart-topper "Turn, Turn, Turn," a song adapted by Pete Seeger from the Book of Ecclesiastes. "I changed the chord structure to be more like, kind of Beatley, and we changed the beat," intimated Roger McGuinn about "Turn, Turn, Turn." "We put a kick, that Phil Spector beat, to it."

Simon and Garfunkel
in concert, c. 1965.
Permission by The Daily
*of The University of
Washington*.

Other groups became successful with the folk-rock formula of electrified renditions of Dylan songs sung in harmony with a Beatles beat. In 1965, the ebullient
Turtles, a band that had switched from surf music to folk the year before, hit the Top
Ten with "It Ain't Me Babe." The same year, a husband-wife team, Sonny and Cher,
released the million-selling, Dylan-sounding "I Got You Babe." Cher, a former backup singer for the Ronettes, scored a solo hit with Dylan's "All I Really Want to Do."
"What do we sing? We call it folk and roll—a sort of folk music with a rocking beat.
But with a smile," gushed Sonny Bono to *Melody Maker*. "Ours is happy music—we
haven't any message to impart."

Paul Simon and Art Garfunkel were two high school friends, who in 1957 had
attracted notice as Tom and Jerry with "Hey! Schoolgirl" and had appeared on
American Bandstand. In 1964, after being influenced by the folk boom, they reemerged
with a collegiate image and an album of soft harmonies, *Wednesday Morning, 3 A.M.*
The album showcased Dylan's "The Times They Are A-Changin" and Simon's composition, "The Sound of Silence," which in January 1966 became a number-one hit
when Tom Wilson, Dylan's producer at the time, remixed the track by adding drums,
percussion, and electric guitar.

Mimicking Dylan by wearing a denim cap and using a racked harmonica, Donovan Leitch of Scotland became the British answer to Dylan. In 1964, Donovan began performing folk music in clubs throughout the United Kingdom. The next year, he landed a spot on the British television show *Ready, Steady, Go!*, on which he appeared with a guitar that had the Woody Guthrie–inspired message: "This guitar kills." "I knew immediately that I would be to the European youth what Bob Dylan was to America, the European Bob Dylan," recalled Donovan. After appearing on the television show, Donovan hit the British singles chart with the acoustic "Catch the Wind," which bore an obvious resemblance to the Dylan title, "Blowin' in the Wind." Later in 1965, Donovan hit the chart with the antiwar "Universal Soldier," written by Native American Buffy Saint-Marie, and a four-song extended play record of the same name that included three more antiwar titles.

After appearing at the 1965 Newport Folk Festival and watching Dylan's rock-oriented performance, Donovan turned to folk rock. "What's wrong with electrified guitar? And drums?" he asked a reporter for *Melody Maker* in May 1965. In 1966, amid the folk-rock boom, Donovan scored his first American success with the chart-topping "Sunshine Superman," which featured cryptic lyrics and a rock band. In three months, Donovan snagged the number-two slot with the equally impressionistic "Mellow Yellow," which featured vocal assistance from Beatle Paul McCartney.

The Lovin' Spoonful joined the folk-rock legion. Formed in 1965 by John Sebastian who had backed several folk groups in Greenwich Village before forming the Spoonful, the group admitted its debt to Dylan. Sebastian insisted that Bob Dylan acted as "a force on our music, just like the 'Star Spangled Banner.' We all heard it." The group also attributed its music to the Beatles, delivering an upbeat electric sound similar to British invasion bands. They called their sound "good-time music." In October 1965, the Lovin' Spoonful hit the Top Ten with "Do You Believe in Magic?" The next year, they followed with the Top Ten hits "You Didn't Have to Be So Nice" and "Daydream," and their blockbuster "Summer in the City."

By the mid-1960s, the escapist Dylan-Beatles amalgam of folk rock had permeated popular music. In September 1965 alone, reported *Billboard*, various folk rockers had recorded snappy versions of forty-eight different Dylan songs, most of them concerned with topics other than protest. According to *Newsweek*, "healthy, cheap, moral or venal, folk rock is what's happening at this moment in the dissonant echo chamber of pop culture."

In 1965, a few members of the folk band, Mother McCree's Uptown Jug Champions, heard the Lovin' Spoonful and became convinced that they needed to swap their acoustic guitars for electric instruments. These musicians bolted from Mother McCree's to form their own band called the Warlocks and eventually the Grateful Dead. However, unlike the Lovin' Spoonful that delivered a bubbly, radio-friendly sound, the Grateful Dead and their compatriots in San Francisco created a hard acid rock that would serve as the foundation for a psychedelic movement, which would confront established culture and call for a revolution.

Acid Rock

66 We have a private revolution going on. **99**

—A handbill distributed from the Blue Unicorn,
a coffeehouse in the Haight

"Everybody's relaxing and not afraid to speak out and not afraid not to wear a tie to work," asserted Marty Balin, one of the founders of the Jefferson Airplane, a group that took off in San Francisco during the mid-1960s. "The one word I can think of is love, even though that sounds like a cliché, but that's where it's at, it's uninhibited, coming-out emotion. It's like the twenties. The twenties were really a start and at the end of it, they had all these great creative different things come out of it. . . . It's the most moving generation since the twenties. In creativity. And out of this are going to come many wonderful artists and people and thinkers."

Speak out, love, creativity, uninhibited, and *happening now* became the bywords of a new era. In the wake of the British invasion, thousands of middle-class, college-educated youths clustered around San Francisco Bay to demonstrate to the country, and eventually to the world, that love could replace war, sharing could replace greed, and community could supersede the individual. These San Francisco visionaries strove for nothing less than a total transformation of America that they demanded immediately. As Jim Morrison, lead singer of the Doors, screamed: "We want the world, and we want it *now*."

A new hybrid of rock-and-roll reflected and helped propagate the new culture. Named after a strange new drug, LSD, acid rock broadcast the word of hippiedom from the epicenter, San Francisco, to the hinterlands. Unlike the working-class British invaders, who used music to entertain, the West Coast bands such as the Jefferson Airplane, the Grateful Dead, Quicksilver Messenger Service, and countless others (1,500 by one count) led a youth movement that consciously withdrew from America's nine-to-five, workaholic society and tried to create an alternative community built upon love. From 1965 to 1967, the vanguard of rock-and-roll had a mission.

The Beats

The social upheaval of hippiedom had its origins with the Beats, who had wandered from their homes in New York City to San Francisco's North Beach more than a decade earlier. In 1951, Jack Kerouac, the Columbia University football star turned writer, planted the seeds of the Beat Generation, when he bummed around the country with the ever-energetic, ever-adventuresome Neal Cassady and told of their travels in his book *On the Road*. That same year, poet Lawrence Ferlinghetti left New York for San Francisco because "it was the only place in the country where you could get decent wine cheap." Two years later, he opened the prime beatnik haunt in North Beach, City Lights Bookstore. Also in 1953, Allen Ginsberg migrated to San Francisco on the advice of his friend Neal Cassady. Two years later, he organized the first public appearance of the Beat Generation—a poetry reading advertised as "Six Poets at the Six Gallery," at which he premiered his controversial poem *Howl*, which the San Francisco Police Department first declared obscene, then banned and confiscated. In 1957, Kerouac finally published *On the Road* to the critical acclaim of *The New York Times*.

The Beats formulated a countercultural philosophy based on tenets of Eastern religion. Their metaphorical name—Beat—suggested the quest for beatitude that could be discovered in Zen Buddhism. It also referred to the patron saints of the movement, the drifters, who shed the trappings of institutional society and gathered in places such as New York City's Bowery. Although appearing "beat down" and downtrodden to "straights," the bums symbolized the freedom that the avant-garde so dearly cherished. As one writer put it, the beatniks "chased the unwashed American dream." Finally, the term alluded to the beat of jazz, especially the be-bop of artists such as Charlie Parker and Dizzy Gillespie and the cool jazz of Miles Davis, Lennie Tristano, and Gerry Mulligan, who were considered cultural heroes by the Beat writers.

Congregating in San Francisco and New York City's Greenwich Village, these countercultural literati lambasted traditional American values. In his once-banned *Naked Lunch* (1959), William S. Burroughs, the literary genius who had inherited the Burroughs adding-machine fortune, wove together powerful, graphic images of a decaying society: "Smell of chili houses and dank overcoats and atrophied testicles. . . . A heaving sea of air hammers in the purple brown dusk tainted with rotten metal smell of sewer gas." Ginsberg penned antiestablishment poems such as *America* (1956), which blasted racism against African Americans and Native Americans and criticized the army and the "sixteen-hour-a-day" work ethic. "America I've given you all and now I'm nothing," the poem begins. "I'm sick of your insane demands."

In place of traditional bourgeois values, the Beats sought fundamental change through cultural relativism. "We love everything," explained Kerouac. "Billy Graham, the Big Ten, rock-and-roll, Zen, apple pie, Eisenhower—we dig it all." Believing that no value was absolute, the Beats emphasized individual feelings. As one Beat argued, "I stay cool, far out, alone. When I flip it's over something *I* feel, only me." Ginsberg contended that the Beats wrote to encourage a "liberating insolence of recognizing one's own feelings and acting on one's own feelings rather than acting on Madison Avenue feelings of careerism. . . . I don't think you can create new structures until you have transformed consciousness," the poet explained. "The experiences through which you've gone, in conjunction with many others, is an indispensable state for reorganizing the system."

Such a radical ethos that was centered around the individual led to experimentation with sex and drugs, especially marijuana and amphetamines, which Kerouac mentioned in *Dharma Bums* and Ginsberg glorified in his poetry. "They had no interest in building a greater America, in fighting Communism, in working at a career to buy $100 suits and dresses, color television sets, a house in the suburbs, or a flight to

Poet Allen Ginsberg, c. mid-'70s. A bridge between the Beats and the Hippies. *Permission by* The Daily *of The University of Washington.*

Paris," observed writer Burton Wolfe. "In fact, they laughed at those goals. Some brew, a few joints, a sympathetic partner in the sack, a walk in the park, an afternoon of lying in the sun on the beach, a hitchhike trip to Mexico—this was all there was."

The Beat challenge to institutional values resulted in attacks from more traditional quarters. Right-wing FBI director J. Edgar Hoover, turning literary critic in 1959, reviewed Lawrence Ferlinghetti's poem *Tentative Description of a Dinner Given to Promote the Impeachment of President Eisenhower*, concluding "it appears that Ferlinghetti may possibly be a mental case." One month later, the Alcoholic Beverages Commission declared North Beach a "problem area" and refused to issue any more liquor licenses there. Other, more violent critics bombed the women's restroom at the Co-Existence Bagel Shop, a favorite gathering spot for the San Francisco Beats, which, along with The Place, closed down shortly thereafter. By the end of 1959, Eric Nord, a visible West Coast Beat writer, told a courtroom that "the Beat Generation is dead. I don't go to North Beach anymore."

The Reemergence of the Beats: The New York Connection

Some of the Beats reappeared on the cultural scene to parent the psychedelic movement during the mid-1960s. On the East Coast, at St. Mark's Place in Greenwich Village in 1965, Beat poets Tuli Kupferberg, Ken Weaver, and Ed Sanders, the editor of *Fuck You: A Magazine of the Arts*, started the Fugs. "We used to read at the Metro, on Second Avenue," recalled Kupferberg. "After the readings, we'd go to the Dom, on St. Marks Place . . . where lots of young people would go. The jukebox had Beatles and Stones albums on it, and some of the kids would dance. Once they started, the other paper-assed intellectuals tried to get up and dance, too. And Ed Sanders got the idea it might be good to try to combine some of our poetry with rock music."

The band caricatured American society, in the process using the verse of William Blake in *How Sweet I Roamed from Field to Field* and the prose of William S. Burroughs in *Virgin Forest*. Allen Ginsberg described the countercultural message of the group in the liner notes on the Fugs' second album, released in 1966. "The United States is split down the middle," he contended. "On one side are everybody who make love with their eyes open, maybe smoke pot and maybe take LSD and look inside their heads to find the Self-God Walt Whitman prophesied for America. . . . Who's on the other side? People who think we are *bad*. . . . Yogies and Beatles say there is no other side. 'We can get along.' Can we? Teenagers rise up and understand. When they scream 'Kill for Peace' they're announcing publicly the madness of our white-haired crazy governments." The poet concluded: "The Bible says that when Christ comes back, 'every eye shall see.' Now every ear can hear, and when the Fugs break thru the monopoly blockade and their image is broadcast on National Television, every kid in America and most white-haired old suffering men will turn them on with Relief at last and every eye shall see."

To some extent, Ginsberg's prophecy came true. Although none of their albums were best sellers, the Fugs appeared on the cover of *Life* and *Look* magazines and snagged a spot on the David Susskind television show. The Fugs used their national forum to propagate a philosophy, which fused the Beat sensibility with a hope for political change. Buoyed by "the tide of expectations created by the Kennedy era still in place," explained Ed Sanders, "[the band] believed that there might be some permanent change, that the country might become a social democracy. There'd be no homelessness, that there was an expectation the economy would be adjusted so everyone could partake in the largess of America."

The Velvet Underground, who performed many times with the Fugs, drew inspiration from the same Beat source. In 1964, at a party in New York City, songwriter Lou Reed met musical prodigy John Cale, who had been performing with an avant-garde ensemble, and they decided to form a band. "When I first met Lou, we were interested in the same things," recalled Cale. "We both needed a vehicle. Lou needed one to carry out his lyrical ideas and I needed one to carry out my musical ideas." They enlisted the help of guitarist Sterling Morrison and drummer Angus MacLise, who the following year was replaced by Maureen Tucker, and began playing at local clubs.

Pop art innovator Andy Warhol helped the band achieve notoriety. Rather than continue with his own rock group of fellow artists such as Jasper Johns, in July 1965 he agreed to manage the band after meeting Reed and Cale through mutual friends and added Hungarian chanteuse Nico to the lineup. Warhol named the band the Velvet Underground, after Michael Leigh's novel about sadism and masochism, showcased the band at his Factory club, and added them to his mixed-media extravaganza, the Exploding Plastic Inevitable. "He was the catalyst," remarked Reed about Warhol years later.

Reed, who wrote the lyrics for the band, derived his ideas from Beat sources. The songwriter, who had studied at Syracuse University with Beat poet Delmore Schwartz, crafted songs that dealt with the down-and-out themes of Beat fiction— heroin addiction in "I'm Waiting for the Man" and the rushing "Heroin," and cocaine in "Run, Run, Run." In a self-titled Velvet album, Reed led the listener through the adventures of a girl named Candy, who roamed the cultural underground assisted by her junkie boyfriend. The sexual and drug-related themes of the Velvet Underground, Reed later mentioned, were "only taboo on records. Let's keep that in mind. Movies, plays, books, it's all there. You read Ginsberg, you read Burroughs."

The Haight-Ashbury Scene

The Beats resurfaced in San Francisco to inspire the hippies, as the *San Francisco Examiner* writer Michael Fallon first called them in September 1965. At the first hippie gathering, held at Longshoremen's Hall near Fishermen's Wharf on October 16, 1965, wrote journalist Ralph Gleason, "long lines of dancers snaked through the crowd for hours holding hands. Free-form improvisation ('self-expression') was everywhere. The clothes were a blast. Like a giant costume party." Amid the revelry whirled a long-haired, bearded Allen Ginsberg.

Three weeks later, on November 6, Allen Ginsberg appeared at the Appeal, a benefit rock concert for the San Francisco Mime Troupe, an avant-garde theater group managed by Bill Graham. He brought his Beat friends, the Fugs, who flew in from New York for the event, mingling with hundreds of free-minded participants who lived in the surrounding Haight-Ashbury district near San Francisco State College. At the end of the evening, Ginsberg chanted as the Hashbury hippies cleaned the Mime Troupe loft.

For three days in late January 1966, Beat writer Ken Kesey, author of *One Flew Over the Cuckoo's Nest* (1962), and his band of free spirits, known as the Merry Pranksters, hosted the Trips Festival, which attracted more than 6,600 people. For the event they enlisted the services of the Grateful Dead and Big Brother and the Holding Company, set up five movie screens, on which they projected a mind-boggling combination of colors and shapes, and spiked the punch with some LSD, a concoction that became known as the Kool-Aid acid test. At the festivities, Kesey stalked the floor dressed in a space helmet and a jumpsuit and periodically composed free-form poetry on an overhead projector. Eyewitness Ralph Gleason saw one man "bandaged all over, with only his eyes peeking out through dark glasses, carrying a crutch and wearing a sign: 'You're in the Pepsi generation and I'm a pimply freak.' Another long-haired exotic dressed in a modified Hell's Angels' leather jerkin that had 'Under Ass Wizard Mojo Indian Fighter' stenciled on his back. Several varieties of Lawrence of Arabia costumes wandered through."

At one point, Neal Cassady, the Beat High Priest who had appeared in Kerouac's *On the Road* as Dean Moriarty and had inspired the Indian in Kesey's *Cuckoo's Nest*, "stood for a while upstairs and then swung out and over the back of the balcony railing, scaring everyone who saw him, as they expected him to slip and fall to the floor." Cassady would reappear at countless Grateful Dead concerts to deliver amazing free-associational monologues as preludes to the performances. He also sat at the helm of the psychedelic bus, which took Kesey and the Merry Pranksters on a symbolic trip across the country. Neal Cassady especially influenced the Grateful Dead, the premier psychedelic band. "There's no experience in my life yet that equals riding with Cassady in like a 1956 Plymouth or a Cadillac through San Francisco or from San Jose to Santa Rosa," remembered Jerry Garcia, lead guitarist for the Dead. "He was the ultimate *something*—the ultimate person as art."

Other Beats helped organize the "First Human Be-In," which took place in Golden Gate Park Stadium on January 14, 1967. Allen Ginsberg, painter Michael Bowen, playwright Michael McClure, and poets Lenore Kandal and Gary Snyder helped stage the multicolored community gathering, which attracted 20,000 people on an unseasonably warm day. Early in the morning, Ginsberg and Snyder opened the proceedings by conducting an ancient Hindu blessing ritual, the dakshina, around the Polo Field to ensure its suitability for the coming pilgrimage. Throughout the day, hippies danced on the grass to the sounds of the Grateful Dead, the Jefferson Airplane, and Quicksilver Messenger Service. "The costumes were a designer's dream, a wild polyglot mixture of Mod, Paladin, Ringling Brothers, Cochise and Hell's Angels' Formal," wrote Ralph Gleason in the *San Francisco Chronicle*. "The poets read. Allen Ginsberg (who may yet be elected president) chanted and Gary Snyder sat on the stage and joined in. Bells rang and balloons floated in the air. A man went around handing out oranges and there were sandwiches and candy and cookies. No one was selling anything." The celebration ended when Gary Snyder blew on a conch shell, the ritual instrument of the

Yamabushi sect of Japanese Buddhism, and Allen Ginsberg led a chant of "Om Shri Maitreya" to the Coming Buddha of Love.

When news of these remarkable events spread to the burgeoning ranks of college-age baby boomers, the psychedelic ranks in San Francisco began to swell. "Like, wow! There was an explosion," remarked Jay Thelin, co-owner with his brother Ron of the Psychedelic Shop, which served as the briefing center for hippie initiates to the city. "People began coming in from all over and our little information shop became sort of a clubhouse for dropouts and, well, we just let it happen, that's all." By 1967, fifty thousand hippies resided in or near the Haight-Ashbury district of San Francisco.

The Hippie Culture

Many who flocked to the Haight were baby boomers, who had grown up in educated, middle-class homes. Most of the hippies, who lived in San Francisco at the time, wrote journalist Hunter Thompson, "were white and voluntarily poor. Their backgrounds were largely middle class; many had gone to college." According to a report by San Francisco State sociologist H. Taylor Buckner, 96 percent of the Haight hippies were between the ages of sixteen and thirty, 68 percent had attended college for a time, and 44 percent had a father who had earned a college degree.

The hippies, as with the Beats, criticized the bourgeois values with which they had been raised. "The standard thing is to feel in the gut that middle-class values are all wrong," remarked one hippie. "It's the system itself that is corrupt," added another. "Capitalism, communism, whatever it is. These are phony labels. There is no capitalism or communism. Only dictators telling people what to do." The hippies, remarked Peter Cohan of the Haight, "are the fruit of the middle class and they are telling the middle class they don't like what has been given them."

The hippies, raised in an age of relative affluence, attacked the materialistic American culture that had been formed and embraced by their Depression-bred parents. "I have no possessions," remarked Joyce Ann Francisco of the *San Francisco Oracle*, the preeminent psychedelic newspaper, which was published by Ron Thelin in the Haight. "Money is beautiful only when it is flowing. When it piles up it's a hang-up." The residents of the Haight, noticed historian Arnold Toynbee when he toured the district during the spring of 1967, "repudiate the affluent way of life in which making money is the object of life and work. They reject their parents' way of life as uncompromisingly as Saint Francis rejected the rich cloth merchants' way of life of his father in Assisi."

Many hippies challenged other dominant values. Morning Glory, a long-haired, twenty-two-year-old hippie, felt that the "human body is a beautiful thing. It should be displayed. I want people to see what I look like, and I want to see what they look like without a bunch of clothes covering them up. Nude, everybody is in the same bag, the same economic class."

Such a freewheeling attitude toward nudity, coupled with the use of the birth control pill by more than six million women in 1966 a decade after its introduction to the general public, led to a rejection of sexual taboos. As early as 1965, Haight residents started the Sexual Freedom League to confront traditional standards concerning sex. Within two years, hundreds of youths engaged in premarital sex with many partners, continuing a trend that had intensified with the Beats. "The '60s will be called the decade of the orgasmic preoccupation," predicted Dr. William Masters, the director of the Institute for Sex Research at Indiana University. "Young people are far more tolerant and permissive regarding sex."

To distinguish themselves from, and many times to antagonize, the middle-class American mainstream, male hippies generally wore their hair long. "As for bad vibrations emanating from my follicles, I say great," wrote James Simon Kunen in the *Strawberry Statement*. "I want the cops to sneer and the old ladies to swear and the businessmen to worry."

By challenging authority, the hippies hoped to create an atmosphere that engendered freedom of individual expression. "We have a private revolution going on," read a handbill distributed by the Blue Unicorn, a coffeehouse in the Haight. "A revolution of individuality and diversity that can only be private."

The hippies turned to mind-expanding drugs to enhance their individual potentials. Most rolled marijuana or the more expensive hashish into joints or smoked the weed Indian style in pipes. In 1965, Haight residents organized the legalize marijuana movement (LEMER), which held meetings at the Blue Unicorn. By the end of the decade, more than 96 percent of the hippies in the Haight had smoked marijuana, and more than ten million youths across the nation had tried the drug.

Another drug, the hallucinogen LSD (lysergic acid diethylamide), defined the hippie experience. Discovered in Switzerland in April 1943 and legal in the United States until late 1966, "acid" fragmented everyday perception into a multitude of melting shapes and vibrant colors. "The first thing you notice is an incredible enhancement of sensory awareness," related Timothy Leary, the ex-Harvard professor who edited the *Psychedelic Review*, organized the LSD-based League for Spiritual Discovery, and became the most visible popularizer and high priest of acid. "Take the sense of sight. LSD vision is to normal vision as normal vision is to the picture of a badly tuned television set. Under LSD, it's as though you have microscopes up to your eyes, in which you see jewel-like, radiant details of anything your eye falls upon. . . . The organ of the corti in your inner ear becomes a trembling membrane seething with tattoos of sound waves. The vibrations seem to penetrate deep inside you, swell and burst there. . . . You not only hear but *see* the music emerging from the speaker system like dancing particles, like squirming curls of toothpaste."

Timothy Leary contended that the drug experience resulted in altered, introspective states that expanded individual consciousness. In September 1966, comfortably lying on a mattress in his headquarters, a sixty-four-room mansion in Millbrook, New York, he outlined the various states of consciousness to *Playboy*: "The lowest level of consciousness is sleep—or stupor, which is produced by narcotics, barbiturates and our national stuporfactant, alcohol. The second level of consciousness is the conventional wakeful state, in which awareness is hooked to conventional symbols: flags, dollar signs, job titles, brand names, party affiliations and the like. . . . In order to reach [the third level], you have to have something that will turn *off* the symbols and open up your billions of sensory cameras to the billions of impulses that are hitting them. The chemical that opens the door to this level has been well known for centuries. . . . It is marijuana. . . . But we must bid a sad farewell to the sensory level of

Timothy Leary, c. mid-'70s, the guru of LSD. *Permission by* The Daily *of The University of Washington.*

consciousness and go on to the fourth level, which I call the cellular level. It is well known that the stronger psychedelics such as mescaline and LSD take you *beyond* the senses into a world of cellular awareness. During an LSD session, enormous clusters of cells are turned on, and consciousness whirls into eerie panoramas for which we have no words or concepts." Leary advised readers to "turn on, tune in, and drop out."

Many heeded Leary's advice. "Grass and LSD are the most important factors in the community," remarked Jay Thelin. "You should acquaint yourself with all of the consciousness-expanding drugs. I turn on every Sunday with acid, and I smoke grass every day, working continuously with an expanding consciousness." Gabe Katz of the *San Francisco Oracle* agreed, "The only way to understand is to turn on. The chemicals are essential. Without them you can ask a million questions and write a million words and never get it." On October 6, 1966, when legislation outlawing LSD took effect, hundreds of residents in the Haight staged a "Love Pageant" to assert the "inalienable rights" of "freedom of the body, the pursuit of joy, and the expansion of consciousness." In 1966, an official from the Food and Drug

Administration estimated that more than 10 percent of all college students had ingested LSD and more than 90 percent of youths in the Haight had taken the drug. Many of the hippies had obtained LSD from chemist Augustus Owsley Stanley III, the grandson of a Kentucky senator, who had produced and distributed an estimated fifteen million acid tabs. He sometimes dispensed them free at events such as the Trips Festival.

With their newfound consciousness, the hippies embraced the beliefs of past, less technology-driven civilizations, real or imagined, to create a counterculture. Some followed the example of the Beats by looking for salvation in the mysteries of the Orient. One San Francisco free spirit expounded that "society feeds us machines, technology, computers and we answer with primitivism: the *I Ching*, the *Tibetan Book of the Dead*, Buddhism, Taoism. The greatest truths lie in the ancient cultures. Modern civilization is out of balance with nature." Many hippies adopted the teachings of Zen popularizer Alan Watts. Others joined Hare Krishna, when in January 1967 the International Society for Krishna Consciousness moved to the Haight, and Allen Ginsberg declared that a Hare Krishna mantra "brings a state of ecstasy."

Attempting to recapture a lost innocence, some embraced the popular image of the noble American Indian. They slipped into moccasins and sported fringed deerskin jackets, headbands, feathers, and colorful beads. Many hippies painted their faces and bodies for festive occasions as did Native Americans during a ceremony. In September 1965, the Committee Theater in the Haight staged a multimedia extravaganza, "America Needs Indians," and a few months later took their show to the acid tests. In January 1967, organizers of the Human Be-In in Golden Gate Park called the event a "Pow Wow" and a "Gathering of Tribes," advertising it with a poster that pictured a Plains Indian on horseback clutching a blanket in one hand and an electric guitar in the other.

Even though most Native Americans such as Robert Costo, president of the American Indian Historical Society, believed that the hippies practiced a "certain insidious exploitation of the Indian which is the worst of all," residents of the Haight created a cult of tribalism. "For one of the yearly Tribal Stomp dances at the Avalon, we gave everyone a little leather thong with a little Indian bell and a long white turkey feather tied to it," recalled Chet Helms, manager of the dance hall. "I can't tell you how effective that thematic favor was. It made everyone a member of the tribe."

Adhering to the notion of tribalism, some banded together in communal living arrangements. At Drop City near Trinidad, Colorado, twenty-two midwestern hippies built and lived in geodesic domes constructed from automobile hoods. Roughly 40 miles from San Francisco near Sebastopol, more than fifty hippies communally farmed the 31-acre Morningstar Ranch. Morningstar founder Lou Gottlieb, who had played in the folk group the Limeliters, envisioned the Ranch as "an alternative for those who can't make it in the straight society and don't want to. . . . for people who are technologically unemployable and for other people it would be a retreat where they could come and recreate, I mean really re-create themselves. I can see ten Morning-stars in every state, where people from straight society would come to live for a while in the 'alternative society,' a whole different culture based on noncompetition." In the Haight itself, reported a San Francisco State sociologist, more than 25 percent of the hippies lived with ten or more people.

Some hippies, believing in a noncompetitive, tribalistic society, shared their resources with others. The Diggers, most of them former members of the San Francisco Mime Troupe, who named themselves after a seventeenth-century society of English agricultural altruists, provided free food, shelter, and transportation to needy hippies in the Haight-Ashbury district. A Digger leaflet distributed at the October 1966 "Love Pageant" advertised "free food, every day, free food, it's free because it's yours." The Prunes in Cleveland, the Brothers in Seattle, and the Berkeley Provos shared the Digger spirit.

Even the shopkeepers in the Haight exhibited a community spirit. On November 23, 1966, the *San Francisco Examiner* told its readers that "the hip purveyors of painting, poetry, handcrafted leather and jewelry along Haight Street, having been blackballed by the Haight Merchants' Association, have formed their own Haight Street Merchants' Association, HIP for short." Once organized, HIP established a job cooperative to cope with the incoming hippies and provided free legal advice. Psychedelic Shop owners Jay and Ron Thelin additionally devoted over one-third of their shop's floor space to a "calm center," where hippies could meditate, talk, or sleep.

The hippies cultivated personal appearances that reflected the elements of their counterculture. In 1966, Janis Joplin, the lead singer for Big Brother and the Holding Company, described Haight fashion in a letter to her family: "The girls are, of course, young and beautiful looking with long straight hair. The beatnik look, I call it, is definitely in. Pants, sandals, capes of all kinds, far-out handmade jewelry, or loose-fitting dresses and sandals. . . . The boys are the real peacocks," observed the singer about the colorful, acid-inspired male attire. "All hair at least Beatle length. And very ultramod dress—boots, *always* boots, tight low pants in hounds tooth check, stripes, even polka dots! Very fancy shirts—prints, very loud, high collars, Tom Jones full sleeves. Fancy print ties, Bob Dylan caps. Really too much." Added Joplin, "the younger girls wear very tight bell-bottoms cut very low around the hips and short tops—bare midriffs," which reflected the ongoing sexual revolution and contributed to the doubling of the sales of Levi Strauss jeans from 1963 to 1966. The hippies had created a fashion that exemplified a counterculture influenced by the Beats, accessed by LSD, and based upon a loose-knit community of individuals that focused on self-expression.

By the mid-1960s, hundreds of newspapers were established to promulgate the countercultural ethos. In 1964, Art Kunkin started the *Los Angeles Free Press*, an underground newspaper, modeled after the *Village Voice* in New York. In late 1966, the *San Francisco Oracle* published the first of thirteen issues, unveiling a non-news, art-oriented format and a psychedelic look of vibrant, random colors and swirling typefaces perfected by hip artist Rick Griffin. Remembered *Oracle* editor Allen Cohen: "We were going to fill our newspaper with art, philosophy, poetry and attend to this change of consciousness that was happening in the Haight-Ashbury and, we hoped, the world." The *Oracle* staff wanted to "serve as vehicles for the forces that were emerging." By 1967, when the Underground Press Syndicate (UPS) was founded, five other major underground tabloids printed stories about sex, drugs, and revolution: *The East Village Other*, *The Paper* in East Lansing, Michigan, the *Berkeley Barb*, the *Seed* in Chicago, and the *Fifth Estate* in Detroit. Two years later, more than

500 underground newspapers printed stories about the counterculture that reached nearly one million readers.

Acid Rock: The Trip Begins

A legion of rock bands, playing what became known as "acid rock," stood in the vanguard of the movement for cultural change. The *San Francisco Oracle* defined rock music as a "regenerative and revolutionary art, offering us our first real hope for the future (indeed, for the present) since August 6, 1945."

"Rock-and-roll," announced *Rolling Stone*, which had been established in 1967 by Berkeley dropout and budding journalist Jann Wenner and well-known music critic Ralph Gleason, "is more than just music. It is the energy center of the new culture and the youth revolution." Ray Manzarek of the Doors echoed, "That was the point of rock-'n'-roll at the time, to become a new tribe, to bring America into a cleaner, purer realm of existence." In January 1966, handbills distributed to promote the Trips Festival hinted that "maybe this is the ROCK REVOLUTION."

Not surprisingly, psychedelic music had its basis in Dylanesque folk. "I began as a folk musician. I went to New York and I heard Dylan when he was at Gerde's. And I was very impressed by . . ., his youth I guess, his exuberance," mentioned Marty Balin (a.k.a. Martyn Buchwald), who had played in the Los Angeles folk group the Town Criers. "So I decided to start [a band] up here [San Francisco]. I went through a million different guys and then I saw Paul [Kantner]. He was walking into a folk club. I just saw him, and I said, 'That's the guy.' I just knew it. He had a twelve-string and a banjo and he had his hair down to here and an old cap." In July 1965, the duo asked a few other musicians to join their band and then, according to lead guitarist Jorma Kaukonen, the group was "thinking of names, trying to think of some sort of name that would imply a whole different way of looking at things." They settled on the Jefferson Airplane.

The Grateful Dead, another major exponent of acid rock, grew from folk roots. "When the whole folk music thing started, I got caught up into that," remembered Jerry Garcia. "When Joan Baez's first record came out I heard it and I heard her finger picking the guitar, I'd never heard anything like it before so I got into that and I started getting into country music, into old-time white music. Mostly white spiritual stuff, white instrumental music and I got into finger style, the folk–music–festival scene, the whole thing. And I was very heavy into that for a long time and I sort of employed a scholarly approach and even went through the South with tape recorders and stuff recording bluegrass bands. I spent about three years playing bluegrass banjo, that was my big thing and I almost forgot how to play the guitar. . . . And then . . . we got a jug band going and I took up the guitar again and from the jug band it was right into rock-and-roll. . . . I was sort of a beatnik guitar player." Garcia continued: "Bob Weir, who plays rhythm, did the whole folk–blues coffeehouse thing. That was his thing. And he also played jug and kazoo in the jug band [Mother McCree's Uptown Jug Champions] when we were playing. And he's a student, you might say. His musical leader was Jorma [Kaukonen]." Garcia concluded: "Here on the West Coast, the guys that are into rock-'n'-roll music have mostly come up like I have . . . up through folk music."

Poster for a Jefferson Airplane show at the Fillmore, San Francisco.
(Artist: Clifford Charles Seeley.) Photo by Neal, Stratford, & Kerr.
Wolfgang's Vault. Bill Graham Presents Poster BG69. © B.G.P. 1967.

In early 1965, folkies Garcia and Weir joined with blues enthusiast Ron "Pig Pen" McKernan, drummer Bill Kreutzmann, and bassist Phil Lesch to form the band the Warlocks, which was renamed the Grateful Dead later that year.

Other acid rockers rose through the ranks of folk. Peter Albin, an impetus behind Big Brother and the Holding Company, had organized folk concerts during the early 1960s and had been a member of a folk group playing "Kingston Trio-type music." James Gurley, another member of Big Brother, began "working in a progressive bluegrass band." David Freiberg, the unofficial leader of Quicksilver Messenger Service, learned guitar in 1963 amidst the folk craze, and one-time fellow band member, drummer Dino Valenti, had worked for several years as a folk singer in Greenwich Village. In 1964, Country Joe McDonald "came to become a folk singer with the beatniks in San Francisco" and formed a jug band with Barry Melton, a friend of Peter Albin, shortly before he teamed up with the Fish to deliver his politically minded brand of psychedelic rock. Likewise, lead guitarist Robby Kreiger of the Doors—which formed in late 1965 with Kreiger, John Densmore on drums, singer Jim Morrison, and organist Ray Manzarek—had started a jug band during his stay at the University of California at Santa Barbara.

Psychedelic music, though based in folk, featured a loud, experimental sound. Unlike the acoustic strummings of early Bob Dylan, the acid rockers amplified their message to glass-shattering levels. Jerry Garcia thought of it as "a sensory overload." The San Francisco bands also favored extended guitar improvisations, sometimes distorted by guitar effects, which combined folk music with some blues riffs, a dash of country-western, and traces of Indian ragas.

Such eclectic experimentation fully utilized the long-play (LP) format of the 12-inch, 33 1/3-rpm record. Introduced by Columbia in 1948, the LP had been used in the pop field to market collections of three- to four-minute songs. During the psychedelic era, rock artists began to improvise on songs that sometimes lasted an entire side, using the LP medium as classical and jazz musicians had done years earlier. Paralleling the rise of the avant-garde in jazz during the mid-1960s, the psychedelic sound exemplified the freewheeling, experimental bent of the counterculture.

Rock-and-Roll Revolution

The new sound of experimentation came from middle-class youths. Grace Slick, the daughter of a Chicago investment banker, attended the exclusive Finch College where, in her words, she became a "regular suburban preppy." Fellow Airplane member Jorma Kaukonen was the son of a foreign service official and graduated from the University of California at Santa Clara; Airplane drummer Spencer Dryden had moved to Hollywood with his father, an assistant film director. Jim Morrison, the son of a rear admiral, had enrolled in the Theater Arts Department at UCLA, where he met keyboardist Ray Manzarek. John Cipollina, the guitarist for Quicksilver Messenger Service, had become interested in music through his mother, a concert pianist, and his godfather, Jose Iturbi, a well-known classical pianist. Peter Albin of Big Brother and the Holding Company grew up in suburban San Francisco, the son of a magazine editor-illustrator.

These middle-class youths wanted to overturn the social order in which they had been raised. Jim Morrison, characterized as "a postbeat poet influenced by Kerouac and Ginsberg" by fellow Door Ray Manzarek, professed an interest "in anything about revolt, disorder, chaos. It seemed to me to be the road toward freedom—external revolt is a way to bring about internal freedom." He told *The New York Times*, "When I sing my songs in public, that's a dramatic act, but not just acting as in theater, but a *social* act, real action." As he sang in one song, he hoped to "break on through to the other side." Grace Slick of the Jefferson Airplane hoped for "a whole turnaround of values." Chet Helms, the transplanted Texan who opened the Avalon Ballroom in the Haight and who became the manager of Big Brother and the Holding Company, "was very interested in the scene's potential for revolution. For turning things upside down, for changing values."

As with the hippies in general, the psychedelic rockers challenged restrictive, middle-class values, especially those dealing with sex. The Fugs, always forthright, belted out "Boobs Alot," "Group Grope," and "Dirty Old Man." Their name itself raised the eyebrows of the sexually inhibited. Reveling in the same theme, the Doors hit the chart with "Love Me Two Times," "Hello, I Love You," "Love Her Madly," and their biggest hit, "Light My Fire." Morrison, who referred to himself as an "erotic politician," faced legal charges when he supposedly exposed himself on stage in Florida. The outspoken Grace Slick, who delivered such songs as "Somebody to Love," confessed that "it doesn't matter what the lyrics say, or who sings them. They're all the same. They say, 'Be free—free in love, free in sex.'" Marty Balin of the Airplane added, "The stage is our bed and the audience is our broad. We're not entertaining, we're making love."

Many psychedelic bands renounced the competitive, corporate structure of American society in general and of the recording industry in particular. Jerry Garcia of the Grateful Dead resented "being just another face in a corporate personality. There isn't even a Warner 'brother' to talk to. The music business and the Grateful Dead are in two different orbits, two different universes." Stephen Stills of Buffalo Springfield, and later of Crosby, Stills, and Nash, added, "The Dead were the first people, I don't know whether it was acid or what, to come to that realization where they really didn't give a shit whether they made it or not." Paul Kantner of the Jefferson Airplane complained, "The record companies sell rock-and-roll records like they sell refrigerators. They don't care about the people who make rock or what they're all about as human beings." Max Weiss, owner of Fantasy Records in the Bay area, characterized the San Francisco bands as "absolutely noncommercial."

Opposed to a faceless commercialism, bands such as the Grateful Dead and the Airplane began to stage free concerts. "We don't do what the system says—make single hits, take big gigs, do the success number," Dead manager Rock Scully told an interviewer. "The summer of 1967, when all the other groups were making it, we were playing free in the park, man, trying to cool the Haight-Ashbury." Guitarist Eric Clapton recalled about his first visit to San Francisco, "The first thing that really hit me hard was the Grateful Dead were playing a lot of gigs for nothing. There is this incredible thing that the musical people seem to have toward their audience: they want to give."

The emphasis on sharing shaped the group concept of the psychedelic band. David Getz, drummer for Big Brother and the Holding Company, said that these bands tried "to consciously avoid making anyone the star, focusing more on the interaction between the audience and the band, and trying to create something together." Acid master Owsley Stanley agreed, "All the bands were tribal and tribal meant you agreed amongst yourselves as to who was momentarily the leader of the team."

Most San Francisco bands felt camaraderie with one another. "All of the bands were very close," remembered Mickey Hart of the Grateful Dead. "We'd be over at each other's houses, see each other all-day long, party at night. There were no hassles about who was going to open the show or close the show. It seemed like when we played with one of our sister bands, our compadres, we always played a little better for each other."

The cooperative feeling within bands sometimes extended to their own living arrangements. The members of the Grateful Dead lived communally in the Haight district at 710 Ashbury Street. Quicksilver Messenger Service roomed together in a house near the Dead headquarters. For a time, the Jefferson Airplane lived together in the Haight at 2400 Fulton Street, and the members of Big Brother and the Holding Company roomed communally in a Victorian house at 1090 Page Street.

Many acid rockers discovered the cooperative alternative to a competitive society through LSD. "Along came LSD and that was the end of that whole world. The whole world just went kablooey," related Jerry Garcia. "It changed everything, you know, it was just—ah, first of all, for me personally, it freed me . . . because I suddenly realized that my little attempt at having a straight life and doing that was really a fiction and just wasn't going to work out."

As well as demonstrating the hollowness of self-centered mainstream values, acid helped Garcia realize the existence of more interconnected social relationships. "To get really high is to forget yourself," he asserted. "And to forget yourself is to see everything else. And to see everything else is to become an understanding molecule in evolution, a conscious tool in the universe."

As the avenue to understanding a new social order, mind-expanding drugs became the centerpiece of acid rock. They inspired the names of many West Coast bands: the Loading Zone, Morning Glory, the Weeds, the Seeds, and the Doors, the last name taken from a phrase of poet William Blake, which had been quoted by Aldous Huxley in a book about a mescaline experience, *The Doors of Perception*.

Many San Francisco bands extolled psychedelic drugs in their songs. The Jefferson Airplane delivered the Haight-Ashbury anthem, "White Rabbit":[1] "One pill makes you larger and one pill makes you small, and the ones that mother gives you don't do anything at all. Go ask Alice when she's ten feet tall," sang Grace Slick while the Airplane churned out a sinister, electric drone in the background. She continued: "When the men on the chessboard get up and tell you where to go. You just had some kind of mushroom and your mind is moving low. Go ask Alice, I think she'll know." Then Slick launched into her piercing vibrato: "When logic and proportion have fallen softly dead, and the white knight's talking backwards and the red queen's lost her head, remember what the dormouse said, FEED YOUR HEAD, FEED YOUR HEAD." By 1969, a distraught Art Linkletter, whose daughter had overdosed on LSD, charged that at least half of all rock songs were "concerned with secret messages to teenagers to drop

---

[1]Lyrics from "White Rabbit." Lyrics and music by Grace Slick, copyright © 1967 Irving Music, Inc. (BMI). All rights reserved—International Copyright Secured.

out, turn on, and groove with chemicals." A year later, Vice President Spiro Agnew complained that much of "rock music glorified drug use."

Drugs defined the purpose of some psychedelic bands. According to Jerry Garcia, "The Grateful Dead is not for cranking out rock-and-roll, it's not for going out and doing concerts or any of that stuff, I think it's to get high."

Light shows at dances in the Haight simulated the LSD experience. The projection of light through liquid pigments in motion to create ever-changing expressionistic light shows had been discovered in 1952 by San Francisco State professor Seymour Locks as he prepared for a national conference of art educators. Through the efforts of beatnik art student Elias Romero, who witnessed some of Locks's first shows, hipsters such as Bill Ham, Anthony Martin, and Ben Van Meter learned the craft and adapted it to the hippie subculture. By 1966 dances in the Haight, normally held in the Avalon Ballroom, the Straight Theater, or the Fillmore Theater, featured light shows of melting colors, which mimicked an LSD experience.

The poster art advertising the gatherings captured on paper the acid-inspired, swirling designs of the light shows. Through recycling motifs and the lettering of Art Nouveau artists such as Alphonse Mucha, the posters featured a unique graphic style of thick, distorted letters that melted together against vibrant, multicolored, pulsating backgrounds, which could only be easily deciphered by members of the hippie tribe. They were crafted by Haight artists such as Wes Wilson, Stanley Mouse (a.k.a. Miller), Alton Kelley, Victor Moscoso, Bonnie MacLean, Lee Conklin, and Rick Griffin, who also designed album covers for the Grateful Dead and Big Brother and the Holding Company. "When I started doing posters," explained Wes Wilson, "I think I selected my colors from my visual experiences with LSD." Poster artist Lee Conklin echoed, "I made it my mission to translate my psychedelic experience onto paper." The resulting graphic art, contended Chet Helms, signaled that "the joyless head-long rat-race to the top was supplanted by the joyful, sensuous curves and gyrations of the dance, expanding in all directions."

Bill Graham, a politically minded, thirty-five-year-old émigré who had changed his name from Wolfgang Grajonca, organized the psychedelic groundswell in San Francisco. In 1965, after staging two benefit concerts as the manager of the San Francisco Mime Troupe, Graham decided to concentrate his efforts on the concert scene, first coordinating the Trips Festival for Ken Kesey and his Merry Pranksters. By March 1966, Graham had secured a three-year lease on the Fillmore, which became a popular dance hall in the Haight. He also began to manage the Fillmore house band, the Jefferson Airplane, and later the Grateful Dead. Although never "a great fan of high volume rock-and-roll, and a lot of it was nonsensical to me," Graham took pride in his organizational abilities. "I was always, 'Well, I took your ticket and you came here expecting something, and I want you to have that,'" he recalled. "I want the food to be hot and the drinks to be cold." Marty Balin of the Airplane asserted, "Bill Graham was the star of the sixties. In the beginning there was great talent, but there were no sound systems. No microphones. Graham came along and changed it. He made the performers a stage. He was what Alan Freed was to the fifties."

The acid-inspired music, organized locally by Graham, reached youths across the country through airplay on FM radio. During the 1940s, the Federal

Communications Commission (FCC) had encouraged AM radio stations to create counterparts on FM bands. In 1964, after issuing a moratorium on new AM licenses, the FCC decided that at least half of the airtime on FM stations in cities of 100,000 or more people had to be original programming.

Psychedelic music appeared in this new FM context. Not produced for the Top-Forty play list of AM radio, the meandering psychedelic sounds first aired on the free-wheeling San Francisco station KMPX on the programs of disc jockeys such as Larry Miller and Tom Donahue. "Somewhere in the dim misty days of yore, some radio station statistician decided that regardless of chronological age, the average mental age of the audience was twelve and a half, and Top-Forty AM radio aimed its message directly at the lowest common denominator," sniped Donahue. "The disc jockeys have become robots performing their inanities at the direction of programmers who had succeeded in totally squeezing blips and bleeps and happy, oh yes, always happy sounding cretins who are poured from a bottle every three hours." To eradicate the "rotting corpse stinking up the airwaves," the San Francisco jockey used FM radio to air songs that lasted more than three minutes, began to spin entire albums, discontinued the breakneck delivery of Top-Forty disc jockeys, and played songs by the new groups in the Bay area. When confronted by an unhappy owner and a strike at KMPX, Donahue and his staff took their hip format to KSAN, which poster artist Alton Kelley described as a "community drum." Soon FM stations in other parts of the country began to adopt Donahue's format and broadcast psychedelia across the airwaves.

Promoted by FM radio, acid rock started to scale the charts. In June 1967, the Jefferson Airplane, the first Haight band signed by a major label, hit number three with *Surrealistic Pillow*, an album that included the guitar of Jerry Garcia in the background. That same year, the Grateful Dead cracked the charts with its self-named debut LP. By the next year, Quicksilver Messenger Service charted with its first album. The Doors, probably the best-selling West Coast band, in early 1967 neared the top of the chart with its self-named debut album and later the same year hit the Top Five with *Strange Days*. In late 1968, they topped the chart with *Waiting for the Sun*. The Doors also scored with singles such as "People Are Strange," "Love Me Two Times," and "Touch Me," as well as the chart-topping "Light My Fire" and "Hello, I Love You."

Other bands jumped on the psychedelic bandwagon. In 1967, the lovable, mop-topped Beatles released two influential number-one albums: *Sgt. Pepper's Lonely Hearts Club Band*, which included the cryptic "Lucy in the Sky with Diamonds," reputedly LSD for short; and *Magical Mystery Tour*, a soundtrack to a movie modeled after Ken Kesey's travels in his psychedelic bus. Later that year, the bubbly Paul McCartney admitted that he had taken LSD. The Beatles began to study transcendental meditation with Maharishi Mahesh Yogi, and George and Pattie Harrison, wearing heart-shaped granny glasses and paisley frocks, took a ceremonial tour of the Haight district. That same year, the Rolling Stones released *Their Satanic Majesties' Request*, a psychedelic album featuring a three-dimensional cover, and Mick Jagger joined the Beatles in transcendental meditation. Eric Burdon of the Animals, after abandoning the blues for psychedelia, told *Melody Maker*, "It wasn't me singing. It was someone trying to be an American Negro. I look back and see how stupid I was." Adorned in vibrantly colored shirts and love beads, Burdon sang such odes to hippiedom as "San

The Doors. Photo by Joel Brodsky. Jeffrey Jampol. Joel Brodsky/Elektra Records.

Franciscan Nights" and "Monterey." Even Dick Clark changed with the times to mastermind the movie *The Love Children*, which starred a young Jack Nicholson.

By 1967, acid rock had spread to youths throughout the country. Philadelphia hippies danced at the Electric Factory. Adherents to the counterculture flocked to acid rock shows at the Tea Party Ballroom in Boston, at the Kinetic Playground in Chicago, and at the Grande Ballroom in Detroit, where Russ Gibb, inspired by Family Dog concerts in San Francisco, coordinated the events and Gary Grimshaw designed flowing psychedelic posters. In New York, hippies frequented the Electric Circus and the Fillmore East, which Bill Graham had designed as an East Coast counterpart to the San Francisco original. Acid rock had become a national phenomenon.

Psychedelic London

The counterculture developed on the other side of the Atlantic in swinging London. In 1966, Michael Hollingshead brought 6,000 tabs of acid to England that he obtained from Timothy Leary, with a mission to turn on London. He opened the World Psychedelic Centre (WPC) in Chelsea and started his work. The same year, Nigel Waymouth opened the alternative clothing store Granny Takes a Trip, stocked with velvet jackets, Native American–styled garb, and wild–colored shirts and trousers. "It was a rebellion against conventional outfits," Waymouth contended. "Why can't things be more androgynous? Why can't men wear flowered jackets with their long hair? Why can't we wear velvet as a kind of aesthetic thing?"

The communication network for the growing London counterculture emerged at the same time. Peter Jenner, a lecturer at the London School of Economics, started the London Free School and hoped to "connect traditional disciplines in a relevant 'modern' manner." In 1966 Barry Miles and photojournalist John "Hoppy" Hopkins launched the underground newspaper *International Times*, which, according to Jenner, "was all about enlightenment and freeing your head from all the old hang-ups."

Simultaneously, acid rock burst on the London scene. In late 1966 Joe Boyd, who had traveled from his native America to the UK branch of Elektra Records in London, met "Hoppy" Hopkins. After witnessing Fillmore shows in San Francisco and looking for a way to raise money for the fledgling *International Times*, Boyd joined with Hopkins to stage concerts. Leasing a club on Friday nights after 11:00 P.M., the duo established the UFO club, which featured light shows, poetry readings, well-known rock acts such as Jimi Hendrix, and avant-garde art by Yoko Ono. They hired the Art Nouveau–inspired Michael English and Nigel Waymouth as poster artists, who called themselves Hapshash and the Colored Coat and designed sinuous, vibrant silkscreen posters that advertised many of the UFO happenings. "We felt like we were illustrating an ideal," remembered Waymouth. "We were trying to give a visual concept of what we were experiencing, which was like hallucinations."

The UFO also featured local house bands such as Pink Floyd. Named after country bluesmen Pink Anderson and Floyd Council, the band began by playing R&B music at the Marquee Club. Fueled by the psychedelic energy of front man Syd Barrett and the vision of their comanager Peter Jenner, Pink Floyd quickly embraced psychedelia. In 1966 they moved toward an airy acid rock and played at a benefit for the London Free School, performed at the Roundhouse to launch the *International Times*, and on December 23 played the first show at the UFO. In March 1967 they debuted with the first British Top-twenty acid-rock single "Arnold Layne," cracked the Top Ten with "See Emily Play," and by the summer introduced a spacey electronic sound to the British Top Ten with *Piper at the Gates of Dawn*. On April 29, 1967, with several other bands, they spearheaded the 14-Hour Technicolor Dream event at Alexandra Palace that attracted more than 10,000 members of the London counterculture, who came to support the underground *International Times* that had been closed on alleged obscenity charges.

The Soft Machine, another free-flowing UFO band, epitomized English psychedelia. The outfit, "all middle-class kids from literary backgrounds" according to cofounder Kevin Ayers, rejected the aspirations of their parents. Prodded by coleader Daevid Allen, they read the American Beats, lifting their name from William Burroughs. The group lived together communally and developed a hippie ethic. "It was just to be nice to each other, and don't step on other people's toes and infringe on their freedom," explained Ayers.

By the end of 1967, London teens had fully adopted the hippie culture. Youths experimented with acid tests, rallied for an underground newspaper, opened alternative clothing shops, boasted their own psychedelic bands, and crowded into their own version of the Fillmore. Most important, they accepted a new way of looking at the world. "The whole movement was about a change in attitude from aggression to peace," insisted Steve Howe, who had played at the UFO with the band Tomorrow and later became the guitarist for Yes. "It was a very euphoric time."

The Decline and Fall of Hippiedom

The counterculture had a short-lived heyday, falling victim to its own drug-based logic. Many hippies, initially using drugs to increase awareness and open alternative realities, became wasted addicts. As some youths repeatedly tried to delve deeper and deeper into their own consciousnesses with LSD, they became isolated and detached from their own bodies. In the street vernacular, these hippies "burned out." Others became hooked on drugs that seemed to promise freedom. By 1967, many Haight residents had become methedrine or "speed" addicts who, according to Dr. Ellis D. ("LSD") Sox, the San Francisco public health director, cost the city $35,000 a month for treatment. "You had a lot of people talking to posts," remembered Travis Rivers, then owner of the Print Mint, which sold psychedelic posters in the Haight. "They were ripping one another off, because it costs a lot of money once you get strung out on speed."

Some of the major figures in the Haight drug culture fell prey to the guns of gangland. On August 3, 1967, John Kent Carter, a dealer known as "Shob," was found murdered with his arms hacked off at the elbows. Three days later, William "Superspade" Thomas ended up in a sleeping bag with a bullet through his head at the bottom of a cliff in Marin County.

The saga of Skip Spence provides a moving testimony to the perils of drug experimentation. Alexander ("Skip") Spence was the original drummer for the Jefferson Airplane, composing "Blues from an Airplane." When he quit the Airplane to form the pathbreaking psychedelic band Moby Grape, he began to overindulge in psychedelics and suffered a mental breakdown. Confided Skip: "Acid was like heaven, a moment of God, inspiring, tragic. I must have taken it a hundred times, a thousand times." One day, Spence reached too high. He woke up in a hospital: "An overdose where I died and was brought back to life." Before his untimely death at fifty-three in 1999, the scraggly, unwashed ex-rock star lived in San Jose, where he spent his $7-a-day allowance from the state. At night, when he did not confine himself to the psychiatric ward of a San Jose hospital, Spence stayed alone in a dingy, rundown room in the Maas Hotel. Sometimes he spoke to Joan of Arc. Once in a while he was visited by Clark Kent, who the drummer/guitarist found to be "civilized, decent and a genius." And on a few thick, intense, San Jose summer nights, Spence met his "master," who materialized with startling revelations. Asserted Spence, delivering his own epitaph, "I'm a derelict. I'm a world savior. I am drugs. I am rock-and-roll."

A passive, accepting psychedelic worldview, unlocked by mind-expanding drugs, also made hippiedom susceptible to co-optation. Most hippies, such as Jerry Garcia, considered themselves to be "conscious tools of the universe," who were directed by "cosmic forces" that bound disparate individuals and events into a logical pattern. They believed in an almost preordained "flow" that would sweep everyone into a cohesive psychedelic community and disregarded outside forces, which undermined their vision.

Businessmen, resistant to the flow of the cosmic community, began to exploit and commercialize the counterculture. During early 1967, more than twenty shops opened their doors in the Haight-Ashbury district to cater to the tourist traffic. The Pall Mall Lounge began to market "love burgers," and one store began to sell hippie costumes to weekenders: scraggly wigs for $85 and beards for $125. Even the Greyhound Bus Company started a "Hippie Hop" in San Francisco, advertised as "the only foreign tour within the continental limits of the United States." "Haight Street is no longer fun," complained Tsvi Strauch, an original hippie proprietor in the Haight. "Many of us are getting away from it because of all the plastic hippies and tourists that are fouling up the whole scene. They've made a mess of it."

On October 4, 1967, Jay Thelin closed the Psychedelic Shop, a hub of the Bay area counterculture, and posted a sign on the front door: "Be Free—Nebraska Needs You More." Two days later, a procession of original hippies in the Haight district loaded a coffin full of beads, peace signs, flowers, and other symbols of their lifestyle and publicly burned it, announcing the "death of hippie, loyal son of media." That same day, the Fugs coordinated a similar procession in the East Village, memorializing the hippie culture. "The tourist buses started coming through. Then they [hippies] left," summarized one Haight resident. "The kids went out to the country. Bolinas, Santa Rosa, Healdsburg, Auburn, Santa Cruz. Basically, they all left the city and it became a very different situation. More drugs came in and it was an angrier crowd. There were some homicides in the Haight-Ashbury. A lot of rapes, many of them unreported, came down. Essentially, there was a dissipation of the environment."

Even acid rock, the music of the counterculture, became subsumed by the recording industry. Though complaining about the corporate structure of the music industry, the psychedelic rockers readily signed contracts with the major record labels that marketed the psychedelic sound with new promotional strategies to reach a national audience. "We found we couldn't sell the Grateful Dead's records in a traditional manner," said Joe Smith, at the time the president of Warner-Reprise. "You couldn't take your ad in *Billboard* and sell a record that way. . . . The packaging was important. The cult was important. Free concerts where you handed out fruit and nuts were important" as well as exposure on the underground club circuit, the campuses, and FM radio. Gil Frieson, then vice president of A&M Records, assembled a Standard American Promotional Package—"billboards on Sunset Strip and Broadway, full-page advertising in the underground press, the trades, and various other outlets; radio spots and a promotional tour with all expenses paid by the label." Bill Siddons, manager of the Doors, complained, "It's funny, the group out there on the stage preaching a revolutionary message, but to get the message to the people, you gotta do it in the establishment way."

By late 1967, acid rock and the counterculture it exemplified had been drawn into the competitive society it attacked. "When the Summer of Love happened, that was it," recalled Bill Thompson, a manager of the Jefferson Airplane. "It had all started happening in the summer of 1965 and it was over by the summer of 1967." The psychedelic baby boomers, armed with flowers and a hopeful spirit, would soon confront the M-1 rifles of National Guardsmen, who would turn the brightly colored hopes of hippiedom into a dark nightmare of war-torn campuses.

Fire from the Streets

❝ Soul is sass, man. ❞

—Claude Brown

Four o'clock on a muggy, steamy Sunday morning in Detroit, July 22, 1967. A crowd of young African Americans clustered around a pack of police squad cars on the corner of Twelfth Street and Clairmount, the heart of the city's West Side ghetto. As two hundred African Americans pressed against one another to get a better view of the action, blue-shirted, white-faced policemen herded eighty-two captives into paddy wagons. The arrested African Americans had been accused of drinking liquor after hours at the United Community League for Civic Action, which hosted a party for two returning veterans from Vietnam. After finishing their job by 5:00 A.M., the policemen jumped into squad cars, revved the engines, and started to move out of the area. Someone in the crowd flung a full wine bottle through the air, shattering the windshield of the car driven by Sergeant Arthur Howison of the Tenth Precinct. Howison slammed on the brakes and leapt onto the street. He was pelted first by a few stones and then by a barrage of rocks and bottles. The police officer ducked back into the car and sped off, followed by the angry mob.

The crowd, recently incensed by the killing of African-American veteran Danny

Thomas by a band of white thugs, multiplied as it made its way down Twelfth Street, until it had grown to three thousand agitated men, women, and youths. Someone grabbed a brick from the pavement and hurled it through the window of a grocery store. People swarmed toward the jagged opening. They poked out the rest of the glass in the window frame with sticks, jumped into the store, and began gathering armloads of meat, bread, and canned goods. One man struggled with an entire side of beef. "I've always wanted to be a butcher," he told an onlooker.

Around daybreak, some teens overturned a line of garbage cans and set the trash on fire. Another man threw a homemade firebomb into a shoe store that already had been sacked. Summer breezes fanned the flames, which spread to adjoining buildings. Within a few hours, columns of fire engulfed East Detroit and spread across Woodward Avenue into the western part of the city. Williams' Drug Store and Lou's Men's Wear, along with hundreds of other buildings, disappeared in flames. "It looks like 1945 in Berlin," reported a dejected Mayor Jerome Cavanaugh, who had been credited with the idea for the Model Cities Program and just a year earlier could boast that *Look* magazine had named Detroit the All-American City.

The rioting and looting continued for the next four days. Enraged African Americans ravaged thousands of stores, searching for food, clothing, furniture, and liquor. They spared only the storefronts that had been marked "Soul Brother" or "Afro All the Way." Fires set by the rioters gutted 19 square miles of Detroit, causing an estimated $40 million in damage. "Man, this is crazy," one older African American told *Newsweek*. "We're burnin' our own houses up. Where are these poor people going to live now?" Another home owner echoed, "This is madness. Why do they have to burn our houses? That's not right. Goddamn. And there's not a house burning in Grosse Point [a white, middle-class suburb of Detroit]. This has got to stop." But other African Americans in the Motor City, unemployed and confined to dilapidated slums, were impatient for the reforms promised by the Civil Rights Act of 1964, and they predicted more trouble. Said one twenty-two-year-old youth, "We're tired of being second class. We've been asking too long. Now it's time to take. This thing ain't over. It's just beginning."

The authorities responded to the rioting with brutal armed force. During the first day of trouble, Mayor Cavanaugh unleashed his 4,000-man police force on the ghetto. When police proved inadequate, Michigan Governor George Romney mobilized 7,300 state troopers and National Guardsmen armed with tear gas, grenade launchers, M-1 rifles, submachine guns, M-48 tanks, and Huey helicopters. "I'm gonna shoot anything that moves and is black," vowed one young Guardsman. The next day, President Lyndon Johnson airlifted Task Force Detroit, a 4,700-man paratrooper unit commanded by Lieutenant General John L. Throckmorton, who had served as a deputy to General William Westmoreland in Vietnam. All told, a 16,000-man army marched into Detroit to quell the tumult. The city had become an armed camp divided into war zones, cordoned off by barbed wire and patrolled by helmeted troops in khakis.

After the fires had been stamped out and the smoke had cleared, the authorities counted 43 dead, 2,250 injured, and 7,200 arrested, the worst civil disorder in twentieth-century America. Most of the casualties were African-American men. On national

A huge pall of smoke pours from a burning building during race riots in Detroit, 1967. Photo by POPPERFOTO. *Permission by Alamy Images.*

television, President Johnson pleaded that the "violence must be stopped—quickly, finally, and permanently. There are no victors in the aftermath of violence. . . . We have endured a week such as no nation should live through: a time of violence and tragedy."

The cause of the Detroit riot stemmed from the poor economic conditions of African Americans in the inner city, which stood in stark contrast to the promise of the Civil Rights Act. As whites fled from the cities to the suburbs, African Americans remained in nearly abject poverty. Despite low national unemployment, nearly 30 percent of the Detroit rioters were unemployed, and many others held low-skilled, low-paid jobs. Most saw few prospects for a better wage and attributed their condition to racism. Only a small percentage owned their own homes, and most lived in fear of being robbed or beaten on the streets and wanted to move from their neighborhoods. After playing an active role in the civil rights movement, some Detroit rioters despaired of change through nonviolence. The Detroiters, remarked civil rights leader Roger Wilkens, "saw Congress pass those laws in 1964 and 1965. When they looked around, they saw that nothing, absolutely nothing, was changing in their lives. They were still poor, they were still jobless, they still lived in miserable housing, their kids still went to lousy schools."

The depressed economic conditions among inner-city African Americans caused riots elsewhere. In August 1965, only days after the passage of the Voters Act, the Watts section of Los Angeles exploded in violence for six days, leaving thirty-four persons dead, 4,000 arrested, and entire blocks burned to the ground. "What we didn't have in Watts wasn't civil rights," related one resident. "It was jobs, housing and education." Nearly 30 percent of African-American males and 50 percent of African-American teenagers could not find jobs, and more than 60 percent of Watts residents lived on government relief. When 30,000 African Americans rioted in Watts, they appropriated a slogan of Los Angeles disc jockey Magnificent Montague by chanting "burn, baby, burn" to white America. "People didn't look at themselves as committing a crime," explained one rioter. "They had lived through all that deprivation, and they were now uplifted."

Disgruntled African Americans rioted in other urban areas. In 1966, trouble erupted in Chicago, San Francisco, and Atlanta. During 1967, in the aftermath of the Detroit riot, problems surfaced in Michigan cities such as Pontiac, Saginaw, Flint, Grand Rapids, Albion, and Kalamazoo. During the last days of July, looters sacked stores in the African-American neighborhoods of Phoenix, Hartford, Passaic, Poughkeepsie, and South Bend. The next month, four nights of violence ripped through Milwaukee, leaving four dead and more than 100 injured. African Americans in nearby Chicago took to the streets, and riots scarred Providence and Wichita. During the first eight months of 1967, race riots had torn apart more than 131 cities and had left a trail of eighty-three dead, thousands injured, and blocks of charred rubble. One government report estimated that 41 percent of the cities with populations of more than 100,000 had experienced racial violence. The press called it the "long hot summer."

On April 4, 1968, another wave of violence swept the country after the murder of Dr. Martin Luther King, Jr., who had become increasingly convinced of the need for economic as well as political equality and had just begun to organize the Poor People's Campaign. "When White America killed Dr. King," sneered African-American militant Stokely Carmichael, "she declared war on us. . . . We have to retaliate for the deaths of our leaders. The executions of those deaths are going to be in the streets."

Carmichael proved to be prophetic. A few hours after the King assassination, Washington, D.C., burst into flames. As described by *Newsweek*, the more than 700 fires in the national capital, the worst conflagration in the city since the British burned it during the War of 1812, "made Washington look like the besieged capital of a banana republic, with helmeted combat troops, bayoneted rifles at the ready guarding the White House, and a light machine-gun post defending the steps of the Capitol." President Lyndon Johnson activated nearly 15,000 troops—more than twice the size of the U.S. garrison that defended Khe Sanh in Vietnam—to quiet the violence. In three days of rioting, the death toll reached ten, and property damage exceeded $13.3 million.

Other African-American populated urban areas exploded after receiving news about the King assassination. In Kansas City, six rioters died and sixty-five were injured. Chicago's riot, quelled by 5,000 federal troops and 6,700 National

Guardsmen, left eleven dead, ninety-one injured, and miles of burned-out buildings. By the end of the week, 168 cities had erupted into violence; 5,117 fires had been started; almost 2,000 shops had been ransacked; $40 million worth of property had been destroyed; and forty-six people, mostly African Americans, had died. It took almost 73,000 U.S. Army and National Guard troops to quell the disturbances.

The urban riots reflected and were in part incited by such firebrands as Malcolm X, Stokely Carmichael, H. Rap Brown, and leaders of the growing Black Panther Party, such as Bobby Seale and Huey Newton, who preached a doctrine of militant African-American pride and self-determination. Carmichael, who coined the term *black power*, had joined the Student Non-Violent Coordinating Committee and reluctantly had worked for change through nonviolent tactics. Radicalized by the Vietnam War and the struggle of African nations to shed their colonial rulers, he increasingly viewed the struggle of African Americans within a colonial context and adopted the tenets of militants such as Malcolm X, who preached a doctrine of political and economic equality without whites rather than integration. After the assassination of Martin Luther King, Jr., Carmichael and others abandoned nonviolence for a militant stance. "If America don't come around, we're going to burn America down," threatened H. Rap Brown. In 1967 and 1968, many African Americans had dramatically reasserted their collective identity, an identity born in slavery and shaped by a century of discrimination. They called their reclaimed identity *soul*.

Soul Music

Soul music reflected the militant search for an African-American identity. The term *soul* had been used by African Americans during the 1950s to suggest the essence of being an African American in the United States. African-American jazz musicians, some of whom had converted to Islam, had soul: In 1957, horn man Lou Donaldson recorded *Swing and Soul*; the next year, saxophone great John Coltrane released *Soultrane*; and several more jazz artists released albums with similar titles over the next few years. During the early 1960s, Eldridge Cleaver noted in *Soul on Ice* that many referred to jazz as "soul music."

Around 1965, as the African-American ghettos of Watts and Harlem erupted in violence, many African Americans started to equate soul with the struggle to reassert African-American dignity in the face of continued discrimination. "Soul is sass, man," wrote Claude Brown, author of *Manchild in the Promised Land* (1965). "Soul is arrogance. Soul is walkin' down the street in a way that says, 'This is me, muhfuh'. . . . Soul is that uninhibited, no, *extremely* uninhibited self-expression that goes into practically every Negro endeavor. That's soul. And there's a swagger in it, man." Writer Arnold Shaw came to the same conclusion in *The World of Soul*: "Soul is black, not blue, sass, anger and rage. . . . It is an expressive explosiveness, ignited by a people's discovery of self-pride, power and potential for growth."

Emphasizing the value of their culture, African Americans began to refer to chitterlings, collard greens, black-eyed peas, candied yams, and sweet potato pie as soul food, and fellow African Americans became soul brothers and soul sisters. After the Detroit riots, "there was a strong sense of brotherhood and sisterhood," noted Detroit bookstore owner Ed Vaughn. "We saw more and more sisters begin to wear natural hairdos, and more and more brothers begin to wear their hair in the new natural styles. More and more people began to wear dashikis." With the newfound African-American consciousness, rhythm and blues became soul music.

Some of the "soul" performers had been involved in R&B long before it underwent a name change. James Brown, "Soul Brother Number One," released his first record "Please, Please, Please" with his Famous Flames in early 1956. "I first dug Little Richard at the Two Spot, down on the corner of Fifth and Walnut," remembered Brown. "Seeing Little Richard sing 'Tutti Frutti' and getting over, I went on to the WIBB studios in 1954 to do a demo of 'Please, Please, Please.'" Two years later Brown scaled the R&B chart with "Try Me" and in 1960 reworked the 5 Royales' "Think" for a hit.

By October 1962, when he recorded the now legendary album *Live at the Apollo*, Brown had perfected a stunning stage act, complete with a backup band and vocal group known as the James Brown Revue. In a typical performance, the singer leapt on stage wearing skin-tight black pants, a half-unbuttoned, dark-blue satin shirt, and a purple cape. Without missing a beat, his head jerking to the music, he suddenly jumped into the air, landed in a perfect split, and bounced back to his feet. Before the audience recovered, Brown was twirling in midair.

Ray Charles, considered the "Genius of Soul" during the mid-1960s, initially gained fame in R&B. Born Ray Charles Robinson on September 23, 1930, Charles

James Brown. The hardest-working man in rock-and-roll. Photo by Matt McVay. *Permission by* The Seattle Times.

traveled from the South to Seattle in 1947 to play cocktail-swing piano in a Nat King Cole style. In 1949, he cut his first disc, "Confession Blues," and two years later followed with the R&B hit "Baby Let Me Hold Your Hand." During the next few years, he toured with blues growler Lowell Fulson, R&B singer Ruth Brown, African-American comic Jackie "Moms" Mabley, and Eddie "Guitar Slim" Jones.

In June 1952, Atlantic Records, a leading company in the R&B field, bought Ray's contract for $2,500. During the summer of 1953, Atlantic president Ahmet Ertegun and vice president Jerry Wexler "ran into Ray at Cosimo's famous small studio, and Ray asked us to please do a session with him. . . . This was the landmark session because it had Ray Charles originals, Ray Charles arrangements, a Ray Charles band." The session produced the single "Don't You Know," his first chart success for Atlantic. The singer-pianist quickly followed with "I've Got a Woman," one of his most notable hits, which reached number two on the R&B chart. During the rest of the 1950s, he scored repeatedly with the R&B audience. In 1955, he hit with "A Fool for You" and "This Little Girl of Mine"; the next year, he scored with "I'll Drown in My Own Tears," and "Hallelujah, I Love Her So." By 1959, Brother Ray reached the *Billboard* Top Ten with "What'd I Say" to firmly establish himself as a major figure in R&B.

Wilson Pickett, although not as prominent in the 1950s as Ray Charles, had roots in early R&B. One day in 1959, as Pickett lounged on his porch strumming a guitar and singing, Willie Schofield, a member of the R&B group the Falcons, happened to pass by. According to Pickett, Schofield walked up to him and said, "'Man, you got a good voice,' and invited me to come to the next rehearsal. That's when I found I could sing rhythm and blues." Pickett joined the Falcons and added lead vocals to their 1962 hit "I Found a Love."

Otis Redding, recognized as "The King of Soul" by some, initially drew his inspiration from Little Richard. In an unlikely success story that took place in October 1962, Redding chauffeured a band, Johnny Jenkins and the Pinetoppers, to the Stax studio in Memphis for a recording session. "They had thirty minutes left in the studio and I asked if I could do a song," remembered Redding, who previously had recorded some unsuccessful Little Richard–sounding songs. "He did one of those heh, heh, baby things," recalled Stax president Jim Stewart. "It was just like Little Richard. I told them the world didn't need another Little Richard. Then someone suggested he do a slow one. He did 'These Arms of Mine.'" Impressed by the song, Stewart signed Redding and released the song, which hit the Top Twenty on the R&B chart and crossed over to the national chart. In early 1964, Redding cut *Pain in My Heart*, a mixture of Little Richard screamers and Sam Cooke–type ballads that nearly cracked the Top 100.

Most soul artists, as with R&B performers of the 1950s, started their careers in the church. Wilson Pickett had sung in the gospel group the Violinaires before joining the Falcons; he described his style as "a gospel melody, not nothing pretty, a funky groove with lines that mean something." Eddie Floyd, who in 1966 hit with the archetypical soul of "Knock on Wood," had helped start the Falcons, who had begun as a gospel group and drifted toward R&B by the time Pickett joined. Percy Sledge had sung with his cousin's gospel group, the Singing Clouds. Garnet Mimms, who charted in 1963 with the Top Ten "Cry Baby," had sung with the Philadelphia gospel groups the Evening Star Quartet and the Harmonizing Four, and had cut his first record with the gospel troupe, the Norfolk Four. As a youngster, Dave Prater, who later teamed up with Sam Moore as Sam and Dave, had sung and recorded with the gospel group, the Sensational Hummingbirds. Sam Moore, the son of a Baptist minister, had been a member of the gospel group, the Melonaires.

Solomon Burke had close ties to the church. He had worked as a boy preacher, had been a broadcaster on the religious show *Solomon's Temple*, and had soloed in his family's own Philadelphia church, The House of God for All People. Before turning to secular music in 1955, he had debuted with the single "Christmas Presents from Heaven."

Otis Redding and James Brown had learned about music in the church. The son of a minister, Redding had sung in the Mount Ivy Baptist Church choir as a young boy. "Otis and I were very close," remembered Katie Webster, who played piano for Redding. "It was a spiritual thing. Both our fathers were ministers, and we would read the Bible together." James Brown had played organ and drums during the 1940s for various gospel outfits. "I sang gospel in prison," recalled the singer. "Once I got out I joined Sarah Byrd's group, the Gospel Starlighters."

Ray Charles's music reflected his religious upbringing, having sang as a youth in the Shiloh Baptist Church in Greenville, Florida. He replaced the Pilgrim Travelers' "I've Got a New Home" with "Lonely Avenue" and shortened "Nobody But You, Lord" to "Nobody But You." He changed the gospel standard "This Little Light of Mine" to "This Little Girl of Mine," switched "I've Got a Savior (Way Over Jordan)" to "I've Got a Woman," and exulted in gospel screams in "Hallelujah, I Love Her So." "Now I'd been singing spirituals since I was three and I'd been singing the blues for just as long," explained Charles. "So what could be more natural than to combine them? It didn't take any thinking, didn't take any calculating. All the sounds were there, right at the top of my head." Added bluesman Big Bill Broonzy about Ray Charles, "He's cryin', sanctified. He's mixing the blues with the spirituals. He should be singing in a church."

Aretha Franklin, the 5-foot-5-inch dynamo dubbed "Lady Soul," had a direct connection to the church. Her father, the Reverend Clarence L. Franklin, served as the pastor of Detroit's 4,500-member New Bethel Baptist Church and recorded more than seventy albums of fiery, blues-drenched sermons. Two white-uniformed nurses commonly stood guard at the aisles of New Bethel Baptist to aid parishioners, who were overcome by the emotionally draining message of the minister. As a youth, Aretha came into contact with gospel greats such as James Cleveland and Mahalia Jackson, and at a funeral of an aunt, she witnessed Clara Ward belt out a powerful rendition of "Peace in the Valley." At that moment, the minister's daughter later recollected, "I wanted to become a singer." Aretha began to learn gospel from James Cleveland: "He showed me some real nice chords and I liked his deep, deep sound. There's a whole lot of earthiness in the way he sings, and what he was feelin', I was feelin', but I just didn't know how to put it across. The more I watched him, the more I got out of it." Soon Aretha joined a family organized traveling gospel troupe, before signing with Columbia Records. The soul of Aretha Franklin had matured in the church.

Atlantic Records distributed most of the gospel-based R&B, which would become known as soul music. The company had been established in 1947 by Ahmet Ertegun, a son of the Turkish ambassador to the United States. An avid jazz and blues record collector, he auctioned 15,000 78-rpm discs to start Atlantic Records with fellow record collector Herb Abramson, who had been a part-time producer for National Records. In 1949, Atlantic scored its first hit with the R&B song "Drinking Wine, Spo-Dee-O-Dee," by Stick McGee. During the next fifteen years, Atlantic produced a variety of jazz and R&B artists, hitting the R&B charts with performers such as former Drifter Clyde McPhatter, Big Joe Turner ("Shake, Rattle, and Roll"), LaVern Baker ("Tweedle Dee"), and Chuck Willis ("C. C. Rider").

Building on their success with Ray Charles, who as early as 1959 had been promoted as a "soul brother" by the company, Atlantic began to produce more soul acts. In late 1960, Ertegun signed Solomon Burke, who in 1965 topped the R&B chart and neared the Top Twenty with "Got to Get You Off My Mind." The year that Burke scaled the charts, Atlantic Records lured Wilson Pickett from the Double LL label. For the next two years, Atlantic had success with Pickett, who charted with "In the Midnight Hour," "634-5789," "Land of a 1,000 Dances," and "Mustang Sally." Percy Sledge, the Alabama farm boy who had chopped cotton as a youth, joined the Atlantic stable and in 1966 topped the singles chart with "When a Man Loves a Woman."

Atlantic also distributed the music of artists on Stax Records. In 1958, the brother-sister team of Jim Stewart and Estelle Axton started the Memphis-based Satellite Records and recording studio, which they renamed Stax three years later. The new label initially recorded local talent such as African-American disc jockey Rufus Thomas and his daughter Carla, who in 1959 dueted for the regional hit "Cause I Love You." In 1961, Carla delivered Stax's first national hit with the Top Ten "Gee Whiz (Look at His Eyes)." After the success of the Thomas duo, the label signed other African-American artists such as William Bell. "We just didn't sit down and say, 'We're going on with the black music,'" mentioned Stewart. "Once we had the success with Rufus and Carla it was as though we cut off a whole part of our lives that had existed previously. We never looked back from there." In 1960, on the strength of their success with local acts, Stax signed an agreement with Atlantic to distribute its records.

Stax gave artists who recorded at its studio on McLemore Avenue a distinctive sound, which was created by the Stax house band, Booker T. and the MGs. The band originally consisted of several high school friends, including Packy Axton, Estelle's son. By 1962, the band had solidified into a racially integrated rhythm section: keyboardist Booker T. Jones; drummer Al Jackson, Jr.; guitarist Steve Cropper, who drew his inspiration from 5 Royales' guitarist Lowman Pauling; and bassist Lewis Steinberg, who in March 1964 was replaced by Donald "Duck" Dunn. The band, who in 1962 hit with its own number-three smash, "Green Onions," played with the Memphis Horns, anchored by Andrew Love and Wayne Jackson, to back virtually every artist who recorded at Stax, including Wilson Pickett, Percy Sledge, Otis Redding, and Sam and Dave.

Sam and Dave, the "Double Dynamite" soul duo from Miami, were discovered by Atlantic vice president Jerry Wexler, who agreed to let the duo record for Stax. From 1966 to 1968, they hit with "I Thank You," and their trademark, "Hold On, I'm Coming."

The gospel-based rhythm and blues, recorded by Atlantic and Stax, became known as soul music during the mid-1960s, when many African Americans discovered a sense of self-esteem. In 1965, station WOL in Washington, D.C., attracting primarily

African-American listeners, began to call itself "soul radio," local disc jockey Fred Correy labeled himself "Soulfinger," and *Soul* magazine began publication. In 1965 and 1966, Otis Redding perfected his style with several albums, culminating in *Otis Blue (Otis Redding Sings Soul)*, which included the hit "Respect."

Around the same time, James Brown began to perfect a new style called "funk," which became part of the soul culture. From 1956, when he began to record secular music, to his breakthrough *Live at the Apollo* album six years later, Brown sang a mixture of gospel and spirited blues. In late 1964, with the single "Out of Sight," he unveiled a new style that featured bursts of dominant, repeating, overpowering rhythm accented by phrase-shouting vocals and the staccato punchy sound of horns. The next year, the singer refined the funk style with "Papa's Got a Brand New Bag," which hit the national Top Ten, topped the R&B chart, and sold one million copies. Later in the year, Brown released the equally successful funk single "I Got You (I Feel Good)."

As Brown shifted from more traditional R&B to funk, he recalled, "I got the name 'Soul Brother Number One.' The word 'soul' by this time meant a lot of things—in music and out. It was about the roots of black music, and it was a kind of pride thing, too, being proud of yourself and your people. Soul music and the civil rights movement went hand in hand, sort of grew up together."

During 1965 and 1966, amid the civil rights movement, African Americans supported soul acts. Otis Redding broke attendance records at shows in Harlem and Watts, and in 1966 he grossed $250,000 on a monthlong rhythm-and-blues tour. He earned enough money to start Jotis Records and helped to promote the career of Arthur Conley, who in 1967 neared the top of the chart with "Sweet Soul Music." James Brown bought a bright red Sting Ray, a fleet of Cadillacs, and a wardrobe of 150 suits and 80 pairs of shoes with the money he had amassed from the sale of records to an audience, which, except for the crossover interest in his *Live at the Apollo* album, consisted almost exclusively of African Americans. During the mid-1960s, while white youths listened to the Beatles, acid rock, or British blues-based bands such as the Rolling Stones, African Americans took pride in a gritty soul sound performed by fellow African Americans. "It's SOUL, man, SOUL," exclaimed African-American disc jockey Magnificent Montague in *Billboard*. "Now what is soul? It's the last to be hired, the first to be fired, brown all year-round, sit-in-the-back-of-the-bus feeling. You've got to live with us or you don't have it. The Black Brothers are the mainstay of our pop music today. Artists like John Lee Hooker, Otis Redding and others are heavy soul—one thing our English friends can't imitate."

Black Soul in White America

The inner-city explosions during the late 1960s made many Americans, especially those raised during the civil rights era, more aware of and interested in African-American culture. Though causing a white backlash in some quarters, the 1967 riots in Detroit allowed many whites to better understand the plight of African Americans. Discrimination "hurts them real bad. I'd probably be rioting right with them," a Texas salesman told *Time* magazine. Mrs. Margaret Lamb, a widow from Owensboro,

Kentucky, told *Time*: "It makes you wonder that they do as good as they do the way people treat them sometimes. You see things that make you wonder why they put up with it."

Sympathizing with African Americans, many young whites tried to adopt an African-American outlook. Radicalized students, protesting the war in Vietnam, embraced the ideology of militant Black Power groups such as the Black Panther Party for Self-Defense, which in October 1966 formed in Oakland, a few miles from the Berkeley campus. "We had captured the imagination of the white radical left in this country to a point that its whole identification became connected with what the Black Panther Party was doing, how it was personifying things," boasted Panther cofounder Bobby Seale. The students also successfully lobbied for ethnic studies classes, which fostered a greater awareness of the contributions of African Americans to fields such as history, psychology, literature, and anthropology.

White youths also started to buy soul records. The year "1967 saw the greatest emergence of the blues in recent pop history. It was the year in which rhythm and blues became the music of the charts and the year in which 'soul' became the popular music of America," exclaimed Jon Landau, rock writer and later manager of Bruce Springsteen.

African-American soul crossed over into white America with Aretha Franklin. In August 1960, Aretha signed with John Hammond, the talent scout for Columbia Records who had discovered Count Basie, Benny Goodman, and Bob Dylan. Mitch Miller, the Columbia executive who had assailed rock during the 1950s, gave Franklin voice lessons, hooked her up with Bob Mersey, the musical arranger for pop singer

Aretha Franklin. Queen of soul. *Permission by Atlantic Recording Corporation.*

Barbra Streisand, and assigned her such pop material as the show tune "If Ever I Would Leave You" and Al Jolson's "Rock-a-Bye Your Baby with a Dixie Melody." By late 1966, a dissatisfied Aretha had found only moderate success and was in debt to Columbia.

When her contract with Columbia expired, Jerry Wexler of Atlantic Records signed the singer. Within a few months, Aretha recorded for Atlantic *I Never Loved a Man (the Way I Love You)*, which included the single "Respect." "Respect," an R&B hit for Otis Redding two years earlier, took on an added importance in 1967. The song, belted out by the Detroit native Aretha Franklin, hit the streets as the ghetto of the Motor City exploded into flames. To whites, it seemed to epitomize the renewed self-pride that African Americans had discovered. The chart-topping song sold more than one million copies in ten months and brought African-American soul into white America. The album reached number two on the chart.

Aretha continued to achieve crossover success. During the next two years, she charted with the million-selling singles "(You Make Me Feel Like a) Natural Woman" and "Chain of Fools" and hit the Top Five with the albums *Aretha Arrives, Aretha: Lady Soul*, and *Aretha Now*. In 1968, Aretha won the Best Female Vocalist of the Year award, and Detroit Mayor Jerome Cavanaugh declared Aretha Franklin Day. *Ebony* magazine characterized the summer of 1967 as "'Retha, Rap [Brown], and Revolt." In July 1968, Aretha solidified her reputation among whites as the soul spokeswoman with her rendition of "Think," which ended with the singer crying, "Oh, Freedom, Freedom, Freedom, ya, Freeeeeedom."

Other soul singers began to attract greater mainstream interest after the rioting. In 1967, Wilson Pickett hit the Top Ten with a remake of Dyke and the Blazers' "Funky Broadway" and spent eight weeks on the album chart with *The Best of Wilson Pickett*. Sam and Dave scored a crossover hit with the number-two "Soul Man." In 1968, James Brown reached the Top Ten with "Say It Loud—I'm Black and I'm Proud." Otis Redding, who died December 10, 1967, when his twin-engine Beechcraft plane plunged into icy lake Monoma outside of Madison, Wisconsin, won posthumous accolades for the chart-topping "(Sittin' On) The Dock of the Bay." The King of Soul, who had received little attention from the white audience during his lifetime until he electrified youths at the 1967 Monterey Pop Festival, hit the Top Five with the album *Dock of the Bay*.

Atlantic Records, which had produced many of the soul artists, began to reap financial rewards. In July 1967, *Time* calculated that "Manhattan-based Atlantic, with such singers as Aretha, Wilson Pickett and Sam and Dave, can now sell more records in a week (1,300,000) than it did in six months in 1950." Remarked Jerry Wexler in 1968: "The young white audience now digs soul the way the black does." Soul had become the music of white America.

Militant Blues on Campus

12

> **" The pop scene has become a roaring, pulsating paradox of sound—the white man singing the black blues. "**
>
> —*Time* magazine

Young college students took to the streets to protest the war in Vietnam as race riots swept across urban America. As the decade came to a close, the hopeful mood of psychedelia changed to a somber resolve and then a dark depression. During the late 1960s, young rock-and-rollers listened to desperate, loud blues that reflected the times.

Campus Unrest

The war in Vietnam triggered disturbances on American campuses. By 1963, President John Kennedy had sent more than 16,000 military advisors to help the South Vietnamese train their troops. Worried about the threat of communism in Southeast Asia, American officials slowly increased the U.S. commitment in Vietnam. In 1965, after Congress passed the Gulf of Tonkin Resolution that gave the president the authority to conduct military operations in Southeast Asia without declaring war, the number of American troops skyrocketed from 23,000 to 184,000. By 1968, the United States had sent 542,000 troops to the war-torn country. The U.S. government also embarked on a bombing campaign to quell the National Liberation Front of the North Vietnamese. Between 1965 when the bombing started and 1968, they dropped more than a million tons of bombs, rockets, and missiles during such campaigns as Operation Rolling Thunder and Operation Flaming Dart. Chief of Staff of the United States Air Force Curtis LeMay vowed to "bomb them [North Vietnamese] back into the Stone Age."

Small groups of youths, clustered in major universities such as University of California at Berkeley, started to protest against the war. In April 1967, in New York's Central Park, more than 100,000 demonstrators gathered for the Spring Mobilization to End the War in Vietnam. On the same day, 75,000 San Francisco protesters came together for the same purpose. Others started a draft resistance movement to "urge that other young men join us in noncooperation with the Selective Service System."

Many of the initial protests such as the October 21, 1967, levitating of the Pentagon were conducted in a hippie spirit. The Pentagon protest was organized by Abbie Hoffman, a civil rights organizer, and his friend Jerry Rubin, a coconspirator in the Youth International Party (Yippie), which, according to Rubin, "merged New Left politics with a psychedelic lifestyle. Our lifestyle—acid, long hair, freaky clothes, pot, rock music, sex—is the Revolution. Our very existence mocks America. The old order is dying." On October 21, Hoffman and Rubin, who had spoken at the Human Be-In, banded together with Allen Ginsberg, Ed Sanders of the Fugs, and others to levitate the Pentagon. Standing outside of the building with 150,000 adherents, the leaders chanted "in the name of the lives of the dead soldiers in Vietnam who were killed because of a bad karma, in the name of the Tyrone Power pound cake society in the sky, out demon out, out demon out." Unsuccessful in their attempt, the exorcising demonstrators were dispersed by the police, who arrested 647 protesters. "We wanted to be stoned, wasted, and free," asserted Ray Mongo, cofounder of the Liberation News Service, who had been arrested at the event. "We were proud of being individuals."

In 1968, student protests against the war became more serious and violent, driving a wedge between the hippies and radicals. After the Viet Cong had launched their Tet offensive and the United States had stepped up aerial bombardment and defoliation efforts, students at Columbia University occupied university buildings to protest the war. "Columbia was seen as part of a power structure linked to the same forces that were waging war in Vietnam," contended Allen Young of the Liberation News Service. "We viewed the disruption of university life as a necessary step. For life to go on as usual in the face of the horror of the Vietnam War was unacceptable and immoral."

In early May 1968, at 2:30 A.M., a thousand New York City policemen approached the Morningside Heights campus of Columbia University. They moved onto the campus in police vans and squad cars, sealed off the entrances to the university, and, on orders from Police Commissioner Howard Leary, marched toward five buildings that had been occupied by student rebels to protest the university's affiliation with the Institute for Defense Analysis. As they began to dislodge student militants, the police encountered resistance. At Fayerweather Hall, they clubbed and kicked angry students and newsmen such as columnist Walter Winchell. By midmorning, the police had dispersed the students from the buildings, arresting 698 and injuring 120. To noted anthropologist Margaret Mead, who had taught at Columbia for forty-eight years, the police action signaled "the end of an epoch."

The protest at Columbia sparked trouble at other colleges and universities. More than 500 students at Princeton demonstrated in support of students at Columbia. At Stony Brook, 50 student militants staged a seventeen-hour sit-in to express their sympathy. More than 200 Temple University students picketed university buildings in the wake of the Columbia protests. By the middle of June, as the inner cities burst into violence, a National Students Association report estimated that almost 40,000 students engaged in 221 major demonstrations at 101 colleges and universities.

In August, student dissent intensified at the National Democratic Convention in Chicago, where the ineffectiveness of the flower-power approach became evident. To protest the war in Vietnam, 10,000 young, peaceful reformers traveled to the Windy City for the opening of the convention on August 26. They were organized by David Dellinger of the National Mobilization Committee to End the War in Vietnam, Tom Hayden and Rennie Davis, cofounders of the Students for a Democratic Society (SDS), and Jerry Rubin of the Yippies, who the year before had won 22 percent of the vote in the Berkeley mayoral race on a platform that included the legalization of marijuana. In the summer of 1968, Rubin announced that "the Democratic Party is dying. While it dies, we will celebrate the Festival of Life. Come to Chicago! We are the politics of the future." He continued: "Join us in Chicago in August for an international festival of youth, music and theater." The Yippies promised "making love in the parks . . . singing, laughing, printing newspapers, making a mock convention, and celebrating the birth of FREE AMERICA in our own time."

As hopeful student militants flooded into Chicago armed with backpacks and flowers, Chicago Mayor Richard Daley readied the city for battle. The mayor, who the previous year had recommended that looters be maimed and arsonists be killed during a race riot, heavily barricaded the Amphitheater, the site of the convention. He activated 6,000 National Guardsmen, requested and received 6,000 federal troops armed with bazookas, barbed wire, and tanks, and placed 12,000 Chicago policemen on twelve-hour shifts. After encountering stiff resistance from the organized students, Daley planned a strategy of confrontation that, according to the subsequent *Walker Report*, created a "police riot." When the Democrats left on August 29, Daley's police force had injured 198 and arrested 641 protesters. Violence at the Chicago convention and the subsequent trial of eight protest leaders, labeled by *Rolling Stone* as the "trial of the new culture," radicalized many hip students who had once believed in the power of example. "I saw the power of flowers wilt, first by gas, then when the guy next to me— a hardened street hippie out of *A Clockwork Orange*—lobbed a trash can through the windshield of a trapped squad car," remembered Abe Peck of the *Seed*, a Chicago underground paper.

Events at Columbia University and the Chicago convention changed the mood of students from a hope-filled ebullience to a dark, protective aggression. "The scene has changed," wrote Steve Dreyer in the Austin *Rag*, "as people realized that you can't build a 'community' of beautiful people in a rotten, capitalist society. And it occurred with Columbia and Chicago—with the death (and co-optation) of 'do your own thing'

Vietnam War protest, Seattle, Washington, 1970. *Permission by* The Daily *of The University of Washington.*

and with the beginning of the revolutionary consciousness." Steve Diamond of the Liberation News Service agreed, "Nobody wanted to know about communal living in the country, about organic food. It was 'Be in the city, in the streets fighting the man.'" In January 1969, *The Rat*, an underground newspaper in New York City, told its readers that "the revolution has come. It's time to pick up your gun."

In 1969, campus violence escalated. In May, 3,000 students at the University of California at Berkeley tried to remove a chain-link fence that university officials had erected around a grassy lot known as People's Park, which students recently had renovated. Ronald Reagan, then governor of California, calling the action "a deliberate and planned attempt at confrontation," activated 2,000 National Guardsmen, who gassed the unsuspecting students from a helicopter and with shotguns killed one onlooker, wounded 30 protesters, and arrested 800 others. Even *Time* magazine called the reaction a "crushing repression."

More of the 7.8 million university students across the country marched in protest. In 1969, disturbances occurred at state universities in Maryland, Delaware, and Minnesota. Students faced the police in major confrontations at San Francisco State, Duke University, Queens College in New York, Dartmouth College, and even at Harvard University, the bastion of academic respectability. At the University of Wisconsin at Madison, students protested the war in Vietnam by building 435 crosses, which they planted in rows on the lawn of the main administration building. The organizer of the demonstration wanted to show that "students really are faced with death." By the end of 1969, millions of students had taken to the streets, and more than 100,000 militants had banded together in 350 chapters of the radical SDS. A few hundred joined the violent Weathermen faction of SDS, bent on destroying the "system."

The war in Vietnam became very personal for American youths with the draft. On December 1, 1969, U.S. officials held the first lottery drawing to draft men into the armed forces since World War II. No longer a distant, philosophical problem, the war became an immediate concern for young men who feared death in combat. The draft helped further mobilize students who now protested for their lives.

The Psychedelic Blues

Radicalized by a war in Vietnam, the militant American youths became interested in a hard-edged rock. Rather than the folk-based, airy, acid rock, they began to listen to the angry, slashing, piercing blues of British and American guitar heroes. Faced with police clubs and tear gas, they turned to the music of an oppressed race. "The blues are bigger now than ever—ten times bigger," John Lee Hooker noticed in late 1968. "You know why it's bigger? Because all the college kids are digging it now. Ten years back the blues was just in a certain area, it was the blues lovers only. But nowadays all the kids are digging the blues—the college kids."

Jimi Hendrix, a poor, part African American, part Cherokee from a broken home in Seattle, reflected the desperate mood of late 1960s' youth through a psychedelic blues. On the cover of his 1967 debut album *Are You Experienced?*, Hendrix and his band appeared to be quintessential flower children. Hendrix wore bright yellow hip huggers and a white vest over a red, pink, and yellow paisley shirt, which had two openings around the chest that let two red eyeballs peek out. Around his neck Hendrix sported a vibrant orange tufted scarf. Bass player Noel Redding favored a double-breasted, yellow felt sport coat with flowers emblazoned on it, and drummer Mitch Mitchell had white-and-blue-striped trousers, a yellow scarf, and a white, red, and yellow tie-dyed shirt. The group stood against a backdrop of blood-red trees.

Hendrix and the Experience also freely experimented with drugs. "I fully admit that drugs controlled our music," Noel Redding later admitted. "Whether it was true or not, we felt we had to be stoned to play properly. Good dope equaled good music." Hendrix, identifying with the drug culture of the 1960s, used titles such as the title song from his first album and "Stone Free" from his first single released in December 1966.

Despite his hippie trappings, Jimi Hendrix unleashed a gut-wrenching electric blues to become rock's greatest virtuoso. The young Hendrix had listened to Chicago blues greats such as Muddy Waters, Howlin' Wolf, and Elmore James. After being honorably discharged as a paratrooper from the 101st Airborne Division in 1962, he and fellow paratrooper Billy Cox began to play around Nashville, backing blues acts such as Nappy Brown and Slim Harpo. For the next two years, he played with R&B performers such as Little Richard, James Brown, Jackie Wilson, and B. B. King. In 1964, Hendrix relocated to New York City, where he performed with the Isley Brothers and soul singer Curtis Knight.

In late 1966, Hendrix formed the Experience and amazed European audiences with an act modeled after former employers such as Little Richard and James Brown. At the Paris Olympia, he twisted, rolled, shook, and writhed in perfect time to every half note of his thunderous electric blues. During the next few months, the guitarist staged similar shows for spectators at Stockholm's Tivoli, the Sports Arena in Copenhagen, and the Saville Theater in London.

Hendrix delivered a loud, angry electric blues that captured the violence of the era. Using various electronic devices such as the wah-wah pedal, the fuzz box, and feedback at almost deafening levels, the guitarist pioneered a harsh, explosive, ripping style of electric blues. Explained Hendrix about the sound: "Lots of young people now feel they're not getting a fair deal. So they revert to something loud, harsh, almost verging on violence; if they didn't go to a concert, they might be going to a riot." Contended Billy Cox, who played with the guitarist in the Band of Gypsys in 1970, "He revolutionized the blues. He took it to another level." The titles Hendrix gave to his songs reflected the desperation of the times. For his 1967 debut, he penned "Manic Depression," "I Don't Live Today," and "Purple Haze."

By 1970, Hendrix shed some of his hippie veneer and replaced it with a politicized aggression. Songs such as "Machine Gun" combined Hendrix's guitar explosions with a growing awareness of social problems. "Jimi told me that what he was trying to express in ["Machine Gun"] was that at every moment there are terrible things going on all over the world—war, destruction, and terror, and that he wanted to open people's eyes," confided Monika Danneman, Hendrix's girlfriend at the time of his death. At a 1969–1970 New Year's Eve concert at the Fillmore East, the guitarist dedicated the song "to all the soldiers who are fighting in Chicago and Milwaukee and New York, oh yes, and to all the soldiers who are fighting in Vietnam." Explained the guitarist in 1970, "That's all I'm singing about. It's today's blues."

Hendrix also exemplified the militant era through his stage show. On June 18, 1967, at the Monterey Pop Festival, where he made his debut in the United States and attracted American acclaim, he finished his set with a thrashing, tortured version of the Troggs' "Wild Thing." As the last notes of the song blasted the audience from a column of nine amplifiers and eighteen speakers, Hendrix ceremonially doused his guitar with lighter fluid and set it on fire. "The Experience's destruction is inevitable rather than accidental, the surfacing of a violent streak," commented *Newsweek*, "the spontaneous and impulsive violence of the young."

Technological advances helped Hendrix deliver his message. On the advice of guitarist Pete Townshend of the Who, electronics wiz Jim Marshall started to work on a

Jimi Hendrix playing his guitar at Woodstock, 1969. © Henry Diltz/Corbis.

more powerful amplifier to suit the needs of sixties' rock-and-rollers. He designed a huge 100-watt amp that could be stacked, allowing rock guitarists to generate a deafening roar accompanied by distortion and feedback. In 1966, Hendrix visited Marshall's shop in London and agreed to exclusively use the new mega-powered amplifiers, which he stacked on top of one another to blast his audiences. The combination of Hendrix's style and Marshall's amps created a new sound for a tumultuous time.

Eric Clapton, the lead guitarist for Cream, regularly practiced in Marshall's shop and also bought the new Marshall stacks to deliver a hard-hitting paisley blues. The members of Cream—also including Jack Bruce and Ginger Baker—had individually started out in various blues units: Drummer Ginger Baker had joined Blues Incorporated and had powered the Graham Bond Organization; Jack Bruce had played his six-string bass with Baker in Blues Incorporated and the Graham Bond Organization, leaving to join John Mayall and Manfred Mann; and Eric Clapton, idolizing blues legend Robert Johnson, had perfected a piercing guitar sound in the Yardbirds and John Mayall's Bluesbreakers before joining Cream. In June 1966, Ginger Baker approached Clapton about forming a group that, upon the guitarist's insistence, included Jack Bruce on bass and vocals. Clapton defined the group's musical approach as "blues ancient and modern."

As with Hendrix, Cream delivered a high-volume, jazz-tinged version of the electric blues. They first released the album *Fresh Cream*, which included Muddy Waters' "Rollin' and Tumblin'," "I'm So Glad" by Skip James, and "From Four Until Late" by Robert Johnson. In late 1967, the group followed with *Disraeli Gears*, their U.S. breakthrough, which contained several blues-based originals such as their signature "Sunshine of Your Love." The next year, they followed with the number-one *Wheels of Fire*, recorded at the Fillmore West, which included the Hendrix-inspired "White Room" and the biting "Politician." After hearing the group, Rose Clapp, Clapton's grandmother who had raised him, felt that Eric had "always been a lonely boy and his music still gives me that feeling about him." Said the guitarist about his music: "Rock is like a battery that must always go back to the blues to get recharged."

Cream played their psychedelic blues at a near-deafening level. "There was, in fact, one gig where Eric and I stopped playing for two choruses," remembered Ginger Baker. "Jack didn't even know. Standing in front of his triple stack Marshalls [amplifiers], he was making so much noise he couldn't tell." After attending a May 1968 concert on the band's final tour, Ian Whitcomb wrote in the *Los Angeles Times* about the "great cataleptic hunks cut from the aged blues and pummeled out, slit up, reshaped, thoroughly examined by the violent guitars and drums."

Though delivering a hard-hitting electric blues, Cream also adopted touches of psychedelia. Despite being "pretty contemptuous of the West Coast rock-and-roll scene as exemplified by the new bands like Jefferson Airplane, Big Brother and the Holding Company and the Grateful Dead," Clapton nonetheless wore extravagant stage costumes purchased at Granny Takes a Trip in London and performed on acid. He also used a full array of guitar devices such as the distortion box and the wah-wah pedal to produce a new variant of the blues that adopted elements from the psychedelic sound.

Steve Miller offered another brand of psychedelic blues. As a youth he met T-Bone Walker, who provided him with "my basic lead phrasing." In 1961, after backing Jimmy Reed in a Dallas bar, Miller traveled from his Texas home with his friend Boz Scaggs to the University of Wisconsin in Madison, where they formed a white blues group, the Ardells. In 1964, he migrated to Chicago, where he backed blues greats Howlin' Wolf, Muddy Waters, and James Cotton and organized a blues band with Barry Goldberg. "Texas and then Chicago," Miller told a reporter, "where I spent some time learning Chicago blues and by the time I got to San Francisco [in 1966] I realized I had picked up a whole lot of Chicago blues."

Steve Miller Band, including Boz Scaggs (left) and Steve Miller (center), 1967. Photo by Platt Collection/Hulton Archive/Getty Images.

Traveling to San Francisco in late 1966, the guitarist formed the Steve Miller Blues Band, which combined Miller's blues experience with the surrounding sounds of acid rock. In October 1967, after appearing at the Monterey Pop Festival, the band signed with Capitol Records and released *Children of the Future*, a hybrid of blues and psychedelia complete with Victor Moscoso album art. The next year Miller neared the Top Twenty with *Sailor*, another hybrid effort, which featured the spacey "Quicksilver Girl" and the Chicago blues of the Jimmy Reed tune "You're So Fine."

Jeff Beck, another guitar hero who had been a veteran of the Yardbirds, produced a hard-edged blues. After splitting from the Yardbirds in late 1966, Beck formed his own group, which included blues shouter Rod Stewart. The guitarist, though dressed in paisley shirts and bell-bottomed, multicolored pants, reworked blues standards such as Willie Dixon's "You Shook Me" and "I Ain't Superstitious" in a tumultuous, shattering style. "We used to take things like John Lee Hooker and Muddy Waters and all the great bluesmen and play them our way," related Beck. "We wanted to mess with them a bit." He characterized his second LP, the Top-Twenty *Beck-Ola*, a 1969 collection of blues-drenched originals and rock standards such as "All Shook Up," as "heavy music."

Alvin Lee, the blues fanatic who fronted Ten Years After, produced a loud, aggressive electric blues. He first drew attention to his guitar mastery, when he backed John Lee Hooker at the Marquee Club in London. By August 1965, Lee had joined with bass player Leo Lyons and drummer Ric Lee in the blues-oriented Jaybirds. Late the next year, the band added Chick Churchill on keyboards and changed their name to Ten Years After. In 1967, the band released their first LP that, though on the cover featuring psychedelic art and a blurred picture of the band in paisley-print shirts, delivered biting renditions of blues such as Sonny Boy Williamson's "Help Me" and Willie Dixon's "Spoonful." The group developed their blues style on Top-Twenty albums like *Ssssh* (1969) and *Cricklewood Green* (1970).

Janis Joplin, propelled to stardom amid the hippie craze, sang the blues. In 1963 she and Chet Helms, the future owner of the Avalon Ballroom, hitchhiked from her home in Port Arthur, Texas, to San Francisco where Joplin sang in various North Beach folk clubs such as the Coffee Gallery, sometimes backed by Jorma Kaukonen, who later would help start the Jefferson Airplane. Joplin returned home but drifted back to San Francisco. In June 1966, Chet Helms recruited the singer to a group that he managed, Big Brother and the Holding Company, who Janis transformed from one of the original psychedelic bands into a blues unit that showcased her razor-sharp cries of anguish. As with so many young American electric blues artists of the late 1960s, Joplin first surprised the rock-and-roll world at the Monterey Pop Festival, held in June 1967. Late next year, the Big Brother album *Cheap Thrills* topped the chart and reached the million-dollar mark in sales within a few months, and Joplin's reputation began to grow.

Within weeks of the *Cheap Thrills* success, Joplin started to shed her psychedelic backdrop. In September 1968, she dumped her one-time psychedelic band to assemble the Kosmic Blues Band, which charted with *I Got Dem Ol' Kozmic Blues Again Mama!*. In May 1970, she hired the rock-blues outfit, the Full-Tilt Boogie Band, that

Jeff Beck of the Yardbirds. Courtesy of Cam Garrett/S.C.V.D. Studio.

hit the top of the chart the next year with *Pearl*. On a visit to the East Coast in August 1970, she participated in a twelve-hour antiwar rally at Shea Stadium. Two days later on August 8, Joplin traveled to the Mount Lawn cemetery in Philadelphia, where she bought a headstone for the unmarked grave of blues great Bessie Smith, probably Joplin's greatest influence. Despite the raves of journalists and her financial success, Joplin continued to feel the blues. "Someday," she confided to an interviewer, "I'm going to write a song about making love to 25,000 people in a concert and then going to my room alone."

The Motor City Five also made the transition from psychedelia to an aggressive, radicalized blues. Formed by five high school friends in Detroit in 1964, the MC5 took off in 1966 while attending Wayne State University, where they met their manager, John Sinclair. According to drummer Dennis Thompson, "Sinclair was in charge of the beatnik community then; he was the head man. Basically [vocalist Rob] Tyner, [guitarist Wayne] Kramer, and [guitarist Fred "Sonic"] Smith realized it would be a good thing to get in line with John, because John was a powerful figure in the beatnik community. This was the same time as things were happening in Frisco, and we were getting vibrations from Big Brother, the Grateful Dead, bands that were forming out there. It was like, 'Hey, let's get something happening back here'" in Detroit.

As with their counterparts in San Francisco, the MC5 lived and worked communally. They roomed together above the office of the underground newspaper the *Fifth Estate*. Believing in cooperation, the band started "trans-love energies," which guitarist Wayne Kramer described as "a communal association that provided all the services that we, as a band, needed. . . . It was like a multicultural collective with a lot of marijuana smoke and LSD thrown in." Though playing a James Brown–type, free-jazz-influenced, blues-based music, the MC5 adopted as a "three-point program" the slogan "dope, rock-'n'-roll, and fucking in the streets."

During the late 1960s, the MC5 became radicalized. According to Kramer, they expanded their three-point program "into a ten-point program that got more overtly political, like Free Economy, Free All Political Prisoners, and the rest of the agenda of the day." The MC5 Social and Athletic fan club became the White Panther Party, and the band played to the rioters at the 1968 National Democratic Convention in Chicago. By 1969, asserted manager John Sinclair, the group was "totally committed to the revolution, as the revolution is totally committed to driving people out of their separate shells and into each other's arms."

In 1969, the MC5 released their first album, *Kick Out the Jams*, which included songs such as "Motor City Is Burning." To open the album, they enlisted the services of Brother J. C. Crawford, who delivered one of the most rousing exhortations in rock history: "Brothers and sisters, I want to see a sea of hands out there, let me see a sea of hands. I want everybody to kick up some noise. I want to hear some revolution out there, brothers, I want to hear a little revolution!" The crowd, clapping when Crawford had begun, became more agitated. "Brothers and sisters, the time has come for each and every one of you to decide whether you are going to be the problem or whether you are going to be the solution," he continued, using a Black Panther slogan. "You must choose, brothers, you must choose. It takes five seconds, five seconds of decision, five seconds to realize your purpose here on the planet. It takes just five seconds to

Janis Joplin belting out the blues. *Permission by* The Daily *of The University of Washington.*

realize that it's time to *move*, it's time to *get down with it*. Brothers, it's time to testify, and I want to know, are you ready to testify? *Are you ready?*" screamed Crawford to a wild crowd that was jumping on the auditorium chairs. "I give you a testimonial—the MC5." The band launched into a near-deafening version of a hard-edged blues called "Rambling Rose."

The debut album included incendiary lyrics—"Kick out the jams, mother-fuckers"—that led to a clamp-down on the group. "They were arresting clerks in stores for selling the record. Certain chains refused to carry our record," bitterly remembered Sinclair, who himself was jailed several times on trumped-up charges, "and our contract with Elektra lasted only six months." He described the political platform of the band as "carrying a bomb up to the front of the door of the White House and knocking on the door and handing it to 'em."

Creedence Clearwater Revival, although flirting with psychedelia, infused the blues with a similar political message. In his home near San Francisco during the Beat era, amid the stirrings of hippiedom, bandleader John Fogerty listened to the records of Muddy Waters, Howlin' Wolf, Lightnin' Hopkins, Elvis Presley, and Carl Perkins. By 1959, he joined with his brother Tom and high school classmates Stu Cook and Doug "Cosmo" Clifford in bands called the Blue Velvets, the Golliwogs, and, finally in 1967, Creedence Clearwater Revival.

The band mixed Chicago electric blues with early rockabilly and a touch of fuzzy psychedelia into a driving concoction that Fogerty labeled "swamp music." In 1968, Creedence gained attention with a cover of Dale Hawkins's "Suzie-Q," which consciously catered to hippiedom. "It was meant to be psychedelic—to fit on underground radio," Fogerty admitted. "Actually, it was originally just a demo tape, and we took it to KMPX, the underground San Francisco FM station, and they started playing it."

Though paying homage to the nearby sound of San Francisco, Creedence emphasized stinging electric blues and rockabilly licks on their 1969 Top-Ten breakthrough album *Bayou Country*, which included Fogerty's "Proud Mary." "I pay homage to my icons. Howlin' Wolf was a big influence on me," remarked the singer-guitarist. "I unashamedly admit that I was influenced by James Burton [Ricky Nelson's guitarist], Scotty Moore [Elvis Presley's guitarist], Chet Atkins." Within eighteen months, the hard-driving rockabilly-blues band topped the album chart twice (*Green River* and *Cosmo's Factory*); placed two other LPs in the Top Five (*Willie and the Poor Boys* and *Pendulum*); and scored with Top-Five singles such as "Bad Moon Rising," "Green River," "Down on the Corner," "Travelin' Band," and "Lookin' Out My Back Door."

Besides swamp classics, which conjured up images of a mythical South, Fogerty turned to social commentary. He penned antiwar songs such as "Effigy," "Fortunate Son,"[1] and "Who'll Stop the Rain," which mirrored the sentiments of young Americans who feared being drafted and shipped to the unpopular and escalating war in Vietnam. "Some folks are born, made to wave the flag, ooh, they're red, white, and blue," sang the gravelly voiced Fogerty in "Fortunate Son." "When the band plays 'Hail to the Chief' they point the cannon at you. Some folks inherit star-spangled eyes, ooh, send you off to war, and when you ask them how much should we give, the only answer's more, more. It ain't me, it ain't me, I ain't no military son. It ain't me, it ain't me, I ain't no fortunate one."

Heavy-Metal Thunder

Some rockers, reflecting the militant mood of the times, delivered a loud, explosive blues unfettered by psychedelia to produce a sound termed *heavy metal*, initially defined by Steppenwolf. The band, coalescing around German-born vocalist/guitarist John Kay (a.k.a. Krauledat), provided an amped-up, aggressive, politicized rock. In 1968, they benefited from the inclusion of two songs from their debut on the soundtrack to the cult film classic *Easy Rider*. The self-named effort neared the top of the chart and yielded an anthem for the late 1960s, "Born to Be Wild," which included the phrase "heavy-metal thunder" that characterized the band's sound. "We play fairly intense, fairly aggressive music," contended Kay, "and when I sing and spit out my lyrics, so to speak, it tends to come out in a sort of intense, and to some people, somewhat intimidating or frightening,

[1]© 1969 Jondora Music, courtesy Concord Music Group, Inc.

kind of way." During the next two years, Steppenwolf amazingly placed five more albums in the Top Twenty, culminating their efforts with the antiwar statement *Monster*, which included the song "Draft Resister." In 1972, the group temporarily disbanded when Kay ran for a slot on the Los Angeles City Council.

If Steppenwolf coined a name for the new music, Led Zeppelin, led by guitarist extraordinaire Jimmy Page, became one of heavy metal's main stars. Page, a poor youth from the London working class, had played brilliant session guitar for the Rolling Stones, the Kinks, and the Who before joining the Yardbirds. After the Yardbirds disbanded in July 1968, Page enlisted the help of session bassist John Paul Jones, drummer John Bonham, and vocalist Robert Plant, who had earned the moniker "wild man of the blues from the Black Country" for his work with groups such as the Delta Blues Band and the Crawling King Snakes. The foursome toured briefly in Scandinavia as the New Yardbirds before changing their name to Led Zeppelin.

In 1968, Led Zeppelin entered the studio to record their blues-based debut. "I've never been so turned on in my life," recalled Robert Plant of the fifteen-hour recording session. "Although we were all steeped in blues and R&B, we found out in the first hour and a half that we had our own identity." On the album they unveiled a slashing, amplified blues, including Willie Dixon's "You Shook Me" and "I Can't Quit You Baby," and a reworked version of Howlin' Wolf's "How Many More Years," called "How Many More Times." By early 1969, Led Zeppelin had hit the Top Ten in Britain and the United States with the album, and later in the year, hit the top of the chart with their second effort, which featured their signature, Willie Dixon–inspired "Whole Lotta Love." The next year, the group topped the charts with *Led Zeppelin 3*, becoming the top rock act in the world.

Black Sabbath perfected the loud, aggressive blues that characterized heavy metal. Formed in 1967 as Earth, four Birmingham toughs initially churned out blues covers. "When we were Earth, we were doing lots of blues stuff, from Howlin' Wolf, Muddy Waters, John Lee Hooker," remembered bassist Terry "Geezer" Butler. "And a lot of the English blues band stuff, like Cream, John Mayall. Eventually [the blues covers] translated into much heavier stuff."

In early 1969, the band changed its name from Earth to Black Sabbath and pounded out a hard-driving, militant sound on its 1970 debut. "I don't profess to be a messiah of slum people," insisted vocalist John "Ozzy" Osbourne, "but I was a backstreet kid, and that little demon is still in there, shoving the hot coal in. The aggression I play is the aggression I know. And it's obviously aggression a lot of people have." The group recorded songs such as "War Pigs" and "Iron Man" on their second album *Paranoid* (1970), which embodied the intense antiwar sentiment of the era.

Prompted at least in part by Geezer Butler's fixation on religious imagery, Black Sabbath fastened on a preoccupation with demons and a hellish otherworld that had tormented many Delta bluesmen such as Robert Johnson, who had recorded "Me and the Devil Blues." The band borrowed their name from the title of a 1963 Boris Karloff movie and chose "Evil Woman," backed by "Wicked World," as their first single. They followed with songs such as "Electric Funeral," "Children of the Grave," and "Sabbath, Bloody Sabbath." "If we come across doomy and evil, it's just the way we feel," contended guitarist Tony Iommi.

Ozzy Osbourne gave a more vivid, expansive explanation for the band's gloomy theme: "Now you consider everyone's all jolly and tip-toein' around, stoned on acid, havin' Woodstock and all love, peace, sex, drugs and rock-'n'-roll, and all that's great," he told an interviewer. "But for us guys that were livin' in this *hole* in the world, it wasn't that way. And Tony [Iommi] thought 'wouldn't it be interesting to put this horror vibe to a musical thing.' And then we started to write doomy music, we used to call it. This death music. Doom music." Such "doom music" struck a chord among youth, who propelled the first six Black Sabbath albums to the British Top Ten and the Top Thirty in the United States.

Deep Purple turned to heavy metal midway through their career. Funded in 1967 by two London businessmen, the band began to chart with a series of remade pop songs such as Joe South's "Hush" and Neil Diamond's "Kentucky Woman." In September 1969, they recorded a *Concerto for Group and Orchestra* with the Royal Philharmonic Orchestra. After *Concerto* failed to sell in the United States, guitarist Ritchie Blackmore steered the band toward a loud, pulsating, dangerous sound on the British Top-Five effort *Deep Purple in Rock* (1970). "I always played every amp I've ever had full up, because rock-and-roll is supposed to be played loud," Blackmore explained. "I also got my amps boosted," he intimated about the music. "I know Jim Marshall personally, and he boosted them for me." The band continued to mine explosive, roaring chunks of sound on their next six efforts, including their classic *Machine Head* (1972), all of which hit the British Top Ten and the upper reaches of the American chart.

The Rebirth of the Blues

The militant, dark mood that fostered heavy metal led to a late 1960s' electric blues revival. Young, white blues performers raised in the American South began to gain popularity. Johnny Winter, raised in Beaumont, Texas, had played the blues for years before attracting national attention. After starting a number of blues-rock outfits with his brother Edgar, Winter traveled to Louisiana and then to Chicago, where he backed local blues greats. He returned to Texas, played the Georgia-Florida blues circuit, and produced a demo tape that included blues standards such as Howlin' Wolf's "Forty-Four," Sonny Boy Williamson's "Help Me," and Muddy Waters' "Rollin' and Tumblin'."

Winter began to reap the rewards of his efforts. In a 1968 *Rolling Stone* review of the Texas blues scene, the guitarist was referred to as "a 130-pound cross-eyed albino with long, fleecy hair, playing some of the gutsiest fluid blues guitar you have ever heard." A few weeks later, Winter was signed by East Coast club owner Steve Paul, who had rushed to Houston after reading the article. In 1969, Johnny Winter debuted on Columbia Records with an electric blues album that neared the Top Twenty. "I'd been put down for years for singing the blues and suddenly everyone liked me and wanted to hear me," shrugged Winter at the time.

Canned Heat, a Los Angeles blues band named after the Tommy Johnson song "Canned Heat Blues," also began to attract fans. Brought together in 1965 by singer Bob ("The Bear") Hite and guitarist Alan Wilson, Canned Heat initially had trouble finding work. "Nobody would hire us because we were blues," complained Hite, who in the 1960s rabidly collected more than 70,000 blues records. After their electric

Johnny Winter. Photo by Ebet Roberts. *Permission by Alligator Records.*

performance at the Monterey Pop Festival, the band began to gain recognition. In 1967, they signed with Liberty Records and hit the chart with their self-named debut, composed mostly of blues standards. The next year, the group neared the Top Ten with the Henry Thomas 1928 blues tune "Going Up the Country" and reached the Top Twenty with *Boogie with Canned Heat* and *Living the Blues.* In 1971, after three more successful, blues-drenched LPs, Canned Heat recorded an album with one of their idols, John Lee Hooker.

The Allman Brothers delivered electric blues from the Deep South. Raised in Florida, brothers Duane and Gregg Allman became young blues fanatics. Late-night radio station WLAC "would play those [blues] tunes and we'd head to the record store, man. We'd run in yelling, 'Who is this guy Lightnin' Hopkins?'" Gregg reminisced. By the time Duane graduated from high school in 1964, the duo had spearheaded blues bands up and down Daytona Beach and had recorded a commercially unsuccessful version of Willie Dixon's "Spoonful." In 1967, they moved to Los

Angeles and signed with Liberty Records as Hourglass. After two LPs, Hourglass disbanded and Duane moved to Muscle Shoals, Alabama, providing background guitar for Wilson Pickett, Aretha Franklin, and Percy Sledge.

In 1969, Duane Allman formed a new band with brother Gregg, Dickey Betts on second guitar, Berry Oakley on bass, and drummers Butch Trucks and Jaimoe Johanson. "Duane and Gregg were students of the urban blues," recalled Betts. "Their thing was like a real honest, truthful chilling delivery of that music, whereas Oakley and I may have been influenced by the blues and were students of it, but we were more innovative. We would try to take a blues tune and, instead of respecting the sacredness of it, we would go *sideways* with it." Concluded the guitarist: "So when we all came together, we gave each other a new foundation." In 1969, the Allman Brothers released their unique electric, jazz-tinged blues on a debut album, which sold well in the South. Two years later, when the band released the commercially successful *At Fillmore East*, they had become the spearhead of what critics termed *southern rock*, paving the way for mid-1970s' boogie bands such as Lynyrd Skynyrd and ZZ Top. At the turn of the decade, with bands such as the Allman Brothers, reported *Time* magazine, "the pop scene has become a roaring, pulsating paradox of sound—the white man singing the black blues."

Woodstock and the End of an Era

The intense mood of American youths, reflected by their interest in hard-edged, high-volume electric blues, changed at the turn of the decade as the militant hope of Woodstock turned into dark fear at Altamont and Kent State. The Woodstock Music and Arts Festival in Bethel, New York, held from Friday, August 15, to early Monday morning, August 18, 1969, seemed to herald a new era. Organized by John Roberts, a young millionaire who had graduated from the University of Pennsylvania; Joel Rosenman, a Yale Law School graduate and the son of a prominent Long Island orthodontist; Michael Lang, organizer of the Miami Pops Festival; and Artie Kornfeld, a seasoned songwriter and manager, the Woodstock Festival symbolized unity of purpose among the swelling ranks of youths, who opposed the war in Vietnam and hoped to assert their own power. "Woodstock signified the coming together of all tribes," remarked guitarist Carlos Santana, who played a mixture of Latin rhythms and the blues to the 400,000 mostly white educated youths who journeyed to the festival. "It became apparent that there were a lot of people who didn't want to go to Vietnam, who didn't see eye to eye with Nixon and none of that system, you know?"

The music at the festival reflected the antiauthoritarian attitude of late 1960s' youth. Though including a motley assortment of sounds from folk rockers such as Melanie to psychedelic bands such as the Grateful Dead and the Jefferson Airplane, Woodstock featured performances by Country Joe and Jimi Hendrix. Dressed in an army fatigue shirt and jeans, Country Joe McDonald took the stage at Woodstock without his band. "I get kind of mystical about my solo performance at Woodstock," remembered McDonald. "I was hanging around, and I was just filling time, singing a few country and western songs and folk songs. Then I did the [anti–Vietnam War song,] 'Feel-Like-I'm-Fixing-to-Die-Rag'—the F-U-C-K cheer—the rest is history.

From the first response to 'Give me an F,' when they all stopped talking and looked at me and yelled, F, I knew there was no turning back."

Jimi Hendrix played the final set of the festival around 9:00 A.M. on Monday. Taking the stage with a group of musicians called the Electric Sky Church, he launched into a series of heavy, ripping electric blues. Near the end of his performance, the guitar hero delivered a powerful version of "The Star Spangled Banner," which featured screaming-rockets and exploding-bomb guitar effects and sounded like a heaving, wounded monster about to die. In his rendition of the national anthem, Hendrix had captured the militant spirit of 1960s' youth who felt alienated, detached, and at the same time enraged toward their country.

The festival at Altamont Speedway near San Francisco, held on December 6, 1969, dashed the sense of power that Woodstock had engendered among many youth. Drawn by a free concert staged by the Rolling Stones, who wanted to repeat their successful Hyde Park performance, more than 300,000 fans flocked to the site. During the event, hundreds required treatment for drug overdoses, including one youth who jumped off of a freeway overpass after ingesting some LSD. Horrified, powerless spectators watched the San Francisco contingent of the Hell's Angels motorcycle gang, hired to keep order in exchange for $500 worth of beer, stab to death an eighteen-year-old African American from Berkeley, one of four deaths at the concert. "Altamont was the end of the sixties," contended Bill Thompson, manager of the Jefferson Airplane. "It was December 1969, and that was the end. Of the whole feeling."

Events at Kent State University in May 1970 destroyed any remaining feeling of militant power that existed among 1960s' youth after Altamont. When President Richard Nixon announced that American troops had been sent into Cambodia, students at Kent State University in northeastern Ohio took to the streets. On May 2, they hurled bottles at police cars, smashed store windows, and doused trees with gasoline, setting them on fire. The next day, 1,500 protesters firebombed the one-story ROTC building on the Kent State campus.

The authorities responded swiftly and decisively to the disruptions. Mayor Leroy Satrom asked Ohio Governor James Rhodes to activate the National Guard. Rhodes, who described the students as "worse than the 'brownshirt' and Communist element . . . the worst type of people that we harbor in America," responded with 900 troops armed with M-1 rifles, submachine guns, and canisters of tear gas. On the third day of trouble, Guardsmen chased a mob of students to a knoll near Taylor Hall. Suddenly, without warning, sixteen National Guardsmen each knelt on one knee and leveled their guns at the crowd. Asserted journalism professor Charles Brill, who witnessed the action: "They all waited and they all pointed their rifles at the same time. It looked like a firing squad." The soldiers pumped thirty-five rounds from their M-1 rifles into the protesters standing 75 feet away. "It's about time we showed the bastards who's in charge," sneered one Guardsman. The gunfire killed four students and wounded ten others. "My God! My God! They're killing us," screamed one Kent State freshman.

The murders at Kent State caused an immediate reaction in colleges and universities across the nation. Students sacked the treasurer's office at the University of South Carolina; they bombed the ROTC buildings at the universities of Utah and

Idaho; and 124 students were arrested in a fight with state troopers at the University of Colorado. Protesters occupied the ROTC building at the University of Nebraska, and a half-million-dollar fire blazed at Colorado State. Three weeks of rioting ravaged the University of California at Berkeley campus, and in a riot at the University of Maryland, state troopers injured 138 and arrested 200. Students at the University of Wisconsin, chanting, "We're gonna open up a second front in Madison," took over the Army Mathematics Research Center and were responsible for at least twenty major fire bombings. More than 75,000 students marched on Washington, D.C., gathering in front of the White House, and more than 200 colleges and universities shut down for at least one day, most for the rest of the academic year. In May and June 1970, more than 508 protests rocked college campuses and drew support from two-thirds of the students.

After the initial outbursts of violence, a sense of helplessness enveloped many American youths. Said one youth at the post–Kent State demonstration in Washington, D.C.: "The people here understand that we are surrounded by fully armed troops and that if we start anything, we'd be destroyed." Recalled Cheryl McCall of the underground newspaper *South End*, "I thought that the war was just escalating, was never going to stop, that Nixon was absolutely crazed, that these people had taken over everything, that the Movement didn't have a chance. They had put up with us protesting, marching in the streets, but now they were just going to kill us." For the first time in a decade, rebellious youths who had hoped for a better world felt that they had reached a dead end.

Government actions deepened the despair of radicalized youths, making future protests seem dangerous and potentially deadly. President Richard Nixon openly called the post–Kent State demonstrators "bums . . . blowing up the campuses . . . burning up the books." Authorities refused to prosecute the National Guardsmen who killed the Kent State students, despite an F.B.I. investigation that found the shootings "not necessary and not in order . . . No Guardsmen were hurt by flying rocks or projectiles and none was in danger of his life." To further squelch student protests, in 1970 Congress passed the Omnibus Crime Act, which prescribed the death penalty for anyone convicted of a fatal bombing.

During the next few months, shocking news of the deaths of several prominent rock figures aggravated the hopeless mood of youth. Jimi Hendrix passed away on September 18, 1970, a victim of complications from an overdose of sleeping pills. On September 3, Al Wilson, lead guitarist for Canned Heat, died of a drug overdose. Only a few weeks later, on October 4, at the Landmark Hotel in Hollywood, authorities confirmed the death of Janis Joplin from an overdose of heroin. On July 3, 1971, Jim Morrison of the Doors died of a heart attack in a bathtub in Paris. By the beginning of the 1970s, many youths who only a few years earlier had vowed to work for sweeping social change listened to the guns of Kent State and retreated to the cerebral music of jazz rock, classical rock, and the soft sounds of a nonpolitical, country-tinged folk revival.

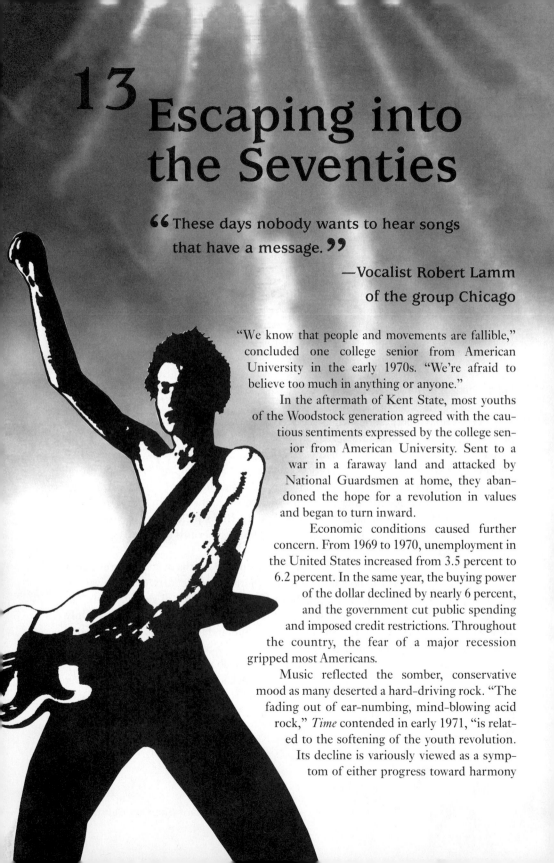

13 Escaping into the Seventies

"These days nobody wants to hear songs that have a message."

—Vocalist Robert Lamm of the group Chicago

"We know that people and movements are fallible," concluded one college senior from American University in the early 1970s. "We're afraid to believe too much in anything or anyone."

In the aftermath of Kent State, most youths of the Woodstock generation agreed with the cautious sentiments expressed by the college senior from American University. Sent to a war in a faraway land and attacked by National Guardsmen at home, they abandoned the hope for a revolution in values and began to turn inward.

Economic conditions caused further concern. From 1969 to 1970, unemployment in the United States increased from 3.5 percent to 6.2 percent. In the same year, the buying power of the dollar declined by nearly 6 percent, and the government cut public spending and imposed credit restrictions. Throughout the country, the fear of a major recession gripped most Americans.

Music reflected the somber, conservative mood as many deserted a hard-driving rock. "The fading out of ear-numbing, mind-blowing acid rock," *Time* contended in early 1971, "is related to the softening of the youth revolution. Its decline is variously viewed as a symptom of either progress toward harmony and thoughtfulness or a tragic slide from activist rage to a mode of 'enlightened apathy.'"

Rather than the pounding, loud sounds of psychedelia, the punchy rhythms of soul, or the wrenching, angry urban blues, rock became serious and introspective. Built on the yen for experimentation fostered during the hippie era, it was fused with more respectable, established musical forms such as jazz, classical, country, and folk. During the early 1970s, rock-and-roll became an apolitical, intensely personal experience.

Miles Ahead

Rock-and-roll has always been a union of diverse types of music. At its inception, it was concocted from an amalgam of electric R&B and country, first joined together by Chuck Berry, Elvis, and the rockabillies. During the mid-1960s, when Bob Dylan plugged an electric guitar cord into an amplifier, rock merged with folk for what critics called folk rock. Later in the decade, the Rolling Stones rediscovered Chicago blues, and African Americans turned gospel-based R&B into soul and funk. The psychedelic bands, dedicated to experimentation, merged 1950s' rock with blues, folk, and exotic-sounding world music such as the Indian raga.

At the turn of the decade, performers continued to fuse rock with other musical forms such as jazz. Blood, Sweat and Tears spearheaded the trend toward a jazz-rock fusion. Organized by Al Kooper, a former member of the Blues Project who in 1965 had backed Bob Dylan, Blood, Sweat and Tears played a blues-based music complemented by the horns of New York jazzmen such as trumpeter Randy Brecker. In 1968, they cut their first LP, the Top-Fifty *The Child Is Father to the Man*. When Kooper quit in early 1969, the band recruited vocalist David Clayton-Thomas, who added a pop element to the jazz rock for the top-selling *Blood, Sweat and Tears*, which included the hits "Spinning Wheel," "And When I Die" and "You've Made Me So Very Happy." They followed with two more top-selling albums, both featuring Clayton-Thomas on vocals and jazz horn men such as Joe Henderson and Lew Soloff.

James William Guercio, who had worked for Blood, Sweat and Tears, successfully promoted and managed another jazz-rock unit, Chicago. Formed in 1966 as the Big Thing by two school friends, guitarist Terry Kath and saxophonist Walter Parazaider, the band changed its name to the Chicago Transit Authority and in 1969 released a political jazz-rock album that included protest chants from the 1968 Democratic National Convention. Under the guidance of manager Guercio, the band shortened its name to Chicago, dispensed with radical politics, and fused their sound with pop to achieve long-standing commercial success. In 1970, they hit the Top Five with *Chicago II*, the next year reached the number-two position with *Chicago III*, and during the next four years topped the album chart five times. As with other rock acts during the early 1970s, Chicago delivered apolitical music with these chart-toppers. "These days nobody wants to hear songs that have a message," asserted vocalist and keyboardist Robert Lamm.

Carlos Santana added Latin rhythms to the jazz-rock amalgam. Raised in Tijuana, Mexico, Santana moved to San Francisco and, in October 1966, started the

Santana Blues Band. By 1968, the band had begun to incorporate different types of influences into their electric blues. "If I would go to some cat's room," remembered the guitarist about the band, "he'd be listening to Sly [Stone] and Jimi Hendrix; another guy to the Stones and the Beatles. Another guy'd be listening to Tito Puente and Mongo Santamaria. Another guy'd be listening to Miles [Davis] and [John] Coltrane. . . . To me it was like being at a university." In late 1969, the band released their first, self-named album, which featured their trademark Latin and jazz rhythms, beginning a series of top-selling releases through 1972.

Donald Fagen and Walter Becker, the cofounders of Steely Dan, drew their inspiration from similar sources. "I met Walter in college and we had very similar musical interests," remembered keyboardist Fagen, who learned piano from Thelonious Monk and Red Garland records. "We kind of combined the [rhythm and] blues thing—which was much simpler but very direct and emotional—with the jazz stuff we knew into a big mess." In 1973, the duo, helped by various session musicians, charted with their debut *Can't Buy a Thrill*, which, according to Fagen, "used devices that I think had formerly been used only by jazz people." The next year, Steely Dan reached the Top Ten with *Pretzel Logic*, which included the hit "Rikki Don't Lose That Number." Throughout the rest of the decade, they produced three more Top-Twenty albums, which helped popularize jazz rock.

Jazz great Miles Davis, who had been present at the inception of bop during the mid-1940s and had helped spearhead the cool jazz movement, provided the framework for many jazz-rock experiments. According to the trumpet master, Columbia Records executive "Clive Davis started talking to me about trying to reach this younger market and about changing."

In 1970, influenced by rock artists such as Jimi Hendrix, Davis blended a raw-edged, slightly dissonant 1960s' jazz with the electric sound of rock, emerging with *Bitches Brew*, his first major chart success. "This music is new," gushed music critic and *Rolling Stone* magazine cofounder Ralph Gleason in the liner notes for the album. "It hits me like an electric shock and the word 'electric' is interesting because the music is to some degree electric music. . . . Electric music is the music of this culture, and in the breaking away (not the breaking down) from previously assumed forms a new kind of music is emerging."

The album included future innovators of the fusion movement: John McLaughlin on guitar, Joe Zawinul's electric piano on some cuts, Chick Corea's electric keyboard on others, and the soprano saxophone of Wayne Shorter. John McLaughlin, playing with the Graham Bond Organization during the early 1960s and later with the Tony Williams Lifetime jazz outfit, formed the jazz-rock Mahavishnu Orchestra, which charted with *Birds of Fire* (1973). Zawinul and Wayne Shorter continued the fusion experiment in Weather Report, and in 1972, Chick Corea brought together Stanley Clarke, Joe Farrell, Airto Moreira, and eventually guitarist Larry Coryell in Return to Forever, which hit the album chart four times during the 1970s. Herbie Hancock, another pianist who had played with Miles Davis, formed the Headhunters, who in 1974 placed a self-named debut and *Thrust* on the chart. These musicians, along with a number of mainstream jazz performers who adopted the new style, defined and shaped the sound of the 1970s' jazz-rock fusion. "The whole atmosphere . . . was one of adventurousness, challenge and experimentation," explained Corea. "Jazz musicians were trying to play all kinds of stuff." "Everybody was dropping acid, and the prevailing attitude was, 'Let's do something different,'" added Coryell. "We love the Beatles but we also love Coltrane. We love the Rolling Stones, but we also love Miles. And out of that came bands like the Mahavishnu Orchestra and Return to Forever."

Sweet Seventies Soul

Just as hard bop and avant-garde jazz surrendered to fusion, the gritty soul of Aretha Franklin and Wilson Pickett drifted into the balladry of 1970s' soul. Though soul singers had offered smooth confections since the early 1950s and throughout the 1960s, the mellow side of soul reasserted itself and dominated the genre at the beginning of the 1970s.

Stevie Wonder reinvigorated the sweet soul sound. The product of Detroit's Motown, Steveland Morris had topped the chart as a teenage phenomenon with the jumping, harmonica-driven "Fingertips (Part 2)" in 1963 to earn the Wonder moniker. After a series of minor hits and three more Top-Ten singles, including "Uptight (Everything's Alright)" (1966), Wonder began to turn from the Motown sound toward softer ballads such as the Top-Ten "I Was Made to Love Her" (1967) and "My Cherie Amour" (1969). In 1971, when Wonder turned twenty-one and received $1 million from his trust fund, he renegotiated his contract with Motown to secure nearly complete artistic freedom with autonomous production and publishing companies.

Enjoying artistic control, Wonder began to craft sensitive, largely personal songs. In 1972, he started with *Music of My Mind*, which hit number twenty-one. His *Talking Book*, recorded late that same year, reached the Top Five on the strength of two number-one singles, the smooth ballad "You Are the Sunshine of My Life" and the funkier "Superstition." The next year, after recovering from an auto accident, he delivered another Top-Five effort, the million-selling *Innervisions*, and in 1974 he topped the chart with *Fulfillingness' First Finale*. By 1976, when he again topped the chart with *Songs in the Key of Life*, the singer/composer/multi-instrumentalist had snagged three consecutive Album-of-the-Year awards by softening and helping redefine soul for the 1970s.

If Stevie Wonder popularized a silky soul, producers Gamble and Huff perfected it. Meeting in the band the Romeos, Kenny Gamble and Leon Huff had produced several minor hits during the 1960s and in 1966 formed Excel Records, which had a regional hit with the Intruders. In 1967, they began to shape their silky sound of smooth vocals embellished with strings and horns on singles such as the Top-Ten "Expressway to Your Heart" by the Soul Survivors and acts such as Jerry Butler. In 1971, with the help of CBS Records president Clive Davis, the duo started Philadelphia International Records, which set the tone for 1970s' soul.

Philadelphia International first hit the charts with the O'Jays. The group first formed in 1958, and signed with major label Imperial in 1963, but failed to find chart success through the 1960s. By 1972, when the O'Jays signed with Philadelphia

International Records, the group had become a trio of Eddie Levert, Walter Williams, and William Powell. Using the Gamble and Huff formula of smooth, sometimes orchestrated harmonies, the O'Jays registered their first chart success with the number-three "Back Stabbers" and a Top-Ten album of the same name. During the next three years, they followed with a string of hits, including their crowning achievement, the number-one "Love Train."

Gamble and Huff also charted with Harold Melvin and the Blue Notes. Formed in the mid-1950s as a doo-wop quartet, the group floundered in roadhouse bars and Las Vegas supper clubs during the 1960s. In early 1970s, after drummer Teddy Pendergrass became the lead vocalist and Lloyd Parks joined to make the Blues Notes a quintet, the group signed with Gamble and Huff. They immediately scored with soft, Top-Ten pop ballads such as "If You Don't Know Me By Now" (1972) and "The Love I Lost (Part 1)" (1973), and the Top-Ten album *Wake Up Everybody* (1975).

Philadelphia International Records even charted with its house band, MFSB. Standing for Mother, Father, Sister, Brother, the almost forty-person MFSB was similar to Motown's Funk Brothers, providing the rhythm background and sometimes the lush backdrop for the label's artists. Asked to create a theme song for the television show *Soul Train*, the band hammered out an instrumental with the vocal help of the Three Degrees for a number-one smash. Gamble and Huff labeled the song "T.S.O.P" (1974), The Sound of Philadelphia, accurately defining 1970s' soul.

Philadelphia International soon became a force within the music business. Within its first nine months of operation, the label sold ten million singles and two million albums. By 1975, Gamble and Huff grossed more than $25 million annually, making their enterprise the second-largest African American–owned business in the United States, second only to Motown.

Thom Bell, a former associate of Gamble and Huff, offered his own lush arrangements of strings, French horns, and light percussion to challenge his former partners. Working as a producer for Atlantic Records during the early 1970s, Bell applied his soothing trademark sound to the Spinners. Started in 1955 by several Detroit toughs, the group attracted the attention of former Moonglow Harvey Fuqua who signed them to his Tri-Phi label. In 1961, they released their debut "That's What Girls Are Made For." For the next eleven years, they struggled with only one Top-Twenty single, the Stevie Wonder–produced "It's a Shame" (1970). In 1972, with new lead singer Phillipe Wynne, the group moved to Atlantic Records and began to record with Thom Bell. Almost immediately, they scored with the lush "I'll Be Around" and "Could It Be I'm Falling in Love" and followed with hits such as the number-one "Then Came You" (1974) with torch singer Dionne Warwick and the Top-Five "They Just Can't Stop It (The Games People Play)" (1975) and "The Rubberband Man" (1976).

Thom Bell also hit with the Stylistics. Banding together in 1968 as a union of two Philadelphia vocal groups, the Stylistics signed to Atlantic in 1971. Led by the falsetto of Russell Thompkins, they hit the chart with the smooth, string-drenched "You Are Everything" (1971), "Betcha By Golly, Wow" and "I'm Stone in Love with You" (1972), and "You Make Me Feel Brand New" (1974).

Seventies' soul did not totally desert the social protest of a few years earlier. Probably the most important album of the era was Marvin Gaye's landmark 1971 release, *What's Goin' On?*, which featured several songs addressing inner-city unrest and the toll of the Vietnam War, particularly on the black minority population. Gamble and Huff provided hard-hitting social commentaries with the O'Jays "Back Stabbers" and "Ship Ahoy," the last about the middle passage of a slave ship. In "Living in the City," Stevie Wonder told about the trials of an African American making his way from home in "Hard Times, Mississippi" to a jail cell in New York City. Even the Spinners sang the Linda Creed–penned "Ghetto Child."

These message songs proved the exception to the rule for 1970s' soul. Most Gamble and Huff and Thom Bell acts sang about personal relationships against the soothing backdrop of strings and horns. "'Love Train,'" explained Kenny Gamble about one of his most successful hits, "was about people uniting, living together in peace and harmony, and having fun." During the first half of the 1970s, a soft, lush, romantic, and hopeful soul dominated the airwaves.

Classical Rock

Some British musicians merged rock with classical music, sometimes adding escapist, fantasy-laden lyrics to create a hybrid, which became popular on both sides of the Atlantic during the early 1970s. Two English R&B bands, the Moody Blues and Procol Harum, became the forerunners of the classical-rock movement. Formed in 1964, the Moody Blues initially delivered a high-powered British R&B, even backing Sonny Boy Williamson on his UK tour. In 1965, they topped the British chart and hit the U.S. Top Ten with "Go Now," a cover of an American R&B song by singer Bessie Banks. "At that time, there were only two bands in Birmingham playing the blues, us and the Spencer Davis Group," explained vocalist and harmonica player Ray Thomas, a founder of the Moody Blues.

In late 1966, with a reconstituted lineup, the band shifted from R&B to an atmospheric, classically driven sound, showcasing Mike Pinder's Mellotron, a keyboard capable of reproducing the sounds of violins, trumpets, cellos, and other orchestral instruments. Using their newfound sounds, the band scaled the chart with *Days of Future Passed*, which featured the London Festival Orchestra and included the Hayward composition "Nights in White Satin." Hayward called the album "a little rock opera." Several more albums of orchestrated rock highlighted by obscure, fantasy-filled lyrics followed, culminating in 1972 with the chart-topping *Seventh Sojourn*.

Procol Harum also presaged the flowering of 1970s' classical rock. The band had its roots in an R&B group called the Paramounts, which enjoyed limited success, most notably with their 1964 remake of the Coasters' "Poison Ivy." After guitarist Robin Trower left the Paramounts, eventually to form a Hendrix-style power trio, vocalist Gary Brooker and lyricist Keith Reid joined the classically trained organist Matthew Fisher, guitarist Ray Royer, bassist Dave Knights, and drummer Bobby Harrison to start Procol Harum. In 1967, the group topped the British chart and reached the U.S. Top Five with "A Whiter Shade of Pale," a surreal poem by Reid set to music adapted from one of the movements in Bach's *Suite No. 3 in D Major*. After several commercially disappointing follow-ups, in 1972 Procol Harum rode the crest of the classical-rock wave for their greatest success with *Procol Harum in Concert with the Edmonton Symphony Orchestra*, which included an orchestral version of "Conquistador."

Jethro Tull also made the transition from blues bashers to classical rockers. Rising from the remains of an earlier blues band, flautist Ian Anderson and bassist Glenn Cornick joined with guitarist Mick Abrahams and drummer Clive Bunker to form Jethro Tull, named after an eighteenth-century English agriculturalist. In 1968, they delivered the blues-drenched *This Was* to modest success and a year later moved away from the blues with new guitarist Martin Barre. In 1971, the band released the Top-Ten *Aqualung*, which abandoned the blues for a rock/folk sound. The next year, Jethro Tull merged English folk, rock, and obscure lyrics with classical flourishes for the number-one *Thick as a Brick* and the next year followed with the classical rock of the chart-topping *A Passion Play*.

King Crimson, fueled by the ideas of Robert Fripp, served as a prototype for 1970s' classical rock. "Well-educated university graduate types were coming in as musicians and band members," reasoned Chris Blackwell, owner of Island Records. "So you were starting to have a different input in the music. Robert Fripp really represented that type of new performer."

In early 1969, the band formed around Fripp, who combined classical guitar technique with screaming rock solos. The group neared the top of the British chart with its debut, *In the Court of the Crimson King*, which included the symphonic sounds of the Mellotron and featured mythical, escapist, fantasy-based lyrics similar to the motifs that would appear on the albums of other classical-rock bands. The next year they followed with the commercially successful *In the Wake of Poseidon*, which included "The Devil's Triangle," based on Gustav Holst's orchestral suite *The Planets*, and continued their fascination with deep-sea mythology.

Genesis used King Crimson as a role model. Meeting at secondary school, the band members started as songwriters who idolized Fripp and his mates. "King Crimson appeared on the scene, and we thought they were just magnificent," explained singer Peter Gabriel. After an unsuccessful debut, Genesis began to gather a following based on their extravagant stage show and an intricate, melodic sound that was accentuated by Mellotron player Tony Banks. Appearing in long dresses and wearing masks, the costumed Peter Gabriel wooed audiences, and from 1972 to 1975 the band hit the British Top Ten with three albums of classically tinged rock.

Banding together backstage at the Fillmore in San Francisco, former King Crimson guitarist Greg Lake, classically trained pianist Keith Emerson, and drummer Carl Palmer made their major debut as Emerson, Lake and Palmer on August 29, 1970, at the Isle of Wight Festival. That year they reached the Top Twenty with their first album, embellished with classical motifs and songs written by ex–King Crimson lyricist Pete Sinfield. In 1971, the trio released a live version of Mussorgsky's composition *Pictures at an Exhibition*, which reached the Top Ten. That same year, they released the best-selling *Tarkus*, which revolved around the concept of a mechanized armadillo that battled a mythical beast, the Manticore. In 1974, after creating their own record label named after the Manticore, the group charted with the three-record set, *Welcome Back My Friend to the Show That Never Ends*, which included "Toccata" by Bach. "We didn't play the blues, and we really didn't play rock-and-roll," related Carl Palmer. "We played classical adaptations."

The Electric Light Orchestra also mined the classics "I had the idea for ELO," explained cofounder Roy Wood. "I thought 'wouldn't it be great to get a band together and instead of advertising for a guitarist, advertise for a French horn player or a cellist 'cause there must be young people around that play those instruments that like rock-'n'-roll.'" Along with guitarist Jeff Lynne, Wood formed the band's first lineup, which released *No Answer*, an album graced with cellos and violins. In 1973, after the abrupt departure of Wood, they enlisted three former members of the London Symphony Orchestra to help with their second effort, which included their first hit, a richly orchestrated version of Chuck Berry's "Roll Over Beethoven." In 1974, the band cracked the U.S. Top Twenty with *Eldorado—A Symphony by the Electric Light Orchestra*, which included their first U.S. Top-Ten hit "Can't Get It Out of My Head," which showcased a thirty-piece string section. "I like the *sound*," insisted Jeff Lynne. "That's all music is for me. Not for putting a message over."

Pink Floyd, a British psychedelic band formed in 1965, moved increasingly toward classical structures during the 1970s. In early 1968, when vocalist-guitarist Syd Barrett became incapacitated because of excessive LSD use, the group hired guitarist David Gilmour, who led the band to a more subtle, classically based experimental sound evident on several atmospheric sound tracks and the albums *Ummagumma*, *Atom Heart Mother*, and *Meddle*, which all hit the Top Five in England. "Syd moving out meant that we had to start writing," explained bassist-vocalist Roger Waters. "In fact, his leaving made us pursue the idea of the extended epic and a more classically constructed idea of music."

In 1971, the group played at the Montreux Classical Musical Festival. "This is what we like," enthused keyboardist Richard Wright. "A lot of people who normally listen to classics will be able to hear us, and a lot of young people will probably be hearing a symphony orchestra for the first time. It will be good for both."

By their 1973 masterpiece *The Dark Side of the Moon*, which took nine painstaking months to produce and sold more than thirteen million copies, Pink Floyd had perfected a Wagnerian electronic sound that provided a backdrop for epic tales of alienation, paranoia, and madness. Rather than a political statement so popular a few years before, "*Dark Side of the Moon* itself is an allusion to the moon and lunacy," explained guitarist David Gilmour. "The dark side is generally related to what goes on inside people's heads, the subconscious and the unknown."

Yes, a band formed in 1968, featured neoclassical structures and three-part harmonies. After adding guitarist Steve Howe and classically trained pianist Rick Wakeman, the group recorded the Top-Five *Fragile* (1971), their U.S. breakthrough, which contained the hit "Roundabout." "That kind of using the classical structure as a basis to make music, rather than pop music, that's where we were heading when we did *Fragile*," explained Yes founder Jon Anderson. The group followed with the Top-Five *Close to the Edge*, which consisted of three extended cuts and a four-movement title suite. Starting with *Fragile*, the Yes albums also highlighted the fantasy-style artwork of Roger Dean that reinforced the escapist lyrics of the classical rockers. By 1974, *Time* gushed over "the complex, educated sounds" of groups such as Yes. "Thus do

barriers fall," the magazine concluded, "and such often enclosed worlds as rock music get a little sunshine in."

Back to the Country

Confronted by the harsh, complicated realities of an unwanted war in Vietnam and events at Kent State, some folk rockers began to move toward a country music that extolled simple living and rural traditions. "Country rock," observed *Time* in 1970, was a "turning back toward easy-rhythmed blues, folk songs, and the twangy, lonely lamentations known as country music." The new musical blend, continued *Time*, was a "symptom of a general cultural reaction to the most unsettling decade that the U.S. has yet endured. The yen to escape the corrupt present by returning to the virtuous past—real or imagined—has haunted Americans, never more so than today." Even *Rolling Stone* labeled country rock the "music of reconciliation."

Country music had always been part of the rock-and-roll gumbo, beginning with Chuck Berry and Elvis Presley. But unlike Berry and the rockabillies, who fused a jumping, gut-bucket R&B with old-style country, the country rock of the 1970s merged a mellow folk rock with bluegrass and country swing. "The folk phenomenon," explained Bernie Leadon of the Flying Burrito Brothers and then the Eagles, "really started in the late fifties. Out of that came many of the late sixties, early seventies folk rockers and, later, country rockers came directly out of *that* folk movement."

Bob Dylan, the most visible protest singer of the 1960s, led youth back to the country. In 1968, Dylan began to lean toward a country sound on *John Wesley Harding*,

which reinterpreted and glorified the Texas outlaw and neared the top of the chart. In May 1969, Dylan made his country influences more obvious on the million-selling *Nashville Skyline*, recorded in the country music capital of Nashville, Tennessee. This album featured a duet with former rockabilly and country music giant Johnny Cash on "Girl from the North Country." On June 7, Dylan appeared with Cash on a television special filmed at the Grand Ole Opry.

As Dylan moved toward country, the Byrds, the folk-rock group that had risen to fame on Dylan compositions, looked to country music for inspiration. Prodded by new Byrds singer-guitarist Gram Parsons, the group released the country-flavored *Sweetheart of the Rodeo* (1968). Gram Parsons, related to Byrds' leader Roger

McGuinn, "took us through a whole country bag, and sort of directed us in it, and then he split." Remembered Byrd Chris Hillman, "Gram reminded me how much I loved country music. We'd always played a little country with the Byrds, but with two of us in the band, the obvious thing was to bring out that influence in our music." Counterbalanced by the more rock-oriented Roger McGuinn, the Byrds fastened on a country-rock sound with the album. Although achieving only moderate commercial success with their new direction, the band signaled the way back to the country. "It's sort of a backlash from the psychedelic scene, which I'm personally saturated with," explained McGuinn at the time.

The Band, Dylan's sometime backup group, began to achieve popularity with its country-based sound. In 1961, guitarist Jaime "Robbie" Robertson, pianist Richard Manuel, drummer Levon Helm, bassist Rick Danko, and organist Garth Hudson coalesced as the Hawks under rockabilly singer Ronnie Hawkins. In 1965 after being noticed by Dylan's manager Albert Grossman, the group backed and toured with Dylan and by 1967 moved close to the reclusive singer in Woodstock, New York.

The Band, as they were now called, recorded their debut at Woodstock in their large, pink-colored house and in 1968 released the countrified *Music From Big Pink*. "Everybody was getting real loud, psychedelic, flashy; and we went the other way," reasoned Band leader Robbie Robertson. The next year they hit the Top Ten with a heavily country-influenced, self-named LP, which included the hit "Up on Cripple Creek." By late 1970, the group reached the Top Five in the United States with their third album *Stage Fright*. The Band, wrote *Time*, perfected a rock hybrid that "comes on mainly as country music full of straight lines and sentiment."

Poco offered a similar brand of country rock. In late 1968, when the folk-rock group Buffalo Springfield splintered into the trio Crosby, Stills, and Nash and a solo career for Neil Young, Springfield guitarist Richie Furay decided to establish a country-rock outfit with his friend Jim Messina. "Richie and I were riding in a cab in Nashville," remembered Messina. "We talked about forming a new band that would be an extension of what we'd been doing with the Springfield, but more country and rock than folk and rock." The duo invited steel guitar player Rusty Young, bassist Randy Meisner, and drummer George Grantham to join them. After two moderately successful efforts, in 1971 the group neared the Top Twenty with *Deliverin'*, which relied heavily on traditional country instruments such as steel guitars, mandolins, and dobros. "I think the most dominating thing was the fact that we had this country sound," Furay remarked about the album. "We were pioneering the country-rock sound at this time with the introduction of the steel guitar, the high, countryish harmonies and all."

The Arizona-born Linda Ronstadt served as the focal point for several other 1970s' country rockers. In 1964, the singer moved to Los Angeles to join the folk trio the Stone Poneys. Though selling few copies of their debut, the group scored with "Different Drum" (1968) before disbanding. After two unsuccessful solo efforts, Ronstadt began to frequent the Troubadour club in Los Angeles. "We all used to sit in a corner of the Troubadour and dream," she reminisced. "It was where everyone met, where everyone got to hear everyone else's act. It was where I made all my musical contacts." At the Troubadour in April 1971, Ronstadt recruited a new band, including

Linda Ronstadt. Photo by Bonnie Lippel. *Permission by Peter Asher Management.*

guitarist Glenn Frey and drummer Don Henley. Ronstadt and her new bandmates quickly recorded an album, which included country standards such as "I Fall to Pieces" and "Crazy Arms."

In 1973, the singer hired as her manager Peter Asher, who had started in the music business as half of the folk-rock duo Peter and Gordon. Helped by her new manager, the singer released *Don't Cry Now*, which remained on the chart for fifty-six weeks and cracked the Top Fifty. In 1975, she followed with the country-rock, number-one classic *Heart Like a Wheel*, which included country and rockabilly classics such as the Everly Brothers' "When Will I Be Loved" and "I Can't Help It (If I'm Still in Love with You)" by Hank Williams. Having set her pattern, during the next two years

Ronstadt recorded a number of top-selling albums that combined sensitive ballads with smooth renditions of country-tinged songs.

Linda Ronstadt professed conservative political beliefs, which had become prevalent during the early 1970s. She hoped for a "real resurgence of patriotism in this country." After campaigning for liberal candidates, the singer felt that "I really didn't know what I was talking about. Who knows who should be president and if anybody should have an interest in determining those things, shouldn't Standard Oil? I mean, they have more to gain and more to lose. If something terrible happens to Standard Oil, a lot of people will be out of jobs. You can say what you want about big multinationals running the country and stuff, but the fact remains that we need that, we need their services, we need jobs from them, and they are in a better position to decide what's going to be good for the economic climate of the country and for the rest of the world."

Ronstadt's one-time tour band, splitting from the singer in August 1971, achieved stardom as the Eagles. Frey and Henley formed the Eagles with bassist Randy Meisner, who had played for Poco, and guitarist Bernie Leadon, who had been a member of the Flying Burrito Brothers. "Glenn [Frey] said we needed to get those guys [Meisner and Leadon] because they could play the kind of country rock we were all so interested in," observed Henley.

In early 1972, the group recorded their self-named debut album, which neared the Top Twenty and included the hits "Take It Easy," "Peaceful Easy Feeling," and "Witchy Woman." The next year, they recorded *Desperado*, a concept album about the Dalton gang and its leaders, Bill Dalton and Bill Doolin. Atlantic President Jerry Greenberg called the album a "fucking cowboy record!" "We grew up wanting to be the cowboys," enthused Leadon. "So much so that we actually wanted to act that out. The album was our chance to do that: a dream come true." In 1975, the Eagles topped the chart with *One of These Nights* and scored their first million-selling single, "The Best of My Love," which exemplified their trademark soft, country-influenced rock.

Jackson Browne, writing songs for the Eagles and Linda Ronstadt, epitomized the country-tinged, West Coast tunesmith of the 1970s. According to the singer, he was influenced by his sister, who "was two years older than me, and she hung around with these guys who wrote songs and did a lot of civil rights stuff. I started hanging around with them and writing songs when I was fifteen. We gravitated toward Bob Dylan, Pete Seeger kind of stuff. This is 1964, '65."

Browne, as did Dylan himself, deserted social protest for an intensely personal, country-flavored folk. After traveling to New York City, where he wrote songs recorded by the Byrds, he signed with the newly established Asylum Records. In 1972, with the help of David Crosby and country guitarist Clarence White, the singer-songwriter released his first LP, which contained the hit "Doctor My Eyes." Later in the year, to promote the album, he toured with the Eagles. As he toured, Browne hit the chart as a cocomposer of the Eagles' hit "Take It Easy," which he wrote with former roommate Glenn Frey. He continued to compose hits for the Eagles, who charted with Browne's "Doolin' Dalton" and "James Dean." By the second half of the decade, he charted as a solo artist with two Top-Five albums of highly personal compositions. Browne called his work "the residue of my life."

Seventies Folk

The disintegration of the American family, coupled with the decline of political activism, gave rise to a less country-based version of folk music that dealt with the loneliness of the single young adult. During the 1970s, as the number of women in the workforce doubled, many Americans, especially the baby boomers, began to divorce their partners at an increasing rate. During the 1950s and early 1960s, only 1 percent of married women divorced each year. In 1970, the yearly divorce rate leapt to 1.5 percent, and five years later it reached 2 percent. Stated in another way, the number of divorces in the United States skyrocketed from 377,000 in 1955 to 1,036,000 by 1975. Adjusting for the population growth, the rate climbed 54 percent, most of the increase coming during the late 1960s and early 1970s with more liberal divorce laws and changing perceptions toward marriage.

Many baby boomers began to question the institution of matrimony in the midst of the burgeoning divorce rate. In one study, conducted in 1971 among college students, more than 34 percent of the respondents believed that marriage was obsolete. Two years later, according to a Rutgers University student survey, 30 percent of the seniors felt that marriage was no longer a viable option.

Divorcing or not marrying, many baby boomers lived the sometimes lonely life of the unmarried young adult. By 1978, more than 1.1 million Americans lived in single households, an increase of 117 percent in one decade. To find companionship, they populated singles bars, singles resorts, and singles housing complexes.

During the early 1970s, singer-songwriters sang ballads about the emotional traumas of divorce, lost love, and loneliness in a plaintive, confessional style that had its roots in 1960s' folk. James Taylor, the prototype of the easygoing, sensitive 1970s' folkster, grew up in Chapel Hill, North Carolina, and spent his summers on Martha's Vineyard off Cape Cod, listening to the records of the Weavers, Woody Guthrie, and Pete Seeger. He began playing with his friend Danny Kortchmar as a folk duo, James & Kootch, who won a local hootenanny contest. In 1966, he joined Kortchmar's band the Flying Machine, which performed in Greenwich Village coffeehouses before disbanding a year later. Taylor, exhausted and suffering from a heroin addiction, in 1968 traveled to England, where he recorded his first LP for the Beatles-owned Apple Records. When his vinyl debut failed to crack the Top Fifty despite background work by Paul McCartney, the singer returned to the United States.

Taylor rebounded from his setback. After appearing at the Newport Folk Festival, he landed a contract with Warner Brothers through manager Peter Asher. In early 1970, he recorded the album *Sweet Baby James*, which reached the Top Five and remained on the chart for more than two years. It included the soul-baring "Fire and Rain" about the suicide of Taylor's friend. The singer followed the next year with *Mud Slide Slim and the Blue Horizon*, which neared the top of the charts in the United States and Britain and included the Carole King–written chart-topper "You've Got a Friend," a soft, reassuring ballad appropriate for the millions of divorced and unmarried baby boomers.

Taylor, as did most early 1970s' singer-songwriters, wrote and performed a collection of acoustic confessions. "I wish I weren't so self-centered or self-referred all the time with the stuff I write," he later complained, "but for some reason that's the window I utilize, hopefully in an open-ended way."

Other 1970s' folk artists, most of them associated with James Taylor, penned self-revelatory paeans of loneliness and confusion. Carole King, the Brill Building sensation of the early 1960s, became intrigued by the New York folk scene after she divorced husband-collaborator Gerry Goffin. She backed the Flying Machine in Greenwich Village and in 1968, with Danny Kortchmar, formed the short-lived band the City.

In 1971, King again vaulted to the top of the chart. Aided by Kortchmar and James Taylor, she released the number-one *Tapestry*, which stayed on the chart for six years and sold more than twenty million copies. It included her own version of "You've Got a Friend" as well as tales of lost love such as "So Far Away" and "It's Too Late."

Carly Simon had a more intimate connection with James Taylor on her road to success. Daughter of the cofounder of Simon & Schuster publishers, Carly left the exclusive Sarah Lawrence College to perform and record as a folk duo with her sister Lucy. In 1965, after the Simon Sisters disbanded, she signed with Bob Dylan's manager, Albert Grossman, who hoped to promote her as a female Dylan and recorded four unreleased tracks. Four years later, Carly met Jac Holzman, owner of Elektra Records, who signed her to his label and in 1971 released the singer's solo debut, which reached number thirty on the album chart. She recorded her second LP, *Anticipation*, which included the Top-Twenty single of the same name that was written for Top-Ten singer-songwriter Cat Stevens. In late 1972, Carly Simon topped the charts with the single "You're So Vain" and the album *No Secrets*, and on November 3, she married James Taylor in her Manhattan apartment. In 1974, the husband-wife team duetted on the Top-Five single "Mockingbird."

Joni Mitchell, collaborating with a number of the 1970s' folk elite, strummed her way to the top. Born Roberta Joan Anderson, she began to play acoustic folk in her native Canada. In 1964, she performed at the Mariposa Folk Festival, and the next year, after moving to Toronto, she met and married Chuck Mitchell, who played with her as a folk duo in local coffeehouses. In 1966, Mitchell moved to Detroit, where she became a sensation on the folk scene. She then began to make appearances in New York City. While in Greenwich Village, Mitchell met folk artists such as Judy Collins, who hit in 1968 with Mitchell's "Both Sides Now."

In 1968, Mitchell signed with Reprise Records and released her debut album, which was produced by ex-Byrd David Crosby and included on guitar Stephen Stills, formerly of the folk-rock band Buffalo Springfield. The next year, she recorded her second LP, *Clouds*, which neared the Top Thirty and earned her a Grammy for the Best Folk Performer of the Year.

During the early 1970s, Mitchell delivered three confessional albums, which focused on the pain of broken relationships and epitomized the sensitive singer-songwriter ethos. In 1971, she enlisted the support of Stephen Stills on bass and James Taylor on guitar, the latter who had Mitchell sing background vocals on "You've Got a Friend," and crafted the archetypical singer-songwriter work, the Top-Fifteen *Blue*, which featured tales of lost love such as "The Last Time I Saw Richard," "This Flight Tonight," and the title song. It also included "Little Green" about the child she was forced to give up for adoption as a young woman. "I made the decision in my emotionally disturbed period, which was when *Blue* was, that I wanted everything to be transparent," she later recalled. "I wanted to present myself as I was. To continue [as a songwriter], I had to show what I was going through." Before moving toward a more jazz-oriented approach, she continued with the self-revelatory *For the Roses* (1972), which neared the Top Ten and the near number-one *Court and Spark* (1974). "When I think of Vietnam or Berkeley, I feel so helpless," Mitchell told *Time*. "I just write about what happens to me."

Crosby, Stills, and Nash, entangled with Mitchell on professional and personal levels, rode the singer-songwriter wave to success. In mid-1968, after the breakup of the folk-rock group Buffalo Springfield, Stephen Stills began to practice with ex-Byrd David Crosby (a.k.a. David Van Courtland) and Graham Nash, formerly of the Hollies. A year later, the folk rockers released a self-titled, Top-Ten album featuring a blend of floating harmonies and acoustic guitars. It featured the hit "Suite: Judy Blue Eyes" about the breakup of Stills and folkster Judy Collins. As their album scaled the chart, the group asked ex–Buffalo Springfield guitarist Neil Young to join. In March 1970, they released *Déjà Vu*, which topped the chart and included their best-selling single, Joni Mitchell's "Woodstock," as well as paeans to lost love.

Crosby, Stills, and Nash. *Permission by* The Daily *of The University of Washington.*

In the early 1970s, rock had turned from a politicized heavy metal to airy ballads of unrequited love. In 1971, Robert Hilburn, music critic for the *Los Angeles Times*, observed that "the creative/influential center of contemporary pop music has shifted during recent months from the loud desperation and exaggeration of such performers as Janis Joplin and Jimi Hendrix to reflective, more reassuring gentleness." He concluded that "for a generation that has been trying to recover some of the balance shattered during the troubled, riot-torn, confrontation-bent late 1960s, Miss [Carole] King and James Taylor have provided direction. They've tried to refocus attention on such simple, classical values as friendship, loved ones and the home."

As Crosby, Stills, Nash and Young and other singer-songwriters lofted their distinctive harmonies about difficult relationships, a wild, hard-edged, and theatrical heavy metal started to emerge to take the self-absorption of the soft rockers to excessive heights. Soon, the soft-spoken escapism of the early 1970s would give way to the excesses of the Me Generation.

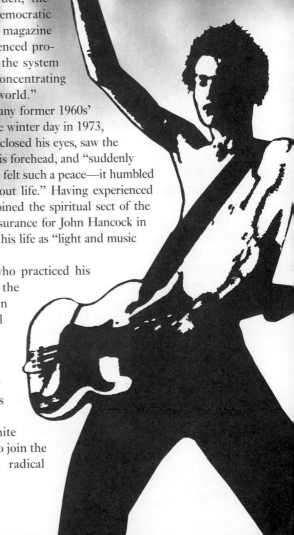

The Era of Excess

14

> 66 You can't make a revolution if
> you have to make a living. 99
> —John Sinclair

"It's a very selfish decade," Tom Hayden, the cofounder of the radical Students for a Democratic Society (SDS), complained to *Newsweek* magazine in 1977. "It's all me. People who experienced profound disappointment trying to change the system are jogging and growing vegetables and concentrating on brightening their own corners of the world."

During the mid- and late 1970s, many former 1960s' radicals turned inward for fulfillment. One winter day in 1973, Rennie Davis, the other founder of SDS, closed his eyes, saw the bright light of the mythic "third eye" in his forehead, and "suddenly I was in a place no words could describe. I felt such a peace—it humbled me and shattered all my assumptions about life." Having experienced transcendental Consciousness Four, he joined the spiritual sect of the guru Maharaj Ji and began selling life insurance for John Hancock in Denver. Four years later, Davis described his life as "light and music and vibration."

Jerry Rubin, the radical yippie who practiced his guerrilla theater of the absurd during the late 1960s, underwent a similar rebirth. In 1970, Rubin began to question his radical beliefs and by 1977 lived in a Manhattan high-rise apartment, feasted on vitamin pills and health food, jogged regularly, and attended seminars about money consciousness. He hoped to be "as Establishment as I can possibly get."

John Sinclair, the head of the White Panther Party who exhorted MC5 fans to join the revolution, became disillusioned with radical politics after a prison term and parenthood. The "Left, man, I'm just not interested anymore," Sinclair, dressed in a suit and tie, told *Newsweek*. "You can't make a revolution if you have to make a living."

The "Me" Decade

An end to the war in Vietnam, disillusionment with politics, and a sometimes booming economy helped transform 1960s' radicals into 1970s' yuppies. The war in Vietnam, escalating steadily throughout the 1960s, ended by the early 1970s. In January 1973, the United States signed the Paris Peace Accord, a formal peace treaty with North Vietnam, leaving behind 56,555 dead American soldiers. Six months later, Congress ended the military draft. By April 30, 1975, the United States had withdrawn all troops and military advisors from Vietnam and Cambodia, an action that satisfied one of the last major demands of college-age radicals.

As the war in Vietnam came to a close, Richard M. Nixon, who had first attracted national prominence for his strident, anticommunist stance during the McCarthy hearings, was reelected to the presidency by voters in forty-nine of fifty states. He defeated George McGovern, the liberal senator and former college professor who had been championed by radicalized college-age youths. Coupled with an end to the war, the reelection of Nixon deflated the rage and blunted the resolve of college radicals. As Rennie Davis contended, "Suddenly that collective energy was gone. The war was over and Nixon had just been reelected. People just found themselves living lives—settling in, getting a job because you had to buy food and pay the rent."

A new crop of college students in the mid-1970s, the last of the baby-boom generation, focused their energies on immediate, material concerns. The students, a senior from Boston University told *Time* in late 1974, were "seeking tangible, not spiritual, returns from their investment in a university." Oriented toward financially rewarding careers, they began to enroll in business administration and engineering classes, bypassing the history, English, and philosophy courses so popular only a few years earlier. "The mood here is, 'I'm here for me,'" remarked senior Steve Ainsworth, editor of UCLA's *Daily Bruin*. During the 1970s, *Time* magazine characterized baby boomers in general as "the Self-Centered Generation."

A growing economy allowed the baby boomers to indulge themselves. Although beset by a temporary economic downturn and inflated prices after the Vietnam War, Americans enjoyed increased real disposable income, which during the 1970s rose 28.5 percent, and allowed many baby boomers, graduating from college and entering the white-collar workforce, to satisfy their fantasies. Having more money to spend, baby boomers embraced the full array of new consumer products introduced during the 1970s. They bought automatic garage door openers, hot tubs, food processors, air-conditioned cars, snowmobiles, and ten-speed bicycles.

Many self-indulgent boomers sought pleasure through drugs, which only a few years earlier had been considered weapons to break down barriers and change the social order. "Drugs have become co-opted by the consumer society," asserted LSD guru Timothy Leary in 1976. "Drugs are now just another thing people can buy to make themselves feel one way or another."

Though by 1975 smoking marijuana had been decriminalized in states such as Alaska and Oregon, baby boomers began to indulge in the more expensive, ego-enhancing cocaine, the drug introduced to the U.S. market in 1886 by John Styth Pemberton, who mixed it with caffeine for a syrup he called Coca-Cola. As early as 1973, more than 4.8 million Americans had sampled the drug, which *Time* magazine labeled "tyrannical King Coke." "Why the fad?" asked the magazine. "For one thing, smoking pot has become commonplace, even passé, and some people look for new thrills."

Some baby boomers sought excitement in their personal relationships, especially through open sexual relations, which had continued to expand since the 1960s. Singles, a category that doubled to 1.3 million during the decade, spent $40 billion a year to meet ready partners. More than a few married boomers discussed open marriage, engaged in wife swapping, and joined free sex clubs such as the Sandstone in Los Angeles, which sought the "membership of stable couples, young middle-class sensualists who believed that their personal relationships would be enhanced, rather than shattered, by the elimination of sexual possessiveness."

Some homosexuals, becoming more open and vocal about their sexual orientation, experimented with many sexual partners. In June 1969, when homosexuality remained illegal in every state except Illinois, gays at the Stonewall Inn in Greenwich Village resisted police arrest and rioted. Spurred by the protest, gays banded together in the Gay Liberation Front and began to publish newspapers such as *Come Out!*, which called for gay power. In December 1969, gays founded the Gay Activist Alliance and the *Gay Activist* to highlight gender politics. At the turn of the decade, homosexuals read other newspapers such as *Gay Sunshine*, *Gay*, and *Gay Power*. By the late 1970s, the Institute for Sex Research discovered that 6 percent of single men considered themselves homosexual, and another 5 percent had at least one homosexual experience after age nineteen. Among single women, 5 percent considered themselves lesbians, and another 13 percent had at least one homosexual encounter as an adult.

Many of these homosexuals, especially men, practiced unrestrained sex. Though 50 percent of gay men enjoyed a steady relationship at the time of the Institute study, gay men confessed to having sex with a stranger 80 percent of the time, 30 percent admitted to "cruising" in parks, and 28 percent contended that they had engaged in sex with more than 1,000 different partners. As with the heterosexual population, many gays became absorbed by their own search for pleasure.

The baby boomers, preoccupied with their own needs, chased the dream of self-perfection. They aimed at "changing one's personality—remaking, remodeling, elevating, and polishing one's very self . . . and observing, studying, and doting on it," wrote Tom Wolfe in his influential essay "The Me Decade." Some trekked to Big Sur, California, where they paid $200 a week to attend the Esalen Institute, which, in the words of Tom Wolfe, promised "lube jobs for the personality." Others flocked to Oscar Ichazo's Arica or Werner Erhard's EST sessions to purge themselves through abuse and self-deprivation. A few expelled personal demons and discovered themselves through primal scream therapy. Unlike the hippies, who informally met with friends to discuss changing the social system, the baby-boom generation in the 1970s paid money for encounter sessions that delved into the individual psyches of the participants. In their material possessions, their intimate relationships, and their self-explorations, 1970s' baby boomers became obsessed with their own desires and sometimes excessive cravings.

Elton John

Elton John mirrored the extravagance of the era, serving as the transitional figure from the early 1970s' sensitive singer to the mid-1970s' excessive rock star. One of the most commercially successful and atypical of the 1970s' acoustic solo acts, pianist John (b. Reginald Dwight) was raised in England and as a teen joined the blues group Bluesology. In 1967, he auditioned for Liberty Records and, at the suggestion of the label, teamed with songwriter Bernie Taupin. Two years later, John released his debut album, and in 1970 charted with a Top-Five, self-titled effort, which featured a gospel-influenced piano sound and the sensitive ballads of Taupin. Throughout the 1970s, he crafted six singles that became number-one hits. Between 1972 and 1975, the singer recorded six number-one albums and became the first act since the Beatles to place four albums in the Top Ten simultaneously.

Unlike the subdued 1970s' singer-songwriters who generally strummed their guitars with few flourishes, Elton John developed a wild stage act that included handstands on the piano and kicking over the piano bench. "I'm pretty much making up for lost time," he told an interviewer. "Not having had a real teenage life, I'm living those

Elton John. *Permission by Cam Garrett.*

thirteen to nineteen years now. Mentally I may be twenty-eight, but somewhere half of me is still thirteen."

John complemented his antics with extravagant costumes. Many times he wore sequined, gaudy jumpsuits, platform shoes, and pink boas. He sported his trademark outrageous glasses, owning more than 200 pairs, including mink-lined glasses, diamond-inlaid spectacles, and a pair with fifty-seven tiny lightbulbs that spelled ELTON. "I love . . . to wear great, feathery costumes—and I do it," revealed the singer. "It's like an actor getting into his costume for his part. I don't really feel that part until I'm into whatever I'm going to wear." Though specializing in sensitive ballads such as "Your Song," played on an acoustic instrument during the early 1970s, John reflected the theatrical extravagance that characterized the "me" generation of the mid- and late 1970s. He confessed, "If I do it, I do it to extreme excess."

Heavy-Metal Theater

A theatrical, glittery, sometimes androgynous heavy metal, exemplified by David Bowie, epitomized 1970s' rock-and-roll excess. Born David Jones, a teenaged Bowie joined a number of rock outfits with little commercial success. In 1966, he changed his name to avoid confusion with Davy Jones of the Monkees and the next year took mime and dance lessons from a theatrical fringe artist. In 1969, amid the furor over the first moon landing, Bowie released "Space Oddity," which hit the Top Five in Britain.

Bowie began to change his image at the turn of the decade. After backing Marc Bolan, who had begun a glitter-rock craze in England as T-Rex, the singer began to affect an androgynous image, appearing in a dress publicly as well as on the album cover of *The Man Who Sold the World*. In January 1972, Bowie declared his bisexuality to the British music paper the *New Musical Express*, reflecting the 1970s' trend toward an openness about different sexual orientations.

Expanding on his image, Bowie created the bisexual, space-age, glittery persona of Ziggy Stardust. On August 16, 1972, at the Rainbow Theater in London, he materialized from a cloud of dry ice, adorned by a tight-fitting, glimmering jumpsuit, high-topped, sequined hunting boots, and orange-tinted hair. "His eyebrows have vanished, replaced by finely sketched red lines. He's wearing red eye shadow which makes him look faintly insectlike," wrote the *New Musical Express*. "The only thing that shocks now is an extreme," explained the singer about his space-age character. "Unless you do that, nobody will pay attention to you. Not for long. You have to hit them on the head."

"We were coming out of the whole hippie thing, which was very much a dressed-down thing, denimy, T-shirts, grungy," suggested Mick Rock, Bowie's photographer at the time. "David was technicolor compared to this gray/blue/brown world. He was also sexual—a very decadent thing that would come to influence even brick layers."

The shocking image of Ziggy Stardust began to sell. After having only limited success with his previous albums, Bowie sold more than one million copies of *The Rise and Fall of Ziggy Stardust and the Spiders from Mars*, which featured a hard-rocking band anchored by guitarist Mick Ronson. The next year he topped the British chart and hit the Top Twenty with *Aladdin Sane* and began to chart with previous albums such as *Hunky Dory*.

The heavy-metal androgyny of Ziggy Stardust gave direction to the careers of other bands such as Mott the Hoople. Begun in 1969 as a hard-rock outfit led by singer Ian Hunter, Mott the Hoople initially released four poor-selling albums and then disbanded. On the eve of their dissolution, in March 1972, they met David Bowie, a longtime fan of the group, who offered them one of his songs, "All the Young Dudes." The band, agreeing to wear 9-inch platform shoes, heavy mascara, and sequined costumes, recorded the hard-rocking song, which hit the charts in both Britain and the United States and became a gay-liberation anthem. "We were considered instant fags," remembered the heterosexual Hunter. "A lot of gays followed us around, especially in America." Reinforcing its image with songs such as "Sucker" and "One of the Boys," the group climbed the charts in 1974 with *The Hoople* and *Mott the Hoople—Live*.

Iggy Pop revitalized his career by following the advice of David Bowie. The young Pop, born James Osterberg, traveled from his native Michigan to Chicago, where he briefly played drums for electric-blues artists. Upon returning to Ann Arbor

Iggy Pop. *Permission by* The Daily *of The University of Washington.*

in 1967, he formed the Stooges, who debuted at a Halloween party, and during the next three years they recorded two slashing, hard-driving, proto-punk LPs that failed to chart. Disconsolate, Iggy moved to Florida, where he cut lawns for a living.

In 1972, on a trip to New York, Iggy met Bowie and manager Tony DeFries, who persuaded Pop to reform the Stooges under DeFries's management and Bowie's guidance. The Stooges, continuing their trademark live performances, unleashed wild theatrical shows. "Iggy had gone beyond performance—to the point where it was really some kind of psychodrama," observed John Sinclair, manager of the MC5. "It exceeded conventional theater. He might do *anything*. That was his act." In April 1973, Iggy and the Stooges released *Raw Power*, which showcased the thrashing guitar of James Williamson and on the cover pictured a shirtless Iggy with bleached-blonde hair, heavy makeup, dark red lipstick, eye shadow, and silver-lamé, skin-tight studded pants. Though disbanding within a year after the album's release, the Stooges served as a model for late 1970s' punk, and Iggy became a collaborator with Bowie, writing "Jean Genie" for the singer.

Lou Reed also collaborated with Bowie for a new direction. After quitting the Velvet Underground in August 1970, the New Yorker went into seclusion at his parents' home in Long Island. In 1972, Reed met Bowie, who encouraged him to pursue a solo career. He began to perform with bleached-blonde hair, makeup, and black fingernail polish. In April 1973, Reed recorded the Bowie-produced album *Transformer*, which on the cover pictured a prominent New York drag queen and included the Top Twenty "Walk on the Wild Side," a song about a transvestite, which became Reed's first pop hit. The next year he earned his first gold album with the live, hard-edged *Rock 'n' Roll Animal*.

The New York Dolls adopted the Bowie-defined image of heavy-metal androgyny. Formed in 1971 and fronted by guitarist Johnny Thunders and singer David Johansen, the group began playing locally at clubs such as the Mercer Arts Center. In 1973, they released their first album, which included thrashing, driving, proto-punk anthems such as "Personality Crisis." On the cover, done in gray and shocking pink with the band's name written in lipstick, the group posed with heavy makeup, jewelry, and ruby lipstick. Johansen, with a shoulder thrust forward, stared wistfully into the mirror of his powder box. The other group members looked straight ahead, attired in 6-inch heeled boots, skin-tight leather or spandex pants, and provocative blouses. "We liked dressing up, which was kind of like a thing that was happening in the Village anyway," explained Johansen, "like mixing and matching and going to thrift stores and wearing man-tailored jackets that were made for Marlene Dietrich."

On stage, the New York Dolls delivered a wild, extreme heavy-metal act. They "were totally outrageous. They were setting the pace," remarked rock photographer Bob Gruen. In one show that Gruen witnessed, the band appeared in "cellophane tutus with army boots. They mixed the genders. . . . The Dolls blew up more equipment than anybody because they were just over the top. They did everything to the fullest, to the maximum."

Kiss tried to outdo the New York Dolls, their cross-town rivals. "In 1972 there was only one impressive band in New York and that was the New York Dolls," remembered Gene Simmons, the former schoolteacher who started Kiss. "I was impressed mostly by their stage presence, and the fact that they didn't look like other American bands." He added: "We were extremely jealous of the New York Dolls and we were going to do them one better."

To grab attention, the band, according to Simmons, "decided to put on bizarre makeup. What came out for me was an expression of the superhero/horror/science fiction sort of genre that I'd always admired. . . . [Guitarist] Paul [Stanley's] was kind of the rock star, Eddie Cochran, I-wanna-be-Elvis routine—magnified. [Guitarist] Ace [Frehley] had his space stuff and [drummer] Peter [Criss] his cat stuff." Like cartoon characters, the face-painted group began to dress in skin-hugging, bejeweled, spandex pants, platform shoes, and black, glittering, leather shirts. Coached by ex-television producer Bill Aucoin, Kiss assaulted their audiences with rockets, police lights, snow machines, smoke bombs, and levitating drum kits. By 1975, when they released the million-selling albums *Dressed to Kill* and *Alive!*, the hard-rock band had become one of America's hottest acts. As with their counterparts in the 1970s, Kiss avoided any political messages. Some bands "get heavily into politics and political issues, which we try to stay clear of," explained Ace Frehley. "We're just entertainers."

Alice Cooper matched Kiss with overtly sexual, heavy-metal, apolitical rock theatrics. Born Vince Furnier, Cooper formed his first band with a group of high school friends. On Halloween 1967 at the Cheetah club in Los Angeles, the band followed the Grateful Dead and the Jefferson Airplane, with Cooper wearing Janis Joplin's gold lamé pants, high-heeled boots, and black mascara. "Everyone was taking acid, and peace and love, but when they got us, we were anything but peace and love," explained Cooper. "We were more sensational. We were the *National Enquirer* of rock-'n'-roll." In the audience, Shep Gordon, the manager for Frank Zappa, attentively watched the spectacle. Gordon told Zappa that Alice Cooper had emptied the club in a few minutes with their act, and an interested Zappa auditioned the group. "Frank loved us," gushed Cooper. "He thought our ability to drive people out of there was great." Zappa signed the band to his Straight Records, which released the largely unnoticed *Pretties for You* (1969) and *Easy Action* (1970).

The band slowly began to attract more attention through sensationalist tactics. In 1971, they released the hard-rock album *Love It to Death*, which included the hit "Eighteen" and on the cover showed Cooper's thumb suggestively thrusting through a 3-inch-wide ring. Late the same year, they released the Top Twenty-Five *Killer*. Having more money and encouraged by new manager Shep Gordon, the group attracted an even larger audience through an elaborate show that included throwing live chickens into the crowd, axing off the heads of dolls, staging mock executions in fake electric chairs, Cooper draping himself with a live boa constrictor, and beating fans over the heads with 6-foot-long, inflated phalluses.

By 1973, when they released the number-one *Billion Dollar Babies*, the group had become one of the preeminent practitioners of rock theater. On a tour that grossed more than $6 million in a few months, they simulated a beheading, a hanging, an electrocution, a dismemberment, and a transformation of Cooper into a bloodsucking vampire. "I didn't feel that people went to rock shows to be preached to," sniffed Cooper. "I go to shows to escape. I hated the idea of going to something, and having people tell me what I should do about Vietnam. What we were doing was saying, 'Go have fun.'" The bandleader added: "I would like to think that Alice Cooper opened the door to theatrics. We were sort of the band that drove the stake through the heart of the love generation."

Queen nearly rivaled Alice Cooper in extravagance. Formed in 1971 by guitarist Brian May and drummer Roger Taylor, the band featured vocalist Freddie Mercury (b. Farok Bulsara), who named the band. "I'd had the idea of calling a group Queen for a long time," he asserted. "It was a very strong name, very universal and very immediate; it had a lot of visual potential." Sometimes Mercury favored dresses, tights, and black nail polish, modeling his demeanor after one of his idols, pop singer Liza Minnelli. In other shows, Mercury wore leather storm-trooper outfits that emphasized the gay connotation of the band's name. The *New York Times* referred to Mercury's act as "strutting and preening, by turns campy and almost militaristic." "Of all the more theatrical rock performers, Freddie took it further than the rest," explained David Bowie, who collaborated with Mercury on the 1981 hit "Under Pressure." "He took it over the edge. And of course, I always admired a man who wears tights."

Queen produced a dramatic music equal to its theatrical stage shows. After securing a following in Britain during 1973 and 1974, the band hit the U.S. Top Five with *A Night at the Opera* (1975), which included the operatic heavy metal of "Bohemian Rhapsody." In 1977, they neared the top of the charts with *News of the World*, featuring the militaristic thump of "We Will Rock You" and the dramatic-sounding, self-important "We Are the Champions." By the end of the decade, Queen had fashioned a sound and an act that reflected the escapist, extravagant "me" generation. "With the revolt long since gone out of the music," observed *Time*, "what is left is really a new kind of vaudeville or sometimes a freak show."

Art Pop in the Arena

The extravagant stage antics of mid-seventies' rock fit well with the venue that became the staple of the "Me Generation": the arena. During the folk boom and the surf craze, acts generally played in small, intimate clubs. British invaders graduated to 1,000- to 5,000-seat auditoriums and only amid the height of Beatlemania did the Fab Four perform at such places as Shea Stadium. Psychedelic bands played at local halls such as the Fillmore and the Avalon ballrooms, where light shows could be projected on the walls and the bands mingled with the fans. By the mid to late 1970s as rock performances became bigger business, shows moved to large sports arenas, where smoke-bomb explosions, fake decapitations, and outlandish costumes appeared apropos to thousands of cheering fans. Like the gladiator contests in ancient Rome, the event had moved to the Coliseum.

These arenas, separating the audience from the performer, gave rise to a new genre of art rock, sometimes disparagingly called arena rock. Suitable to a larger-than-life, flashy era, this music abandoned the intricate, sometimes muted textures and piano stylings of the original art rockers for the slick production of hook-laden, melodramatic songs about lost love and bygone eras. High-pitched vocalists beckoned their listeners with an exaggerated art pop that included flourishes of classical accents.

Assaulting and capturing the Top Ten near the late 1970s, art-pop bands played in venues such as Madison Square Garden, dominated the airwaves, and sold millions of records. Kansas, signed by music mogul Don Kirshner in 1973, patiently played small venues until early 1977, when they reached the Top Ten with *Leftoverture* and the single "Carry On Wayward Son." They achieved their greatest success with *Point of Know Return* (1977), which included the smash "Dust in the Wind." After four chart failures, the Chicago-based Styx hit the Top Ten in 1977 with *The Grand Illusion*. In quick succession, they added three more Top-Ten efforts, including the chart-topping *Paradise Theater*. Led by former Santana guitarist Neal Schon, Journey turned from a jazz-tinged art rock by enlisting the help of Queen producer Thomas Baker, who in 1978 produced the slick platinum pop of *Infinity*. Supertramp similarly replaced intricate soundscapes with the irresistible pop gem *Breakfast in America* (1979), which topped the chart and sold eighteen million copies. Boston, the brain-child of basement-studio wizard Tom Scholz, filled coliseums with the expansive pop of two top-sellers, including the number-one *Don't Look Back* (1978). By the end of the seventies, the radio-friendly art-pop snagged listeners, leading them to immense arenas that accommodated art pop's full-blown, enveloping sound.

Funk from Outer Space

During the mid-1970s, George Clinton covered funk with heavy-metal glitter. Funk, the stripped-down gospel blues that featured an insistent rhythm, punchy horns, and repetitious, drumlike vocals, had been unveiled by James Brown. In 1964, Brown shifted from a gospel-drenched soul to a minimalistic funk on "Out of Sight" and the next year perfected his new style with "Papa's Got a Brand New Bag." After 1967, Brown completed his transition to funk when he hired musical director Albert Ellis and new musicians such as bassist Bootsy Collins, drummer Clyde Stubblefield, saxophonist Maceo Parker, guitarist Jimmy Nolan, and horn man Fred Wesley. "I emphasized the beat, not the melody, understand?" explained Brown. "Heat the beat, and the rest'll turn sweat." The singer charted with funky singles such as "Cold Sweat," "Get Up, I Feel Like Being a Sex Machine," and "Hot Pants." "Funk," observed bassist William "Billy Bass" Nelson, "comes from James Brown. And James Brown got it from the blues."

Sly Stone (a.k.a. Sylvester Stewart) combined funk with rock-and-roll. As a child, Stewart moved with his family from Texas to San Francisco, where he sang in gospel groups and studied trumpet. During the flowering of hippiedom, he landed jobs as a disc jockey on station KDIA and as a producer for Autumn Records, where he mixed the psychedelic music of the Mojo Men and the Great Society, which included Grace Slick. In 1966, Stewart formed the racially integrated Sly and the Family Stone with his brother Freddie on guitar; his sister Rosie, who added gospel-inflected vocals; trumpeter Cynthia Robinson, his cousin; bass player Larry Graham, Jr., who had played with the Drifters, John Lee Hooker, and several gospel groups; and cousins Jerry Martini on saxophone and Greg Errico on drums.

Sly and the Family Stone combined their rock and funk influences with a psychedelic sensibility to top the charts. Though flopping with their debut, the band hit with "Dance to the Music" (1968). The next year, Sly and the Family Stone topped the chart with "Everyday People," hit number two with "Hot Fun in the Summertime," and neared the Top Ten with the politically charged *Stand!*, which included "You Can Make It If You Try," and "Don't Call Me Nigger, Whitey (Don't Call Me Whitey, Nigger)." "It was just a recognition of all the racial tensions that were happening," recalled Martini. During the next two years, after an appearance at Woodstock, the group again reached the top of the charts with the funky classics "Thank You (Falettinme Be Mice Elf Agin)," "Family Affair," and *There's a Riot Goin' On*. "It was Sly who first cracked the barrier between black-and-white rock," observed funkmaster George Clinton.

George Clinton took Sly's funk rock into the extravagant mid-1970s. In 1955, a fifteen-year-old Clinton started the Parliaments, a doo-wop group that performed on the streets of New Jersey. Eight years later on the urging of Clinton who had landed a job as a staff writer for Berry Gordy, Jr.'s Jobete Music, the group relocated to Detroit, where they recorded unreleased tracks for Motown. In 1967, amid the soul explosion, the Parliaments finally hit the Top Twenty with "(I Wanna) Testify."

On the road to promote the hit single, Clinton changed the direction of his band. The leader, forced to use the equipment of a rock band, "went out and bought Jimi Hendrix's *Are You Experienced?*, Cream's album, a Richie Havens record, and Sly's *A Whole New Thing*. I gave them to Eddie [Hazel, guitarist] and Billy [Nelson, bassist] in the band." After fusing hard-rock sounds to their funky base, Clinton created a stage show similar to the onstage antics of fellow Detroiters Iggy and the Stooges. "It was like the Stooges!" Clinton remembered. "I had a head with a dick shaved onto it right down the middle with a star on one side and a moon on the other and bald all around that. I was crawling all around on the floor sticking my tongue out. We were James Brown on acid. . . ."

During the 1970s, Clinton solidified the funky rock sound of his band. Threatened with a lawsuit over the name Parliament, he began to call the group Funkadelic and added ex–James Brown sidemen such as William "Bootsy" Collins, Fred Wesley, and Maceo Parker. By the mid-1970s, when he had regained the right to the Parliament name, Clinton had created a hard funk-rock amalgam with Parliament and, to some extent, with Funkadelic, which he continued as a more rock-oriented outfit. "We got Fred [Wesley] and Maceo [Parker] on the horns and Bootsy [Collins] and all that power in the bass. They had been with James Brown." recalled Clinton. "And then on the other side we had doo-wop, Motown, Jimi Hendrix, rock-'n'-roll white groups."

In tune with the times, Clinton changed his stage image during the mid-1970s. "By the time I got the name Parliament back, I knew the psychedelic thing was all but gone. So I went with glitter." Touring to promote his breakthrough *Mothership Connection* (1976), Clinton and his band appeared Bowie-like, garbed in leather space-suits, gogglelike sunglasses, and jewel-studded boots. He hired Jules Fisher, who had designed overblown stage sets for Bowie and Kiss, to create a huge spaceship that descended to the stage from a denim cap. "Black [audiences] have never experienced a really loud group, let alone all these theatrics," enthused Clinton. "You cannot make sense and be funky. We take the heaviness out of being profound." Several years earlier, he already had instructed his listeners to "Free Your Mind and Your Ass Will

Follow." The funk-rock master had accurately gauged the rock audience, who bought millions of Top-Twenty Parliament albums such as *The Clones of Dr. Funkenstein* (1976), *Funkentelechy vs. the Placebo Syndrome* (1977), and *Flash Light* (1978).

Disco

Disco, a simplified version of funk, epitomized 1970s' excess. It began in New York City at African-American, Latin, and gay all-night clubs such as the Sanctuary, the Loft, and the Gallery, where disc jockeys played nonstop dance music with an insistent, funky, thumping beat. Favoring Philadelphia soul sounds, jockeys such as Francis Grosso, David Mancuso, and Nicky Siano expertly mixed records with new techniques to bring dancers to a fever pitch. They hoped to create an underground community centered around the music. "I view the whole scene as a spiritual congregation," DJ David Rodriguez said. "You've got hundreds of people in a room, and their bond is the music. There isn't any tension between gays and straights; the common denominator is the music."

Gradually disco incorporated the antiseptic, rock-steady, electronic beat of European synthesizer groups such as Kraftwerk, which, according to group founder Ralf Hutter, consisted of "industrial music; not so much mental or meditative music, but rhythmically more primitive." Gloria Gaynor, one of the first disco recording stars, felt that "it was kind of hard for white people to get into R&B music because the beat is so sophisticated and hard for the kind of dancing that white people are used to doing. This clearly defined beat that is so apparent in disco music now makes it easier to learn to do our kind of dancing."

By the mid-1970s, disco emerged from the New York underground to become a commercialized, theatrical event for self-obsessed baby boomers, who yearned for center stage. "A few years ago, I went into clubs, and I realized people needed mood music," remarked Neil Bogart, then president of Casablanca Records. "They were tired of guitarists playing to their amplifiers. *They* wanted to be the stars."

Disco, unlike most rock-and-roll, allowed the participants to assume primary importance. Not involving musicians standing on stage, it centered on the audience. "It's like an adult Disney World. We really give people a chance to get off on their fantasies," explained Steve Rubell, co-owner of one of the premier discos, Studio 54 in New York City. "I think the theater atmosphere has a lot to do with it. Everybody secretly likes to be on stage, and here we give them a huge space to do it all on." Discos should let "everyone feel like a star," echoed Mark Hugo, manager of a Boston disco.

The various elements of the popularized disco culture embodied the narcissism of the mid- and late 1970s. Discotheques, *Time* told its readers in 1977, offered "a space-age world of mesmeric lighting and Neroian decor." Studio 54, once the baroque Fortune Gallo Opera House, featured theatrical lighting, flashing strobes, and more than 450 special effects, including plastic snowfalls and 85-foot backdrops. Zorine's in Chicago offered members rooms of mirrors, twisting staircases, balconies, and secret nooks. In Los Angeles, Dillion's boasted four floors, which were monitored on closed-circuit television. Pisces in Washington, D.C., had old movie sets, a 1,000-gallon, shark-filled aquarium, and exotic flora.

The clothing of the dancers reflected glittery opulence and a freewheeling attitude toward sex. Men sported gold chains, gold rings, patent leather platform shoes, tight Italian-style pants, and unbuttoned shiny satin shirts. Women wore low-cut, backless, sequined gowns, spiked heels, long gold necklaces, and gold lamé gloves. "The new boogie bunch dress up for the occasion—with shoulders, backs, breasts, and midriffs tending to be nearly bare," observed *Time*. In a disco, where the participants became the stars, remarked photographer Francesco Scavullo, "the dress becomes your dancing partner."

The dances, notably Le Freak, which was popularized by a song of the same name by premier disco group Chic, exhibited an unrestrained sexuality. The exotic dance consisted of two people spreading their legs, bending their backs backward, and thrusting their pelvises against each other in time to the music. Disco, reasoned Nile Rodgers, who cowrote "Le Freak" for Chic, "was the most hedonistic music I had ever heard in my life. It was really all about Me! Me! Me! Me!"

The sexual openness of disco began in gay clubs. "It was definitely R&B dance music. That's where it originated," remembered Nile Rodgers. "Then it took on more blatant overtones because of the gay movement."

As part of gay culture, disco served as a focal point for gay liberation. "The music is a symbolic call for gays to come out of the closet and dance with each other," explained Nat Freedland of Fantasy Records. It allowed gays, who many times owned and worked as the disc jockeys and lighting crews at prominent New York discos, to become highly visible and respected for their creative achievements. It also allowed gay musicians such as Sylvester to step into the limelight.

The disco culture involved the use of drugs, especially cocaine. When asked about drug use at Studio 54, Steve Rubell replied, "What can I tell you? We look the other way. Anyway, so many people are taking pills these days how do I know if it's an aspirin or something else?" As one of its special effects, the New York disco displayed a man in the moon with a spoon uplifted to his nose.

The discos, trading in excess, tried to lure celebrities to their doors. Studio 54 hired socialite Carmen D'Alessio to entice her rich and famous friends to the club. "It's all the celebrities," explained Rubell. "You have to have them first. They draw business in." He successfully added Cher, actress Farrah Fawcett, actor Warren Beatty, Christina Onassis, Woody Allen, and David Bowie to the guest list. Pisces in Washington, D.C., attracted stars such as Elizabeth Taylor and actor Gregory Peck. In Los Angeles, Pip's lured actors Paul Newman, Peter Falk, and Tony Curtis as well as singer Frank Sinatra.

The star-studded disco became a craze near the end of the decade. In late 1977, Robert Stigwood, owner of RSO records, filmed the movie *Saturday Night Fever*, which showed the transformation of a poor, trouble-ridden, Italian teenager, played by John Travolta, into a white-suited disco star. He built the soundtrack of the film around songs written and performed by one of his groups, the Bee Gees. By 1978, the record executive had scored a major success with the movie and had sold more than thirty million copies of the soundtrack worldwide.

Discomania spread across the country in the wake of *Saturday Night Fever*. In New York, more than 1,000 discos opened their doors for business. The Holiday Inn motel chain added more than thirty-five discos on its premises. A $100,000 disco even opened in the small town of Fennimore, Wisconsin (population: 1,900). High schoolers went to disco proms and disco roller-skating rinks. One disco in Dubuque, Iowa, provided a disco wedding service complete with smoke-machine effects. Throughout the country in 1978, more than thirty-six million Americans danced on the floors of 20,000 discos.

John Travolta's famous arm-thrusting pose in his all-white suit from *Saturday Night Fever*, 1977. Photo by Paramount. *Permission by Picture Desk, Inc./Kobal Collection.*

Records especially made for disco, first popularized in 1975 with "Never Can Say Goodbye" by Gloria Gaynor, began to sell. The acknowledged queen of disco, Donna Summer, almost topped the chart in 1976 with the suggestive "Love to Love You Baby," which was punctuated by Summer's sighs and groans, and followed with a series of disco smashes. The Village People, named after a gay enclave in Greenwich Village in New York City, consisted of a costumed band of actors and singers portraying stereotypes of the rugged American male. The band, manufactured by French producer Jacques Morali, hit the chart in 1978 and 1979 with the million-selling gay anthems "Macho Man" and "Y.M.C.A." Even established artists such as Rod Stewart and the Rolling Stones released disco-influenced songs. In 1978, *Billboard* categorized more than 20 percent of songs on the singles chart as disco. "Disco will be the major force in the music marketplace for some time," predicted Nat Freedland of Fantasy Records.

By the end of the decade, disco had become a lucrative business. Besides record sales, it involved products such as spandex pants, magazines like *Discothekin'*, disco dresses slit to expose the thighs, more than 200 disco radio stations from Los Angeles to Miami, and undersized disco purses. Discos such as Studio 54 netted yearly profits of $800,000. "The profits are astronomical," enthused Steve Rubell. "Only the Mafia does better." By 1979, disco, a mirror for the excesses of the rock generation, was a $5 billion industry.

Corporate Rock

The record business, buttressed by the increasing number of materialistic, disco-crazed baby boomers, consolidated into a few highly profitable international companies, which dominated the marketplace. During the 1950s, American business in general started to consolidate. By 1955, the fifty largest corporations controlled 27 percent of the national market and sold more than $86 billion of manufactured goods, a figure equal to more than one-fourth of the gross national product. The trend to merge continued, until by 1970 the market share of the 600 largest companies increased to 75 percent, and the share held by the top 200 corporations rose to more than 60 percent. The 102 giants on top of the corporate pyramid, holding assets of $1 billion or more, controlled 48 percent of the U.S. market and made 53 percent of the profits.

The record industry followed the pattern of consolidation. Though influenced by a number of viable independent companies such as Chess and Sun during the 1950s, by 1973 the record business was almost completely controlled by seven majors: CBS, Capitol, MCA, Polygram, RCA, A&M, and Warner Communications. The top four companies accounted for more than 52 percent of all record and tape sales, and the leading two—CBS and Warner-Elektra/Asylum-Atlantic—sold 38 percent of the total product manufactured by the industry.

These companies, as with other American conglomerates during the decade, had interests in fields other than music. MCA owned Universal Films, various television stations, Arlington and Mount Vernon cemeteries, a bank in Colorado, and the Spencer Gifts novelty chain. RCA, the twentieth largest corporation in the country, operated NBC television and radio, owned the Hertz Rent-A-Car company, Banquet Foods, the Cushman and Wakefield real estate firm, and Random House and Alfred Knopf publishers. It also served as a prime defense contractor.

These giant corporations built rock-and-roll, which by 1975 accounted for 80 percent of all record sales, into a multibillion-dollar enterprise. In 1950, record companies sold $189 million of product, increasing their gross revenues five years later to $277 million. By 1971, in the United States alone, the industry sold $1.7 billion in records and tapes. Two years later, it grossed $2 billion, which surpassed the gross revenues of Broadway ($36 million), professional sports ($540 million), the film industry ($1.3 billion), and network television ($1 billion). By 1978, the record industry grossed approximately $4 billion.

Many companies posted healthy profits. In the summer quarter of 1978, MCA made a profit of more than $5.5 million, CBS cleared $48.5 million, and Warner netted $19.8 million. "Records are where the big money is in the entertainment business these days," observed *Forbes* in July 1978.

Profits came from around the world. In 1973, the companies sold $2 billion worth of records and tapes in the United States, a per capita expenditure of $9.70. That same year, they sold more than $555 million worth of records and tapes in Japan; $454 million in West Germany; $441 million in the Soviet Union; $384 million in the United Kingdom, controlled largely by the British Electrical Manufacturing Industries (EMI); and even $16 million in Poland. Per capita expenditures amounted to $7.57 in West Germany, $6.91 in the Netherlands, $7.69 in Sweden, and $5.14 in Japan. By the end of the decade, the corporate rock establishment had penetrated nearly every world market to amass excessive profits in an excessive age.

Some 1970s' rock stars eagerly embraced the international music business. Gene Simmons of Kiss equated a "successful rock-and-roll band" with "a well-oiled machine. It's a good business." Observed Columbia Records talent scout Greg Geller as he compared 1960s' and 1970s' rock performers, "Now artists are more up front about admitting that they are interested in selling some records. This is not an ivory-tower age: there's some recognition that we're involved in commerce."

Some of the performers worked with the music corporations to become millionaires. For Alice Cooper, "The idea all along was to make $1 million. Otherwise the struggle wouldn't have been worth it. . . . I am the most American rock act. I have American ideals. I love money."

Many rock stars realized their financial goals. In 1973, *Forbes* estimated that at least fifty rock superstars earned between $2 million and $6 million a year, with each musician accumulating from three to seven times more than the highest-paid executive in the United States.

Many successful 1970s' stars invested their earnings. The Bee Gees, one of the largest draws of the 1970s, established their own merchandising company, which sold "things like nice T-shirts," according to Barry Gibb, who with his twin brothers Maurice and Robin started the band. "We deal in jewelry but only real gold plate. We're doing a little electronic piano with Mattel Toys that'll be available soon." They also marketed "a cute Andy Gibb doll" to promote the career of their younger brother. Alice Cooper financed films such as *Funny Lady* and *Shampoo* for tax shelters and invested in art, antiques, and tax-free municipal bonds. Ted Nugent, the guitarist who scaled the charts during the 1970s with a heavy-metal sound and Neanderthal costumes, owned a mink farm and a trout operation. Said Bob Weed, Nugent's financial manager, "all of this fits in with Ted's plan for acquiring land. Sure, we're involved in some oil and gas-lease tax shelters, but when I tell him about property, that's something he understands." Rod Stewart, the blues singer turned disco star, adopted a similar investment strategy. "I've always said that Rod isn't a rock star. He's a growth industry," remarked Billy Gaff, Stewart's manager. "Rod is essentially very conservative. He doesn't invest in football clubs or crazy movie- or record-financing schemes. The tax shelter scams are all a little scary, so we stick to art and real estate." By the end of the decade, rock-and-roll had become a big business dominated by millionaire rock stars who provided extravagant entertainment to self-absorbed baby boomers. Soon it would be challenged by the rebellious music of a new generation.

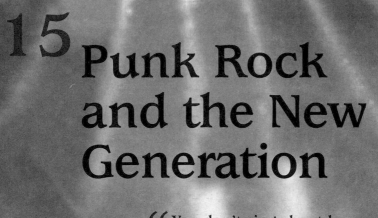

15 Punk Rock and the New Generation

66 You don't sing about love
to people on the dole. 99

—Johnny Rotten

"Punk is so constipated it should be called hemorrhoid rock," snapped Linda Ronstadt to an interviewer. "All that punk singers can bring to the presentations of their songs is the gesture of sexual obscenity or of impotent rage. There is a lot of caged simian gibber," wrote Anthony Burgess, author of the futuristic *A Clockwork Orange*, in 1977. "British youth, like American and French and Upper Slobovian youth, needs a good kick in the pants and a bit of solid education." The *London Times* declared that "punk rock is the generic term for the latest musical garbage bred by our troubled culture. It features screaming, venomous, threatening rock sounds." And Bernard Brook Partridge, a member of the Greater London Council, snarled in late 1976, "What is punk music? It's disgusting, degrading, ghastly, sleazy, prurient, voyeuristic and nauseating," articulating the sentiments of the establishment toward punk rock.

A new generation of rock-and-rollers inspired this outrage. Punk originated with a small group of literary, Beat-influenced musicians in their twenties such as Patti Smith and Richard Hell, who congregated in New York City's seedy Bowery.

Within a year, the pained posture of an artistic punk had been transformed into an anarchic, sometimes political rage by angry British teens who felt that they had nothing to lose. Opposed to the excessive corporate rock of the mid-1970s, they created a minimalistic, angry music that threatened their materialistic baby-boom elders. In 1976, a new generation had arisen to lay claim to a rebellious rock-and-roll heritage.

New York Punk

CBGB's, a small bar in the Bowery section of New York City, served as the birthplace of punk rock. Established in December 1973 by ex–U.S. Marine Sergeant Hilly Kristal, the bar first catered to Bowery bums. "When I first opened it as Hilly's on the Bowery," recalled the proprietor, "I ran it for a while as a derelict bar, and bums would be lining up at eight in the morning when I opened the doors. They would come in and fall on their faces even before they had their first drink." In a few months, Kristal changed the name of his bar to CBGB-OMFUG, which stood for "country, bluegrass, blues, and other music for uplifting gourmandizers."

In 1974, bands such as Television, influenced by the New York avant-garde of Andy Warhol, the Velvet Underground, and the free-jazz improvisations of John Coltrane and Albert Ayler, began to play regularly at CBGB's. Formed in late 1973, Television originally included bassist Richard Hell (b. Richard Myers), who had traveled to New York City to "become a real sophisticated writer"; guitarist Richard Lloyd; drummer Billy Ficca; and vocalist-guitarist Tom Verlaine (b. Tom Miller), who renamed himself after the French symbolist poet. After debuting at the New York Townhouse Theater, the band convinced Andy Warhol associate Terry Ork to manage them. Through the efforts of Ork in early 1974, the group landed a permanent job at CBGB's.

Terry Ork, persuading his artist friends to hear Television, created an avant-garde artistic scene at CBGB's. "He brought in a lot of theater and poetry people from this area, since he lived around here and knew them all," remembered Hilly Kristal. "It wasn't really so much his bookings, but because he knew so many things about theater, film, and art, and he knew all those people. He also had the energy, and he was very excited about the whole thing, and he excited me about it. . . . the whole scene wouldn't have happened without him."

Fellow students at the Rhode Island School of Design, David Byrne, Tina Weymouth, and Chris Franz traveled to New York and in late 1974 began to play together as the Talking Heads, a name found in an issue of *TV Guide*. "We started rehearsing our songs, the songs I had written," remembered Byrne. "I was writing these things, but I didn't know what they were for. I didn't have any plans to put a band together, but there were the songs." Living in an apartment only a few blocks from CBGB's, the Talking Heads auditioned for Hilly Kristal and in May 1975 began to play at the bar. In 1977, the group invited keyboardist Jerry Harrison to play with them and released their debut album, which included the eccentric minor hit "Psycho Killer." "The Heads were great and Television were great, but on a sort of intellectual level," recalled Kristal. "The Heads were so quirky and weird that they set much of the stylistic tone. Not punk, but a transition period."

Patti Smith brought national attention to the literary avant-garde rock that CBGB's had begun to feature. The daughter of a New Jersey factory worker, Smith herself worked in a factory until moving to New York City. Once in town, she worked with photographer Robert Mapplethorpe and playwright Sam Shepard and began to write a William Burroughs–Arthur Rimbaud style of poetry. She regularly read her work at the Mercer Arts Center, publishing two books of poetry, *Witt* and *Seventh Heaven*.

A diehard fan of Jimi Hendrix and Jim Morrison of the Doors and a former writer for the rock magazine *Creem*, Patti Smith combined her poetry with a rock sound. In early 1971, she read her poetry at St. Mark's Church in New York, accompanied by guitarist/rock writer Lenny Kaye, who had assembled the 1960s' proto-punk record compilations, *Nuggets*. "I had this little poem called 'Ballad of a Bad Boy,' which ends in a stock car crash," she related. "And I was thinking that it would be really cool not only to deliver this emotionally, but to illustrate this car crash sonically, with feedback or some Hendrix style of guitar playing."

By March 1974, she had invited pianist Richard Sohl to help Kaye provide an improvisational rock backdrop to her readings. "Of course it was still more of an art thing," Kaye pointed out. "It wasn't even a club circuit. We played with Television." Three months later, Smith recorded the independently produced single "Hey Joe/Piss Factory," which convinced Sire Records to sign the fledgling group. After club dates on the West Coast, Smith added guitarist Ivan Kral and drummer Jay Dee Daugherty to form the Patti Smith Group. "As soon as we [added Kral and Daugherty], we became more of a rock band," observed Lenny Kaye.

In early 1975, the Patti Smith Group brought attention to the emerging scene at CBGB's during a seven-week stint at the club. "What happened was that [as] we played there more and more people came down," said Lenny Kaye. "CBGB's became not only a place for them to come and check us out, but it sort of got into the New York consciousness." Kristal added, "Patti's stay here was one of the most memorable seven-week periods the club ever had. Clive Davis [of Arista Records, which signed Smith in January 1975] came a number of times and a lot of the record people came, but mostly it was newspapers and a lot of people on the periphery of theater and the arts. Those first dates put us on the map." A few months later, the Patti Smith Group released their debut *Horses*, produced by former Velvet Underground leader John Cale, which combined rock history with avant-garde poetry in songs such as "Gloria" and the William Burroughs–inspired "Land of a Thousand Dances." The 1976 follow-up *Radio Ethiopia* similarly featured hard-driving improvisational numbers such as "Pumping (My Heart)" and "Ask the Angels."

Like other New York punks, the poet adopted the vague, Beat-inspired populist stance of the 1960s. She admired "all the great sixties guys" who "had sort of a political consciousness." With her music, Smith was "determined to make us kids, us fuck-ups, us ones who could never get a degree in college, whatever, have a family, or do regular stuff, prove that there's a place for us." Neither a hippie nor a punk, Smith later "thought one could call us a sacrificial bridge between the two. We anticipated the future and sort of encapsulated the past."

RICHARD HELL
& THE VOIDOIDS

BLANK
GENERATION

YOU MAKE ME

Richard Hell. King of New York Punk. Photo by Roberta Bayley. Courtesy of Richard Hell and Sire Records.

Richard Hell helped define the emerging, artistic, do-it-yourself New York rock, which centered around Patti Smith. As a member of Television, Hell created a minimalist, populist image that would characterize punk rock and contrast starkly with the glittery image of David Bowie. Modeling himself after French poets such as Rimbaud, he cut his hair in a short, spiky style and wore ripped T-shirts. "My look was a sort of a strategy," explained the bassist. "I wanted it to look like do-it-yourself. Everything we were doing . . . had that element, from having ripped up clothes to not knowing how to play instruments. The whole thing was partly a reaction to the hippie stadium music." He continued, "I wanted the way we looked to be as expressive as the material on the stage. It was all of a piece. The ripped T-shirts meant that I don't give a fuck about stardom and all that or glamour and going to rock shows to see someone pretend to be perfect. The people wanted to see someone they could identify with. It was saying, 'You could be here, too.'"

Richard Hell also adopted a populist attitude in his songs. He delivered the New York punk anthem "Blank Generation," which he wrote in 1975 and recorded two years later with the Voidoids after leaving Television. "To me, 'blank' is a line where you can fill in anything. It's positive," he told an interviewer. "It's the idea that you have the option of making yourself anything you want, filling in the blank. And that's something that provides a uniquely powerful sense to this generation."

The Ramones, atypical of the artistic CBGB's crowd, added a buzz-saw guitar attack and a 1950s' sensibility to the populist stance and ripped T-shirt fashion of Richard Hell to make a transition from the avant-garde to punk rock. Banding together after playing at a private party in late 1974, Johnny Cummings, Dee Dee Colvin, Jeffrey ("Joey") Hyman, and Tommy Erdelyi adopted the surname Ramone. They first performed in public at CBGB's, appearing in black leather jackets, black

Joey Ramone. A CBGB's original. *Permission by Cam Garrett*.

pegged pants, torn jeans, and ripped T-shirts. "We wanted to do punk rock and decided the punks were people from the fifties like Eddie Cochran and Elvis Presley. You would always see them walking around in motorcycle jackets. We thought that was the coolest thing, to have a motorcycle jacket, to really prove you were in the groove," enthused Joey.

The Ramones cared little for the artistic avant-garde. On one tour with the Talking Heads, remembered then-manager Danny Fields, "The Ramones hated Europe. They didn't like the idea that people didn't speak English. The Talking Heads adored it. It was really yuppie chic at work. The Ramones were like Archie Bunker at the Vatican. They were not amused. They hated the food and just looked for hamburgers everywhere." On a Talking Heads–planned side trip to Stonehenge during the tour, the Ramones refused to leave the bus. "It's really nothing to see," explained Dee Dee. "It's not like going to see a castle."

The Ramones reflected their populist attitude in a thrashing sound borrowed from the New York Dolls. "What really kicked it off was seeing the New York Dolls in clubs around Manhattan," recalled Dee Dee Ramone. "It was so inspiring to see a bunch of young people playing rock-and-roll that we wanted to do it too. It took off from there."

Unlike the more meandering art groups, which looked to literary and free-jazz sources, the Ramones sped through eight-song, seventeen-minute sets at CBGB's, defining the punk sound on their first LP, which featured "Blitzkrieg Bop," "Beat on the Brat," and "Now I Wanna Sniff Some Glue." "Rock-'n'-roll was a hodgepodge of Pink Floyd and ELP and all this crap," explained Joey Ramone. "What we did was we stripped it right down to the bone and we disassembled it and reassembled it and put all the excitement and fun and spirit, raw energy and raw emotion and guts and attitude back into it." After attending a Ramones concert, writer Norman Mailer raved, "For me it was like I was an old car and I was being taken out for a ride at 100 miles an hour."

The CBGB's Rock Festival Showcase Auditions in mid-1975 brought international attention to the emerging New York punk scene. Featuring the Ramones, the Talking Heads, and Television, the festival attracted major U.S. and British music and mainstream journalists. "The coverage of the festival started making things happen," maintained Hilly Kristal. "The record companies started coming down, mainly Sire Records, but also others."

Promoted by the British press after this showcase, the Ramones unveiled their thrashing sound in England. In 1976 they released the British version of their first album, which impressed the British critics and gave some English punks direction. "I heard the Ramones' first record and I thought that it was fucking brilliant," remembered Billy Idol, who started the British punk band Generation X and was a member of the Bromley Contingent that followed the Sex Pistols. "We got that first record and every song was under two minutes and it was like a revolution! We were playing normal speed until we heard the Ramones, and because of them, [we] revved everything up. Everybody did, 'cause the Ramones really had their groove and we were still searching for ours."

On July 4, 1976, the Ramones brought their live show to British youths. They celebrated the U.S. Bicentennial by performing in London at the Roundhouse, which, contended Hilly Kristal, "started the whole thing going. All the other groups saw them and realized they could do it too." Joey Ramone asserted, "I feel we were responsible for the whole punk revolution. We signed to Sire in 1975 and our first album came out in 1976. It came out in England about six months before it came out in America. That's sort of what inspired the English bands to start up. When we first went over there the big thing was pub rock." Though overstating his influence, Joey and the other Ramones mirrored and, to some extent, shaped the music that would explode from Britain later the same year.

The Sex Pistols and British Punk

Unemployed British youths infused New York punk with a venomous anger. Between 1974 and 1977, unemployment in Britain shot up from 3.4 percent to nearly 6 percent, increasing by more than 200 percent among the young. To cope with the crisis, the British government suspended wage increases. In 1976, the rate of inflation ran rampant at a staggering 22.7 percent and increased another 16.7 percent the next year. By 1977, the beleaguered British government took a loan from the International Monetary fund to cope with the economic crisis.

The economic instability especially affected British youths. "It's not much fun to be young today. If you think otherwise, take a look at yesterday's jobless figures," instructed the *Daily Mirror* on June 22, 1977. "Is it any wonder if the youngsters feel disillusioned and betrayed? A brave new generation of talent and purpose is turning sour before our very eyes."

Guided by manager Malcolm McLaren, the Sex Pistols embodied the desperate rage of unemployed British teens and combined it with the do-it-yourself attitude of the New York avant-garde to create British punk. The transition from a literary New York scene to an explosive, politically charged British punk began in early 1975, when clothing store owner McLaren traveled to New York to manage the fashion-conscious New York Dolls. Returning six months later when the Dolls disbanded, McLaren agreed to manage the Swankers, a group of lower-class London schoolmates, consisting of Paul Cook, Steve Jones, and Wally Nightingale, who were joined by Glen Matlock, an assistant in McLaren's shop, called Sex. He suggested the group move Jones to guitar and dispense with Nightingale, who appeared too clean-cut.

As a lead singer, McLaren proposed Richard Hell, who in 1975 had begun to play with ex–New York Doll Johnny Thunders in the Heartbreakers and who had impressed the store owner during his brief stay in the States. "I just thought Richard Hell was incredible," enthused McLaren. "Here was a guy all deconstructed, torn down, looking like he just crawled out of a drain hole, looking like he was covered in slime, looking like he hadn't slept in years, looking like he hadn't washed in years, and looking like no one gave a fuck about him. And looking like he didn't give a fuck about you!" He admitted, "There was no question that I'd take it back to London. These are the two things I brought back: the image of this distressed, strange thing called Richard Hell. And this phrase, 'the blank generation.'"

Confronted with opposition from the Swankers over an American addition to the band, McLaren asked John Lydon, nicknamed Rotten, to come to the manager's shop. In August 1975, wearing an "I Hate Pink Floyd" T-shirt, Lydon successfully auditioned for the band by singing along to Alice Cooper's "School's Out," which played on the jukebox. "It really didn't take off 'till John got involved," remarked bassist Matlock. "We knew what we wanted, but we didn't have the gift of gab. John did. He put his words out on sort of a gut-level sensibility."

Johnny Rotten also fit the band's image better than Richard Hell because of his age. In 1976, Richard Hell and Tom Verlaine were twenty-seven, Patti Smith was thirty, Johnny Ramone was twenty-five, and Joey Ramone was twenty-four. Like their fellow British punks, the Swankers had barely finished school: Johnny Rotten, Glen Matlock, and Paul Cook were twenty, and Steve Jones had just turned twenty-one.

Finding themselves in the dire situation of most British teens, the Swankers had few options other than forming a band. Johnny Rotten characterized the group as

The Sex Pistols. Anarchy in the U.K. *Permission by* The Daily *of The University of Washington.*

"a collection of extremely bored people. I suppose we'd come together out of desperation. There was no hope as far as any of us were concerned. This was our common bond. There was no point in looking for a normal job because that would be just too awful. There was no way out. It was a very, very squalid period, massive unemployment, class warfare rampant, quite literally no future."

By 1975, Malcolm McLaren had the ingredients for his new rock-and-roll hybrid. "I was taking the nuances of Richard Hell, the faggy pop side of the New York Dolls, the politics of boredom and mashing it altogether to make a statement," he related. The manager renamed the band the Sex Pistols: "It came about by the idea of a pistol, a pinup, a young thing, a better-looking assassin—a sex pistol," he explained.

The Sex Pistols combined the energy of the New York Dolls, Iggy Pop, and the Ramones for an aggressive, pumping sound. Playing their first show in November 1975 at St. Martin's School of Art in London, the group featured a frenzied, buzz-saw attack anchored by guitarist Steve Jones. "I'd wake up in the morning," related Jones, "and play along with an Iggy Pop record and the New York Dolls' first album. I would listen to them over and over again and play guitar to them." Johnny Rotten agreed, "*Funhouse* by Iggy and the Stooges was my kind of music. Our sound was pretty damn close to that." Chrissie Hynde, the singer/guitarist who followed the Sex Pistols and later founded the Pretenders, recalled: "Sid learned how to play guitar playing with the Ramones albums for two or three days. He fucking loved the Ramones!"

Besides adopting the sound of American punk, the Sex Pistols created an onstage image that at least partly derived from the Stooges and New York punks. Like Iggy Pop, they taunted, shouted, and spat at the audience, blurring the distinction between the artist and the fan. Band members appeared in ripped, graffitied shirts and pants, black boots, and leather jackets that flashed with metal studs and zippers. As with Richard Hell, they cut their hair in a short, spiky style. To reinforce their image, in February 1977, the band fired bass player Glen Matlock because, according to Rotten, "he was so clean and had that look, like he had never gone without a meal," and replaced him with Sid Vicious (a.k.a. John Ritchie) who, like Iggy, mutilated himself onstage with broken beer bottles.

The rebellious band offered this furious music to a new generation of rock-and-rollers. "The millionaire groups were singing about love and their own hang-ups," sneered Rotten. "That's stupid. You don't sing about love to people on the dole. We're totally against apathy of any kind. We have got to fight the entire super band system. Groups like the Who and the Stones are revolting. They have nothing to offer the kids anymore."

The Sex Pistols even rejected their arty New York predecessors who at least on some level had provided them with inspiration. A day after Patti Smith played the Roundhouse in London, the Sex Pistols performed in a small club on Oxford Street. "Before they even play the first song," remembered Jay Dee Daugherty of the Patti Smith Group, "John Rotten says, 'Did anyone go to the Roundhouse the other night and see the hippie [Patti Smith] shaking the tambourine? Horses, horses, HORSE-SHIT.'"

The Sex Pistols substituted an angry anarchism for 1960s' hippiedom and the theatrical excess of 1970s' superstars. In 1976, they recorded their first single, "Anarchy in the U.K.," which warned of impending chaos in Britain. The band next blasted royalty in "God Save the Queen," releasing the single to coincide with Queen Elizabeth's Silver Jubilee in June. The Sex Pistols followed with other songs such as "Pretty Vacant," their adaptation of Richard Hell's "Blank Generation," and "Holiday in the Sun," which described the hopeless plight of many British youths. "There'll always be something to fight—apathy's the main thing," asserted Rotten. "The Pistols are presenting one alternative to apathy and if you don't like it, that's just too bad. Anarchy is self-rule and that's better than anything else." Rotten later observed that "the Pistols projected that anger, that rock-bottom working class hate."

An outraged, threatened establishment aimed a barrage of criticism at the anarchistic Sex Pistols, reminiscent of the outcries against Elvis Presley in 1956. On April 10, 1976, the British music paper *Melody Maker* told its readers that "the Sex Pistols do as much for music as World War II did for the cause of peace." Robert Adley, a Conservative member of Parliament, called the group "a bunch of ill-mannered louts, who seem to cause offense wherever they go." One vicar of the Anglican Church, his face muscles tightened and his head raised high, planted himself outside of a club, where the Sex Pistols were scheduled to play, and warned concertgoers: "Keep out of there! They're the devil's children." Almost every local government in Britain banned the Pistols, publications refused to print ads publicizing the band, and in June 1976, after the release of "God Save the Queen," royalists attacked both Johnny Rotten and Paul Cook with razors, knives, and iron pipes.

The record industry offered little help to the Sex Pistols. EMI first signed the band for a £40,000 advance. After packers in its record plant refused to handle "Anarchy in the U.K.," and drunken band members had been prodded into using profanities on the live BBC TV broadcast of the Bill Grundy–hosted *Today* show, the company criticized the Pistols for "aggressive behavior" and terminated the band's contract. In a ceremony outside Buckingham Palace on March 10, 1977, A&M Records signed the Sex Pistols; six days later, the company terminated the contract. Two months later, Virgin Records offered a deal to the band and released the British version of *Never Mind the Bollocks—Here's the Sex Pistols*.

Despite opposition, the Sex Pistols' records topped the charts. "God Save the Queen," even though banned by British radio, sold 150,000 copies in five days and shot to the number-two spot on the chart. "Pretty Vacant" hit the number-six slot, and "Holiday in the Sun" reached number eight. In November 1977, the band's first and only studio album topped the British chart.

As well as a new rock sound, the Sex Pistols created an alternative do-it-yourself culture for British youths. Carefully cultivated by manager and fashion-monger Malcolm McLaren, they wore clothes that appeared disheveled, dirty, and menacing. "We'd take brand new T-shirts, make them look old, stamp on them, throw them around in the garden . . . cut them up, dye them the grungiest colors so they went from being clean white to dirty gray," remembered McLaren. They also stenciled such slogans as "Destroy" and "Anarchy" in bold letters on the refashioned shirts. Within months, McLaren saw his antifashion statement, borrowed in part from New York punks, spread to British teens, who sported ripped T-shirts with stenciled slogans, spray-painted pants, studded leather, and spiked hair. "They wear with snarling pride the marks of the downtrodden," wrote Anthony Burgess about British teens in 1977. "Hair is cropped because long hair holds lice. Clothes are not patched, since patching denotes skill and a seedy desire for respectability; their gaping holes are held together with safety pins."

McLaren contacted the politically minded Jamie Reid, a friend from his days at Croydon Art College, to create posters and record-cover art for the Sex Pistols that provided punk culture with a graphic style. Much like the swirling, psychedelic poster art had reflected the acid rock of hippiedom, Reid's cut-and-paste, ransom-note style captured the threatening anger of British punk. "The Pistols were just the perfect marriage between the images I was creating and the music," remembered Reid. "I was messing about with design, but because we had no money, I was cutting up newspapers and doing collage. It was from there that the look for punk came." An outgrowth of "twentieth-century collage agit-prop art, including early Russian Revolutionary artists" such as Malevich, Tatlin, and Rodchenko, Reid's graphic design style of sharp, piercing lines against stark backgrounds helped define the look of a generation.

By 1976, the Sex Pistols and their manager had unleashed a revolutionary culture on an unsuspecting Britain and, eventually, the Western world. "Getting into the Sex Pistols wasn't like, 'Oh, I like this new band.' It really was a lifestyle choice," explained Mark Perry, the editor of the influential punk fanzine *Sniffin' Glue* and later a founder of the band Alternative TV. "If you got into the Pistols, you changed your life. That's how dramatic it was."

The British Punk Legion

Driven by the forces of cultural change that had been created by the Sex Pistols, some British youths followed the Pistols by forming punk bands. After hearing the Sex Pistols at the 100 Club in London, Joe Strummer quit his pub-rock band and joined with guitarist Mick Jones and three other musicians to form the Clash. The group asked Bernie Rhodes, a regular at Malcolm McLaren's boutique, to be their manager. On July 4, 1976, they first performed in Sheffield, backing the Sex Pistols, and that December joined the Pistols' "Anarchy in the U.K." tour. The next month, the Clash signed with CBS and in March debuted with the single "White Riot," followed a month later by their first, self-named LP. The album hit the British Top Twenty and included punk anthems such as "I'm So Bored with the U.S.A.," "Career Opportunities," and "London's Burning." Though ignored by distributors in the United States, in 1978 the Clash followed with the sobering *Give 'Em Enough Rope*, which hit the number-two slot in Britain. "You write about what affects you," explained Strummer. The Clash sang about the "dissatisfaction among the young people, the way that everyone seemed to be going nowhere."

The Damned began their career backing the Sex Pistols. Formed in 1976 by Dave Vanian, Brian James, Captain Sensible, and Rat Scabies, the group also played on the Pistols' "Anarchy in the U.K." tour. Trying to "play as fast and as loud and as chaotically as possible," according to bassist Captain Sensible, the band released the first British punk single, "New Rose," in October 1976. Nearly four months later, they hit the streets with the first British punk LP, *Damned, Damned, Damned*, which climbed to number thirty-six on the English chart.

Siouxsie and the Banshees began as part of the Bromley Contingent, a group of fans that religiously followed the Sex Pistols. On September 20, 1976, at the 100 Club Punk Festival headlined by the Pistols, Siouxsie Sioux (b. Susan Dallion), Sid Vicious, Marco Pirroni, and Steve Havoc (b. Steve Severin) jumped on the stage and performed an extemporaneous, twenty-minute punk version of "The Lord's Prayer." At the end of the year, Siouxsie appeared with the Sex Pistols on the British television show *Today*, and later the next year the fledgling band backed Johnny Thunders in concert. On June 9, 1978, the Banshees signed with Polydor Records and in two months released their first single, "Hong Kong Garden," which hit the number-seven spot on the British singles chart. They quickly recorded *The Scream*, which by the end of the year climbed into the British Top Fifteen.

Generation X was started by two Bromley Contingent fans, Billy Idol (b. William Broad) and Tony James. In late 1976, the band was the first punk group to perform at The Roxy, which became a punk hangout. Within a year, the band released the single "Your Generation," an answer to the Who's baby-boom anthem "My Generation." In March 1978, the group released their first LP, which charted at number twenty-nine in Britain.

The Buzzcocks banded together after witnessing a Sex Pistols show in Manchester. Although a Stooges fan, guitarist Pete Shelly confessed that "we were floundering around. We just weren't moving in any kind of musical world. We *needed* to see the Sex Pistols." Within weeks of the Manchester show, the Buzzcocks snagged their first gig, supporting the Sex Pistols. Later in the year, they participated in the "Anarchy in the U.K." tour. By January 1977, they released the EP *Spiral Scratch*, which featured such punk gems as "Boredom," and early the next year reached the Top Fifteen with *Another Music in a Different Kitchen*.

Marion Elliot, soon to become Poly Styrene, also grabbed the punk banner after a Sex Pistols show. "The Pistols," she remembered, ". . . sparked me to realize that there was something happening that was a little bit more of my generation. I thought, 'Oh, if they can get a band together, I should be able to do that too.'" In 1976, Poly Styrene formed X-Ray Spex and blasted consumer culture with the ranting "Oh Bondage, Up Yours!" "It was about being in bondage to material life," she explained. "A call for liberation. I was saying, 'Bondage? Forget it, I'm not going to be bound by the laws of consumerism.'"

By 1977, the Buzzcocks, the Clash, the Damned, Siouxsie and the Banshees, X-Ray Spex, and a raft of other outfits had followed the Pistols to create a punk movement. "The Pistols had changed the whole musical scene," recalled Rotten. "Everyone started doing it the way the Pistols did it."

Rock Against Racism

Rock Against Racism united many of the British punk bands in a fight against the racism rampant in Britain. It began after an August 14, 1976, concert in Birmingham at which a drunken Eric Clapton lectured concertgoers about Britain "becoming a black colony within ten years." "Musicians were coming out with the 'Blame the Blacks bit,'" recalled one organizer. "Bowie and Clapton were the last straws—how dare they praise Hitler or want to repatriate the race that had created the music they profitably recycled? We loved music, hated racism and thought it was about time rock-and-roll paid back some dues." Rock Against Racism tried to "fight back against the creeping power of racist ideas in popular culture" and attacked the right-wing, neo-Nazi National Front. By early 1978, the coalition had organized fifty-six chapters.

The antiracist group appealed to punkers such as the Clash, who supported a more focused political agenda than the anarchistic Sex Pistols. "If you wanna fuckin' enjoy yourself, you sit in an armchair and watch TV," goaded the Clash's Mick Jones, "but if you wanna get actively involved, rock-'n'-roll's about rebellion." More specific about his political agenda, Clash vocalist Joe Strummer asserted that "we're hoping to educate any kid who comes to listen to us, just to keep 'em from joining the National Front when things get really tough." To back their words with action, on April 30, 1978, the Clash headlined an Anti-Nazi League Carnival in London that attracted more than 80,000 fans.

Elvis Costello headed another Rock Against Racism benefit. The son of band-leader Ross McManus, Declan McManus played at local folk clubs under his mother's maiden name, Costello. In 1976, he signed to Stiff Records, owned by Jake Riviera, who suggested that he rename himself Elvis. In April 1977, Elvis released his vinyl debut "Less Than Zero," a song attacking Oswald Mosley, a 1930s' British fascist who inspired the organization of the National Front. Costello then recorded the ballad "Alison," which blunted the hard-edged punk sound and became a model for the post-punk new wave. "What I really wanted to do was approach the music with the same attitude, the same attack as punk, without sacrificing all the things I liked about music—like, say, tunes," Elvis remembered. In the summer of 1978, Costello played at a Rock Against Racism concert in Brixton.

In June 1978, the Clash, the Tom Robinson Band, and Sham 69 played to 50,000 young punks who attended a Rock Against Racism concert. Tom Robinson, who had formed his band in early 1977 and had hit the Top Five in Britain with "2-4-6-8-Motorway," shouted to the audience that the National Front must be confronted "at school and at work." "If music can erase even a tiny fraction of the prejudice and intolerance in this world, then it's worth trying," he told an interviewer. "Through my lyrics," agreed Morgan Webster of Sham 69, "I want to show the National Front that they're fucking assholes." Joe Strummer of the Clash declared, "We're against fascism and racism." By the end of summer 1978, more than 250,000 youths had rocked against racism in thirty-six concerts held across England.

The Jamaican Connection: Reggae and Ska

Reggae, the music of the downtrodden in Jamaica, was championed by British punks dedicated to racial equality. It served as an essential element of the Jamaican Rastafarian religion, which emerged as early as the 1930s, when the rotund American Marcus Garvey urged Jamaican blacks to return to the Ethiopian kingdom of Haile Selassie, who was considered the Lion of Judah. Garvey's back-to-Africa message appealed to the many unemployed Jamaicans, about 35 percent of the working-age population during the 1960s, who congregated in the slums of West Kingston.

Trapped in this poverty-stricken existence, many Jamaicans adhered to Rastafarianism's coherent set of beliefs: Selassie, embodying the second coming of Christ, became God, or Jah, to the Rastafarians; the Ethiopian colors—yellow, green, and red—were adopted as the Rasta standard; Western society became the corrupt Babylon; by 1935, many Rastas sported a plaited hairstyle known as dreadlocks, inspired by East African warriors; they smoked ganja, or marijuana, to reach a higher level of consciousness; Rastas ate organic, or I-tal food, following Old Testament kosher laws, and they abstained from salt, tobacco, and alcohol consumption. In the late 1960s, reggae, which combined African and indigenous Jamaican rhythms, replaced the westernized R&B–based rock steady to become the music of the counter-cultural religion. Peter Tosh, one of the fathers of reggae, explained that, "Reggae, the word, means 'king's music,' and I play the King's music. The King put many princes on earth, and the music is given to those who praise Him. You have to be spiritually inclined to deal with this kind of talent."

Reggae originated in the slums of the Jamaican capital. "When I came to Kingston at about sixteen years of age," Tosh remembered, "Nine out of ten singers found themselves in poverty in Trenchtown, the ghetto. It was me, Bob Marley, Bunny Livingstone, Joe Higgs, the Maytals—we'd sit around every night and just sing. At that time, me and Joe Higgs were the only ones who could play the guitar. Finally Joe Higgs helped to get us into the studio with [Clement] Sir Coxsone Dodd producing, and that was the start of recording for me and Bob and Bunny."

In early 1965, Tosh and his friends, calling themselves the Wailing Wailers, hit the Jamaican charts with "Simmer Down," a song about gang violence. The song combined Jamaican and Western influences in a music called ska. A year later, they recorded another ska song, "Rude Boy," which immortalized the outlaws of Kingston's shantytown and reached the number-one spot. Changing with the times, the Wailers next recorded a series of songs with a rock-steady beat, a style heavily indebted to the soul music that was exploding from urban America. In 1971, the Wailers benefited from the success of the film *The Harder They Come*. The movie chronicled gang life in Trenchtown and featured the music of Jamaican star Jimmy Cliff. The film became an international hit and created a worldwide market for reggae music.

Chris Blackwell of Island Records, who had helped promote *The Harder They Come*, became attracted to the image of the Wailers and signed the band. Bob

Steel Pulse. *Permission by Cam Garrett.*

Marley, "Bunny and Peter Tosh. They all had this fuck you–type attitude," related Blackwell, "just like *The Harder They Come.*" By the time they signed to Island, the Wailers had abandoned ska and rock steady for a new music that was rooted in Rastafarianism and became known as reggae. In 1973, the group released the reggae LPs *Catch a Fire* and *Burnin'*, the second including "I Shot the Sheriff," a song covered by Eric Clapton. Two years later, the Wailers cut *Natty Dread*, a testament to the Rastafarian culture.

The Wailers, along with other reggae groups such as Toots and the Maytals, Burning Spear, Black Uhuru, and Steel Pulse, lambasted the racism and capitalism that Britain had imposed on Jamaica. Burning Spear (b. Winston Rodney), using a Rastafarian dialect, contended that everyone should "be equal or I-qual and get an equal share. An' everyman entitled to Dem share an' should get Dem share. . . . The work is to bring the whole world together. See. That is naturality. Nonviolence, less pollution, more togetherness, more industry, less institutions like prisons; more schools, more hospitals. These things come through the music. And the music is those things and those things is the music." Lee Perry, who produced bands such as the Wailers, claimed that reggae "denounces the very heart of the system on which much of the capitalist world is built." Not just voicing rhetoric, reggae bands such as Bob Marley and the Wailers actively backed the government of socialist Prime Minister Michael Manley. At one 1976 rally for the prime minister, Marley barely escaped an assassination attempt.

By mid-decade, Bob Marley gained international fame. "Bob really broke strong in England in 1976 or '77," remembered Blackwell. "He did a concert in London that really broke him. It was also big in America." The recorded album of the 1975 concert, titled *Live!*, hit the Top Forty in Britain. Marley, who by this point had split with Peter Tosh and Bunny Wailer, reached the Top Ten in the United States and the Top Fifteen in Britain with *Rastaman Vibration* (1976) and the next year reached the Top Twenty with *Exodus*.

Discontented British punks, attracted to Marley's rebel image, championed the activist reggae bands. "I was heavily into reggae," recalled Johnny Rotten. In 1976, the Clash remade Junior Murvin's reggae hit "Police and Thieves." "You see, there wasn't enough good punk records around. So, to supplement it, we filled it out with a lot of reggae records," explained Mick Jones of the Clash. "It was like punk's other 'chosen music.'" Many British youths supported reggae bands such as Steel Pulse, Aswad and Matumbi, who regularly played with British punks at Rock Against Racism concerts. "Everybody loved reggae music," commented Chrissie Hynde about the English punks.

Some British youths took ska—the light, happy Jamaican music that predated reggae—and fused it with the radical message and energy of punk. "We were the first band who wanted to combine punk and reggae because we liked them both," recalled Jerry Dammers of the racially integrated Specials, one of the most influential of the new ska groups. "I was aiming for revolution, of racial harmony, of peace and unity." In 1979, the band borrowed £700 to record "Gangsters," a tribute to the Prince Buster ska classic "Al Capone," which was released on the group's 2-Tone label. They followed a few months later with a debut album, produced by Elvis Costello, which cracked the British Top Five.

The Selecter recorded on the Specials' 2-Tone label. Living in Coventry, as did the Specials, the racially integrated Selecter delivered a politically charged version of punk-ska. Featuring the vocals of Pauline Black, the band chronicled the tense racial and political situation in Britain with singles such as "Three Minute Hero," "Too Much Pressure," and "Murder." "2-Tone came to light exactly when Margaret Thatcher and Ronald Reagan came to power," explained Black. "We had two years before they sucked both countries dry, which the music scene reflected."

The English Beat, the other major 1970s' ska band, produced a similar sound for a similar purpose. Guitarist Dave Wakeling rediscovered ska because "it said what a terrible world this was—with a smile on its face." In 1979, the Birmingham group created its own Go Feet label and released its near top-selling debut, which included "Stand Down Margaret," aimed at Conservative Prime Minister Margaret Thatcher who had been elected only a few months before.

The Independent Labels

Other independent labels arose to distribute the politicized punk and ska, taking over the music from the large record companies with a do-it-yourself (DIY) ethic. "Punk was always about having control, seizing the means of production, instead of waiting for the record company idiots to make the decisions," insisted Pete Shelley of the Buzzcocks.

Created from a record shop owned by Geoff Travis, Rough Trade Records put the do-it-yourself ethic into action. "Punk gave everyone on the scene the impetus to do things for themselves," asserted Travis. "If that hadn't happened, perhaps we wouldn't have started."

In 1978, the new label began pressing discs. In the words of staffer Allan Sturdy, the label hoped to "provide an alternative to the music establishment so that a record could be available that otherwise wouldn't." The twenty-five staffers at Rough Trade democratically made decisions about material, rejecting songs that were sexist or racist. "I wouldn't sign a band that was racist or sexist or fascist or anything like that," Rough Trade's Howie Klein told a reporter.

Enforcing his standards, Rough Trade first recorded the debut LP of the politically minded Ulster band Stiff Little Fingers, who delivered charged anthems such as "Alternative Ulster," "Suspect Device," "Law and Order," "Rough Trade," and "White Noise," the last lambasting white Britain's racism toward blacks, Pakistanis, and the Irish. The label featured subsequent releases by all-female punk bands such as the Slits and Girls at Our Best and the gender-integrated Delta 5, who called for both racial and sexual equality. "Women were relatively empowered by punk," contended Geoff Travis. "I don't think I'd ever seen a band like the Slits before—I think punk gave them the impetus. We just had respect for women. We didn't see any reason why women couldn't be equally good at making music as their male counterparts."

The new independent record company based its operations on cooperation with the musicians, because, as Klein commented, most "record companies are part of an antisocial movement in Western society, part of the industrial complex that enslaves people." They split profits 50–50 between the company and the artist, keeping the prices as low as possible and funneling their share of the net revenues back into the company. The company staff also collaborated with one another. "It was a cooperative collective from the beginning," explained Travis, "in the sense that it wasn't a traditional workplace. There weren't bosses and a hierarchy. People were paid equal amounts of money."

The collaborative ethic of Rough Trade spread. Factory Records opened a cooperative venture in Manchester, Fast Product did the same in Edinburgh, and Graduate Records started in Dudley. Although a few independents such as I.R.S., Virgin, and Stiff became small versions of the majors, many followed the example of the cooperative Rough Trade.

Some punk bands, though lauding the independents, signed with major labels for better distribution of their records. Tom Robinson, facing the contradiction between his leftist politics and the moneymaking goals of his label, asserted that one has "to use the capitalist media to reach the people. And I do feel that pop music is the way to reach people. Ideally, I'd like to be played on AM stations rather than FM stations, rather than the rarefied atmosphere. I'd rather be played in taxis, in factories, for housewives working at home." The Clash, explained vocalist Joe Strummer, "is trying to do something new, we're trying to be the greatest group in the world, and that also means the biggest. At the same time, we're trying to be radical—I mean, we never want to be *really* respectable—and keep punk alive." Guitarist Mick Jones of the Clash, who had signed with CBS, added, "We realized that if we were a little more subtle, if we branched out a little, we might reach a few more people. We finally saw we had been reaching the same people over and over. This way if more kids started hearing the record, maybe they'd start humming the songs, they'll read the lyrics and learn something from them."

Right-Wing Reaction

The National Front attempted to destroy politicized bands such as the Clash. In 1977, the *British Patriot*, the magazine of the National Front, warned its readers that the Clash was "the most left wing of the contemporary groups." To diffuse their influence, it instructed its members to keep "an eye out for posters that advertise Clash concerts so that they may be removed from walls and boardings and reconsigned to the gutter where they will reach the most appropriate clientele."

The Clash met with resistance on other fronts. During their first tour of Great Britain, police repeatedly stopped their tour bus for little or no reason, and the band members were arrested and fined for forgetting to return hotel keys. In the United States, Epic Records executives at first refused to issue the group's debut *The Clash*, branding it "too crude" for American consumption. They released the album more than two years later in an altered form.

Other punk bands also met with opposition. In July 1978, the National Front burned down two auditoriums used for Rock Against Racism shows. A year later, British police stormed into the Southall Musicians Cooperative—the home of punks and reggae musicians—and wantonly smashed instruments and sound equipment. Benefit concerts for the Cooperative, organized by the Clash and Pete Townshend of the Who, generated enough money to replace the damaged goods.

Throughout the late 1970s, the new Teddy Boys and the skinheads attacked punks in gangland fashion. These two groups of youth, maintained Pete Townshend, were "fascist. They despise everybody who isn't like them. It's a kind of toy fascism, fed by organized fascism; fed by Martin Webster and the National Front." In 1979, right-wing teens organizing into the Young National Front launched a Rock Against Communism movement to counterbalance Rock Against Racism. They also formed rock groups such as Ventz, Column 44, and Tragic Minds to disseminate songs such as "Master Race," "White Power," and "Kill the Reds."

The Decline of Punk

Businesses on both sides of the Atlantic undermined punk by selling punk style without its substance. As early as June 1977, *Newsweek* observed that "both Saks on Fifth Avenue and Bonwit Teller carry gold safety pins at prices up to $100, and noted British designer Zandra Rhodes recently created a collection of gowns for Bloomingdale's that incorporate stylized rips and glitter-studded safety pins—at $345 to $1,150 a gown." The June 1980 issue of *Mademoiselle* offered its readers the choice between "punk or prep" fashion in a four-page spread. Richard Hell began to lament that "punk was intended to be a whole kind of consciousness. But then it got corrupted into being simply a style or a fad."

Some 1970s' rock acts began to co-opt the punk image. Linda Ronstadt appeared with spiked hair on the pink-and-black album cover of *Mad Love* (1980) and covered "Alison" by Elvis Costello. Billy Joel, the piano man who topped the charts in 1977 with *The Stranger*, posed in a leather jacket with a rock in his cocked arm for the cover of his *Glass Houses* (1980) album. Even Cher, the folk singer turned disco queen, surfaced in full punk regalia as the lead singer of the short-lived punk/heavy-metal band, Black Rose. In 1979, Sandy Pearlman, producer of the Clash's second album, complained that "no one's really very scared of punk, especially the record companies. They've sublimated all the revolutionary tendencies this art is based on."

Its image being assimilated into the rock mainstream, aggressive British punk rock began to abandon the buzz-saw guitar sound for different styles of music. In 1979, Tom Robinson confessed to *Melody Maker* that "after two and a half years, [punk] has become a bit tame and predictable. It's time to move on and try something fresh." He opted for the electronic pop of Sector 27. Amid a 1980 European tour, a disgusted Joe Strummer of the Clash complained to *New Musical Express* that "punk rock has just hit Europe in a big way, but it's totally worthless. . . . It's just another fashion. It's become everything it wasn't supposed to be. I was emotionally shattered." The Clash, always interested in Jamaican rhythms, moved further and further from the boisterous sound of their first album. By the triple album *Sandinista* (1980) and *Combat Rock* (1982), they sounded very little like the snarling punks of 1976.

John Lydon (a.k.a. Johnny Rotten). *Permission by Cam Garrett.*

Even the Sex Pistols deserted punk rock. On January 14, 1978, after completing an American tour, the group was disbanded by Johnny Rotten, who felt that the band had extended rock to its outer limits. "The Pistols finished rock-and-roll. That was the last rock-and-roll band. It's all over now," he told an interviewer. "Rock-and-roll is shit. It's dismal. Granddad danced to it." Paul Cook and Steve Jones played briefly with Johnny Thunders before starting more pop-oriented ventures. On February 2, 1979, Sid Vicious, the archetype of the punk image, died from a drug overdose in New York City. Johnny Rotten reclaimed his original surname, Lydon, and started the "antirock-and-roll" band Public Image Ltd. (PiL). Extending the minimalistic tendencies of the punks, PiL produced a dissonant, jagged electronic sound perfected on *Metal Box* (1979). "I've grown very far away from human beings," Lydon told *Trouser Press* magazine. "I like being detached; I don't even like shaking hands. I don't like sweat. I think everyone is ugly. Faces disgust me, and feet really make me reek. I think the human body's about one of the most ugly things ever created." Rather than people, the ex-Pistol found solace in "machines. Lots of buttons on record players. Knobs and gadgets, electrical equipment of any kind."

Postpunk Depression

Though beginning to disintegrate by 1978, punk shattered the monopoly of corporate rock. "Imagine in your mind an ELP [Emerson, Lake and Palmer] number," suggested Joe Strummer of the Clash. "Then imagine punk rock like a blow torch sweeping across it. That to me is what punk rock did." Punk rock paved the way for other bands that played music to a post-baby-boom generation. "I did it. I did it," boasted Johnny Rotten. "I made doors open. I made it easier for up-and-coming bands. It was a Rolling Stones–type of monopoly of the entire business. Record companies would not sign new acts. I opened that up."

Some postpunk bands, following the model of Rotten's PiL, delivered a cold, dissonant, minimalistic music. Formed in late 1975 by Genesis P-Orridge, his girlfriend/guitarist Cosey Fanni Tutti, tape manipulator Peter "Sleazy" Christopherson, and keyboardist Chris Carter, Throbbing Gristle abandoned rock music for synthesizer drones, tape samples, and depraved performances to paint a picture of a society in decline. "We need a new music," asserted P-Orridge. "The slaves no longer work in cotton fields. They work in scrap yards and factories with conveyor belts, just doing repetitive, noisy jobs with frequencies of all these machines and technology around them."

The band debuted with a show that featured tape loops, synthesizer improvisations, gloomy lyrics, and a bevy of strippers that the *Daily Mirror* referred to as "distasteful and inartistic." Though performing sporadically during the punk era, in late 1977 the band released its first album *Second Annual Report* on its own Industrial Records, just before the Sex Pistols disbanded. A year later, Throbbing Gristle released *D.o.A. (The Third and Final Report)* at a concert, which also unveiled their latest film *After Cease to Exist*, which included a castration sequence. By the end of the decade, the *Daily Mail* referred to the band as "wreckers of civilization."

An outfit from Sheffield also expressed their vision of social disintegration through a harsh, intense electronic sound. Banding together in 1973, Chris Watson, Stephen Mallinder, and Richard Kirk named themselves Cabaret Voltaire after the experimental Parisian Dadaist performances of pre-1920s' France. The trio used tape samples, slide shows, distorted vocals, and electronics to deliver a chilling, minimalist, disjointed primativism. "We've taken the standard rock or beat music and stripped it bare," contended the band. The group released their debut *Extended Play* (1978) on Rough Trade and gained notoriety after the demise of the Sex Pistols. The next year the group released its first full-length album, the experimental din of *Mix-Up*.

Joy Division offered a more accessible sound of gloom. In 1976, friends Peter Hook and Bernard Albrecht decided to form a band. "We were both twenty-one when we started and had never played an instrument before in our lives. It was straight after seeing the first Sex Pistols gig in Manchester," recalled Hook. "We thought they were so bad, but yet it was so exciting. God! We could have a go at that." A few months later, Hook, Albrecht, and their friend Steven Morris met singer Ian Curtis who, according to Hook, "introduced us to Lou Reed and the Velvet Underground, to Iggy Pop and the Stooges and the Doors."

By mid-1977, the foursome began to produce a droning, Velvet Underground–inspired sound punctuated by Curtis's gloomy lyrics. They named themselves Joy Division after the prostitute wing in a Nazi concentration camp. In June 1979, the band signed with the newly established Factory Records owned by Tony Wilson, who used his life savings to finance the group's first LP, *Unknown Pleasures*. Joy Division hit the British Top Twenty with the single "Love Will Tear Us Apart" and started to gain momentum before Ian Curtis hanged himself on May 18, 1980, on the eve of an American tour. The posthumous *Closer* reached the British Top Ten.

The Cure reflected the postpunk pessimism. Formed in 1976, the band debuted with the single "Killing an Arab," inspired by a passage in the Albert Camus novel *The Stranger*. In May 1979, they released their first LP, the pop-oriented *Three Imaginary Boys*, which reached number forty-four on the British chart. The band turned to pessimistic themes such as "The Funeral Party" and "The Drowning Man" on subsequent albums such as *Faith*. In April 1982, the Cure released the downbeat classic *Pornography*, which reflected the deep pessimism of some postpunk bands. "I suppose doing an album like *Pornography* and coming to those depths and coming out of it proves that something can come out of nothing," observed singer-lyricist Robert Smith after the band had returned to a pop sound in the mid-1980s.

Bauhaus gave Gothic rock, as it came to be called, its theme song. Forming in 1978 from the remains of the punk band Submerged Tenth, Bauhaus released the brooding single "Bela Lugosi's Dead." Written initially as a joke by lyricist and singer Peter Murphy, the song captured the postpunk gloom of many youths and created a following for the band. In 1980, their debut topped the British independent chart, and by 1982, they hit the British Top Five with *The Sky's Gone Out*.

The Cure. *Permission by Cam Garrett.*

The New Wave

Some refocused punk bands such as the Police offered a bright, pop alternative to postpunk depression that music industry advertisers labeled "the new wave." In January 1977, Stewart Copeland and Gordon Sumner, nicknamed Sting because he often wore a black-and-yellow striped jersey, met at a jazz club and began rehearsing with guitarist Henri Padovani. The next month, the trio released the punk single "Fall Out," and in March toured with Johnny Thunders and the Heartbreakers. "All I could see in punk was a very direct, simple image of power and energy," recalled Sting, who had been enamored of jazz as a youth. "I could relate to that. I could

The Police. *Permission by Cam Garrett.*

easily ally myself with that, and forget about changes, chords with flatted fifths, forget all that."

The Police quickly changed musical direction. They replaced Padovani with guitarist Andy Summers and in April 1978 released the single "Roxanne," which blended the energy of punk with a reggae-influenced, jazz-tinged sound. "I'm an opportunist," admitted Sting. "I saw this vacuum between punk, which was unschooled, and the horrible corporate rock on the other side. I saw this thing in the middle that was clean and simple. That's what 'Roxanne' is; it's so simple and bare. It's not the energy of *Never Mind the Bollocks*, nor is it corporate rock. It's right in between them."

The new pop sound of the Police led to superstardom. The album *Outlandos D'Amour* (1978), which included "Roxanne," hit the Top Ten on the British chart. "Message in a Bottle" and "Walking on the Moon," singles from the band's second album, both topped the U.K. chart. In 1980, *Zenyatta Mondatta* hit the top of the British chart and became the group's first Top-Ten effort in the United States. The next year, *Ghost in the Machine* climbed to number two in America and again topped the chart in Britain, yielding hits such as "Every Little Thing She Does Is Magic" and "Spirits in the Material World." *Synchronicity* (1983) provided the band with its first number-one album on both sides of the Atlantic, making the Police a pop phenomenon. "I don't think pop music is a pejorative term," Sting told an interviewer in 1987. "I want to be proud of being a pop singer when I turn forty."

Billy Idol channeled his punk energy into a bouncy pop. After quitting Generation X in 1981, the singer hired ex-Kiss manager Bill Aucoin and recorded pop songs such as "White Wedding" and "Hot in the City," which fused the persistent beat of punk with snappy melodies. In 1983, he released the Top-Ten album *Rebel Yell* and three years later followed with the million-selling *Whiplash Smile*.

The Cars rode the punk-pop combination to success. Banding together in Boston in 1976, the group hit the Top Twenty two years later with a shiny, upbeat debut. "We knew there was a scene called punk," mentioned vocalist/guitarist Ric Ocasek. "We were certainly liking the rawness of the music that was coming out of that. And we also liked pop. How many people liked both?" The Cars continued to roll up the chart with the Top-Ten *Candy-O* (1979), *Panorama* (1980), and *Shake It Up* (1981) with a sound that Ocasek called "disposable pop."

Chrissie Hynde jumped on the new wave with a combination of hard-edged punk and soul. After attending Kent State University in Ohio, she journeyed to London, where she modeled, sold leather handbags, and wrote for the rock paper *New Musical Express*. In 1974, Hynde worked part-time for Malcolm McLaren in his clothing shop Sex; two years later, she tried unsuccessfully to form a band with guitarist Mick Jones, who had just joined the Clash. Hynde then briefly played guitar for the Malcolm McLaren–managed band Masters of the Backside, who eventually became the Damned.

In March 1978, Chrissie Hynde formed the Pretenders with bassist Pete Farndon, James Honeyman-Scott on guitar, and Martin Chambers on drums. During the next three years, the band released two top-selling albums, which expanded the sound of punk by infusing it with elements of soul. "I didn't quite fit into the London punk scene because I'd been listening to too many Bobby Womack albums," Hynde insisted.

Adam Ant (b. Stuart Goddard) transformed punk energy into pop hits. In 1977, after leaving Hornsey Art College, he formed a punk band named the Ants, who recorded a series of unsuccessful singles. Two years later, he enlisted the help of

Malcolm McLaren, who encouraged the Ants to split from Adam and form Bow Wow Wow with Annabella Lwin.

Deserted by McLaren, Adam Ant began to adopt a different image. He abandoned the ripped T-shirts and safety pins of punk for foppish scarves, embroidered, double-breasted jackets, skin-tight leather pants, and sashes. Enlisting the help of ex–Siouxsie and the Banshees guitarist Marco Pirroni, he formed a pop version of the Ants that featured an upbeat, drum-based sound. From 1980 to 1983, Adam and his Ants hit the chart with four albums, which were promoted by videos of the photogenic group. In 1985, Adam disbanded the group, deciding to concentrate exclusively on his acting career. Adam Ant had been transformed from an angry punk into a video star, who became popular on MTV, an American music channel that would irrevocably change rock music into a visual medium.

I Want
My MTV

❝ Video will be the way to keep time
with the future. **❞**

—*Time* magazine

"Increasingly, and perhaps irreversibly, audiences for American mainstream music will depend, even insist, on each song being a full audiovisual confrontation," observed *Time* in 1983. "Why should sound alone be enough when sight is only as far away as the TV set or the video machine?" Concluded the magazine, "Video will be the way to keep time with the future."

MTV, a music television channel established only two years earlier, was the subject of this *Time* article. During the early 1980s, MTV began to replace radio among a generation of teens born during the 1960s, youngsters who had no personal recollection of Elvis, the Beatles, or Vietnam and who sought their own musical identity. MTV helped create the visual rock of Duran Duran and pop metal and played a major role in the mania over Michael Jackson. In the 1980s, MTV designed and delivered rock to the TV generation.

MTV and the Video Age

Americans of the 1980s became obsessed with a video technology that had first been introduced to the mass market with the television set. By the end of the decade, 98.2 percent of all American households watched television, most had at least two sets, and 85 percent owned a color TV. Americans also purchased video-cassette recorder-players, first mass marketed in 1976 by the Victor Co. of Japan (JVC). In 1981, Americans purchased 1.3 million units, a 69 percent increase from the previous year. In 1981, Americans spent $9.2 billion on video products; four years later, they purchased more than $15 billion in video hardware and accessories. By 1989, more than ninety-seven million Americans owned JVC-manufactured VCRs. In 1990, Americans bought more than 200 million prerecorded video tapes and 280 million blank videocassettes, and most American consumers had become part of the expanding video culture.

American teenagers who had been raised on television embraced the video craze. The post–baby boomers, on average, watched television from three to four hours a day. By high school graduation, they had spent more time watching commercial television than sitting in the classroom. In a 1981 survey of eighth graders, the youths named TV personalities as their Top-Ten role models. The post–baby boomers even stared at television sets in their schools that had become increasingly equipped with instructional TV.

American teenagers of the 1980s, accustomed to the television screen at home and at school, became entranced by video games. They first began to play Space Invaders at the turn of the decade. By 1981, the TV generation dropped more than twenty-five billion quarters into video game machines at local arcades, which grossed more than the combined television revenues of baseball, football, and basketball, and the combined income of all of the casinos in the country. Teens, mostly male, spent an average of $4.30 per week on coin-operated video games, and in 1981, spent the equivalent of 75,000 years playing Pac-Man, Asteroids, Space Invaders, and other video games. By the early 1980s, they also began to play video games at home. In 1982, the Atari Corporation, owned by Warner Communications, grossed approximately $1.3 billion in home video game console and cartridge sales. By the end of that year, more than 8 percent of all households owned home video games.

Warner Communications applied video technology to the pop music field. Aided by the advent of stereo TV and the deregulation of the airwaves, which encouraged the growth of cable television, Warner and American Express invested $20 million to launch Music Television (MTV) on August 1, 1981. They broadcast a nonstop format of three-minute video clips, focusing primarily on Warner artists, which initially appeared on 300 cable outlets in 2.5 million homes.

Music Television, headed by twenty-eight-year-old Robert Pittman, targeted its programming to the under twenty-five-year-old generation, who had been neglected by radio. "Where is the Woodstock generation? They're all old and bald," reasoned Pittman. Recycling the 1960s' ad campaign for the once-popular breakfast cereal Maypo into "I Want My MTV," he stalked the "TV babies," who seldom read newspapers, books, or even the rock press.

The New Romantics

MTV attracted the TV generation with young, visually exciting bands from the dance clubs of England. Opened as a reaction to the austerity of punk, English dance clubs such as the Blitz in Covent Garden provided working-class youths with escapist entertainment. "Most kids who actually live there are sick of the street," contended Gary Kemp, the founder and guitarist of Spandau Ballet, a prominent dance club band. "They want to be in a club with great lights, and look really good and pick up girls."

As with its American counterpart, English disco focused on a fashion-conscious audience. "Discos are always parties because you have to make your own visual entertainment," commented Kemp. "The most important thing in a club is the people, not the music they listen to. You become the most important person. You become the visual aspect of the evening, rather than the band." Discos, he continued, appealed to "people who like being looked at—that's why dancing is so important, and why people try and beat each other at dancing. It's also why clothes are so important."

Gary Kemp linked the excessive concern over fashion to British culture. "The attitude behind it has always been there; Mods, skinheads, and the soul kids—just kids who want to dress smart and enjoy themselves. My dad was a Teddy Boy and my older cousin was a mod. I guess it's hereditary."

The music played at the clubs, a combination of the steady disco beat and the atmospheric sounds of the electronic synthesizer, originated with groups such as Roxy Music. Formed in early 1971 by singer Brian Ferry and named after the popular chain of Roxy cinemas in England, the band wore stylish, sometimes flamboyant, futuristic costumes designed by Anthony Price. One member of the group, wrote *Music Scene*, "has been seen traveling the Underground wearing heavily applied brown eye shadow, thick mascara, lipstick, black glitter beads, pearly nail varnish, and violent purple streaks in his blonde hair."

Unlike most glam rockers of the 1970s who delivered hard rock, Roxy Music featured the synthesizer, which in the hands of Brian Eno added an almost ethereal element to the music. The band released its debut, self-named album in 1972. It reached the Top Ten in Britain and included the smash British single "Virginia Plain." The next year, Roxy Music refined its distinctive style with the synthesizer-drenched *For Your Pleasure*, which reached the British Top Five, and the next year topped the British chart with *Stranded*.

Brian Eno, who shaped the unique Roxy sound, left the group in 1973 to, in his words, "pursue a partially defined direction—probably involving further investigations into bioelectronics, snake guitar, the human voice, and lizard girls." The band replaced him with the teenage multi-instrumentalist Eddie Jobson and began to deliver a quieter, smoother sound that showcased Brian Ferry's vocals. By 1976, a year after the band scored its first U.S. hit single, "Love Is the Drug," Roxy Music disbanded.

Ultravox continued the tradition of Roxy Music and became the direct precursor of the New Romantic movement. Brought together in 1976 by John Foxx (b. Dennis Leigh), who had dabbled in tapes and synthesizers while in school, the extravagantly bedecked band recorded two albums of electronica, punctuated by the violin and keyboards of Billy Currie. In 1978, the band enlisted the help of producer

Conny Plank, who had worked with experimental electronic groups such as Can and Kraftwerk to release *Systems of Romance*, which offered listeners a sparse, crystalline, electronic sound that defined the electro-pop of the New Romantics.

In early 1979, keyboardist Billy Currie joined fashion-conscious Steve Strange, synthesizer player Midge Ure, and some members of the group Magazine to form a side project, which they called Visage. As with Ultravox, the band emphasized outrageous fashion. "Fashion," commented Steve Strange, "has been missing from the scene since the early seventies with Bowie and Roxy, so what we're part of is just an upsurge in fashion."

Visage expanded the Ultravox sound, featuring two synthesizers and guitars supported by a heavy, repetitive drumbeat. "We were trying to get away from the

Gary Numan and synthesizer. *Permission by Cam Garrett.*

obvious disco sound," explained Strange. "I messed around with synthesizers and found sounds which were really different from the traditional guitar and bass. We wanted to create a danceable beat. I know you can do that with drums and a bass, but it was a new sound that we wanted to use."

Gary Numan popularized the sound of electro-pop that Ultravox and Visage had developed. Born Gary Webb in 1958 and taking his pseudonym from the *Yellow Pages*, Numan first played in the punk-influenced Tubeway Army. He soon abandoned the guitar for the synthesizer, donned futuristic outfits, and, on May 4, 1979, released the synthesizer dance number "Are 'Friends' Electric?" Two weeks later, Numan and his band, which included Billy Currie, appeared on the British television show *Top of the Pops*, and by the end of July, the single and the album *Replicas* hit the top of the British chart. "Gary Numan just released "Are 'Friends' Electric?" when everyone thought synthesizer bands were just junk or something or that anyone who used a synthesizer was just a bit of a joke," remembered Midge Ure. "At the time it was very unfashionable, but six months later because of Gary Numan it became very fashionable to be a synthesizer band."

The ease of mastering the synthesizer contributed to its popularity. "In some ways it's quite strange that synthesizers were so hated in the punk era," remarked Andy McClusky of the successful electro-pop band Orchestral Manoeuvres in the Dark, which formed in 1978. "They're the ideal punk instrument if you believe in the ethic of 'anybody can do it.' Someone who's been playing synth for ten minutes can easily sound as good as someone who's been playing for years, provided the ideas are there." Andy Fletcher confessed in 1982, two years after his all-synthesizer band, Depeche Mode, was formed, "We couldn't hardly play at all then; we can't play very well now. In pop music nowadays you don't need technical ability, you need ideas and the ability to write songs."

By the beginning of the 1980s, portable synthesizers had become relatively inexpensive. Unlike the cumbersome, sometimes stationary Moog models of the previous decade, easy-to-handle portables could be purchased for as little as $100 to $300.

The electro-pop sound of the synthesizer, easily attainable and affordable, embodied the digital, push-button 1980s. "Not a day goes by when you don't press a button, whether it's for a cup of coffee or to turn on the stereo or video," observed David Ball of the two-man synthesizer group Soft Cell. "People are so surrounded now by electronics, of course there's electronic music."

MTV Goes Electro-Pop

MTV, searching for videos of new bands to air on its twenty-four-hour-a-day format, promoted the electro-pop of fashion-obsessed New Romantics such as Duran Duran. Begun in 1978 as a duo and named after a character in the science fiction movie *Barbarella*, within two years the group had become a quintet that featured an airy-sounding synthesizer, the insistent drumbeat of disco, and a pop sensibility for what keyboard player Nick Rhodes dubbed "entertainment music." The group reached the British Top Five with its first, self-named effort and then subsequently scored with three Top Ten albums on both sides of the Atlantic through the imaginative use of videos on MTV. "Videos are incredibly important for us," asserted Rhodes. "It's a way of expressing a song in visuals. It gives another dimension." He added, "MTV was instrumental in breaking us in America." Norman Sammick, senior vice president of Warner Communications, put it more succinctly: "I think Duran Duran owes its life to MTV."

The music channel helped other electro-pop bands such as the Human League reach the record-buying American public. The group, formed in Sheffield in 1977, first produced icy, dense electronic music modeled after European outfits such as Kraftwerk. In 1980, vocalist and synthesizer wiz Philip Oakley disbanded the Human League because of its reliance on taped music during concerts, and with Adrian Wright and four new members reformed the band. The next year, the revamped group hired producer Martin Rushent, who infused the band's synthesizer-based music with a toe-tapping, pop sensibility. "I wanted to make a pop electronic album," remembered Rushent. "Not a DAF or a Kraftwerk, but something that was accessible to everybody. The Human League just walked through the door at the right time." The producer replaced the traditional keyboard synthesizer with a Roland Microcomposer sequencer, added the flawless beat of a drum machine, and in 1981 produced *Dare*, which included the single "Don't You Want Me" that immediately topped the British chart. After MTV placed "Don't You Want Me" in heavy rotation in 1982, the song became a number-one single and the album hit the number-three position in the United States.

MTV lifted other wildly garbed, British electro-pop bands up the American charts. Through repeated showings of selected videos, it successfully promoted the London quintet Spandau Ballet, which hit the Top Five with "True" (1983). Soft Cell

Duran Duran. Photo by Mike Owen. *Permission by Capitol Records.*

scored with a remake of the obscure soul song "Tainted Love" (1982), which stayed on the chart for forty-three weeks, and A Flock of Seagulls reached the number-three slot with "I Ran (So Far Away)" (1982). MTV also marketed the Thompson Twins' club hit "In the Name of Love" (1982) and Depeche Mode (translated: "fast fashion"), which had the dance smash "People Are People" (1985).

MTV refurbished the career of David Bowie, the 1970s' icon who had helped lay the groundwork for electro-pop. Bowie, the king of glitter rock who served as a model of fashion for the foppish New Romantics, began to abandon a hard, guitar-based rock sound for the synthesizer around 1976, when he released a collection of techno-pop songs, *Station to Station*. The next year he began a three-album collaboration with synthesizer wunderkind Brian Eno, who produced a sometimes-fragile, sometimes-dense synthesizer sound that he had pioneered as a member of Roxy Music. In 1983, at the height of New Romantic success, the ever-visual Bowie recorded *Let's Dance*, which, with the help of MTV and a world tour, neared the top of the American chart.

By 1983, the electro-pop sound, largely introduced to America by videos on MTV, had swept across the United States. It dominated the charts, filtered into mainstream pop, and captivated the TV generation. Pursuing this new sound, devotees bought an unprecedented number of synthesizers in place of guitars, which declined in sales by 37 percent in one year. MTV, created in the decade of technology, sold a visually interesting, electro-pop dance music to a generation raised on glitter rock, disco, and television.

MTV measured its success by a meteoric increase in viewers. Initially broadcast to 2.5 million households in late 1981, by 1983 the music channel reached more than 17 million homes on 2,000 cable affiliates. The average MTV viewer was less than twenty-three years old and watched the network for one hour a day on weekdays and ninety minutes on weekends. "They're watching it," said MTV vice president Les Garland in early 1983, "not in front of their homework, not as background. They're watching it."

Attracting the under-twenty-three-year-old bracket, MTV appealed to many corporate sponsors that manufactured products for the youth market. "MTV is very attractive," asserted Joseph Ostrow, executive vice president of the ad agency Young & Rubicam. "It allows you to target very discreetly to a particular segment of the population. For youth-oriented companies, that's terrific." John Lack, executive vice president of Warner Amex, agreed when his company started the network, "We are a company that believes in specialized entertainment and if you are a Budweiser or Kawasaki motorcycles or Pepsi-Cola, you want our audience." During its first year of operation, MTV convinced more than 100 companies to spend $1,500 for a thirty-second spot and grossed $20 million. By 1984, revenues had jumped to $73 million.

Music Television provided a much-needed boost to a formerly radio-dependent U.S. record industry that in 1978 had peaked with roughly $4 billion in gross revenues before declining sharply next year. The network created a style of music for a new generation that radio had neglected. "Groups are chalking up huge sales on songs [through MTV] that have never been played on radio," boasted Les Garland. In 1983, *Billboard* estimated that exposure of mostly new bands on MTV resulted in sales increases of 15 to 20 percent. "We were there for the industry," explained John Lack.

"We found we could help a business in trouble and it's worked, and they've responded. Ask anyone at CBS or RCA or Arista."

MTV and Michaelmania

MTV continued to support the U.S. recording industry by promoting a Motown-style revival, which followed naturally from electro-pop. Though using synthesizers, the New Romantics created a discolike dance music that had its foundation in the slick, fashionable Motown. As a youth, Steve Strange of Visage "used to go to these northern soul clubs," which featured Motown-type bands. "Our direction came from the soul/disco/dance side, not rock," agreed Gary Kemp of Spandau Ballet.

As the synthesizer craze began to fade in 1982, MTV capitalized on the renewed interest in Motown by airing videos of former Motown star Michael Jackson. Growing up in Gary, Indiana, during the 1960s, Jackson and his siblings Tito, Jermaine, Jackie, and Marlon practiced songs and dance steps at home. "When I found out that my kids were interested in becoming entertainers, I really went to work with them," recalled father Joe Jackson. "I rehearsed them about three years before I turned them loose. That's practically every day for at least two or three hours. When the other kids would be out on the street playing games, my boys were in the house working—trying to learn how to be something in life." Under the strict and sometimes harsh tutelage of Joe Jackson, the boys entered and won talent contests in Indiana and Illinois and played at Chicago clubs. "This was on weekends," remembered the elder Jackson. "I had a Volkswagen bus and I bought a big luggage rack and put it on the top and had everybody on the inside of the bus."

Joe Jackson approached Motown about his family musical act. In 1967, he "sent Berry Gordy a tape. They kept it about three months and then sent it back." Two years later, the persistent father convinced Gordy to sign the Jackson 5, who had impressed Gladys Knight when she performed on the same bill as the boys in 1967 at a civic Soul Weekend in Gary.

Berry Gordy, following his formula for success, began to groom the boys. "We provide total guidance," a Motown vice president explained. "We provide their material, set their basic sound, and work out the choreographic routines." The company gave special attention to the ten-year-old Michael, who was taught to mimic James Brown's frenzied dancing and the romantic pleadings of Smokey Robinson. In late 1969, Motown featured Michael on the first Jackson 5 release, "I Want You Back," which by January 1970 hit the number-one slot on the singles chart and sold more than two million copies. "We're labeling it soul-bubblegum," declared Berry Gordy.

The Jackson 5 became the last major recording act signed by Motown. They followed their first hit with thirteen consecutive Top-Twenty singles, including the number-one hits "ABC," "The Love You Save," and "I'll Be There." By March 1976, when they left Motown, the Jackson 5 had received a commendation from Congress for their "contribution to American youth," inspired a Saturday morning network television cartoon show, and become the most successful African-American pop vocal group, selling more than 100 million records worldwide.

The Jackson 5, Gordy's crossover dream, appealed to all races, genders, and ages. "The Jacksons' music," stated Joe Jackson, "is a type of music that the young kids like, and as you know, the older people like, too. It's music to send a message to all the people whether they're black or white. It's music for rejoicing, whether you're black or white. It's music for the whole world."

When the Jackson 5 signed with Epic Records, the group changed their name to the Jacksons and continued to churn out hits. Using the songwriting team of Kenny Gamble and Leon Huff, they scored with the Top-Ten "Enjoy Yourself" and then began charting with their own material.

Michael Jackson enjoyed a successful solo career as well. In 1971 and 1972 he hit the chart with the Top-Ten singles "Got to Be There," a reworking of "Rockin' Robin," and the number-one "Ben." In 1978, he played the scarecrow in the movie *The Wiz*, an all-African-American version of *The Wizard of Oz*, starring Diana Ross. While filming the movie, Jackson met producer Quincy Jones, who arranged the music for the soundtrack. The next year, assisted by Jones, Jackson recorded *Off the Wall*, which sold eight million copies and included the hit singles "Don't Stop 'Til You Get Enough," "Rock with You," "Off the Wall," and "She's Out of My Life."

In 1982, Jackson again teamed with Quincy Jones on *Thriller*. Trying to appeal to both African-American and white audiences, he chose as the first single "The Girl Is Mine," a duet with former Beatle Paul McCartney, a choice that ensured a wide audience. He then released "Beat It," which included an Eddie Van Halen guitar solo that assured play on rock radio stations. To further market his product, Jackson filmed slick videos of several songs on the album.

Video provided an ideal medium for Jackson, who had been trained at the Motown school. "Rock videos have transformed the music industry, providing a showcase for Jackson in much the same way as musical comedy did for Fred Astaire in the 1930s," *Maclean's*, the Canadian counterpart to *Time* magazine, told its readers in 1984. "Videos have revived the demand for old-fashioned entertainment skills, an ideal situation for Jackson, who has been perfecting his act from the age of five."

First encouraged by Motown, the singer perfected dazzling choreography unlike most other rock acts. Gene Kelly, the popular dancer of the 1940s, raved about Jackson's "native histrionic wit. He knows when to stop and then flash out like a bolt of lightning." "I think he's terrific," enthused Bob Fosse, the director-choreographer who became known for his work on the movie *Cabaret* and the Broadway smash *Pippin*. "Clean, neat, fast with a sensuality that comes through. . . . It's the style. That's what Michael Jackson has." Even Fred Astaire, probably the best-known dancer in American history, complimented Jackson: "My Lord, he is a wonderful mover."

MTV, criticized for only airing videos of white artists, played the visually stunning, expertly choreographed Jackson videos and helped create Michaelmania. Though Jackson's records had always sold well, *Thriller* began to sell at an amazing rate after it was promoted on MTV. At the height of the mania, it sold one million copies every four days. It stayed on the Japanese album chart for sixty-five weeks, sold on the black market in the Soviet Union, and even topped the chart in South Africa. "Jackson, you might say, bridges the apartheid gap," observed one record executive.

Michael Jackson and Dave Navarro perform during the Democratic National Committee's "A Night at the Apollo" show at Harlem's world-famous Apollo Theater in New York City. Photo by Kevin Mazur/ WireImage. Getty Images—WireImage.com.

Crazed fans around the globe began to snap up Michael Jackson paraphernalia. They bought posters, buttons, and T-shirts, which most rock acts sold by the 1980s. Michael Jackson fanatics also purchased *Thriller* caps, key chains, duffel bags, bubblegum cards, an 11-inch Michael Jackson doll that could be twisted into various dance poses, and replicas of the single, white sequined glove that Jackson wore onstage. They even bought a video that chronicled the making of the video for the song "Thriller."

When the mania subsided in early 1985, Jackson had achieved singular success. He had released seven of the ten songs on the album as singles that reached the Top Ten. The twenty-five-year-old singer had sold forty million copies of *Thriller* worldwide, topped the U.S. charts in both 1983 and 1984 and won 150 gold and platinum awards as well as a record-breaking eight Grammy awards. "Jackson," asserted *Time* in March 1984, "is the biggest thing since the Beatles. He is the hottest single phenomenon since Elvis Presley."

Michael Jackson, the most important rock star of the early 1980s, ostensibly epitomized the growing conservatism in America. He did not smoke, drink, or take drugs. He even refused to utter the word *funky*, preferring *jelly* instead. A devout adherent to the Jehovah's Witnesses, the singer attended meetings at a Kingdom Hall four times a week and regularly fasted on weekends. "Such pop superstars as Elvis Presley, Bob Dylan or the Beatles have traditionally posed a sexual or political challenge to the status quo," contended *Maclean's* magazine, "but Michael Jackson is by contrast an establishment figure, perfectly in tune with the conservative America of Ronald Reagan." In 1984, Jackson received a public-service award from the president, a former 1940s' actor, who himself had become one of the most popular U.S. presidents through his use of video.

Jackson amassed a fortune from his success. By the end of 1984, he had earned more than $30 million from the sales of *Thriller* and had grossed another $50 million from the burgeoning industry of Michael Jackson products. The singer increased his personal net worth to $75 million in 1985, becoming one of the richest men in America. As jazz great and *Thriller* producer Quincy Jones observed, "MTV and Michael rode each other to stardom."

The Jackson Legacy

The success of Michael Jackson paved the way for other soul-pop artists, including British bands such as Culture Club, who merged the English concern for fashion with a Motown-influenced sound to climb the charts. Formed in 1981 by singer Boy George (b. George O'Dowd), the group dressed in outlandish costumes. "I used to dress up from the age of thirteen or fourteen, and George is the same," related the group's guitarist Mikey Craig. "Dressing up in different styles and going to the clubs is a big thrill for kids. You follow the fashion changes and get caught up in it."

The extravagantly bedecked, video-ready Culture Club played, in the words of Boy George, "imitation soul." In 1982, they released the soul-pop album *Kissing to Be Clever*, which included the warm, bouncy, Top-Ten "Do You Really Want to Hurt Me" and "I'll Tumble 4 Ya." Scaling the charts on the coattails of Jackson's *Thriller* the next year, the group produced the number-two *Colour by Numbers*, which employed signature Motown riffs. "'Plagiarism' is one of my favorite words," admitted Boy George. "Culture Club is the most sincere form of plagiarism in modern music—we just do it better than most."

The Eurythmics also scored with an updated Motown sound. Formed in 1980 by Dave Stewart and the photogenic, classically trained Annie Lennox, the duo first recorded electronic experimental music that failed to chart. Amid Michaelmania in 1983, the twosome earned international acclaim for *Sweet Dreams (Are Made of This)*, which featured the sultry, Motown-influenced vocals of Lennox over the insistent beat of a drum machine. "I identify my vocal style very much with black soul music," explained Lennox at the time. "Not with blues, but with 1960s soul. It really struck a chord in me, and I can't get away from that." Stewart agreed, "What she really loved was Tamla/Motown material." During the next two years, the duo followed with the Top-Ten, soul-tinged *Touch* and *Be Yourself Tonight*.

Wham!, another sharply dressed duo from Britain, hit the charts with African American–inspired dance music. Wham!'s Andrew Ridgeley and George Michael (b. Georgios Panayiotou) met as young teens and frequented local clubs, dancing to the soundtrack of *Saturday Night Fever*. "There was disco before *Saturday Night Fever* but after that it all caught fire," George Michael wrote in his autobiography. "It revolutionized dance music. And us."

In 1982, the two friends formed Wham! and scaled the British chart with a series of singles, including "Young Guns" and "Bad Boys." In late 1984, amid the furor over Michael Jackson, Michael and Ridgeley released a second album, *Make It Big*, which, after being promoted through videos aired on MTV, yielded three number-one singles in the United States and Britain: "Wake Me Up Before You Go-Go," "Careless Whisper," and "Everything She Wants." When Wham! disbanded in 1986, George Michael continued to offer spunky dance hits on the chart-topping *Faith* (1987), which yielded four number-one singles.

On the other side of the Atlantic, Madonna combined a decadent sex appeal with African-American dance rhythms to attain stardom. Born of Italian-American parents in Detroit in 1959, Madonna Louise Ciccone won a dance scholarship to the University of Michigan. After her freshman year, she left school to pursue a career as a dancer in New York City, briefly studied at the Alvin Ailey Dance Theater and moved to Paris, where she began to dance with the revue of disco star Patrick Hernandez. In 1979, Madonna formed a band with drummer Steve Bray, and the next year she gave a tape of the band to Mark Kamins, a disco disc jockey, who helped Madonna land a record contract with Sire.

In 1983, Madonna released her first record, which presented the singer's breathy vocals over a disco beat. Propelled by videos of songs on the album that accentuated her sexually aggressive, Marilyn Monroe–like image, including her trademark attire of lace wear, she hit the Top Ten. The next year Madonna attained national stardom with the number-one *Like a Virgin*, a dance album that included the hook-laden singles "Material Girl," "Like a Virgin," and "Dress You Up," and on its cover pictured Madonna in a flimsy lace bodice cinched by a belt that carried the inscription "Boy Toy." By 1986, Madonna had sold more than nine million copies of her first two albums, had hit the top of the chart a second time with *True Blue*, and, based upon her initial exposure through MTV, had snagged a leading role in the feature-length movie *Desperately Seeking Susan*.

The success of Michael Jackson's brand of Motown dance music also helped the careers of African-American soul-pop performers. "It inspired black artists not to look at themselves in a limited way," noted producer Quincy Jones. "Before Michael, those kinds of sales had never happened for a black artist. Michael did it. He did it for the first time."

Motown artist Lionel Richie followed Jackson to the top of the charts. In 1968, Richie joined with five other freshmen at the African-American Tuskegee Institute in Tuskegee, Alabama, to form the Commodores, a name randomly picked from the dictionary. Three years later, the band signed with Motown and for two years served as the opening act for the Jackson 5. In 1974, the Commodores recorded their first album, *Machine Gun*, characterized by a raw, sharp-edged sound. After two more albums, Lionel Richie convinced the group to record his softer, soul-pop ballads such as "Three Times a Lady" and "Sail On," which hit the top of the singles chart. In 1982, the Motown performer released his first solo album, which contained the chart-topping single "Truly." In the midst of Michaelmania the next year, he recorded *Can't Slow Down*, which, with the help of MTV, hit the top of the chart and transformed Lionel Richie into *Billboard*'s Top Artist of 1984.

MTV helped the youngest member of the Jackson family. In 1982, before the success of *Thriller*, Janet Jackson released a self-named debut, which barely cracked the Top Seventy-Five. She followed with the even less successful *Dream Street*. In 1986, promoted by a series of videos and amid the Motown-influenced craze that had been created by her brother, Janet Jackson hit the top of the chart with *Control*, and three years later duplicated her feat with *Janet Jackson's Rhythm Nation 1814*. "Janet's a video artist," reasoned Roger Davies, who managed the singer.

Whitney Houston achieved similar success through video. The daughter of Cissy Houston, who had anchored the Aretha Franklin backup group the Sweet Inspirations, Whitney began performing in a gospel choir at age eight. She continued her signing career, backing dozens of artists in the studio, including Jermaine Jackson on "Take Good Care of My Heart," and appeared as a model in fashion magazines like *Glamour*, *Cosmopolitan*, and *Seventeen*. In 1983, Houston signed with Arista Records, which, as Motown had done with its young talent, groomed the young singer.

In 1985, Houston released her first album, which featured upbeat ballads in the Motown tradition. As the first two singles from the LP climbed the chart, she filmed a video of "How Will I Know," which, according to Peter Baron, Arista's associate direc-tor of video production and promotion, "helped build her image. She's become a superstar in a year." The singer had three consecutive number-one singles and sold fourteen million copies of the album, the biggest-selling debut in history. In 1987, Houston recorded a follow-up, *Whitney*, which shot to the number-one spot and yielded four chart-topping singles.

Prince grafted rock guitars and overtly sexual lyrics onto a soul-pop sound for an innovative hybrid of the Michael Jackson formula for success. Born in Minneapolis to a bandleader father, Prince Rogers Nelson taught himself piano, guitar, and drums by age fourteen and began to play a mixture of rock and soul. "I never grew up in one particular culture," Prince related. "I'm not a punk, but I'm not an R&B artist either—because I'm a middle-class kid from Minnesota, which is very much white America."

In 1976, Prince met Minneapolis sound engineer Chris Moon, who suggested sexually explicit lyrics. "It was amazing to see," recalled Moon. "Here was this very quiet kid, but once he'd discovered the notion of sex as a vehicle for his writing, it was as if a door unlocked for him." Within a year, Prince signed with Warner Brothers and in 1978 recorded *For You*, which included the suggestive "Soft and Wet." Late the next year, he hit the top of the R&B chart with "I Wanna Be Your Lover."

In 1982, after only moderate commercial success with his recordings, Prince released *1999* and filmed a video of the song "Little Red Corvette," one of the first clips by an African–American artist aired on the music channel, which slowly lifted the single to the Top Ten. Through constant promotion by MTV, Prince sold fourteen million copies of *Purple Rain* (1984), the soundtrack for the movie of the same name, which won an Oscar and a Grammy award. In 1985, Prince followed with the number-one *Around the World in a Day*. As with other African–American and white soul-pop artists in the wake of the mania over Michael Jackson, Prince had attained international stardom through video.

Pop Goes the Metal

MTV ensured its preeminent place among the cable networks during the decade by creating a craze for pop metal bands. As it had done with electro-pop and soul-pop, the music channel delivered a visually exciting, largely inoffensive heavy metal to the post–baby boomers.

Van Halen served as the archetype for the metal bands of the 1980s. The sons of a jazz musician, Alex and Eddie Van Halen grew up in the Netherlands, where they received extensive classical music training. In 1965, they moved with their family to Pasadena, California, where they discovered and began to play rock-and-roll. By 1974, the Van Halen brothers joined with bassist Michael Anthony and singer David Lee Roth to form a band, which for three years performed at Los Angeles bars such as Gazzarri's on Sunset Strip in West Hollywood.

The members of Van Halen each contributed a different element to their unique sound. "I think the only true rocker of the bunch is Al," related guitarist Eddie Van Halen. "He's the only one who listens to AC/DC and all that kind of stuff. Dave will walk in with a disco tape, and I'll walk in with my progressive tapes, and Mike walks in with his Disneyland stuff." At home, Eddie preferred the "progressive stuff" and "a lot of Chopin, piano. Very little rock-and-roll."

Unlike the blues-rooted heavy-metal artists of the late 1960s and early 1970s, the eclectic Van Halen presented a more polished, smooth sound. The band favored a variety of tempos; rapid-fire, arpeggio guitar solos much shorter than the extended guitar breaks of the original heavy-metal groups; fast-paced, light bass lines; and periodic harmonies that reinforced the hooks in the songs. In addition, Van Halen featured frequent falsetto screams by the photogenic, acrobatic David Lee Roth, who added a wry sense of humor to the lyrics. "Van Halen is entertainment," contended singer Roth. "Van Halen is entertainment delivered at maximum impact, but it's entertainment."

In 1976, the band recorded a demo tape financed by Gene Simmons of Kiss, who spotted them at the Starwood club in Los Angeles. A year later, they signed a contract with Warner Brothers and in early 1978 released their first album, which hit the Top Twenty and sold more than two million copies. Van Halen followed with four Top-Ten albums, the last of which, *Diver Down* (1982), reached the number-three slot. After Eddie Van Halen received mass notoriety for his guitar work on Michael Jackson's "Beat It," the band neared the top of the chart with *1984*, receiving constant support from MTV.

Def Leppard perfected the pop metal that Van Halen had originated. Raised in the factory town of Sheffield in the midlands of England, Joe Elliott, guitarists Steve

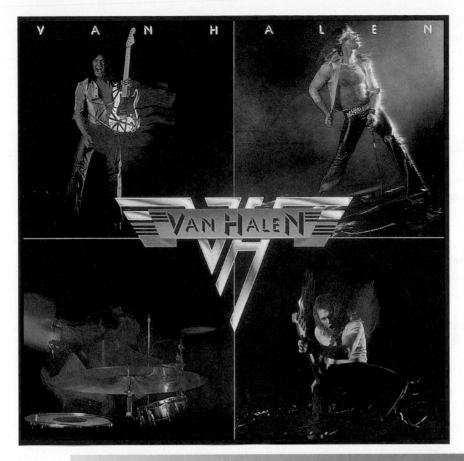

Van Halen. The first album cover. *Permission by Warner Brothers Records/Reprise Records.*

Clark and Pete Willis, and bass player Rick Savage worked in blue-collar jobs before founding the band. They drew their inspiration from a combination of heavy metal and pop. "We always loved the heavy bands of the early seventies, obviously Zeppelin, Uriah Heep, Deep Purple even, but other than that we also were very influenced by what was happening in the pop charts," related bassist Rick Savage. "I suppose if you analyzed it, it was some sort of cross between the two forms." He added, "We always want to have that commercial aspect that's pleasing on the ear, while the seventeen-year-olds can still get off on the power of it."

In 1981, after two commercially unsuccessful releases, the band joined with producer Robert ("Mutt") Lange, who began to help Def Leppard refine their pop-metal sound. "I heard those vocal harmonies and thought, 'Wow, an English band doing that stuff,'" remembered Lange. "Since they had the looks and they had the riffs I knew that with me as an extra member, so to speak, we could pull the songs together." The group released the Lange-produced *High and Dry*, which entered the U.S. Top Forty.

By 1983, after Phil Collen replaced guitarist Willis, Def Leppard had perfected its sound. The group featured tight vocal harmonies and dramatic guitar work accentuated by Lange's production. Joe Elliott called the sound "nice, youthful, melodic rock-'n'-roll."

The band members penned catchy, unobtrusive lyrics. "Because the whole idea of Def Leppard is escapism," asserted Rick Savage, "we hate singing about unemployment and such, and we hate bands that do sing about it. Everybody knows it's tough. A band can't change anything. Who wants to go to one of our shows to hear how bad life is?" Joe Elliott echoed, "It's all wine, women and song. Nothing annoys me more than records about politics this, Greenpeace that. Someone has to be the opposite, and that's us. All we are is total escapism."

MTV promoted the photogenic, escapist pop metal of Def Leppard through performance videos. Offering heavy rotation to clips of such songs as "Photograph," the music channel broadcast the band to its young viewers. Coupled with constant touring, it successfully marketed *Pyromania* (1983), which sold more than nine million copies. "1983 was our year," enthused Cliff Burnstein, comanager of the group.

The music channel also contributed to the success of other pop-metal bands, some of which favored the outlandish costumes and antics of 1970s' glam rockers. In 1981, Motley Crue played a West Coast version of video-ready glam rock. Nikki Sixx (b. Frank Ferranna, Jr.) on bass, vocalist Vince Neil, guitarist Mick Mars (b. Bob Deal), and drummer Tommy Lee (b. Tommy Lee Bass) began performing together around Los Angeles. Setting fire to their extravagant clothing and chain sawing mannequins on stage, the band gained a loyal following for their theatrical heavy metal.

The band identified Kiss as its major influence. "When I first saw Kiss I stood in line for six hours at the Paramount Theater in Seattle, Washington," recalled Nikki Sixx. "I was sitting in the front row, and when they took the stage I knew then that I wanted to have a band that was nothing less than what I saw. The theater bug bit me. Rock-'n'-roll from then on had to have an element of theater to excite me."

In May 1983, after an unsuccessful debut, Motley Crue signed to Elektra Records. Five months later, they released *Shout at the Devil*, which through heavy rotation on MTV entered the Top Twenty. By the end of 1984, the readers of *Hit Parader* and *Circus* magazines voted the band Rock Act of the Year. The glam rockers followed with the Top-Ten *Theater of Pain* (1985).

Ratt came from the same Los Angeles heavy-metal scene. Banding together in 1982 around guitarist Robbin Crosby and singer Stephen Pearcy, the group played an escapist pop metal. "We have more melody in our music," noted Crosby as he compared the group to heavy-metal pioneers such as Led Zeppelin. "We talk about love and sex and reality and fantasy—just down-to-earth, fun stuff."

The band members affected a glam image to increase their popularity. "When we first got together, we were a real heavy-metal band—black leather, studs, the whole thing," admitted Robbin Crosby. "We showed up at our first gig—and everybody else had the same stuff. Me and Steve were going, 'This is not cool. We've got to do something to get away from this.'" Crosby continued: "We started wearing more fashionable clothes. Started dressing real sharp. A lot of the metalers said, 'Whoa! These guys are faggots!' But it's more of a mass appeal kind of thing."

The band proved its popular appeal with the help of MTV. In 1984, Ratt released *Out of the Cellar* with accompanying videos for the music channel. By the next year, the group had cracked the Top Ten and had sold more than two million copies of their debut. The next year, the band repeated its success with million-selling *Invasion of Your Privacy*.

MTV also began to show clips of Bon Jovi. Formed in 1983 by singer Jon Bon Jovi (b. John Bongiovi) and quickly signed to Mercury Records, the pop-metal band toured extensively to promote its first two LPs, which both failed to crack the U.S. Top Thirty. Three years later, the group released *Slippery When Wet* and filmed matching videos, which MTV aired ceaselessly. By late 1987, Bon Jovi had sold more than twelve million copies of its chart-topping album. They followed with the number-one *New Jersey* (1988). "The success of such current hot groups as Bon Jovi," observed *Time*, "is largely traceable to the saturation airplay given their videos on MTV."

The MTV-based success of acts such as Bon Jovi opened the doors for a pop-metal explosion during the late 1980s. "The majors are now going nuts. Everyone's out there trying to sign up a metal band," reported Bob Chiappardi, co-owner of the metal-oriented Concrete Marketing. The major labels signed acts such as Poison, Kix, Kingdom Come, and countless others. Established pop-metal acts continued to sell. In 1986, Van Halen topped the chart with *5150* and followed with the number-one *OU812* (1988), both of which benefited from videos that received continual play on MTV. After a four-year hiatus, Def Leppard topped the charts with *Hysteria*, which sold more than five million copies. In 1987, Motley Crue neared the top with *Girls, Girls, Girls* and topped the chart with *Dr. Feelgood* (1989).

The success of pop-metal and electro-pop bands and the unparalleled achievements of Michael Jackson indicated the importance of MTV. "At any one time, 130,000 homes are watching MTV, according to Nielsen," observed Len Epand of Polygram Records. "If the video is in power rotation—fifteen or sixteen plays a week—and that audience tunes in ten times, that's 1.3 million people hearing the record and deciding whether they like it or not. If they like it, they'll buy it." Director of marketing for RCA video productions, Laura Foti added, "There isn't a national radio station. That's where MTV comes in. That's where they have their power: immediately showing everyone in the country this new band." Joe Jackson, the singer who hit the chart in 1979 with *Look Sharp*, complained about the dominance of MTV: "Things which used to count, such as being a good composer, player, or singer, are getting lost in the desperate rush to visualize everything. It is now possible to be all of the above and still get nowhere simply by not looking good in a video, or worse still, not making one."

The marketing clout of MTV translated into profits. In the first half of 1984, after the *Thriller* hysteria had started to abate, MTV registered $8.1 million in profits from sales of $30.3 million. In 1986, after Viacom International purchased the network from Warner Amex, it grossed $111 million and turned a profit of $47 million. Though its ratings began to decline in 1986, MTV tied with the USA Network and the Cable News Network for first place among the cable channels.

MTV, broadcast on more than 5,000 cable outlets to more than forty-six million viewers in 1989, had helped define 1980s' rock-and-roll. It had fostered and successfully promoted electro-pop and pop metal, and had created a frenzy over Michael Jackson's *Thriller*. To a large extent, the music network had replaced radio as the preeminent trendsetter in rock. As *Billboard* noted in its wrap-up of the decade, "MTV is singularly responsible for one of the most basic changes in the current music fan's vocabulary: Where somebody might have said ten years ago, 'Yeah, I've heard that song,' that same person now might likely say, 'Yeah, I saw that video,' or, even more revealing, 'Yeah, I saw that song.'" During the 1980s, MTV had packaged and delivered rock-and-roll to the TV generation.

The Promise of Rock-and-Roll

> **❝** In the '80s, which is a barren era, we look back at the '60s as a great reservoir of talent, of high ideals, and of the will and desire to change things. **❞**
>
> —Bono

"I'm a romantic," Bruce Springsteen confessed to a reporter in 1980. "To me the idea of a romantic is someone who sees the reality, lives the reality every day but knows about the possibilities, too. You can't lose sight of the dreams. That's what great rock is about to me, it makes the dream seem possible." Rock, added Springsteen, is "a promise, an oath."

The romanticism of Bruce Springsteen, rooted in a 1960s' idealism, became prevalent from the mid-1980s into the 1990s. It appealed to baby boomers, who during the 1960s had protested against the war in Vietnam and now confronted the most severe economic recession since the Great Depression of the 1930s, which their parents had experienced as youths. The return to a 1960s' sensibility led to numerous benefit concerts, which revived the careers of some 1960s' rockers and revitalized the rock industry. It also influenced a

1990s' country-rock boom, which captured the attention of the baby-boom generation. From the mid-1980s and into the 1990s, baby boomers embraced a 1960s-
inspired, cause-oriented rock that provided a stark contrast to the entertaining, glossy,
sexy images on MTV.

Trickling Down with Ronald Reagan

The return to 1960s' ideals occurred around mid-decade, when the policies of
President Ronald Reagan plummeted the country into a dire economic recession and
increasingly stratified the American people into rich and poor. Taking office in January
1981, Reagan hoped to roll back the innovative social programs of Franklin Roosevelt's
New Deal through conservative economic policies and subsidies to businesses. Using
"trickle down" logic, he believed that government aid to corporations would lead to
increased profits, and in their largess businesses would channel these new revenues
into expansion that would translate into higher wages and increased employment.
Misunderstanding the basic profit motive of capitalism, for eight years Ronald Reagan
offered corporate incentives, slashed domestic programs, and padded the military
budget to drive the nation into an economic tailspin.

A determined Reagan tried to decrease the involvement of the federal government
in social welfare programs. During his tenure as president, he cut spending for such programs as job training, college loans, food and medical aid, disability services, and child-
care centers for working mothers. Opposed to any programs that sought to provide
equality to disadvantaged groups, in 1981 Reagan lashed out against affirmative action by
ending the requirement for contractors on federally funded projects to adhere to affirmative action laws; during his administration he reduced efforts by the Justice
Department to enforce laws that prohibited job discrimination and encouraged fair
housing.

While abandoning poor, disadvantaged Americans, Reagan catered to the interests of business. He crushed the trade unions, first targeting the air traffic controllers.
In the summer of 1981 when the Professional Air Traffic Controllers Organization
(PATCO) declared a strike, Reagan threatened that if the strikers did "not report for
work within 48 hours, they have forfeited their jobs and will be terminated." Two days
later on August 5, 1981, Reagan fired 11,359 controllers.

In addition to neutralizing unions for businesses, the president pushed through
the Economic Recovery Act (1981), which provided a series of tax breaks to businesses and wealthy individuals. The act further stratified American society by cutting the
highest tax rate from 70 percent to 28 percent, effectively decreasing the taxes of the
wealthiest 1 percent of Americans by 6 percent while increasing the taxes of the poor-
est 1.6 percent of wage earners by 10 percent. Just as Reagan cut taxes for the rich and
lowered the governmental revenue, he escalated spending for the military to defeat the
Soviet Union, which he called the "evil empire." From 1980 to 1988, Reagan bal-
looned defense spending from $134 billion to $290 billion.

The twin policies of tax reduction for corporations and high tax-bracket
Americans and skyrocketing funding for the Pentagon dramatically increased the
national debt. When Reagan assumed the presidency, the United States had a national

debt of approximately $995 billion. By September 1984, the debt increased to $1.6 trillion, and near the end of the Reagan presidency in late 1989 the United States had a debt load of nearly $3 trillion.

Reagan's Darwinian, free-market policies led to a crisis in the domestic banking industry. Intent on deregulating banks and savings and loans, he supported a new law that gave savings and loans the ability to expand their portfolios into lending for risky real estate deals just as the real-estate market began to soften. Caught with billions of dollars in bad loans, many banks began to fail. In 1983, 49 banks failed—more than the failure rate in the worst year of the Great Depression—and another 540 banks teetered on the brink of closing. Between 1980 and 1983, 118 savings and loans with assets of $43 billion became insolvent. Fearing the effect of the banking debacle on the economy and his popularity, Reagan eventually spent $160 billion to rescue savings and loans and in 1984 engineered a $4.5 billion bailout for the Continental Illinois National Bank and Trust Company, the seventh-largest bank in the United States. Despite these government subsidies, the insolvency of the banking industry arose from Reagan's basic deregulation philosophy and was only reversed at the end of Reagan's second term with the Financial Institutions Reform Act (1989).

Reagan's pro-business stance led to economic distress for many average Americans. In 1981 when Reagan took office, the unemployment rate stood at 7.1 percent. Within two years, it had swelled to 9.7 percent, and only significantly decreased in 1987, when it sharply declined to 6.2 percent. Excepting the 1988 to 1989 period, the Reagan legacy of high unemployment persisted until 1995 when a variety of factors lowered the rate to less than 6 percent.

By the midpoint of the Reagan years in 1984, the economy stood in shambles, and many Americans struggled to survive. According to a Census report, nearly sixty-six million Americans in thirty-six million households were forced to rely on government benefits in the third quarter of 1983. Of the total, which represented nearly 30 percent of the U.S. population, about forty-two million Americans used food stamps, welfare, subsidized housing, or Medicaid to meet their most basic needs.

Many baby boomers who expected the prosperity of their youth to continue especially felt the effects of the recession. "When we grew up in the '50s and '60s, we were told the world would be our oyster," explained Richard Hokenson, a forty-six-year-old demographer in New York City. "Now life's turned out to be more of a struggle than we were told it would be." In 1984, *U.S. News and World Report* referred to the baby boomers as "the disillusioned generation, people in their 20s and early 30s who wonder whatever happened to the American dream."

The Boss

Bruce Springsteen, nicknamed the Boss, sang about Americans who felt the hard times. The son of a bus driver, Springsteen grew up in Freehold, New Jersey. At age fourteen, he learned guitar, which, as with many other rockers, provided Springsteen with solace. "Music saved me," he told an interviewer. "From the beginning, my guitar was something I could go to. If I hadn't found music, I don't know what I would have done."

Bruce Springsteen and the E Street Band. From left to right: Garry Tallent, Bruce Springsteen, Nils Lofgren, Danny Federici, Clarence Clemons, Roy Bittan, and Max Weinberg. Photo by David Gahr. Shore Fire Media. *Permission by David Gehr/Columbia Records.*

Armed with a guitar, Springsteen joined a series of bands, beginning in his high school years. Working with a variety of local musicians, in 1971 Springsteen finally formed the ten-piece Bruce Springsteen Band, which included David Sancious on keyboards, bassist Garry Tallent, Steve Van Zandt on guitar, drummer Vini Lopez, keyboardist Danny Frederici, and Clarence Clemons on saxophone.

Working as a solo act by early 1972, the Boss signed a contract with manager Mike Appel, who arranged an audition with Columbia Records talent head John Hammond. "The kid absolutely knocked me out," recalled Hammond, who had discovered Bob Dylan, Aretha Franklin, and Billie Holiday. "I only hear somebody really good once every ten years, and not only was Bruce the best, he was a lot better than Dylan when I first heard him." Within a week, Hammond had signed Springsteen to the label.

Springsteen initially failed to fulfill Hammond's expectations. In January 1973, he and a reformed version of the Bruce Springsteen Band released a folk-tinged debut, *Greetings from Asbury Park, N. J.*, which, though touted by Columbia as a masterpiece by the "new Dylan," in the first year sold only 12,000 copies, mostly to fans on the Jersey shore. The band toured to promote the album, mismatched as an opening act for the group Chicago. In May 1973, Springsteen made a disastrous appearance at the CBS Records Annual Convention in San Francisco. "It was during a period when he physically looked like Dylan," recalled Hammond. "He came on with a chip on his shoulder and played too long. People came to me and said, 'He really can't be that bad, can he, John?'" At the end of the year, Springsteen and his group, renamed the E Street Band after a road in Belmar, New Jersey, released *The Wild, the Innocent and the E Street Shuffle*, which sold only 80,000 copies in nearly a year.

The next year Springsteen received some encouragement. In April 1974, at Charley's, a small bar in Harvard Square, Cambridge, Massachusetts, the guitarist was spotted by *Rolling Stone* journalist Jon Landau, who wrote: "I saw the rock-and-roll future and its name is Bruce Springsteen." Springsteen remembered, "At the time, Landau's quote helped reaffirm a belief in myself. The band and I were making $50 a week. It helped me go on. I realized I was getting through to somebody." Within a year, he hired Landau to coproduce his third album, *Born to Run*.

Springsteen displayed his many influences on *Born to Run*. Besides the obvious Dylan elements that surfaced in his rapid-fire lyrics and harmonica playing, he borrowed the dramatic stylings of Roy Orbison, the wails of Little Richard, and the operatic sweep of Phil Spector that he labeled "the sound of universes colliding." The Boss also adopted the pounding piano of Jerry Lee Lewis, the intensity of R&B exemplified by the honking sax of Clarence Clemons, and Chuck Berry's chugging guitar sound and his preoccupation with girls and cars. "I was about 24 and I said, 'I don't want to write about girls and cars anymore,'" recalled Springsteen, who cherished his own 1957 yellow Chevy convertible, customized with orange flames. "Then I realized, 'Hey! That's what Chuck Berry wrote about!' So it wasn't my idea. It was a genre thing." Within one record Springsteen had incorporated several aspects of the history of rock-and-roll to produce a signature sound.

Executives at Columbia Records decided to launch an unprecedented promotional campaign to market *Born to Run*. They spent $40,000 on radio spots in twelve major geographic regions to promote Springsteen's first two albums, and in mid-August, Columbia Records and Appel organized an exclusive performance by Springsteen at the Bottom Line in New York City, reserving almost 1,000 of the 4,000 tickets for the press and radio disc jockeys. After releasing *Born to Run* in September 1975, they spent an additional $200,000 to advertise the record in the press and on the radio and $50,000 for television spots. "These are very large expenditures for a record company," admitted Bruce Lundvall, then vice president of Columbia. The Columbia brass also engineered cover stories in the October 27 issues of both *Time* and *Newsweek*.

The promotional blitz had mixed results. *Born to Run*, though hailed by the critics and reaching the number-three slot, sold fewer than one million copies in the first year after its release. The title cut from the album peaked at number twenty-three on the singles chart. *Darkness on the Edge of Town*, Springsteen's next album, released in 1978 after a lengthy legal dispute with manager Mike Appel, stalled at number five on the chart. A single from the album, "Prove It All Night," failed to crack the Top Thirty.

After his thirtieth birthday in 1979, Springsteen began to change along with other baby boomers. "I'm a different person now," he told a rock critic in late 1980. "When you're in your 30s or late 30s, the world is different. At least it looks different."

Springsteen's music reflected his changed attitude. Rather than focusing exclusively on cars, girls, and images of street toughs, his music began to deal with the plight of average Americans trapped by circumstances. The transition started with *Darkness on the Edge of Town*; in addition to Beach Boys–like paeans such as "Racing in the Street," the album included songs such as "Factory" that, in the words of the Boss, described people "who are going from nowhere to nowhere." The double album *The River* (1980) continued to combine car-and-girl-oriented songs such as "Cadillac Ranch," "Crush On You," and "You Can Look (But You Better Not Touch)" with the title song, which told about a factory worker who lost both love and his job because of a collapsing economy.

The 1982 stark, acoustic album *Nebraska* completed the transition. It chronicled the alienation of aging baby-boom Americans who had abandoned their 1960s' idealism. "I think what happened during the seventies was that, first of all, the hustle became legitimized. First through Watergate," Springsteen told *Musician* magazine. "In a funny kind of way, *Born to Run* was a spiritual record in dealing with values. *Nebraska* was about a breakdown of all those values. . . . It was kind of about a spiritual crisis, in which man is left lost. It's like he has nothing left to tie him to society anymore. He's isolated from the government. Isolated from his job. Isolated from his family."

In 1984, Springsteen fused his vision with the infectious rock-and-roll of the E Street Band to create his masterpiece *Born in the U.S.A.* He sang in "Downbound Train" about a lumber worker, who had lost his job and his wife when hard times hit. In the brooding "My Hometown,"[1] the Boss detailed the bleak changes affecting a town located in the depressed heartland of industrial Middle America: "Now main street's whitewashed windows and vacant stores/Seems like there ain't nobody wants to come down there no more/They're closing down the textile mill across the railroad tracks/Foreman says these jobs are going boys and they ain't coming back/to your hometown." Springsteen made a powerful statement in the title song, wailing about the dead-end fate of a working-class Vietnam veteran ten years after the war. In "Glory Days," he sang about the aimlessness of an ex–high school baseball star and a divorced ex–prom queen.

The album dealt with the loss of innocence experienced by an aging baby-boom generation facing the grim realities of the Reagan era. "I think *Born in the U.S.A.* kind of casts a suspicious eye on a lot of things. That's the idea. These are not the same people anymore and it's not the same situation," the Boss remarked. "It certainly is not as innocent anymore. But, like I said, it's ten years down the line." He continued: "I wanted to make the characters grow up. You got to. Everybody has to. It was something I wanted to do right after *Born to Run*. I was thinking about it then. I said, 'Well, how old am I?' I'm this old, so I wanna address that in some fashion. Address it as it is, and I didn't see that was done a whole lot [in rock lyrics]."

Despite an unadorned realism, Springsteen sought a renewed commitment to a 1960s' social consciousness. "We've abandoned a gigantic part of the population—we've just left them for dead. But we're gonna have to pay the piper some day," he insisted. "I mean, I live great, and plenty of people do, but it affects you internally in

---

[1]Lyrics from "My Hometown." Words and music by Bruce Springsteen, copyright © Bruce Springsteen Music. Used with permission of Bruce Springsteen Music.

some fashion, and it just eats away at whatever sort of spirituality you pursue." In an interview with *Rolling Stone*, Springsteen pledged a return "to the social consciousness that was part of the '60s," which during the 1970s seemed to become "old-fashioned." "I wanted the band to come out to be an alternative voice of America that was being presented by the Reagan administration," the Boss explained. "There's people who the trickle down theory of economics ain't trickling down to."

The Boss backed his words with action. As early as September 23, 1979, on his thirtieth birthday, he performed at Madison Square Garden in New York City in a concert organized by Musicians United for Safe Energy (MUSE), which protested against the proliferation of hazardous nuclear power plants. A year later, he played six benefit concerts for Vietnam veterans.

Springsteen intensified his benefit appearances on the *Born in the U.S.A.* tour. He plugged and donated $5,000 to Washington Fair Share, which forced the cleanup of an illegal landfill in Washington State. "This is 1984 and people seem to be searching for something," he told the sellout crowd at the Tacoma Dome. In Oakland, California, he urged listeners to donate to the Berkeley Emergency Food Project; in New Jersey, he donated $10,000 to a soup kitchen. He sent money to unemployed steelworkers, striking copper miners, and food banks across the country. In January 1985, he contributed lead vocals to a USA for Africa benefit disc, "We Are the World," to help starving, famine-plagued Africans. "One of the things I can do is play benefits and help people out that need help, people that are struggling, you know, trying to get something goin' on their own," he contended in December 1984.

Born in the U.S.A., reflecting Springsteen's social awareness, appealed to many baby boomers who had protested the war in Vietnam and during the 1960s had hoped for a better world. Snapped up by thirty-something baby boomers, the album reached the top of the U.S. and British charts and remained there for two years. The LP yielded five Top-Ten singles and by the end of the decade had sold eleven million copies.

The Benefits

Benefit concerts given by other rock performers demonstrated the reawakened interest in improving the world. Bob Geldof launched the first major benefit of the 1980s. Geldof, the leader of the British rock band the Boomtown Rats, saw a graphic BBC television report about the devastating effects of famine in Ethiopia. Moved by the catastrophe, on November 25, 1984, he contacted thirty-five fellow rock musicians and recorded a single, "Do They Know It's Christmas?" The British rock stars called their effort Band Aid. "If you don't like the music, buy the record and throw it to the rubbish. You don't need to like the music, but we need you to buy the records to save lives," he pleaded. Geldof and his fellow musicians donated the $13 million proceeds directly to the starving victims in Ethiopia.

Spurred by their British counterparts and joined by Geldof, several American superstars, including Michael Jackson, started United Support of Artists for Africa, or simply USA for Africa. On January 28, 1985, nearly forty rock luminaries such as the Motown stable of Michael Jackson, Diana Ross, Lionel Richie, and Stevie Wonder, R&B giant Ray Charles, Bob Dylan, Bob Geldof, and Bruce Springsteen got together in the A&M studios in Los Angeles to record the single, "We Are the World." The song became a blockbuster hit and raised American awareness of the plight of thousands of starving Ethiopians. The nonprofit group asked their listeners to "buy the single, album, video and related USA for Africa merchandise. If you buy a sweatshirt or T-shirt, wear it. Whatever the medium, the message remains the same: people need help."

Not content with his successes and those of his American counterparts, Bob Geldof hatched another venture to aid Ethiopia and dubbed his effort Live Aid. He planned two coordinated televised concerts, one in Philadelphia's JFK Stadium and the other in London's Wembley Stadium. He captured the imagination of artists of all types, including stalwarts Crosby, Stills and Nash, the Beach Boys, David Bowie, Santana, the Who, Elton John, ex-Beatle Paul McCartney, singer Mick Jagger of the Rolling Stones, and folk legends Bob Dylan and Joan Baez. He also attracted heavy metalers Judas Priest and Black Sabbath, blues rocker Eric Clapton, Robert Plant of Led Zeppelin, and blues legend B. B. King. Besides his own band, the singer snagged such new acts as U2, Dire Straits, and Madonna. He even convinced the rap group Run D.M.C. to participate. Airing on July 13, 1985, the two concerts lasted more than seventeen hours, reached 140 countries and 1.5 million people, and generated more than $140 million in pledges. "I think Live Aid and Band Aid were the beginning of an awareness," observed Jackson Browne, the 1970s' singer/songwriter who helped organize the MUSE benefit concert.

Other rock-and-rollers, most from the 1960s, organized benefits. The Grateful Dead, having played countless free concerts during their heyday, organized a benefit to protect the world's rain forests. "It's a problem we must address if we wish to have a planet that's capable of supporting life," explained the Dead's Bob Weir. Several rock stars, including former Police members Sting and Stewart Copeland, staged a concert and recorded an album to raise money for cancer research. Peter Gabriel, formerly of Genesis, united with Bruce Springsteen to tour in support of Amnesty International, which sought to free political prisoners around the world. Springsteen, who donated more than $200,000 to the charity, told one sellout crowd on the tour, "The great challenge of adulthood is holding on to your idealism after you lose your innocence."

Steve Van Zandt, nicknamed Little Steven, organized rock-and-rollers against racism in South Africa. In late 1985, after leaving the E Street Band for a solo career, he established Artists United Against Apartheid, an organization that lashed out against the brutal discrimination toward blacks in South Africa, particularly the $90 million, white-only Bophuthatswana resort, Sun City, which had hosted Rod Stewart, Linda Ronstadt, and Queen. Little Steven released an album, a book, and a video to combat apartheid, enlisting the support of rock luminaries such as Springsteen, Pete Townshend, Ringo Starr, Bob Dylan, Keith Richards, and Lou Reed. Taking the civil rights movement into the international arena, Little Steven donated nearly a half-million dollars to causes supporting the antiapartheid struggle.

The antiapartheid furor among rock musicians peaked with Paul Simon's *Graceland*. After participating in USA for Africa, the former folk rocker traveled to

South Africa to record with South African musicians. "To go over and play Sun City, it would be exactly like going over to do a concert in Nazi Germany at the height of the Holocaust," Simon reasoned. "But what I did was go over and essentially play to the Jews." He hoped the record, featuring the South African choir Ladysmith Black Mambazo, would serve as a "powerful form of politics" that would attract people "to the music, and once they hear what's going on within it, they'd say, 'What? They're doing that to these people.'" In 1986, *Graceland* topped the British chart and climbed to the number-three slot in the United States.

Children of the Sixties

The renewed interest in social causes shaped a number of new bands, notably U2. Formed in Dublin by schoolmates Bono (Paul Hewson), The Edge (David Evans), Adam Clayton, and Larry Mullen Jr., the band won a talent contest sponsored by Guinness Harp Lager in March 1978. After two years of local gigs, it released the

U2. Photo by David McIntyre. *Permission by D.M.B.B. Entertainment.*

debut single "11 O'Clock Tick Tock," which failed to chart. The group recorded two albums, *Boy* (1980) and *October* (1981), which attracted critical attention but sold only moderately.

U2 began to infuse its music with a political message. In October 1982, during a concert in Belfast, Northern Ireland, Bono introduced the song "Sunday Bloody Sunday," which detailed the historic political troubles in Ireland and called for peace. A few months later, the band released *War*, combining an anthem rock with various strands of punk. "Punk had died," recalled The Edge. "We couldn't believe it had happened, and *War* was designed as a knuckle buster in the face of the new pop." The guitarist continued: "We loved the Clash's attitude early on and Richard Hell and the Voidoids, the Pistols. We wanted love and anger. We wanted a protest record, but a positive protest record." Right for the times, *War* topped the British chart and neared the Top Ten in the United States.

The band continued to demonstrate its commitment to 1960s' ideals. Though beginning to replace hard-driving guitars with more ethereal, echo-laden sounds engineered by producer Brian Eno, U2 dedicated its 1984 hit "Pride (In the Name of Love)," to Martin Luther King, Jr. In July of the same year Bono sang "Blowing in the Wind" as a duet with Bob Dylan at a Dylan concert in Ireland. U2 contributed to Band Aid, played at the Live Aid spectacular in Wembley Stadium, appeared on the anti–Sun City project, and performed on Amnesty International's twenty-fifth anniversary tour. In 1986, the band raised funds for the unemployed in Dublin and performed in San Francisco for Amnesty International's "A Conspiracy of Hope" tour. By the next year, when it hit the top of the charts on both sides of the Atlantic with *Joshua Tree*, U2 had become spokesmen for change. As Bono remarked in 1987, "In the '80s, which is a barren era, we look back at the '60s as a great reservoir of talent, of high ideals and of the will and desire to change things." As with his counterparts in the 1960s, the singer was interested in "a revolution of love. I believe that if you want to start a revolution you better start a revolution in your own home and your own way of relating to the men and women around you."

The 1960s' spirit also inspired R.E.M. who delivered a socially conscious message through a brand of jangly, folksy rock. Formed in 1980 in Athens, Georgia, by vocalist Michael Stipe, guitarist Peter Buck, bassist Mike Mills, and drummer Bill Berry, the group perfected a Byrds-influenced, guitar-driven sound. Starting in 1983, they released four albums that garnered a cult following and moderate sales. In 1987 the band entered the mainstream with the Top Ten *Document*, which directly confronted Reagan through such songs as "Welcome to the Occupation" and "Exhuming McCarthy." The next year, they followed with *Green*, which lambasted the war in Vietnam in "Orange Crush" and blasted Reagan's foreign policy in "World Leader Pretend." R.E.M. lobbied for Greenpeace, voter registration, a clean environment, and human rights causes. "In the late '80s, I was influenced and politicized to the point that I felt like I wanted to try to make some of these things [songs] topical," remembered Michael Stipe. "Our political activism and the content of our songs was just a reaction to where we were, and what we were surrounded by, which was just abject horror." The singer concluded that "in 1987 and 1988 there was nothing to do but be active."

Classic Rock and the Compact Disc

A return to 1960s-style protest, coupled with the advent of the compact disc, led to a nostalgic rebirth of 1960s' rock. *Billboard* noted that "one of the more notable trends of the late '80s was the commercial success of many bands that made their commercial debut more than twenty years ago." *Time* added in late 1989, "And, as the fairy tales say, it seemed that it might be time again for legends. Twenty years later, there was suddenly on every side the familiar sound of the '60s."

Radio helped promote 1960s' rock. Largely ignoring the TV generation, which preferred the rapid-fire video bites of MTV, it programmed oldies for the baby boomers, who still purchased the greatest number of records and served as the prime target of most advertisers. In 1988, of the roughly 10,000 stations in the country, more than 500 radio stations broadcast oldies exclusively. The next year, contended Ken Barnes, editor of the trade magazine *Radio and Records*, at least 40 percent of all radio programming fell into the "classic rock" or "oldies" categories. In early 1990, oldies station WCBS-FM grabbed the number-one spot in the New York market. Radio, observed CBS Records president Al Teller, seemed to be "chasing the yuppie generation to its grave."

Along with oldies radio, the compact disc helped revive an interest in classic rock and rescued a troubled music industry. Introduced to the mass market in late 1982, it provided record buyers with a high-quality, digital, durable, long-lasting format. The compact disc, commonly called the CD, contained millions of digitally encoded pits, which held musical information that could be converted into almost noise-free sound through a low-powered laser beam. Less than 5 inches in diameter, the polycarbonate plastic disc only warped at temperatures over 220 degrees Fahrenheit, could not easily be scratched like a vinyl record, and produced up to seventy-five minutes of music with a dynamic range of 90 decibels.

The silver platter quickly became more popular than its vinyl counterpart. During its first two years on the market, the CD appealed primarily to jazz and classical music fans, who appreciated its expanded dynamic range. As the price of compact disc players plummeted from about $900 in 1983 to less than $150 in 1987, and as the cost of a compact disc declined from $18 to $14 during the same period, the convenient CD began to sell to the rock record buyers. In 1985, 16.4 million CDs were purchased worldwide. Three years later, more than 390 million compact discs were sold internationally to account for sales of more than $6 billion, compared to 295 million vinyl LPs that sold for $2.8 billion. Cassette tapes, becoming the most popular format for music during the late 1970s and registering even greater sales after the introduction of the portable Walkman cassette player in 1981, outperformed both with sales of more than $6.7 billion for 787 million units sold. However, by late 1990, the CD even began to outsell the popular cassette.

At the end of the decade, many industry executives predicted the demise of the vinyl LP. "I assume the death knell has been sounded, and there's not much we can do about it," mused Joe Smith, president of Capitol Music-EMI. "It's gasping for breath," agreed Russ Solomon, founder and president of the Tower Records chain. "We'd like to hold on, but unfortunately the world is not going that way." Bob

Sherwood, senior vice president of Columbia Records, predicted, "Our little flat friend the record is what drove the business for a long time, but we're going to be out of the business."

Industry predictions became reality. In 1989, the Camelot Music chain of 229 stores dropped vinyl albums from its inventory; other retailers, such as the 85-store Disc Jockey chain, the 119-store Hastings Books and Records, and the 60-store Music Plus group, severely limited vinyl selections. By 1992, vinyl records, which only ten years earlier had accounted for more than 42 percent of music sales, had shrunk to 2.3 percent of the U.S. music market. "They're just not a factor anymore," explained Stan Goman, senior vice president of retail operations for Tower Records. "You just don't think about LPs. They're just not there."

The new compact disc format and the disappearance of vinyl encouraged many baby boomers to replace their old, scratched LPs with CDs. In early 1990, *Billboard* observed, "If the CD did anything in the '80s, it convinced consumers that they needed to buy their favorite albums all over again. Little wonder, therefore, that artists such as the Beatles were charting all over again in the '80s with records they'd recorded twenty-five years earlier." *Time* magazine called the compact disc "the technology most likely to bring Elvis back to life. With revolutionary speed, music lovers are replacing their favorite old scratched-up 45s and 33s with shiny compact discs." By 1992, purchases of previously released rock-and-roll accounted for more than 40 percent of record sales.

A slumping U.S. recording industry was revitalized by the geometric growth in the sales of compact discs, created in part by baby boomers who rebought the music of their youth. After hitting a high point with sales of $4.13 billion in 1978, the U.S. record industry experienced a sharp decline. In 1979, it sold only $3.67 billion in records and tapes despite a high rate of inflation, a downturn that resulted in the loss of 2,500 music industry jobs. Over the next four years, the industry stabilized, but by 1983 it reported only $3.81 billion in total sales, despite price hikes, MTV, and the phenomenal success of Michael Jackson.

The U.S. record industry experienced a boom after the introduction of the CD, which cost about 90 cents to manufacture, excluding packaging. In 1986, it exceeded its previous record, shipping $4.65 billion worth of CDs, records, and tapes. "The rise in profitability," wrote one reporter, "is attributed primarily to the soaring sales of compact discs which carry a retail price of $12 to $20 as opposed to the $8.98 or $9.98 for records and cassettes." A year later, the industry sold $5.57 billion and in 1988 $6.25 billion in records, tapes, and discs. In 1989, the industry registered $6.57 billion in sales of more than 800 million units, bolstered by a 38 percent increase in CD shipments compared to the previous year. The next year, sales peaked at $7.5 billion and continued to rise meteorically in 1992 to more than $9 billion. According to one report, the recording industry registered the highest rate of pretax operating income growth in the communications industry, expanding 26 percent from 1983 to 1987. "It was like this week your paycheck got doubled; it was like 'whee!,'" enthused longtime Warner executive Stan Cornyn. "Everything about CDs cost like LPs: the same cost to record, the same cost to market, soon, the same cost to make." Yet the

CD cost nearly twice as much for the consumer and yielded phenomenal profits for the record companies.

The record industry grew at the same dizzying pace internationally, dominated by six corporations—Time-Warner (WEA), Sony/CBS, Bertelsmann Music Group (BMG), MCA-Matsushita, N.V. Philips of Holland, and Thorn-EMI (CEMA)—which by 1990 sold more than 93 percent of the records in the United States. After a drastic downturn from 1979 to 1986, by 1988 the industry sold more than $14 billion and a year later nearly $17 billion in records, tapes, and CDs. Japan, dominated by the Sony/CBS giant, increased sales to $2.4 billion in 1987, a 10 percent gain from the previous year. In West Germany, dominated by BMG, which had purchased RCA during the decade, sales skyrocketed to $1.56 billion in 1987 and exceeded $1.82 billion by 1989. "The German music market is in a healthy state of growth, and with East Germany opening up, it will develop even more," predicted Manfred Zumkeller, president of the Federation of German Phonographic Industries, in early 1990. In 1989, the United Kingdom, the fourth largest market in the world, had sales of $1.5 billion.

The increased sales translated into profits. In 1988, Warner Communications, the largest company in the field, posted sales of $2.04 billion and profits of nearly $319 million. The next year, after merging with Time Inc., Warner generated music revenues of $2.54 billion and profits of nearly $500 million. In 1987, CBS earned $202 million in profits on $1.75 billion in total sales. The next year, EMI, the British conglomerate, sold $1.2 billion in products for a profit of $70.3 million. BMG showed remarkable growth, building sales from $663 million in 1986–1987 to $1.1 billion in 1989–1990 and increasing profits from $56 million to $85.4 million during the same period. "The ultimate shot in the arm the record industry was craving, the CD allowed companies to rake in the bucks on a product that, in some cases, was one step away from actually being deleted," observed *Billboard* in late 1989.

Country Boomers

In the early 1990s, baby boomers flocked to a sometimes issue-oriented version of country rock, further fueling the record industry upswing. During the first four years of the decade, more than twenty-one million Americans, mostly baby boomers, became country music fans. By 1994, many of the nearly half of all Americans who listened to country music fit the baby-boom profile: 42 percent owned a house, 40 percent had a college education, and 36 percent lived in households with incomes of more than $60,000 a year. "By their sheer demographic weight, the nation's seventy-six million baby boomers continue to determine America's musical preferences," observed *Time* in 1992. "And what America currently prefers is country."

These country boomers caused an upsurge in all formats of country music. In 1985, only sixteen country releases sold more than 500,000 copies. Seven years later, fifty-three country discs went gold, and nearly thirty sold more than one million copies. In 1992, sales of country discs and tapes reached $660 million, more than a 50 percent increase from the previous year. In 1980, about 1,534 radio stations played country music; twelve years later, more than 2,500 stations catered to country listeners. On television, The Nashville Network (TNN) grew from 7 million viewers at its inception in 1983 to 54.5 million subscribers in 1992, and from 1990 to 1992, the magazine *Country America* doubled its subscriptions to almost 1 million.

To some extent, Bruce Springsteen paved the road to country success. The Boss's anthemic tales of the working class and the downtrodden popularized a genre that neo-traditionalists in country embraced. Raised on rock-and-roll and country, singers such as Steve Earle, Travis Tritt, Dwight Yoakam, and Clint Black delivered the traditional populist message of country against a backdrop steeped in honky-tonk, country, and rock influences. They produced an energized, hard-hitting country rock with an outlaw image that grabbed the attention of baby boomers.

Steve Earle hoisted the populist banner with a country-rock sound. Growing up near San Antonio, Texas, Earle wrote songs in Nashville during the 1970s for stars such as Carl Perkins. In 1986, he released an album of heartland rock gems in his major label debut, *Guitar Town*, which appealed to country and rock audiences and cracked the popular chart. He followed with the progressively rock-oriented efforts *Exit O* (1987) and *Copperhead Road* (1988), the last of which neared the Top Fifty and included a collaboration with the punk-folk band the Pogues.

Dwight Yoakam had similar success as a neo-traditionalist country crossover artist. A diehard fan of the Bakersfield honky-tonk style of Buck Owens, Yoakam also unashamedly identified his rock roots. "I listened to country and to rock, everything from Haggard to the Grateful Dead. I was interested in country rock, because it suggested there might be a place I could go." Rejected by the Nashville hierarchy, the singer traveled to California and opened for punk bands such as X, delivering his distinctive blend of honky-tonk rock. In 1986, Yoakam struck a chord amid the Springsteen fervor with the million-selling *Guitars, Cadillacs, Etc. Etc.* and the next year neared the Top Fifty with *Hillbilly Deluxe*. By 1990, he again hit platinum with *If There Was a Way*, which crossed over to the rock audience.

Riding an outlaw image up the charts, Travis Tritt melded traditional country with the southern rock stylings of Lynyrd Skynyrd and the Allman Brothers. He first hit with the 1990 *Country* and then made the Top Twenty-Five with *It's All About to Change*. By 1992, Tritt scored with the country rock of *T-R-O-U-B-L-E*, and its roaring "Blue Collar Man," which included the guitar work of Gary Rossington of Lynyrd Skynyrd. The singer called his songs "country music with a rock-'n'-roll attitude."

The popularity of the neo-traditionalists, cracking the *Billboard* pop chart, presaged the mega-breakthrough of Garth Brooks, who owed a musical debt to rock and reflected the social concerns of the baby boomers. The son of a former country singer, Colleen Carroll Brooks, the college-educated Garth drew his inspiration from rock-and-roll. After attending a Queen concert, Brooks became convinced that he wanted to perform. "My ears are still ringin' from that concert," he enthused. "I was thinking, one day I'm going to feel this feeling—only it's gonna be me up there on that stage." He hoped to duplicate "the seventies-arena-rock thing" in country music.

Folk rock also shaped Brooks. He listened to "a sixties wave of singers: Peter, Paul, and Mary, Tom Rush, Townes Van Zandt, Arlo Guthrie, Janis Joplin, Janis Ian, Rita Coolidge, that kind of music. It was very warm, but you had to step inside it to see what was going on. From that moment on, that's the kind of music I was attracted to. Off that, I went to James Taylor, Dan Fogelberg, the more writer-type artists."

Brooks combined folk rock and 1970s' theatrics with his country roots for superstardom. In 1989, he released a self-titled debut, which sold well. The next year, the singer hit the Top Ten with *No Fences*, which eventually sold more than sixteen million copies. Brooks followed with the blockbuster number-one of *Ropin' the Wind*, which became the first country album to hit the top of the pop chart, and in two years sold ten million copies. During the next two years, he hit the Top Five with a Christmas album and topped the chart with *The Chase* (1992) and *In Pieces* (1993). By early 1993, Brooks had sold more than thirty million discs and tapes to create a country rock craze.

In his music, Garth Brooks addressed current social concerns. He supported gay rights in "We Shall Be Free" and chose antiwar songs such as "Last Night I Had the Strangest Dream" for his concerts. In "The Thunder Rolls," he sang about the effects of domestic violence, and his "Face to Face" condemned date rape. In 1992, after a riot in Los Angeles, Brooks performed a benefit concert that raised nearly $1 million to help rebuild the inner city. Garth Brooks, fashioning a rock-based country that explored socially relevant issues, had created music for early 1990s' baby boomers.

Brooks led the way for other country rockers, none more successful than Shania Twain. Twain grew up near Ontario, Canada, on the Mattagami Indian Reservation and supported her siblings by singing at a resort after the tragic death of her parents in 1987. In 1995 after meeting and marrying rock producer Robert John "Mutt" Lange, who had produced such acts as AC/DC and Def Leppard, Twain released the megahit *The Woman in Me*, which fused country fiddles and steel guitars with Lange's trademark slick, hard-rock sound "Country audiences are capable of stretching, and we can take them with us," Twain insisted. The album sold more than twelve million copies. Two years later, Twain sold even more discs with the radio-friendly *Come on Over* to extend the crossover success of Garth Brooks.

The country boom even extended to a group of bands labeled alternative country or Y'alternative, epitomized by Uncle Tupelo. The brainchild of singer-songwriters Jeff Tweedy and Jay Farrar, the group solidified in 1987 to combine their country and punk rock roots. In 1990, they issued their influential debut *No Depression* that overlaid punk madness on top of a country twang. After three subsequent albums, the band splintered when Tweedy formed Wilco and Farrar put together Son Volt.

During the early 1990s, various strands of country rock reigned supreme on the charts. "A lot of people turned to country because it's more like [early] seventies rock-and-roll," observed Neil Young, who twenty years earlier had released a series of revelatory country-tinged folk-rock discs and in 1985 cut the unadulterated country album *Old Ways*. "Pop and rock have just changed their name to country." From the mid-1980s to the early 1990s, the baby-boom generation tuned in to socially charged rock, recycled oldies, and country rock. This optimistic, sometimes majestic, change-oriented music contrasted sharply with the harsh, rebellious, desperate sound of a new generation.

18 The Generation X Blues

> **66** We had to grow up with this idealization that was never going to fucking come true. **99**
>
> —Courtney Love of Hole

A post–baby-boom generation created an angry rock, which reflected their rage and alienation. Whether listening to hardcore punk, thrash metal, industrial, or grunge, youths in the mid-1980s to the early 1990s vented their frustration over their bleak prospects through music.

The post–baby-boom generation in the United States faced a grim economic reality. In 1992, the average American worker earned $391 a week, $18 less than the average worker brought home in 1979 after adjusting for inflation. As wages declined, unemployment rose. During much of the 1950s and 1960s, the official unemployment rate vacillated between 3.5 percent and 5 percent. In 1984, the rate of unemployment stood at 7.5 percent. By 1992 the official unemployment rate had not improved and did not even reflect an additional 13 percent of nonworking Americans whom the government classified as underemployed and discouraged workers. Many of the remaining jobs shifted from manufacturing to the service sector, which during the 1980s did not pay as well and accounted for more than three-quarters of all new jobs. "The economy is failing nearly every American," contended Lawrence Mishel, chief economist at the Economic Policy Institute, in late 1992.

Post–baby boomers, nearly 50 percent of the population by the early 1990s, especially felt the economic squeeze. In 1992, 20 percent of teens not in school could not find jobs, and more than 11 percent of young men and women between ages twenty and twenty-four were officially unemployed, compared to a 6.7 percent unemployment rate among the baby-boom generation.

The new generation, called Generation X by the press, found little stability in their families. Although fewer people divorced by the mid-1980s, the baby boomers had separated from their partners in record numbers during the 1970s, leaving many post–baby boomers in single-family households. In 1970, single-parent households accounted for only 11 percent of homes with children. By 1992, households headed by one parent comprised more than 26 percent of the total.

The turbulent American family caused frustration, pain, and fear among Generation X. "I spent my life believing that I had this perfect family and making my friends believe we had this perfect family," confessed Nina Gordon of the band Veruca Salt. A "huge and miserable divorce rewrote my entire life." Jesse Malin of D Generation explained, "The bottom line is that most of us come from broken homes. We have this self-destructive thing: We'd get a kick out of breaking up the band. And we do it with a lot of relationships, with girlfriends and everybody, because that was our first impression from when we were seven years old: seeing people split."

Adding to their personal problems, many youths suffered abuse, often within the family. In 1991, reported the National Committee for the Prevention of Child Abuse, 2.7 million children, or 4 percent of all youths under age eighteen in America, were abused. That number represented a 40 percent increase in only six years.

"I do think that having no family structure, having no sense that there's shelter from the storm, drives people insane," contended Elizabeth Wurtzel, the young author of *Prozac Nation: Young and Depressed in America.* "The level of uncertainty we function under in a personal realm is daunting. And, obviously, economically, things are very uncertain. So altogether, this is not a pretty way to live."

Confronted with few economic prospects and a painful, sometimes brutal home life, many youths became violent. Most post–baby boomers had witnessed violent actions daily on television. According to the American Psychological Association, in the 1980s the average child had watched 8,000 murders and 100,000 other acts of violence by the sixth grade. In the 1980s and 1990s, many youths followed the celluloid images by carrying guns. "For youth today, I don't care where you live, what class you are, or whether you're white, black, or Hispanic, it's cool to carry a gun," complained Colonel Leonard Supenski of the Baltimore County Police Department. "Owing to a lot of things, primarily the entertainment industry, it's a macho thing to do." In 1990, more than 4 percent of all high school students surveyed by the Centers for Disease Control had carried a gun, especially the semiautomatic 9-millimeter pistol, at least once in the previous month.

Many of the youths used the guns they carried. In the Seattle city school system, 6 percent of high school juniors confessed to carrying a gun into school, and one-third of the gun-toting students fired their weapons at another person. In the United States, during 1987, almost 1,500 youths aged ten to nineteen died from gunshot wounds, usually inflicted by another youth. Two years later, nearly 2,200 youths died as a result of gun violence.

Many gun-carrying youths banded together in urban gangs across the country. By 1985, nearly 45,000 Los Angeles youths had formed together in more than 450 gangs, an increase of 25 percent in gangland activity in just five years. By 1992, in Los Angeles, 150,000 disgruntled youths joined more than 1,000 gangs. Though highly visible due to press coverage, the Los Angeles gangs reflected a national trend. Seeking security in an insecure world, 1980s' youths started gangs in such disparate locales as Davenport, Iowa; Chicago; New Haven; Jackson, Mississippi; and Portsmouth, New Hampshire. By 1994, gangs existed in 187 U.S. cities. "The kids are all on the edge," warned Chicago social worker Sharon Brown. "Brush against them, and they're ready to fight."

The desperate generation, which followed the baby boomers, was drawn to a loud, aggressive, angry music. "A lot of people our age and younger have been brought up with these notions of Reagan-era fueled affluence," noticed Jonathan Poneman, co-owner of Sub Pop Records, in 1992. "Then when you suddenly see a lot of those dreams subside because of this particularly brutal recession, and class warfare, race warfare, it makes you very angry, very fearful, very alienated. And those are qualities that lead to an unusually rebellious, passionate rock."

The Hardcore Generation

Rock-and-roll music, especially hardcore, thrash, industrial, and grunge, reflected the alienation of the post–baby-boom generation. The desperate, angry, and extreme version of punk known as hardcore fittingly began during the late 1970s in Hollywood, the smog-filled, make-believe fairyland steeped in excess and corruption. Los Angeles punk started with bands such as X, which fused the hyperactive roar of English punk with lyrics, describing a society that had degenerated beyond repair. In late 1977, X began performing a version of punk characterized by the thunderous drumming of Don Bonebrake, the rockabilly-tinged, Ramones-influenced guitar of Billy Zoom (b. Tyson Kindell), and the Charles Bukowski–beat-inspired lyrics of John Doe (b. John Duchac) and poet Exene Cervenka. "I saw the Ramones. That made me decide to play the kind of music we play now in X," Zoom explained at the time.

On their 1980 debut, *Los Angeles*, released by Slash Records—which had evolved from the punk-rock fanzine of the same name—X applied the energy of the Ramones to tales of despondency such as "Nausea" and "Sex and Dying in High Society." "In 1979 or '80, people realized everything was fucked up, and they couldn't do anything about it, and they didn't want to," recalled Doe. "We wrote about how estranged we were," agreed Cervenka.

X set the desperate tone for other punk bands from Los Angeles. The Germs, first performing at the Orpheum Theater in Los Angeles in 1977, featured the staccato fuzz guitar of Pat Smear (b. George Ruthenberg) and the barking vocals of Darby Crash (b. Paul Beahm). In concert and on their first LP (*GI*), they sang sobering songs such as "We Must Bleed." "The Germs were much darker than most of the other bands," explained John Doe. Germs followers ceremoniously burned themselves with cigarettes. "Self-destruction is a means of showing, if you're cutting up your body and marking or whatever, it's your own, it's one thing that you can call completely and totally your own," reasoned one Germs fanatic. On December 7, 1980, Crash symbolically committed suicide as a tribute to his hero, Sid Vicious.

X and the Germs, the leaders of the scene, were joined by other punk outfits such as the Weirdos, the Zeros, the Dils, and the Zippers, who played to the growing throngs of discontented youths in Los Angeles at clubs like the Orpheum and the Masque. "We were into a punk-rock revolution to destroy the way things were, to destroy the status quo," explained Tony Kinman of the Dils.

By 1978, Los Angeles punk had moved from the city into the suburbs and had turned from self-destruction to violence toward others. Former surfers and skateboarders from Huntington Beach and Costa Mesa went to punk shows looking for fights, encouraged by suburban punk bands such as Black Flag and the Minutemen. "We were riled up and protesting against what was going on socially and musically," explained Black Flag singer and Circle Jerks leader Keith Morris. "We reacted in a very aggressive, energetic, hateful, spiteful manner. Because we're from SoCal and we've grown up surfing and skating and skiing, we have a bit of aggressiveness to us." The up-and-down pogo dance of Los Angeles gave way to bodies slamming against each other near the stage in a slam pit, which eventually became known as the "mosh pit." Youths began to rush and jump on the stage and dive off onto the slamming masses below. "Right around the time of our first album, around '81," explained Lee Ving of the Los Angeles hardcore band Fear, "it changed from the pogo bullshit into the real slam stuff."

The pace of the music also changed from Hollywood's fast tempos to the hyperkinetic, blinding speed of hardcore kids hell-bent on violence. "The focus changed from Hollywood toward the beaches, and the idea of speed and the slam pit had its birth," Lee Ving remembered. "We started playing as fast as you could fucking think and the crowd would go berserk, pounding the shit out of each other in the pit." The new version of punk, added Ray Farrell of the aptly named hardcore label SST, "replaced the arty stuff [of Hollywood] with an injection of extreme energy, to the point of where being a faster band was the equivalent of playing a faster solo in the 70s." Though disdained by most of the original Los Angeles punk bands such as X, this new suburban punk, known as hardcore, muscled out its urban counterpart.

Generally young middle-class male suburbanites fueled the hardcore explosion. "When the hardcore thing really took off, it became more of a macho testosterone overdrive thing, the stage diving and the slam pits," remembered Keith Morris. "Most girls didn't want to have anything to do with it." Ray Farrell agreed, "Hardcore made it more like a sporting event than music—with like the worst jocks you've ever seen. It excluded women . . . because it was violent."

The hardcore ethos of violence led to a new punk fashion. Rather than the Mohawk haircuts of British punk, hardcore youths shaved their heads to avoid someone grabbing their hair in the mosh pit. They favored tattoos of the names and logos of their favorite bands and sometimes pierced themselves in various parts of their body. Keeping some of the original punk style, the hardcore wore T-shirts, worn-out jeans, combat boots, and leather jackets, which sometimes had rows of pointed studs. As a total look, the hardcore youth dressed like they were preparing for war. As Jack Grisham of the band punk band TSOL (short for True Sounds of Liberty) explained, "We were into the combat thing—we'd go to an Army Surplus and get black combat gear. We'd go on missions."

These violent males many times came from dysfunctional families nestled in the ultraconservative conclave of Orange County, California. Mike Ness, leader of the Fullerton band Social Distortion, came from a welfare home plagued by alcohol abuse. Mugger, a roadie for Black Flag, characterized hardcore fans as "kids whose families didn't care about them . . . and they just got crazy. It was basically a full-on white suburban rebellion."

Tony Cadena of the Adolescents typified the type of youth that joined the hardcore ranks, growing up in the "very suburban right wing, white middle-class stifling environment" of Orange County. "There was no father in my family," he confessed. "We were dysfunctional, a welfare family living in an upward middle-class neighborhood. Punk came along at just the right time. It gave me a chance to reject everything I couldn't have anyway. I started bringing bands into my garage to rehearse. It was exciting to tip that 'hood on its ear. It was the final fuck you."

Henry Rollins of Black Flag. *Permission by Cam Garrett.*

Black Flag, named for the symbol of anarchy, became the prototypical band for this violent, angry hardcore scene. They fused early American punk with themes of desperation. Guitarist Greg Ginn first became interested in music when he "read in the *Village Voice* what was happening at Max's and CBGB's and thought, 'maybe this is something that is going to open it up again.' That's when I started getting interested in having a band." Singer Dez Cadena echoed, "I hooked up with people who were getting into the Dolls, the Stooges, MC5, and all of a sudden we read about these bands playing CBGB's and Max's."

Unlike the lower-class British punks, the band consisted of suburbanites from middle-class, sometimes dysfunctional, families. Henry Rollins (b. Henry Garfield), who joined Black Flag in 1981 and wrote many of the group's lyrics, contended that, "I've always been privileged, I've got it all going for me." But as with many of the band's fans, Rollins confessed he was "a classic product of a typical dysfunctional family. I don't know jack shit about love, or about feeling a relationship with a blood relative. That shit means nothing to me."

Black Flag delivered songs about personal dysfunction over a thrashing, fuzzy, chaotic, speed-guitar sound. In 1978, the band recorded *Nervous Breakdown*; three years later, it released the album *Damaged*, which included the hardcore anthem "Rise Above" and such despair-ridden songs such as "Depression" and "Life of Pain." "Pain is my girlfriend; that's how I see it," explained Rollins. "I feel pain every day of my life. When you see me perform, it's that pain you're seeing coming out. I put all my emotions, all my feelings, and my body on the line. People hurt me, I hurt myself— mentally, physically." In contrast to the politicized British punk, explained Rollins in 1983, "There are no songs telling you to do anything. There are no political songs, there are no songs that speak out on some topic." Black Flag founder Greg Ginn added, "We were an extrapolation of the blues."

The Los Angeles media began to promote such pain-filled music. Rodney Bingenheimer, calling himself Rodney on the ROQ, played punk and then hardcore on his regular show on radio station KROQ that was broadcast from 8:00 P.M. until midnight on Sundays. In 1981, filmmaker Penelope Spheeris released *The Decline of Western Civilization*, which documented the seamier sides of the lifestyle and live performances of hardcore bands. Punk fanzines such as *Slash*, *Flipside*, and *Maximum RocknRoll*, patterned after English predecessors such as *Sniffin' Glue*, became the bibles of the new scene.

Local independent record companies were established to record and distribute hardcore. Lisa Fancher, a former employee at the Los Angeles–based Bomp Records, started Frontier Records in 1980. She initially recorded the Circle Jerks, a group of young, middle-class teens from the suburbs, who included Keith Morris. "As it happened," Fancher recalled, "no one wanted to put out the Circle Jerks' LP *Group Sex*. It was total providence. I said, 'I'll do it.'" She continued: "It's a classic, classic punk record, and it's what made everything else fall into place for me. After them I did the Adolescents' [first album] and TSOL. I was on a roll." In 1983, Fancher recorded the Suicidal Tendencies single "Institutionalized" and their first album, which, according to the label owner, sold "absolute shitloads: five hundred thousand copies to date [1993]."

Other labels in California specialized in hardcore. Posh Boy recorded Red Cross (later Redd Kross), the initial TSOL release, and punk compilations selected by Rodney Bingenheimer. Brett Gurewitz, bassist for the "melodic" hardcore outfit Bad Religion, started Epitaph to record his own band and, within a decade, hit the Top Ten with Offspring, who sold seven million copies of *Smash*. Two founding members of Black Flag, guitarist Gregg Ginn and drummer Gary McDaniel (who renamed himself Chuck Dukowski in honor of beat poet Charles Bukowski) started their own label, SST, to record their band. Almost immediately, they began to press the music of other local hard-core punkers such as San Pedro's Minutemen, who debuted with *Paranoid Time* (1980).

Ginn and Dukowski also documented the burgeoning national hardcore scene, which spread from California to other urban areas across the nation. They recorded Husker Du from Minneapolis. When guitarist Bob Mould "heard the first Ramones' record," he said "I gotta get back into music. This is something." In 1979, he joined with drummer Grant Hart and bassist Greg Norton in Husker Du, who played loud, fast songs of alienation, reflected in the title of their 1983 studio debut *Everything Falls Apart*. As with Black Flag, Husker Du delivered songs of personal angst. "I don't write about politics because I'm not an expert," commented Bob Mould in 1985. "We're sort of like reporters in a way. Reporters of our own mental state."

In Minneapolis, Husker Du shared the hardcore spotlight with the Replacements, who drew their inspiration from the punk that blasted forth from Southern California. "We were spawned by power-pop and hardcore, which were both offshoots of punk, so we were a product of that environment," pointed out singer Paul Westerberg. In May 1980, Westerberg dropped off a demo tape at the Oarfolkjokeopus record store for manager Peter Jesperson, who since 1978 also had co-owned Twin/Tone Records. "I know it sounds like a fairy tale," remembered Jesperson, "but I knew how special it was the minute I heard it." The band signed with the label, which late the next year released *Sorry Ma, Forgot to Take Out the Trash* that included the hyperactive "Shut Up," "Kick Your Door Down," and "I Hate Music." Westerberg characterized the follow-up, *Stink*, as an "excursion into hardcore to try and compete with Husker Du." Though eventually turning to a more mainstream rock, the early Replacements delivered a memorable version of 1980s' hardcore.

Hardcore contingents arose in other cities. In Washington, D.C., Minor Threat carried the hardcore banner. In 1978, recalled singer and leader Ian MacKaye, "I heard the Clash and the Sex Pistols." Hooked on punk, he formed the Teen Idles and, with friend Henry Rollins, later of Black Flag, "thought California was where it was at. We had heard Black Flag's single, it was our favorite, and *Slash* and *Flipside* were like our Bible." In the fall of 1980, MacKaye and Teen Idles drummer Jeff Nelson started their own label, Dischord, to release their first single. They also decided to document the expanding Washington, D.C., hardcore community, first recording Rollins's band, SOA [State of Alert], and following with the first single of their renamed band, Minor Threat. Dischord continued to record local hardcore outfits such as Youth Brigade and Government Issue. "We thought, 'This is so cool, we'll do a little label, and everyone will get their own seven-inch.'"

Though certainly as aggressive and violent as their Los Angeles hardcore coun-terparts, Minor Threat eschewed drugs, wanton sex, and alcohol in a philosophy that they termed "Straight Edge." MacKaye and his bandmates tried "to get away from a really corrupted music, you know, basically your heavy-metal bands that were into heroin, cocaine, just a lot of drinking. We just drank a lot of Coke and ate a lot of Twinkies." Nathan Strejcek, who had played in the Teen Idles and then sang in the D.C. Straight Edge band Youth Brigade, explained, "Since we weren't allowed to legally drink, we said, 'Fine, we don't want to,' just to piss the lawmakers off. This is where we established a new place in modern society for ourselves . . . clear-minded thinking against the most evil of all, the adults!"

The premier hardcore band in San Francisco, the Dead Kennedys were older than the teens in the Washington, D.C., hardcore scene and cared more about overt leftist politics than abstention from the rock-and-roll lifestyle. Leader Jello Biafra (b. Eric Boucher) had attended the University of California at Santa Cruz. By 1980, when he was twenty-two, Biafra had become enamored of a politicized British punk. As he told it, "Punk was an outbreak of new talent that . . . opened the door to a whole new generation of people who had ideas to replace the bankrupt swill that was being regurgitated [by people] who blew a lot of their talent and shot their wads in the sixties, but who maintained a stranglehold on the airwaves in the seventies."

The Dead Kennedys, formed in June 1978, embraced the message of British punk, merging a buzz-saw guitar sound with lyrics that lambasted U.S. imperialism, the Moral Majority, and the creeping fascism among some hardcore youths, who began to wear Nazi armbands. In 1979, on their own Alternative Tentacles label, they released their first single "California Über Alles," which criticized California Governor Jerry Brown and other "Zen fascists." On their first LP, *Fresh Fruit for Rotting Vegetables* (1980), the Dead Kennedys blasted U.S. involvement in Southeast Asia in "Holiday in Cambodia" and tackled the issue of poverty in "Let's Lynch the Landlord" and "Kill the Poor." The band continued to deliver social commentaries such as "Terminal Preppie" and "Nazi Punks Fuck Off!" until they disbanded in 1986, amid a controversy over censorship of the album cover to the LP *Frankenchrist*. "I think what we are witnessing in this country is the slow but inevitable fall of an empire that got too comfortable," asserted Biafra.

The Dils, a band that garnered a following in San Francisco alongside the Dead Kennedys, also embraced a politicized version of punk. "We believed in punk-rock revolution," explained Chip Kinman of the group. "I mean, punk rock to change the world." The Dils delivered two hard-hitting singles, "I Hate the Rich" and "Class War," which embodied their philosophy and contrasted starkly with many of the Los Angeles hardcore punkers. "San Francisco was the more serious punk town, into punk revolution," Kinman mentioned. "Whereas L.A. was more into the nihilistic punk-rock vibe. It was a constant battle with those two towns, and the philosophies."

The San Francisco hardcore became disillusioned with the embittered generation of Los Angeles punks who exhibited a violent, nihilistic aggression. "[We] had talked for years about how great it would be for us to get our music to younger kids and how once they saw the energy they'd automatically like it," Jello Biafra explained. "But what we didn't realize is that they might not like it on our terms. So when younger people did start coming to shows in droves, they brought the arena rock mentality with them, including fights, jumping off the stage just to see if you could hit people."

Thrash Metal

The aggressive, dissatisfied youth of the 1980s also began to listen to the equally speedy thrash metal, which originated with the New Wave of British Heavy Metal (NWBHM). The NWBHM stemmed from the conditions that helped foster English punk. Poor British youths with no apparent future formed bands to express their frustration through a violent, explosive sound. In 1976, four working-class youths from Stourbridge in the West Midlands near Birmingham—an area that had produced original heavy-metalers Black Sabbath and Led Zeppelin's Robert Plant and John Bonham—banded together as Diamond Head. "We started on June 26th, 1976. It was the last year of our school, about to leave to get jobs or go on the dole, whatever," recalled lead guitarist Brian Tatler. Around the same time, other heavy-metal bands arose with names that indicated a dark militancy: Saxon, Venom, Tygers of Pan Tang, Angel Witch, and Iron Maiden. These bands owed a musical debt to the heavy metal of the early 1970s. Iron Maiden favored the Led Zeppelin sound. Venom and Angelwitch leaned more toward Black Sabbath. Diamond Head, remembered Tatler, first learned Black Sabbath's "Paranoid 'cause we thought it'd go down well."

Though modeling themselves on a blues-based style, the new wave of heavy metal delivered a harsh-sounding, fist-pumping music that shared the spirit of its British punk counterparts. "What people were looking for in punk is what they are looking for in heavy rock," observed Saxon vocalist Biff Byford. "We were the ones breaking down the barriers between band and audience, and we were doing it with complete honesty and no b.s."

The new wave of metal coalesced with the help of disc jockey Neil Kay. Kay constantly promoted the albums of struggling bands such as Iron Maiden at his heavy-metal club, London's Soundhouse. In May 1979, he helped stage a concert that featured many of the new metal acts, which prompted Alan Lewis and Geoff Barton, editors of the British music magazine *Sounds*, to coin the phrase, New Wave of British Heavy Metal. In August 1980, the British television show *20th Century Box* aired a special on the new music.

Heavy-metal magazines such as *Kerrang* also helped create an underground of metal fans who helped spread the word. "The number one source [of support] is fanzines," contended Bret Hartman, manager of A&R at MCA. "Getting demos with good songs is the bottom line, but the sources to expose the band are word of mouth, fanzines, and magazines, especially for metal." Metal fans, remarked Roadrunner Records executive Michael Schnapp, "print fanzines, they talk to each other all the time on the phone, they are pen pals; you have that family type of atmosphere."

By the turn of the decade, the new metal bands began to offer records to the swelling ranks of the metal underground. In 1980, Diamond Head, mirroring the do-it-yourself punk attitude, released their first album on their own Happy Face label. That same year, Tygers of Pan Tang cut the British Top Twenty *Wildcat*. Saxon debuted in 1979 and during the next three years provided fans with four more British Top Twenty albums. In 1980, Angel Witch cut its debut, and the next year Venom released *Welcome to Hell*.

AC/DC, the blues-powered Australian band that formed in 1973 and struggled for popular acceptance during the mid-1970s, benefited from the exposure given to the NWBHM. In 1977, they first charted in Britain with *Let There Be Rock*. Two years later, amid the furor over the NWBHM, the band hit the British Top Ten and the Top Twenty in the United States with *Highway to Hell*; the next year, they topped the British chart and reached the Top Five in the United States with *Back in Black*. In 1981, they topped the U.S. chart with *For Those About to Rock (We Salute You)*.

During the early 1980s, Iron Maiden, another commercially successful NWBHM band, gained a following. In early 1979, the band distributed by mail order their first effort, *The Soundhouse Tapes*. Early the next year, they unveiled their self-named, major label debut, which hit the British charts. During the early 1980s, Iron Maiden continued to chart with *Killers* (1981); *The Number of the Beast* (1982), which topped the British album chart; and the million-selling *Piece of Mind* (1983). By the end of 1983, readers of the NWBHM magazine *Kerrang* voted *Piece of Mind* and *The Number of the Beast* the best two heavy-metal albums of all time.

Motorhead stood at the vanguard of the new metal explosion. Banding together in 1975, the group consisted of guitarist "Fast" Eddie Clarke, drummer Philthy Animal (b. Phil Taylor), and bassist and vocalist Lemmy Kilmister, a former member of Hawkwind and an ex-roadie for Jimi Hendrix. Boasting that "We're the kind of band that if we moved next to you, your lawn would die," the trio played a fast, aggressive, loud brand of metal. After a self-named debut in 1977, they continued their vinyl career with *Overkill* and *Bomber*, which suggested the destructive intent of the music. In 1980, the band hit the British Top Five with *Ace of Spades*. The next year, as the NWBHM swept across the United Kingdom, Motorhead reached the top of the chart with the live album *No Sleep Till Hammersmith*.

Metallica combined the different elements of the NWBHM to create a new genre called "thrash" or "speed metal," which swept across Britain and the United States during the mid-1980s. The band initially grew from a passion for metal that drove Danish-born Lars Ulrich. In 1980, Ulrich, the son of a professional tennis player, moved to Los Angeles with his parents. "I got very pissed off being in L.A.," related Ulrich, "so the summer of '81 I just upped and went back to Europe, kind of a hang-out trip. So I'd go hang out with Diamond Head for a while, and then try and find Iron Maiden, or try and find Motorhead, and sit outside of Motorhead's rehearsal room and wait." After returning to the United States, continued the drummer, "I wanted to get a band together in America that had some of those qualities I [had heard in Europe]." Ulrich placed an ad in a Los Angeles newspaper and found guitarist and vocalist James Hetfield, who "listened to a lot of Black Sabbath in the early days." The duo added lead guitarist Dave Mustaine and bassist Ron McGovney, Hetfield's roommate, to form Metallica.

The band first mimicked the NWBHM. "When we started doing clubs," recalled Hetfield, "we were doing mostly covers of the new wave of British metal bands, and because nobody had heard these records [in the United States], all the bangers thought we were doing our own songs." Prodded by California crowds who were embracing a moshing West Coast punk, Metallica began to speed up the already

Metallica. Left to right: Lars Ulrich, Kirk Hammett, James Hetfield, and Jason Newsted. Photo by Anton Corbijn—1998. *Permission by Q-Prime/Elektra Records.*

fast, loud, propulsive metal music. "That whole fast tempo thing started with a lot of the songs we had for the first album," explained James Hetfield. "When we started writing our own songs, they weren't fast at all. Then we got a few more gigs, and we got a little more pissed off at the crowd and how people weren't appreciating our stuff. So they gradually got faster and faster as we got more aggressive. Instead of going, 'Please like us,' we were like . . . 'AAAHH! Fuck you!'"

The speeded-up sound of Metallica became known as thrash or speed metal. "Metallica really created a form of music," contended Brian Slagel, the metal enthusiast who started Metal Blade Records. "When they came out, there was no speed metal or thrash metal. They were doing something new." *Rolling Stone* magazine called the new sound "a marvel of precisely channeled aggression."

Metallica, which now included bassist Cliff Burton and guitarist Kirk Hammett, who took the place of McGovney and Mustaine, respectively, snagged a record contract through the metal underground. The band recorded a demo tape of its songs that Ulrich, an avid metal tape swapper, sent along the underground. "All we wanted to do was to send it out to the traders, get mentioned in some fan magazines," mentioned Ulrich. "The cool thing about the metal scene is that you could pass out ten copies of your tape to people who were really into it and within a week know that 100 people would have it, and another 100 a week later." In 1982, the tape landed in the hands of John Zazula and his wife Marsha, New Jersey record store owners who recently had started the label Megaforce. By the next March, Metallica had signed with Megaforce and had traveled to New York to record *Kill 'Em All*, originally titled *Metal Up Your Ass*. The next year, they cut *Ride the Lightning* for Megaforce.

The band began to attract a national following by mid-decade, at a time when seminal California punk bands such as Black Flag and the Dead Kennedys disbanded. In early 1986, they released *Master of Puppets* and embarked on a six-month tour behind metal legend Ozzy Osbourne. Osbourne "told us, 'Man, you guys remind me of Sabbath in their early days—hungry, all the energy,'" enthused James Hetfield. With little radio play and virtually no support from MTV, which characterized thrash metal as "very polarizing music," Metallica slowly climbed to the U.S. Top Thirty. As the metal army grew, the band hit the Top Ten on both sides of the Atlantic with . . . *And Justice for All* (1988). They topped British and U.S. charts with *Metallica* (1991), which registered more than nine million in sales, and *Loaded* (1996), which sold 600,000 copies in its first two weeks. "It's a cultlike audience," claimed Geoff Mayfield, director of retail research for *Billboard*. "A record like *Metallica* can sell without airplay and without MTV."

Metallica delivered a somber, angry message, similar to the desperate rantings of Southern California punk. "*Puppets* was about manipulation, *Ride the Lightning* was about death and dying, and *Justice* talked about the American dream and how that doesn't always work out anymore," explained James Hetfield. "Our music," agreed Kirk Hammett, "it's grim, based in reality. Our music mirrors modern life as much as Motown's mirrored the romance of falling in love. It says, 'You're being manipulated, man, by the big corporations, by the media.'"

Capturing the alienation and frustration of post–baby-boom youth, Metallica paved the way for a legion of thrashers. In 1988, Megadeth, fronted by ex-Metallica guitarist Dave Mustaine, who listed Motorhead as a major influence, hit the Top Thirty with *so far, so good . . . so what!* The same year, Anthrax, the New York thrash band influenced heavily by Iron Maiden, AC/DC, and the Ramones, hit the Top Thirty with *State of Euphoria*. Slayer, fronted by shredder Kerry King, joined the thrash pantheon by cracking the chart in 1986 with the speed-metal classic, *Reign in Blood*. "The thing is," explained vocalist/bassist Tom Araya, "we apply all our anger to our music and lyrics."

Megadeth, Anthrax, and Slayer banded together in the 1991 Clash of Titans tour and played to wild-eyed, enthusiastic throngs of metalers. "I tend to think of that tour as the pinnacle of the thrash movement in general," fondly remembered David Ellefson, the bassist for Megadeth, "because it proved to everybody how big the whole thing really was." By the beginning of the 1990s, even *Time* magazine admitted that "heavy metal is white hot."

Death Metal and Grindcore

Within a few years, some bands revved up the speed metal of Slayer and fused it with violent, slasher-type lyrics, nearly incomprehensible growls and abrupt tempo, key, and time signature changes to create an even more aggressive music called death metal. Starting in Florida, the genre had its origins with the band Death. The brainchild of guitarist and vocalist Chuck Schuldiner, Death started in 1983 and helped define the genre in their debut *Scream Bloody Gore* (1987) and the follow-up *Leprosy* (1988). By 1991, Schuldiner and his rotating crew of bandmates had toned down their gory lyrics and honed their guitar prowess to deliver *Human*, which attracted a greater number of followers and even landed some MTV airplay. Their success continued through *Philosophy* (1995), with the title song getting exposure on the TV show *Beavis and Butt-Head*.

Two other Florida bands were arguably originators of death metal along with Death. Fronted by guitarist Trey Azagthoth, Morbid Angel came together in 1983. After pounding out several seminal death-metal efforts, the band signed to Giant Records in 1992 and the next year released *Covenant*, which entered the *Billboard* Heatseekers chart and snagged a spot on *Beavis and Butt-Head* for the song "God of Emptiness." Amid the death-metal mania of the early 1990s, they released their best-selling album *Domination* (1995). Obituary, coming from Tampa and founded in 1985, signed to the extreme metal label Roadrunner in 1989, releasing *Slowly We Rot* that featured the low-pitched growls of John Tardy. By 1992, they hit the American Heatseekers chart and cracked the British Top 100 with *The End Complete* and the follow-up *World Demise* (1994).

Once death metal rose from the roots of thrash, a multitude of death-obsessed headbangers proliferated. Deicide, also from Florida and headed by vocalist and bassist Glen Benton, enjoyed moderate chart success with 1992's *Legion* and their second album *Once Upon the Cross* (1995). "I've always seen this kind of music as a progression from rock and roll, from early on to where it is now," reasoned Benton. "You're getting kids who in the early Eighties were getting into thrash and from there, slowly, they just get more aggressive and aggressive and aggressive."

Coming from Buffalo, New York, Cannibal Corpse offered the most vividly violent, gory lyrics imaginable. Their big break came when their music appeared on the 1994 soundtrack for the film *Ace Ventura: Pet Detective*. "So many people have come up to us since [the release of the film] and said, 'man, I never heard of you guys or death metal, and I saw you in the movie, and now I'm into death metal,'" explained drummer Paul Mazurkiewicz about the impact of their part in the film. By the mid-1990s, death metal had become a staple among the rock legions.

A few bands took death metal to even greater extremes. They adopted the gutteral growls of death metal, combining them with the speed of thrash and the energy of hardcore punk to create a style they called grindcore. The British band Napalm Death headed the grindcore movement. After producing a series of militant efforts on their own Earache label, the band finally hit the chart amid the death-metal craze. They inked a distribution deal with Columbia Records for Earache albums and charted with *Utopia Banished* (1992) and *Fear, Emptiness and Despair*

(1994), which summed up the mood of the Generation X crowd. They reached their commercial apex, when their song "Twist the Knife (Slowly)" from *Fear, Emptiness and Despair* hit the Top Ten as part of the soundtrack to the movie *Mortal Kombat* (1995). Carcass, a grindcore project fronted by former Napalm Death guitarist Bill Steer, signed with Sony Records in 1994. They quickly climbed the chart in America and the United Kingdom with the thrashingly savage *Heartwork* (1994). "I think cheezy music weakens us," contended Steer. "We're to take music to its heaviest, most ludicrous extremities." Along with Napalm Death, Carcass defined the exteme metal of grindcore.

Death metal and its grindcore offshoot, as with other extreme musical styles of the period, exemplified the anger and hopelessness of a generation. Openly embracing violence and death in one genre, the bands reflected the aggression and depression of youths during the late 1980s and early 1990s. Some of the album titles clearly displayed the hopelessness of a generation: *Entangled in Chaos* by Morbid Angel, *Slowly We Rot* and *World Demise* by Obituary, and *Gallery of Suicide* by Cannibal Corpse. Others such as *Butchered at Birth* and *Bloodthirst* by Cannibal Corpse showed the violent bent of youth.

Not confined to song titles, violence surfaced at death-metal and grindcore concerts. Like their hardcore punk counterparts, death metalers formed mosh pits in front of the stage and pummeled each other throughout the shows. Sometimes, the mosh pit jostling led to serious consequences. "I've seen people killed. I've seen people with their heads completely fucking cracked open and their brains laying out," remembered Glen Benton of Deicide. "I've seen fingers snapped back. I've seen broken arms. I've seen fucking gashes in faces and heads—I've seen it all," he asserted.

Benton attributed the violence to broader social trends operative during the 1990s. "Society is becoming more and more violent," he contended. "You can't let your ten-year-old kid go off with his buddies to go see a movie or even ride his bike around the block. You just can't. Things are getting worse," he concluded.

Benton blamed this growing violence on the breakdown of the family. "We live in the age of divorce, where 80 percent of the kids at school come from divorced households," he observed. The youth seemed "lost" without a stable family, and social values seemed to be breaking down. By the early 1990s, Generation X headbanged to the extreme metal of death and grindcore to relieve their frustrations.

The Industrial Revolution

Industrial music, the wild buzz-saw abandon of thrash metal combined with harsh, dissonant vocals and electronic samples and synthesizers, also reflected and captured the mood of alienated youths in the late 1980s and early 1990s.

The 1980s' industrial sound had its roots in the postpunk pessimism that enveloped England in the wake of the Sex Pistols. Post-Pistols bands such as John Lydon's PiL, Cabaret Voltaire, and Throbbing Gristle combined taped music, synthesizer moans, and distorted vocals to reflect the grim life of postindustrial England.

By the mid-1980s, industrial music had begun to surface on the other side of the Atlantic with outfits such as Skinny Puppy and Foetus. Originating in Vancouver, British Columbia, Skinny Puppy owed its sound to multi-instrumentalist cEvin Key, lyricist/droner Nivek Ogre (b. Kevin Ogilvie), and producer Dave "Rave" Ogilvie. After a British synthesizer-sounding debut, the outfit enlisted the help of sample master and synthesizer player Dwayne Goettel and began to churn out a harsh, dissonant industrial music on efforts such as *Cleanse Fold and Manipulate* (1987) and the overtly political *VIVIsectVI* (1988).

The various incarnations of Foetus, the brainchild of Jim Thirlwell, enhanced the cacophonic din with tinges of melody. On mid-1980s' releases such as *Hole*, the band used automatic weapons, symphony orchestras, clanging metallic objects, and tape samples to capture the intense chaos of the times.

Other American outfits such as Ministry and Nine Inch Nails added a thrashing heavy-metal guitar to the mix, making industrial music more accessible to the masses of disenchanted youths. The brainchild of Wax Trax label co-owner Al Jourgensen, Ministry abandoned funky dance music in 1986 on *Twitch* for a sound they labeled "aggro": sheets of guitar music broken by tape samples and angry vocals. By 1988, the group had perfected their sound on the genre-breaking *The Land of Rape and Honey*, which added guitars to the industrial din and brought industrial music into the mainstream. "Guitars and sequencers just seemed a natural combination," recalled Jourgensen. The next year, Jourgensen combined forces with Skinny Puppy's Dave Ogilvie on the guitar-steeped *The Mind Is a Terrible Thing to Taste* to complete the marriage between thrash metal and industrial samples. By 1992, Ministry hit the U.S. Top Thirty with *Psalm 69: The Way to Succeed and the Way to Suck Eggs*.

Trent Reznor, a Pennsylvania farm boy, classically trained pianist, and former synthesizer-band member, created Nine Inch Nails (NIN) just as Al Jourgensen introduced industrial music to the heavy-metal masses. Formed in 1988, NIN became the

Nine Inch Nails poster. (Artist: Jeff Kleinsmith.) *Permission by Jeff Kleinsmith Design.*

popular embodiment of industrial music. Reznor first added guitars to his industrialist mix in *Pretty Hate Machine* (1989), which encapsulated the doomy negativity of youth at the outset of the 1990s. According to Oliver Stone, who commissioned Reznor to record the soundtrack to his film *Natural Born Killers*, NIN reflected "that agony, that pain, that overwhelming sense of suffering." Though initially selling slowly, *Pretty Hate Machine* picked up momentum, charted in 1990, and by the 1991 Lollapalooza tour, it had turned Reznor into an underground rock icon.

After a battle with his label, Reznor followed with the Top-Ten *Broken* (1992), characterized by the industrial mastermind as "just one big blast of anger. Not necessarily a well-rounded record—just one ultrafast chunk of death." In 1994, the gloom spread with NIN's aptly titled *The Downward Spiral*, which debuted at number two on the chart. "When I'm writing songs," explained Reznor at the time, "I deliberately try to explore incredibly black emotions—combining personal experience with imaginative projection—to see how far I can get. I often end up bumming myself out pretty good." By mid-decade the commercial success of NIN encouraged a spate of other industrialists such as Cop Shoot Cop, My Life with the Thrill Kill Kult, Front 242, Nitzer Ebb, and Marilyn Manson, the last signed to Reznor's fittingly named label, Nothing.

Grunge

Grunge, growing in the Seattle offices of the independent Sub Pop Records, combined hardcore and metal to top the charts and help define the desperation of a generation. In 1979, Bruce Pavitt moved to Olympia, Washington, to attend the experimental Evergreen State College, where he worked at the alternative radio station KAOS and started the fanzine *Subterranean Pop*. After graduating in 1983, he relocated to nearby Seattle, where he wrote a column for the local music paper *The Rocket* and landed a job as a disc jockey on the University of Washington radio station KCMU, hosting a show called *Sub Pop U.S.A.* In 1986, after unsuccessfully launching a record store, Pavitt expanded his concept of regional band cassette compilations, which had accompanied his *Subterranean Pop* fanzine, into a record label. "I could always see that the real essence of the punk work was the Dead Kennedys putting stuff out themselves," reasoned Pavitt, "and people taking control of their own culture." To inaugurate the label, he released a collection of local Northwest bands, *Sub Pop 100*, and followed in June 1987 with an extended play by local punk band Green River. After the initial releases, Pavitt joined with fellow KCMU jockey Jonathan Poneman to launch Sub Pop Records as a joint venture. In an early catalog, the label owners referred to their music as "ultraloose GRUNGE that destroyed the morals of a generation."

Sub Pop scored its first success with Soundgarden. In 1987, Pavitt and Poneman borrowed money to record *Screaming Life* by the band, which included vocalist Chris Cornell and guitarist Kim Thayil. The band fastened upon a new sound, which Poneman characterized as "a bastardization of the '70s revisionist guitar thing, with a healthy dose of punk-rock aesthetic. It wasn't orthodox metal, and it wasn't a bunch of people moshing in the pit either." The Soundgarden sound melded elements of the

Nirvana, 1993. (Left to right) Dave Grohl, Kurt Cobain, and Krist Novoselic. Photo by Charles J. Peterson/Time & Life Pictures/Getty Images.

New York Dolls, the Sex Pistols, the Ramones, the MC5, and the avant-garde jazz of Ornette Coleman for a "nervous, angry, wound-up, tense" feeling, according to guitarist Thayil. Attracting fans with their musical hybrid, Soundgarden began to gain the attention of other record labels. In 1988, they recorded *Ultramega OK* with SST, the company owned by Black Flag members Greg Ginn and Chuck Dukowski, and the next year they released *Louder Than Love* on A&M Records.

Encouraged by their success with Soundgarden, Sub Pop signed other grunge bands, including Nirvana, who would become the pacesetter of new music. Nirvana vocalist and guitarist Kurt Cobain had grown up in Aberdeen, Washington. The musical impetus behind the band, Cobain first became enraptured with the Beatles and then 1970s' metal bands such as Led Zeppelin and Black Sabbath. By his teens, remembered the singer, "I was looking for something a lot heavier, yet melodic at the same time, something different from heavy metal, a different attitude."

Cobain found his niche with punk rock. He became friends with Buzz Osborne, leader of the Aberdeen punk band the Melvins. When he heard the Melvins for the first time, recalled Cobain, "it just blew me away, I was instantly a punk rocker. I abandoned all my friends, 'cause they didn't like any of the music. And then I asked Buzz to make me a compilation tape of punk-rock songs, and I got a spiky haircut." Osborne also took Cobain to his first rock concert, a show by Black Flag.

By the mid-1980s, Cobain had decided to start a band that would showcase his musical influences. He joined with fellow Aberdeen resident and bassist Krist Novoselic. Cobain observed that the band "sounded exactly like Black Flag, totally abrasive, fast, punk music. There were some Nirvana elements, some slower songs, even then. And some heavy, Black Sabbath–influenced stuff. I can't deny Black Sabbath. Or Black Flag."

In 1987, Cobain, Novoselic, and drummer Chad Channing, now named Nirvana, signed a record contract with Sub Pop. In late 1988, the trio released the 7-inch single "Love Buzz/Big Cheese." The next spring, they released their first album, *Bleach*, recorded for $606.17, which combined hardcore and metal influences.

The group added a new musical dimension as they entered the studio to record their second Sub Pop album. Recording the songs that would become *Nevermind*, Nirvana added a melodic, Beatlesque element, which had shaped Cobain, Novoselic, and new drummer Dave Grohl. "We might as well just play Beatles covers for the rest of our careers," joked Novoselic. "They started it, they did it best, they ended it." Grohl agreed, "When it comes down to pop, there's only one word—the B word, Beatles." Cobain enthused at the time, "I had finally gotten to the point where I was mixing pop music and the heavy side of us in the right formula."

As Nirvana moved toward a pop/metal/punk hybrid, the Seattle scene began to garner media attention through the efforts of Sub Pop. From its inception, Sub Pop had tried to market the Northwest scene. "The thing that we've done here is we've taken a number of bands that sound similar," remarked Poneman in 1989. "We've given them a similar marketing look in terms of dynamic, live, portrait-oriented covers. We're using a precedent set by Tamla/Motown and Stax, where you have the scene that is being born in a particular region and then you just have a machine that you use to refine and perfect your product. You create a sensation, like Great Britain in 1962 through 1965. All of a sudden there are all these bands coming out of this part of the world, there's good press, it's romantic."

Rather than the slick Motown image of suits and dinner gowns, Sub Pop helped create a downtrodden punk/metal fashion unique to the Northwest. They signed bands who dressed in faded flannel shirts or T-shirts, ripped jeans or baggy shorts, and worn boots or tennis shoes. The mostly male band members favored long hair underneath woolen caps, which had become a trademark among heavy-metal fanatics. In 1992, Poneman wrote the copy for a *Vogue* article about grunge fashion that featured the Northwest look.

Sub Pop marketed their acts through a singles–of–the–month club. They introduced their bands to the metal/punk underground by starting a subscription service, modeled after the cassette compilations Pavitt had included in his *Subterranean Pop* fanzine, to interest diehard fans and collectors. For $20, the label sent to subscribers six limited–edition singles such as "Room a 1,000 Years Wide" by Soundgarden.

To promote their bands, the label also courted the press. In 1989, they paid for a visit from journalist Everett True, who wrote for the British music magazine *Melody*

Maker, which subsequently called Sub Pop the "life force to the most vibrant, kicking music scene encompassed in one city for at least ten years." Within a year, the label attracted the attention of the national press. *The New York Times* referred to the Northwest as "America's latest music mecca," and articles about Sub Pop appeared in the *Los Angeles Times, Wall Street Journal*, and other newspapers and magazines across the country. "At long last, Seattle is suddenly hot," observed *Billboard* in November 1990.

By the end of 1990, Sub Pop had helped create the image of Seattle as the site of an exciting, emerging music scene. "Bruce and I like to compare what's going on here in Seattle with what happened in San Francisco in 1967," Poneman told the *Seattle Times*. "People are moving out here to become part of a scene," added Pavitt. "No matter how silly it sounds, Seattle has become a mecca."

Television and film helped solidify the image of Seattle as a new mecca. In April 1990, David Lynch premiered the ABC television show *Twin Peaks*, which was filmed in Snoqualmie and North Bend, Washington, and popularized an image of flannel-clad, coffee-drinking Northwesterners. *Northern Exposure*, starting as a replacement series in 1990 and quickly becoming one of the most popular shows on television, extolled the virtues of the Northwest and was filmed a few miles from Seattle. In early 1991, director Cameron Crowe started to film the movie *Singles* about the punk/metal Seattle scene that included the music of Northwest bands and featured band members in cameo roles. The film revolved around a Seattle grunge band, which recorded the single "Touch Me I'm Dick," patterned after "Touch Me I'm Sick" by the Seattle grunge outfit Mudhoney. By early 1992, when *Singles* aired in theaters across the country, the national media had embraced Seattle as the newest hip locale. "I really wanted the movie to have a real private kind of feel to it," remarked Crowe about *Singles*. "Now you get people going, 'Oh, it's about Seattle? How trendy.'"

Just as Sub Pop and the media lionized the Northwest, Nirvana signed to a national label and became a national phenomenon. By 1990, the band realized that Sub Pop had fallen into financial difficulties and used their demo tape to search for a new label. In August, they signed to David Geffen's DGC label, which paid Sub Pop $75,000 for the Nirvana contract.

The band released their major label debut *Nevermind* on September 24, 1991, amid the Northwest frenzy. Even before MTV placed their video of "Smells Like Teen Spirit" in heavy rotation, the album went gold, and in January 1992 Nirvana hit the top of the chart in the United States and the Top Ten in Britain. The band appeared on *Saturday Night Live* and was featured in *Rolling Stone, Spin*, and many other music publications. Within a year, the band had sold ten million copies of their major label debut and had entered the chart at the number-one position with their follow-up, *In Utero*.

Pearl Jam followed Nirvana to the top of the chart. The band had been established in Seattle by hardcore/British heavy-metal fans Jeff Ament and Stone Gossard, who had been members of Green River, the first band to record for Sub Pop, and had played together in Mother Love Bone. They added Black Sabbath–influenced guitarist Mike McCready, vocalist Eddie Vedder, and eventually drummer Dave Abbruzzese to complete the lineup. In late 1991, Pearl Jam released their first album, *Ten*. After waiting twenty weeks to crack the Top 200, the band topped the chart in the wake of Nirvana's success and eventually sold twelve million copies of the album. The next year, matching Nirvana's track record, the band entered the chart at number one with *Vs.*

Other Northwest metal/punk bands scored similar successes. In 1992, Alice in Chains, described by the band's guitarist Jerry Cantrell as "not entirely metal, not entirely grunge, but all of the above," released the million-selling, Top Ten *Dirt*. Two years later, they topped the chart with the more pop-sounding *Jar of Flies*. In early 1994, Soundgarden, the first Seattle band to land a major label deal, topped the chart with *Superunknown*. Mudhoney, formed by Mark Arm and Steve Turner, who had played in the influential Green River, charted as well, and their *Every Good Boy Deserves Fudge* (1991) became Sub Pop's biggest seller after Nirvana's *Bleach*. By early 1994, Seattle bands dominated the national album chart.

These bands played music for a post–baby-boom generation. "There's millions and millions of people in their 40s who think they're so fucking special," railed Kim Thayil of Soundgarden. "They're this ultimate white-bread, suburban, upper-middle-class group that were spoiled little fuckers as kids 'cause they were all children of Dr. Spock, and then they were stupid, stinky hippies, and then they were spoiled little yuppie materialists. They thought they had a monopoly on rock-'n'-roll," Thayil sneered, "and all of a sudden they realize they don't. It belongs to someone else now."

Seattle bands articulated the fears and frustrations of their many post–baby-boom fans. Kurt Cobain suffered through the divorce of his parents at age eight and drifted in and out of his mother's home as a teenager. "It just destroyed his life," lamented his mother. "He changed completely." The young boy scrawled, "I hate Mom, I hate Dad, Dad hates Mom, Mom hates Dad, it simply makes you want to be sad" on his bedroom wall. Cobain explained that "my story is exactly the same as 90 percent of everyone my age. Everyone's parents got divorced, their kids smoked pot all through high school." He continued, "The majority of bands you interview would have divorced parents. I think there's a universal display of psychological damage that everyone my age has acquired." In the case of Cobain, he projected his pain on himself and expressed it in such Nirvana songs as "Negative Creep."

Eddie Vedder, who grew up believing that his biological father was his uncle, wrote about similar feelings of parental neglect in "Jeremy." "I think the seventies and eighties were a really weird time for parenting, especially in the middle class," reasoned Vedder. "Was that the 'Me Generation' or something? Parents were looking for their things, which meant a lot of kids got left behind."

Soundgarden similarly mirrored the concerns of Generation X. Chris Cornell's lyrics "deal with inner struggles he's gone through, but a lot of people can relate to them," remarked former Soundgarden and Pearl Jam drummer Matt Cameron about the band's songs. "I think the angst this generation is experiencing is very valid, and I think it's a pretty important change that this generation of bands is actually dealing with those issues." Cornell noted, "I guess the music industry didn't predict that this generation of songwriters was going to plug in so accurately and so unanimously to the group of people who were buying records. It's a representation of the generation that wasn't being accurately represented."

The marketing of Sub Pop reflected the mood of a new generation. In 1989, the label dubbed a showcase of Sub Pop bands as a "Lamefest" and billed the event as "Seattle's lamest bands in a one-night orgy of sweat and insanity." The label owners followed with three more annual Lamefest events. They sold Sub Pop T-shirts emblazoned with the word "loser." "That shirt really hit home," explained Poneman. "There were an incredible number of young people out there who weren't making it. It was a real anti-yuppie statement." Guitarist Kurt Danielson of the Northwest grunge band Tad stated, "The loser is the existential hero of the 90s."

The poster art of the grunge era also reflected the desperate mood of youth. Artists such as Derek Hess, Ward Sutton, and Coop drew cartoonish images of a society in decline. Frank Kozik, probably the most well-known poster artist of grunge, pictured naive, happy cartoon characters shooting heroin or tormenting one another. "I prefer gallows humor, black humor," explained Kozik.

As Northwest grunge enveloped the music industry, the angst spread to nearby San Francisco as Green Day popularized California hardcore by grafting snappy melodies onto punk's speedy, muscular sound and its message of frustration. Formed in 1989 by singer/guitarist Billie Joe Armstrong and bass player Mike Dirnt, the band signed with the pop-punk label Lookout. After releasing their debut and adding drummer Frank "Tre Cool" Wright III to complete its lineup, the band delivered a soundtrack for the alienated Generation X with *Kerplunk*.

Sighted by the major labels in the grunge-band signing frenzy, in 1993 Green Day inked a deal with Warner-Reprise and early the next year released *Dookie*, which offered listeners lyrics of hopelessness behind a snappy, bright 1990s' punk sound. The threesome snagged listeners with the cynical "Welcome to Paradise," the despondent "Longview," the apathetic "Burnout," and the self-deprecating "Basket Case." "I think it's a sign of the times to be way more self-destructive, way more apathetic," reasoned Armstrong. "Basically it's yet another generation falling down the shithole. I just think about the whole American culture and go, Why?" With help from MTV and an appearance at Woodstock 1994, the album sold fifteen million copies worldwide.

Green Day opened the floodgates for a spate of other Southern California pop-punk bands that reflected the feelings of their generation. The metallic-tinged skate punk of Offspring hit the Top Five in late 1994 with *Smash*. "Punk was really abrasive, and a lot of the topics the songs dealt with were alienation, not fitting in, and being disillusioned with what American values were supposed to be," asserted singer/guitarist Dexter Holland. "Nowadays, it seems like mainstream America is identifying with those kinds of feelings."

Rancid cracked the chart amid the pop-punk explosion. The Northern California quartet grew up in broken homes and poverty. "I remember my mom trying to raise two kids on her own in the eighties and Ronald Reagan being in power, and having her hours cut so she could barely make the fucking rent," Lars Frederiksen bitterly recollected. "I remember eating fucking Raisin Bran for Christmas dinner." Though banding together in 1991 and debuting two years later, the politicized group first charted in 1994 with *Let's Go* and . . . *And Out Come the Wolves* the next year. "As long as America is the way it is, punk is never going to die," explained Rancid front-

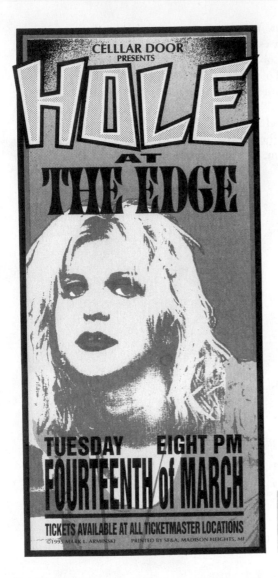

Hole poster. (Artist: Mark L. Arminski.) *Permission by Mark Arminski.*

man Tim Armstrong. "Kids are always going to be going through shit, and will be using guitars as vehicles to express how fucked up they feel."

By mid-decade, rock-and-roll bands expressed the disillusionment that gripped many post–baby boomers and ultimately sowed the seeds of grunge's demise. "We had to grow up with this idealization that was never going to fucking come true, and it turned us into a bunch of cynics—or a bunch of drug addicts," complained Courtney Love, who fronted the grunge band Hole. The early 1990s' overdose deaths of Mother Love Bone singer Andrew Wood, Hole bass player Kristen Pfaff, and guitarist Stefanie Sargent of Seven Year Bitch emphasized the effects of heroin, which had appeared to provide an escape from a hopeless situation. The April 5, 1994, shotgun suicide of Kurt Cobain, probably the most important figure in Northwest grunge and the husband of Courtney Love, highlighted the angry desperation of a generation. "I think there's gonna be more and more people who just give up hope," predicted Chris Cornell. "I mean, that's the way I feel. I'm successful in what I do, but I don't really have a clue where I'm going or how I fit into the rest of society." As had happened during the late 1960s with the deaths of rock musicians such as Jimi Hendrix and Janis Joplin, the anger, frustration, and disillusionment of a new generation had become lethal.

The Rave Revolution and Britpop

> 66 Our music doesn't reflect the times, it ignores them. 99
>
> —Alex Paterson of the Orb

British youths in the 1980s and 1990s confronted even harsher conditions than their American counterparts. But unlike American youths, who crafted a desperate music of disillusionment, British teens followed their Mod and New Romantic forebears, who took to the dance floor to escape their problems. Enjoying few prospects, they chose to blissfully crowd the dance floor with drug-induced smiles on their faces.

In the postpunk era, British youths experienced grim economic realities. In Great Britain during 1984, nearly 12 percent of the adult population searched for work. Ten years later, the unemployment rate still hovered at 10 percent, not including the "economically inactive" who had given up hope of ever finding employment. The number of teens without jobs during the same period stood at roughly double the overall unemployment rate, indicating the headlong decline of the British economy.

Coupled with a crippling inflation rate that slashed the purchasing power of the pound by more than 315 percent from 1975 to 1988, joblessness in Great Britain, especially among British youths, created a sobering, sometimes hopeless attitude.

House and Techno

Faced with a nearly untenable situation, many British youths decided to escape reality through a rave dance culture, which had its origins in the house music of Chicago and the techno clubs of Detroit.

Disc jockey Frankie Knuckles began to transform disco by reediting his records, intensifying the four-to-the-floor disco beat, and extending certain parts of a song to work his dance crowd to a fevered pitch. Moving from New York to Chicago, Knuckles realized that he needed to improvise because of the lack of new disco records. "By '81 when they had declared disco dead, all the record labels were getting rid of their dance . . . or their disco departments, so there were no more up-tempo dance records, everything was down tempo," recalled Knuckles. "That's when I realized I had to start changing certain things in order to keep feeding my dance floor." Using a tape recorder and then a Roland TR-909 drum machine, he began splicing preprogrammed rhythms into his act to intensify the bass or connect one song to another. Just as New Yorkers such as Afrika Bambaataa cut, spliced, and scratched, Knuckles unveiled his new sound at a gay, three-story Chicago club called the Warehouse, which gave this Chicago variant of funk the name "house."

When Knuckles left the Warehouse in 1982 to start his own club, the Power Plant, the Warehouse owners retaliated by renaming their club the Music Box and hiring Chicago DJ Ron Hardy, who challenged Knuckles by pushing disco into a new realm with loud, hard bass beats and booming percussion. Excited clubgoers began to "jack," a dance that consisted of a full-body, random, prolonged shake.

In 1983, Jesse Saunders and Vince Lawrence brought house to vinyl with "On and On," released by local record plant owner Larry Sherman. Impressed with the selling power of the new music, Sherman started Trax Records. By the mid-1980s, Trax, along with DJ International Records, posted a series of minor hits such as Farley "Jackmaster" Funk (b. Farley Williams), Jesse Saunders's "Love Can't Turn Around," and Ron Hardy's "Sensation."

Some disc jockeys such as DJ Pierre (b. Nathaniel Pierre Jones) added the wobbly, multiple-frequency buzz of a Roland TB-303 baseline synthesizer to create a refinement on house, tagged "acid house." Collaborating with Earl "Spanky" Smith and Herb Jackson, in late 1985 DJ Pierre experimented with the Roland TB-303 and ended with the fuzzy bleeps of "Acid Trax," which became a sensation after Ron Hardy introduced it to dancers at the Music Box. By the 1980s when New Yorkers began to rap over their sampled beats, Chicago DJs established the beat-solid, instrumental house and acid house as underground phenomena.

In nearby Detroit, other turntable wizards combined house music with spacy European electronica into a concoction they called "techno." Juan Atkins, the son of a concert promoter, became enamored with the industrial, metallic sound of the German experimental band Kraftwerk. "I just froze in my tracks. Everything was so clean and precise," he explained. Two of Atkins's longtime friends, Derrick May and Kevin Saunderson, became equally fascinated by Chicago house during their visits to the Windy City. "Some people took me to the Power Plant where I heard Frankie Knuckles play," enthused May. "Frankie was really a turning point in my life." Looking for an escape from the sobering realities of the Detroit streets, the threesome joined together to fuse space-age electronic music and bass-heavy house into techno, a minimalist yet romantic funk with thundering drumbeats. May likened this marriage of music to "George Clinton and Kraftwerk stuck in an elevator with only a sequencer to keep them company." This fusion was not unlike New York hip-hopper Afrika Bambaataa's 1982 "Planet Rock," which sampled Kraftwerk's "Trans-Europe Express" and "Numbers" as the background for his rap.

Unlike Bambaataa and his fellow New Yorkers, who wove raps in and around hip-hop beats, techno emphasized the machine-perfect sounds of a futuristic European electronic music over a hard funky bass. From the perspective of Juan Atkins, "Berry Gordy built the Motown sound on the same principles as the conveyor belt system at Ford's. Today their plants don't work that way—they use robots and computers to make the cars. I'm more interested in Ford's robots than Berry Gordy's music." He characterized himself as "a warrior for the technological revolution." He declared, "I want my music to sound like computers talking to each other."

In 1981, as Cybotron, Atkins and techno colleague Rick Davis launched the Detroit techno scene on their own Deep Space label with the single "Alleys of Your Mind" and followed with "Cosmic Cars" and the *Enter* album. When the Cybotron duo split after Davis wanted to pursue a more rock-oriented direction, Atkins soloed as Model 500 with "No UFOs" on his own Metroplex label, which also featured tracks such as Kevin Saunderson's "Triangle of Love," Derrick May's "Let's Go," and Eddie "Flashin" Fowlkes's "Goodbye Kiss." Saunderson, Atkins, Fowlkes, and a few others also collaborated on "Big Fun." "It was real tight," remembered Fowlkes about the 1980s' Detroit techno scene. "Everyone was helping each other out, there were no egos, and nobody could compete with Juan because he had already done stuff as Cybotron and knew where he wanted to go. We were like kids following the Pied Piper."

A Rave New World

The sampled four-to-the-floor funk of house and the pristine, electronic techno carried over the Atlantic to British youths, who hoped to escape from the numbing effects of the conservative Margaret Thatcher government by dancing the night away. The party began in the summer of 1986 with unemployed British youths who had traveled to Ibiza, one of the four Balearic Islands in the Mediterranean off the east coast of Spain. "From the age of sixteen," explained clubber Marie Marden, "they left home because they didn't have careers or anything, and basically they were just thieves," who would rob tourists and then dance to a musical amalgam that included acid house and techno in clubs such as Amnesia, Pasha, and Ku.

In 1987, after Paul Oakenfold hosted a twenty-sixth birthday party for himself with friends Danny Rampling and Nicky Holloway in Ibiza, the acid house/techno scene shifted to London clubs such as the Project and then the Future and Spectrum, operated by Oakenfold and his partner Ian St. Paul; Shoom, started by Rampling; and the Trip, established by Holloway. Soon teens began to frequent the clubs to dance to the new music. "London clubs had always been about people drinking, trying to chat up girls, looking good but not dancing," recalled Oakenfold, forgetting about the long-standing British dance tradition starting with the Mods and continuing to the early 1980s with the New Romantics. "All of a sudden we completely changed that—you'd come down and you'd dance for six hours. The idea was 'if you're not into dancing, then don't come down.'"

The dancing teens favored a fashion that resembled their Ibiza counterparts. In order to dance furiously, they wore baggy pants and T-shirts, brightly colored headbands, and casual shoes. In time, the girls began to sport tight-fitting lycra outfits that allowed maximum movement.

As well as common clothing, the hedonistic dance scene revolved around a drug called Ecstasy. Ecstasy, or MDMA, had been first synthesized in Germany in 1912. Therapeutically, psychiatrists used the drug to break down barriers and to enhance intimacy and communication. Though outlawed in Great Britain by 1977, the drug had become so entrenched in the house clubs of Chicago and the gay culture of New York City that 1960s' drug guru Timothy Leary called Ecstasy "the drug of the eighties" before the Drug Enforcement Agency banned it from the United States in 1985. British youths, finding themselves jobless and insecure about their future, imported Ecstasy in an attempt to capture the intimacy and security that eluded them. Between 1990 and 1995, the amount of Ecstasy shipped into Britain increased by 4,000 percent, and the drug economy grew by 500 percent, with an estimated worth of £1.8 billion by 1993.

Unlike the serious-minded American hippies, who twenty years earlier had used drugs to create a new world order by expanding their collective consciousness, British youths ingested Ecstasy for pure pleasure. "In some ways it was a throwback to the '60s, but it was very much something else," commented club owner Tony Colston-Hayter. "It was totally nonpolitical. It was the ultimate leisure activity. It was about going out and having a good time."

Propelled by the hallucinatory, speedy warmth of Ecstasy's first glow, good-time British youths spouted endlessly about love and positivity and adopted the 1970s' smiley face as their logo. "I liked the energy and the visual side of punk, but it was all just saying 'no, no, no,' whereas now everybody's saying 'yes, yes, yes,'" gushed keyboardist Adamski (b. Adam Tinley) in 1990 when he scored with the electronica hit "Killer." "I much prefer the positivity thing we have now."

By 1988, thousands of British teens embraced the new baggy, Ecstasy-fueled subculture and streamed into clubs. Not content with dancing until closing time, they began to demand and frequent illegal after-hour venues such as RIP. Some became more adventurous and met in abandoned warehouses to dance until dawn in what became known as "raves." The press began to label the movement of pleasure-driven, dance-crazy teens as a new Summer of Love.

The ravers danced to a hybrid music with a base of acid house and techno. Sometimes they resurrected acid house and techno pioneers. At one early rave, Juan

Atkins hosted the music. "When I first went to Europe, the first big party I played was in London for 5,000 kids at a rave in a big film studio," he remembered. "Kids were going crazy for the records."

Soon exhausting American imports, the new subculture inevitably demanded homegrown heroes. In 1988, D-Mob's "We Call It Acieed" hit number three, "Acid Man" by Jolly Roger cracked the chart, and the British house outfit 808 State hit with their *Newbuild* and the next year followed with their acid house classic "Pacific State." Gerald Simpson, leaving 808 State, hit the chart with "Voodoo Ray" as A Guy Called Gerald.

Two bands, the Happy Mondays and Primal Scream, became the stars of British rave culture through the efforts of skillful DJs. Starting as a funk/rock band in 1980, the Manchester-based Happy Mondays began to incorporate acid house into their mix of funk, up-tempo, Motown-based northern soul, and straight-ahead rock as they played in Ecstasy-infested Manchester clubs such as the Hacienda. By 1988, their sound had permanently changed from a more traditional rock/funk to a rave dance machine that featured a lazy groove pieced together with 1970s' R&B, washes of psychedelic guitars, the rantings of vocalist Shaun Ryder, and an insistent heavy bass and drumbeat. The Happy Mondays, contended Daniel Ash of Bauhaus and later of Love and Rockets, pioneered "a mixture of guitars and dance beats instead of rock beats." In 1988, producer Martin Hannett helped transform the band from an ordinary-sounding dance-rock outfit to an underground rave sensation with the album *Bummed*, one of the first rave smashes. Next, DJs Paul Oakenfold and Steve Osborne helped complete the band's transition to a house trance-dance unit with their work on the extended play *Madchester Rave On* (1989), which hit the British Top Twenty, and on *Pills 'n' Thrills and Bellyaches*, which neared the top of the British chart the next year.

Primal Scream enjoyed an even more complete makeover to briefly abandon rock for rave success. Formed in 1984 by the Jesus and Mary Chain drummer Bobby Gillespie and guitarist Jim Beattie, the band initially cut several singles of jangly rock. After two harder-edged albums, the group turned to rave. "Contemporary rock ceased to excite us," explained Gillespie. "At raves, the music was better, the people were better, the girls were better, and the drugs were better." The band asked DJ Andrew Weatherall to remix their song "I'm Losing More Than I'll Ever Have." The newly ordained producer stripped most of the instrumentation from the original and replaced it with heavy bass beats and samples to create the rave classic "Loaded" (1990). Adding the programming expertise of Hugo Nicholson, the next year Primal Scream hit the British Top Ten with *Screamadelica*, which married rock guitars with the throbbing beat of dance music to carry acid house into the mainstream.

By 1989, the dance parties had become large-scale events in open areas with a music stage, lights, multiple DJs, huge sound systems, and vendor booths. Youth jumped into their cars and headed out to the country to massive raves organized by groups such as Sunrise, World Dance, and Biology. On June 24, 1989, a Sunrise event attracted 11,000 youths to an empty aircraft hangar in Berkshire. Less than two months later, on August 12, the Sunrise/Back to the Future Dance Music Festival, held on a farm outside the village of Longwick, drew 17,000 ravers. On September

30, in the pouring rain, another 4,000 youths congregated in a plowed field in Oxfordshire at the Helter Skelter Party. The retro-hippie rave scene continued to grow and in 1992 peaked with Castlemorton, which brought together a reported 40,000 rave fanatics.

By 1990, the music began to change with the growing size and commercialization of raves as well as with the continued use of Ecstasy, which left habitual users with the speedy amphetamine rush but without the communal glow. Like the transition from the Sex Pistols to American hardcore punk, the music became faster and more intense. Hardcore rave featured a tremoring sub-bass roar introduced by Unique 3 in "The Theme" and by LFO (short for Low Frequency Oscillation) in *Frequencies* (1991), both released by Warp Records. "There were definitely loads of detailed conversations about how you could get the bass heavier," related Steve Beckett, co-owner of Warp. "The track 'LFO' was actually shaking the bar. That was when we knew we'd got it right." The four-to-the-floor house rhythm gave way to frenetic breakbeats, the percussion-only parts of a record. Hardcore outfits such as Orbital added blasts of Euro-techno noise and freely sampled using computerized sequencers that had become more affordable and user friendly during the early 1990s.

Orbital, the creation of brothers Phil and Paul Hartnoll, became one of the most popular hardcore acts among the large numbers of speeded-up ravers. Starting

Orbital (Paul Hartnoll and Phil Hartnoll).
Permission by London Records.

to record together in 1987, the Kraftwerk-inspired duo named themselves after the London freeway that led British clubbers to countryside raves. They first cut the bass-heavy, harsh techno of "Chime" (1989), which hit the Top Twenty. Building support with live appearances that included light shows, visuals, and electronic improvisations, the brothers slowly attracted ravers to their pounding sound. By 1993, they hit the Top Thirty with *Untitled* (*Orbital II*). The next year, Orbital reached the Top Five with the sonically varied *Snivilization*. With techno tour mates such as Moby and Richard "Aphex Twin" James, by the mid-1990s the brothers had helped move rave to the hardcore.

Chillin' Out

By the early 1990s, hardcore ravers speeded out of control. As British youth became exhausted from the pace of the hardcore scene and as the Ecstacy-propelled teens began to suffer from the effects of a drug-focused culture, many left the dance floor and turned to a somber, escapist music of lilting vocals and atmospheric rhythms called ambient techno.

The ambient scene started in the back rooms of rave clubs, where club owners created chill-out rooms for hardcore dancers who collapsed in cushy sofas and listened to Brian Eno–like soundscapes laced with house music and intricate rhythms. Techno champion Mixmaster Morris of Irresistible Force characterized this "intelligent techno" as the direct "opposite of the stupid hardcore." The new sound, declared Ken Dowie of the hardcore-turned-ambient trio Black Dog, filled "a hole in music."

The music had its origins during the mid-1980s with KLF. In 1986, former A&R man for Warner Records Bill Drummond and guitarist Jimmy Cauty formed the Kopyright Liberation Front, or KLF. In 1990, the duo fashioned a seminal atmospheric techno album, the aptly named *Chill Out*, which failed to chart but provided a direction for future ambient experiments. In 1992, after nearly topping the chart with *White Room*, which included acid house gems such as "3 A.M. Eternal" and "What Time Is Love?," KLF abruptly disbanded, publicly burning one million pounds in cash and vowing not to return until the governments of the world declared world peace.

Before disappearing from the music scene, Jimmy Cauty joined with synthesizer wiz Alex Paterson in his project the Orb, one of the most successful of the new ambient outfits. In 1988, Paterson, who had disc jockeyed at the Land of Oz, the chill-out room for the Paul Oakenfold club Heaven, joined with Cauty for the extended play *Kiss*, which pieced together radio samples from New York's KISS-FM station. The same year, the duo crafted the twenty-two-minute single "A Huge Ever Growing Pulsating Brain That Rules from the Center of the Ultraworld," which boasted Cauty's samples, acid-house dance grooves, and languid, ambient soundscapes. After recording engineer Thrash (b. Kris Weston) replaced Cauty, in mid-1992, Paterson's the Orb hit the Top Ten with "Blue Room," at nearly forty minutes, the longest single in history to chart. On the strength of the single, *U.F.Orb* soared to the top of the chart to the glee of the growing throngs attracted to ambient techno.

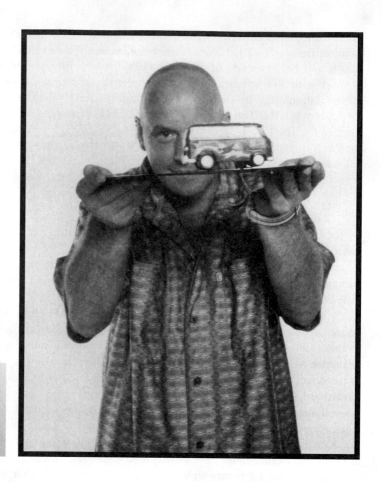

The Orb (Alex Paterson). Photo by Evan Spencer. Universal Island Records, Ltd.

In 1992, the influential Warp Records released *Artificial Intelligence*, a compilation that helped launch the genre by featuring the sounds of soon-to-be ambient stars such as the Manchester-based Autechre, electronic wizard Richard "Aphex Twin" James, Alex Paterson of the Orb, and Black Dog. "Are you sitting comfortably? Artificial Intelligence is for long journeys, quiet nights and club drowsy dawns. Listen with an open mind," the album sleeve stated.

A few bands such as Massive Attack took the dreaming, somber sounds of ambient techno and added some hip-hop rhythms and sultry melodies to create what critics termed "trip hop." Originating in Bristol, Massive Attack—Andrew "Mushroom" Vowles, Grantley "Daddy G." Marshall, and Robert "3-D" Del Naja—began to perform as the Wild Bunch. According to 3-D, they would "just throw basic parties where we'd play other people's music. You'd play some track over and over, but add different vocalists and rappers and toasters on top of the music." By 1987, they had formed Massive Attack and soon added the smooth soul vocals of Shara Nelson.

In early 1991, Massive Attack released its seminal album *Blue Lines*, which mixed ambient music, pop, hip-hop, and a trancelike soul into a beautiful but disturbing concoction. The songs consisted of a bass line or drumbeat, which expanded into a sonic landscape, replete with pop melodies and samples of reverberating guitars. 3-D rapped, reggae dub legend Horace Andy lent his falsetto, and the sultry, silky vocals of Shara Nelson floated above the entire mix, giving the music a trippy, otherworldly feel. The album hit number thirteen in Britain. Though Nelson departed for a solo career after the release of *Blue Lines*, Massive Attack recruited two more divas, Tracey Thorn and Nicolette, to keep their distinctive sound intact. The group released *Protection* (number four, Britain, 1994) and the next year followed with *No Protection* (Top Ten, Britain).

Tricky (b. Adrian Thaws) extended the ambient, trippy genre. He started as a member of the Wild Bunch collective and lent his raps to Massive Attack's pivotal *Blue Lines* and *Protection*. In 1994, he signed a solo contract, releasing the breakthrough single "Aftermath," which had been recorded two years earlier with his musical partner, vocalist Martina. The next year, the trip-hopper released the brooding *Maxinquaye* (number three, Britain), which featured the smooth vocals of Martina over Tricky's raps, hypnotic, sullen, and disjointed rhythms, odd noises, and samples.

Massive Attack laid the groundwork for the success of Portishead. Geoff Barrow grew up in the West Coast English shipping town of Portishead and worked in the Coach House recording studio. He met Massive Attack there and began working along similar lines. By 1993, the programmer/synthesizer wizard had joined with vocalist Beth Gibbons and jazz guitarist Adrian Utley to near the top of the British chart with the lilting film-noir vibe of *Dummy*, which the British rock newspaper *Melody Maker* named Album of the Year. In 1997, the outfit again neared the top of the British chart and brought their sound to the U.S. Top Twenty-Five with the self-named *Portishead*.

Ambient techno, like rave before it, provided escapist music for teens hoping to flee an unappealing reality. "Our music doesn't reflect the times, it ignores them," asserted Alex Paterson of the Orb. "Society today is so suppressed, you can only make music that is escapist."

The Dark Side of the Jungle

The popularity of the ambient sounds of the Orb and Portishead, peaking between 1991 and 1993, gave way to another, harsher version of hardcore called drum 'n' bass, which reflected a desperate mood among British ravers who confronted problems with drugs and a police crackdown.

As with most subcultures revolving around drugs, the rave scene became littered with habitual users and organized criminals. "The initial phase of taking Ecstasy, the pleasure of it is so unexpected, you just keep doing it," related journalist Jack Barron. The Ecstasy-crazy youths soon took handfuls of the drug in an attempt to recapture the initial warm glow of first contact. "You'd see people who were completely abusing it," related one raver. "Seven or eight pills on a Friday, ten pills on a Saturday, and half a dozen on a Sunday." Unable to perfectly rekindle or intensify their initial high, they turned to other similar drugs such as LSD and amphetamines to at least reach the frenetic speed and hallucinogenic state realized through Ecstasy.

As soon as drug intake became widespread and more varied, thugs entered the scene to service a drug-addicted clientele. "You'd come out of a club at the end of the night feeling like you were going to change the world," related Ian Brown, the leader of the Stone Roses, the Manchester band that hit the Top Ten with the guitar-funk of "Fool's Gold" (1990). "The guns come in, and heroin starts being put in Ecstasy. It took a lot of the love vibe out."

When drugs became big business, the police began to crack down on the rave scene. As early as 1989, they combed for clues about the next rave and many times successfully blockaded disappointed ravers from their dance events. As the raves evolved to include more and more people and drug activity, police actions intensified. The antirave vigilance climaxed with the passage of the Criminal Justice and Public Order Act of late 1994 that gave police the authority to disperse a rave, defined as 100 or more people playing music "with a succession of repetitive beats." Authorities also received the power to stop and detain anyone within a mile perimeter of a rave and to order ten or more people suspected of organizing a rave to disperse with the threat of a £2,500 fine and a three-month jail sentence.

Confronted by police action, the happy-go-lucky ravers became more somber. Hardcore rave units such as 4 Hero, with their *In Rough Territory* (1991), and Doc Scott, with his "Here Come the Drumz," became drum 'n' bass pioneers by grafting the frenetic pace of hardcore on jagged backbeats and gloomy bass lines inspired by the soundtrack to *Blade Runner*. They also eliminated the hyperspeed vocals and melodramatic strings of hardcore to create a sound defined by fast, pounding drums 'n' bass. "'Dark' came from the feeling of breakdown in society," jungle pioneer Goldie later explained about the change in music that began to take place by the early 1990s. "It was winter, clubs were closing, the country was in decline."

The "darkcore" music, as some critics labeled it, quickly morphed into a complex drum 'n' bass or jungle genre. Originally labeled "jungle" by racist detractors who disdained its working-class, black origins, the music featured hard, fast, fractured breakbeats that appeared and then disappeared from a song to create an intense, surging polyrhythmic dynamic. The complex, computer-generated rhythms of jungle chattered over multiple bass lines, usually with one traveling at hyperkinetic speed and the other inching along at a much slower rate. Combining rave, techno, and hip-hop, drum 'n' bass artists pushed listeners to new heights with brash, rapid, stop-and-start beats.

The drum 'n' bass subculture had little resemblance to rave. The baggy look gave way to stylish dress, and marijuana and alcohol replaced Ecstasy and speed. Some drum 'n' bass outfits such as 4 Hero, led by Dego (b. McFarland) and Mark Mac (b. Mark Clair) who operated the influential drum 'n' bass label Reinforced Records, warned their fans about the drug problems of the declining rave scene. The duo released "Mr. Kirk's Nightmare," which sampled a policeman telling a father that his son had died of an overdose. They delivered a similar message in "Cookin' Up Ya Brain." Maybe most important, few danced to the complex jungle rhythms in stark contrast to hardcore, which pulled youths to the dance floor in droves.

Jungle became even less dance friendly by mid-decade as it mutated by layering atmospheric vocals on top of the scattering, complicated rhythm patterns for an "intelligent" drum-and-bass style popularized by Goldie (b. Clifford Price). First attracted to hip-hop culture, Goldie began to frequent the London hardcore rave club Rage to dance to the frantic, upbeat, hardcore sounds flying from the turntables of DJs Grooverider and Fabio. He entered the scene as an engineer and an A&R man for 4 Hero's Reinforced Records. In late 1992, Goldie combined hardcore rave with heavy bass beats, deconstructed samples, and haunting vocals for his extended play *Terminator*. Two years later, he unleashed his first full-length effort *Timeless* (Top Ten, Britain), which featured frenetic samples that spun around the seductive vocals of Diane Charlemagne.

LTJ Bukem (b. Danny Williamson) offered a more jazz-oriented variant of drum 'n' bass on his own Good Looking/Looking Good Records. Steeped in fusion jazz, house, techno, and hip-hop, Bukem joined with DJ Fabio in 1991 to open the

Goldie. *Permission by London Records.*

West End London club Speed, where the duo spun high-energy, lightning-fast break-beats under MC Conrad's vocals. For the next few years, Bukem produced sides for jungle spinmeisters such as Goldie and Grooverider. After drum 'n' bass hit the British mainstream with Goldie's *Timeless*, in 1995 he released *Mixmag Live!, Vol. 3*, a collection of material by himself and label mates PFM.

The frenetic drum 'n' bass hit the mainstream on both sides of the Atlantic with Prodigy who offered a guitar-driven blend of acid house, hardcore, and drum 'n' bass. In 1990 amid the rave craze, Liam Howlett formed the group with dancers Keith Flint and Leeroy Thornhill and reggae/house MC Maxim Reality (b. Keith Palmer). A year later, they released their debut album, the extended play *What Evil Lurks*, which included songs such as "Android." Howlett described it as "a pretty hard song. It's more four to the floor, but it does have a breakbeat, and was about 128 beats per minute. It was quite techno-y, and actually quite melodical at points." The group followed a few months later with the single "Charly," which sampled a TV public-service spot for children, which generated some negative publicity. In 1992, Prodigy crafted the album *Experience* (number twelve, Britain), which solidified their position among dance-crazy hardcore ravers. In 1994, Prodigy released the drum 'n' bass–flavored *Music for the Jilted Generation* (number one, Britain), directly confronting the Criminal Justice and Public Order Act with such songs as "Their Law."

Prodigy began to add rock elements to the mix of acid house, hardcore, and drum 'n' bass. "Before Nirvana and those sorts of new rock bands," declared Howlett, "rock just wasn't cool. Dance music and hip-hop came along and were much cooler than rock ever was. Then when Nirvana arrived, in the street rock again was cool." Changing with the times, on their number-one British hit "Firestarter" (1996), the group sampled the grungy Breeders.

Despite their British triumphs, Prodigy did not initially score in the States. Touring America three times during the early 1990s, the band met with lukewarm responses at best. "After going back a few times," Howlett recalled, "it became evident that it wasn't the same as what was going on in Europe. I guessed, in a way, that we'd never really catch on here [in America]."

During the late 1990s, U.S. teens warmed to Prodigy's rock-influenced drum 'n' bass amalgam. In March 1996, the group first cracked the American Top Thirty with the single "Firestarter," which featured a wild-haired Keith Flint spitting out vocals over harsh, exploding drums and heavy bass beats. The next year, Prodigy's *The Fat of the Land* topped the British and American charts, selling more than two million copies in the States.

Britpop

While some British youths escaped sobering social conditions through the many forms of techno, others took to the dance floor with a new version of British pop simply called "Britpop" by the press. Building on the success of the mid-80s' popdom of the Smiths, groups such as Suede, Pulp, Blur, and Oasis dominated the British charts during the late 1990s.

Many of these bands had been inspired by the Smiths. Formed by guitarist Johnny Marr and singer Stephen Morrissey, or just Morrissey, the band successfully combined Morrisey's morose lyrics with Marr's upbeat guitar work. In 1984, they hit the number-two slot with their self-named debut, reached the Top Ten the same year with *Hateful of Hollow* and the next year hit the top of the chart with *Meat Is Murder*. In 1987, they followed with the near chart-topper *The Queen Is Dead* before disbanding.

Suede had formed in 1989 in the wake of the Smiths' demise, well before the Britpop mania of the mid-1990s. Inspired by the Smiths, vocalist Brett Anderson and guitarist Bernard Butler took their name from a Morrissey single, "Suedehead." They developed a dark, guitar-based sound that, in 1993, kicked off the Britpop craze. Their self-titled debut reached number one and the follow-up, *Dog Man Star*, nearly equaled the success of the first album. In 1996, they earned top honors for *Coming Up*.

Pulp rode the British pop wave started by Suede. Cemented together by vocalist/guitarist Jarvis Cocker, the band made its recording debut in 1983 to lukewarm reviews. As the Britpop craze began to take hold, their version of pop-rock climbed the British chart. In 1994, they hit with the Top-Ten *His 'N' Hers* and the next year topped the album chart with *Different Class*.

Grouping together in 1989, Blur initially mined the sound of the Manchester scene with *Leisure* (1991). The next year, the band changed its musical direction toward a more guitar-pop sound but it took two more years for them to break through to pop stardom. They released two successive number-one albums, *Parklife* (1994) and *The Great Escape* (1995). The band paved the way for a spate of British guitar-based popsters such as Menswear, the Boo Radleys, Supergrass, and Gene.

In 1994 during the Britpop explosion, Oasis seemed to rise from obscurity to international stardom. Headed by lyricist/guitarist Noel Gallagher and his brother Liam, the group burst on the scene with the number-one *Definitely Maybe*, which sold 500,000 copies in a day and holds the record for the fastest-selling debut in history. The next year the Manchester outfit again topped the chart with *(What's the Story) Morning Glory?* Unlike the other British pop bands, Oasis also crossed over into America, hitting the Top Five with *Morning Glory*, which also topped charts in Europe and Asia. In 1997, the band just missed the top spot in America with *Be Here Now*, which shattered sales records in Britain.

The more experimental pop of Radiohead also garnered success on both sides of the Atlantic. Fronted by singer Thom Yorke and featuring a three-guitar lineup, the band debuted with *Pablo Honey* in 1993, which hit the Top Twenty-Five in Britain and approached the U.S. Top Thirty. Two years later they followed with *The Bends*, which scaled the chart in their homeland. Within another two years, they released their masterpiece, the eclectic, progressive pop of *OK Computer*, which topped the British chart and neared the Top Twenty in the United States.

From 1994 to 1997, Britpop swept Britain and invaded America. Radiohead, Oasis, and other Britpop bands created their sounds from many borrowed sources, including the Beatles who spearheaded the first, most successful British invasion. Radiohead, one of the most stylistically diverse acts, incorporated aspects of the Beatles, U2, and Pink Floyd. They also cited Miles Davis and Italian film composer

Tom Yorke performs with Radiohead in London in 2006. Photo by Jo Hale/Getty Images.

Ennio Morricone as important to their music. Noel Gallagher of Oasis cited the Smiths as a major influence. "When the Smiths came on the *Top of the Pops* for the first time, that was it for me," he confessed. "From that day on, I wanted to be Johnny Marr." He also paid homage to the ultimate British pop band, the Beatles. The guitarist called the Beatles more than "an obsession. It's an ideal for living." Blur bassist Alex James identified the same Beatlesque influence. "We made a very deliberate attempt to embrace classic British songwriting values and imagery," he explained.

The Britpop bands proudly displayed their pop roots as a reaction to American grunge. "Grunge? People in shorts and socks and pumps with guitars and stickers jumping up and down screaming," Liam Gallagher sniffed. "Not having it. Far too smelly for me." His brother Noel added, "The grunge thing was all about eating your parents and all that shit." Though he secretly enjoyed some of the grunge bands, Graham Coxon, guitarist for Blur, said he would take his "Walkman to his bunk on the tour bus and listen to it in secret, because we had to be proud of being British at that point."

Unlike the starkly realistic grunge, Britpop helped British youths dance away their troubles much like techno did. As Noel Gallagher described it, "we just came along and it was like, if fuckin' 'cow' rhymes with 'now,' and it goes with a good tune, you know, who cares. It's all about escapism," he explained, "a pint in one hand, your best mate in the other, whoever that may be, and just having a good time." This British escapist attitude contrasted sharply with the rapid-fire raps, which sounded from destitute urban areas of the hip-hop nation.

The Hip-Hop Nation

> **66** Hip-hop has proved itself to be the rock-'n'-roll of the 90s. **99**
>
> —Brian Taylor, President, Priority Records

African-American youths, facing greater hardships than their white counterparts on both sides of the Atlantic, responded with a hard-edged hip-hop music to chronicle their plight and to generate community support. They created an adaptable vehicle that constantly changed and merged with other music, becoming an innovative, distinctive, nearly ubiquitous sound in the late 1980s and 1990s and into the twenty-first century.

African Americans generally experienced hard times despite the civil rights movement of the 1960s. By 1980, more than 31 percent of African Americans lived in poverty, nearly three times the percentage of impoverished whites. Six years later, 14 percent of African-American families earned less than $5,000 a year, compared to 9.6 percent in 1970, and more than 30 percent had a yearly income of less than $10,000.

African-American youths especially confronted forbidding economic prospects. The percentage of African-American males under the age of twenty-four who had never held a job increased from 9.9 percent in 1966 to 23.3 percent in 1977. By 1987, more than 34 percent of African-American teens were unemployed, compared to 17 percent of white teens; more than 21 percent of African Americans between the ages of twenty

and twenty-four could not find jobs, compared to less than 10 percent of their white counterparts. Five years later, nearly 40 percent of African-American teens and 24 percent of African Americans in their early twenties found themselves on the unemployment rolls.

Many of these poor, unemployed youths lived in single-parent, single-income households, usually headed by a mother. In 1964, roughly 25 percent of African-American children lived in female-headed homes. Abetted by a welfare system that rewarded fatherless families, in 1980 that figure increased to 40 percent. In 1984, the number of female-headed, single-parent African-American families skyrocketed to more than 50 percent, compared to 14 percent among white families. By 1992, the number of fatherless families increased to 59 percent among African Americans.

To gain the support usually provided by a stable family, many African-American youths joined gangs such as the notorious warring Crips and Bloods in Los Angeles. By the mid-1980s in Los Angeles, 24,000 young African Americans belonged to more than 260 gangs. By 1992, just the membership among the Bloods and Crips numbered around 40,000.

Many of the new gang members found the support they sought. "There's a lot of admirable qualities in gang membership. A guy will look at you and say, 'If something happens to you, I'll be the first one to die.' There's a lot of love," suggested rapper Ice-T. "The gang was like your family," said rap pioneer Afrika Bambaataa, who had been a member of the Black Spades in New York City. "Sometimes a gang is more your family than a real family is, and that's what a lot of people don't understand," added B-Real (b. Louis Freese) of Cypress Hill. "Why do you want to be in a gang? Well, because my homeboy loves me more than my fuckin' mother or father does."

Many gangs warred against one another. Unlike the gangs in previous decades that wielded clubs, knives, and chains, gang members during the 1980s and 1990s carried guns for protection. As rapper Coolio explained about the need for a gun, "They say on the radio and TV that you have a choice, but it's bullshit. If you're getting your ass whipped every day, you've got to have some protection."

Gang members, sporting some of the most modern handheld weaponry available, contributed to a dramatic growth in street violence and death. From 1986 to 1989, the number of African-American teen homicide victims increased from under 1,000 to more than 1,600. By 1992, homicide had become the leading cause of death among African-American teenagers. "The other day I was looking at an old picture from back when I used to play Pop Warner football," said rapper and Crips member Snoop Doggy Dogg (b. Cordozar Calvin Broadus, Jr.), who would later be charged with murder, "and like of twenty-eight homies on the team, twelve are dead, seven are in the penitentiary, and three of them are smoked out."

A burgeoning, competitive cocaine industry among poor, out-of-work African Americans, especially the sale of an inexpensive type of cocaine called "crack," intensified the violence. Without many options, some inner-city African-American youths sold crack. "When a nigga sells drugs around here," observed the rapper OMB of the group OFTM [Operation from the Bottom], "he ain't selling for no big thing, 'cause his family is starving, he's starving, so he's gotta make some kind of move to get what he gotta get, and I mean dope [crack] is the most popular and quickest way he can get money. If you don't have no way out, you would do the same muthafuckin' thing."

As crack sales became more competitive and lucrative, gangs became involved and violence escalated. "In 1984," remembered Manuel Velasquez, a gang counselor in Los Angeles, "coke became cheap and it wasn't just a white, rich thing anymore. Everybody on each block wanted to sell the shit. When you have too many of one product on one block, the guy with the biggest gun is gonna end up selling it. Because of that, gang-related homicides shot up."

The violent, economically bleak conditions that faced inner-city African-American youths created a sense of despair. "We not living no American Dream," remarked rapper Kam. "We in a nightmare. Like I said, this is hell for us. Anything else would be an improvement, you know what I'm saying, we can't get no lower, we can't get no farther back."

The Old School

Rap music arose from and helped shape the African-American desperation in the inner cities, many times decrying poverty, drugs, and gang-inspired violence. The music originated in the ghettos of New York City. As disco started to become popular in New York during the early 1970s, some disc jockeys in the Bronx and Harlem began to play at parties. Rather than use an entire song, some record spinners such as Kool Herc (b. Clive Campbell) began to play, or sample, short fragments, usually the percussion breaks, which the dancers requested. Starting in 1973, he "took the music of Mandrill, like 'Fencewalk,' certain disco records that had funky percussion breaks and he just kept that beat going," recalled Afrika Bambaataa, who began spinning records three years after Herc. "It might be that certain part of the record that everyone waits for."

The rap pioneers sampled all types of music. As Afrika Bambaataa explained, "The music itself is colorless 'cause you can't say, I don't like R&B, I don't like heavy metal, when half the shit that's out comes from all the different styles of records that's out there."

Though having eclectic tastes, rappers favored polyrhythmic funk over the more simplistic disco. "We was against the disco that was happenin', we had the funk back 'cause they wasn't playing James, Sly, or Parliament no more," remarked Bambaataa. "How the funk came back on the scene was through hip-hop, through the street," agreed Jazzy Jay, a member of one of Bambaataa's groups. "All of them—James Brown, George Clinton, Parliament, all that—that was almost dead. Disco was in, everybody was hustling, and the disco deejays were taking over. Well, what happened, the kids just rebelled. They wanted something that they couldn't hear on the radio and everything. They wanted something else."

Kool Herc started to add special effects to the samples of the funky music. Following the lead of his fellow Jamaican, reggae producer King Tubby (b. Osbourne Ruddock), he removed most vocals from the track to create a "dub" version of the song and then added echo and reverb to the altered rhythm track. Using a special

Afrika Bambaataa around 1980. Photo by Michael Ochs. *Permission by Getty Images, Inc.—Michael Ochs Archives.*

stylus, other spinners such as the teenaged Theodore Livingston rotated, or scratched, the records back and forth to produce a unique rhythmic pattern. Kool Herc sometimes mixed the beat with two turntables, quickly fading one song into another. Through these methods, he wove together intricate polyrhythms into a staccato sound that mimicked the short, abrupt changes that had become commonplace on commercial television.

Building on the African oral history tradition and copying Jamaican U-Roy, who had spoken, or toasted, to the dubs of King Tubby, Kool Herc began to talk along with the halting, polyrhythmic sounds. Afrika Bambaataa remembered that "Herc took phrases, like what was happening in the streets, what was the new saying going round the high school like 'rock on my mellow,' 'to the beat y'all,' 'you don't stop,' and just elaborated on that."

Soon, other disc jockeys such as rap pioneer Bambaataa and DJ Hollywood, who played disco records at the Apollo Theater during breaks, started to rap to their sampled music. "To attract their own followings, some of these DJs would give little raps to let the crowd know who was spinning the records," explained rapper Kurtis Blow (b. Curtis Walker). "As time went by, these raps became more elaborate, with the DJ sometimes including a call-and-response 'conversation' with the regulars in the house." Bambaataa summarized, "We just took the Jamaican style and put it to American records."

To allow themselves greater dexterity and creativity with the funk-based music, some disc jockeys enlisted the help of friends to rap, or emcee, for them. Kool Herc asked his high school friend Coke La Rock to accompany him, "saying little poems on the mike, or saying something in a joke-ified manner." Related Lil Rodney Cee of the rap duo Double Trouble, "The first MC that I know of is Cowboy [Keith Wiggins], from Grandmaster Flash and the Furious Five. He was the first MC to talk for Grandmaster Flash [b. Joseph Saddler] and say how great Flash was—you know, 'the pulsating, inflating disco shaking, heartbreaking, the man on the turntable.'" Grandmaster Flash then enlisted the help of Mel Melle (b. Melvin Glover). "I was just trying to take off from where Coke La Rock had left it," he remembered.

During the 1970s, the number of disc jockeys and their friends who rapped to the funky samples of effect-laden music began to multiply. "After myself, Herc, and Flash, crazy amounts of DJs started springing up everywhere," recalled Bambaataa. "They always wanted to challenge or battle somebody. It was no joke. . . . If you lost you could kiss your career goodbye."

Most of these DJs started to display their skills on the streets of New York by wiring their sound systems to the base of a street lamp they had broken. Despite the danger of electrocution, they took the chance. "Playing music was more important than our lives," remembered Charlie Chase, the DJ for the Cold Crush Brothers.

A few of these dedicated disc jockeys, ready for sonic battle, began to perform at prominent disco clubs. By September 2, 1976, Grandmaster Flash, nicknamed for his speed on the turntable, had progressed from parties on Fox Street, parks such as Mount Morris, and small clubs such as the Back Door to the Audubon Club, which held a maximum of three thousand patrons. "The pinnacle of a DJ group's career, before it was recording, was who can make it to the Audubon," indicated the Grandmaster. "Once you played there you were famous throughout the five boroughs" of New York City. By the late 1970s, popular jockeys such as Afrika Bambaataa had found jobs at well-known downtown discos. After playing the Mudd Club, Bambaataa performed at Negril. "Then it got too big for Negril. One time the fire marshals closed the whole place down so we moved to the Danceteria," he related. "Then it got too big for Danceteria. Finally, we made home at the Roxy. It started slow, building at the Roxy, and [soon] Friday nights always [attracted] three thousand, four thousand."

A youth culture partly based on disco began to develop around rappers such as Grandmaster Flash and Afrika Bambaataa. "Not only did our fans want to talk like we did," remembered Kurtis Blow, a onetime collaborator with Grandmaster Flash, "but they dressed like we did, and seemed to be trying to live out the fantasies we were kicking in our raps." Calling themselves b-boys and fly girls, the rap fanatics in the inner cities of New York, Philadelphia, and Baltimore wore discolike heavy gold chains and oversized gold rings. They extended disco by perfecting break dancing, a complex form of dance that hit the public with the films *Flashdance* (1983) and *Breakin'* (1984) and was perfected by dancers such as Crazy Legs and the Rock Steady Crew.

In reaction to the extravagance of disco, the poor, urban rappers grafted a street element to their counterculture, which they called hip-hop after a common phrase chanted at many Bronx dance parties. They adopted a low-brow fashion that included baseball caps with upturned bills, Adidas or 69er Pro Keds tennis shoes, and T-shirts. Mimicking the rappers, the b-boys and fly girls used a street language that reflected their everyday concerns and included words and phrases such as "chill" (calm down), "sweat" (hassle), "dope" (great), "posse" (gang), "def" (good), and "wack" (bad). Using subway trains and building facades as their canvases, individual artists and groups such as Lee Quinones, who appeared in the film *Wild Style* (1982), the Vanguards, Magic, Inc., the Nod Squad, the young Jean-Michel Basquiat, and Keith Haring employed cans of spray paint to perfect a low-budget form of hip-hop visual art called graffiti.

The hip-hop culture engendered a sense of community and self-worth among the poor African Americans in New York. "I'm wearing my suede Pumas. I got the whole thing with my Gazelle spectacle frames and Kangol hat with my gold watch going on. In short, I'm fresh," explained hip-hop performer KRS-ONE. "In this community, I can *win*. Now, if I step out of this community dressed like this, not only will I be thrown up against the wall and asked what drugs I got, but I also can't get a job and I'm ridiculed in school. So this community, the block parties, was an escape."

As with the 1980s' heavy-metal underground, the hip-hop community spread as a growing number of fans bought and traded tapes of their favorite performers. "Cassette tapes used to be our albums before anybody recorded what they called rap records," Bambaataa pointed out. "People started hearing all this rapping coming out of boxes. When they heard the tapes down in the Village they wanted to know, 'Who's this black DJ who's playing all this rock and new wave up in the Bronx?'" Added Jazzy Jay, "I mean, we had tapes that went platinum before we were even involved with the music industry."

Independent companies eventually heard the tapes and recorded the new music. In 1979, Sylvia Robinson, a former R&B vocalist who in the 1950s had been half of the Mickey and Sylvia duo, heard several rap tapes that her children played at home. "Hey, if my kids like this, all the kids around the world will like this!" she reasoned. With her husband Joe she started Sugarhill Records and recorded the Sugarhill Gang's "Rapper's Delight," which reached the Top Five on the R&B chart and cracked the national Top Forty.

Grandmaster Flash and the Furious Five, the next Sugarhill signing, infused rap with a social awareness. The group was comprised of disc jockey Flash, Cowboy, Melle Mel and his brother Kid Creole (Nathaniel Glover), Scorpio (Eddie Morris), and Rahiem (Guy Williams). In 1981, following in the path of African-American performers such as the Last Poets ("Niggers Are Scared of Revolution," "When the Revolution Comes," and "White Man's Got a God Complex") and Gil Scott-Heron ("The Revolution Will Not Be Televised"), they released the socially charged "Freedom." The next year, the group recorded "The Message," a bleak tale of life on the streets, which hit the charts in Britain and the United States. In November 1983, before fracturing into different bands, they produced the anticocaine "White Lines (Don't Do It)." Rap, asserted Kurtis Blow at the time, provides "a way for the people of the ghetto to make themselves heard."

The Second Wave

Leading a second wave of rap that replaced the initial Old School sound, Run–D.M.C. brought inner-city rap to the masses of American teens by combining it with hard guitar rock. In 1982, the group banded together after graduating from St. Pascal's Catholic School in New York City. The next year, disc jockey Jam-Master Jay (Jason Mizell) and rappers D.M.C. (Darryl McDaniels) and Joseph "Run" Simmons (who had worked as a disc jockey behind Kurtis Blow) released their first LP, which after a year on the chart became the first gold rap album.

The group followed its initial success with *King of Rock*, which reached number fifty-two on the chart through the use of the heavy-metal guitar of Eddie Martinez. "Run–D.M.C. used to rap over rock records a lot," mentioned Jam-Master Jay Mizel. "I used to mix rock tunes, and have the guitar come in a little bit, and then play the drum over and over again. *Toys in the Attic*, Aerosmith, that was the best." The band secured airplay on MTV for its videos of "King of Rock" and "You Talk Too Much,"

Run-D.M.C. From left to right. D.M.C. (Darryl McDaniels), Jam-Master Jay (Jason Mizell), Joseph "Run" Simmons. Photo by Frank Micelotta. *Permission by Getty Images—Entertainment. Frank Micelotta/Getty Images, Inc.*

two of the first rap videos aired on the network. Through its heavy-metal rap, Run-D.M.C. began to appeal to white teens. "Does the band have white crossover fans?" rhetorically asked Bill Adler, who helped manage the group. "I'll tell you, a typical letter we get is from someplace like North Dakota. They say, 'I'll bet I'm the only white person ever to write to you, but I love Run-D.M.C.' All the white people think they're alone, but they're not."

Run-D.M.C. increased its white audience by collaborating with Aerosmith, a mid-1970s, Rolling Stones–influenced, hard-rock outfit that neared the top of the chart with *Rocks* (1976) and rebounded with two number-one albums in the 1990s. In 1986, Run-D.M.C. combined the polyrhythms of rap with hard rock to nearly top the singles chart with a remake of Aerosmith's "Walk This Way," which featured Aerosmith's Joe Perry on guitar and Steven Tyler helping with vocals. Run-D.M.C. sold more than three million copies of the Top Five *Raising Hell*, the album that included the hit single and, according to Darryl McDaniels, "put rap into a lot of people's living rooms." Explained rap promoter Silk, "It was what took rap to the next level. 'Walk This Way' was the door opener." By the end of the year, observed Fred Durst, who a decade later headed the rock/rap outfit Limp Bizkit, "All the white kids jumped on the rap thing hard, dude. Suddenly everybody's walking around trying to rap like D.M.C."

If Run-D.M.C. introduced rap to white teens, the Beastie Boys opened the floodgates. Originally members of fledgling New York City punk bands, the white, middle-class threesome—Adam "MCA" Yauch, Michael "D" Diamond, and Adam "King Ad-Rock" Horovitz—became friendly with Rick Rubin, who had partnered with Run-D.M.C. manager Russell Simmons to establish Def Jam Records. In October 1984, the Beastie Boys signed with Def Jam and the next year toured with Run-D.M.C. Only a few months after Run-D.M.C. scored with "Walk This Way," the trio released *Licensed to Ill*, which featured raps over Led Zeppelin and AC/DC heavy-metal riffs. One of the fastest-selling albums in history, *Licensed* sold seven million copies, largely on the strength of the Top-Ten heavy-metal/rap anthem "(You Gotta) Fight for Your Right (To Party!)" and brought rap into the white rock mainstream. It became the first rap album to top the U.S. chart and reached the Top Ten in Britain. "By making our rap records sound more like pop songs, we changed the form," boasted Rick Rubin. "And we sold a lot of records."

Gangsta

As the Beastie Boys partied, another wave of African-American rappers highlighted the sobering conditions that confronted young, urban African Americans by graphically describing the violent life in the inner cities with "gangsta rap." Schoolly-D (b. Jesse Weaver, Jr.), a former member of the Parkside Killers in North Philadelphia, started the trend with the shocking description of gang warfare in "P.S.K. What Does It Mean?" (1986). "The first record that came out along those lines was Schoolly D's 'P.S.K.,'" explained Ice-T (b. Tracy Marrow) who scored in 1991 with the Top Ten gangsta classic *O.G. Original Gangster*. "All he did was represent a gang on his record."

Formed in 1986 by Eric "Eazy-E" Wright, N.W.A. [Niggaz with Attitude] perfected gangsta rap. They sold one million copies of their second album, *Straight Outta Compton* (1988), which included the genre-defining "Gangsta Gangsta." In 1991, they stood atop the chart with the harsh number-one *Niggaz4Life*. Ice Cube (b. O'Shea Jackson), the rhymer who split from N.W.A. in 1990, rapped about the consequences of gang violence in his debut *AmeriKKKa's Most Wanted* (1990) and "Dead Homiez" and "The Product" on *Kill at Will* (1990). He followed the next year with *Death Certificate*, which included "How to Survive in South Central" and "Steady Mobbin'."

The angry gangsta rappers, though sometimes glorifying a streetwise, misogynist, gun culture, considered themselves reporters on the urban African-American beat. "I show white America about the black community, and I hold a mirror up to the black community to show them about themselves," contended Ice Cube. "I just look at it as, if there wasn't rap, where would the voice of the eighteen-year-old black male be?" asked Ice-T. "He would never be on TV, he ain't writin' no book. He is not in the movies. They call it gangsta rap, I call it reality-based rap." Tupac Shakur, who scaled the charts with five gold gangsta rap albums, similarly wondered why the "raps that I'm rapping to my community shouldn't be filled with rage? They shouldn't be filled with the same atrocities that they [white America] gave to me? The media, they don't talk about it, so in my raps I have to talk about it, and it just seems foreign because there's no one else talking about it."

Many of the gangsta rappers focused their sights on the American legal system, considering the disproportionate number of African Americans in jail. In 1999, African Americans comprised 49 percent of the inmate population in U.S. jails but accounted for only 13 percent of the population. On any given day, one in fourteen (7 percent) African-American males were in prison compared to just 1 percent of Caucasian men. Put in another way, an African-American male born in 1991 had a 29 percent likelihood of spending some time in prison compared to only a 4 percent chance of their Caucasian counterparts. "You got to remember that half the people in the ghetto got somebody who's in jail," observed Ice-T.

Some African Americans landed in prison due to the racist practices of police, referred to as racial profiling. For example, during 1995 in Volusia County, Florida, African Americans accounted for nearly 70 percent of the drivers who police stopped on the roads even though they made up 12 percent of the county population. The "Driving While Black" detentions and arrests engendered a fear of uncontrolled police action among some African Americans. "When I'm alone and driving, coming from the studio, if I see a cop pull up behind me, I really am afraid that they might just decide they don't like me and pull out that backup gun they carry and shoot me," Ice-T confessed. "The only way you can run around with a gun is to be a cop."

Gangsta rap understandably and bluntly lashed out against racial profiling and police brutality. N.W.A. released "Fuck Tha Police," a reaction to Los Angeles Police Chief Darryl Gates's Operation HAMMER that led to the booking of more than 1,500 African-American youths for "looking suspicious." They followed with "Sa Prize, Pt. 2" (1990), which continued their antipolice message. The Geto Boys penned

"City Under Siege" (1990) about police harassment, and Cypress Hill included "Pigs" on their 1991 self-titled debut. Ice-T mined the same theme with the controversial "Cop Killer," which he wrote in 1990 and released in early 1992 with the heavy-metal band Body Count backing him. "I'm singing in the first person as a character who is fed up with police brutality. I ain't never killed no cop. I felt like it a lot of times," contended the rapper. The song sparked protests and a boycott of Warner Records, Ice-T's label, from police organizations throughout the country until the rapper voluntarily removed the song from the *Body Count* album.

During late April and early May 1992, the truth behind the gangsta rappers' songs became starkly evident, when rioting erupted in Los Angeles after the acquittal of the police officers who had brutally beaten African-American taxi driver Rodney King. For four days, angry African Americans took to the streets in response to the actions of a nearly all-white jury who had seemingly disregarded videotaped evidence of police brutality. They burned and looted buildings until dispersed by 2,000 National Guardsmen and 4,500 federal troops dispatched by President George Bush. When the smoke cleared, the riots had caused nearly $1 billion in damage and had resulted in 53 deaths, 2,383 injuries, more than 7,000 fire responses, and 3,100 businesses damaged. One of the worst riots in U.S. history, the disturbance in Los Angeles sparked rioters in other cities such as Las Vegas and Atlanta. "When rap came out of L.A., what you heard initially was my voice yelling about South Central," remarked Ice-T. "People thought, 'That shit's crazy,' and ignored it. Then N.W.A. came out and yelled, Ice Cube yelled about it. People said, 'Oh, that's just kids making a buck.' They didn't realize how many niggas with attitude are out there on the street. Now you see them."

Young, Gifted, and Black

Besides reporting the stark realities of the African-American community, rappers such as the militant Public Enemy delivered an updated version of the late 1960s' soul message of African-American pride. "Black men and women are treated like bullshit," declared Chuck D (b. Carlton Ridenhour), who started Public Enemy while a student at Adelphi University on Long Island. During a concert at Riker's Island prison, he said, "You've got to know the rules of the game so we won't be falling into traps and keep coming back to places like these! Our goal in life is to get ourselves out of this mess and be responsible to our sons and daughters so they can lead a better life. . . . My job is to build 5,000 potential black leaders through my means of communication in America. A black leader is just someone who takes responsibility."

By the end of the 1980s, Public Enemy had sold more than one million copies of *It Takes a Nation of Millions to Hold Us Back*, a pointed discourse about drugs, inner-city poverty, and African-American self-determination. They also contributed the song "Fight the Power" to director Spike Lee's controversial, popular film *Do the Right Thing*, which pictured life in the inner city. In 1990, the group hit the Top Ten on both sides of the Atlantic with *Fear of a Black Planet*, released by Def Jam Records, which was the largest African American–owned label since Motown, started by Russell

Simmons, brother of Run-D.M.C.'s Joseph Simmons, and white producer Rick Rubin. "We represented a combination of self-empowerment, nationalism, and militancy from the combined influences of the Black Panther Party and the Nation of Islam," explained Chuck D.

Arrested Development scaled the chart with its call for African-American self-respect. "We wanted to recognize all the bad things going on—the killings, the shootings, AIDS, and everything that's crushing the communities," insisted Speech (b. Todd Thomas), who had been a gangsta rapper before forming the group. "But we wanted to make people understand that you've got to still be alive in order to change it." In 1992, they released their debut album, *3 Years, 5 Months and 2 Days in the Life of . . .*, which included hopeful songs such as "Raining Revolution," hit the Top Ten, and sold two million copies. Based on their effort, the group snagged Artist of the Year honors from both *Rolling Stone* and *Musician* magazines.

Public Enemy. Clockwise from bottom left: Flavor Flav, Professor Griff, Terminator X, Brother Roger, and Chuck D, c. late 1980s. Photo by Michael Ochs. *Permission by Getty Images, Inc.—Michael Ochs Archives.*

During the late 1980s and early 1990s, others used rap to convey a sense of African-American self-worth. The Jungle Brothers fused rap, jazz, and drum 'n' bass "to bring about peace and unity." "We always felt that spreading a message was the way to go," related the group's Mike G. (b. Michael Small). In 1990, the group embarked on the "Politics of Nature" tour, which included speaking engagements about African-American consciousness. In 1989, Big Daddy Kane rapped about African-American pride in "Young, Gifted and Black" and "Ain't No Stoppin' Us Now."

As African pendants replaced gold chains, female rapper Queen Latifah (b. Dana Owens) emphasized an Afrocentric "show of pride for ancestors from whom we descended" to create a sense of unity among African Americans. In September 1990, LL Cool J (b. James Todd Smith III) released *Mama Said Knock You Out*. "It's about truancy, drug abuse, teenage pregnancy," he explained. "It's about knocking out all the ills of society." Eric B. (b. Eric Barrier) and Rakim (b. William Griffin) rapped about African-American pride in "In the Ghetto" (1990), and the rap duo Erick "E" Sermon and Parrish "P" Smith, known as EPMD, addressed the same topic in "So What Cha Sayin'." Even rap pioneer Kool Moe Dee, who had been a member of the Treacherous Three, which in the early 1980s recorded for Sugarhill, switched from boasting to rap about African-American unity in the Top Twenty-Five *Knowledge Is King* (1989).

Having pride in their race, some rappers warned against the damaging effects of drugs on the African-American community. De La Soul, for example, delivered the sobering "My Brother's a Basehead." "We guide a lot of kids," mentioned Queen Latifah. "When kids constantly hear rappers saying, 'don't do drugs, don't do drugs,' there's a chance it will sink in."

KRS-One, an acronym for Knowledge Reigns Supreme Over Nearly Everyone, organized rappers into action. After abandoning gangsta rap, in 1988 KRS (b. Lawrence Krisna Parker) helped organize Stop the Violence movement. By the next year, he had convinced a number of leading rappers such as Chuck D and Flavor Flav of Public Enemy, Just-Ice, Heavy D, Kool Moe Dee, and MC Lyte to denounce gang warfare on the inner-city streets in the single "Self-Destruction," which sold a half-million copies. He donated the $500,000 in royalties to the National Urban League, which used the money to combat illiteracy. "We wanted to reach the kids most affected by black-on-black crime" that many times resulted from "unemployment which can be the result of illiteracy," noted Ann Carli, Jive Records vice president of artist development, who helped KRS-One organize Stop the Violence. "Rap records," added Carli, "can be a tool that can be used in education today; young adults will listen to rap and what rap artists have to say."

KRS-One continued his educational efforts. In 1991, with the help of Queen Latifah and Run-D.M.C., he started H.E.A.L. Yourself and released a video. The rapper gave profits from the video to Human Education Against Lies, which printed and distributed books to high schools. The next year, he joined with Rutgers-educated rapper and activist Sister Souljah (b. Lisa Williamson) to advocate a ten-point program to empower African Americans. The program "addresses all areas of African-American life, economics, education, culture, spirituality, defense, and everything," explained

Sister Souljah. "It's not a militant message but one of truth and common sense. We have to be educated on our own ethnicity."

Many rappers followed the socially active path of KRS-One and Sister Souljah. In 1990, Michael Conception, a former gang member and Grand Jury Records president, organized rap performers such as Eazy-E., MC Hammer, Ice-T, and N.W.A. for the antiviolence rap single and video project "We're All in the Same Gang." "I hope it generates a lot of money and we can get it to the people who really need it," Conception told *Billboard*. "If anyone can convince the black gangs, it's somebody who was in one." Female rapper Yo-Yo (b. Yolanda Whittaker) started the Intelligent Black Woman's Coalition. LL Cool J visited schools to advise students about drug abuse, and the New York hip-hop collective X-Clan organized voter registration drives and anticrack seminars. MC Hammer (b. Stanley Burrell), who in 1990 sold six million copies of the chart-topping *Please Hammer Don't Hurt 'Em*, which blended rap with melodic hooks, worked with inner-city school children in his hometown of Oakland. "I make an active role model to kids," he explained. "They need people to show them there's another way." By the 1990s, rappers had directly faced the problems that confronted African-American youths and had made efforts to change them.

The militant message of rap, though sometimes including a Black Muslim–inspired separatism, reached discontented white teens. "Rap music in the '90s is developing a more socially aware conscience. For example: Public Enemy, [the KRS-One-led] Boogie Down Productions, X-Clan and Harmony," observed Troi Torain, R&B alternative promotion director for Virgin Records, in late 1990. "These artists are committed to broadening the state of awareness, which is being acknowledged by more and more young people." Ernie Singleton, president at MCA Records, agreed, "Now more than ever the rap market had reached a level of acceptance [among white teens]."

The white teens became aware of rap through television, the medium that had helped expose previous generations to rock-and-roll. In 1987, MTV began to air more rap videos and on August 6, 1988, premiered a special two-hour program on rap, "Yo! MTV Raps," hosted by Fab 5 Freddy (b. Fred Brathwaite). "That wall between rock and hip-hop is falling down, especially with our younger audience," explained Andy Schuon, senior vice president of MTV. "We've created an environment where Aerosmith can be programmed right next to Snoop [Doggy Dog], and people will accept that." Filling a void created by radio, which seldom played rap, other networks programmed rap shows such as Fox's "Pump It Up" and the Black Entertainment Television network's "Rap City." Advertisers began to use hip-hop rhythms and rap rhymes in commercials. By 1991, noticed Rick Rubin, cofounder of Def Jam Records, "rap has moved into the suburbs. Ice Cube, N.W.A., Public Enemy—I'd say 90 percent of their audience is white."

As rap moved into the suburbs, it served once again to integrate America. "The Black kids, they listening to the beat. The white kids are listening to the words," noticed Ice-T. "The kids are not only listening to it, but they're becoming allies and they're going back to Harvard. They're going back to their colleges and they're saying, 'Yo! This is injustice.' And they're stepping to their parents, saying . . . 'What makes John Wayne such a great man?' you know. 'He killed Indians.' And, 'Why did the Hispanics start a solo? Went to the Alamo, Mexico, to be a rich country.' And, 'What makes Orientals the enemy? What did they do?' And 'Why should I dislike somebody from Iran?—ain't done nothing to me!' They're questioning all these authoritarian hate figures, because of rap, because rap is saying, 'Yo! Check this!'"

The Return of *Shaft*

As hip-hop evolved during the nineties, an overblown version of gangsta overtook rap's socially responsible messages to scale the charts and pave the way for the rebirth of 1970s' blaxploitation.

Starting in the early 1970s, filmmakers featured African-American actors in violent action movies such as *Shaft* (1971), *Superfly, The Mack, Dolemite*, and *Trouble Man* (all 1972) that critics termed "blaxploitation." On one hand, the films offered African Americans one of their first chances to star in leading roles and play heroes. "From 1970 to 1976, the Black actor being the winner, being the hero was really happening," asserted film star Fred Williamson, who starred in such films as *Black Caesar* (1973). "In my films, I was trying to say, 'Hey, we're tired of seeing the train porters, the waitresses, the maids, we're tired of seeing that.'" Issac Hayes, who had co-written many soul hits such as "Soul Man" and "Hold On, I'm Coming" and in 1971 composed the soundtrack to *Shaft*, thought that "it was fun to see, at least, the brother on the screen being a hero, being a sex symbol, having the upper hand, and winning for a change." The movies, contended Jack Hill, the director of *Coffy*, "brought Black subject matter and Black characters into the mainstream of film."

Though they provided African Americans with a chance to star in the movies, the blaxploitation films portrayed African-American life as violent, drug-obsessed, and ghettolike without a hint of a stable family. The heroes toted guns, cavorted with pimps and drug dealers, and shot their opponents at will. Objecting to the recurring themes of violence, African-American leaders such as Jesse Jackson, Roy Innis of CORE (Congress for Racial Equality), Roger Wilkins of the NAACP (National Association for the Advancement of Colored People), and Ralph Abernathy of the SCLC (Southern Christian Leadership Council) lashed out against the films and called for more positive role models for African Americans. After 200 movies in the genre, in 1977 the blaxploitation craze started to ebb.

During the late 1990s, gangsta rappers reintroduced the themes and sentiments of 1970s' blaxploitation as crime and the prison life become more commonplace among African Americans. In 1980, the Bureau of Justice Statistics reported that 330,000 Americans were in prison. By 1994 with an intensified war on drugs, the number had skyrocketed to more than a million, and by 2006 more than three million Americans wasted away behind bars.

African Americans and Hispanics comprised a disproportionate number of this burgeoning prison population. Though only accounting for approximately 25 percent of the general population at the turn of the century, they comprised more than 60 percent of the prison population. In a staggering statistic, the Bureau of Justice reported that in 2002 more than 12 percent of all African-American males between the ages of twenty-five and twenty-nine were in prison. Four years later, the Bureau indicated that nearly 1.2 million inmates, or 38.7 percent of the prison population, were African Americans. For a young African-American man, the prison life or fear of imprisonment became an everyday reality, which gangsta rap graphically captured.

Similar to the 1930s, when gangsters such as Al Capone, John Dillinger, and "Baby Face" Nelson became national heroes to youngsters, rappers created and embodied a new gangster chic. They boasted about their gats and ho's and with puffed chests challenged the world to a fight. Rather than simply report about the atrocities of the ghetto, they embraced a materialistic, misogynist, violent culture and bragged about their subservient women, guns, sexual prowess, and wealth. As break dancing, graffiti, and the DJ faded from hip-hop culture, the rapper became the central cultural figure, who posed as a gangster preoccupied with a macho ethos and a quick dollar.

The gangsta culture turned its violence inward with the chilling murders of two prominent gangsta rappers. During the evening of September 7, 1996, on the Las Vegas strip, gunmen opened fire on a car, driven by Death Row Records President Suge Knight, which had several passengers, including rapper/actor Tupac Shakur. Though Knight survived a head injury, six days later four gunshot wounds in the chest proved fatal to the twenty-five-year-old Shakur, who had scored with three straight number-one albums: *Me Against the World* (1995), *All Eyez on Me* (1996), and *Don Killuminati: The 7 Day Theory*, released eight weeks after the rapper's death. A few months later, on March 9, 1997, the Notorious B.I.G. (b. Chris Wallace), reputedly the East Coast rival of Shakur, who had ironically hit the chart in 1994 with the million-seller *Ready to Die*, was murdered in a drive-by shooting.

Gangsta rap continued to sell to mainstream America after these brutal shootings, including the Notorious B.I.G.'s chart-topping, posthumously released *Life After Death* (1997) and Snoop Dogg's number-one *Da Game Is to Be Sold, Not to Be Told* (1998) and a number-two effort *No Limit Top Dogg* (1999). Master P (b. Percy Miller) hit with two number-one efforts, *Ghetto D* (1997) and *MP Da Last Don* (1998). DMX (b. Earl Simmons) delivered five consecutive number-one efforts, starting with *It's Dark and Hell Is Hot* (1998). The Game (b. Jayceon Taylor), a Dr. Dre protégé and a member of the Blood gang, topped the chart with *The Documentary* (2005).

Eminem (b. Marshall Mathers III), the white protégé of Dr. Dre, also grabbed the top spot on the chart with his white gangsta raps. He snagged the number-two slot with *The Slim Shady LP* (1999) and followed with three number-one efforts: *The Marshall Mathers LP* (2000), *The Eminem Show* (2002), and *Encore* (2004). All told, the rapper sold twenty million albums and become one of the best-selling and most well-known rappers. His movie *8 Mile* grossed more than $116 million and won an Academy Award for Best Original Song ("Lose Yourself"), and his record label, Shady Records, hit pay dirt with the number-one gangsta hip-hop of 50 Cent (b. Curtis Jackson III) who created the multimillion-selling *Get Rich or Die Tryin'* (2003) and *The Massacre* (2005). By the new century, the braggadocio of gangsta rap translated into commercial success and kept the record labels afloat, much like the blaxploitation films

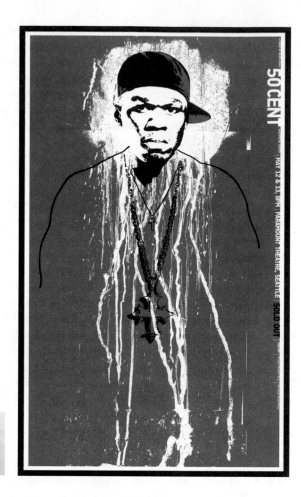

50 Cent. *Permission by Modern Dog Design Co. 2003/Michael Strassburger.*

of the early 1970s had saved Hollywood by providing astounding returns on modest investments.

These chart successes preached a message of violence, misogyny, and hedonism. Popular songs such as Jay-Z's (b. Shawn Carter) infectious "Big Pimpin'" (2000), Juvenile's (b. Terius Gray) Top Twenty "Back That Azz Up" (1998), and white rapper Eminem's "Kim" (2000) portrayed women as g-stringed, big-breasted playthings from the pages of *Playboy* who could be commanded at will, slapped around, and even killed. In the gangsta world, the rappers themselves became gun-toting, drug-dealing sex machines who roamed the streets for their next conquest and their next big deal. Through their street smarts, they hoped to grab the women and the cash, or the "bling-bling," as rapper B.G. (b. Christopher Dorsey) insisted in a song of the same name. "What else can you rap about but money, sex, murder or pimping?" reasoned Queens, New York, rapper Ja Rule (b. Jeffrey Atkins) who hit the top chart spot with *Rule 3:36* (2000) and *Pain Is Love* (2001).

The gangsta image, similar to blaxploitation, unwittingly resulted in a minstrel-like portrayal of African Americans to white teens in the suburbs. "The endorsement of thugs is white people's fantasy of what they want us to be," complained Public Enemy's Chuck D. "That's what white people want to believe about us," agreed rapper Mos Def, "that it's about money, cash, ho's for all of us." Almost as a capstone of the gangsta era, which dominated the charts during the late 1990s and the first years of the new millennium, New Jack Swing pioneers La Face remade the film *Shaft* (2000), which promulgated the unfortunate but lasting caricature of African Americans as unsavory characters from the underworld.

Even though gangsta rap promulgated a stilted, racist image of African Americans, it ironically helped to integrate young America. "If there's one music that could break down racist barriers, it's hip-hop," explained Eminem. "When I do shows, I look out into the crowd and see black, white, Chinese, Korean people—I see all nationalities there for one thing. You don't see that shit at a country show, you don't see it at a rock show. It's hip-hop that's doing it."

Similar to the blaxploitation film stars, gangsta rappers hoped to use their crossover success to achieve independence in a white-dominated entertainment business. Sean "Puffy" Combs, the rapper and owner of Bad Boy Entertainment, which recorded and marketed the Notorious B.I.G., urged the participants at a *Vibe* music seminar to "focus on handling a business, creating a business plan" in order to "build up the economic power of your race and your community." His own success—as well as the examples of such African American–owned labels as Master P's No Limit, Roc-A-Fella Records co-owned by Jay-Z, Russell Simmons's Def Jam, and LaFace owned by Antonio "L.A." Reid and Babyface—provided role models to young black youths who wanted to break into the American mainstream on their own terms. "We try to continue the tradition of Black entrepreneurship," instructed Puffy. "It gives you a sense of independence."

Many swaggering gangsta rappers followed Puffy's advice and became successful entrepreneurs through ancillary business ventures. Master P, who had studied business at Oakland's Merritt Junior College, became a $50-million-dollar industry with a successful record label, a clothing line, a property company, sports agent services, and a film company that released *I Got the Hook Up* (1998) with Master P as one of the stars. *Fortune* magazine featured Master P on a 1999 cover to celebrate his business success. In 2002, Eminem inked a deal with Macy's to feature his Shady Ltd. Clothing line. His protégé 50 Cent launched a new footwear line with Reebok as part of his G-Unit Clothing Company, marketed his own line of watches and condoms, released an autobiography, endorsed a video game, *50 Cent: Bulletproof*, starred in a feature-length film, and endorsed the grape-flavored Formula 50 Vitamin Water drink. "50 is a promo man's wet dream," enthused manager James Cruz. "He's a conglomerate." Jay-Z, the Brooklyn rapper who vacillated between a hip-hop pop and gangsta with the million-selling *Vol. 2 . . . Hard Knock Life* (1998), owned a fashion line (Rocawear) that grossed $200 million in 2002, a production house (Roc-A-Fella Films), a record label, a sports bar, and part of the NBA basketball team, the New Jersey Nets. "This music is just a stepping stone," he told *Vibe*. "We used this music to get our foot in the door."

Hollywood helped the gangstas achieve even greater monetary success and stardom. Capitalizing on the popularity of hip-hop, Hollywood fully embraced rap stars as actors. In 1991, the major studios first found success by casting Ice-T as a policeman in *New Jack City*. His acting career flourished through the new century, with *Johnny Mnemonic* (1995), *The Heist* (1999), *Judgment Day* (1999), *Gangland* (2000), and numerous episodes of the television series *Law and Order: Special Victims Unit*. Another early film pioneer was Ice Cube, who appeared as a gang member in the critically acclaimed *Boyz n the Hood* (1991), followed by *The Glass Shield* (1994), *Friday* (1995), *BarberShop* (2002), *All About the Benjamins* (2002), and *The Longshots* (2008). Tupac Shakur appeared in *Juice* (1992), *Poetic Justice* (1993) with Janet Jackson, and *Above the Rim* (1994).

Within a few years, Hollywood opened the floodgates to rap artists. Snoop Dogg snagged roles in the award-winning *Training Day* (2001), *Baby Boy* (2001), *Soul Plane* (2004), and *Starsky and Hutch* (2004). Miramax Films gave Master P a two-contract deal, and DMX acted in several films, including *Cradle 2 the Grave* (2003) and *Never Die Alone* (2004). Atlanta rapper Ludacris (b. Christopher Bridges) who scored with five straight multiplatinum albums starting with *Back for the First Time* (2000), appeared in *2 Fast 2 Furious* (2003) and *Hustle and Flow* (2005). Fellow Atlantan Andre [Benjamin] 3000 from OutKast, which hit with the multiplatinum albums *Aquemini* (1998) and *Stankonia* (2000), appeared in such films as *Four Brothers* and *Be Cool* (both 2005). By the new century, gangsta rap dominated the charts, filled the silver screen, and accounted for a billion-dollar clothing industry. The *New Yorker* contended that "over the past ten years, 'corporate rock' has been upstaged by 'corporate rap.'"

Hip-Hop Pop

A new generation in the late 1990s began to dance to a more melodic, less violent permutation of hip-hop. Enjoying better times, teens on both sides of the Atlantic began to abandon hardcore gangsta rap and grunge for a sound that fused hip-hop rhythms with sweet 1970s-style R&B into a hip-hop pop.

Hip-hop pop appealed to a growing legion of teens. In 1977, four years after the postwar baby boom had ended, the birthrate in the United States again began to increase. By 1989, the number of yearly births topped four million and continued at a steady pace until the new boom subsided in 1993. In 1998, nearly thirty million teenagers vied for center stage with Generation X, who either went to college or somehow disappeared into mainstream America with jobs and families. The 2000 U.S. census counted nearly sixty million members of Generation Y, the age-group between six and twenty-one years old, which became the second largest generation in history after the seventy-two million baby boomers.

These "boomlet" children, as some called them, lived in an increasingly favorable economic climate. In 1993 during the height of grunge, the unemployment rate in the United States stood at 6.9. By April 1998, it had decreased to a respectable 4.3 percent, a hallmark that had not been achieved since the early days of rock-and-roll. Even in Britain, which had been racked by a stifling unemployment for nearly two decades, the jobless rate declined by nearly half from 10.5 percent in 1993 to 5.9 percent in late 1999.

Teens benefited from the economic boom. Using earnings from part-time jobs and allowances, American youths spent about $109 billion a year. Unlike older Americans, they considered about 90 percent of their money disposable income, which they spent primarily on clothes, health and beauty aids, and entertainment, including CDs and music concerts. One 2000 study found that teenaged girls spent on average nearly $100 a week for clothes, cosmetics, and music. These youth also influenced their parents to buy another $139 billion in goods annually, making this boomlet an economic force that determined marketing strategies and the economic well-being of countless American businesses.

New Jack Swing

Near the end of the 1990s, this new, more economically advantaged generation of teens began to desert the hard-edged music of the previous few years. They turned to hip-hop pop, which had its roots in the New Jack Swing of the late 1980s. Producers such as Teddy Riley and the team of Antonio "L.A." Reid and Kenneth "Babyface" Edmonds masterminded New Jack (and Jill) Swing, which used hip-hop beats and replaced raps with smooth, romantic R&B to update 1970s' soul. Riley produced hits with the romantic stylings of Keith Sweat on the Top Five "I Want Her" (1987), probably the first New Jack Swing single, and the multiplatinum albums *Make It Last Forever* (1987) and *I'll Give All My Love to You* (1990). Riley also scored with his own group Guy, who in 1988 hit double platinum with their self-named debut and reached the Top Twenty with *The Future* (1990), which yielded three Top-Ten R&B hits.

L.A. Reid and Babyface scored the biggest New Jack Swing success with Bobby Brown. A former member of the teenage sensation New Edition, Brown hooked up with the two producers, who grafted hip-hop beats onto Brown's ultra-soothing vocals for the 1988 chart-topping effort *Don't Be Cruel*. The album spawned five Top-Ten singles, including the Teddy Riley collaboration "My Prerogative," and sold seven million copies. Brown's remix album *Dance! . . . Ya Know It!* (1989) and *Bobby* (1992) also neared the top of the chart.

Three other former members of New Edition—Ricky Bell, Michael Bivins, and Ronnie DeVoe—banded together in 1988 as Bell Biv DeVoe to craft hard-edged New Jack Swing. Their debut album, *Poison* (1990), reached the Top Five and sold three million copies. However, the next two Bell Biv DeVoe albums showed the waning influence of New Jack Swing as they barely edged into the Top Twenty, and by 1994, the threesome had drifted apart.

Despite the dominance of grunge and gangsta rap during the early and mid-1990s, the harmonies of Boyz II Men kept hip-hop pop alive throughout the entire decade. Meeting at their high school in Philadelphia in 1988, the quartet combined hip-hop beats with harmonies reminiscent of doo-wop and 1970s' soul. Discovered by Michael Bivins of Bell Biv DeVoe, they signed with the Motown label and in 1991 revitalized the near-dormant label with *Cooleyhighharmony*, which reached the Top

Ten in the United States and Britain. Three years later, they followed with the chart-topping *II*, which sold seven million copies and included the single "I'll Make Love to You," which topped the chart for over two months. In 1997, the foursome sold two million copies of *Evolution*, which led the way for a chart onslaught of a hip–hop/R&B fusion that *Rolling Stone* called a "distinctive, nonthreatening, and video-friendly" form of hip-hop.

The hip-hop harmony group Jodeci offered their mixture of R&B and hip-hop. During the late 1980s, Cedric "K-Ci" Hailey and his brother Jo-Jo had joined with brothers Donald "DeVante Swing" and Dalvin DeGrate to form the group. The foursome, gaining their experience in different North Carolina gospel choirs, hit the Top Twenty with their debut *Forever My Lady* (1991), an example of hip-hop-tinged soul, which sold more than three million copies. After exposure on MTV, they hit the Top Five with their combination of soul and New Jack Swing, *Diary of a Mad Band* (1993). After a number-two effort, *The Show, The After Part, The Hotel*, the Hailey brothers split from the group to reach the Top Ten with *Love Always* (1997), which sold three million copies.

Bone Thugs-N-Harmony offered a harder-edged version of hip-hop harmony. Raised in a tough Cleveland neighborhood, Bizzy Bone, Wish Bone, Krayzie Bone, and Layzie Bone practiced their sound in Gordon Park. Wearing baggy pants, braids, and other rap fashions, they sang about the hard realities of street life with sweet harmonies. "Growing up we loved Michael Jackson and Run-D.M.C.," explained Krayzie Bone. "We couldn't decide if we wanted to rap or sing, so we did both."

In 1993, N.W.A. rapper Eazy-E signed the group to his Ruthless Records. Two years later, they released the innovative chart-topping single "Tha Crossroads" from *E 1999 Eternal* that eulogized Eazy-E who had died of AIDS earlier in the year. By 1997, the group delivered their third album, the multiplatinum, number-one *The Art of War*. The next year, Bizzy Bone climbed to number three in the chart with his solo effort *Heaven'z Movie*. By the late 1990s, *Newsweek* enthusiastically called the hip-hop singers "one of the most successful and innovative groups in rap."

Mary J. Blige rode the New Jack Swing wave with the up-tempo, soul/hip-hop of the Top Ten *What's the 411* (1992). Helped by the production of Sean "Puffy" Combs, she sold three million copies of the album and earned the title of "queen of hip-hop soul." In 1994, she followed with the triple-platinum success of *My Life*, and in 1997 resurfaced to top the chart with *Share My World*, produced by a spate of soul/hip-hop producers including Babyface, Jimmy Jam, and Terry Lewis.

Lauryn Hill and her compatriots in the Fugees epitomized the success of the late 1990s' hip-hop gumbo. Formed in 1992 by Hill, Prakazrel "Pras" Michel, and Wyclef Jean, the threesome combined hip-hop beats, reggae, and 1970s-style funk and soul. Their 1994 debut *Blunted on Reality* turned critical heads but failed to chart on either side of the Atlantic. As hip-hop pop took root, their follow-up, *The Score* (1996), became one of the hits of the year, selling eighteen million copies and reaching number one in the United States and number two in Britain. The Fugees' hip-hop renditions of Roberta Flack's "Killing Me Softly" and Bob Marley's "No Woman, No Cry" exemplified the evolution of hip-hop in the 1990s. "The Fugees created a poetic

Pras, Lauryn Hill, and Wyclef Jean of the Fugees at the 1996 MTV Movie Awards. Photo by Jeff Kravitz. *Permission by Getty Images.*

hybrid that has become hip-hop's universal amalgam," pointed out Elektra Records CEO Sylvia Rhone. "It's the new definition of pop."

The Fugees also scored with solo efforts. In mid-1997, Wyclef Jean hit the Top Twenty with *Wyclef Jean Presents the Carnival Featuring Refugee All Stars*. The next year, Lauryn Hill topped the chart with a mixture of hip-hop and soul in *The Miseducation of Lauryn Hill*. "With my record, I wanted to merge the two—old school soul and hip-hop," explained the singer. By the end of the year, fickle critics began to call Hill, who as a child "wanted to be Whitney [Houston]," the "queen of hip-hop soul," taking the title from Mary J. Blige, who sang a duet with Hill on the multiplatinum *Miseducation*.

In the late 1990s, other artists scaled the charts with hip-hop beats grafted to R&B. Usher Raymond signed to Babyface's LaFace label and sold eight million copies of *My Way* (1997). The Baltimore singing group Dru Hill hit the Top Ten with their second effort *Enter the Dru* (1998). Sean "Puff Daddy" Combs, who had produced hits for Mary J. Blige, Usher, Boyz II Men, and Jodeci, topped the chart with his own *No Way Out*. TLC, the trio that had combined rap and R&B for success with *Crazysexycool* (1994), in 1999 topped the chart with the million-selling *FanMail*. Destiny's Child, fronted by Beyoncé Knowles and managed by her father, cracked the *Billboard* chart with their self-named debut in 1998 and the next year hit the Top Five with *The Writing's on the Wall*. In 1998, even New Jack Swing pioneer Keith Sweat reappeared in the Top Ten with the aptly titled *Still in the Game*.

Spice World

The most heralded and surely the most commercially successful version of hip-hop pop came from across the Atlantic with the Spice Girls. Just as the Monkees had been formed nearly twenty-five years earlier, in 1994 the quintet banded together as a result of a newspaper advertisement for volunteers who were "street smart, extrovert[ed], ambitious and able to sing and dance." The five young women—Geri "Ginger Spice" Halliwell, Melanie "Scary Spice" Brown, Victoria "Posh Spice" Adams, Emma "Baby Spice" Bunton, and Melanie "Sporty Spice" Chisholm— dumped the managers who had assembled them a few months after they had formed and fought to secure a recording contract. Searching for a manager to mount their career ascent, in 1995 the group signed with veteran Svengali Simon Fuller and started to work on their debut.

The Spice Girls perfected a feminist philosophy sprinkled with a rave flavoring for their preteen fans. They projected the persona of scantily clad 1990s' feminists, who spouted a philosophy of "girl power, an equalization of the sexes" to an army of preteen and teenage girls. The group also brought an element of the rave culture to the world with their constant lip service to "positivity" and their smiley demeanor.

The masses of "tweens" and teenage girls transformed the Spice Girls into the most visible musical phenomenon of the 1990s. Featuring a bright, bouncy R&B sound laced with hip-hop beats, their debut *Spice* quickly scaled the charts. Their hit "Wannabe" became the first number-one single in Britain by an all-female band and topped the charts in twenty-one countries, including the United States, when it reached American shores in January 1997. The album sold seven million copies in the United States and fifteen million worldwide and spawned several other hit singles. The Spice Girls followed with *Spiceworld* and a movie of the same name. Though the movie did poorly at box offices around America, videos of the film sold briskly, and the sophomore album sold more than three million copies in the United States. By the end of 1997, the Spice Girls had earned nearly $70 million, and the two Spice Girls albums amazingly still charted in the U.S. Top Sixty-Five by the end of 1998. Remembering another British invasion by mop-tops from Liverpool, the press referred to the hip-hop pop delivered by the first female teen idols as the "Spice Girls revolution."

The Backstreet Boys and 'N Sync delivered the male equivalent of the Spice Girls' hip-hop-tinged R&B. Formed during the late 1990s, the Backstreet Boys— Nick Carter, Howie Dorough, Brian Littrell, A.J. McLean, and Kevin Richardson— added their smooth harmonies and light hip-hop beats to Jive Records' production and songwriting. Their self-titled 1997 American debut jumped to the Top Five and, by the end of 1998, still stood at number five with more than nine million copies sold in the United States. The next year, their *Millennium* entered the chart at number one and within a year had sold eleven million copies.

'N Sync, citing Boyz II Men as their main influence, neared the top of the chart with a similar sound. Banding together in Florida in 1995, the group formed around Justin Timberlake and JC Chasez who started together on the Disney Channel's

Mickey Mouse Club. In 1998, the quintet harmonized to create a smooth, hip-hop-tinged R&B effort with their multiplatinum, self-titled debut. At the end of year, *NSYNC* still held the number-three slot with U.S. sales of more than five million, and the group's *Home for Christmas* hit number seven. In 2000, the group scored again with *No Strings Attached*, which sold more than 2.4 million copies in the first week and eventually sold more than fifteen million units worldwide. The next year, they topped the chart with *Celebrity* before disbanding.

With the mega-sales of R&B hip-hop pop acts such as 'N Sync, the Backstreet Boys, the Spice Girls, and Lauryn Hill, hip-hop achieved a greater commercial viability. In 1995, rap captured 6.7 percent of all sales. By 1998, hip-hop accounted for 10.3 percent of sales, and R&B snagged another 11.2 percent of the market. Hip-hop pop helped fuel a record industry that in the late 1990s had grossed more than $12 billion a year in the United States and more than $40 billion worldwide.

By the end of the 1990s, hip-hop pop had become the new music for a new generation. *Newsweek* smugly called the shift from gangsta rap to hip-hop R&B a transition from "raunch to romance." *Time* characterized it as "a creative time in hip-hop history." Whatever the perspective, rap had mutated into a new strain for the upcoming millennium.

Hip-Hop Pop Grows Up

Kanye West delivered a more mature hip-hop pop in the new century as the fans of 'N Sync, the Backstreet Boys, and the Spice Girls went to college and landed jobs. Taking the chart by storm with the mega-platinum *The College Dropout* (2004) and the subsequent number-one efforts *Late Registration* (2005) and *Graduation* (2007), West combined the beats and samples of rap with a wholesome demeanor and a social conscience to craft hip-hop pop for young adults.

On one hand, Kanye projected a clean-cut image, which contrasted with the gangsta rap culture of guns, baggy pants, and loose women. Raised in a middle-class suburb of Chicago by his mother, a Ph.D. who was the chair of the English department at Chicago State University, he sported polo shirts, white pants, and checkered sports jackets. When he first walked into the offices of Roc-A-Fella Records, remembered Damon Dash, then CEO of the company, "Kanye wore a pink shirt with the collar sticking up and Gucci loafers. It was obvious that we were not from the same place or cut from the same cloth." "To my knowledge Kanye has never hustled a day in his life," confessed Jay-Z who gave West his break in 2001 when he allowed him to produce several of the songs on his *The Blueprint*. Rather than brag about his sexual conquests, West told the press about a steady girlfriend and his plans for marriage. He professed a belief in God, releasing the hit single "Jesus Walks." "My [future] is in God's hands. If He wants me to make another album, then He'll give me the inspiration to do so," the rapper asserted. "It was a strike against me that I didn't wear baggy jeans and jerseys and that I never hustled, never sold drugs," he complained.

Though seemingly squeaky clean, Kanye offered crisp rhymes and reintroduced samples of soul and gospel music into hip-hop to reinvigorate a general interest in rap music, which had become stultified by gangster braggadocio. Besides his own work, he scored hits as a producer for Talib Kweli ("Get By"), Ludacris ("Stand Up"), Common ("Be," "Go!," and "Faithful"), and The Game ("Dreams"). "I stopped listening to hip-hop years ago," remarked Darryl McDaniels of Run-D.M.C. "This past decade seems like hip-hop has mostly been about parties and guns and women." Kanye West rekindled an interest in rap in McDaniels: "When I heard [Kanye], I just stopped in my tracks."

The rap sensation also offered a political message. He rapped against Ronald Reagan's alleged introduction of crack cocaine into the inner cities in "Crack Music" and addressed an inequitable health care system in "Roses." West blasted the rap community for their homophobia on an MTV special in August 2005 and attacked George Bush at a benefit for Hurricane Katrina relief. He also addressed the human toll of the African diamond trade with the video for "Diamonds in Sierra Leone." All told, the politically conscious, clean-cut rap innovator updated hip-hop pop for a maturing audience. "He combines the superficialness that the urban demographic needs with conscious rhymes for the kids with backpacks," observed Damon Dash. "It's brilliant business." Referred to as a "genius" by the press, Kayne West had updated hip-hop pop for the twenty-first century.

Metal Gumbo: Rockin' in the Twenty-First Century

21

> ❝ Metal is resurging back, coming out of the underground. Metal is like a roller-coaster. It has its peaks, it goes down—and stays down for a while—but I think it's going up the big hill right now. ❞
> —Meegs Rascon, guitarist for Coal Chamber

As the new century unfolded, a multidimensional, metallic rock resurfaced and slowly began to replace hip-hop as the dominant sound. Teens, who had listened to the hip-hop pop of 'N Sync and the Spice Girls turned to a harder-edged music as they became older. Rather than rap, some favored what critics termed "nu-metal," which grafted hip-hop, grunge, funk, punk, thrash, and other elements of rock history onto a heavy-metal base. Though not totally displacing rap, this metal gumbo slowly began to dominate the charts and became the first musical trend of the twenty-first century.

Nu-Metal Pioneers

Early in hip-hop's history, a hybrid sound emerged that combined hip-hop with a hard-edged rock. A few rock groups, thrash metal shredders, and grunge bands joined with angry rappers to create a united front of a desperate generation. In February 1985, ex–Sex Pistol John Lydon and hip-hop pioneer Afrika Bambaataa started the trend toward a rap-rock fusion with their collaboration on "World Destruction." The next year, rockers Aerosmith joined with rappers Run-D.M.C. for the classic rap-rock version of Aerosmith's "Walk This Way," and guitar thrash master Kerry King of Slayer provided the guitar on the Beastie Boys' anthem, "(You Gotta) Fight for Your Right (To Party)." Thrash metal kings Anthrax combined with Chuck D to record a thrash/rap version of Public Enemy's "Bring the Noise" (1991) and subsequently toured with the hip-hoppers. "These two kinds of music have always been similar in attitude; I never understood why there wasn't more of a crossover," explained Anthrax guitarist Scott Ian. "Heavy metal and rap music are both defiant forms of music," echoed Chuck D of Public Enemy.

Faith No More, coming together in Los Angeles in 1982, welded together hip-hop, funk, and metal into an original sound. Guitarist Jim Martin paid homage to such metal gods as Black Sabbath, Led Zeppelin, and Jimi Hendrix. "If it wasn't for Sabbath, I wouldn't be sitting here," added drummer Mike "Puffy" Bordin. Keyboard player Roddy Bottum cited hip-hop as an inspiration. "We really liked the Run-D.M.C. thing that was going on at the time—'Rock Box' and all those big rap songs with heavy guitars." Other band members such as theatrical singer Mike Patton added funk to the metal/hip-hop mix. Characterizing the group's music as funk-rap-metal, Martin explained that "I was playing a metal guitar style and Bill [Gould] was playing a funky bass." After a commercially unsuccessful debut, the band added rap to their funk-rock mix on *Introduce Yourself* and in 1989 almost hit the U.S. Top Ten with their next effort, *The Real Thing*.

The Red Hot Chili Peppers reinforced the power of the funk-metal-rap connection. Cemented by singer Anthony Kiedis and funk master bass player Michael "Flea" Balzary, the band coalesced in 1983 in California. After several groundbreaking but commercially unsuccessful albums, the Peppers added guitarist John Frusciante and drummer Chad Smith to crack the chart in 1989 with *Mother's Milk* and finally broke through to the mainstream with the 1991 classic *Blood Sugar Sex Magik*, which hit the number-three slot. They followed with the Top-Ten release *One Hot Minute* (1995) and showed their staying power with the more subdued hits *Californication* (1999) and *By the Way* (2002). Inspired by diverse musicians such as "Parliament/Funkadelic, Sly and the Family Stone, Run-D.M.C. and the Beastie Boys," Kiedis thought, "you can definitely make a case for us being a big part of what became nu-metal or rap metal. When I meet those bands today that are along the rap-metal vein—nu-metal or whatever you want to call it, they often say they enjoyed us when they were beginning."

The Red Hot Chili Peppers. Photo by Sonya Koskoff. *Permission by Warner Brothers Records/Reprise Records.*

In 1991, Ice-T married rap and heavy metal by linking with the band Body Count. On his *O.G. Original Gangster*, he used the heavy-metal band as the background for his angry rhymes about prison, drug addiction, and police abuse. Ice-T admired the "more evil sounds" of metal bands such as Black Sabbath and the "punk energy" of Black Flag and the Dead Kennedys. He chose Body Count because he "wanted a group that has the attack of [thrash metal band] Slayer, the impending doom of Sabbath, the drive of Motorhead and groove-oriented . . . like what Anthrax does." As the rapper observed, "Rock-and-roll's not dead—it's just gotta open its doors and realize where it came from. I'm trying to get rap kids to realize that it's all rock-and-roll. When rock-and-roll first started, it was black and white kids together—I'm trying to get it back together."

Rob "Zombie" Straker, the frontman of the band White Zombie as well as a solo act during the late 1990s, drew similar inspiration from the rap-rock wellspring. After an initial foray into the art-noise, no-wave New York scene of bands such as Sonic Youth, White Zombie mixed the energy of metal, punk, and rap into a potent amalgam. As Rob explained it, "I loved the power of metal guitar, but so many times, it was too stiff. I also loved rap music like Public Enemy, when it was high powered and almost seemed like metal with this insane wall of sound. That was my main inspiration, loving Public Enemy and Slayer at the same time but not wanting to sound like either of them." The sound of the band, characterized by Rob Zombie as "rhythmic guitars locked into these heavy beats," propelled White Zombie into the Top Thirty with the 1992 *La Sexorcisto: Devil Music Vol. 1* and three years later into the Top Ten with *Astro-Creep 2000.*

Rapper Method Man (b. Clifford Smith) of the Wu-Tang Clan saw a similar connection between rap and rock. "There was a time when I had nothing but Soundgarden in my goddamn CD player, you know?" he told a journalist. "'Black Hole Sun' was my shit!" Method Man and his compatriots in the nine-man Wu-Tang Clan collective hit the chart near the end of the grunge craze with *Enter the Wu-Tang (36 Chambers)* (1994). Three years later, they soared to the top in Britain and the United States by selling two million copies of *Wu-Tang Forever.*

Other rappers and rockers united to deliver the rap-rock sound. In 1993 on the soundtrack to *Judgment Night*, the grunge-metal outfit Pearl Jam recorded "Real Thing" with hip-hoppers Cypress Hill. "We listen to that kind of music anyway," insisted B-Real of the rap group, "so it wasn't hard to click with them." Sen Dog of Cypress Hill added, "The Pearl Jam shit is dope because we put hard B-boy rhymes on top of some heavy-metal-sounding shit." On the same soundtrack, Slayer joined with Ice-T on "Disorder," and Sir Mix-a-Lot (b. Anthony Ray), the Seattle hip hopper who had released a rap version of the Black Sabbath classic "Iron Man" with Metal Church, rapped over the grunge band Mudhoney in "Freak Momma." "I was wondering when we'd bring rap and rock together in a big way," remarked Mix-a-Lot, "because the fans are a lot alike."

The Rap-Rock Explosion

Shown the experimental path by pioneers during the 1980s and early 1990s, in the late 1990s rock-rap hit its stride with bands such as Rage Against the Machine, who climbed to the top of the chart with an incendiary mixture of heavy-metal riffing and hip-hop beats. Formed in 1991, the band featured guitarist Tom Morello, the son of a Kenyan Mau Mau revolutionary and the great-nephew of radical Kenyan President Jomo Kenyatta, and rapper/vocalist Zack de la Rocha, the son of a Chicano artist. They first charted in 1993 with an overtly political, self-titled album that contained a Public Enemy–like "Take the Power Back," raged against American authority in songs such as "Know Your Enemy," and envisioned a revolution that would engulf cities from South Africa to Los Angeles in "Township Rebellion." "The goal of the first record was to document our experimentation with hip-hop and punk, but also to destroy the boundaries between art and politics," asserted Tom Morello. Living their convictions, they railed against the British right-wing National Front and made the video "Freedom" to protest the unjust imprisonment of Native American leader Leonard Peltier, who had been jailed in 1977 on flimsy evidence for allegedly killing two F.B.I. agents.

Three years later, the band topped the U.S. chart and hit the British Top Five with *Evil Empire*, which featured Morello's rap-influenced guitar. "In Rage Against the Machine, I am the DJ," he asserted. "Scratching" a guitar like a hip-hop DJ scratches records on a turntable, "I can cite [Run-D.M.C. DJ] Jam Master Jay and [Public Enemy DJ] Terminator X and now, to a certain extent, [Wu-Tang Clan DJ] RZA as influences on my six-string instrument, giving me a different perspective." In 1999, the rap-rock of Rage Against the Machine again hit number one on the chart with *The Battle of Los Angeles*.

A number of bands kept the aggressive sound but dropped the political venom of Rage Against the Machine to scale the charts with their own version of a bass-heavy rap-metal. The California-based Korn, fronted by singer Jonathan Davis, formed in 1993 to deliver a hip-hop and funk-inflected version of a monstrous rock sound. In 1996, they reached number three on the album chart with *Life Is Peachy* and followed with two number-one efforts, *Follow the Leader* (1998) and *Issues* (1999).

The band incorporated hip-hop into their metal core through bassist Reginald "Fieldy" Arvizu. "He's a hip-hop fanatic," explained singer Davis. "When he plays his bass lines he gives everything a hip-hop feel. He turned the rest of us on to a lot of hip-hop, too." Added Korn guitarist James "Munky" Shaffer, "We were kinda influenced by the whole hip-hop thing, so we wanted all of the tones on the verses and stuff to sound very hip-hoppish."

Limp Bizkit, the Florida band led by volatile singer Fred Durst and anchored by guitarist Wes Borland, found similar success with hip-hop heavy metal. Getting together in 1994, they first cracked the Top Twenty-Five with *Three Dollar Bills, Y'all$* (1997). The band hit the top of the chart in 1999 amid the rap-rock rage with the million-selling *Significant Other*, which included collaborations with Eminem and Method Man of the Wu-Tang Clan and guest vocals from Korn's Jonathan Davis. The next year, they followed with another chart-topper, *Chocolate Starfish and the Hot Dog Flavored Water*.

Limp Bizkit relied heavily on 1980s' metal and hip-hop for their signature sound. Asked to describe his influences, Wes Borland pointed toward "the first crossover thing that happened with Anthrax and Public Enemy." He idolized Anthrax, "Megadeth and Metallica and Testament and all the other heavy-metal bands." Like "all of the long-haired heavy-metal kids," the guitarist was "introduced to the whole hip-hop world through Anthrax and [Public Enemy's collaboration on] the *Attack of the Killer Bs* album. All of a sudden I realized, 'Wow! This is really cool stuff!,'" he enthused. Together with his band mates, including turntablist DJ Lethal, Borland delivered a hard-hitting version of late 1990s' hip-hop metal.

The Deftones, fans of Korn, Faith No More, and Rage Against the Machine, launched their own rap-metal mix. Formed in 1988 in Sacramento, after years of constant touring, they finally neared the top of the chart with *White Pony* (2000), which included turntablist Frank Delgado. "It's funny that we're considered nu-metal," mused guitarist Stephen Carpenter. "I feel like I've been playing metal the whole time! But the rap was there all along. I mean, Anthrax was doing that, like, a decade ago. We're *all* caught up in the rap game now."

Kid Rock and his band, Twisted Brown Trucker, concocted one of the more sonically varied versions of the hip-hop/rock mixture. After a series of commercially

Linkin Park. Photo by Brad Miller. *Permission by Warner Brothers Records/Reprise Records.*

unsuccessful efforts, Kid Rock (b. Bob Ritchie) hit pay dirt with a musical stew of sounds. The Michigan-born leader cited a variety of influences from hard-rock icons Creedence Clearwater Revival to southern rock gods Lynyrd Skynryd. He also "got into hip-hop 'cause I thought it was the best sounding music at the time that it came out," listening to pioneers such as the Sugarhill Gang, Run-D.M.C., and the Beastie Boys. "I wanted to sing on some songs. I wanted to rap on some songs. I wanted to do it all," he explained. His twin-guitar attack featured Kenny Olson with some "country pickin' or some blues-based stuff" and Jason Krause "with the pretty straightforward metal stuff," according to the Kid. In 1999, the band scored with its melting pot of heavy sounds in the smash million-seller *Devil Without a Cause.*

Hip-hop rock carried into the new millennium with the mega-success of Linkin Park. The band, signed by Warner in 1999, tried to break down "the boundaries between different genres," according to guitarist Brad Delson. "The idea of Linkin Park is to make every part a mixture of everything, so that you can't pull apart the influences." The group especially fused hip-hop to heavy rock sounds. In addition to Delson and a rhythm section, Linkin Park included vocalist Chester Bennington, MC Mike Shinoda, and DJ Joseph Hahn. In 2000, the band released a flurry of guitar riffs, hip-hop beats, and well-timed scratches on *Hybrid Theory*, which sold more than twenty-four million copies worldwide. They followed with the number-one, multiplatinum sellers *Meteora* (2003) and *Minutes to Midnight* (2007).

Progressive Metal

One band took the 1990s' penchant of combining metal with other musical styles in another direction. Formed in 1990 in Los Angeles, Tool started as a hard rock outfit with their debut *Opiate* (1992). They slowly started to incorporate other elements into their sound and by 1993 with their album *Undertow* created progressive metal, which combined the pile-driving guitar attack of heavy metal and thrash, experimental rock, and grunge like lyrics of personal angst. Their new sound matured with *Aemina* (1996), which nearly topped the *Billboard* chart; in the new century they released two number-one albums, *Lateralus* (2001) and *10,000 Days* (2006).

The band attributed its change in direction to the progressive art rock group King Crimson, with whom they toured in 2001. "A lot of our fans weren't really aware where we were coming from, what inspired us," explained Tool singer Maynard James Keenan. "I think to share the stage with King Crimson was important. It showed where are roots are . . . For me, being on stage with King Crimson is like Lenny Kravitz playing with Led Zeppelin, or Britney Spears onstage with Debbie Gibson."

Nu-Metal Anthems

Some youths turned to a more straight-ahead rock-and-roll in the new millennium. Usually combining grunge, 1970s' metal, and only sometimes a dash of funk or thrash, guitar-driven units from Creed to Nickelback assaulted the charts. Though hard rock had never disappeared, nu-metal anthems became the favorite music of American and British teens, who had abandoned boy bands and pop chanteuses, when they became older and confronted grim realities.

The baby-boom echo had grown up from the days of hip-hop pop. From 1998 to 2002, the number of teens aged fourteen to seventeen increased by more than a half million. The number of young adults in the United States grew even more dramatically, swelling by more than 8 percent to a total of 27.5 million. While the number of American preteens remained about the same, the total population between the ages of fourteen and twenty-four skyrocketed by 11.5 percent to more than 42.5 million.

These youths braced for a harsh future after the dot-com meltdown and its accompanying recession. From 1995 to 2000, the country enjoyed a wild boom, fueled by an information-technology bubble that led to a declining unemployment rate, which reached a low point of 4 percent in 2000. Americans flocked to start-up companies with get-rich-fast hopes of well-paying jobs and stock options for anyone who learned basic computer programming. After peaking in March 2000, the dot-com bubble burst and within a year the NASDAQ stock exchange, which carried many of the technology firms, plummeted from a high of 5,132 to a pre-boom level of 2,000. In the same period, 862 e-commerce, Internet-content, and other information-technology companies failed. When the dot-com recession hit, unemployment headed upward and reached nearly 6 percent by 2002. At the same time, corporate scandals led by the bankruptcy of energy and communication giant Enron further torpedoed American confidence in the economy, and within less than two years the Web boom had been replaced for many by the quest to find a job and economic security.

The bleak mood intensified in late 2001. On September 11, teens and other Americans experienced the horrors of an attack on the United States. In the early morning, nineteen terrorists hijacked four planes and successfully crashed two of them into the World Trade Center in New York City and another into the Pentagon outside Washington, DC. The incidents resulted in nearly 3,000 deaths and caused a wave of fear, which rolled across the nation. To many youths, the event defined the new millennium. "I think that the images of that day," intimated one teen, "will stay with me for the rest of my life. I cannot even begin to describe the anticipation, the dread, the uncertainty, and the sadness that I felt."

As a generation grew older and faced the panic of 9/11 and challenge of an economic downturn, they turned to the crashing sounds of nu-metal acts such as Creed. Put together by Florida high school buddies vocalist Scott Stapp and guitarist Mark Tremonti, the band delivered a hard-hitting mixture of 1970s' rock and 1990s' grunge. Tremonti defined the group's music as "old-school rock." He wanted Creed's performances to harken back to "bands like Kiss or Nugent that blew everything up." At the same time, the guitarist identified grunge bands such as Soundgarden as inspirations. Signed to Epic in 1997, the outfit debuted with *My Own Prison*, which rose slowly on the chart, peaked a year later, and eventually sold seven million copies. In 1999, Creed released the multiplatinum chart-topper *Human Clay*. As hard rock's popularity escalated in the new millennium, the group continued their success with the number-one *Weathered* (2001), which included the rock anthem "My Sacrifice."

Staind also waved the hard-rock banner. Heralding from Springfield, Massachusetts, the group started in late 1995 by covering songs by Pearl Jam, Alice in Chains, Rage Against the Machine, and Korn with a sprinkling of their own material. The band was spotted by Fred Durst of Limp Bizkit, who helped them snag a deal with Flip Records in 1998 and added them to the influential Family Values Tour. Promoted by a label with national distribution, Staind cracked the Top 100 with *Dysfunction* (1999). Amid the nu-metal craze, they followed with the number-one, multimillion-selling albums *Break the Cycle* (2001) and *14 Shades of Grey* (2003), both of which combined heavy guitars with the tormented grunge-style lyrics of singer Aaron Lewis. "People talk about this resurgence of rock," explained guitarist Mike Mushok in 2001, "but to me, rock never went away."

Fred Durst similarly helped Puddle of Mudd bubble up to the top of the rock heap. Signed to Durst's own Flawless Records label, the band cited grunge as a major inspiration. "We were definitely at an impressionable age when bands like Smashing

Pumpkins, Soundgarden, Pearl Jam, and Nirvana first came out," noted guitarist Paul James Phillips. "We were all heavily influenced by grunge, and we all love it." Guitarist/vocalist Wes Scantlin echoed, "I feel honored to bring grunge back a little bit, maybe give it another chance and have another generation experience that kind of music." In 2001, when Durst released the band's major-label debut *Come Clean*, Puddle of Mudd's grunge-flavored hard rock cracked the Top Ten and eventually sold five million copies.

The Canadian outfit Nickelback joined the hard-rock vanguard of the twenty-first century. Learning to play by "jamming along with Metallica, Megadeth, and Testament records," guitarist/singer Chad Kroeger characterized his band as "four guys who stand up there in cowboy boots and play rock-and-roll." The group formed in the mid-1990s, toured ceaselessly, and released two self-financed records before licensing their independently released *The State* to a major label in 2000. The next year, amid the nu-metal renaissance, Nickelback teamed with producer Rick Parasher of Pearl Jam fame to near the top the chart with the melodic hard rock of *Silver Side Up*, which sold more than ten million copies worldwide.

Disturbed hit the chart with a rock sound that featured soul-purifying lyrics. Forming during 1996 in Chicago, they first scored with the multimillion-seller *The Sickness* (2000) and two years later hit the top spot with *Believe*. According to singer David Draiman, the hard-rocking band used their music "as therapy. The songs are cathartic. They've ways of dealing with life experiences and the world around you."

Most nu-metalers and their forebearers, reflecting the disturbing world around them, owed a debt to heavy-metal god Ozzy Osbourne. Many of the twenty-first-century metal men paid homage to the king of dark, foreboding rock-and-roll. Kid Rock guitarist Kenny Olson and guitarist Dan Donegan of Disturbed cited Black Sabbath as a prime influence. Singer Serj Tankian of System of a Down, the quartet who hit the top of the chart with *Toxicity* in late 2001 amid the rock revival, cited Ozzy as the "godfather" of nu-metal. Guitarist Brian "Head" Welch of Korn enthused that Ozzy "got me interested in music back when I was a little lad." As Kerry King, guitarist for Slayer, pointed out, "anybody that plays heavy music and doesn't cite Sabbath as an influence is lying, because that's where it all started."

In addition to the musical inspiration he provided to nu-metal, Ozzy Osbourne helped propel many twenty-first-century metal acts to stardom through his annual concert tour, Ozzfest. Started by the Black Sabbath leader in 1996, Ozzfest provided instant visibility to struggling new bands in search of a national audience. In 1998, Limp Bizkit played the Ozzfest main stage. In 1998 and 1999, System of a Down joined the tour and three years later reconnected with the metal festival. In 2000, Disturbed made their first Ozzfest appearance and played the festival two more times. The next year, Linkin Park debuted on Ozzy's concert tour. Not surprisingly, the influential Ozzy Osbourne and his family served as the focus of a real-life MTV series *The Osbournes*, which became the hit of the 2002 television season and won an Emmy award.

By the start of the new century, nu-metal bands had swept through the charts. "Metal is resurging back, coming out of the underground," contended Meegs Rascon, the guitarist for the gothic-looking metal outfit Coal Chamber, which hit the Top

Twenty-Five in 1999 with *Chamber Music* and played Ozzfest three times. "Metal is like a roller coaster: It has its peaks, it goes down—and stays down for a while—but I think it's going up the big hill right now." Even *Time* magazine carried the headline, "Rock at the Top," in a late 2001 story and begrudgingly admitted that nu-metal acts such as Creed and Staind "may prove to be a lesson in Rock 101 for the Britney [Spears] generation."

The recording industry looked toward a rebounding hard rock as its salavation. In 2000, the Recording Industry Association of America reported that the "'modern rock' category registered the greatest gain in listeners among all music genres compared to the previous year. The interest in rock, especially nu-metal acts, showed a remarkable 24 percent annual increase among teenagers, with 57 percent of all teens citing it as their favorite music." Internationally, rock music experienced a similar rebirth. "The year 2000 was a 'comeback' year for rock music in many markets," asserted the International Federation of the Phonographic Industry. "In the U.S. alternative/modern rock increased its share of sales by 11%. In the U.K. rock sales accounted for 26% in 2000, up from 22% in 1999, driven by the popularity of 'nu-metal' acts." As the century unfolded, rock-and-roll metal bands had made a comeback.

The Internet, Jam Bands, and Three Shades of the Blues

The Internet irrevocably changed rock-and-roll. Like other defining technologies such as the electric guitar, the 33 1/3 LP, and the compact disc, it altered the way people found, listened to, and approached popular music. By 2007, online digital files had become a ubiquitious part of the music experience that allowed youths to download a wide variety of musical genres and carry thousands of their favorite songs with them on a new device called the iPod.

Though having access to a seemingly unlimited number of songs and musicians, youths preferred several styles that reflected their lives. They favored three shades of the blues—music by socially conscious singer-songwriters; a stripped-down, raw, bluesy, garage rock; and an extreme black metal—that mirrored their deep-seated concerns about a war in Iraq and the terrifying prospects of global warming.

The Age of the Internet

The Internet, introduced for mass consumption during the early 1990s, had become an

Apple made special iPods, such as this U2 model, that came preloaded with all of the group's songs. *Permission by Apple Computer, Inc.*

essential part of every office and home by 2007. In 1995, only 7 percent of all Americans had access to the Internet. At the turn of the century, nearly 60 percent of Americans surfed the Net. By 2007, more than 70 percent had access to the wide variety of information and services on the Internet.

American teenagers, a prime demographic for the record industry, went digital more than the average American. By 2000, approximately thirteen million or 68 percent of American teens logged time online and spent an average of 303 minutes on the Internet per month. By 2007, according to the Pew Internet and American Life Project, 93 percent of all teens in the United States surfed the Web.

Many of these youths used the Internet to communicate with one another. Nearly 75 percent of online teens embraced instant messaging, spending almost eight hours per week conversing with their friends online. Forty-eight percent stated that they improved current friendships through their online activity, and 32 percent reported that they made new friends from instant messaging. Overall, 70 percent of the wired teens found the Internet "exciting." In 2002, the Cyber Atlas survey group contended that "the Internet is now the primary communication tool for U.S. teenagers."

By 2007, broadband access—the ability to download material from the Internet at a faster rate than a dial-up connection through a normal phone line—swept the United States and allowed teens and their parents to engage in more activities than communication. In 2003, only a third of active Internet users had broadband. By early 2006, 68 percent of Americans connected to the Web had purchased either a Digital Subscriber Line (DSL) or the faster but more expensive broadband cable connection. These 95.5 million Americans spent an average of 30.5 hours a month on the Web, up from 25.5 hours a month just three years earlier.

Broadband connections permitted Americans to play and download complex video files quickly and easily, fueling the online video-game craze. The software game industry started in 1972, when a tavern in Sunnyvale, California, installed the first Pong game. Four years later, companies began to sell consoles to allow people to play games in their own homes through their television sets. These game consoles slowly evolved into computers such as Sony's PlayStation, Xbox from Microsoft, and Nintendo's GameCube and Wii to allow for more graphically rich, artificial-intelligence-based games, which in 2004 averaged $10 million each to develop.

The gaming environment began to change further at the turn of the century. In 2000, only 19 percent of gamers indicated that they played online. By 2007 the majority of gamers used the desktop computer to play their video games, aided by the introduction of ever-faster central processing units (CPUs), enhanced graphical processing units (GPUs), and increasing bandwidth with broadband. In 2005, 13 percent of all broadband users subscribed to a gaming service. Though a majority of the games purchased and the revenue generated in the industry still came from the console business, in 2006 retailers sold nearly 40 million online games such as World of Warcraft and the Sims 2 for nearly $1 billion. Overall, the $7.4 billion game industry moved from 74 million units sold in 1996 to 241 million units ten years later and provided a challenge to the record industry for the discretionary income of Americans.

The Download Mania

Broadband enabled Americans to engage in another new venture that directly affected the record industry: downloading music files. Plugged-in teens logged onto central and peer-to-peer sites such as Napster, Morpheus, Freenet, and Gnutella to access their favorite music for free. In 1999, Americans racked up more than one billion music downloads, helped by MP3 technology, a standard, universal compression format for Internet audio files. Three years later, the Ipsos-Reid market research group estimated that sixty million Americans over the age of twelve—especially teens and young adults, who historically had accounted for nearly half of all sound recording purchases—had downloaded music from the Internet. In 2006 as broadband became more widespread, BigChampagne, a file-sharing analyst firm, found that ten million people globally used peer-to-peer services at any given moment and had a choice of thirteen billion song files. Half of these file swappers resided in the United States.

Many of the people who downloaded these files had no ethical concerns over accessing copyrighted material without a charge, feeling entitled to any material on the Internet. In a Pew Internet and American Life Project study, conducted in late 2000, 78 percent of the downloaders did not consider the digital capture of copyrighted songs for free as stealing. Sixty-one percent of the survey sample did not even care about whether a digital file had been copyrighted or not. In another study the same year, Quicktake.com found that 80 percent of all file swappers did not consider their behavior to be unethical.

Others rationalized away their actions. In 2007, one writer for *Time* magazine used a typical excuse. "Most of us are really criminals," he contended. "Sure, O.K., I ripped the audio of the Shins' *Phantom Limb* off a YouTube video. But on the strength of that minor copyright atrocity, I legally bought two complete Shins albums and shelled out for a Shins concert. The legit market feeds off the black market."

Some rock musicians used the same rationale, claiming that free online music resulted in increased purchases by allowing teens to sample the music. David Draiman, lead singer of Disturbed, told an interviewer that "I can't tell you how many kids have come up to me and said, 'I downloaded a couple of tunes off Napster and I went out and bought the album.'" Other musicians agreed with the singer. In a 2004 study by the Pew Foundation, "when asked what impact free downloading on the Internet had on their careers as musicians, 37% say free downloading has not really made a difference, 35% say it has helped and 8% say it has both helped and hurt their career. Only 5% say free downloading has exclusively hurt their career."

A 2002 study by the market research firm Ipsos-Reid confirmed the Pew survey. It found that "81 percent of downloaders claimed that their CD purchases have stayed the same or even increased since they began downloading music from the Net." Nearly half of the respondents replied that they had "purchased a CD from an artist because of something they read or listened to on the Internet." In 2005, the market research firm The Leading Question concluded that downloaders purchased four and a half times more CDs than the average music fan. Aram Sinnreich, analyst for Jupiter Media Metrix, argued that "it is safe to say that active usage of online music content is one of the best predictors of increased consumer purchasing."

A new technology, the digital audio player (DAP), encouraged the digital-download practice. Introduced in 1998, the first DAP, called the MPMan, allowed users to download digital music files into a small handheld device for storage, organization, and playback. The Rio PMP300 quickly followed within a few months. Though the Recording Industry Association of America (RIAA) sued its maker, contending that the MP3 Rio player encouraged illegal digital downloads, the court ruled against the RIAA to sanction digital audio players in the marketplace.

Introduced in October 2001, the iPod popularized and commercialized the use of the digital audio player. Masterminded by Apple Computer, the iPod enabled music listeners to download thousands of songs, and eventually videos, on a device that weighed less than a pound. Teens could download Internet files or music from physical compact discs into iTunes software developed by Apple to transfer digital audio and video files to the iPod. By 2008, Apple had sold more than 120 million iPods, which became a new way to store and listen to rock-and-roll. A 2007 Pew Research Center study found that more than half of all teens owned an iPod.

Apple entrenched its market position by creating a for-pay music subscriber service for the iPod legions and in the process revolutionized the distribution of popular music. In 2003, Apple created iTunes Store, a service that allowed listeners to download their favorite songs for 99 cents each. Some campuses across the country paid Apple a flat fee for unlimited use of the service, trying to decrease illegal file sharing. By January 2005, Apple Computer's iTunes Store had sold more than 250 million songs in fifteen countries and reported downloading more than 1.25 million songs a day. Within another year, the iTunes Store had moved one billion songs online, "representing a major force against music piracy and the future of music distribution as we move from CDs to the Internet," according to Apple CEO and founder Steve Jobs. By mid-2008, Apple had sold 5 billion songs and controlled 80 percent of the legal digital download market with Amazon.com a distant second in market share.

Digital audio players such as the iPod created new possibilities for the music fan. Most chose to download songs rather than albums, returning to the Elvis-era days of the 45-rpm single rather than embracing the long-play album, which became indispensable during the 1960s' psychedelic era when the focus on extended songs made the 45 obsolete. The new digital files offered the best of both worlds: the ability to select only the best cuts from an artist and the chance to hear songs of any length. The downloaders could also shuffle songs in any way to customize their music and make their own versions of albums if they chose to burn the music on a physical CD. By 2006, more than 95 percent of digital music lovers downloaded songs rather than complete albums to change the focus of the recording process for many artists.

Music fans found a much wider choice of styles than they had ever previously been able to explore with new developments on the Internet such as Internet radio, MySpace, Facebook, and YouTube. Internet-only radio began in 1995, when Radio HK started to broadcast online a program of music by independent bands. Within a few years, hundreds of stations had appeared. Unlike traditional commercial radio that played a limited number of artists in a very tight programming format, Internet-only radio catered to the interests of listeners who wanted to hear nonmainstream acts. A Web surfer could find programs that focused exclusively on the blues, jazz, progressive rock, death metal, ethnic music, and almost any other type of genre imaginable. In 2000, Tim Westergren started the Music Genome Project, which broke down songs by their characteristics and permitted anyone, free of charge, to create a personal radio station based on his or her musical tastes. He wanted to let listeners "explore their musical universe." By 2007, the Music Genome Project had more than six million subscribers. Though a 2007 copyright royalty change threatened to tax the Internet-only stations into oblivion, the Internet continued to provide an almost dizzying array of musical styles to online fans.

MySpace also allowed listeners to become familiar with a range of artists that would have been inconceivable in the past. Created in 2003 by eUniverse and two years later purchased by media mogul Rupert Murdock as part of his Fox corporation, MySpace encouraged anyone to establish an interactive "social network," which included photos, personal profiles, music, videos, blogs, and other material. The third most popular Website in the United States, by late 2007 it boasted 200 million accounts.

This interactive site enabled unknown and unsigned bands to play their music and air their videos in a cost-effective manner to an audience of potentially millions. In a success story, Soulja Boy (b. DeAndre Way) created a MySpace site and in 2004 aired a music video, which featured his dance, the "Superman," and his single "Crank Dat." Hearing the buzz from MySpace, Interscope Records signed the sixteen-year-old and released his CD *Tell 'Em*, which neared the top of the *Billboard* chart. "A year ago, I was just making songs in my house and putting them online," shrugged Soulja Boy. Similarly, teen singer Colbie Caillat posted her music on MySpace, attracted fourteen million hits, and snagged a record deal with Universal Republic. In 2007, her album *Coco* hit the *Billboard* Top Five. "Labels were signing fewer acts, giving them less time to prove themselves," explained MySpace CEO Chris DeWolfe. "We saw a need to develop a community of artists to get their music to the masses." By 2007, 800,000 artists had registered on MySpace. "MySpace is the blueprint for the new record business," contended Chris Clancy, the co-head of marketing at Interscope.

YouTube offered similar exposure to unsigned artists. Created in 2005 and bought the next year by Google, it allowed users to upload, view, and share their videos with others. By 2007, the site had more than 56 million videos and more than 500,000 accounts. "Other video sites were making decisions on what was entertaining," contended Chad Hurley, a founder of the site. "We removed that barrier by allowing everyone to participate and add content. It's really the users of the community that decide what's entertaining and what rises to the top."

The Internet assisted fledgling rock critics. With the introduction of blogs, self-appointed rock experts such as Scott Lapatine started to sway the musical choices of teens. Launching his initial blog, Stereogum, in 2003, he quickly became "the blog-sphere's most influential music tastemaker" and hired five staff writers to help him. "A&R [artist identification and development] is happening on the Internet now," Lapatine remarked, "because blogs constantly look for new bands—championing them and watching them grow."

Social networking sites such as iLike.com, Last.fm, and Mog.com extended the music-critic role to the fans. They recommended tunes to listeners and allowed like-minded fanatics to connect with each other to share their discoveries. By March 2008, iLike.com had twenty-three million subscribers, Last.fm snagged twenty-one million unique users per month, and Mog.com played host to a million moggers per month.

The Internet also provided established artists a new way to promote themselves, make money, and break loose from the once ironclad grip of the record industry. At the turn of the century, artists earned two-thirds of their money from the sale of pre-recorded music and a third from the sale of merchandise and concert tours. By 2007, the situation had reversed, and many bands expected to make the bulk of their earn-ings from T-shirts, endorsements, and the sale of concert tickets, which had nearly doubled in price from the previous decade.

A nonprofit corporation called Merlin, launched in January 2007, gave artists and independent labels the expertise to maximize their nonalbum revenues. The com-pany negotiated digital-download contracts for artists. According to Merlin CEO

Charles Caldas, it "removes the cost of negotiating and managing individual contracts for each online music site." Merlin quickly signed a deal to collaborate with SNOCAP, a company founded in 2002 by Napster inventor Shawn Fanning, which created an online retail service for artists to upload, sell, and monitor the sales of their music from their MySpace pages and other Websites.

With the new focus on digital downloads, concerts, and merchandise, some artists began to look at physical CDs as promotional devices. Prince, who had consistently made more money from concert tickets than CDs, shocked the music industry by giving away copies of his album *Planet Earth* to anyone who bought a ticket to a concert on his 2007 tour.

Some bands such as Radiohead eliminated physical CDs altogether and developed a new business model for the sale of their music. The experimental/progressive rock act Radiohead had always supported file sharing, feeling, in the words of singer Thom Yorke, that it served as "a nice way of spreading the word around." In a bold move in 2007, the band released their album *In Rainbows* in a digital format available only on their own Website and asked their fans to decide on the price of a download. "It's up to you," read a message on their site. "Warner/Chappell fully supports Radiohead in their desire to find new ways to present their music to their fans and to the wider world," remarked Richard Manners, the managing director of their music publishing firm in the United Kingdom. "These new ways are iconoclastic in nature; they acknowledge the realities of a digital society and they challenge existing commercial assumptions."

Colbie Caillat performing in 2008. Photo by Brian Ach. *Permission by Getty Images.*

A few weeks later, Trent Reznor of Nine Inch Nails followed the Radiohead example. On October 8, 2007, he informed readers of his Website that "as of right now, Nine Inch Nails is a totally free agent, free of any recording contract. . . . I have been under recording contracts for 18 years and have watched the business mutate from one thing to something inherently very different, and it gives me great pleasure to be able to finally have a direct relationship with the audience as I see fit," he concluded. In 2008, he released his new album *The Slip* free of charge on his Website only. Within two months, 1.4 million fans had downloaded the files from his site.

The Reinvention of the Music Industry

The seismic changes in the record industry caused by the Internet directly affected the sales of compact discs. At the beginning of the century, four major companies controlled the music industry and accounted for more than 80 percent of prerecorded music sales. Sony BMG, the Warner Music Group, EMI, and the Universal Music Group had a tight lock on music manufacturing, promotion, distribution, and sales.

The Internet changed the business paradigm in the industry with the commercialization of digital files, and CD sales of the Big Four companies started to decline for the first time in decades. During the 1990s in the United States, the number of CD sales had risen steadily. In 1991, the record industry shipped 333.3 million full-length compact discs at a value of $4.33 billion. By 1995, it shipped 723 million CDs worth nearly $9.4 billion and four years later sold almost 939 million silver platters for $12.8 billion. Despite the introduction of digital downloads, the sale of CDs in the United States expanded in 2000 to an all-time high of 942 million units worth $13.2 billion and accounted for 92 percent of all music industry sales.

After the turn of the century, the sale of audio CDs started to plummet in the United States, slipping to 881 million units worth $12.9 billion in 2001 and declining further two years later to 745 million units worth $11.2 billion. In 2007, the sale of audio CDs bottomed at 511 million units valued at just more than $7.4 billion. From 2000 to 2007, the number of CDs sold skidded 46 percent, and retail sales slipped by 44 percent.

The international music market experienced declining revenues during the same period. In 1999, the record industry worldwide grossed nearly $36 billion. By 2003, the global music industry saw a decrease in revenues to $32.3 billion that the International Federation of the Phonographic Industry (IFPI) blamed on a "global economic downturn." Even with an improved global economy, in 2007 music sales continued to free-fall to $29.9 billion, totaling a 17 percent loss in eight years.

The decline in the sale of CDs sounded the death knell for many retail outlets. On December 22, 2006, Tower Records closed its 89 stores in the United States and most of its worldwide locations. Started by Russ Solomon in Sacramento, California, Tower had been in operation for 46 years. Overall in the United States during 2006, more than 800 record stores ceased operations. In the United Kingdom, the Fopp chain of 100 stores closed its doors in June 2007. Though general retailers such as Wal-Mart and Best Buy had taken some of the business from these outlets, the overall decline in the sale of physical CDs amid the download revolution served as the main explanation for the closures.

Faced with severely declining sales, music executives first lashed out against free online music providers. "Many are concerned about the continued use of CD-Rs [compact disc recordables]," warned Hilary Rosen, president and CEO of the RIAA. Jay Berman, the CEO and chairman of the IFPI, similarly linked "disappointing [sales] figures" to "mass CD copying." Using the same arguments the entertainment industry had mustered against cassette and VCR taping, RIAA and IFPI contended that the "digital piracy" of free downloads posed a dire threat to the financial solvency of the record industry.

The music industry, reeling from the effects of digital downloads and attempting to protect its market share, vigorously attacked the free music providers on the Web. The RIAA sued file-sharing pioneer Napster, which by late 2001 capitulated, discontinued its free service, and started a subscription online music business. The music industry used a different approach against peer-to-peer online services such as Morpheus, SoulSeek, WinMx, Grokster, EDonkey, Ares Galaxy, and Kazaa, which did not have central servers for music downloads like Napster but provided free, nearly undetectable software that allowed music fans across the globe to easily share files from their desktop computers. Unable to shut down the networks from central sites, the music companies tried to infiltrate their enemies by planting users on the peer-to-peer sites to disrupt the networks with nonfunctioning versions of music files.

As the number of illegal downloads increased despite these tactics, the music industry realized that it could not control peer-to-peer networks and began to attack individual file sharers. In 2005, the IFPI filed 2,100 lawsuits against illegal downloaders in sixteen countries. The next year, it increased its efforts and leveled 8,000 suits against defendants in seventeen countries. From 2003 to late 2007, the RIAA filed more than 26,000 lawsuits in the United States against people who used peer-to-peer network software to download free music. Defendants such as Jammie Thomas of Minnesota were found guilty and ordered to pay $9,250 to six record companies for each of the twenty-four songs she downloaded for a total fine of $222,000. "The case has put [file-sharing] back in the news," boasted RIAA president Carey Sherman in 2007.

In 2006, the music industry even pressured the U.S. House of Representatives to pass a bill that imposed a longer prison sentence for illegal song swapping. "The Internet has revolutionized how Americans locate information, shop and communicate," argued Texas Republican Representative Lamar Smith, a sponsor of the Intellectual Property Protection Act. "We must not let new Internet technologies become a haven for criminals." Despite these efforts by the music business, the downloading continued unabated. The number of American households that downloaded music each month increased from 6.9 million in April 2003 to 7.8 million households in March 2007.

The sluggish U.S. revenue figures of the music industry, though partly attributable to free music downloads, originated from several other factors as well. Mega-retailers such as Wal-Mart, which by 2004 sold 20 percent of all CDs in the United States, insisted on lower prices on wholesale product, driving down music industry revenues despite sizable CD sales. The cassette tape format, which in 1991 had accounted for half of all revenues, by 2003 had plummeted to less than 1 percent of music sales.

The record industry faced increased competition from other entertainment sectors. By 2003, movie DVDs accounted for nearly $24 billion in sales. The same year, three giants of network television—Viacom, Disney, and NBC Universal—posted $31.9 billion in television-associated revenues. Three years later, the burgeoning computer and video-game market hit the $7.4 billion gross revenue mark. In 2007, theater box office receipts from filmgoers worldwide hit an all-time high-water mark of $26.7 billion. "Music is mature," explained Eric Garland, the CEO of BigChampagne in March 2008. "The growth is in TV shows, movies, and gaming."

Caught off balance by entertainment-industry competitors and unable to stop the onrush of digital downloads, the record companies scrambled and tried to muscle into existing markets. Noticing the wild success of the iTunes Store, they jumped into the for-pay download business. In addition to Napster, they encouraged the launching of Rhapsody and Peer Impact in the United States and online services in Australia, Europe, Latin America, and Asia. Music companies also inked deals that bundled their music with the sale of other products to bring revenue to the music industry. In 2007, Universal Music signed an agreement with Nokia that enabled Nokia mobile phone users to have free twelve-month subscriptions to Universal's music catalog in the "Comes with Music" plan. Omniphone worked with other music giants to establish MusicStation, which permitted their customers to have access to 1.4 million songs on their cell phones.

Through such tactics, legal downloads increased exponentially. In 2003, the legal download business accounted for less than 1 percent of the music business. Four years later, the number of digital downloads exceeded all physical formats (CDs, cassettes, vinyl and music DVDs) sold in the United States, and legal downloads accounted for 23 percent of the U.S. music revenues and 15 percent of worldwide sales. "Steve Jobs [CEO of Apple Computer] understood Napster better than the record business did," contended music mogul David Geffen. "iPods made it easy for people to share music, and Apple took a big percentage of the business that once belonged to the record companies. The subscription model is the only way to save the music business." Though the new digital product line did not initially compensate for the sharp decline in CD sales because many favored the relatively inexpensive download of single songs rather than an entire album, music executives such as Geffen believed that it provided the best chance of survival.

The record industry leaders also tried to grab the artist management business, hoping to convince new artists to give them a share of their concert and merchandising rights as well as their sound recordings. They tried to sell "360-degree contracts," which offered a slightly increased signing bonus in exchange for a percentage of the revenues from touring and merchandise sales. "It's a discussion you have with every new artist," explained Jeanne Meyer of EMI Records. In 2007, Warner tried to enhance its profitability by acquiring Front Line Management, the largest artists management firm. "The record industry used to be focused on the record and all the rest was promotions. Now it's a more balanced business where you have records, TV shows, merchandise, touring revenues and so on," explained Vivendi CEO Jean-Bernard Levy.

By 2007, the business model for the music industry had undergone a fundamental shift. The traditional plan of signing new acts, promoting them, pressing their CDs, and selling their albums in retail outlets had changed almost completely. Rick Rubin, the mastermind behind Def Jam Records and most recently the co-head of Columbia Records, described the paradigm shift in the music business. "Until very recently there was a handful of channels in the music business that the gatekeepers controlled," he observed in 2007. "They were radio, Tower Records, MTV, certain mainstream press like *Rolling Stone*. That's how people found about new things. Every record company in the industry was built on that model . . . and that's how the music business functioned for 50 years. Well, the world has changed." Nicholas Firth, chairman and CEO of BMG Music Publishing Worldwide, added, "The one prediction I will make is that in 10 years record companies will be like publishing companies. They will not be in the manufacturing business."

Jam Bands

The pervasive changes in the music industry brought about by the Internet and the shuffle-and-play capabilities of the iPod created and responded to the eclectic tastes among many twenty-first-century youths. Some of them downloaded metal, rap, folk, Motown, and '60s' psychedelia on their digital audio players, listening to them one after another. They favored songs that caught their interest from MySpace or other download sources, combining them for their own soundtrack to life. Many of these youths with catholic musical tastes favored bands that incorporated multiple influences to deliver a progressive, experimental rock for the digital age. They used the Internet to discover new bands, which otherwise might not easily be found through the traditional distribution channels of radio, MTV, and in-store promotions.

Jam bands, characterized by long improvisational guitar solos, a mixture of musical influences, and a focus on the audience, swept the nation during the mid-to-late 1990s with the help of constant touring, word-of-mouth promotion and, most importantly, Websites on the Internet. Taking their cue from their progenitor, the Grateful Dead, these bands attracted thousands of fans to their shows without the aid of MTV, radio play, or record label marketing and employed the Internet to create a sense of community among their adherents.

Probably the archetype of the jam bands, Phish formed at the University of Vermont in 1983 by guitarists Trey Anastasio and Jeff Holdsworth, bassist Mike Gordon, and drummer Jon Fishman. In late 1985, keyboard player Page McConnell joined the band, and the next year Holdsworth left as the band's personnel solidified. Playing a combination of jazz, rock, folk, country, and blues, the group attracted a following by strategic use of the Internet. In 1991, Phish became one of the first rock acts to establish a Usenet newsgroup on the Web, encouraging their growing fan base to trade downloaded files of Phish concerts with one another. This online activity replaced

Trey Anastasio (left) and Mike Gordon of Phish performing in Santa Cruz, California, in 1993. Photo by Tim Mosenfelder. *Permission by Getty Images.*

the more laborious and complex practice of trading cassette tapes that Deadheads and metal fans had used for years. Phish also bolstered their popularity through audience-friendly antics at concerts, sometimes throwing a beach ball into the audience and composing a song by adding a new note each time the ball bounced. They headlined such festivals as H.O.R.D.E. (Horizon Of Rock Developing Everywhere), which started in 1992 and continued through 1998 to showcase the eclectic style of the jam bands.

After growing their fan base slowly, Phish hit the mainstream in 1994, when *Hoist* reached number thirty-four on the chart. After Jerry Garcia of the Grateful Dead passed away in 1995 and the Dead disbanded, the legion of Phish adherents—known as phans, phamily phriends, and Phishheads—continued to expand. The band hit with the Top Twenty *A Live One*, followed with the Top Ten efforts *Billy Breathes* (1996) and *The Story of the Ghost* (1998). Knitting their fans together through the Web, the band delivered an intoxicating stylistic mixture with extended solos to increasing large crowds, which reached 80,000 by the mid-1990s.

Dave Matthews served a similar musical gumbo to a carefully cultivated fan base. Matthews, born in South Africa and ending up in Charlottesville, Virginia, by 1991 banded together with several jazz musicians to deliver a concoction of jazz, blues, rock, and folk. The band's sound reflected the wide-ranging tastes of its leader. "I got into different kinds of music," explained Matthews who as influences cited the

Beatles, Led Zeppelin, Joan Baez, Cat Stevens, Bob Marley, and jazz pianists Abdullah Ibrahim and Keith Jarrett.

Like Phish, Matthews toured constantly, appeared at H.O.R.D.E., and allowed fans to tape his shows and trade the files online. By 1994, the same year that Phish entered the chart, the Dave Matthews Band released *Under the Table Dreaming*, which nearly cracked the Top Ten and proved to be the first among many top-selling albums. They neared the top with *Crash* (1996) and *Live at Red Rocks 8.15.95* (1997), hit the top spot in 1998 with *Before These Crowded Streets*, and continued to churn out hit albums for the next ten years.

Providing a similar blend of musical styles, Blues Traveler used the same method to ascend the chart. Formed in 1987 in New Jersey by harmonica whiz John Popper, the band moved to New York City and played in local clubs. In 1992, they founded the H.O.R.D.E festival and toured constantly, featuring the jam-band trademark of extended guitar improvisations. Like their jam-band compatriots, they urged their followers to tape their shows and trade them online. By 1995, they reached the *Billboard* Top Ten with *four* and neared the top with *Straight on Till Morning* (1997).

Widespread Panic followed the same path to success. They came together during the mid-1980s in Athens, Georgia, named after their leader and guitarist Michael "Panic" Houser. The band toured constantly, participated in the first H.O.R.D.E festival, and created a file-trading Website for their fans. In 1994, the group entered the chart with *Ain't Life Grand* and two years later with *Light Fuse Get Away*. By 2001, a year before the untimely death of Houser from pancreatic cancer, they had become one of the top-twenty concert attractions in the country without radio play, MTV, or much major record label help. Through the Internet, they had created a community of devotees who during the mid-to-late 1990s streamed by the thousands onto fairgrounds to their concerts, which became shared cultural celebrations.

Life in Wartime

As a new century unfolded, the full flowering of possibilities for music provided by the Internet allowed youths to uncover a series of blues-influenced styles that reflected the grim realities of their lives. As much as any other event, the U.S. invasion of Iraq defined the beginning of the twenty-first century. Launched by the George W. Bush administration on March 20, 2003, on the unfounded pretext of Iraq's possession of weapons of mass destruction, the war at least partly sought to secure Iraqi oil fields. Tagged "Operation Iraqi Freedom," the invasion was led by General Tommy Franks and involved 300,000 U.S. and British troops. The coalition forces quickly swept through Iraq, captured Baghdad on April 9, and within another week declared military victory.

Despite the military triumph and the discovery that no weapons of mass destruction existed in the country, the United States occupied Iraq and fought a protracted war against insurgents who used guerilla tactics against their opponents. On average, the rebels initiated more than 70 attacks a day against U.S. troops, contractors, and Iraqi supporters of the coalition. By August 2007, nearly 4,000 U.S. troops had been killed, and another 28,000 had been wounded. More than 230 U.S. contractors had died. On the opposing side, approximately 30,000 Iraqi soldiers and insurgents had been killed. Including civilians who had died violently from car bombs, aerial bombing, war-related accidents, and random blasts, the death toll stood at 1.2 million. Another 3.9 million Iraqis—16 percent of the total population—became refuges, fleeing their country.

As the seemingly endless conflict continued unabated, many questioned the prolonged U.S. presence in Iraq and urged withdrawal. An Iraq Study Group Report headed by former secretary of state James Baker and former congressman Lee Hamilton concluded in late 2006 that "the situation in Iraq is grave and deteriorating," and "U.S. forces seem to be caught in a mission that has no foreseeable future." In a poll conducted the same year, 72 percent of the U.S. troops stationed in Iraq contended that the United States should withdraw within a year. A late 2006 poll of Iraqis found that 70 percent wanted a withdrawal of U.S. troops, and 78 percent believed that the U.S. presence seemed to be "provoking more violence than it's preventing."

Worldwide opinion turned against the United States due to the ongoing war. In a January 2007 poll of people in twenty-five countries, 73 percent disapproved of the Iraqi occupation by the United States. Later in the year, a British Broadcasting Corporation poll yielded the same results. Despite the casualty rate and worldwide sentiment against the occupation, in 2007 President Bush commissioned more military personnel and initiated a "surge" strategy by increasing the tour duties of the current troops. As British forces withdrew from the country under orders from Prime Minister Gordon Brown, American troop levels increased with no end to the war in sight.

The Iraq invasion both repelled and frightened American youths. In a June 2007 poll conducted by CNN, *The New York Times*, and MTV, the majority of Americans under twenty-one years of age identified the Iraq war as the "most important issue facing people of [our] generation" by more than a 2 to 1 margin. Nearly 58 percent thought that the United States never should have entered the conflict. Worried about their own safety, 42 percent of those surveyed feared that the war would lead to a reinstatement of the military draft.

Not only concerned about an unpopular war, American youths also confronted long-term environmental issues, especially global warming. Global warming refers to the increase in the average temperature of the earth due to heightened water vapor, carbon dioxide, methane, and nitrous oxide levels in the atmosphere that create a "greenhouse effect." Naturally occurring greenhouse gas emissions maintain an atmospheric temperature that can support humans. However, elevated levels of carbon dioxide, nitrous oxide, and methane beyond a stable point trap additional solar heat to cause further increases in the temperature of the earth and the oceans and lead to an increase in extreme weather events such as hurricanes and tornados, changes in food production, extinction of certain species, and the spread of diseases.

After engaging in a heated debate about global warming and its causes during the 1980s, by the turn of the century scientists almost universally believed that significant global warming had already occurred and would continue unabated unless the amount of human-produced carbon dioxide and methane emitted into the environment decreased. They called for an end to deforestation and a reduction in the use of fossil fuels, which together had increased the atmospheric concentration of carbon dioxide by 31 percent and the amount of methane by 149 percent since the industrial revolution. Scientists found that the heightened greenhouse gas levels had especially risen at an alarming rate since 1975 and pointed toward the ongoing retreat of glaciers and the rise in the level of the oceans as physical evidence of their findings. Taking heed from the scientific community, in 1997 more than 160 nations pledged to reduce greenhouse gas emissions in the Kyoto Protocol.

Most Americans, believing their government and the media, seemed unconcerned about the issue despite the overwhelming evidence of an increase in the earth's temperature. Pressured by major oil companies and automobile manufacturers, the U.S. government refused to sign the Kyoto Protocol and actively manipulated scientific reports to downplay the existence of global warming. In 2002, George Bush declared that he would never impose limits on carbon dioxide emissions. The American press generally supported this short-sighted view by providing equal time to pro- and anti-global warming advocates. They presented climate change as an unresolved issue and implicitly reassured Americans that global warming existed as only a scientific debate. As a result, by the turn of the century most Americans had little concern about global warming. Though "the new paradigm of an abruptly changing climatic system has been well established by research over the last decade," a 2001 report by the National Academy of Scientists in the United States contended that "this new thinking is little known and scarcely appreciated by the wider community."

Hurricane Katrina changed the American sentiment. Battering and decimating New Orleans, the 2005 hurricane seemed to indicate beyond a doubt the existence of global warming to the press and the American public. A cover of *Time* magazine asked "are we making hurricanes worse" and on another cover warned "be worried. Be very worried." The Public Broadcasting System, the Turner Broadcasting System, and the conservative Fox News Network all aired specials about global warming in the wake of Katrina. Former Vice President Al Gore also campaigned ceaselessly for the mitigation of global warming and in May 2006 released the award-winning documentary film *An Inconvenient Truth*, which gripped Americans. By a September 2007 poll conducted by the Associated Press and Stanford University, 77 percent of those surveyed rated the current environmental condition as fair to very poor. More than half indicated that the environment seemed worse than ten years ago and would deteriorate further after another ten years. All told, 79 percent of the respondents considered global warming a "serious problem," and 61 percent had "personally taken steps to reduce energy consumption." In 2007, even the conservative *Wall Street Journal* reported that "the global warming debate is shifting from science to economics. The biggest question going forward no longer is whether fossil-fuel emissions should be curbed. It is who will foot the bill for the cleanup."

American youths who would suffer most from long-term environmental problems exhibited the growing concern of the majority. When asked about the importance of global warming in 2007, 89 percent considered it serious. More than half of young Americans between the ages of thirteen and twenty-four felt that global warming existed now, and 81 percent wanted immediate action. These youths characterized global warming as "the most important problem my generation will have to deal with."

The Singer-Songwriters

Confronted by a prolonged conflict in Iraq and the realities of climate change, American youths turned to several variants of the blues. Some of them, especially the rapidly expanding number of college students, embraced a group of socially conscious singer-songwriters who delivered a blues-tinged and jazz-influenced folk-pop, railed against the war, and supported environmental causes.

During the first few years of the twenty-first century, the number of college students began to increase. In 1970, 7.4 million students attended American colleges and universities. In 1985, the number rose to 12.5 million and in 1994 grew to 15 million, remaining relatively stable for the next several years. By 2004 as the baby-boom echo became older, the number of American college students had mushroomed to 17.4 million.

Many of the students favored the cerebral music of singer-songwriters such as John Mayer. Mayer, first inspired by blues guitar master Stevie Ray Vaughan, started playing in local Connecticut bars. In 2001 he signed with Aware Records and released the Internet-only album *Room for Squares*. Noticing the Web interest generated by the release, Sony signed Mayer and rereleased the album, which cracked the *Billboard* Top Ten.

During the next several years, Mayer used jam-band techniques to garner a large college-aged following. He toured, allowed audiences to tape and share files of his performances, and incessantly communicated with his fans through four blogs that he personally wrote. In the next three years, Mayer neared the top of the chart three times with *Inside Wants Out* (2002), *Any Given Thursday* (2003), and *Heavier Things* (2004). By 2006, Mayer added a discernible blues influence to his sound and infused his music with a social message. "Waiting on the World to Change," the lead song on *Continuum*, lashed out against war, and "Belief" directly blasted the war in Iraq. The singer-songwriter also launched "Another Kind of Green" on his blog to convince his fans to reverse global warming by designing, manufacturing, and selling "products that are cheap, easy alternatives to cut down on plastics."

Jack Johnson, a former professional surfer turned singer-songwriter, exhibited a similar sound and social conscience. Starting with *Bushfire Fairytales* (2002), Johnson crafted a mixture of the blues, jazz, and soft folk to lure his listeners into songs directed against the media and its portrayal of violence ("News" and "All Understood"). He followed with two near number-one efforts, *On and On* (2003) and *In Between Dreams* (2005), which attacked the war in Iraq ("Crying Shame"), war in general ("Traffic in the Sky"), American materialism ("Gone"), and the media ("Good People," "Fall Line," and "Cookie Jar"). He also lobbied for environmental issues. His Website indicated that "Jack Johnson and his crew are collaborating with local and national non-profits around the world in the realms of climate change, water quality, community and school gardens, land preservation, environmental education, and more." It instructed his fans to give "1% to the Planet" by contributing 1 percent of their income to one of dozens of environmentally focused nonprofit groups.

Fellow singer-songwriter Ben Harper offered an even more direct political message. Combining folk-blues with jazz and funk on a slide guitar, Harper started in 1994

John Mayer performs at the 2008 Milwaukee Summerfest. Photo by Paul Warner. *Permission by Getty Images*.

with *Welcome to the Cruel World* and the politically charged *Fight for Your Mind*. Though scoring some success and attracting a following, Harper first hit the Top Twenty in 2003 with *Diamonds on the Inside* during the rise in popularity of the singer-songwriter. He followed with the Top Ten *Both Sides of the Gun* (2006) and *Lifeline* (2007). By 2007, Harper featured Bob Dylan's "Masters of War" in his concerts as a statement against the Iraq war. "The opposite of activism is inactivity, and I would rather be active in a social way," he explained.

James Blunt mined his personal experience for his antiwar songs. A former British soldier stationed in Kosovo, Blunt turned to songwriting immediately after his discharge. He nearly topped the chart with his 2005 debut *Back to Bedlam*, which featured the anti-war "No Bravery," and the next year hit the Top Ten with *All the Lost Souls*. Summing up the concerns of most twenty-first-century singer-songwriters, Blunt fastened on the "remarkable state of the world, when there are important things that we should be dealing with. There are wars going on. There are people dying. There's climate change."

Blues from the Garage

Dogged by sobering issues, other youths preferred a rawer, more minimalist and rock-influenced version of the blues epitomized by the White Stripes. In 1997 the band formed in Detroit, when guitarist Jack White (b. Gillis) linked with drummer Meg White. They snuck onto the *Billboard* chart with their 2002 debut *White Blood Cells* and the follow-up *De Stijl* named after the minimalist movement in painting headed by Piet Mondrian. In 2003, the duo scored with the Top Ten *Elephant* (2003), followed by the equally successful *Get Behind Me Satan* (2005), and nearly topped the chart with the more musically varied *Icky Thump* (2007).

On one hand, the twosome found inspiration in fellow-Detroiters Iggy and the Stooges who Jack initially discovered, when he unearthed the first Stooges album in a dumpster behind a neighbor's house. "I mean, I'm in debt to the Stooges for life and I'm never going to say no," confessed Jack. Even more important than the proto-punk of the Stooges, Mississippi Delta blues motivated the band. According to Jack, he became "transformed" after listening to Son House, and "I kept on digging to Charley Patton." In the end, asserted Jack, the White Stripes wanted to be remembered "just as being part of the blues canon, 100 years since the blues started. I'd like to think that we were the first male/female two-piece attack on it in the electric world." Like the original Mississippi Delta sound, the band hoped to create a powerful music through a minimalist approach. "We're trying to keep it as simple as possible," explained Jack.

The Strokes joined the blues-based garage rock movement in 1999, when they cracked the *Billboard* Top Fifty with their raw debut *Is This It* (2002) and toured with the White Stripes. They followed with the slicker *Room on Fire* the next year and *Impressions of Earth* (2006), which both hit the Top Five. Like the White Stripes, the Strokes paid homage to the 1960s' proto-punkers. In their case, they incorporated the sound of the Velvet Underground. "The Velvet Underground is probably one band that they mention that *was* influential for us," admitted guitarist Nick Valensi. The guitarist also stressed the importance of the blues. He listed a long line of possible influences on the band, including Texas guitarist Freddie King.

The Hives, a Swedish band who also played a stripped-down version of garage rock, cited as major influences punk and the garage bands of the 1960s. "We got into American punk and hardcore like the Dead Kennedys and stuff like that," remembered guitarist Nicholas Arson. "They were a big influence. And then we listened to the Saints, the Sex Pistols, the Damned, Bad Brains—just good punk rock music, something with an energy." Band members paid special tribute to the 1960s' Seattle garage rock of the Sonics and Wailers. "I think the Sonics were one of the first garage bands we listened to," second guitarist Mike Carlstroem told an interviewer in 2002. "I like the Wailers. I like all that '60s stuff."

Forming in 1993, the group initially released several Swedish-made CDs. In 2000, they recorded their album *Veni Vidi Vicious*, which included the single "Hate to Say I Told You So." After repeated tours, a reissue of their initial efforts, and amid the furor over the White Stripes, in 2002 the band hit the U.S. chart with *Veni Vidi Vicious*, which made it into the Top 100. During the first years of the new century, a blues-based, minimalist garage music rocked the youth of America.

Black Metal

More brutal, direct, and aggressive than the new version of garage rock, black metal rose with a vengeance from an underground cult to prominence during the new century and delivered a somber, edgy, furious sound, which reflected a world racked by the war in Iraq and the specter of global warming

The roots of black metal can be traced to the thrash of the New Wave of British Heavy Metal that captured youth in the 1980s. Bathory, named after sixteenth-century Hungarian "Blood Countess" Elizabeth Bathory, was assembled in 1983 in Stockholm by leader Thomas "Quorthon" Forsberg. The band gave black metal its sound and fury with screeching vocals, low-fi production, a frenetic, distorted buzz-saw guitar attack, blast-beat drumming, and demonic lyrical themes. "My reason for forming Bathory was I wanted to create a mix of the atmosphere of early Black Sabbath, the energy of early Motorhead, and the pace of early [British hardcore punkers] G.H.B.," explained Quorthon. He characterized his music as "primitive and dark extreme metal," exemplified by a self-titled debut, *The Return* (1985), and *Under the Sign of the Black Mark* (1987). Together with Venom that gave the genre its name with their second release *Black Metal* (1982) and Celtic Frost of the *Morbid Tales*–era (1984) that offered an experimental thrash, Bathory laid the groundwork for the next generation of black metal.

Mayhem served as the hub of the second wave, which coalesced in Norway, and defined black metal of the 1990s. Coming together in 1984 in Oslo around leader and guitarist Oystein "Euronymous" Aarseth, the band took its name from a Venom song "Mayhem with Mercy." They fused the major elements of the early Bathory sound with a pagan, anti-Christian ethos and the medieval look of leather, spikes, armor, and weaponry. The group painted their faces white to emulate corpses, showing their fascination with death and a disdain of the temporal world. Also including bassist Jorn "Necrobutcher" Stubberud, drummer Kjetil Manheim, Per Yngve "Swede Dead" Ohlin, and Jan Axel "Hellhammer" Blomberg, Mayhem brutally assaulted listeners with their *Deathcrush* extended play (1987) and the pivotal *De Myseriis Dom Sathanas (Lord Satan's Secret Rites)* (1994). At the same time, "Euronymous" started a record store, Helvete, which specialized in black metal, and established a black-metal record label Deathlike Silence with a mail-order business to promote the new music.

Following Mayhem's lead, other Norwegian black metalers arose during the late 1980s and mid-1990s. In 1987 Darkthrone joined forces in Kolbotn, Norway. After hearing Mayhem, the group abandoned the growling vocals and violence-obsessed lyrics of death metal and turned to black metal. They began to wear corpse paint, adopted the thrash guitar and screams of Bathory and Celtic Frost, and assumed pseudonyms. In 1993, Darkthrone released the landmark black metal album *Under a Funeral Moon* and followed with *Transylvanian Hunger* the next year.

Satyricon, brought together by Satyr (b. Sigurd Wongraven) and Frost (b. Kjetil-Vidar Haraldstad), offered the same satanic concoction of black metal. In 1993, they started with *Dark Medieval Times* and continued with *Shadowthrone* (1994) and *Nemesis Divina* (1996). "The music is rock based but more extreme," contended Satyr on his homepage. "It is black metal pushing the boundaries that began with bands like Venom and Bathory; reinventing ourselves based on a foundation of rock-oriented black metal is our philosophy."

Changing their style to black metal on the advice of "Euronymous," in 1991, the Norwegian band Immortal emerged in corpse paint with a thrashing, screaming black-metal sound, which focused on a mythical world plagued by war and suffering. They released a series of genre-defining albums including their debut *Diabolical Fullmoon Mysticism* (1992), *Pure Holocaust* (1993), and *Battles in the North* (1995). Drummer Kolgrim referred to Immortal's music as "pure holocaust metal."

Just as it rose to prominence in Norway from 1993 to 1995, the second wave of black metal began to unravel through its inherent aggression. Varg Vikernes, who had founded the black-metal band Burzum and had periodically played with Mayhem, stabbed "Euronymous" to death in 1993. Two years earlier, Mayhem vocalist "Dead" committed suicide by a self-inflicted shotgun wound. Just as important, some of the black-metal band members and fans put their pagan beliefs into action, setting fire to more than fifty Christian churches from 1992 to 1996. By mid-1997, the black-metal originators had either been killed ("Euronymous" and "Dead"), jailed for murder (Vikernes and Bard "Faust" Eithun of the band Emperor), or incarcerated for arson (guitarist Jorn Tonsberg of Immortal and Emperor members Samoth and Tchort), and the Norwegian black-metal movement receded into the background.

Black metal persisted into the twenty-first century with a worldwide underground movement. From Sweden came bands such as Watain, Marduk, Dark Funeral, and Dissection. Finland boasted Beherit and Impaled Nazarene, and France hosted Mütiilation and Deathspell Omega. Destroyer 666 hailed from Australia, and Moonblood started in Germany. In Poland, Graveland surfaced, and Nokturnal Mortum emerged from the Ukraine.

Fans became a secret cognoscenti, trading limited-edition vinyl albums of their favorite bands. As the hippies had done during the psychedelic era, they deciphered the intricate cover and poster art of the bands that had been created only for the true believers. Some of them became familiar with theories of paganism and the occult, and others became enthralled with medieval times. During the 1990s, black metal remained a cult with a disdain for the masses.

The Internet pushed black metal from its cult status into the mainstream. For the first time, the Web allowed American youths to easily learn about and hear international black-metal bands through digital downloads. Obtaining black-metal records became possible on eBay, and MySpace enabled fans from around the world to discuss the music among themselves and sometimes with band members. As Satyr observed as early as 1999, "the Internet [is] replacing the old correspondence of the underground, the slow mail, and now you have the Internet replacing the whole underground [methods of communication]."

By 2003 through the help of the Internet, black metal began to infiltrate the American music scene. The extreme-metal band Cradle of Filth formed in England in 1991 and released their black-metal debut *The Principle of Evil Made Flesh* (1994). Adopting other influences throughout the 1990s, by the new century the band preached to a broad audience. They joined the Ozzfest lineup, landed their videos in heavy rotation on MTV, signed a deal with Sony Records, and launched a merchandising unit, Vamperotica. In 2003, Cradle of Filth cracked the *Billboard* Top 200 with *Damnation and a Day*, which guitarist Paul Allender characterized as a "black metal symphony about the expelling of Lucifer from heaven." The next year, they hit the Top 100 with *Nymphetamine* and in 2006 reached number sixty-six with *Thornography*. Singer Dani Filth considered the success "a fantastic opportunity for us to reach a totally new and bigger crowd."

The symphonic black metal of Dimmu Borgir also climbed the *Billboard* chart. Founded in 1993 by Norwegians Stien "Shagrath" Thoresen and Sven Atle "Silenoz" Kopperud, the band churned out a series of albums during the 1990s. Using a number of media, Dimmu Borgir slowly attracted a sizable fan base. They appeared on MTV and Fuse TV, communicated with their fans on their Website, and joined Ozzfest for a North American tour. In 2003, they entered the Top 200 with *Death Cult Armageddon* and even cracked the Top Fifty with *In Sorte Diaboli* (2007). The commercial breakthrough allowed Silenoz to finally quit his day job and concentrate on his music. Despite their other influences, "Shagrath" insisted that the music was "still black metal . . . I mean, Dimmu Borgir is more like a second-generation black metal band."

Behemoth, a Polish band that vacillated between black and death metal, also experienced mainstream acceptance during the same period. Founded in 1994, the group released several albums and toured with Satyricon. In 2007, they neared the top of the Heatseakers *Billboard* chart with *The Apostasy*, which had been leaked on the Internet a month before its official release. "This genre is doing really well at the moment, man," observed Behemoth front man Adam "Nergal" Darski in late 2007.

A troubling conflict in Iraq and the dire prospects of global warming, coupled with the newfound accessibility of underground music through the Internet, led some American youths to an extreme form of the blues. Trying to explain the success of his band in 2007, Darski conjectured that "I think that it has a lot to do with the state of the world around us. It's not becoming a better place, unfortunately, and anytime you switch on the television or you read the news, there's a lot of fucked-up shit happening all around us, and causing a lot of frustration. The music is just a perfect expression of that." As the new century progressed, youths listened to three shades of the blues, including an extreme metal, which mirrored the extremely precarious world around them.

Bibliography

This bibliography consists of the material that I found most useful in the preparation of this book. I also relied on the interviews and articles in the following periodicals: *Billboard, Chronicles of Chaos.com, Furious.com, Goldmine, Guitar Player, Guitar World, Living Blues, Musician, Newsweek, Perfect Sound Forever.com, Performing Songwriter, Playboy, Q,* and *Rolling Stone.*

Books

ARNOLD, GINA. *Route 666: On the Road to Nirvana*. New York: St. Martin's, 1993.

AZERRAD, MICHAEL. *Come As You Are: The Story of Nirvana*. New York: Doubleday, 1993.

———. *Our Band Could Be Your Life*. New York: Little Brown, 2001.

BARNES, RICHARD. *The Who: Maximum R & B*. New York: St. Martin's, 1982.

BERTRAND, MICHAEL T. *Race, Rock and Elvis*. Chicago: University of Illinois, 2000.

BLUSH, STEVEN. *American Hardcore: A Tribal History*. Los Angeles: Feral, 2001.

BLUSH, STEVEN, and GEORGE PETROS, eds. *45. Dangerous Minds: The Most Intense Interviews from Seconds Magazine*. New York: Creation, 2005.

BREWSTER, BILL, and FRANK BROUGHTON. *Last Night a DJ Saved My Life: The History of the Disc Jockey*. New York: Grove, 1999.

CLAPTON, ERIC. *Clapton: The Autobiography*. New York: Broadway, 2007.

CLARK, DICK. *Rocks, Rolls, and Remembers*. New York: Popular, 1978.

CLAYTON, ROSE, and DICK HEARD, eds. *Elvis Up Close: In the Words of Those Who Knew Him Best*. Atlanta: Turner, 1994.

COLLIN, MATTHEW. *Altered State: The Story of Ecstasy and Acid House*. London: Serpent's Tail, 1997.

DALTON, DAVID. *The Rolling Stones: The First Twenty Years*. New York: Knopf, 1981.

DAVIES, HUNTER. *The Beatles*. New York: McGraw-Hill, 1968.

DAVIS, STEPHEN, and PETER SIMON. *Reggae International*. New York: R & B, 1982.

DOGGETT, PETER. *Are You Ready for the Country: Elvis, Dylan, Parsons and the Roots of Country Rock*. New York: Penguin, 2001.

ERLEWINE, MICHAEL et al., eds. *All Music Guide to Rock*. San Francisco: Miller Freeman, 1997.

ESCOTT, COLIN, and MARTIN HAWKINS. *Sun Records*. New York: Quick Fox, 1975.

FERNANDO, S. H. *The New Beats: Exploring the Music, Culture and Attitudes of Hip-Hop*. New York: Anchor, 1994.

GEORGE, NELSON. *Where Did Our Love Go? The Rise and Fall of the Motown Sound*. New York: St. Martin's, 1985.

George, Nelson, Sally Barnes, Susan Flinker, and Patty Romanowski. *Fresh: Hip Hop Don't Stop*. New York: Random, 1985.

Girl Groups. (Film). Steven Alpert, director, MGM, 1983.

Goldrosen, John. *Buddy Holly*. New York: Putnam, 1979.

Graham, Bill. *Bill Graham Presents: My Life Inside Rock and Out*. New York: Doubleday, 1992.

Greene, Bob. *Billion Dollar Baby*. New York: New American Library, 1974.

Greenfield, Robert. *Dark Star: An Oral Biography of Jerry Garcia*. New York: Morrow, 1996.

Guitar One Presents Legends of the Lead Guitar: The Best of the Interviews 1995–2000. New York: Cherry Lane, 2001.

Guralnick, Peter. *Feel Like Going Home*. London: Dutton, 1971.

——. *Last Train to Memphis: The Rise of Elvis Presley*. New York: Little, Brown & Co., 1994.

——. *Lost Highways*. New York: Vintage, 1982.

——. *Sweet Soul Music*. New York: Harper & Row, 1986.

Hampton, Henry, and Steve Fayer. *Voices of Freedom: An Oral History of the Civil Rights Movement*. New York: Bantam, 1990.

Henderson, David. *Jimi Hendrix: Voodoo Child of the Aquarian Age*. New York: Doubleday, 1978.

Hendler, Herb. *Year by Year in the Rock Era*. Westport, CT: Greenwood, 1983.

Hewitt, Paolo, ed. *The Sharper Word: A Mod Anthology*. London: Helter Skelter, 2000.

Heylin, Clinton. *From the Velvets to the Voidoids: A Pre-Punk History for a Post-Punk World*. New York: Penguin, 1993.

"History of Rock-and-Roll." ABC television series.

Holt, Sid. *The Rolling Stone Interviews: The 1980s*. New York: St. Martin's, 1989.

Hopkins, Jerry. *Elvis: A Biography*. New York: Warner, 1971.

Hotchner, A. E. *Blown Away: The Rolling Stones and the Death of the Sixties*. New York: Simon & Schuster, 1990.

Jones, Landon. *Great Expectations: America and the Baby Boom Generation*. New York: Coward, McCann & Geohegan, 1980.

Kiefer, Kit, ed. *They Called It Rock: The Goldmine Oral History of Rock 'N Roll, 1950–1970*. Iola: Krause, 1991.

Kiersh, Edward. *Where Are You Now, Bo Diddley?* New York: Dolphin, 1986.

Kitts, Jeff, Brad Tolinski, and Harold Steinblatt, eds. *Guitar World Presents Alternative Rock*. Milwaukee: Hal Leonard, 1999.

Kozak, Roman. *This Ain't No Disco: The Story of CBGB*. Boston: Faber & Faber, 1988.

Lazell, Barry, ed. *Rock Movers and Shakers*. New York: Billboard, 1989.

Lydon, John. *Rotten: No Irish—No Blacks—No Dogs*. New York: St. Martin's, 1994.

Martinez, Gerald, Diana Martinez, and Andres Chavez. *What It Is . . . What It Was!: Black Film Explosion of the '70s in Words and Pictures*. New York: Hyperion, 1998.

McNeil, Legs, and Gillian McCain. *Please Kill Me: An Uncensored Oral History of Punk*. New York: Grove, 1996.

O'NEAL, JIM and AMY VAN SINGEL, eds. *The Voice of the Blues*. New York: Routledge, 2002.

PALMER, ROBERT. *Deep Blues*. New York: Penguin, 1982.

PECK, ABE. *Uncovering the Sixties: The Life and Times of the Underground Press*. New York: Pantheon, 1985.

PEISCH, JEFFREY. "History of Rock-and-Roll." Television series, 1995.

PERRY, CHARLES. *The Haight-Ashbury*. New York: Vintage, 1984.

POLLACK, BRUCE. *When the Music Mattered: Rock in the 1960s*. New York: Holt, 1983.

REES, DAFYDD, and LUKE CARMPTON. *VH1 Rock Stars Encyclopedia*. New York: DK, 1999.

Report of the National Advisory Commission on Civil Disorders. New York: Bantam, 1968.

REYNOLDS, SIMON. *Generation Ecstasy: Into the World of Techno and Rave Culture*. Boston: Little Brown, 1998.

RO, RONIN. *Gangsta: Merchandizing the Rhymes of Violence*. New York: St. Martin's, 1996.

Rolling Stone, editors. *The Rolling Stone Interviews*. New York: Paperback, 1971.

————. *The Rolling Stone Interviews*. Vol. 2. New York: Warner, 1973.

ROWE, MIKE. *Chicago Blues: The City and the Music*. New York: Da Capo, 1981.

SCADUTO, ANTHONY. *Bob Dylan*. New York: New American Library, 1979.

SCHAFFNER, NICHOLAS. *The British Invasion*. New York: McGraw-Hill, 1983.

SHAW, ARNOLD. *Honkers and Shouters: The Golden Years of Rhythm and Blues*. New York: Macmillan, 1978.

————. *The Rock Revolution*. London: Collier, 1969.

SHELTON, ROBERT. *No Direction Home: The Life and Music of Bob Dylan*. New York: Ballantine, 1986.

SINKER, DANIEL, ed. *We Owe You Nothing—Punk Planet: The Collected Interviews*. New York: Akashic, 2001.

SMITH, JOE. *Off the Record: An Oral History of Popular Music*. New York: Warner, 1988.

SPITZ, MARC, and BRENDAN MULLEN. *We Got the Neutron Bomb: The Untold Story of L.A. Punk*. New York: Three Rivers, 2001.

SPITZ, ROBERT. *The Making of Superstars*. New York: Doubleday, 1978.

STRONG, MARTIN. *The Great Rock Discography*. 5th edition. Edinburgh: Mojo, 2001.

TARABORRELLI, RANDY. *Motown*. New York: Doubleday, 1986.

UNTERBERGER, RICHIE. *Unknown Legends of Rock 'n' Roll*. San Francisco: Miller Freeman, 1998.

————. *Turn! Turn! Turn!: The '60s Folk-Rock Revolution*. San Francisco: Backbeat, 2002.

VIORST, MILTON. *Fire in the Streets: America in the 60s*. New York: Touchstone, 1979.

WENNER, JANN. *Lennon Remembers: The Rolling Stone Interviews*. San Francisco: Rolling Stone, 1971.

WEST, DARRELL, and JOHN ORMAN. *Celebrity Politics: Real Politics in America*. Upper Saddle River: Prentice Hall, 2003.

WHITE, CHARLES. *The Life and Times of Little Richard*. New York: Harmony, 1984.

WOLFE, BURTON. *The Hippies*. New York: New American Library, 1968.

Photo Credits

Chapter 1

p. 1: Elvis Presley, RCA Victor Ad from Billboard, December 3, 1955. RCA Records, Inc. Estate of Elvis Presley.

Chapter 2

p. 29: Elvis Presley, RCA Victor Ad from Billboard, December 3, 1955. RCA Records, Inc. Estate of Elvis Presley.

Chapter 3

p. 55: Ronnie Spector of Ronettes, c. 1970. Photo by Michael Ochs Archives. Getty Images, Inc.—Michael Ochs Archives.

Chapter 4

p. 72: Ronnie Spector of the Ronettes, c. 1970. Photo by Michael Ochs Archives. Getty Images, Inc.—Michael Ochs Archives.

Chapter 5

p. 82: Bob Dylan (live performance shot). The Daily of The University of Washington.

Chapter 6

p. 96: Photo of Diana Ross from the Supremes, c. 1960. Photo by Michael Ochs Archives. Getty Images, Inc.—Michael Ochs Archives.

Chapter 7

p. 106: Photo of Paul McCartney grinning in a tailored suit. Capitol Records.

Chapter 8

p. 126: Photo of Paul McCartney grinning in a tailored suit. Capitol Records.

Chapter 9

p. 140: Bob Dylan (live performance shot). The Daily of The University of Washington.

Chapter 10

p. 147: Jimi Hendrix playing his guitar during his set at the Woodstock Music and Art Fair. Photo by Henry Diltz. CORBIS-NY. © Henry Diltz/CORBIS All Rights Reserved.

Chapter 11

p. 169: Jimi Hendrix playing his guitar during his set at the Woodstock Music and Art Fair. Photo by Henry Diltz. Permission by CORBIS–NY. © Henry Diltz/CORBIS All Rights Reserved.

Chapter 12

p. 181: Jimi Hendrix playing his guitar during his set at the Woodstock Music and Art Fair. Photo by Henry Diltz. Permission by CORBIS–NY. © Henry Diltz/CORBIS All Rights Reserved.

Chapter 13

p. 200: Photo of Sid Vicious from The Sex Pistols. Permission by The Daily of The University of Washington.

Chapter 14

p. 217: Photo of Sid Vicious from The Sex Pistols. Permission by The Daily of The University of Washington.

Chapter 15

p. 234: Photo of Sid Vicious from The Sex Pistols. Permission by The Daily of The University of Washington.

Chapter 16

p. 259: Joey Ramone. Permission by Cam Garrett/S.C.V.D. Studio.

Chapter 17

p. 277: Joey Ramone. Permission by Cam Garrett/S.C.V.D. Studio.

Chapter 18

p. 292: Joey Ramone. Permission by Cam Garrett/S.C.V.D. Studio.

Chapter 19

p. 315: Radiohead performs at Carling Apollo Hamnmersmith, London, May 18, 2006. Tom Yorke performs with Radiohead. Photo by Jo Hale. Permission by Getty Images.

Chapter 20

p. 329: Run-D.M.C. From left to right: D.M.C. (Darryl McDaniels), Jam Master Jay (Jason Mizell), Run (Joseph Simmons). Photo by Janette Beckman.

Chapter 21

p. 353: Radiohead performs at Carling Apollo Hammersmith, London, May 18, 2006. Tom Yorke performs with Radiohead. Photo by Jo Hale. Permission by Getty Images.

Chapter 22

p. 363: Radiohead performs at Carling Apollo Hammersmith, London, May 18, 2006. Tom Yorke performs with Radiohead. Photo by Jo Hale. Permission by Getty Images.

Index